Parvéz Dewân's

Jammû, Kashmîr and Ladâkh

Ladâkh

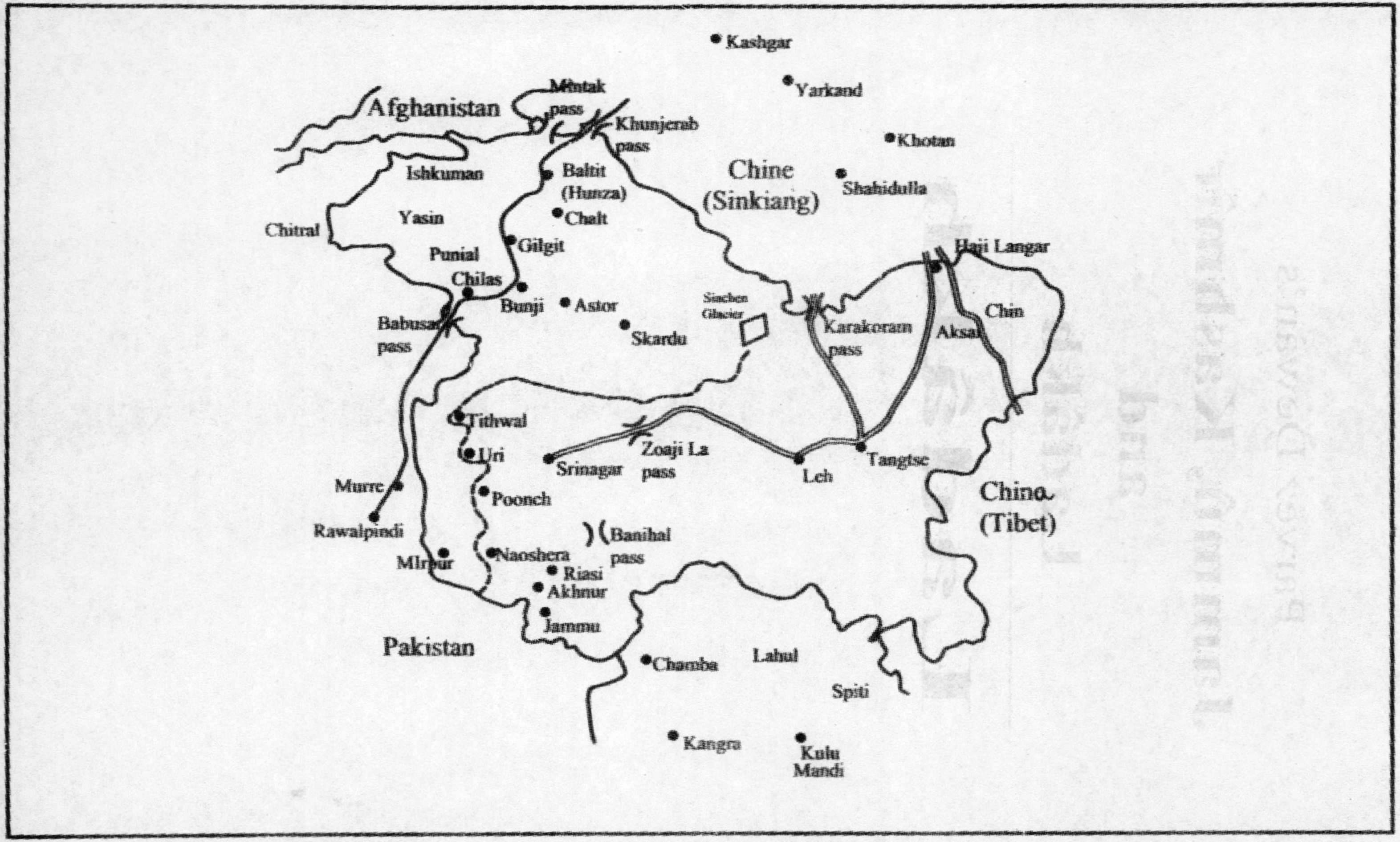

Jammu & Kashmir (including Ladakh)

Parvéz Dewân's

Jammû, Kashmîr and Ladâkh

Ladâkh

Parvéz Dewân, IAS

2nd Updated Edition

Manas Publications
New Delhi-110 002 (INDIA)

MANAS PUBLICATIONS
(Publishers, Distributors, Importers & Exporters)
4402/5-A, Main Ansari Road, (Opp HDFC Bank)
Darya Ganj, New Delhi - 110 002 (INDIA)
Ph.: 23260783, 23265523 (O); 23842660 (R)
Fax: 011 - 23272766
E-mail: manaspublications@vsnl.com
Website: www.manaspublications.in

Second Edition, ***2008*** *(First published, 2004)*

ISBN 81-7049-200-9 (Ladâkh)
ISBN 81-7049-099-5 (Set)

Rs 995/-

Typeset at
Manas Publications

Printed in India at
Shakti Printing Press
and Published by Mrs Suman Lata for
Manas Publications, 4402/5-A, Main Ansari Road
(Opp. HDFC Bank), Darya Ganj,
New Delhi - 110 002 (INDIA)

For

Saroj Dewân

From whom I have inherited our ancestral love for Ladâkh-Gilgit

Books by the author

Hiñdî-Urdû: A language Survival Kit (Lonely Planet, Australia)
The Civil Services (20/ 20 Publications, Delhi)
India's Western Himâlayas (co-authored; APA, Singapore)
The Hanûmân Châlîsâ (Viking-Penguin)
The Names of Allâh (Viking-Penguin)
Jammû, Kashmîr, Ladâkh: Kashmîr (Manas)
Jammû, Kashmîr, Ladâkh: Jammû (Manas)
The Book of Hanumân (Viking-Penguin)
Ladâkh: Buddhism and Monasteries (Viking-Penguin: under publication)

Cover Illustrations

Front and back-cover spread: 'The Thiksey monastery, Leh district,' a painting by Suman Gupta.

Inset at the top of the spine: 'Jammu, Kashmîr, Ladâkh,' a painting by Suman Gupta, representing the three regions are—the Raghunâth temple (Jammu city), the old Tsrâr é Sharîf shrine (Budgâm district, Kashmîr) and the Thiksey monastery (Leh district).

Preface

Ladâkh is the only place in India—and one of the few in the world—which has learnt how to balance modernity with tradition. Private residences in Leh are still being built as they always were-that is, the exteriors are. Inside they now have many modern conveniences. Teenaged girls wear synthetic quilted jackets—brought in from the west—to protect themselves from the cold. But under these jackets there normally are elegant traditional clothes.

Far from destroying the culture of Ladâkh, tourism is actually strengthening it. For example, tourists are helping revive local theatrical traditions—which are fast disappearing in the rest of India for want of patronage.

The government spends more on Ladâkh, in per capita terms, than on any other district of India. Tourists and NGOs supplement this. Leh is now the third most-literate district of Jammu and Kashmîr. The per capita availability of high quality primary schools might even make it the number one. What a radical change from the extremely poor infrastructure of the 1960s. Transformation has been even more dramatic in Kargil. Educational standards there have leapfrogged from the 13th position among the fourteen districts of the state to the fifth from the top, almost on a par with Srînagar.

Today the public in Leh and Zâñskâr is more 'international' than all other Indian peoples—except the Goans. But till just three decades ago Ladâkh was the most isolated part of India. Most Ladâkhis had never seen a Punjabi, leave alone someone from South Korea or Taiwan. (East Asia is the most rapidly emerging market for Ladâkh tourism.)

As a result, the international NGO (non-governmental organisation) culture has caught on like nowhere else in the state. And so has an extremely sophisticated awareness of issues concerning the ecology and environment. I was the first District Magistrate to ban the use of polythene bags. This was in Jammu in 1990-91. The ban faded away because the public was not bothered. Five years later my colleague P.K. Tripathi imposed a similar ban in Leh. The people were so enthusiastic about it that plastic bags have almost disappeared from Leh.

The people of Leh (and Kashmîr valley) adapt new ideas and technologies as quickly and as well as few South Asians do. The attitude of the common man in Leh—and not just the tourist trade—is very positive, very 'can do.'

This probably is because of the extremely hostile physical environment that the Ladâkhis find themselves surrounded by the bitter cold, the low levels of oxygen in the air, the shortage of water, the virtual absence of greenery and wood, and the enormous distances that they have to travel though uninhabited deserts to get anywhere.

The people of Ladâkh seem to have decided that modern science is their best defence against the harshness of nature.

In the rest of India the government has been doling out huge subsidies to get the people to give up agricultural practices that are uneconomical, cooking methods that are fuel inefficient, lifestyles that are bad for the health and architecture that needs improvement. The government also subsidises new technologies in Ladâkh, as elsewhere in India.

However, the 'glass room' caught on like wildfire throughout Ladâkh in the 1970s, without any governmental prodding whatsoever. (The government only provided the idea and set an example.) This is a room that has glass on the walls that face the south and the east. The Ladâkhis saw how effective it was in saving heating costs at least during the day. Almost every new house built after the late 1970s has a 'glass room.'

Levels of public hygiene in Leh, as most international tourists observe, are quite good. The streets are clean, though there certainly is room for improvement. And while the hotels might seem overpriced in their category and class, according to every survey tourists rank Ladâkhi hotels and guest houses in the top rungs in terms of service, friendliness and hospitality.

The district administration of Leh is one of the most advanced in the state when it comes to office automation, knowledge of computers and internet-connectivity. What a far cry from even 1990, when it was almost impossible to make a phone call to Leh, and Zâñskâr had no phones at all.

It is this vibrant land that I have tried to chronicle. The task has been daunting because of the formidable list of luminaries who have done this before me. Europeans have written about Ladâkh-Baltistân more copiously than about most other parts of India. This tradition began at least as far back as in A.D. 1715, if we don't count stray references to the region in Ptolemy's works. [See the chapter 'Europeans in Ladakh (And the books that they wrote).']

Today there are more Western (which term includes Australia) guidebooks about Ladâkh than about any other part of India. This is a humbling thought for anyone who aspires to write yet another book about the world's highest inhabited region. My only hope of getting noticed amidst all these excellent works is the unique position that I occupy—when I write about Ladâkh (or Kashmîr) I am both an insider and an outsider.

I am still wonderstruck by the excellence of the culture, the people, the mountains, the lakes and wildlife of Kashmîr-Ladâkh. Ethnic Ladâkhis and Kashmîrîs take the uniqueness of their glorious traditions for granted. Only an outsider like I can remain in perpetual awe.

On the other hand, having spent my entire adult life in this great state, I have acquired an insider's perspective. Though I am not an ethnic Ladâkhi, I am perhaps the first to write a comprehensive book in English about the Ladâkh-Gilgit-Baltistân region from the indigenous point of view.

The reader might notice that the chapter on Buddhist monasteries is not as detailed as the rest of the book. That is because of a conflict of interest. I am under contract to write a book on 'Ladâkh: Buddhism and Monasteries' for another publisher. I submitted that manuscript for publication well before I completed this book.

I also realise that the same name has sometimes been spelt somewhat differently at different places. This is partly because the English spellings of many names (notably Shyok and Shayok; Thikse, Thiksay and Thiksey; Astor and Astore; Khapalu and Khaplu) have still not been standardised.

Above all, I would like to submit that I try to keep my life as a civil servant and that as a writer in two separate compartments. Therefore, the views expressed in this book (and statistics given) are purely the result of my own research. The government is in no way responsible for either.

Parvéz Dewân

Pronunciation

This book has used diacritical marks to double the value of three vowels: a, i and u.

'a' is as in 'c*a*thedral'

'â' is as in 'f*â*ther'

'ao'= 'a' + 'o', much as in 'c*ow*'

'e' is as in 'g*e*t'

'é' is as in 'caf*é*'

'i' is as in '*i*t'

'î' is as in '*ea*t'

'ñ' is a brief, almost silent 'n,' much as in 'mo*n*k.'

'o' is always as in 'g*o*'

'u' is as in 'p*u*t'

'û' is as in 'f*oo*d'

'ts' is much like the 'z' in 'Mozart'. Most English-speaking people settle for the 'ch' sound. They thus turn 'Tséwâñg' into 'Chéwâñg,' which the people of Ladâkh find quite acceptable.

Acknowledgements and Credits

Credits

Photographs: Mohd. Ashraf, IAS, and his team at J&K Tourism, led by Amar Singh, obtained colour slides from the department's archives. These pictures had been taken by some of India's best-known professional photographers, on behalf of the department. Had their names been available, I would have gladly mentioned them.

Neelam Mohata is the photographer of all the brilliant panoramic photographs used in the book.

Shishu Pal photographed the two paintings that appear on the cover of this book. Both are by Suman Gupta and are part of the Raj Bhawan collection. (I had, in the mid-1990s, the honour of commissioning these paintings on behalf of His Excellency Gen. K.V. Krishna Rao, the then Governor of Jammû and Kashmîr, whose Principal Secretary I then was.)

Mr. Lobzâng Thinles, Deputy Director, Tourism Department, shot the photographs of Chumâthâñg. Tsomo Riri and Karzok

The mugshot of me on the inside cover, which makes me look presentable, is by Afshan Jeelani.

Maps: Tufail Ahmed Bhat and his colleagues at Autocadd Centre, Jawahar Nagar, Srînagar, prepared some of the maps that have been used in this book.

Cover notes: The opening lines are by Renuka Narayanan.

Acknowledgements

My deepest debt of gratitude for help with this book is to Sonam Dorjay, Kâchu Sikander Khân 'Sikander' and Kâchu Asfandyâr Khân, KAS (Kashmîr Administrative Service).

Kâchu Sikander Khân 'Sikander' presented me with a copy of his memoirs, as well as his encyclopædic Urdu-language book, *Qadeem Ladâkh: Târîkh o Tamaddan*. The Kachu is the most thorough chronicler, and greatest votary of the composite culture of Ladâkh—in an age when barriers are being erected between the various communities.[1] I have tried to carry the Kachu's mission forward by taking some of his insights to English-speaking people.

His worthy son, Asfandyâr, helped me at every stage, including after his transfer from Kargil, of the administration of which district he had been the very able head.

If, despite being a Delhiite, I have to some small extent acquired a Ladâkhi perspective when it comes to matters concerning the culture of the region, it is in part because of countless conversations with Sonam Dorjay, the knowledgeable and resourceful Deputy Director, Tourism.

Mr. C. Phonsog, IAS (Indian Administrative Service), very kindly went through the first draft of this book and suggested some changes and additions. Dr. Motup Dorjé and Spalzes Angmo, too, scanned every word of that draft and corrected me wherever I had gone wrong.

I am grateful, for their inputs, to Shaleen Kabra, IAS, and Dr. Muhammad Deen, IAS (the two had, at different times, been the District Development Commissioners of Kargil), Brig. RE Williams, Mona Bhan (who is working on a doctoral thesis for Rutgers) and SDS Jamwal of the Indian Police Service. Thanks to conversations with them I have been able to pepper this book with little factoids and insights that have never been published before.

Feroz Ahmed, IAS, helped me update the census figures.

Sonam Dolma, Senior.Asstt., enabled me to polish up my Ladâkhi vocabulary.

After the main body of the book had gone to the printers, my friend and colleague Rup Lal Bharati of the Indian Forest Service referred me to Jigmet Takpa, the brilliant Director, Wildlife, Ladâkh. Jigmet had maintained some personal notes about the flora of Ladâkh, which he gave me. Suddenly the chapter about Flora doubled in length and also acquired greater depth.

1. There are some equally great visionaries in Baltistân—people like Kazmi and Hasnain—whom I have never met but about whose works I keep reading on the internet. In the chapter about the history of Balâwaristân I have referred to their touching efforts to deepen the bonds of love between the Buddhists and Muslims of the Balâwaristân-Ladâkh-Western Tibet belt.

Acknowledgements of a different kind

Because of my long association with Ladâkh, first as the head of the Zâñskâr administration and, later, as the Tourism Commissioner of the state and the Commissioner/ Secretary (Ladâkh Affairs), my publishers and I have at several places in this book referred to 'my' work and 'my' contributions.

But 'my' work was not mine alone. So many other people, both senior and junior to me, helped me make my dreams for Ladâkh come true. I would be failing my duty if I did not acknowledge their contributions.

The opening up of restricted areas

The opening up of seven thitherto 'prohibited' parts of Ladâkh to tourists is generally credited to me: (These areas include much of Nubrâ, Nyomâ, Dâ-Hânu and the great lakes-Tsomo Riri and Pangong.) However, my efforts would have come to nought had the then junior Home Minister of India, Mr. Rajesh Pilot, not brushed aside the objections of people who hadn't the foggiest idea about these areas.

The Indian Army, on the other hand, knows the area most thoroughly. I am grateful to the then Army Commander and Corps Commander for convincing the ignorant that tourists in these seven areas were not a security risk.

We were proved right as far as national security was concerned. However, the impact of tourism on the wildlife and ecology of the region is another matter altogether.

The Ladâkh Festival

The Ladâkh Festival was born in September 1993, under rather grim circumstances.

A militant organisation (not in Ladâkh) threatened to kill every employee of the Tourism Department who helped organise the festival. A threat to this effect was published on the front page of one of the largest selling dailies (of a place well away from Ladâkh).

I was appointed the Tourism Commissioner (and Secretary) of Jammu and Kashmîr in 1992. At the time Leh's tourism industry was doing badly. That of Kargil had been almost wiped out.

I spent several months studying Ladâkh's potential for tourism as well as how much of it had actually been realised. The highest number of tourists to have visited Ladâkh in a year was just under twenty-five thousand. That was in 1989. Things got disturbed in neigbouring Kashmîr later that year. The number of tourists visiting Ladâkh immediately dropped by a third, that's right, by around 33%. It stayed that way for the next several years. This told us that a third of those who were likely to visit Leh (and ninety per cent of those planning to go to Kargil) would actually make that trip only if they could do Kashmîr as well.

So, a third of the hotel beds in Leh (and more than ninety per cent in Kargil) were lying vacant. In any case, twenty-four thousand plus tourists a year is an extremely small figure. The holy shrine of Srî Mâtâ Vaishno Devî jî (in Jammu) attracts that many pilgrim tourists in a single day.[2] No, I did not want to crowd Ladâkh with tourists. I only wanted to spread their visits evenly throughout the year, so that we never had an 'off-season,' so that we never had empty hotel beds.

But Ladâkh has an extremely limited tourist season. (Actually that should have been 'had'-in the past tense.) Till then Ladâkh's tourist season began in late June and started tapering off around the 22nd August.

Clearly something had to be done.

At the time the overwhelming majority of tourists in Ladâkh were international, had received a good education, were youthful, physically fit and wanted to go boldly where few had ever been before. In a word, people like I. If we wanted to fill those empty hotel beds we also needed to attract Indians with a similar background. PLU. People like us.[3]

And that is why the Ladâkh Festival was created. We had to convince people that there were no terrorists in Ladâkh. We had to extend the 'tourist season' into September. And we had to persuade well-heeled Indians[4] to come to Ladâkh.

I firmly believe that it is not the job of a Tourism Department to organise concerts (in Jammu and Kashmîr it is the Cultural Academy which does such things) or polo matches (that's the turf of the Sports Department).[5] District administrations (in Leh and elsewhere in Jammu

2. True, these pilgrims don't spend as much. Nor do they stay on as long.
3. That phrase is not mine own. It is from a Booker Prize-winning novel. However, shouldn't that, instead, have been PLW? People Like We.
4. Why this emphasis on Indian tourists? Firstly, a state government rarely has the means to launch an international campaign. At least in 1993, we did not. Only the national government did. Besides, even without the image problem that Ladâkh then had-it was so unfairly being associated with terrorism by half a dozen foreign governments and one influential guidebook-even at the best of times the international market had been growing extremely slowly. For any dramatic increases we had to look within India.
5. Those who know me as the author of every single extant Tourism Festival in Jammu and Kashmîr (and some extinct ones, too) -except the Navarâtra Festival-might think that this contradicts my actual administrative practice. It doesn't. And I continue to hold this view.

and Kashmîr) sporadically host district-level festivals that showcase the local culture whenever the head of the district has a talent for such things. When he gets posted out, the festival dies a natural death.

And yet I felt that in the circumstances the most cost effective option would be to organise a festival in Ladâkh. Adverstising guru, David Ogilvy, had little faith in the effectiveness of paid advertisements. He believed that 'one inch of [column space by way of] editorial endorsement' was more potent than several pages of paid advertisements.

We could easily have bought space in the press and on television. However, mere advertisements would have convinced no one that Ladâkh was absolutely free of militancy. I decided to put Ogilvy's theory into practice (and have since developed it into a hugely successful commercial formula).

September, into which month we wanted to extend the 'season,' was very far away. So, I began my experiment with the Mansar Festival (Jammu) in March 1993. That Festival did not go on to become a household name like the Ladâkh Festival later did, but the publicity that we generated (measured in column inches and television minutes) was worth perhaps five or six times what we had spent. (And I spend incredibly little money on my festivals. That's another trademark of mine.) In May 1993, I repeated the formula at Jammu's Mattalai. Once again the publicity that we received was well worth the expenditure, even though in both cases only some of the press and television crews that we had invited actually accepted our invitation.

Buoyed by these moderate successes, I decided to go in for the big one, the Ladâkh Festival. (I feel awkward using the first person singular while writing about this particular project. It isn't normally my style to do so, but a plural is just not possible.) At least one major hotel owner in Leh was not at all keen to attract Indian tourists. But that was a very minor hiccup.

The real problem arose when a non-Ladâkhi newspaper front-paged the terrorist threat to the employees of the department. Meanwhile, every single major newspaper, magazine and TV station in English, Gujarati, Bengali and Hiñdi agreed to cover the festival. We needed staff to cope with this massive media contingent, which had to be looked after in a region that imported all its requirements of consumer goods and foodstuffs from the rest of the country.

To cope with the situation I requested Mr. Manwati, our Deputy Director in Bombay-a model of thoroughness and efficiency-to fly in to Srînagar. We also appealed to some senior staff from Jammu to help out, even though Ladâkh was outside their jurisdiction. I will always remain grateful to them for helping out the dynamic local staff, who were extremely undermanned.

One of the mediapersons who came for the festival was a superstar of the world journalism. He had been to college with me. He noticed how I was flitting in and out of the three media coaches, trying to make our guests from the media comfortable. He sarcastically quipped, 'Why doesn't Parvéz act like the head of the state's tourism department? Why is he behaving like a bus conductor-cum-tourist guide?'

If only he had the sagacity to understand why.

In the event we spent a mere six or seven lakh (six or seven hundred thousand) rupees on the festival itself, and an equal amount on our guests. The festival earned us column space and television time worth more than two crore (twenty million) rupees in the first three months alone. (Many of our guests from the media continued to write about Ladâkh for several years thereafter.[6]) I want to use this occasion to thank all those fabulous mediapersons. I am tempted to single out some publications for having given us publicity of a kind that we couldn't even

6. One of my most strongly held theories about tourism is that people living in distant lands don't suddenly decide, "Hey, there's this great article/ advertisement/ TV feature about Ladâkh. Therefore, let's go to Ladâkh for a vacation next week/ month [or even next year].'

I was five or six when I fell in love with Egypt, Greece and Switzerland-and, at age ten, with Guatemala. I would have been perfectly happy if these were the only countries that I ever vacationed in (apart from going to Oxbridge for an education, that is).

Therefore, if a national tourism authority wants to have international tourists craving for their country they should plan long—really long. Target five to ten-year olds, and hope for results twenty years later. That is what I have done for Ladâkh. I have planted countless stories on television (about thirty on Doordarshan's 'Surubhi' alone; and more on the travel shows of privately owned satellite channels). The results are beginning to show a decade later, and should continue for quite a while. In fact, after a while the government can stop spending money on publicity. If the place is any good, private film crews will start coming on their own, as has happened in Ladâkh.

The glossy magazines *Society* and *Savvy* have a feature that is divided into two columns. One column is labelled 'What's hot' (or 'What's in') and the other is called 'What's not' (or 'What's out'). In August or September 1993, these magazines gave us a one word mention (that's right, exactly one word). They listed 'Ladâkh' as the hot new destination. Several tourists told us that they decided to go to Leh because of that one word endorsement.

I wish I could do similar things for the tourism industry of Gilgit-Baltistân-Hunzâ-Chitrâl and the other occupied areas. This book is a humble step in that direction.

have dreamt of getting. However, that would be impolitic. So, I will restrict myself to thanking the wonderful contingent from Mumbai.

India Today gave us nine pages spread over three issues. *The Illustrated Weekly of India* (which folded up soon after it wrote some extremely kind things about me) covered Ladâkh (and Kashmîr) in as many pages, but of a much bigger size. Thank you once again.

The festival succeeded in all its objectives, and achieved a lot more as well, especially a renewed pride in the culture of the land. The tourist season now starts tapering off when the Festival ends, that is, around the 10th September. A twenty-day prolongation of the season means so much to our economy.

Before the festival, Filmistân[7] had visited Ladâkh just once—to shoot a war film. The floodgates opened after the Festival. We have since lost count of the number of Indian feature films, rock videos, documentaries and advertising films that have been shot in Ladâkh. Not to mention shoots for the print media. And the very hotel owners who had been too superior to receive Indian guests are the biggest beneficiaries.

Within two years, the Ladâkh Festival became a household name in India—and in the travel trade of the target countries. I knew that the Festival had arrived when I saw Filmistân superstar Shah Rukh Khân wandering about Leh town in the Hiñdî-Tamil blockbuster *Dil Se* (1998). He was asking everyone he encountered, 'Where is the Ladâkh Festival [being held]?'

The makers of that film did not feel the need to add a parenthesis to that, to explain what this Festival was. They assumed that everyone knew.

Sindhu Darshan

The Sindhu Darshan festival is the brainchild of Mr. L. K. Advani, who was the Deputy Prime Minister of India at the time (1999-2004). He very kindly allowed the state Tourism Department to have a major role in the organisation of the festival from its third year onwards.

Having succeeded in extending the tourist season into autumn, I requested the Government of India to allow me to take advantage of the Sindhu Darshan festival to advance the tourist season by a few weeks.

Ideally the Ladâkh Festival should start around the 22nd August every year, when the 'season' begins to wane. And yet I took the risk of giving it the dates 1-10 September because those dates are easy to remember. For the same reason I suggested that the Sindhu Darshan festival should commence on the 1st of June every year. I am grateful that the Government of India accepted my suggestion.

7. Better known by that slavish term 'Bollywood.'

Not all passes in Ladâkh open by the 1st June. Therefore, it hasn't been as easy to bring the season forward ('prepone' being the Indian word for it) by as many as three weeks. All the same, we benefit enormously from the Sindhu Darshan festival. It generates crores of rupees worth of publicity for Ladâkh in the first fortnight of June, and thus heralds the season. It reminds would be travellers to start making their reservations. And it ensures that almost all available hotel beds in Leh are filled up for the duration of the festival.

The Baudh Mahotsav

Sonam Dorjay and I then decided to use the same formula to promote Nubrâ through the Baudh Mahotsav ('the Great Festival of Lord Buddha'), also sponsored by the Government of India. This time our success was somewhat limited because Sonam had, by then, been transferred from Ladâkh (on promotion) and I wasn't able to nurse the Mahotsav beyond the first year.

The Kargil Festival

We started a festival in Kargil in 1993, as a part of the overall festival of Ladâkh. There was resistance in the town. Therefore, unlike the Ladâkh Festival, this one doesn't have a single focal point. It has been a big hit at Mulbek and Bodh Kharboo, as well as in all-Muslim areas like Trespon, Sâñkoo and Pânikhar.

These are dispersed villages. For that reason, the Kargil Festival is peripatetic. The idea to delink it from the Ladâkh Festival and hold it in June, as a 'season heralder,' was born during a discussion with Shaleen Kabra and some elders from Kargil.

Between us we came to the conclusion that Leh was now a byword in the world of international tourism. It did not need to be 'sold' as a destination any more. Its promotional needs were very different. Kargil needed to remind the world of its existence every year. For that reason the Kargil festival was carved out of the Ladâkh Festival and is now being held in June. (It commences on a nice round date-the 15th or 25th June-by when the passes would have opened.) In any case, any publicity generated for Kargil benefits Leh as well, because one has to pass through Leh (or Kashmîr) to reach Kargil.

Wangchuk Chhenmo: The Amarnath of Ladâkh

The idea to promote the holy Wangchuk Chhenmo cave as the Amarnath of Ladâkh (see the chapter on 'Trekking in Ladâkh') was born during a discussion with Mr. Tsetan Namgyal, the then junior Tourism Minister of Jammu and Kashmîr.

This is perhaps the first book to have made an effort to project the cave, which is on one of the Zâñskâr-Leh trekking routes, as a Hiñdu-Buddhist pilgrimage. With a couple of years of careful 'nursing,' the holy Wangchuk Chhenmo cave is bound to become a household name in India. It has the potential to attract at least seventy-five thousand pilgrims a year—in the first place.

The Gigantic Maitreya of Kartsé Khar

I did not discover this seven-metre tall, seventh-century Chambâ/ Maitreya idol. The people of the Suru Valley have always known about it. I am grateful to the elders of Sankoo and Trespon for having told me of its existence.

I was merely the first to promote this sculpture. I took the Indian and international media to Kartsé Khar, to show them 'India's own Bâmiyân,' within weeks of the Taliban's blasting of similar sculptures in Afghânistân.

There is a large icon of Lord Buddha, carved, almost impossibly, into the middle of a sheer mountain near Lâmâ Yûrû. It can be seen from the Srînagar-Leh Highway. Thousands of people pass it every day. Therefore, only a very foolish 21st century man will claim to have 'discovered' it. However, for some reason none of the many books that I have read about Ladâkh mention it.

I believe that I am the first to notice a pattern a 7th century A.D. trend, that runs through this amazing icon and that at Kargah/Naupura (Gilgit, Occupied Kashmîr). I am grateful to Tsering Angmo (Station Director, All India Radio, Leh) for allowing me to test my theory on her—and for sharing my excitement about the 'discovery'.

The war sites

I believe that the negative publicity that Kashmîr and Kargil have received can be turned into a good thing. Mr. M. Ashraf, the then Director General, Tourism, and I (as the Commissioner and Secretary) patiently waited for the Kargil war of 1999, to come to an end. The very next day we launched a campaign to attract tourists to Kargil, and its celebrated war sites. I believe that the sight of people flocking to the war sites gives the brave soldiers of the Indian Army the feeling that their sacrifices are appreciated by the nation. We met with immediate success and received bookings from places as far away as Vijaywada (in Andhra Pradesh, South India).

Posters

You will find two kinds of posters about Ladâkh (and Kashmîr and Jammu) when you visit the state. If the name of the site has been mentioned in small letters above the word 'Ladâkh' (or 'Kashmîr' or 'Jammu'), and if there is a matter-of-fact, prosaic, one-line explanation below, then the copy and design of the poster are mine. All such photographs were collected by Mr. M. Ashraf. The two of us selected the ones to be used as posters.

At college I had done two prize-winning hoardings for India's biggest advertising agency, Hindustan Thompson Associates (an affiliate of J. Walter Thompson). That gave me the confidence to design all the posters for Jammu & Kashmîr Tourism that have been printed after 1990, eliminating ad agency fees.

Failed dreams

Not all dreams succeed. I wanted to create an artificial lake at Sânkoo (Kargil). For three years running I sanctioned funds for the purpose, but the engineers felt that water would not hold in the lake. I deferred to their superior knowledge.

For Trespon (also in Kargil) I designed a tower—at the request of the local people. This was to have been a statement, a tourist landmark with no function. It cost very little. Hassan (of the Tourism Department) and I spent several days on the Internet and came to the conclusion that an Afghan-style tower suited the area best. And for three consecutive years I sanctioned generous funds. (Mrs. Asha Murthy, Joint Secretary, Tourism, helped generously.) I am very unhappy that the field staff (which did not report to me) did not spend the funds.

Some dreams were realised only in part.

It has been my cherished goal to bring scholars and artistes from all Himâlayan Mahâyân communities together on one platform, at least once a year, somewhere in Ladâkh. In addition to Leh, Kargil and Pâdar in Jammu & Kashmîr, these communities live in the Indian states of Himâchal Pradésh (Lahaul Spiti and Dharamshâlâ), Sikkim, Arunâchal Pradésh and West Bengal (mainly Darjeeling). They also live in Bhutân and Nepal, as well as Karnâtaka (South India). The idea of getting them together is not merely idealistic. I have seen nations vy with each other to get multilateral bodies to set up their headequarters (or host the Olympics or Commonwealth or Asian games) in their country. I want Ladâkh to similarly become the unofficial headquarters of the various pan-Himâlayan Mahâyân peoples.

To this end I sent out invitations to the governments of the various countries and states involved (and to the Tibetan government in exile) for the Ladâkh Festival 2000 and the Baudh Mahotsav 2001 and even offered to pay the fare of their delegations. Each time, eighty per cent of the governments sent delegations. Therefore, this idea still needs nurturing. I am confident that it has a great future. Indeed, its time has come. It is inevitable.

Similarly, I have given friends working in NGOs a blueprint for an annual literary and cultural get together of all the people of the Kârâkorams i.e. the people of the regions that this book is about. It is, for instance, unfair that the Baltis and Dards of Kargil and Gilgit-Baltistân never get to meet each other. This idea of mine might never materialise because most of these wonderful people live in the parts occupied by Pâkistân. Perhaps they will have to meet in a third country.

An endorsement by `Time'

In my keenness to promote the first Ladakh Festival within India and abroad. I visited several newspaper offices in Delhi in 1993. (That was how every single major newspaper, magazine and TV channel covered it.) At the Delhi bureau of *Time* magazine I was referred to a very handsome young journalist, Meenakshi Ganguly. In most parts of India parents give their children matching names. So, I hazarded a guess. Was she my friend Eenakshi's sister, I asked. She was. That broke the ice. However, *Time* could not write about the Festival, she explained. Her arguments were extremely reasonable, but I was naturally, disappointed. So, Meenakshi offered to do one better. She got *Time* to endorse Ladakh as a destination. This was a huge coup for us, because till then no regional tourism authority in India had ever received such a positive approval from *Time.* It was Meenakshi who made this possible.

Above all...

Mr. Thupstan Chewang, MP, very kindly helped identify monuments from some photo captions. Thanks to Mr. Nawang Tsering, Cultural Officer, Leh, we were able to get Mr. Ghulam Mustafa's beautiful water colours.

Glossary

chhang: Barley beer made and drunk by people in Leh, Zâñskâr, Padar and parts of Lahul Spiti (HP). In other Himalayan regions chhang is brewed from rice.

chomo: Buddhist nun.

crore: Ten million. See also 'lakh' below. Both are Hiñdî words. The Indian practice is to give Indian figures in lakhs and crores, and international ones (especially when it comes to money) in millions and billions. Indians talk of so many crore rupees but $xxx,xxx million. For that reason Indians put commas differently between the zeroes. Thus, one crore rupees are expressed in figures as Rs.1,00,00,000. Ten million pounds sterling on the other hand are £10,000,000. Same number of zeroes, but the commas are differently placed.

district: India is divided into around thirty states. Each state is divided into districts. In the year 2004, Jammu and Kashmîr has 14 districts. Ladâkh now consists of two districts, Leh and Kargil. Till 1979, all of Ladâkh was just one district. The areas occupied by Pâkistân were part of either the old Ladâkh district or of Gilgit district.

gompâ: Buddhist monastery.

HP: Himâchal Pradésh, the mountainous state that neighbours the Jammû and Ladâkh regions to the east and south.

J&K: Jammû and Kashmîr; the name of the state that Kashmîr is a part of.

jeepable road: A track on which only rugged sports utility vehicles can ply.

jû-lé: Good morning, good evening, hello, goodbye. An all-encompassing greeting.

khar (both suffix and prefix): Fort.

KKH: The Kârâkoram Highway.

lâ: A mountain pass.

lakh: A hundred thousand.

lâmâ: Buddhist monk.

lé: A polite sound. Refined people say lé at the end of every sentence.

LoC: Line of Control. This is the 'line' (on maps) that separates the areas illegally occupied by Pâkistân from those actually administered by India. It is not an 'international border' (IB) because neither side accepts it as one. It serves the same purpose as a border but lacks the legal status of one. The international community, however, treats it as the border between India and Pâkistân. When Pâkistân forces crossed the LoC in 1999, the G-8 nations condemned the action and spoke of the 'inviolability' of the LoC.

Pâkistân has illegally occupied 35.15% of the state of Jammû and Kashmîr. India actually administers 45.62% of the state. (China is in the illegal occupation of the rest.)

motorable road: 'Motorable' means that in theory a car (or bus) can drive on that road. In practice most 'motorable' roads are only 'jeepable.' A 'motorable stretch' (or motorable distance) is one on which you can travel in a vehicle. You don't have to walk on that stretch, except for the exercise.

Names like Leh and Kargil: Leh is the name of a town, as well as of the district in which it is located. The same is true of Kargil. However, there is no town or village called Zâñskâr (the HQ is called Padum), Nubra (Deskit is the main village), Baltistân (Skardu is the HQ) or Hunzâ (Baltit/ Karîmâbâd is the HQ).

pass(es)/ mountain passes: What is a pass? A pass, more precisely a mountain pass, is a gap between two mountains. It the highest point on a segment of a mountain road. There might be more than one passes on a road, and the next pass might be higher still.

There always are mountains on the right and left of a pass. These mountains are much higher than the pass. The job of a pass is to help you cross from the place behind you to the place in front, without having to climb all the way to the top of the mountains on the sides. A pass is called a galli in Urdu/ Kashmîri, a galla in Dogri and la in Ladâkhi.

pbuh: Peace be upon him. This is an expression that is written (or spoken) after the name of Prophet Muhammad, whenever the name is written (or spoken).

perâk: Long female headdress made of leather and studded with precious stones.

POK (Pâkistân Occupied Kashmîr): These are areas of Jammu & Kashmîr that are under Pâkistân's illegal occupation. Pâkistân has divided these areas into three: i) AJK (Azad Jammu & Kashmîr): This is a narrow strip that begins in Jammu district and goes through Poonch district to Muzaffarabad. ii) The Northern Areas ('Shumâli Ilâqâjât'): This mostly consists of the occupied areas of Ladâkh. iii) The Shaksgâm area of present day Leh district that Pâkistân has carved out of the state and gifted to China. Because this particular segment is now with China, it (along with Aksai Chin) is referred to as COK (China Occupied Kashmîr).

roadhead: A 'roadhead' is the last point to which you can drive up in a vehicle. There are no 'motorable' or 'jeepable' roads beyond this point. (On the return trek, this is the point where the motorable road begins.)

trekker: A trekker is someone who treks.

tso: Lake

UP: Uttar Pradesh (a central Indian state; India's largest).

List of maps

Contents

History

Place of Tourist Interest

Gilgit-Baltistan-Hunza-Chitral-Aksai Chin-Shimshal: The paradise across the line of control

Religion

Culture

People

Wildlife and Nature

Trekking, Mountain climbing, River Rafting

Everything *(almost)*

Leh, Zanskar, Suru Valley

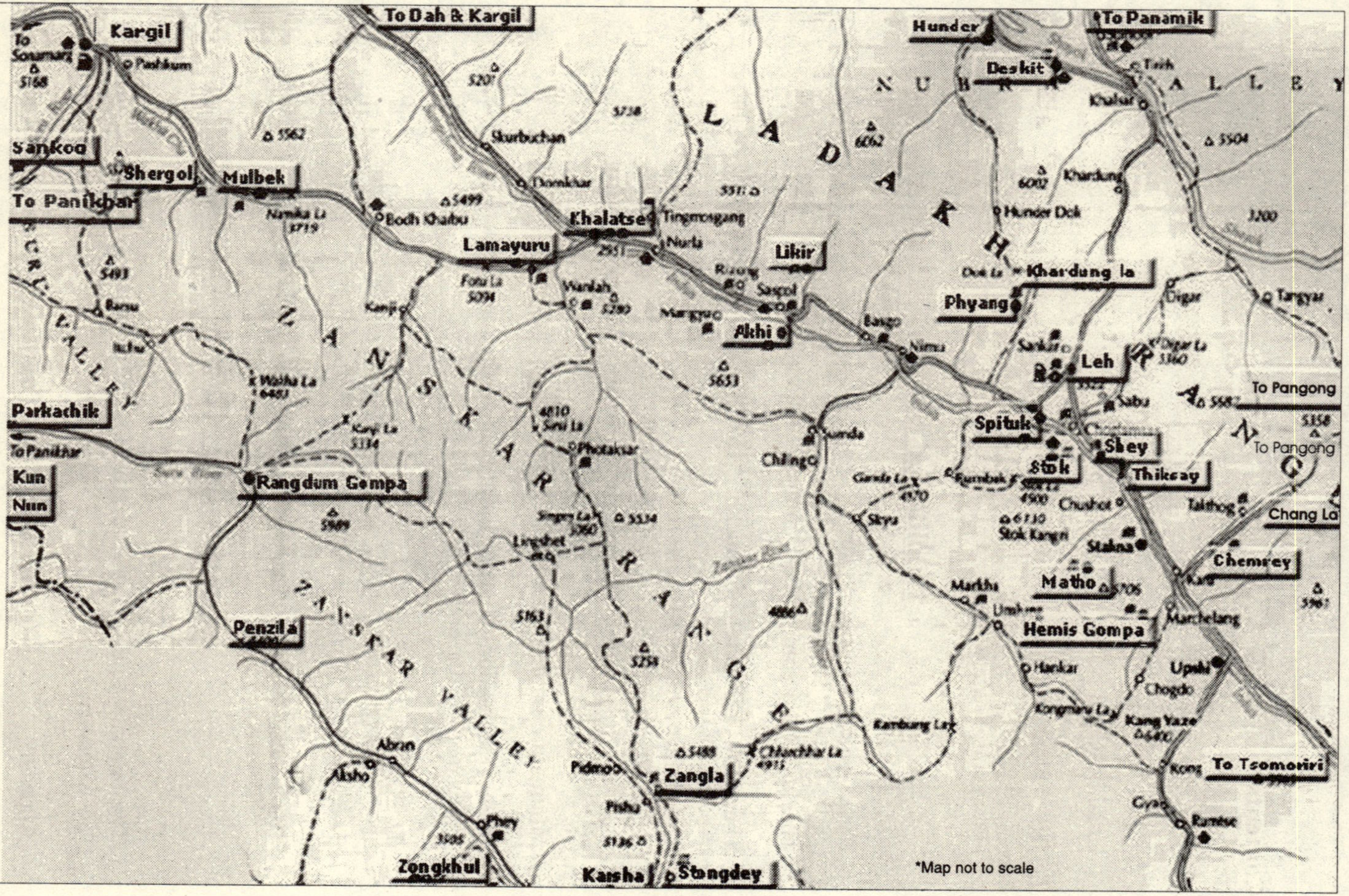

*Map not to scale

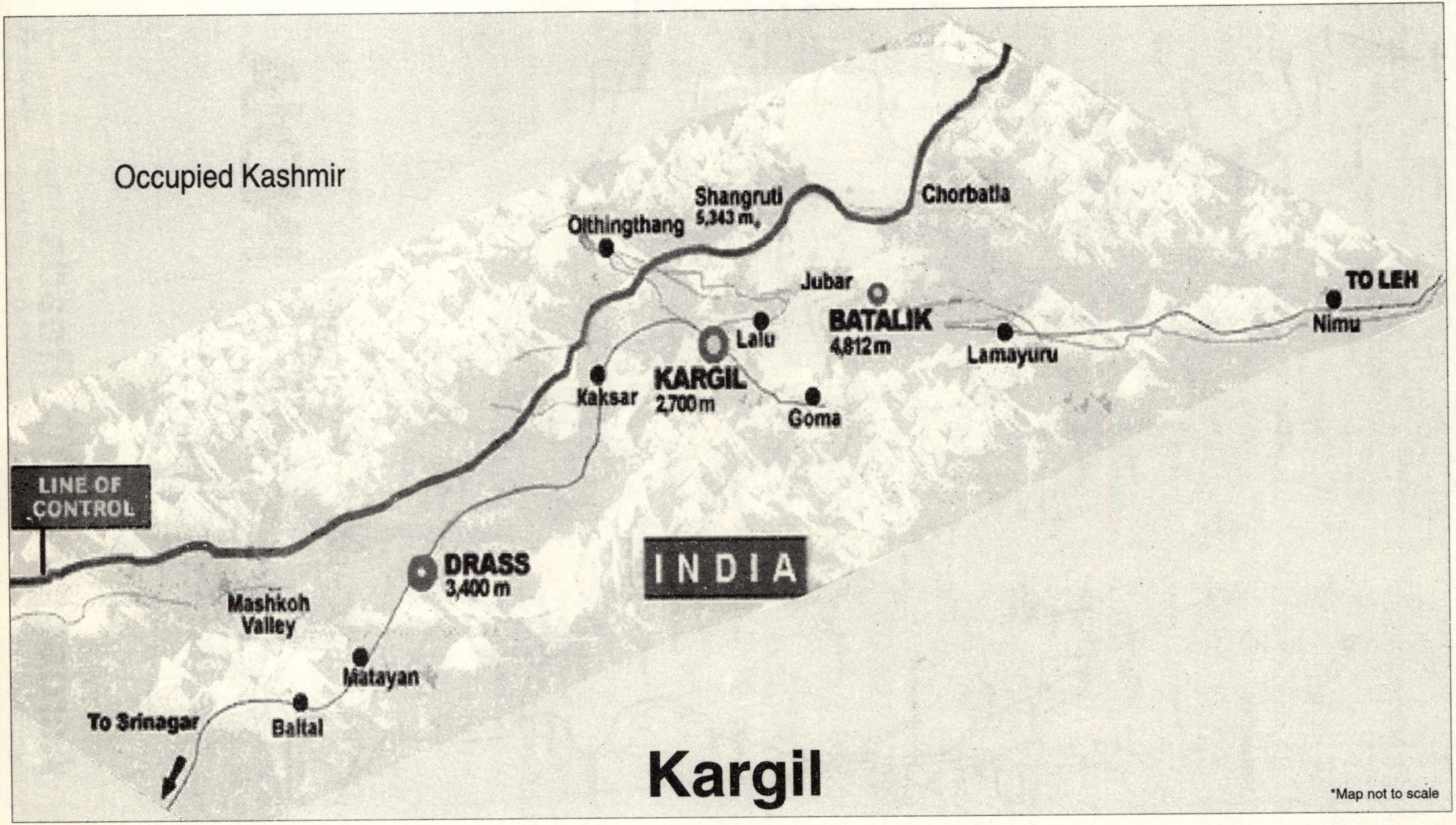
Occupied Kashmir
Olthingthang
Shangruti
5,343 m.
Chorbatla
Jubar
BATALIK
4,812 m
Lalu
KARGIL
2,700 m
Goma
Kaksar
Lamayuru
TO LEH
Nimu
LINE OF CONTROL
DRASS
3,400 m
INDIA
Mashkoh Valley
Matayan
Baltal
To Srinagar
Kargil
*Map not to scale

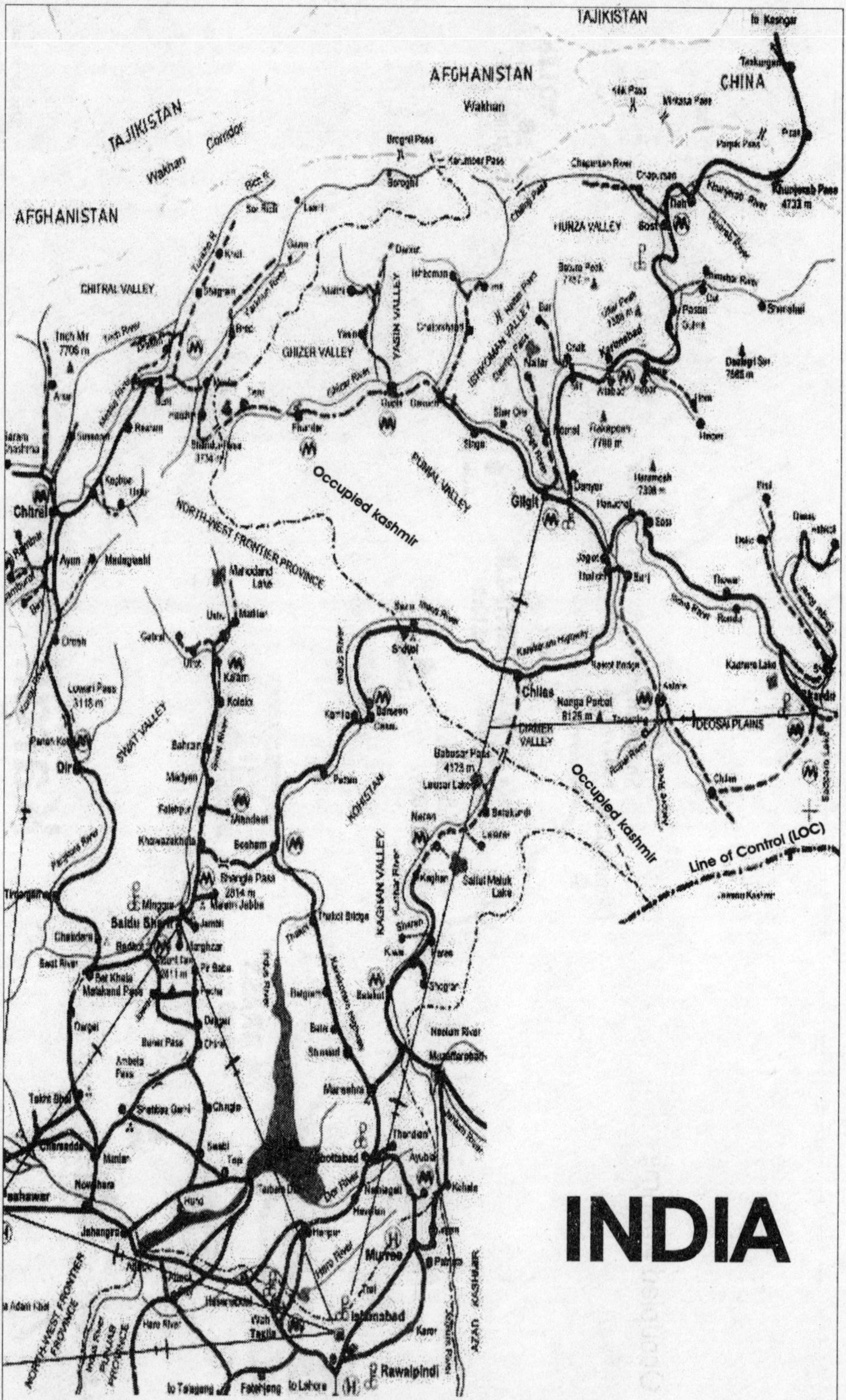

Across the LOC: Roads

*Map not to scale

History

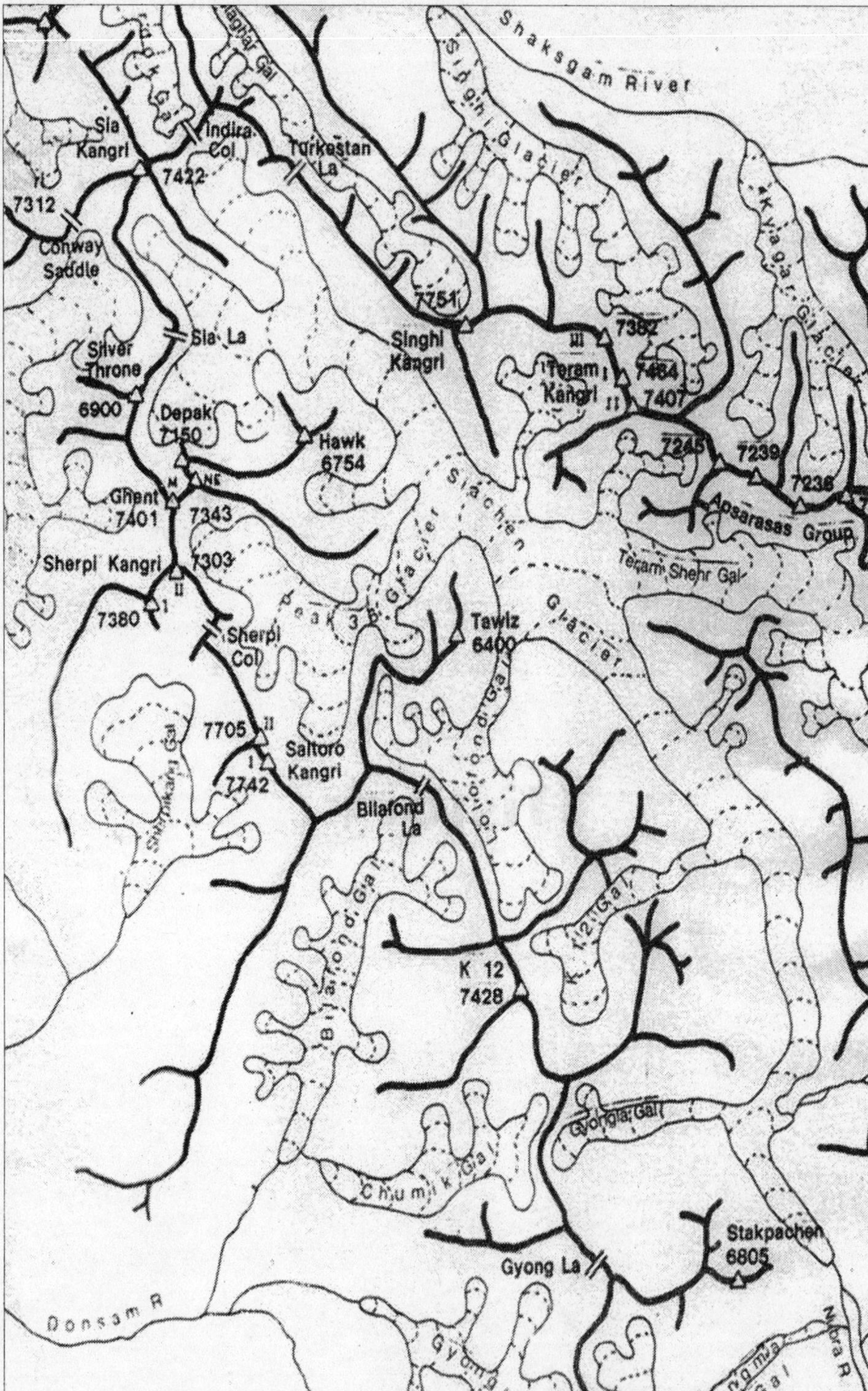

Siachen

*Map not to scale

'A ***Chorten.***' (Painting by Ghulâm Mustafâ of Leh)Chortens (called stûpas in central India) are sometimes dedicated to Sâkyâ Thubbâ or one of the incarnations of the Buddha. There are eight kinds of chortens, one for each stage of the Lord's life. Chortens often contain the ashes of an incarnate monk, king or, rarely, important citizen, in which case they are called *dungtens*

The **Phugtâl** monastery of Zâñskâr is partly inside the cave shown. The eighteenth century Hungarian mystic-scholar Csoma Körös wrote his famous *Zâñskâr Chronicles* here. (Painting by Ghulâm Mustafâ of Leh)

The **Drokpâ** community of Dards migrated to Dâ-Hânu from Gilgit-Dardistân (Pâkistân Occupied Kashmir). Some European 'Aryan Supremacists' believe that as far as bloodlines go, the **Drokpâs** are 'the purest Aryans in the world.'(Both paintings are by Ghulâm Mustafâ of Leh)

'*A Ladâkhi lady wearing a gem-studded* ***pérâk***.' (Painting by Ghulâm Mustafâ of Leh). This head-dress has a base made of leather and passes down from mother to eldest daughter. Each generation tries to add a few jewels to it. Ladâkh's most celebrated pérâks are several hundred years old. A girl called Angmo once told this author, 'The antiquity and class of a pérâk is measured by the grime in the crevices. Only an upstart family will purchase a brand new pérâk from the market.' In case there is no daughter, the pérâk goes out of the family and is often (but not always) donated to a monastery, rather than being given to a daughter in law or cousin. The best pérâks have gems worth several lakh (hundred thousand) rupees

'A Ladâkhi potter': (Painting by Ghulâm Mustafâ of Leh). The Government of India spends more, per capita, on Leh and Kargil than on any other district of India. Tourism adds to this. As a result, the daily wage for labourers has traditionally been three times the all-India average. Since the late 1980s, manual labourers from the poorer parts of India have performed most of the low-end jobs. Barbers, tailors. shoe- and watch-repairers, construction labour for all public (and many private) buildings and, yes, beggars, all come from the plains of central India. There is very little pottery in Ladâkh and hardly any potters

'A group of priests sacrifices an animal': *a rock carving found near* **Warsu** (on the **Dâ-Hânu** road). On the chest of each priest is a shining spot, which represents his spiritual elevation. SDS Jamwal, IPS, writes, 'This is a unique rock carving the like of which has not been reported from anywhere else in the world'

"Demi-god': a rock carving found near **Warsu** (on the **Dâ-Hânu** road). Courtesy: SDS Jamwal, IPS

'Male horses (all right, studs) with massive erections': a rock carving found along the **Sasomâ** route, near River Siachen, in **Nubrâ Valley**. SDS Jamwal writes, 'This is probably the only place in India where horses have been depicted.' Not correct. There are huge, mediæval stone reliefs of horses in Ghora Galli ('the mountain pass of the horses') in Gool-Gulâbgarh, Jammû.

A country bridge on a stream in the **Châñgthâñg** area.
Standing left to right are Bhâvnâ Singh, Kathak dancer
Anâmikâ Singh and Parvéz Dewân

Bhâvnâ, Parvéz and Anâmikâ near an ancient pit linked
to hot-water springs in **Chumathâñg**

Chortens inside **the Thiksey monastery, 20km. south of Leh town**.
This twelve-storeyed monastery, built in the 11th century,
is arguably the world's oldest extant skyscraper

The Namgyâl Tsemo Monastery, Leh town.
A three- storey idol of the Maitreya Chambâ Buddha in a sitting posture

The venue of the Kâl-chakr ceremony of His Holiness the Dalâi Lâmâ.
Nyomâ is 168km. from Leh, in the direction of Hânlé

Two lâmâs (monks) play gigantic woodwind instruments in winter.
The Spituk monastery is 9km. southwest of Leh

Inside the Japan-inspired Shâñti Stûpa (built in A.D. 1985), near Châñgspâ, Leh town

Large sculpture of Lord Buddha at the Thiksey monastery

Monks outside **the Sañkar monastery, 3km. from Leh**

The **Shargol(e) monastery**, 35 km. east of Kargil town, juts out of a brown, granite cliff and appears as if it is suspended in the middle of the mountain

The Likir monastery, **61 km. west of Leh**

A pair of dzos pulling a plough on a Ladâkhi field.
The Zo (or dZo) is what is born when a cow mates with a yâk.
It is male and sterile. The female is
called Zomo or dZomo and is perfectly fecund

Buddhist sculptures, possibly from the eighth century A.D.,
on the National Highway, at **Stekbu (near Drâss)**

Top: **A rope bridge**: The 150m. Rope bridge near Zâñglâ (Zâñskâr) is the longest in Ladâkh and yet one of the easiest and least scary to walk on. That it has a 2" thick steel rope to place toes on helps. *Zampâ* bridges are found in the entire Himâlayan belt, from Hunzâ (occupied Kashmîr) in the west to Arunâchal Pradésh in India's extreme east. The bridge in the picture is almost straight and has a very mild sag. The truly scary ones look like a 'U,' and have a very deep sag

Lake Tsomo Riri, which is one of the highest located wetlands in the world. Parvéz Dewân is on an island within the lake. The Bar-headed Goose and the Brown-headed Gull set up their nests on this island. The rare and endangered Black-necked Crane is the lake's star attraction. The Craig Martin, the Horned Lark, the Red-billed Chough, the Tibetan Snow-finch and several kinds of Wagtail come visiting every summer

A rock formation. There are several rock formations on the Leh-Kargil National Highway. Though created by the winds, and such rain and snow as the region receives, they look like man-made installation art

A **village** on the way to Hemis in the month of May. The fields have been freshly prepared for agriculture

Frescoes at the **Hemis monastery** (*gompâ*)

Lake Pangong: which is 144 kilometres (90 miles) long.
The misty mountains at the centre of the photograph lead the lake first to the areas illegally occupied by China and then to Tibet, where the eastern banks of the lake are

Châñgspâ village, which is on the outskirts of Leh town
(in the neighbourhood where some upmarket hotels are). The greenery is all man-made

Fresh snow on mountains near the Châñg La pass

The Hemis monastery's galleries: as seen from the courtyard

The 7th century A.D.**Buddha of Naupur, at the mouth of the Kargah Nallah, Gilgit**. The most awesome thing about this 10' (3m.) tall sculpture in relief (and its equally amazing counterpart on the National Highway to Leh) is the mystery of how it was crafted on that sheer cliff. It is enclosed within a niche that has an arch at the top (much like an Islâmic mehrab). The 'Kargah Buddha' was sculpted in the era of Srî Pramod-vajr. The Buddhist monastery and stupa at the bottom of the cliff are now in ruins. The now-famous Gilgit Manuscripts were discovered in a cave here in A.D. 1934

A mosque in **Hunzâ**. Most Hunzâkuts are Muslims who belong to the Ismâili sect. They are locally known as Mughlî Shiâs (the Mughal Shiites)

Fresh snow at **Aksai Chin**

Shaksgam: A camel caravan near the bed of the river. The Silk Route used to pass through Shaksgam. Trade caravans are a living tradition to this day

The Shimshal valley.A wood-and-stone culvert is being built on a country road

Heap of slate stones, **Shimshal**

Shimshal Valley

An island within **Lake Tsomo Riri.**
Parvéz Dewân, standing on a marsh.

Lake Saif ul Muluk

Flowering trees in **Hunzâ.** The valley has a haunting mien. The wind that wafts through the poplars smells sweet

Shepherds in **Hunzâ**

Khaplu (above and below) is famous for its stunning Muslim shrines. It won the UNESCO Heritage Award, 2003 for the restoration of the Âstânâ (tomb) of Syed Mîr Muhammad. Syed Muhammad Shâh founded the Khânqâh Sofiâ Nûrbakhshîâ in 1712 A.D. The Chaqchan mosque was built by the Shâh é Hamadân, around 1370

Rakaposhi peak Hunzâ

River Bridge, **Chitrâl**

The **Khunjerab Pass (4,733m.)** links Pasu in occupied Kashmîr with China's Xinjiang province. A chairlift takes passengers across the icy waters of melting glaciers. Few passes in the Himâlayas are as picturesque as this. The endangered Marco Polo sheep (Ovis ammon polii) lives in this area

The 15th century Baltit Fort, **Hunzâ**

The meadows of **Kâghân** Valley are similar to those in Sonamarg (Kashmir)

The Rock Tower (6,257m.), **Hunzâ**. Very tall mountains surround Hunzâ, The Berber range, which rises to 25,000' at places, is to the north of Hunzâ. The Budalas hill (c.15,000') is in the west and the Shimshal range (c.22,000' at places) in the east

K-2 or Mt. Godwin Austen ((8,611 m/28,253') is the world's second highest mountain peak

A village in **Balâwaristân**

The wooded **Kâghân** valley is often called 'the little Kashmîr'

The melting waters of an ice field in **Kâghân**
(as elsewhere in Kashmîr and Ladâkh) form a stream

Polo was invented in Baltistân and is the favourite sport of all of Ladâkh

Khaplu

Shaksgam Valley

The Siachen glacier. At some stage in 1986 or 1987 the Pakistani army walked into an undefended stretch that was at 21,153' above the sea. By deciding to station soldiers there, the Pakistanis made it the world's highest army 'post.' As few as 3% of the Indian and Pakistani soldiers stationed at Siachen have died because of enemy firing. 97% of the soldiers die because of the biting cold, the altitude and the terrain. More than 1,000 kg. of human refuse is deposited in these glacial crevices annually. Because of the extreme cold, there is no bio-degradation. The melting snow washes this waste into the Indus River, which feeds India and Pâkistân. By the year 2050 there will be very little of the glacier left to melt.

The Latok Mountain.The mountain has a number of celebrated peaks. The one and a half mile long Walker Spur of **Latok I** (7,145m.) has been unsuccessfully attempted by many. A barrier of very loose rocks has thwarted them all. A team from the USA went within 45 metres of the peak

Latok II: The French retreated from around 7,000m. Some Germans were the first to scale the 6,250m. **South Pillar**

The **Nañgâ Parbat** ("the naked mountain") At 8,125m. this is the world's ninth highest mountain, and the westernmost peak of the Himâlayas. Called the 'killer mountain' because of what it has done to climbers, it was first scaled by Herman Bohl in 1953

1

A History of Leh

Ladakh—and the writing of its history

The Ladakhis have very precise calendars and Twelve-Year cycles. Their system is called Rabjung. It is similar to the system that the Tibetans and the Chinese follow.

Each year (*lo*) is named after an animal. Each cycle of twelve years is called a *Loskor*. Every decade is divided into five groups of two years each. Each two-year group is named after one of the 'five elements.' (The Ladakhi elements are similar to those of the Hindus: fire-sun, water, wood, iron and wind-air.) However, the Ladakhis think in terms of twelve-year cycles, and not decades. Thus each *Loskor* consists of one decade and one more two-year group.

The Ladakhis do not think in centuries either. They have sixty-year *Lorgans* instead. Each Lorgan consists of five Loskors. The first half of the 21st century corresponds to the 17th cycle of the present Ladakhi era. This era began around the end of the 10th century AD.

It is, therefore, surprising that the various histories of Ladakh are rather short on dates, even centuries. These include histories written by contemporary Tibetans as well as early 20th century Europeans.

Among the oldest available records are inscriptions, attributed to the second century BC, in the Brahmi and Kharoshthi scripts of the Indian plains. Unfortunately, they reveal little of historical interest.

Post-1947 historians have painstakingly tried to figure out which event took place in which century. Janet Rizvi has identified the centuries. The State government's Gazetteer Department has tried to date kings to the nearest quarter century. It has obviously not been easy for them, because entire generations are missing from the traditional histories.

This may please be kept in mind whenever the reader finds no dates given against the events mentioned. And where dates have been mentioned, please assume that they could be askew by a century or even more.

Herodotus' gold digging ants

The oldest available reference to the region is in the works of Herodotus, the Greek historian. He wrote of gold-digging ants that were as big as foxes. These ants would dig deep into the earth and throw up gold in the process. AH Francke examined this belief and published his conclusions in 1907. He discovered that in Khaltse, too, there were legends about such ants. However, in Khaltse they were merely supposed to have been as big as normal ants. (There is some alluvial gold in the rivers of Chang Thâñg and the sands of Shyok. The people of Ladakh used to wash these sands to recover gold from them. However, they gave up when they found that the amount of gold obtained thus was worth less than the effort that they had put in.)

Archæologist B.R.Mani feels that these gold-digging ants were, in fact, 'cat-size rats,' the colour of whose skin was a 'combination of orange and black' and who 'occasionally whistle and live in double mouth holes.' Dr. Mani is obviously referring to marmots. What he is saying is that the Greeks mistook marmots for gold-digging ants. Who knows? Maybe they did.

And maybe they did not.

My own theory is that microbes, which are smaller than even ants, did the digging. Therefore, Herodotus might well have been right. He didn't have a word for microbes, so he called them ants. The theory is based on the work done by Derek Lovley of the University of Massachusetts, Amherst (USA). Dr. Lovley studied metal-eating bacteria for about twenty years before publishing his results in the July 2001 issue of *Applied and Environmental Microbiology*.

These bacteria attack the dissolved ions of metallic elements. They then convert the ions from one electrical state to another. Energy is released during this conversion. The bacteria live on this energy. Which is why they keep converting (or reducing) the ions.

Dr. Lovley placed some bacteria inside a solution of gold chloride. Bacteria normally find compounds of gold toxic. However, Dr. Lovley discovered that the bacteria had separated metallic gold from the rest of the compound.

Therefore, scientists now accept that it is possible that gold deposits have a bacterial origin. Microbes probably go to sources like volcanic springs, locate compounds of gold, extract gold from them and then concentrate the gold into forms that can be mined.

Race and Religion

It is possible that 'Aryan' Dards originally inhabited all of Ladakh. For the first few hundred years they followed Bon Chos (the Bon religion). Later, some Dards of Dâ-Hânu (which is in the lower Indus region of Ladakh) converted to Buddhism, while the majority accepted Islam.

Several rocks with Bon Chos engravings have been discovered near Khaltse and in the Kargil district. The ibex looms large in these carvings.

According to this theory, the Dards were later squeezed in from the east by a Mongoloid people from Tibet.

The animist Buddhism of the Buddhist Dards is distinct from that of other Ladakhi Buddhists. It still bears the imprint of the pre-Buddhist religion called Bon Chos. In their Bono Na festival, held in two out of three years, are seen features not found in other Ladakhi Buddhism.

Muslim Dards live in the Gilgit and Astor regions of Pakistan Occupied Kashmir. The (Muslim) Dards of Drâss speak a dialect of the Dardi language.

From the north and west came Islam, to which almost half the people now subscribe. If we include the parts of Ladakh that are currently under the illegal occupation of Pakistan and China, the Muslims are overwhelmingly in a majority.

An alternative theory: Reeve Heber (1923), for one, feels that Tibetan nomads were the first to come. They were shepherds and followed the old Bon Chos (religion) the demon worship of which was later absorbed by Lâmâism. Since they were nomads, they did not found towns or villages. Thus, though they came first, they were the last to settle.

The Mon people of north India were the next. They probably came here to propagate Buddhism. They are best known for the castles that they constructed. They also developed the ancient irrigation system. The Mons ruled over Stot and Muryul before the Tibetans displaced them. Ruins of their forts still exist at Chemray, Sâkti and rGyâ. (See also 'Migration from the Indian plains' in 'A History of Kargil'.)

The Mons have ever since formed a substantial portion of the population. They are carpenters, masons and musicians. (According to a writer of non-Ladakhi origin, the Mons are smiths and weavers as well. Since at least the 20th century, they have not been smiths, though some might be part-time weavers.)

The Dards were the third group of settlers. They introduced agriculture and polo in Ladakh. They also carved figures on rocks. Francke surmises that there were marriages between the Tibetan nomads and Dard agriculturists. A mixed race was the result.

In any case it is difficult to say when the first Tibetans came to Ladakh to settle. Seasonal migration from Tibet to Ladakh has perhaps always have been there, and continues to this day in areas where Tibet's borders meet India's.

Folklore: tales of warfare

Several Ladakhi folksongs, translated mainly by Francke, speak of wars and armies. The soldiers rode on horses when they went to war. If the songs are to be taken literally then there were separate contingents of men, women and even lâmâs, each of which would ride to war. The Mons, Bhedas and smiths were obviously seen as separate communities or castes. Each clan, gender and professional group had a contingent or regiment of its own. Together they formed a united army.

From Ladakhi folklore we also learn that the army of, say, Togmaching, would, in full armour, turn up at Khaltse to steal the harvest. A few days later, Francke tells us, the young men of Khaltse would raid Togmaching 'to pay [its] people back in their own coin'.

Early Chinese references

The oldest available historical references to Ladakh are in the histories of its Central Asian neighbours.

A state government publication says that 'the travel accounts of Fa-Hian (400 AD) and Hieun Tsang (640 AD) [mention that Ladakh had] close relations with the northern kingdoms of India'.

The Chinese scholar Hui Ch'ao journeyed through Central Asia around AD 727. We know that at least by then the 'three kingdoms' of Ladakh were 'under the suzerainty of the Tibetans.' We also learn from Hui that the people of these kingdoms were of Hu stock, that they were 'believers' (in Buddhism) and that at that stage Buddhism was 'unknown' in Tibet. (The Hu people were probably the Dards and almost certainly were 'Aryans' of the Indo-Iranian variety.)

Buddhism reaches Ladakh and Tibet, separately

It is difficult to accept that Buddhism was 'unknown' in Tibet in AD 727. Only a few decades before, King Srong-tsan Gam-po, who unified Tibet, had accepted it as the state religion. Hui Ch'ao might have been more accurate, though, when he wrote that 'there [were] no monasteries at all' in Tibet.

Even by the ninth century Buddhism was not the dominant religion in Tibet. The ancient Bon religion was still quite popular. Its believers were in political conflict- at times bloody- with the Buddhists.

It first comes from Kashmir

What Hui Ch'ao's account indicates is that Buddhism had reached Ladakh several centuries before Indian saints took it to Tibet. (This taking of Buddhism to Tibet is known as the 'first spreading' of Buddhism in Tibet. In AD 747 the northern Indian Buddhist monk and scholar Padma Sambhav went to Tibet. There he set up the first order of *lâmâs,* or monks. It was after this that Buddhism spread rapidly in Tibet.)

We also have (unrelated) evidence that in ancient times Kashmir used to be a flourishing centre of Buddhism. We further know that the eleventh or twelfth century murals on the walls of the Alchi monastery are the creations of Kashmiri painters. (These murals alone in all of Ladakh are purely Indian, with no Tibetan influence.)

Pre-Tibetan Buddhist rock engravings can be seen near Drâss and in Zâñskâr. At Mulbek, next to the highway, and in Kartse Khar are sculptures of the Bodhi-Sattva Maitreya (c. eighth century). These carvings are in much deeper relief than those of the post-Tibetan period.

So when did Buddhism reach Ladakh? Possibly in the first century after Christ, and certainly by the second. Equally certainly it came through Kashmir, even though a millennium later Tibetan Buddhism would overwhelm the indigenous variety.

Lalitaditya

Lalitaditya (AD 725-753), king of Kashmir, probably conquered Ladakh in the eighth century. Tibet itself had been unified only in the seventh century. Therefore, that would be the earliest when Ladakh could have come under Tibet's sway. In any case, this control from Tibet was short lived and started almost certainly *after* Lalitaditya's reign.

Tibet revives Buddhism with Indian assistance

Lang Dar Ma (also spelt Glan Dharma), a descendant of King Srong-tsan Gam-po, was the king of Tibet in the first half of the ninth century. He replaced Buddhism with Bon as the state religion and strained to exterminate Buddhism from his kingdom.

Conflict between the followers of the two faiths ensued and a monk murdered the king. In 842, the Tibetan monarchy disintegrated and Tibet itself started breaking into autonomous provinces. Almost a century later, Skitde Nemagon (975-990), a descendant of the assassinated king, migrated from Tibet to a region that borders Ladakh on the east. This region probably was Guge, which he started ruling independently. Evidently he did not subscribe to his forebear's anti-Buddhist views. Some ranking Tibetan nobles accompanied him.

Nemagon, Atisa etc.- the second spreading

Buddhism had suffered a setback in Tibet proper. So, Skitde Nemagon and his grandson Yesh-es Od initiated its revival by sending young scholars like Rinchen (b)Zâñgpo and Atisa to the centres of Buddhism in India, especially in Kashmir. This phase is known as the 'second spreading' of Buddhism in Tibet.

Lotsawa Rinchen

Rinchen (born c. AD 985, in the Guge area) is known as *lhotsawa,* or the translator. He either founded or inspired the foundation of the Tabo (Himachal) and Nyarma (near Thiksey) monasteries, as well as perhaps half a dozen other gompas in present day Ladakh, Himachal and Western Tibet. These gompas include those at Alchi, Guge and Purang.

Rinchen went on to become the biggest propagator of Indian culture in Tibet. He translated *sutr* and *tañtr* literature from Sanskrit into the Tibetan language. He also took Kashmiri artists, architects and craftsmen over to Tibet.

According to one account even Atisa, then a scholar at the Vikramshila University (in Central India), went to Tibet at Rinchen's invitation. Kashmiri artists gave to West Tibetan monasteries brilliant frescoes, as well as stucco and wooden sculptures. Monasteries in Tibet, Ladakh and Himachal which reveal Kashmiri workmanship include Alchi, Tsaparang, Tholing and Tabo.

Lalit Gupta, a journalist writes[1] 'The murals of Manan temples are the only surviving frescoes of the Kashmiri idiom known today.' (Not true. The ones at Alchi, too, have survived. Besides, Mr. Gupta has not indicated where Manan is. All the same, this is important information. It must be in Western Tibet, because there is no such place of any significance in Ladakh.)

Atisa founded, in Tibet, the mystical Vajrâyan school of Mahâyân Buddhism. Steeped in *tañtr*, this form gained mass acceptance in Tibet.

1. I chanced upon a newspaper clipping titled 'Rin-chen-bzan-po—Tibetan envoy of Buddhism' by Lalit Gupta. The clipping had no details of date or even name of newspaper. I suspect it was from *The Indian Express* Newsline and was published between November 1998 and February 1999. The mention of Manan is too important for art historians to ignore.

Tibet invades Ladakh in AD 975

As a scion of the Tibetan royal family, Skitde Nemagon assumed that suzerainty over Ladakh (and Zâñskâr, Lahaul and Spiti) had passed on to him. It is a different thing that none of the various Ladakhi kings shared this assumption. So, Skitde's eldest son, Lhâ-chen sPal Gyi Gon (c.990-1020), went over with an army to make them do so.

At that stage Ladakh was split into several independent kingdoms, two of them of significance. Of these upper Ladakh was the biggest and was ruled by a hardy dynasty that claimed descent from the legendary King Gyâlam Kesar. (Ladakh's best-known epic poem is called Kesar-lû, or 'the song of Kesar.' Lû means 'song.')

Some believe that it was Nemagon himself who invaded Ladakh, which was till then also called Muryul, the red country, because of the colour of its soil. Muryul could also mean 'the lowland', because the plains of Leh are lower than the huge mountains surrounding them. Nemagon is supposed to have come to Ladakh with a tiny army of a few hundred men. Since Ladakh was divided into principalities, often at war with each other, Nemagon's force met with little resistance.

However, even in those days some concept of a single Ladakh, albeit divided into two broad provinces, certainly existed. Shey- fifteen kilometres from Leh town- was considered the capital of all Ladakh. This was so even in the 10th century when Ladakh had no central authority and was better known as Nariskorsoom, or the country of *three* provinces. Guge [western Tibet] was the third province. Off and on, Shey would continue to enjoy this status for several centuries thereafter.

Nemagon was a man of taste and culture. The sculpture at Shey is attributed to him, as is the practice of covering royal dishes with large napkins.

The empire of his grandson Yesh-es Od possibly included Zâñskâr in Ladakh, as well as Spiti and Kinnaur in Himachal Pradesh. This must have been around the eleventh century AD.

It was left to *his* great grandson, King Lhâ-chen Otpal (c.1125-1150), to conquer Kulu (Himachal), as well as portions of present day Baltistan. Otpal is known to have built castles and, possibly, the Likir monastery.

Tibetan Buddhism replaces the Kashmiri variety

When did Tibet begin to replace Kashmir and central India as the source of Ladakh's Buddhism? Perhaps around the beginning of the thirteenth century. It had certainly taken over by the reign of the Ladakhi king Lhâ-chen Ngo Rub (c.1300-1325). The reason was obvious: by then Buddhism had disappeared from the Indian plains.

Some argue that Tibetan Buddhism had reached Ladakh by the eighth or ninth century AD. However, there is no archæological evidence to support this claim. B.R. Mani writes, 'Widespread traces of cultural impacts of Tibetan Buddhism and art forms of the tenth and eleventh centuries AD have been found throughout Ladakh.' On the other hand, the Alchi monastery was built some time between the 10th and 12th centuries AD. This shows that Kashmiri Buddhism was the dominant form till then.

By Ngo Rub's time, institutional links had been forged between the monasteries of Ladakh and those of central Tibet. Tibetan Buddhist texts- many of which had been copied in gold during this and the immediately preceding era—were brought to Ladakh. Ngo Rub got the huge Tibetan Encyclopædia, as well as a book of secret chants and spells, copied.

More significantly, the Ladakhis started sending young monks to central Tibet for advanced monastic training. This system continued till the 1950s, when the Chinese drove Tibet's top religious leadership out. (To this day many Ladakhi lâmâs aspire to be trained in Tibet. A few actually make it, despite the difficulties involved.) After the 15th century, all new *gompas* in Ladakh were founded as representatives of one Tibetan monastic order or another.

Around the 14th century Ladakh's spiritual connection with Kashmir took a new turn- one which could not have been anticipated by the events that had gone before. Ngo Rub's descendant[2] Rinchen went over to Kashmir, of which he became the king. He converted to Islam and thus became the first Muslim king of Kashmir. The wheel had thus turned a full circle. Thitherto Kashmir had been exporting its Buddhism to Ladakh, rooting out the region's pre-Buddhist religion. Now a Ladakhi prince established Muslim political rule in Kashmir, aiding the Turkistani saint Bulbul Shah, who took Islam to the masses. This process would, over the centuries, result in almost 95% of the population of Kashmir accepting Islam. (See also the volume 'A History of Kashmir'.)

Kashmir and Central Asia attack Ladakh

Between the fourteenth and sixteenth centuries, Ladakh was raided and invaded several times by armies from Kashmir, Central Asia and Baltistan. Some of these invasions took place in the reign of Dragspâ Bum Lde (1400-40), king of Ladakh. (He is also referred to as Lhâ-chen Trags Bum De, Gragspâ Bum-Lde and just Lde.)

2. European scholars, writing in the early 20th century, assumed that Rinchen was Ngo Rub's son. However, Janet Rizvi convincingly argues that Rinchen was probably his great-great-grandson instead.

Lde built several important monuments. His Spituk monastery as well as the ruins of his Triple Temple and Red College can still be seen. He also tried to cleanse Ladakhi Buddhism of Bon Chos influences such as animal sacrifice. This proved unpopular at the time. A contemporary engraving reads, 'King Lde's order is too difficult to implement.' However, he succeeded in the long run. Leave alone animal sacrifice, the Buddhists of present-day Ladakh are reluctant to even kill for food. They prefer to let Muslim butchers do the job instead.

What happened between Ladakh and Kashmir depends on whose point of view gets reflected in the histories you read. Tibetan (and Ladakh-based European) historians see Kashmir's invasions as raids for the sake of plunder and tribute.

Sultan Shihab ud Din (1353-74) wrested Baltistan from the ruler of Kâshghar. His army also overran Leh, without much resistance. It withdrew to Kashmir after the king of Leh agreed to pay an annual tribute in the form of wool, mainly pashmina. The role of pashmina in the politics, and destiny, of Ladakh is at least as old as that. Two generations later, the then king of Leh defaulted on the tribute. So, Shihab's nephew, Sultan Sikander (1389-1413), sent an army under Rai Magrey to Leh to, um, collect the arrears.

Viewed from the Valley of Kashmir, this was empire- building of the highest order. Sikander's son, Zain ul Abedin (1420-70), brought most of Ladakh, as well as Guge (Western Tibet), under his sway. He is considered the greatest Kashmiri king ever. He also ruled over the biggest Kashmir-based empire.

Either way, the support of Kashmir helped the rulers- and internal unity- of Leh. Lde's son, Lodros Chog Ldan (1440-70), could keep the tiny principalities of the region under his sway as long as Zain ul Abedin backed him. On the Kashmir emperor's death, not only did the Leh kingdom start disintegrating, Bhagan, the grandson of the Basgo king, put him in jail and brought the first Ladakhi dynasty to an end.

This also happened to be a time when not just Kashmir but also Baltistan and Central Asia had started converting to Islam, because of the efforts of mystics and saints. In the latter half of the 16th century so did parts of Ladakh- especially those now in Kargil district and the so-called Northern Areas. These parts included Pashkum, Mulbek, Shakar Chiktan and the Suru valley[3]. This region was made up of semi-independent principalities that accepted the overlordship of the Ladakhi kings. Many

3. And, according to one authority, Bodh Kharbu as well. However, this seems doubtful.

of the newly converted chiefs- for instance, those of Chiktan and Kartse- started calling themselves Sultan.

Islam was not the only new faith to enter Ladakh in the 15th century. So was the reformed Ge Lugs Pâ ('yellow hat') monastic order.

The Namgyâl dynasty

The Namgyâl (lit.: victorious) dynasty- the second to rule Ladakh- was founded, by Bhagan (c.1470-1500) of Basgo. It continued to reign till the 19th century merger of Ladakh with the rest of Jammu and Kashmir. Bhagan took the name Lhâ-chen Kuñ-gâ Namgyâl. (The dates of his reign- and those of his successors—could be off by twenty or thirty years.)

Present-day Leh district got partitioned between two royal brothers into as many kingdoms: Leh- Shey and Basgo- Tingmosgang. This perhaps was in the 15th century The descendants of King Trags Bum De, based in Shey, were generally accepted as the true inheritors. The Basgo line did not quite enjoy the same stature. However, Bhagan somehow got rid of his Shey based cousin, who is said to have been the son of Trags Bum De- though it is more likely that he was a great-grandson. Thus Bhagan united most of Ladakh all over again. At least for the while.

It is likely that around the 1520s today's Leh district once again got divided into two kingdoms. However, Bhagan's son, Tashi Namgyâl (1500-1532), reunited Leh. He also brought Guge (western Tibet) as well as large, recently Islamised, tracts of the present Kargil district under his control.

Tashi was a cruel man. He eliminated his elder brother, Lhâwang, from succession to the throne by getting his eyes gouged and imprisoning him near Zâñskâr. He took equally drastic measures against invaders from Central Asia and Kashmir. He neutralised a weak attack from Kashmir, after which the Kashmiris did not attack Ladakh ever again. He not only defeated Hor (Central Asian invaders), he put the bodies of the killed enemy soldiers beneath the icons of Mahâkâlâ, the Lords of the Four Quarters. He had got these icons constructed on the Namgyâl Tsemo Hill (in present-day Leh town).

Tashi Namgyâl, as Mrs. Rizvi points out, is the first king of Ladakh whose portrait is extant. 'It is a court scene,' she writes, 'on a tiny scale besides the huge representations of the Guardians, which adorns one wall of his Temple of the Guardian Deities on Namgyâl Tsemo peak. This temple is part of a complex, including a fort, probably the whole of which was built by Tashi; it is also the first recorded royal residence at Leh.'

Dughlat and Ali Mir conquer Ladakh, separately

Among the Central Asian invaders was Mirza Haidar Dughlat. Around 1532, this Mughal of royal stock overran Kargil's Suru valley. He ruled over parts of Leh district (certainly over Nubra) as well.

Dughlat executed Tashi when he started a resistance movement against the Kâshghar army. Tashi had no children. So Tsewang Namgyâl, Tashi's nephew and the eldest son of the blinded brother, became the next king. Dughlat invaded Ladakh again in 1545 and 1548, this time from Kashmir.

Janet Rizvi argues that 'the Ladakhi king, whoever he may have been [almost certainly it was Tsewang], seems to have reached an agreement with the invader, for Haidar used Ladakh as a base for an invasion of Tibet about 1533.' She adds that the Mirza 'was forced to retreat when within eight days' march of Lhâsâ by the difficult terrain and the bitter cold; he stayed for two more years in Ladakh, making his headquarters at Shey, before pulling out in 1536…A nominal administration in Mirza Haidar's name was set up [in 1548], but it did not survive his death in 1551.'

Tsewang (1532-1555) continued his uncle's empire building drive. He conquered, though only for a short while, areas as far apart as Mustang, Kulu (in neighbouring Himachal Pradesh) and Baltistan. Tsewang took Tashi's hard line against the Turks even further, wanting to wage war on their soil. However, traders from Nubra (which was on the silk route) dissuaded him from doing so, because war would disrupt trade and thus ruin Nubra's economy.

It was Tsewang who got the Maitreya Temple of Basgo built.

Jamyang Namgyâl (1555-90) was Tsewang's brother and successor. We first hear of a European, Diogo d'Almeira[4], a Portuguese trader, visiting Ladakh during his reign. He spent two years there and noted that Ladakh was a rich country.

Around the same time, Jamyang travelled with his army to tackle Balti ambitions in Chiktan. His army was ambushed and defeated. He was taken prisoner by Ali Mir (or Ali Sher Khan), king of Skardu. An army from Baltistan accompanied Ali. It looted and destroyed the treasures of Ladakh—according to Mrs. Rizvi 'with iconoclastic zeal.' She adds, 'Thus, apart from Alchi … and a few others in remote villages in the mountains, the *gompa* buildings and their treasures that we see today all date from after this period.'

4. d'Almeida, according to Mrs. Rizvi

The defeat in Baltistân shattered Jamyang's morale. Leh had in the process lost many territories that had thitherto been under its control. Worse, Jamyang had to accept someone else as his overlord—even if it was his own father-in-law. He lost all appetite for tightening Leh's control on the principalities that were supposed to be under its sway. Jamyang's kingdom was now limited to the stretch from Tâñgtsé (near the Pangong Lake) to the border with Purîg. (This corresponds roughly to present-day Leh district.)

The life and loves of Jamyang

According to Ladakhi folklore, during his imprisonment at Skardu, Jamyang fell in love with Ali Mir's daughter Gyâl Kâtûn. It is a fact that Jamyang married the Balti (Muslim) princess. Her father, the most powerful emperor of the era in all of Ladâkh-Balâwaristân, gladly agreed to the match. Gyâl was promptly accepted by the Ladakhis as an incarnation of the White Târâ, a Buddhist goddess. If you've seen the women of Baltistân- or the Baltis of Kargil- you'll know why.

The Baltis vacated Ladakh and released Jamyang only when he agreed to i) recognise Ali Mir as his suzerain; ii) marry Gyâl Kâtûn; and iii) disinherit his two sons from a previous marriage. (This, thus, was perhaps the only period in history when a Muslim king exercised control over Ladakh.)

Jamyang's love life is certainly the stuff of legends: for more see 'A History of Kargil'. For more about the misadventure in Baltistân see 'A History of Baltistân.'

Jamyang did all that he could to promote Buddhism. He got religious books copied in gold, silver and copper. He also invited Stag Tsang Ras Pâ, the celebrated Tibetan priest, known as the rainbow-bodied Buddha, to Ladakh. Above all, Jamyang exempted the Buddhists from taxes.

Sometimes he managed to combine the promotion of Buddhism with the side effects of his active love life. He decided to send expensive gifts to the most important monasteries of Tibet. He chose the sons born to his first wife to deliver these presents personally. The journey to Tibet and back took several months. So, this was a subtle method of getting the older sons out of the way, in fulfillment of the promise that he had made to his newfound father-in-law.

Senge Namgyâl, the lion king

Jamyang died perhaps in 1590 (in 1616 according to some historians) when his son Senge ('the lion') Namgyâl was still a minor. His mother, Gyâl Khâtûn, was the regent for a while. Senge Namgyâl (1590-1620 or

1570-1642[5]) went on to become the greatest of all Ladakhi kings-combining in his person king and clergy, 'church' and state.

This happened partly by accident. For a year, maybe two, Senge's younger brother Norbu Namgyâl seized the kingdom from him. During this interregnum Senge took to religion and moved to Hanle[6], an extremely remote village on the Tibetan border. There, at Stag Tsang Ras Pâ's behest, he got constructed a massive monastery affiliated to the Tibetan master's Drug Pâ (red hat) sect.

Upon Norbu's death, a year or two after the palace coup, Senge was back as king. Following the footsteps of uncle Tsewang and grand-uncle Tashi he started annexing neighbouring areas like Zâñskâr and Guge. Ultimately he presided over the biggest Ladakhi empire ever, which extended to the Mayum Lâ in the west and Spiti in the south. It also included Purang, Sedakh, Rudok and Shâkyancho. The Mayum pass is in Guge. Senge's empire thus included the Mansarovar lake and the Kailash mountain.

Senge's army then headed towards Lhâsâ. The terrified people of Tibet rushed towards Senge with entreaties and peace offerings of gold and silver, which he accepted and abandoned the planned invasion.

Señgé married Skalzang Dolmâ, a princess from Rupshu. Their children and she have been spoken of very glowingly in the numerous inscriptions of that period. Francke has wondered why of all the queens

5. Thus far this author has followed the dates assumed by the Gazetteer department of the state government. However, we have the evidence of the Jesuit Father de Azevedo that Senge was the king in 1631 when the cleric visited Leh. Therefore, it is not possible to agree with the Gazetteer department's dating of Senge's reign to 1590-1620. Both Janet Rizvi and Snellgrove & Skorupski state, with good reason, that Senge died in 1642. So, two sets of dates have been given for Senge and some of his successors. The dates mentioned first are those provided by the Gazetteer department. Mrs. Rizvi feels Senge's reign began in 1616. S&S date Senge's period at 1570-1642. But we know that he died young. Therefore, Mrs. Rizvi's estimate seems the best. Kachu Sikander Khan dates Senge's reign at between 1569 and 1594, which can't be right in view of the Jesuits' evidence. The Gazetteer department has obviously followed Francke's dating of Senge's reign. Mrs. Rizvi seems to agree with Luciano Petech. The Kachu and Gergan concur with each other. Hashmatullâh Khân believes that Senge ruled from 1610 to 1645. 'Gyalrabs,' which perhaps is the most authentic source of them all, gives the dates as 1590-1635. Because the 'Gyalrabs' dates accommodate de Azevedo's visit, it is at least as good as the Petech-Rizvi dating, if not better.

6. Today Hanle is best known for the astronomical observatory built there by the Government of India in 1996. This sparsely populated village has since renewed its Tibetan connection. In the 1950s some Tibetans fled to Hanle, seeking refuge from the Chinese. They continue to live there.

of Ladâkh, she was 'one of the few who acquired some real fame.' I believe that the explanation is simple. Most of the other queens were mere consorts. Skalzang, as we will see, ruled as a regent for a while.

Two Jesuit priests, Fathers Francesco de Azevedo and Giovanni de Oliveiro visited Ladakh in 1631. They came from Tsaparang (the capital of Guge), where they had set up a mission. They stayed in Ladakh only briefly. However, de Azevedo has left for us a detailed description of King Senge Namgyâl, who granted the two an audience.

The Jesuits must have sought the audience because the previous year (1630) Senge had conquered Guge. This annexation had put an end to the state patronage that the king of Guge had been giving the Jesuits.[7] (Guge's former ruler had since been exiled to Ladakh and replaced by one of Senge's younger sons.)

Ban on Kashmiri traders: 'Economic suicide'

The Mughals of central India had conquered the Valley of Kashmir by 1586. In 1639, they (and thus the Indian nation) found themselves claiming suzerainty over Ladakh. This happened when Senge set out to conquer Purîg (the areas around today's Kargil town, the adjacent part of Baltistan, the Suru valley, and the tract between Kargil and Leh). His invasion was resisted by a joint Mughal-Balti army at Bodh Kharbu. (See also 'A History of Kargil'.)

Ladakhi historians claim that Senge's army won. However, no one else- not even Tibetan historians- back this claim. Indeed, it is certain (from Mughal as well as French sources, the latter being the traveller Francois Bernier who visited the neighbourhood in 1663) that Senge was defeated. He agreed to pay the Mughals a tribute through their Kashmir-based governor. However, immediately thereafter Senge renegued on the agreement that he had made at Bodh Kharbu.

Because the Mughal army had come from Kashmir, Senge also banned the entry of people from Kashmir into Ladakh. Since traders from Kashmir would use trade routes that went through Ladakh, this was meant to spite them. However, it hurt Ladakh's own economy even more. This meant that Ladakh would lose its pivotal position, and thus the many economic benefits which went with that position, on a large number of trade routes. Scholars attribute the subsequent economic (and political) decline of Ladakh to this set of decisions. Officially the trade

7. The Jesuit mission in Guge closed down in 1635. The next attempt by the Goa-based Jesuits to resume missionary work in Ladakh-Guge was in 1715, when two Jesuits reached Leh through Delhi. Which, incidentally, indicates that the present trend among Western tourists to do Goa-Delhi-Ladakh as a circuit has a pedigree going back to at least 1715.

route was closed from 1639 to 1663. It was reopened- under Mughal pressure- by Senge's successor in 1663. However, by that time the damage had been done. Substitutes had been found for many of the routes.

Senge: The greatest Ladakhi king?

Then why is it that Senge is always referred to as 'the great'? He occupies the same position in the history of Ladakh as Zain ul Abedin does in Kashmir and Akbar and Ashok do in all of India.

For one he built the biggest ever Ladakh-based empire. His contributions to Buddhism are regarded as even more important. He helped Stag Tsang Ras Pâ construct the Hanle[8] monastery, the massive idol of Buddha at Shey. a large number of *maaney* walls and, above all, Hemis, the biggest and richest monastery in all of Ladakh-Kishtwâr-Himachal. (The Chemrey monastery was built for Senge's funeral, but not by him.)

Señgé's real claim to greatness is the prosperity that his subjects enjoyed. It has been recorded that thanks to him, all of Ladâkh was full of yaks and sheep. He seems to have launched a major drive to rear cattle and sheep. Since the results of the drive were so significant, he must have imported the 'parent' cattle and sheep from neighbouring regions.

Senge was a great builder. (See 'Leh palace' in the chapter on 'Leh town.')

His government sent extravagant religious missions to Tibet, with gifts of gold, silver and turquoise. He gave each 'tiger-lâmâ' gold (300 grams), pearls (one string), ponies and yâks (100 of each), cash (the equivalent of Rs.1000), sheep (1000), silk (25 scarves), brocades and large weapons. He also got the *Kahgyur* copied in gold.

All this, coupled with his building spree, was to cost Ladakh dear. It bled the economy dry. As Senge's son Deldan would later learn, it also reduced Ladakh's ability to defend itself against attacks from its neighbours.

Senge died in his youth, in 1642, at Hanle. At the time he was returning with his army from Tsang, one of his Tibetan possessions east of Guge, which the Mongols had temporarily wrested from him. This happened three years after his defeat at Bodh Kharbu.

Deldan, the Mughals and Islam

None of Senge's three sons was old enough to succeed him. So his widow, Skalzâñg Dolma, was the regent till around 1647, when the

8. Pronounced aan-lay

Buddhist areas of Ladakh were divided among the three. The present day Leh district went to Deldan the eldest (1642-1670s), Indrabodhi, the middle son, a lâmâ, got Guge, while Demchong, the youngest, got Zâñskâr and Spiti (HP).

(By now, certainly after Senge's 1639 defeat at Bodh Kharbu, the Muslim areas of Kargil- which means almost all of the present day Kargil district, minus Zâñskâr- were no longer under the kings of Leh. However, Deldan recovered much of Purîg around 1673. He also conquered Khapalu and Chhorbat, thus angering the chieftain of Skardu.)

In 1663, the Mughal emperor Aurangzeb visited Kashmir. He was reminded that Senge had gone back on his agreement to pay the Mughals a tribute. Deldan Namgyâl had inherited the largest territory. He was thus seen as Senge's main successor.

Therefore, it devolved on Deldan to go through the motions of assuring the Mughals that he accepted their suzerainty, that he would get coins struck and the *khutba* (Islamic sermon) read in Aurangzeb's name, that he would get a mosque built, and so on. He agreed to all this. However, like his father and another Ladakhi king who was (Sultan Sikander's contemporary) before him, Deldan had no intention of actually implementing any of his promises.

The Mughals sent over an army contingent to show that they were serious. In all this the Mughals received the enthusiastic support of Skardu, which had accepted their overlordship. Thus the first mosque in Leh town was built around 1666. (See also 'Shey' and 'Islam in Leh' in the chapter on 'Leh' district.) Some historians say that it was the chief of Skardu who asked the Mughals to help him against Deldan.

However, Deldan showed few other signs of acknowledging Mughal suzerainty. As mentioned, around 1673, he recovered most of Purîg- the areas around Kargil town. But when he tried to repeat his success in Baltistan, the Mughals sent a medium sized army (around 5,000 men) through Kashmir, and defeated the economically enfeebled Ladakhis.

Defeat, Decline and Loss of Independence

Around this time the 'yellow hat' Ge Lugs Pâ monastic sect was on the ascendant in Tibet. The fifth Dalai Lâmâ had accepted it as the official sect. On the other hand its rival Drug Pâ sect was receiving royal patronage in Ladakh- and Bhutan. This created some tension between Tibet on the one hand and Ladakh and Bhutan on the other.

At some stage in the last quarter of the 17th century, Tibet attacked Bhutan, and was beaten back. The king of Leh wrote to Tibet protesting its treatment of Bhutan, a Drug Pâ country like Ladakh. (It is not clear who this king was. Some historians say that it was Deldan. Others say that it was his son Deleg.) This incensed the Dalai Lâmâ, who, in 1679 and 1680, sent his army to subdue Leh.

After some initial reverses, the Tibetan army overran Guge and all of Ladakh's western territories till it was stopped at Basgo. The Tibetans laid siege to Basgo for three years.[9] They were pushed back only when the Mughals based in Kashmir sent an army to help Deldan, at his request.

Now, for the first time, there was a Mughal army inside Leh.[10] It had no intention of withdrawing till the king of Leh fulfilled all the pledges that Senge and Deldan had made to the Mughals. In addition he had to concede to Kashmir a monopoly on the purchase of pashmina wool. Some say that Ibrahim Khan, the Mughal governor of Kashmir, helped Leh against Tibet only to ensure that Ladakh, and not Tibet, remained in control of the pashmina trade. This way the wool would continue to reach Kashmir. Pashmina wool was then obtained mainly from Chang Thâñg on Leh's border with Tibet.[11] Equally, it was also in the itnerest of Leh that the wool reached Kashmir through its territory.

Deldan also found it expedient to convert to Islam- at least for the sake of appearances. He sent a son to Kashmir for training as a Muslim. Deldan was now called Aqibat Mahmud Khan. However, there do not seem to have been many other conversions to Islam in Leh around that time, or even later. (According to some, it was his son Deleg who converted.)

Deldan's conversion to Islam greatly disturbed the rulers of Tibet. (The fifth Dalai Lâmâ had recently died and his successor had not yet taken over.) Tibet's regent sent the highest-ranking Drug Pâ monk (lâmâ) to Ladakh to draw up ground rules for the changed situation.

This resulted in the Treaty of Tingmo(s)gang (1684), named after the palace (near Khaltse) where the lâmâ had received Deldan. The

9. Knowledgeable Ladakhis say that it was the Mongol, and not Tibetan, army that had surrounded Basgo. For proof they point out that the dried hand of General Sokpos, of the Sosko Mongol tribe, is still preserved in the Deskit monastery. And yet all the books that I have consulted insist that it was the Tibetan army. There is no real contradiction between the two versions. The Oelot Mongols supported the fifth Dalai Lama. They could have had a military alliance, too. The particular detachment that invaded Deskit must have been led or manned by Mongols.

10. It was also the first recorded army in Leh from mainland India.

11. Rudok, a village in Chang Thâñg, was and is an important centre of the pashmina trade.

weakened Ladakhi king succumbed to almost all of Tibet's demands. It was this treaty that drew up the present day borders between Ladakh and Tibet (and thus India and China). Guge was wrested from Ladakh, never again to return to the Ladakhi/ Indian fold. Thus the Pangong Lake[12], the world's highest brackish water lake, got partitioned between Ladakh and Tibet.

The Drug Pâ lâmâ, whose sect Deldan's dynasty favoured, also extracted an assurance from the king that the rival Ge Lugs Pâ sect would receive more or less equal treatment in Ladakh. He was further assured that the King of Ladakh would not allow an Indian (i.e. Mughal) army to go through Ladakh to attack Tibet.

In turn, Ladakh received favourable terms in the trade of tea. As part of the treaty, Kashmiri traders were settled in Spituk from where they would buy up all the raw pashmina produced in Chang Thâñg as well as Rudok. The treaty also gave Ladakh a monopoly over the pashmina trade, including the pashmina produced in western Tibet.

Ladakh was never to recover from the concessions made during Deldan's fateful reign to the Tibetans in the east and the Mughals/ Kashmiris in the south. Its sovereignty was diluted forever, to be lost altogether a century and a half later. However, Kashmir did not interfere in Ladakh's internal affairs after that and Tibet did so only once. This was partly because it was (and to an extent still is) so difficult to reach Ladakh. In any case, after Aurangzeb the Mughals went into their own decline.

External affairs were a different matter altogether. Kashmir and Tibet ensured that Ladakh ceased to have any. Well, more or less. No more conquests of Guge or even of Kargil or Spiti, leave alone going deeper into Tibet, to places like Tsang. And no more dealings with Tibet as an equal.

The only battle we hear of after this was on the border with the Baltis. The Namgyâls had married someone from the family of the chieftain of Khapalu in Baltistan. This chieftain had problems with his Balti neighbours. A small battle ensued, in which the Ladakhis helped Khapalu. (Ladakhi historians claim that their army won, after which they helped sort out the problem through negotiations and diplomacy.)

Lahaul and Kinnaur (now in Himachal Pradesh) had often been part of Ladâkh. It was during the reign of Deleg(s) Namgyâl that Leh lost these territories, never to recover them again.

12. The Ladakhi word for 'lake' is 'Tso.' Therefore, you will sometimes come across usages like 'Pangong Tso.' The 'Tsomo Riri,' on the other hand, is invariably referred to by its full Ladakhi name and never as Lake Moriri.

Religious tolerance

By now Ladakh was a little less than half Muslim, with the Buddhists enjoying only a slight majority. The Buddhists of Leh district and Zâñskâr would send monks for training to Tibet. The Shiite Muslims of Kargil (and the areas now in the illegal possession of Pakistan) sent their novices to Iran and Central Asia.

However, as far as day-to-day life was concerned there was harmony between the two communities. There are no records (or even memories) of riots or physical violence because of religious differences. At least in the villages where Leh district meets Kargil, till the 1980s, the young would marry partners from the other community. Till the 1990s, one could come across people with names like Tsering Muhammad, because one parent was a Muslim and the other a Buddhist.

So much so that in the 17th and 18th centuries the Lo Pchak religious and trade mission would be managed by Ladakhi Muslims, even though its official head was a Buddhist monk. (This mission would travel from Leh to Lhâsâ once every three years carrying presents for the ranking lâmâs of Lhâsâ. This was a requirement of the Treaty of Tingmosgang.)

Deleg's son Nima Namgyâl ruled around 1685-1720. He established the first printing press in Ladakh. His wife, Zizi Khâtûn, later dominated the administration during the reign of her stepson Des-kyoñg (1720-1739). It was at her behest that Purîg was prised away from Des-kyoñg's territories and given to his brother Trashi. Kishtwâr was under her son-in-law, whom she got murdered.

The mess and the imperfect solutions

Around 1720, the Chinese laid claim to Tibet and to an extent brought it under their sway. The then king of Leh (perhaps Des-kyoñg) sent his compliments to Beijing. After this some kind of an alliance between China and Ladakh seems to have taken place, with the Ladakhis keeping an eye on Yarqand on behalf of the Chinese.

Internally, however, Ladakh had gone into a sharp decline. Members of the Namgyâl family took to fighting and killing each other for the sake of the throne. Des-kyoñg's son, Phuntsog Namgyâl (1739-52) grabbed power by shunting his elder half-brother, Shes-kyoñg to the Hemis monastery as a monk. (Shes-kyoñg went on to earn a name for himself in Ladakh as well as Tibet as an outstanding lâmâ, better known as Gyâlras Rinpoche.) Phuntsog's uncle Trashi, who ruled Purîg, started creating problems for both Kashmir and Leh.

Things got so bad that in the middle of the 18th century the Dalai Lâmâ had to send a top-ranking lâmâ to Leh to mediate. It was he who got the claimants to agree that the eldest son would always inherit the throne, the second son would always become a lâmâ (monk) and the kingdom would never again be divided between princes. (Other historians say that the elders and wise men of the kingdom had taken these three historic decisions. However, the group had got together at the Hanle monastery to sort the mess out. Hanle is close to Tibet. Therefore, this must have been done at the Dalai's behest.)

Because of this agreement the mentally diseased Tsewang Namgyâl II (1752-82), succeeded Phuntsog- and Trashi- to the united kingdom of Leh and Purîg (plus Zâñskâr and Spiti). In his madness Tsewang was sometimes cruel. This caused the people to revolt against him and install his eldest son, the teenaged Tsetan (perhaps 1782-1808), in his place.

An outstanding polo player, Tsetan introduced the system of progressive taxation (a concept unknown in most parts of the world at the time), which meant that the rich would pay more taxes than the poor. This earned him the love of the people. Some historians say that Tsetan died when he was just 23. In any case he was childless and very young when he died. His incompetent brother Tsespal (1808-30) succeeded him. Power went into the hands of his ministers.

The leadership of Ladakh got fragmented and the kingdom, in decline for more than a century, was ripe for the plucking. Every tiny neighbour and former vassal felt so bold as to attack this once mighty kingdom. Rattan Sher Khan, the Raja of tiny Pâdar, looted Zâñskâr. The people of Kulu ransacked the Spiti valley. In 1821, the Balti army plundered Ladakh. Each time Tsespal refused to intervene. He was the last king of independent Leh. Naturally.

The fugitive prince from Kokand

Around 1825, Ladâkh received an unusual group of visitors. These were fugitives from neighbouring Kokañd, led by Prince Abdus Sattâr Adijan. They requested Ladâkh's King Tsespel Tondup Namgyâl for asylum, which was granted. Apparently they were fleeing the Chinese.

However, the Chinese were unhappy at this grant of asylum. They started leaning on the administrators of Leh to hand the runaways back to them. After a while the rulers of Leh succumbed. In 1828[1] they handed the prince over to the Chinese.

First contacts with the (British) East India Company

In 1819, Kashmir was taken over by rulers who happened to be Sikh, and incorporated into the empire of the great Mahâraja Ranjit Singh. William Moorcroft, a veterinary surgeon employed by the (British) East

India Company (EIC), happened to be in Ladakh. He was on his way to Yarqand, from where he was to purchase horses for the EIC. After a three-year wait in Ladakh he was denied permission to go to Yarqand. He used this time not only to record the history of Ladakh but also to influence it.

Moorcroft argued with Tsespal that Ladakh was better off under the distant, Calcutta-based EIC than under the 'oppressive ...(and) insolent' Sikhs, what with their 'exactions'. He described the EIC as the 'legitimate representatives' of the Mughals. Tsespal agreed and made an offer of allegiance to the EIC.

Moorcroft thus divided two Indian peoples, the Sikhs and the Ladakhi Buddhists, ostensibly to protect the latter from the former. However, as he would later write, he 'secured for [his] country... a strong outwork against an enemy from the north [i.e. Russia].'

In this we see the beginnings of the Ladakh chapter of the Great Game between England and Russia. (The Game existed mainly in the minds of some paranoid British administrators of the Raj, who were convinced that the Russians' fondest desire was to 'dip their toes in the warm waters of the Indian Ocean.' After India and Pakistan became independent in 1947, India's officials inherited most of the foreign policy of the Raj, minus this particular paranoia, which Pakistan has appropriated instead.)

Moorcroft, being a middle ranking technical man, was obviously not aware of the policies of the EIC. The EIC had, through a treaty signed in 1809, accepted that the areas north of the Sutlej were under Ranjit Singh's sphere of influence.

Kashmir's own economy was in deep trouble around this time: especially the pashmina trade, the fortunes of which were knit inextricably which those of Ladakh and western Tibet. Upon Kashmir's annexation by Mahâraja Ranjit Singh, a famine engulfed the land.

The British had first eyed the lucrative pashmina trade in 1774. A few decades later they started encouraging a covert dilution of Ladakh's (and thus Kashmir's) pashmina monopoly. They began to offer higher prices. More significantly, they allowed some pashmina to leak to the plains of the Punjab, through Spiti and Kinnaur, both being British territories in what now is today's Himachal Pradesh (HP). Thus Kashmir as well as most of the inhabited areas of Leh were sought to be bypassed.

For many in Kashmir, weaving delicate (and expensive) shawls out of raw pashmina was the only way to earn a living. They followed the wool to Amritsar and Ludhiana in today's Punjab and Nurpur in HP. All three towns, which were under Mahâraja Ranjit Singh, benefited from this highly profitable trade with its fat profit margins. (To this day all pashmina shawls made in Basohli (Jammu) are sent to Amritsar for 'calendering'.)

Jammu annexes Ladakh

At this juncture most of today's Jammu province was ruled by Raja Gulab Singh, a Dogra ally and subordinate of Ranjit Singh. He, too, wanted a piece of the pashmina cake trade.

He first tried to ensure that at least some of the trade passed through his territory, via Kishtwâr (which borders not only Kashmir but also Zâñskâr in Ladakh). This move was aborted by Ranjit Singh's Srinagar-based (Sikh) governor. So, in the summer of 1834, Gulab sent Zorâwar Singh Kahluria, his legendary army chief, to get the golden hen itself—Ladakh.

Officially Gulab was conquering Ladakh for his Mahâraja. However, he sought (and received) the blessings of the British to annex Ladakh to Jammu. The alarmed king of Ladakh sent numerous messages to the British that he would ally with them. He was ignored.

Zorâwar's army travelled to Ladakh through Kishtwâr and Kargil. The Ladakhi army had not fought a proper war since Deldan's time. Therefore, almost a hundred and sixty years later, Ladakh did not have an army worth its name: just a civil defence system, for which every family did its bit.

And at Sankoo in the Suru valley (Kargil) they did just that. Volunteers got together and offered some resistance. The Dogra army brushed them aside. By the time that the invaders reached Pashkum, Kargil's dreaded winter announced itself. The Dogras of the boiling plains sent word to the king of Ladakh that they would withdraw if he paid them Rs.15,000. The king rejected the offer, on his wife Zizi's advice. That's destiny for you.

Zorâwar had not learnt about Zizi's views. He sent a complement of soldiers to collect the money. The Ladakhi army killed some of the Dogra soldiers by attacking them from the rear. Ladakhi soldiers tied some of the Dogras by their hands and feet and tossed them into the river. The Ladakhis chased the remaining members of the Dogra contingent to Langkartse.

Snubbed, Zorâwar retreated to a place near Sankoo, where his army and he decided to camp for the winter, biding their time. The Ladakhi army waited till the next April to attack Zorâwar's men, when the Ladakhis were defeated. (Mrs. Rizvi rightly argues that the Ladakhis could have taken advantage of Ladakh's incredible cold, with temperatures falling way below zero, to attack the Dogras during the winter. Inexplicably, they didn't. As I said, you can't fight destiny.)

As Zorâwar marched towards Leh, people from the villages en route- Nyimo, Likir, Alchi and Sespol- came out with tributes for the conqueror. (Most of these villages are on the present National Highway between the Kargil and Leh towns.)

King Tsespal himself met Zorâwar at Basgo. He agreed not only to pay Rs.50,000- more than three times the original demand- but also to accept the suzerainty of Mahâraja Ranjit Singh. This led to a revolt within the Ladakhi establishment, aided by the Srinagar-based Sikh governor, Mehan Singh. The establishment temporarily managed to overthrow Tsespal, who died shortly after his restoration. (For the record, Tsespal was succeeded to a decimated throne by his eightl-year-old grandson, Jigmet.)

According to other accounts, as soon as the victorious Zorâwar withdrew to Jammu, senior Ladakhi officials persuaded Tsespal to sack all Ladakhi officers who were pro-Dogra. Tsespal also put Gulab Singh's representative in Leh, Munshi Daya Ram, under arrest. Governor Mehan Singh got Tsespal to close all the roads through which the Dogras and businessmen patronised by them would thitherto enter Ladakh.

This enraged the Dogras. Zorâwar returned to Leh in 1836, this time through Zâñskâr. He replaced Tsespal with his brother-in-law and Prime Minister, Nurab Stanzin. Tsespal was reinstated when he agreed to pay reparations.

How cruel were the Dogrâ-Sikhs?

How rapacious had the Dogrâ-Sikh soldiers been during their conquest of Ladâkh? This question has often been asked since the 1970s, when modern histories started being written by historians from within the state.

Ladâkhi historians like S.S. Gergan[ii] (writing in 1977) and Abdul Ghani Sheikh (2002[iii]) talk of the 'vandalism perpetrated by Wazir Zorâwar Singh, Diwan Hari Chand, and the Dogrâ military forces.' In fact they are angry that Francke, whose history was published in 1907, and Hashmatullâh Khân (1930) had 'ignored' the atrocities of Zorâwar and his forces.

The oldest account about that era was written by Basti Ram, one of the highest-ranking Dogrâ-Sikh officers of the time. Sheikh calls Basti's memoir 'biased' and that it might well be. Sheikh feels that Hashmatullâh did not write about these incidents because he was 'an official of the Dogrâ regime.'

So, if the three oldest histories of the period—written by a European and a Muslim, in addition to a 'biased' Dogrâ—don't mention these 'atrocities' then what reason do we have to believe that they had taken place at all?

This author has been to some Buddhist monasteries in Ladâkh where he was told that such and such corner of the monastery was empty because Dogrâ-Sikh soldiers had looted its contents in the 1830s.

Zorâwar's forces might well have plundered these monasteries. However, I have gone into considerable detail about similar 'collective memories' concerning 'plunder' by the other community/ caste in the rest of India, especially in Ayodhya where, as in Ladâkh, contemporary records do not mention atrocities but much later histories do. In the case of the Kashmîr of the 1990s, too, I have learnt to be wary of 'collective memories,' what with Delhi-, Jammu- and Srînagar-based journalists often unanimously reporting the version believed by their respective community. 'Collective memories' in much of South Asia often tend to be collective prejudices.

However, in the case of the Sikh-Dogrâ invasion, S.S. Gergan has brought to light some contemporary records. Lama Kondog Nima Rangdol was a monk as well as the private secretary of the last three kings of Leh. The Lâmâ has recorded some cruel actions of the Dogrâ army.

I believe that Francke, who had no axe to grind either way, should have the last word on the subject. He did not slur over Zorâwar's harsh actions at all. I agree with Francke that having been excessively harsh with Sukamir of Purîg, Rahîm Khân of Chiktan and Hussain of Pashkyum, of whom he made spine-chilling examples, Zorâwar did not need to terrorise other Ladâkhis or Baltis.

Zorâwar's nemesis

Zorâwar next conquered Baltistan. Having restored Ladakh's borders on the west, he then set his sights eastwards—on Guge. The motive was not merely territorial. The Dogras wanted to prevent the by then large-scale diversion of pashmina to the plains of the Punjab, which was a clear violation of the Treaty of Tingmosgang.

Mahâraja Ranjit Singh died in 1839, and the Sikh empire began to unravel. Flush with its military successes in Ladakh and also in the Jammu hills, Jammu under Gulab Singh had become much too strong to remain in the Punjab empire. The British, too, started worrying about Gulab's next move, apprehensive that he might ally with Nepal to form a powerful Himalâyan axis.

Gulab knew that this was the best time to invade Tibet. He was on a winning streak whereas Tibet's suzerain, China, was suffering reverses in the Opium War. So, in October 1841, Zorâwar, accompanied by ten thousand Dogra, Ladakhi and Balti troops, marched from the Indus valley, through Hanle, into Guge.

Hutchison and Vogel say, 'There are only three or four months in summer that are suitable for mountain warfare, and the Dogra army did not leave Leh till October, when the favourable season was nearly over.'

All the same, Zorâwar took control of the Taklakot fort, the Mayum Lâ (pass) and all areas in between- including the Mansarovar and Rakas Tal lakes, and Mount Kailash, all three revered by the Hindus.

The Dogras succeeded in plugging the leakage of pashmina- for a while. Conquering Guge was one thing, retaining it quite another. If you are reading these pages while in Leh you must be aware of the breathing difficulties which people from the plains face when they first reach that oxygen-starved land, which is all of 3.5 kilometres above the sea level.

Zorâwar's army, mostly from the plains, fought in Tibet at 4,500 metres- then the highest battlefield in the world. Winter was far more severe than that in Leh town. And China, despite being pummelled by the British on its eastern coast, had enough forces to defend Tibet.

Hutchison and Vogel, writing around 1930, put it thus, 'The Tibetans fell back before the invaders, well knowing that every day's delay was in their favour. As soon as winter set in with the snow and intense cold, to which they were accustomed, but which the Dogras could not bear, they became benumbed and helpless. At length on 10th December, the [10,000-strong] Tibetan army gave a battle, and in two days fighting was over. [Three days, according to the other authorities.] The battle took place on a plain 15,000 feet above the sea. The cold was extreme, hail and snow had fallen during the night. The Dogras suffered severely, and many died from the cold. On 12th December, Zorâwar Singh was wounded in the right shoulder, but he changed his sword to the left hand and fought. At last a rush was made by the Tibetans on the Dogra trenches, and Zorâwar Singh was killed by a spear- thrust in the breast... We have heard it said that the upper portion of Zorâwar Singh's skull is still used as a bowl in one of the Tibetan Monasteries.'

A 'draw' with the Tibetans, and a treaty

A 10,000-strong Tibetan army fought the Dogras for three days. Zorawar died and the outnumbered Dogras were routed—in Guge. The Ladakhis and Baltis, however, assumed that the Dogras' defeat was total. In 1841-42, they revolted against the Dogras. They were joined by a detachment from Tibet. However, the battle-hardened, 7,000-strong Dogra force rose to the occasion despite the loss of Zorâwar's leadership. The combined Ladakhi-Balti-Tibetan force gave in without any significant resistance. The Tibetans scampered towards Guge, taking young Jigmet Namgyâl, the nominal king of Ladakh, with them.

The Dogras chased them and caught them at Tangtse, which was (and is) one of the last Ladakhi/ Indian outposts on the border. There the Dogra force defeated the Tibetans decisively.

On the other hand, say Hutchison and Vogel, 'only about a thousand [Dogra soldiers] reached Leh. The rest were either taken prisoners or died from exposure... The prisoners were on the whole kindly treated, and after a time set at liberty.'

This meant that on the one hand the Dogra vs Tibetan score was now even. On the other, the Dogras' victory was limited, and successes were on Dogra/ Ladakhi soil, not in Guge. So there was no territorial gain for them. However, this did chasten the Tibetans. On the 17th September, 1842, the two sides signed the Treaty of Leh, which essentially formalised the reality—that while Ladakh would now be under the Dogras, the latter should forget about Guge. The borders fixed under the Treaty of Tingmosgang were accepted by both.

The Namgyâls were allowed to stay on in Ladakh. They settled in Stok, where a part of their residence is now a museum. However, after 1842, they were to become one of the many *jagirdars* of the Dogras. (A *jaa-geer* is an estate, a fief, which normally consists of a couple of villages and lots of farmland. A jagirdar is thus a hereditary feudal lord.) They were permitted to continue sending the Lo Pchak (lo= year) religious tribute to Lhâsâ once every three years.

And pashmina? It is considered one of the main reasons (some say, *the* reason) why the Dogras needed to annex Ladakh. Trade in this expensive goat-wool would once again be conducted as established by custom, meaning the Tingmosgang treaty. The tea trade, too. So the Dogras did get what they really wanted.

The concept of district administration is introduced

Till the Dogrâ conquest, Leh was run like a traditional Himâlayan kingdom. The Dogrâ era in Ladâkh coincided with the British era in much of India. The Dogrâs introduced into Ladâkh the Anglo-Indian concept of district administration, which is essentially the administrative structure that obtains to this day. They got conducted Ladâkh's first ever land settlement.[13]

The highest Dogrâ administrator in Ladâkh was called a Thânédâr. Magna and Mehta Basti Ram were some of the more distinguished heads of the Ladâkh administration. They built the present Leh bazar as well as a fort near the town. They also got plantations pitched so that there was an assured supply of firewood. They built and repaired bridle roads leading from Leh to Srinagar in the southwest, Lahaul in the southeast and Yârqañd in the north. They also built a road to Gartok. The Dogrâs got surveyed Ladâkh's traditional border with Tibet.

Initially there was a separate Thânédâr for Baltistân, with his headquarters at Skardu. Later, Ladâkh and Baltistân were merged and placed under one administrator.

Ironically, it was an outside power, the Dogras, which gave Ladakh its biggest map in recorded history. It now included Baltistân, Gilgit and Hunzâ.[14] Leh was the economic and cultural capital of this huge new unit, which was bigger than many sovereign nations. However, the administrative capital would shift from Leh to Kargil and thence to Skardu for a few (specified) months every year. Leh was the summer capital and Skardu the winter capital.

The British have their own ideas

The same Dogras- Mahâraja Gulab Singh to be precise- entered into an agreement with the British in 1847, to detach Spiti from Ladakh. Spiti was then merged with Kulu, a British-administered district.

In 1870, the British leaned on the Dogras to sign a 'commercial' treaty which gave them a major say in the administration of Ladakh. Thitherto a Wazir e Wazarat appointed by the Dogra Mahâraja would administer Ladakh. He was the equivalent of the British Deputy Commissioner, Collector and District Magistrate. However, as happens even today, the officer so posted must have perceived his appointment as the Wazir of Ladakh as a major punishment. So, he would normally look for a way out. The Wazir would appoint a deputy to actually stay in Ladakh while he, the Wazir, would spend most of his time in Jammu.

13. In a land settlement, every inch of inhabited and cultivated land is measured and mapped and the name of its owner is recorded. Uninhabited forest and state land, too, is mapped, though not in the same detail.

14. These three areas have since 1948 been in what Pakistan now calls the Northern Areas. They are administered directly from Islamabad and are not part of the so-called Azad Jammu and Kashmir.

Some Wazirs, like Mehta Mangal (1861-66), brought about real change. Mangal introduced the plantation of poplars and also reorganised agriculture.

Not all Wazirs were from the state- or even from the country. A.F. Fredric Drew was the first European to be appointed thus. A very junior British officer, a former corporal called Jonson, impressed the Mahâraja, who appointed him the Wazir from 1871 to 1883. Through his fairness he won the respect of the local people. He also got some canals dug.

The 'commercial' treaty gave the British the authority to post a Joint Commissioner, theoretically next in rank to the Wazir. However, because he was actually stationed at Leh often he was the real administrator of Ladakh.

The Moravian Mission

The Moravian church and hospital were set up in 1885, when Shive Saran was the Wazir. The number of Ladakhis who converted to Christianity and the physical size of the church, was small. It still is a very modest mission. However, its impact has been far reaching. It brought quality Western schooling to Ladakh. (It is no coincidence that the first two Ladakhi officers to join India's elite civil services, in the 1950s, were Christians from this church and educated at its school.)

Though originally from middle-class families, the Christians are now part of the elite of Ladakh. This is unlike much of north and central India (and Pakistan) where the majority of Christians are converts from the formerly 'untouchable' castes. Like their counterparts in, say Kerala, missionaries did not come here in the wake of a colonial government. Therefore, Christianity in Ladakh is not synonymous with westernisation. Also, as in Kerala, Ladakhi Christians dress the same way, eat the same food and live in the same type of houses as their Buddhist counterparts.

Almost all Christians in Ladakh belong to the Moravian church, even though the Jesuits had arrived almost three hundred years before. Perhaps the Jesuits did not try to proselytise, or maybe they did not stay on long enough.

The missionaries brought with them the seeds of vegetables like potatoes, tomatoes and cauliflower, thitherto unknown in Ladakh. They also introduced 'Western' skills such as baking and knitting. (Most Ladakhis still weave their own tweed—called *pattoo*—at home and knitting is still a rarity in much of rural Ladakh.) As Mrs. Rizvi points out, 'The first radio in Ladakh belonged to the mission, in the 1940s.'

1947 to the present: India's independence and thereafter

1948: The Pakistani invasion

In 1947, India was partitioned between Islamic Pakistan and secular India. The Hindu Mahâraja of the Muslim-majority Jammu and Kashmir vacillated between the two. He even considered remaining independent.

Pakistan decided to annex the state. It engineered what it charmingly described as (but its own historians no longer accept) a 'tribal invasion.' The fiction was that some tribals had, on their own, decided to invade this Indian state, and that the Pakistani army and government had nothing to do with the 'raid.' ('The raid' is the name that *all* Kashmiris remember this event by.)

In the summer of 1948, the Gilgit Scouts invaded Ladakh- the Indus valley to be precise. (Though named 'scouts' by the British, such regiments consist of adult soldiers and are now a formal part of Pakistan's armed forces.) They captured Skardu and Kargil and proceeded towards Leh. They reached Taru, just twenty kilometres short of Leh town. A handful of raiders even sneaked into the town, but were too few to cause any major damage.

Having enjoyed almost a century of peace the last thing that the Ladakhis (or their Dogra rulers) had in mind was the need for an army to defend the land. Leh at least had a platoon of the volunteer 2nd Dogras. Kargil did not even have that (which is why it was taken without resistance). As in Kashmir, a militia was raised in Leh, under the leadership of the Kalon (pron. kuh-lone) clan, descendant of the hereditary prime ministers of Ladakh. (Today, politically the Kalons are greatly respected and count for far more than even the Namgyâl scions.)

Sonam Narboo, a Sheffield University-educated civil engineer and the first Ladakhi to be educated outside India, got an airstrip constructed. It was a remarkable feat because the Leh airfield (expanded on several subsequent occasions) remains the highest in the world. Some Indian troops arrived by air, landing on this airstrip, while a battalion of Gurkhas came up from neighbouring Manali, climbing very difficult mountains in the process. (Manali is now a part of Himachal Pradesh.)

(Sonam Narboo went on to become a legend in his own right—as an engineer who built roads on the world's highest mountains, as an incorruptible civil servant and as a leader of men. That Ladakh's finest hospital is dedicated to his memory indicates that the people of Leh consider him the most outstanding Ladakhi of the 20th century.)

Indian troops, helped by the Ladakhi militia and the 2nd Dogra Regiment, defended Leh and repulsed the raiders. Then, in the legendary dZoji Lâ operations, they used tanks to beat the raiders back from Kargil as well. (The best account of this battle is Dr. S.S. Bloeria's 1997 book, *The Zoji Lâ Operations,* Har Anand Publications.)

Thus the people of Ladakh, Buddhist as well as Muslim, voted with their blood to join India, rather than Pakistan. It has remained so ever since.

In 1948, a ceasefire was ordered before Baltistan could be similarly rescued. The word 'rescued' is used advisedly, for the Baltis would much rather be united with the people of Kargil, with whom they share culture, language and religion, than be submerged in Pakistan, which does not give this federally administered area the rights that it gives its four states.

Landlocked Zâñskâr too was taken by the raiders. When snow fell and blocked the Penzi Lâ (pass) in October-November 1948, Kargil was still with the Pakistanis, and the raiders were in control of Zâñskâr. However, soon thereafter the Indian army liberated Kargil, but it could not enter Zâñskâr because of the snow.

It took this news several weeks to reach Zâñskâr, where the raiders found themselves in an odd position. On the one hand, their control of Zâñskâr was absolute, for they had guns while the unarmed Zâñskâris' only weapon was the (fairly lethal) slingshot. On the other they knew that the Indian army had liberated all the areas surrounding Zâñskâr and would easily regain Zâñskâr as soon as the Penzi Lâ reopened in June.

So, the raiders put on a brave face and ruled Zâñskâr till a few weeks before the passes were to reopen in 1949. They then started slinking away through emergency routes used by the Zâñskâris in spring.

The cease-fire agreement also meant that the Pakistani army was allowed to keep a picket on a hilltop overlooking Kargil town, hardly three kilometres from the heart of the town. This enabled the Pakistanis to pound the civil population of Kargil at will. So, during the September 1965 war, in order to protect the people of Kargil the Indian army set itself the task of recovering this picket, which it did. However, under the agreement signed by the Prime Ministers of India and Pakistan at Tashkent (then in the USSR) in January 1966, the picket was handed back to Pakistan, which resumed its nuisance. During the 1971 war, the Indian army captured the picket again and pushed the Pakistan back to about twelve kilometres away from the town.

That's the way it's been ever since. However, the range of the Pakistani weapon range seems to have improved because in 1998, they started shelling the town and the highway more frequently than ever before. (For the tourist this meant that till the Pakistani army stopped behaving like some primitive force, the safest route to Kargil during that period was from Leh town. The road from Zâñskâr/ Suru valley was equally safe, though.)

The Chinese invasion

Pakistan was not the only neighbour to covet the territory of this fabled frontier province. So did China. To begin with the Pakistani government gifted to its Chinese masters a substantial chunk (5,180 sq.km.) of the Ladakhi territory it had obtained through the 1948 cease-fire. (India and Pakistan are the two mothers who went to King Solomon for a decision on who the baby's real mother was. Solomon would have decreed that the woman who allowed the state of Jammu and Kashmir to be carved up could not have been its mother.)

In 1949, the Chinese snapped Ladakh's centuries- (perhaps a millennium-) old road link with Central Asia. Ladakh's position as the centre of those trade routes, already damaged by King Senge Namgyâl, was thus lost forever.

The Chinese annexed Tibet in 1950. The events that followed resulted in the exile to India of the highest ranking Mahâyân Buddhist, His Holiness the Dalai Lâmâ. Hundreds of thousands of Tibetans—scholars, priests and laymen—accompanied him.

Some of these refugees came to Ladakh. They settled in places as far apart as Hanle on the Tibetan border and Choglamsar near Leh town. China's treatment of His Holiness, senior Buddhist monks and Tibetan monasteries has resulted in hostility for that country in Leh and Zâñskâr in particular.

Then in 1962, the Chinese army walked through India's unguarded Ladakh borders. China helped itself to the huge, but mostly uninhabited, Aksai Chin plateau. The Indian Army had not been posted at the border because the Indians and the Chinese were supposed to be 'brothers' those days. The Chinese incursion was noticed several months later by some junior ranking policemen of India's central government.

Later that year India was formally attacked by China, in Ladakh as well as in what is now known as Arunachal Pradesh. In Ladakh, the Chinese army came up to Chushul (near the Pangong lake). It fought the Ladakh Scouts and other regiments of the Indian army. India lost that war, and even more territory.

Another chunk of the Pangong lake was taken by China (in addition to the portion of the lake legally held by Tibet under previous treaties). In all, China has since been in possession of 37,555 sq.km. of Ladakh.

After the 1962 war, the border between India (i.e. Ladakh) and China (i.e. Tibet) was closed. Ladakh's links with Tibet were snapped, perhaps forever.

(Today the easiest—and only legal—way to travel between Ladakh and neighbouring Tibet is via Delhi. The traveller has to fly from Delhi to some Chinese city such as Beijing, and thence to Lhâsâ. In 1993, this writer had, as J&K's Tourism Secretary, submitted a proposal for allowing Indian pilgrims to travel through Dem Chok in Ladakh to the sacred Mansarovar lake in Tibet. The Government of India has taken the matter up with the Chinese.)

Improved communications

Each war- three with Pakistan and one with China- has brought the people of Leh and Kargil closer to India. Emotionally, as well as physically. Till the mid 1960s the only way to travel from Ladakh to the rest of India was on foot (or horseback) through very difficult, cold and high mountain passes. (Unless one got a lift on an Indian Air Force aeroplane, that is.)

India lost to the Chinese in 1962, mainly because there were no roads on which the Indian army could transport its men and materials into or through Ladakh. So the Indian government got a highway built between Srinagar and Leh. It is rather rough even by Indian standards. However, it is an awesome feat considering it is the world's highest road, considering India's meagre resources and considering the difficulty of building roads at those altitudes and in that freezing climate. Several engineers of the Indian army died while constructing the road.

Suddenly Ladakh was linked to regions quite different from itself—in terms of terrain, climate, race, religion, language and even levels of development. These contacts intensified when in 1974, many parts of Ladakh were thrown open to tourists. (Nine picturesque areas, including the Pangong and Tsomo Riri lakes, as well as Dâ-Hânu, continued to be restricted till 1993. In that year this author managed to overcome the objections of various paranoid organisations that opposed such opening up. Among other things I argued that since the Chinese allowed tourists to go to their part of the Pangong, why shouldn't we. The Army supported me. Mr. Rajesh Pilot, then India's junior Home Minister, accepted our argument. We succeeded.)

Unprecedented prosperity

All over the world tourism departments aim at receiving tourists equal to one percent of the population of the land. In 2004, foreign tourists equal to 0.25 percent of India's population visited India as a whole. In contrast, in 1988, the year tourism peaked in Ladakh, Leh received tourists equal to 35% of the population of the district and perhaps 120% of the population of the town. And that is not even the main reason why Ladakh is so prosperous.

The labour wage in Ladakh is almost three times as high as the rate laid down for India as a whole. There is *no* unemployment in Ladakh at the labour level, or at any other level. Indeed, Ladakh imports labour from the poorer states of India to build its roads. It also 'imports' skilled labour to repair its watches and shoes, sew its clothes, cut hair and cook Indian sweets. Very few of the waiters in Ladakh's many hotels are Ladakhi. The managers are almost all from Bengal. The owners, of course, are entirely Ladakhi.

How did Ladakh, impoverished till the 1960s, suddenly get so prosperous? Among Indian states, in per capita terms Nagaland gets the highest funds from New Delhi for the expenses of its government (for salaries as well as for roads, hospitals, etc.). Among all Indian districts Ladakh receives the highest. And this does not include what is spent on the army or what the army and its officials spend in the markets of Ladakh.

The people of the Valley of Kashmir are far more open to new ideas than the people of, say, Jammu or Uttar Pradesh or Bihar. This is evident from the fact that between 1900 and 1989, the majority of new ideas,[15] in the government and in the private sector, took root in Kashmir before they did in these other places. This could have to do with Kashmir's greater exposure to tourists from Western Europe and the USA. Leh is even more open to new ideas. The concept of guest-houses, for example, caught on in in the 1970s and '80s in Leh and Zâñskâr but not in, say, the rest of Kargil[16].

Solar photovoltaic cells, passive solar heating and, especialy, the south- and east- facing 'glass room' caught on in Leh and Zâñskâr (the glass room in the rest of Kargil, as well), as soon as the government (and non-governmental organisations) introduced them. As the Deputy Commissioner of Jammu, I banned polythene in that district in 1991. The ban did not work. One of my younger colleagues, PK Tripathi, banned it in Leh a few years later, and the people of the district helped him

15. Hostility to new ideas was most notable in the case of allopathic medicine and the railway line, both of which were initially resisted in the towns of Jammu province.
16. The first guest-house in the State was established around 1920- in Srinagar. This culture reached in Jammu city in the 1980s. Guest-houses are found all over rural Leh and Zâñskâr, but nowhere in rural Jammu or Kargil.

enforce the ban strictly. Since the late 1990s, attitudes towards technological change have begun changing in Kargil, as well.

Put together all this has resulted in rapid prosperity for the people of Ladakh, though tourism has mainly benefited parts of Leh and Zâñskâr.

Rapid change

The architecture of houses has changed, certainly for the better. More glass being used on the southern and eastern walls to let in the sun (and thus provide badly needed heat). This in turn owes to the example of the eco-friendly houses and offices built for the government (mainly the army) in the 1970s.

After the 1960s the government went in for a massive plantation of trees. By the mid-1970s Ladakh's climate had begun to change[17] . This cold desert had never known a flood before, but in 1977, just one inch of rainfall caused a flood of sorts. The little snow that the plains of Leh receive is dry and flaky. But in the autumn (not winter) of 1998 parts of Leh received snow that was at the same time wet, plentiful (almost a foot) and unusually early. This snow damaged many buildings, notably the Spituk monastery.

Society, too, has changed, rapidly in Leh town, slower elsewhere. Till the early 1980s everyone in Zâñskâr, without exception, wore red *gonchas* (gowns) made of the local *pattoo* tweed. Even in those days in Leh town people wore gowns of all kinds of colours and materials. Polyandry was on its way out in Leh town then, but still quite common in Zâñskâr. By the end of the 20th century, polyandry (like red gonchas made of pattoo) was fading out even in Zâñskâr.

Some changes are almost imperceptible. The Ladakhis, for instance, do not have surnames. (Not that other Indians have always had them. However, in the 20th century, especially after independence in 1947, most Indians started using the names of their clan/ sub-caste as a surname.) Few Ladakhis would admit to having a caste system. In any case, except for royalty, Ladakhis do not have family names of any kind.

All Ladakhis have two names (e.g. Sonam Dorji). Both Sonam *and* Dorji are *given* names. Sonam Dorji's father would *not* be a Dorji. A

17. The enormous increase in the number of trees since the 1960s is a fact. So is the change in the climate. And yet there might be no connection between the two. According to one school of thought, the climate begins to change only after 30% of an area has been covered with trees. Neither Leh nor Kargil is anywhere near that figure. The change in climate in both districts could possibly be part of the overall change that has taken place in the Indian Himalayas and parts of central Asia, especially since 1998.

person called Jigmet Angchuk would name his son *not* XYZ Angchuk but something totally different and chosen quite at random. Say, Rigzin Dorji.

However, since the 1960s children from some of the better off families of Leh town in particular have been given their father's second name (which, I repeat, was originally not a surname) to use as their own second name. The children of the legendary (and aforementioned Sheffield-educated) Sonam Narboo were among the first to do so. Thus, Narboo became their surname.

Political trends

Buddhist-Muslim relations, too, are no longer what they used to be. In the early 1990s, there was a politically motivated social boycott of a minority community by some people in Leh. This was the result of acrimony that had been building up since the late 1980s.

Following a series of agitations, in 1994 New Delhi conceded Leh a measure of autonomy vis a vis the Srinagar-Jammu based state government. In turn, the previous year the agitationists had agreed to lift the boycott of the minority. The district administration was thitherto headed by civil servants, answerable to Srinagar/ Jammu. Since 1994, the administration has started reportng to the elected Ladakh Autonomous Hill Development Council. The Congress swept the 1995 elections to the LAHDC.

The (Indian National) Congress first contested elections in the state in 1967. (Between the 1930s and the 1960s, the Congress had felt no need to have a presence in the state. That's because the National Conference had a similar ideology and was also friends with the Congress.) Leh has since invariably voted for the Congress. However, in 1996 the (Jammu & Kashmir) National Conference won three of the four seats that Ladakh has in the state legislative assembly.

The Congress was back in form in 2000 when it won 20 of the 26 seats of the LAHDC.

In elections to the national parliament held in 2004, the Ladakh Buddhist Association (LBA), won. Many of its members had been in the Congress.

References

i 1928 according to Sheikh, 'History of Leh- A New Perspective,' *New Hope*, Srînagar. November-December, 2002, p.40.

ii Introduction to *A History of Ladâkh* by A.H.Francke, Sterling Publishers, New Delhi. (1977)

ii 'History of Leh- A New Perspective,' *New Hope*, Srînagar, November-December, 2002, pp.38-39

2

A History of Kargil

'The Kargil-Khaltse area was a lake'

There is reason to believe that much of Kargil was a big lake once. The lake went all the way up to Lama Yûrû and Khaltse. It was formed when a large boulder fell into River Indus at Kachora in Baltistan. To this day there is alluvial soil on both sides of the Indus. This is said to be proof that a lake once existed there.

Bryophite (plant) fossils, perhaps five million years old, found in large numbers in the Khaltse-Lama Yûrû area are said to be further proof for this theory. The clincher is the fact that mollusc fossils have been found near Nîraq and Wan Lâ. These include the fossils of lobsters, horse shoe crabs, some varities of fish, and snails.

This theory, encountered in Kashmir and Kishtwar as well, simply has to be true. The fossils of whales have been found on hilltops in Pakistan's Salt Mountains, which are further south.

People began to settle in the area after the waters of the lake got drained off. The first settlers were the Dards, an Indo-Aryan people from Central Asia, who came through Gilgit and Astor. The Tibetans might have come even before but they were nomads, and were late in settling down. The Mons were the third group of settlers.

Purîg

Much of present day Kargil district was once known as Purîg. The region called Purîg included the area around Kargil town, the Suru valley, Shagh(k)ar Chiktan, Pashk(y)um, Bodh Kharbu and Mulbek(h).

We have almost nothing to go by when we try to study the history of Purîg (pron. pu-reeg). However, two 20th century historians, Moulvi Hashmat Ullah Khan and Kachu Sikandar Khan[1], have been able to piece

1. This account relies largely on the Kachu and, to a lesser extent, on the Maulvi.

together a fairly satisfactory history. They have mostly relied on oral sources- and some references contained in Tibetan chronicles. Of course, 'satisfactory' means sometimes accepting dates that are accurate only to the nearest 1200 years.

The name 'Purîg': There are four theories about the name Purîg itself. One is that it is a contraction of the Tibetan phrase 'pot reeks', which means 'of Tibetan stock'. In that case, the name probably dates to the era when a Tibetan dynasty first established a government in most of Purîg. (The people of Purîg are known as Purîg-pâ. They speak a language that is closer to Tibetan than is the language of Leh district. Racially, too, they are closer to the Tibetans than are the people of Leh. Incidentally, in most Ladakhi languages the suffix '-pa' means 'of-,' exactly the same as the '-walla' of western India and '-wal' of North India. Thus 'Purîg-pâ' means 'of Purîg.')

Another interpretation is that Purîg means 'tube' and refers to the tubular valleys that make up the inhabited parts of the region. Scholars like Francke feel that the word has been derived from 'burig', which means 'the brave race'. The 'race' in question is the Dards.

The fourth theory is that the Tibetans were the first to rule here. They came from Purang. Therefore, they named the region Purig.

The ancient period

The early settlers: Dard and Lone

Human habitation seems to have been late in coming to this incredibly cold and rugged district- perhaps as late as 500-0 B.C. (Drâss, for instance, is the world's second coldest inhabited place, after Siberia.) The Dards were perhaps the first to settle here. They came from the various little valleys of Gilgit, the Pâmîrs, Hunzâ, Nagar and Chîlâs. They mostly belonged to the so-called Aryan 'race'. Some were Scythians. Gilgit is in Dardistan, now in POK.

Khan Bahadur Ghulam Muhammad Khan, a senior civil servant of the Dogra Mahârajas, had this belief investigated in the first few decades of the 20th century. He concluded that the original home of the Dards of Da and Drâss was the Bagrot valley of Gilgit. The Dards of Drâss are certainly from the Sheena (Shina) tribe. The people of Da speak a similar language.

The Dards travelled to Kargil through Baltistan and Deosai, some of them staying on in Baltistan itself. They ruled over Purîg till the Tibetan attack on Zâñskâr- and the Tibetan rule that followed in Purîg. They also ruled over much of the present Leh district. (When did the attack on Zâñskâr take place? Moulvi Hashmat Ullah Khan says 180 BC. Kachu

Sikandar Khan says 9th or 10th century AD. But then, what's eleven or twelve hundred years between friends?)

The anicient language, customs, racial characteristics and religious practices of the Dards can still be found in some areas like Da-Hanu and Chiktan-Garkun, and to some extent in Shanghu-Shaghar. However, by and large, most of the Dards- including some of their most ancient tribes- got assimilated with the Tibetans.

(The Government of India had, in the 1970s, restricted the entry of tourists into the Dâ-Hânu area. This was partly to preserve the purity and antiquity of these 'Aryan' practices and partly because the area had begun to attract neo-Nazis. Several (Western) guidebooks have written about the incident that triggered off this ban. Around 1976, two young (West) German women landed up in Dâ-Hânu to, er, receive the seed of this '100% pure Aryan people'. However, in 1993, during my first stint as the Tourism Secretary of the state, I was able to get the ban lifted for one half of this area.)

The Dards were not the first people to settle in Shanghu-Shaghar and Drâss. The pioneers here were the seven sons of Poyen Lone. They came over from the Chilâs region (near Nanga Parbat) through Deosai. Members of this clan spread themselves all over the Kharmang valley (Baltistan, POK). They mostly settled in the Barsachal, Targon and Tarkati villages. Their culture and language are different from that of the Dards of, say, Dâ-Hânu or Garkun.

The Dards of Dâ-Hânu had migrated there from the Yanding and Sachal areas of ancient Gilgit. Their language, Brushaski, is the same as that spoken in the fabled Hunzâ valley (also in POK). Hunzâ is considered the original Shangri Lâ by many because of the very high life expectancy of the region.

The early Dard settlers spread right up to Khaltse, Rong Chhorgyot and Skindiyang in Leh district. Within the Dards there seems to have been a core group which controlled all of Purîg till the Tibetan conquest. This group owed nominal allegiance to Kashmir.

Tibetan migrants

Around 150 BC there lived in Purang (Tibet) a noble or chieftain called Thigum Champo. One Lumpo-Longnum killed him. Thigum had three sons, all of who fled to what is now called Kargil. One of the sons, Naithichan, is said to have founded the first kingdom in Kargil. This was in Purig.

Migration from the Indian plains

Around the same period a handful of people from the Indian plains, too, migrated to Purîg. They rapidly assimilated with the Dards. Dastak Paldan and Seergaya Motik led them. (Sikandar Khan feels that the latter name corresponds to the Sanskrit Suryamati.)

Apparently they set up their first colony in a cave in the Shakolchey hill near the Dodu hamlet of present day Pashkum. They constructed a house in Maazanthâñg. The house came to be known as Sargyâmotik-khar. They also constructed canals in Khurbâthâng- the very place being developed for agriculture even today- and Saskot.

Around the same time (the eighth century AD according to Sikandar) Lâmâ Nâropâ and Guru Urgyen Padmâ (i.e. Padma Sambhav) came from Zâñṣkâr. They took Seergaya Motik and Dastak Paldan with them to Kashmir. Kargili historians like Kachu Sikandar claim that these four 'established the first human habitation in Kashmir, at Pampore, this being the era in which the great lakes of Kashmir were being drained and habitable land was emerging on their beds'.

Now, this does seem a bit too much. I have no problems with accepting that the first humans in Kashmir might have come from Kargil and Zâñskâr. Nor even that these four could have been the saints referred to in Kashmir's own histories as the first humans to have lived there. However, by the eighth century AD we have evidence of a very sophisticated civilisation in Kashmir. We have precise details beginning 1184 BC about which king ruled Kashmir when, and for how many years, months and *days*. Therefore, even Hashmat Ullah's 120 BC seems late by a thousand years.

However, it is possible that it was Seergaya Motik who constructed the fort near the Indus river in Stakna (Leh).

Later, some people migrated to Purîg from Leh. Among them were Teesug and Gañgâsug, who were considered goddesses by some. They built a fort on the Tolon hill near the Indus. Sikandar says that they were Dards but according to Hashmat they were Mons. They also founded the Achinâthâng village. Ruins of that ancient settlement can still be seen. This fort was then called the Tolonkhar. It was later taken over by the rulers of Chiktan, who also founded the Stakshan hamlet.

Teesug-Gañgâsug, and their colleagues Cho Paldan and Chocho Kunzum, decided to settle in Stakchey[2]. At that stage all of Purîg was ruled by the Dards. The Tibetans controlled only Kateeka Phokar. (The

2. Mr. C. Phonsog has doubts about the Mons having ever ruled upper Ladakh. I have made this assertion on the authority of Kachu Sikander Khan.

house that the 'goddesses' and their colleagues got constructed at Chiktan Khar was later subsumed by a 16th century AD building. However, on the ground floor there is an ancient, decaying window that is said to have been a part of the ancient original.)

Historians like the Kachu Sikandar feel that the history of Purîg/ Kargil is really the history of these two dynasties and clans—the Dards and the Tibetans. For reasons of brevity we will only look at the fortunes of the central section of Kargil, leaving out the branches.

The story of Shaghar-Chiktan and Sot-Pashkum

Gasho Thâ-Thâ Khan

In the eighth (or maybe early ninth) century AD, Gasho Thâ-Thâ Khan started a dynasty that would rule over the Shakar and Chiktan area for almost a thousand years. He was a scion of the royal family of Gilgit (now in POK).

There are two theories about him. One is that he was an infant child when hunters found him atop a hillock. When he reached manhood they decided to make him their king, to replace the cruel man who was ruling over them. An oracle had told the unpopular king about the man who would one day wrest the throne from him. Since the description fitted Thâ-Thâ Khan, the king ordered his assassination.

The other tradition speaks of a Gilgit prince called Thakan whom his stepbrother Shri Bagor Tham wanted killed. This led to a civil war between the supporters of the two brothers. ('Thakan' sounds suspiciously like a contraction of 'Thâ-Thâ Khan'.'Shri' is a part of the latter's name.)

Either way, the story goes, our friend Thâ-Thâ was sitting in a large hall watching a dance. Thâ-Thâ's rival, the king, sent his men to kill him. The king thought that Thâ-Thâ would be too busy enjoying himself to be able to resist the soldiers.

However, the musicians, who loved Thâ-Thâ, got to know of the plot. They started singing a song that warned him of the impending attack. Thâ-Thâ pulled out his sword and planted it firmly on the ground. He then stepped on the hilt of his sword to reach the chimney, through which he escaped.

(Sounds like something out of a classical opera, what? Well, that's how the story travelled down over more than a thousand years. 'Remembrancers' sing out such epic stories, serialised over a week of dinners around a brazier, in the winters, after snow has blocked the passes and there's little else to do. This way history gets mixed with folklore, but at least we have something to go by.)

Thâ-Thâ travels through Kargil

Thâ-Thâ fled to Baltistan (POK). He was accompanied by his 'milk father' Saati Tam and his 'milk brother' Booti Tam. (Milk brothers are men who have shared the same wet nurse or foster mother.) They entered Kargil through the Chhorbat Lâ (pass). On the banks of the Indus river they found an uninhabited but fertile place, with a natural spring. There was no bridge to cross the river on. However, since the river was frozen they walked across on the ice. Thâ-Thâ had a walnut seed in his pocket, which he planted there.

They next went to Kokashu, which, too, they noticed, was fertile. The staff that Thâ-Thâ carried had been taken from a *bhoj* tree and was still green. He planted it in the centre of the plains of Kokashu.

The three decided not to settle in any of these uninhabited villages. They sought the waters of the Indus at Chey Chey Thâñg instead. After that they went to Blârgo where cats sitting on a rock welcomed them with a dance. A wealthy Brokpa had already settled there and had erected a tower made of broken utensils of china and clay. (This is an East Asian tradition.)

Their next stop was Brolmo. There a senior female citizen warned them about a man-eating 'lion' that lived in the rocky mountains of Kharol, at the point where the Drâss and Suru rivers met. She also taught Thâ-Thâ how to kill this animal, which he did. (Lions have probably never lived in Ladakh. Therefore, this could have been a leopard. The Ladakhi language has different words for the two big cats. In this case 'lion' has been specified.)

Tales of Thâ-Thâ's bravery spread throughout the land. These stories continue to be told to this day. In particular, his moustaches inspired fear and awe among the people. (Not just in Kargil but in most of North India rural people seem to be impressed by ferocious looking rulers.)

After that our heroes went to Sot, where a wealthy Dard clan called Sot Saaral gave them jobs. The older man was employed as a tiller and the two youths as shepherds. (Sot rhymes with 'coat', except that the 't' is soft.) Thâ-Thâ once told his boss about a dream that he had seen. The employer interpreted it as indicating that one day Thâ-Thâ would be the emperor.

After a while the three returned to Kokashu and Dargo. The bhoj and the walnut had by then blossomed into mature trees. (These trees would later grow into full-fledged forests, which exist to this day. The tree that Thâ-Thâ had planted remained there till Zorâwar Singh's time (around 1850). The spot where it had stood has been marked with stones.) Thâ-

Thâ considered this a good omen. He got houses constructed at both these sites, at Totokhar for himself and at Patokhar for his companions.

The trio then climbed the peak of the Neen Dum hill. From there they could see parts of Drâss in the west, the Suru valley in the south, and the Indus valley and Khaltse in the east. They prayed that some day they should rule over it all. Before long they did.

Thâ-Thâ becomes the king

During Thâ-Thâ's reign several people migrated to Purîg Kargil. The first was the Ahmed-pâ family. (Interesting name. It helps fix dates. It indicates that these events took place after the founding of Islam.) Then came Teesug and Gañgâsug. These 'goddesses' were given the house in Chiktan mentioned earlier. They later ruled over that area, briefly.

The other contemporary sovereigns who though ruled in what is now Kargil district were Cho Paldan and Chocho Kunzum.

From well before this era, the people of Turkmenistan were in the habit of attacking and raiding the Mon rulers of upper[3] Ladakh. This time they took Teesug-Gañgâsug, Cho Paldan and Chocho Kunzum back with them as hostages. Thâ-Thâ moved into the vacuum that was thus created and added their territories to his.

Sot and other principalities are united

The ruler of Sot found himself caught between two aggressive, expansionist powers- the minority Tibetans and the majority Dards. He realised that he could not resist both- or even either. So, he simply handed his kingdom over to Thâ-Thâ.

Now, many of Thâ-Thâ's supporters in Gilgit started migrating to Sot. Thâ-Thâ shifted his capital to Kokashu and built his palace where the former ruler's house had stood.

After establishing power in Sot, Thâ-Thâ diverted his attention to development. He got forests cleared to establish the villages of Kargil and Poeen Shalikchey, where he persuaded people from Ladakh and Skardu to settle. (In that age the clearing of forests was considered an achievement.) Kargil, according to this version, was named after its pioneer, a noble called Kargeel. Thâ-Thâ also established the Oma Chak Thâñg, village where his descendants still own land. After that he gradually brought Baru, Minji and Gund under his control. In time he also conrolled the Dard rulers of Khaltse.

3. Kachu Sikandar Khan variously refers to the invaders as 'Turks' and 'Turkmens.' Kâshghar is in the Xinjiang province of China, which local separatists call 'Eastern Turkistan.'

Thâ-Thâ then established Trespon (lit. 'the village of djinns'). I have a particular fascination for the grand Imam Bara (Shiite place of worship) of Trespon because of its spiritual power as well as its picturesque hilltop location and colourful architecture. Ruins of what Thâ-Thâ built can still be seen at Seemo Khar, near the Imam Bara.

He next turned to Suru-Kartse (Karchey), which were then ruled by the Tibetans. Their capital was at Phokar. The Tibetans' administration had begun to show signs of decay. Thâ-Thâ assigned this area to his son, NavLde. In turn, NavLde sent his son Chorazi Astan to establish an autonomous principality there, with its capital at present day Sangrâ. Their dynasty came to an end a few generations later, with the immensely popular ruler, Lde Cho.

(NavLde's eldest brother, Boti Khan alias Moi Gasho, was granted the main Sot-Shaghar-Chiktan territory. Their third brother was settled in Gund.)

Thus, according to 9th century folksongs, did Thâ-Thâ subdue and annex independent principalities. This was at a time when the ancient Dard empire was crumbling but the Tibetans were in the ascendant in Baltistan and lower Ladakh, and in power in Purîg (Kargil). However, as historian Sikandar Khan puts it, after Thâ-Thâ, the Dard, established his new kingdom, 'the Tibetans no longer had the courage to interfere' (in Purîg).

Thâ-Thâ's successors: AD 825-1050

Dates start getting somewhat clearer after Thâ-Thâ's reign. However, even now they are only approximate, and have been rounded to the nearest half-decade.

Thâ-Thâ's son Boti Khan had an eventless reign (circa AD 825 to 850). He seems to have been a contemporary of Nemagon of Leh. (See 'A history of Leh'.) The next five rulers were equally colourless.

Jadeem Beig (c. 975-1000) was the eighth king of the dynasty. He conquered Lâmâ Yûrû, Bodh Kharbu, Lingshet, Wân Lâ, Stakchey and Kanji, extending his kingdom to the Khaltse bridge. Apparently Khaltse was either partitioned between the Sot and Khaltse rulers or ruled by both. Both kings collected taxes in Khaltse.

Drâss had thitherto been loosely subject to Kashmir. Jadeem's son Abd(a)al (c.1000-1025) conquered the Drâss area, right upto the dZoji Lâ (pass). He met with no resistance, because the people of the area were mostly fellow Dards.

The spread of Buddhism

A significant development during the reign of Abdal's grandson Chhabza(a)ngs Cho (c. 1060-1090) was the spread of Buddhism. Lâmâ Lotsâvâ Rinchen Zâñgpo was on his way back from the Indian plains to his native Guge (Western Tibet). He preached the Buddhist gospel wherever he passed. He got Lhâ Khangs (Buddhist temples; Lhâ= God) constructed at Chiktan and Wâkhâ (near Mulbek). Several scholars suggest that it was he who got the stone idol of Chambâ built at Mulbek. (The Chambâ is the future Buddha.)

The medieaval (or medieval) era

The advent of Islam

The next important era is that of Amrood Cho, also known as Mureed Khan (c.1450-1475). This was when Islam first spread in Purîg, through the efforts of the saint Ameer Kabeer Syed Ali Hamadani and his disciple Syed Muhammad Noor Bakhsh. (According to some historians, Syed Muhammad was a disciple of Khwaja Ishaq of Khatlan and that it was the Khwaja who had been a *khalifâ* or disciple of the Ameer Kabeer.)

That Amrood Cho had an alternate, Islamic, name seems to indicate that he, too, had converted to Islam, or followed two religions (as twelve per cent of India does even today). Khan, incidentally, is *not* an Islamic surname. (Genghis, to take a particularly celebrated example, was not a Muslim. The word is variously spelt and pronounced Qâ'an, Khân and Hân in various Central Asian languages. In the Mongolian language, the word means 'king.')

The 15th century: Disintegration

The people gave Amrood's elder son and successor Dooroo Cho the nickname Ald-dor Cho, meaning the 'lax and incompetent one'. He was cruel as well. Not surprisingly, under him the administrative structure of the state collapsed.

So, the Gyâpo of Tingmo(s)gang annexed the areas between the Khaltse bridge and the Kanji nallah. The king of Astor, possibly Maqpon Shah Sultan, helped himself to Drâss. Gyal Bum Lde Raja Phokar took Suru and Kartse. That left just Chiktan and Sot with Dooroo. His angry subjects punished him for his incompetence. They ensured that he was allowed to eat only half as much as he used to before. (He was under some kind of house arrest.)

Dooroo died childless. He was succeeded by his younger brother Habib Cho (c. 1490 to 1510). During Habib's reign, Mir Shams ud Din propagated Islam in Purîg and Baltistan. Some historians say that the Mir advocated the Imamiya or Shia school in particular. The Mir was a saint from Iraq and a disciple of the son of the great Syed Muhammad Noor Bakhsh of Khurasan. Habib Cho accepted Shia (Shiite) doctrine. His father had already converted to Islam.

(Other missionaries from Kashmir and Baltistan carried the message of Islam from village to village. Their descendants are known as the Aghas, or the exalted ones. Till, say, the 1950s, before elections began to be held in Kargil, the district was informally divided into turf controlled by two major and several minor Aghas. The Aghas were religious as well as temporal leaders. On festivals each Kargili family would present a small tribute to the Agha that it owed allegiance to. This would be in cash, a tithe to wit. The system still continues but the hold is quite informal now, and much weaker. Real power has shifted to the state, which pumps more money into Ladakh, per capita, than in any other part of India.)

Habib allied with the kings of Khapalû, Shaghar and Skardu. Together they attacked Leh, in order to recover the territory that Dooroo had lost to the Gyâpos. The Gyâpo agreed to pay a heavy tribute. However, this tribute was paid mostly to the King of Shaghar, and not to the other three allies.

Habib's son Ahmed Malik Khan (c. 1510-1535) succeeded him. During his reign, Sultan Abû Saeed Khan Waai, of Kâshghar, who was a Turkmen[4], attacked Leh, Zâñskâr, Suru and Sot. (His army also invaded Kashmir. Mirzâ Haider Dûghlât/ Gurgân was his Commander in Chief.) Ahmed accepted the Sultan's superiority.

The Turkmens must have stayed in Purîg for a while, because they left some major landmarks behind. Among them is the Hor Lam, the Turkmen road that runs between Gund, Mangalpur and Seliskot. The Turkmens left a deep imprint on the culture of Ladakh, including its songs and folktales. (In this context a Turkmen really means a Mughal[5] directly from Central Asia, rather than one who came from Delhi-Agra.)

4. Were the Turkmens Mughals at all? Legitimate doubts have been expressed about this. My main reason for classifying them as 'Central Asian Mughals' is that Dûghlât in particular was a Chughatâî Mughal and a cousin of Emperor Bâbar. Sultan Abû Saeed Khan Waai, too, was his kinsman. Therefore, the leadership of at least this army was Mughal. Unlike Bâbar, who entered India through Afghanistan and present day Pakistan, Sultan Abû Saeed's army came in through Leh. It exited through the Chhorbat Lâ (pass), in the Hanu Lâ area, and crossed into Baltistan.

5. Except that the Kargilis are indeed fussy about the meat they eat. They won't eat meat slaughtered by or food cooked by a non-Muslim. Nor uncooked meat that has been touched by a non-Muslim.

The ambitious Tsering Malik

Khokhor Baghram (c.1535-1555) inherited the throne from his father Ahmed. He made friends with Gyâpo Tsewang Namgyâl in order to buy peace for his eastern borders. His younger son Tsering Malik was the governor of Chiktan. Tsering was an ambitious young man. A bit too ambitious. He wanted to be the king. So, he started going to the court of Gyâpo Jamyang Namgyâl.

Now Jamyang fancied Tsering's wife. So, Tsering divorced her and handed her over to Jamyang, who made an honest woman of her. She is best known by the hybrid name, Tsering rGyâlmo (lit.: Queen Mother Tsering). The historian Maulvi Hashmatullah says that she was pregnant (presumably by Jamyang) when she married the Gyâpo. The child thus born was Nawang Namgyâl.

The sordidness didn't end there. In exchange, Jamyang gave his own daughter in marriage to Tsering, promised to help him and asked him to go home. Jamyang was happy that he had now obtained a foothold in Purîg.

According to a tradition, en route the Gyâpo got Tsering imprisoned at Matho and jailed Tsering's new queen at Stok. Tsering's supporters resorted to arms, attacked Leh and got the royal couple freed. Subsequently perhaps the Gyâpo and Tsering patched up.

On his return to Purîg, Tsering declared Chiktan independent. This could have led to a civil war between Tsering and his brother rGyâl Malik. Their father, Khokhor Baghram, acted wisely and saved the kingdom from ruination by partitioning it between the two.

Around this time, Ali Sher Khan, the heir apparent of Skardu, conquered parts of Baltistan. In those days the Gyâpo of Leh would post a representative (a 'resident' of sorts), as well as soldiers, at Kartakhsha (Baltistan). Ali Sher personally chased both the Resident and the soldiers out of Baltistan.

Now, Tsering controlled the Chiktan area and rGyâl the Sot area. Relations between the two were tense. Tsering, ever the ambitious one, got in touch with Ali Sher. Ali attacked Sot and, thus, formalised Chiktan's independence. In return, Tsering gifted Bodh Kharbu and some neighbouring villages to Ali Sher. Ali stationed his soldiers at the Bodh Kharbu fort and left. On its way home his army burnt and destroyed several Ladakhi villages.

An enraged Jamyang Namgyâl and his army suddenly showed up at Bodh Kharbu. They had travelled through the Fatu Lâ. It was a Friday. The Balti soldiers were offering prayers at Chhorbas Spang. The people of Bodh Kharbu were Buddhists, like Jamyang. They helped him seize the Bodh Kharbu fort. The area was thus liberated from Ali Sher.

The Gyâpo received Tsering at Bodh Kharbu. He wasn't particularly angry with his son-in-law. He even allowed Tsering to retain his independence.

Just then Ali Sher was told about the defeat of his soldiers. He allied with Balti princes and attacked Leh. So, Jamyang had to rush back. (See also 'Losar' in the chapter on 'The Buddhist Festivals of Leh and Zâñskâr'.)

In the event, both Jamyang and Tsering retained their thrones, and kept their kingdoms intact. Indeed, Tsering added Pashkum to his territories, by intervening in a dispute that centred on a love affair. Encouraged by his closeness to the Gyâpo, he also annexed villages like Skambo Yocham, Kostey, Tacha Karat, Kargil, Baru, Manji and Kannaur. These villages had thitherto been under Pashkum.

Sot, Pashkum and Chiktan are united- for a while

Sultan Malik (c.1600-1610) inherited from his father rGyâl Malik both the throne of Sot and the grudge against Tsering. He attacked and annexed Chiktan and Pashkum. Tsering and his son Sankhan fought bravely, but both were killed. Sultan imprisoned Sankhan's minor sons, Adam and Chhosaraang Mailk, at Yukma Kharbu.

Most of the people of Chiktan were Buddhists. Some of them were related by blood to the kings of Leh. They started agitating against the people of, and control by, Sot. They sent a delegation to Ali Sher Khan, who, by then, was the Maqpon of Skardu. They also contacted Senge Namgyâl of Leh, who did not seem interested in helping them.

Ali Sher did.

In those days there lived in Skardu a doctor from Chiktan. His name was Chhozaang Kashi. He had cured Ali Sher's queen of some disease. Instead of a reward all that he asked of Ali Sher was that the delegation from Chiktan be listened to sympathetically. The Maqpon did just that. He even sent his vizier and nobles to Sultan Malik, who freed the two minor princes.

Under pressure from the Baltis of Skardu, Sultan even restored Adam to his ancestral throne. Once again Pashkum and Chiktan became independent of Sot.

Now Senge Namgyâl attacked Purîg, ostensibly to avenge the then recent invasion of Chiktan. He wrested Wâkhâ and Mulbek and, after a while, Kartsey (Kartse/Karchey) and Suru, from different kings.

Senge then prepared to attack Sot. Sultan Muhammad (c.1610-1650), the son of Sultan Malik, was the King of Sot by then. He sought the help of Skardu's Adam Khan. At Adam Khan's request, Ali Mardan Khan, the Mughal governor of Kashmir, sent a detachment of the Mughal army to help out Purîg.

The Mughal-Balti force met Senge at Karpokhar. By most accounts- at least according to the credible ones- the Mughals won. Thus Suru and Kartse (Karchey) were freed from the control of Leh. However, Wâkhâ and Mulbek continued to remain under Leh. (So, the historians of Leh were at least partly right when they claimed that the Leh army had got the better of the Mughal-Balti combine.)

The Kargilis believe that when the Turkmens (Mughals) invaded Kargil at Pasri Khar, Muhammad Sultan repulsed their attack- in alliance with the Leh army. (So, the historians of Leh- and Bhaderwah- are not alone in claiming victory over the Mughals for their kings.)

This was the first time that the Mughals of Delhi-Agra or any other Indian power had sent its forces into Ladakh.

The last independent kings

Muhammad Sultan's son Mirza Sultan (c.1650-1660) was the next king of Sot. Mirza Sultan's throne, in turn, passed on to his descendants Mirza Beig, Baghram Beig, Jangeer Beig and Yahya Khan, in that order.

If folk-songs are to be believed, then of all these kings, Arbab Shah was the best. Peace and prosperity marked his reign. During Baghram Khan's tenure, Sot and Kartse allied against Leh. Together they captured Kharol, Chhotok and some neighbouring villages. However, some influential people of Sot were secretly working for the Gyâpo of Leh. The Gyâpo launched a counter-attack with their help. Baghram Khan had to surrender the gains that he had made only recently. (When the history of this period- the late seventeenth/ early eighteenth century- is viewed from Leh it appears that Leh exercised some kind of control over Kargil. The historians of Kargil do not mention this.)

Yahya Khan (c.1780-1810) succeeded his father Jangeer Beig. His mother was perhaps the sister of the king of Kartse. His son, Salaam Khan (1810-1834) was the next- and last- king of Sot. It was during Salaam's reign that the Dogras conquered Purîg, Baltistan and Leh. (For more details, see 'A History of Leh'.)

The modern age

The Dogra conquest

In the summer of 1834, Raja Gulab Singh of Jammu sent Vazîr Zorâwar Singh, his legendary army chief, to annex Ladakh.

Officially Gulab was conquering Ladakh for the Mahâraja of Punjab. However, he sought (and received) the blessings of the British to add Ladakh to Jammu. An alarmed king of Ladakh sent numerous messages to the British that he would ally with them. He was ignored.

Zorâwar's army travelled to Ladakh through Kishtwâr and Zâñskâr.

Ladakh did not have a proper army at the time: just a civil defence system. At Sankoo in Kargil's Suru valley volunteers got together and offered some resistance. The Dogra army brushed them aside. By the time the invaders reached Pashkum, Kargil's dreaded winter announced itself. The Dogras sent word to the king of Leh that they would withdraw if he would pay them Rs.15,000. The king rejected the offer, on his wife's advice.

Snubbed, Zorâwar retreated to a place near Sankoo, where his army and he decided to camp for the winter, biding their time. The Ladakhi army waited till the next April to attack Zorâwar's men. The Ladakhis were defeated.

In 1839, rebellion broke out against the Dogras. Sukamir Rahim Khan of Chigtan and Hussain of Pashkyum led the resistance. Zorâwar rushed to Kargil and subdued the movement with an enormous show of force.

He then set up a joint command of Dogra and Ladakhi forces. Together they conquered Baltistan, reuniting that area with the rest of Ladakh after a gap of several centuries.

Kargil joins Kashmir and Jammu

The Dogras appointed Salaam Khan, the defeated king, as the chief administrator of the areas that his father- and their ancestors before them had ruled. (His descendants continued to occupy senior positions in the government even in the second half of the twentieth century, after the state acceded to India.)

The fortunes of Purîg, indeed of all Kargil, now merged with those of Leh and Jammu. Soon Kashmir would join them. Therefore, the history of Kargil after that would substantially be the same as that of Leh, Kashmir or Jammu.

In independent India

(See also 'A History of Leh' for this period.)

In August 1947, as soon as Pakistan came into being, it wanted to annex Jammu and Kashmir, the multi-ethnic state that the Dogras had forged. So, on the 22nd October, the Pakistani army sent irregular tribal soldiers into Kashmir and Ladakh. The state acceded to India on the 26th October, 1947. The Pakistani army helped itself to Baltistan, Gilgit, and Hunzâ, which it now administers under the name 'the Northern Areas'. It denies these Areas political representation, despite directions from its own Supreme Court.

1972: A line of control is drawn

On the 10th December, 1972, a 'line of control' was demarcated by the Indian and Pakistani authorities. This is a border, without calling it that. The agreenent was reached at Mini-marg, a vilage near the dZoji Lâ.

The LoC runs somewhat thus: From the Karobalgali passes it goes to Neeral (on the Indian side) and Brelman (under Pakistan's control). It then proceeds northwards to Chet (in Kargil), the Chhorbat Lâ (in Turtuk) and finally Thâñg (also on the Indian side).

Pakistan punishes Kargil

In every war imposed by Pakistan, the people of Kargil have supported India, for which they have paid a heavy price.

Pakistan has not forgiven the all-Muslim Kargil for this: nor for spurning the Pakistan-inspired secessionist movement of the 1990s.

During each war, and often in peacetime as well, the towns and villages of Kargil have been shelled by the Pakistani army, which is stationed on hilltops overlooking Kargil. Once in every few years (as in 1965, 1971 and 1998) it vents its anger by hitting Kargil town and the villages near it with rockets and mortars, killing people and destroying property.

In 1998, Pakistan fired rockets from its side of the line of control several hundred times. It would routinely shell vehicles travelling on the Kargil section of the national highway. It also destroyed the Kargil district hospital, an upmarket hotel and, more ominously, two Shia mosques. I don't believe that even Pakistan would deliberately have tried to destroy Shia mosques. But during the 1999 war the Pakistani army officially boasted of the accuracy of its artillery. Does that mean that the mosques had been targeted, and not hit by mistake?

And yet, as I have repeatedly emphasised in this book, and in its companion volumes, interpretations of history in terms of one religion versus another or one sect versus the other are never correct. It is true that the Shias of Kargil have always stood by India. Alexander Evans, a British researcher, told me that when he visited the camps in Muzaffarabad (POK) where Kashmiri militants are trained, there was not a single trainee from Kargil.

The people of Turtuk in Leh district, on the other hand, were not so immune. (Turtuk, incidentally, was under Pakistani occupation till 1971, when it was liberated by the Indian Army.) The people of Kargil have acted the way they did out of principle and conviction, and not merely because of Pakistan's sectarian bias against them. And God has rewarded the Kargilis for this- generously.

Kargil: the peace dividend

Ask any informed person from Jammu and Kashmir as to which the most backward, the most illiterate district of the state is. Chances are that you will be told 'Kargil'- or, may be, 'Kupwara'. (Both answers are wrong. Budgam has, at least since 1981, been the most illiterate. In that year, Kargil was eleventh among the fourteen districts of the state in terms of literacy.)

Kargil has this image of a people crippled by superstition and feudal lords, and of women subjugated by a malign interpretation of Islam. It is supposed to be a district where the most regressive social customs thrive. I have known, and loved, Kargil and its people since 1982. Since then I have been plied with endless propaganda about Kargil. However, I have seen very little of these supposedly mediæval practices.

When the results of the 2001 census came in, Kargil was the biggest surprise: for everyone except me. In terms of literacy its rank zoomed from no.11, close to the bottom, to no.5, almost on a par with Srinagar, which, till 1989, had been the seat of the finest education in the state. This was the biggest jump for any district.

This sudden change was the result of the work of dedicated civil servants and massive government funding. However, none of it would have worked had the people themselves not been determined to develop their district in every respect.

Every teenaged girl I know in Kargil says the same two things, 'I have a very long way to go [in order to achieve the high goals that I have set myself],' and 'I want to be a doctor.'

In 1993, I started the Ladakh Festival- in Leh as well as Kargil. It was a grand success in Leh, but a virtual non-starter in Kargil. 'The people of Kargil are followers of [the austere, arch conservative] Ayatollah Khomeini,' my juniors told me, year after year. 'They are not into festivity and festivals.' When they saw me determined to hold a festival in Kargil, they offered me a lollipop. 'We can have a children's painting contest,' one of them said.

I had wanted a festival to showcase Kargil's culture before tourists, to boost employment. 'But they don't like tourism,' a Kargili now settled in Leh insisted. 'They think that tourism corrupts society. They don't want to set up "paying guest accommodation" [bed and breakfast] inside their own houses. They feel it will corrupt their girls.'

But equally, year after year, the elders of Kargil would tell me that they wanted tourists, as well as festivals. One of these elders has been campaigning for the extension of the paying-guest scheme to Drâss and some other parts of Kargil: something we had not done all these years because some of my juniors had painted this ultra-orthodox picture of Kargil.

So I decided to bypass the hierarchy below me and reach out directly to the people of Kargil. In June 2000, I piloted the first independent Kargil Festival and it was a great hit.

Earlier that year, the State decided to focus on Kargil during the Republic Day celebrations in New Delhi. Unexpectedly, parents agreed to let their teenaged daughters spend a month and a half in Delhi for this as well as the Surajkund Mela. At the Mela we again emphasised the culture of Kargil.

One of the fixtures of the Surajkund Mela is a 'fashion show' where models wear costumes from the region being highlighted. I was told that there was simply no way that the girls from Kargil would participate in the fashion show. And if they did, they would be lynched when they went back home if the fashion show was shown on television.

In the event, the girls from Kargil agreed, without much prodding, both to the fashion show and its telecast. And they weren't lynched either. True, the clothes that they wore were extremely demure. But the poses the girls and boys from Kargil, who all looked very Central European, struck on the ramp revealed something important. All those years they had been watching professional models on television, and dreaming of the day when they'd be on the catwalk themselves.

The Kargil War

In May 1999, Pakistan dragged Kargil into the international limelight by capturing some territory and by 'shelling' several towns and villages. This forced much of Kargil town to relocate to places outside the range of Pakistan's artillery.

In the preceding months, around 1,500 Pakistani soldiers had infiltrated into Indian territory in Mashkoh valley, Drâss, Kaksar and Batâlik.

Pâkistân tried to pretend that the infiltrators were Kashmîrî *mujâhidîn* (holy warriors). However, these young men were professional soldiers from Gilgit-Baltistân, had nothing to do with the troubled Valley of Kashmîr and could not speak a word of Kashmîrî. Many of them were martyred later.

Their bereaved parents knew the truth about where they were really from. (See 'A history of Balâwaristân.') So did Mr. Bill Clinton, the then President of the USA. He states unambiguously in his memoirs,

My Life,[i] that Pâkistân's 'dangerous standoff with India [began] when *Pâkistâni forces* under the command of General Pervez Musharraf crossed the Line of Control...By crossing the Line of Control, *Pâkistân had wrecked the rules*.' (Emphases mine.[1])

According to the Pakistani press, their aim was to dominate the National Highway between Srinagar and Leh and, thus, cut Siachen and Leh off from Srinagar.

General Anthony Zinni,[ii] the chief of the US Central Command from 1997 to 2000, saw it thus: 'The Pâkistânis waylaid the Indians and penetrated all the way to Kargil.' This threatened Indian communications and support for Siachen. The Indians, as he points out, hit back 'with a vengeance.'

Personally I don't understand why Pâkistâni and American analysts keep emphasising that through its actions in that war Pâkistân was poised to cut Siachen off from the rest of India.

Siachen, according to one assessment, is of 'no strategic value.' This kind of talk (which is quite common on seminar tables in India) goes to the other extreme. (See the chapter on 'Siachen.')

The fact is that the Siachen glacier is the helmet—no more, but also no less—that protects India's head (i.e. Ladâkh and, at one remove, the state of Jammu and Kashmîr). Getting the helmet at best gives you bragging rights. The prize is always the head. Had Pâkistân's ploy in Kargil succeeded it would have sliced off the head itself. Naturally, the helmet would have fallen off, too.

The battle to liberate the unguarded territory that had been stealthily captured by the Pakistanis lasted 74 days (May-July, 1999), during which 407 Indians and 696 Pakistanis were killed. (According to figures published later,[iii] 527 Indian defence personnel died. Pakistan's Prime Minister Mr. Nawâz Sharîf was told that 2,700 Pâkistânis were killed. He admits that 'regular Pâkistân forces also [fought] the Indian forces' in that war.[iv]) *India Today* estimates that the war cost India Rs.1,110 crore ($250 million). Pakistan's finance minister put the cost to his country at $700 million.

Pakistan has officially claimed, and several times at that, that the motive behind its intrusion was to 'internationalise' the Kashmir issue, and that Pakistan had 'succeeded' in doing so. Absolutely. Kashmir was 'internationalised' like never before. On June 20, 1999, eight of the world's richest nations, the G-8, asked the intruders to withdraw to the Pakistani side of the line of control. They thus gave the LOC the same sanctity as an international border.

1. All emphases in quotes from Mr. William Clinton's book used in this chapter hereafter have been added by this author.

China gave its faithful ally, Pakistan, no comfort either.

The four Pâkistâni generals who initiated the war kept their Prime Minister in the dark. When the Indian Prime Minister, Mr. Atal Behâri Vâjpayee, called Mr. Sharîf to protest the attack, the Pâkistâni Prime Minister 'express[ed his] desire to settle the matter directly with Mr. Vâjpayee.' However, Gen. Musharraf 'was keen that [Sharîf should] meet Mr. Clinton and come to a settlement, so that *hamârâ bharam reh jâyegâ*' (our honour will remain intact).

Mr. Sharif would later say, 'Mr. Vâjpayee says that [I] had stabbed him in the back. I think, he is absolutely right.'

Meanwhile, Mr. Bill Clinton sent a special representative to Pâkistân's capital, Islâmâbâd, to persuade the Pâkistâni government to vacate Kargil. This was Gen. Zinni, whom Mr. Sharîf described as a 'close friend of Musharraf.' Zinni met Pâkistân's top leaders on the 24th and 25th June. Zinni records in his memoirs, *Battle Ready*, that he had told the Pâkistânis that unless they withdrew their soldiers from Kargil they would 'bring war and nuclear annihilation down to [their] country.'

The Pâkistânis concurred with his assessment. However, the Pakistani Prime Minister, Mr. Nawâz Sharîf, and his civilian advisors were not amenable to the suggestion that Pâkistân should retreat from Kargil. Mr. Sharîf said that such a withdrawal would be 'political suicide' for him. 'His problem,' Zinni notes, 'was maintaining face.'

However, the then Army Chief (and, a few months later, military dictator), Gen. Pervez Musharraf, did not have elections to face. (Not that any incumbent Pâkistâni Prime Minister has had to either.) Gen. Musharraf advised the PM to hear Zinni out. The Prime Minister agreed.[2]

Pâkistâni journalist Khâlid Hasan writes, 'In other words the man who brought about [the] Kargil [conflict; i.e. Gen. Musharraf] was prepared to back down… Zinni's account reveals that the army pulled out willingly and not because of Sharîf. In fact, if there was any resistance to [the] pull back, it was on the part of the prime minister not the army.'

2. Given Pâkistân's power structure, perhaps he had to. Only a year before, Mr. Sharîf had been overruled by the then Army Chief, Gen. Jehâṅgîr Karâmât. In June 1998 the Americans had wanted to send a team of top officials to Pâkistân to dissuade Mr. Sharîf's government from testing its nuclear bombs. Like a self-respecting, patriotic Pâkistâni Mr. Sharîf told the Americans not to send the team. Gen. Karâmât decided otherwise, and the US team (which, too, had included Gen. Zinni) flew to Pâkistân on schedule.
   Mr. Clinton has openly speculated that Mr. Sharif allowed the Pâkistâni army to invade Kargil 'in order to avoid a confrontation with Pâkistân's powerful military.' (Op. cit., p. 865.)

Mr. Sharîf felt that at the very least the US President should give Pâkistân a face-saver. This was by giving him (Mr. Sharîf) an audience. *after* which a withdrawal from the newly occupied parts of Kargil could be ordered. However, Zinni claims, 'after I insisted, he finally came around and he ordered the withdrawal.'

Mr. Sharîf called Mr. Bill Clinton and requested for an audience on the 4th of July. ('There goes yet another holiday,' the dashing leader at the other end of the line must have thought. 'Can't a guy have at least one day for his family and interns?') Mr. Sharif was worried that 'the situation *Pâkistân had created* was getting out of control.' Mr. Clinton later noted for the record. He sensed that Mr. Sharîf was hoping that he (Clinton) would help him get off the tiger—or off the hook. (Choose whichever metaphor you will. On his part, Mr Clinton saw a man who had 'gotten himself into a bind with no easy way out.'[v])

Mr. Clinton writes that he told Mr. Sharîf that he was welcome to fly in to Washington '*even* on July 4' (meaning that he would have preferred to celebrate that national holiday differently). However, Mr. Sharîf was also informed that he should not expect the USA to mediate with India on Kashmîr, 'especially under circumstances that appeared to reward Pâkistân's *wrongful incursion*.'[vi]

A dejected Nawâz Sharîf, went to Washington hoping that the USA would give some support to his country. Significantly, Gen. Pervez Musharraf went to the Islâmâbâd airport to see Mr. Sharîf off.

Mr. Clinton, received Mr. Sharîf at Blair House—and not the White House—on the Fourth of July. He noticed that the Pâkistâni Prime Minister was hoping to use American pressure as an excuse to rein in his own wayward—but 'powerful'—army.

Strobe Talbott, who was the USA's Assistant Secretary of State at the time, was one of the people present at the meeting. He recalls that Mr. Sharif told President Clinton, "I am prepared to help resolve the current crisis in Kargil but India must commit to resolve the larger issue [i.e. Kashmîr] in a specific time-frame."

'Clinton came as close as I have ever seen to blowing up in a meeting with a foreign leader,' Mr. Talbott writes.

Mr. Clinton said to Prime Minister Sharif, "If I were the Indian Prime Minister, I would never do that. I would be crazy to do it. It would be nuclear blackmail. If you proceed with this line, I will have no leverage [left] with them." The US President added, "I am not—and the Indians are not—going to let you get away with blackmail and I will not permit any characterisation of this meeting that suggests that I am giving in to blackmail."

President Clinton also asked Mr. Sharif if he "knew how advanced the threat of nuclear war really was? Did he know, for example that his military was preparing to use nuclear missiles?" Mr. Sharif indicated that he was unaware of his military's moves. (Levy, Adrian and Scott-Clark, Catherine, *Deception: Pakistan, the United States and the Global Nuclear Weapons Conspiracy*, Atlantic, 2007)

According to Talbott, 'Clinton also refuted Sharif's accusation that the Indians were the instigators of the crisis and intransigents in the ongoing standoff. When Sharif insisted he had to have something to show for his trip to the US beyond unconditional surrender over Kargil, Clinton pointed to the danger of nuclear war if Pâkistân did not return to its previous position.' [vii]

Mr. Clinton asked Mr. Sharîf to pull the intruders out of Indian territory immediately. Mr. Sharîf complied—well, more or less.

Pakistani scholar M.P. Bhandara notes that the above mentioned 'Washington Accord [of July 1999, between the USA and Pakistan] commits Pakistan to the "inviolability" and "sanctity" of the Line of Control. The use of these strong terms gives the LoC nearly an international-border status. This may not be the way Pakistan interprets it, but this may well be the interpretation of the Security Council members and the world at large.' (The *Dawn*, Karachi, Pakistan, August 1999.)

It certainly was that of the USA—and also its President's reading of how the LoC was regarded by the world at large. Mr. Clinton was of the opinion[viii] that since 1972, the LoC 'had been the *recognized* and *generally observed boundary*' between Pâkistân and India in Jammu and Kashmîr.

Country after country, including the USA, praised India for its military 'restraint' during the 1999 war, and for not having retaliated by attacking Pakistan.

India, thus, won the war on the military as well as diplomatic fronts. And the people of Kargil won the peace.

References

i Clinton, William J., *My Life* (2004), Alfred A. Knopf, New York. Pages 864-865.

ii ANI, 'Generally speaking: Musharraf wanted retreat from Kargil' *The Times of India*, June 5, 2004. ANI is a news agency.
Hasan, Khalid, 'Gen. Zinni on Gen. Musharraf and Pâkistân,' *The Kashmîr Times*, June 9, 2004. Mr.Hasan is a senior Pâkistâni journalist based in Washington.

iii 'Kargil air strikes may hit House hard.' *The Times of India*, June 8, 2004.

iv All quotes attributed to Mr. Sharîf have been excerpted from "Nawaz Sharif Speaks Out', an interview with Raj Chengappa, *India Today*, July 26, 2004.

v Clinton, op. cit., p. 865.

vi Clinton, op. cit., p. 865.

vii 'Clinton snubbed Sharif for linking Kargil crisis with Kashmîr,' a Press Trust of India item published in the *Daily Excelsior* of the 13th July, 2004. The news agency has drawn excerpts from Mr. Talbott's book *Engaging India—Diplomacy, Democracy and the Bomb* (2004).

viii Clinton, op. cit., p. 864.

3

A History of Zâñskâr

The 8th to 13th centuries AD: sketchy details

Pre-historic sculptures in Zâñskâr, notably in Padam, behind the office of the Sub-Divisional Magistrate, suggest that Zâñskâr has been inhabited for a long time. My guess is that these rectangular slabs were etched in the eighth century, because that's the date ascribed to similar intaglios at Stekbu (Drâss). Intrepid historians like Kachu Sikander Khan have managed to piece together a fairly satisfactory history of Zâñskâr by examining the fate of ruling dynasties.

As we have seen in 'A History of Leh,' as early as in AD 727, 'the three kingdoms' of Ladakh were 'under the suzerainty of the Tibetans.' The great King Skitde Nemagon ruled over Guge (Western Tibet) around AD 975-990. He is the first Tibetan king known to have asserted his clan's claim to Ladakh (including Zâñskâr). The empire of his eleventh century grandson, Yesh Es Od, almost certainly included Zâñskâr.

Guru Padma Sambhav toured Zâñskâr in the 8th century AD. It was through his efforts that Buddhism spread throughout Zâñskâr and wiped the Bon religion out. He is said to have got a number of Buddhist chortens constructed in Zâñskâr. These include the Nânam Gurû Chorten Châsling, the Nânam Gurû Chorten and a chorten at Sani.

Regaining Zâñskâr, with Kashmir's help

Kachu Sikander Khan writes that the oldest known ruling dynasty of Zâñskâr was founded in the 14th or 15th century AD. That is when Shâkya Thokba was made the king of this region. He was a descendant of Nemagon and was from the royal family of Guge (Western Tibet). There is reason to believe that he married the princess of Skardu (Baltistan).

In those days there was a king who belonged to the Segbo dynasty. Shortly after their marriage, Shâkya and his pregnant wife decided to go to Skardu. Segbo's agents murdered Shâkya on his way to Skardu. Segbo abducted Shâkya's queen, who gave birth to a son in captivity. Segbo knew that this was the slain Shâkya's child. So he turned the queen out.

The little boy took to wandering from place to place. Many years later he found himself in Kashmir. One day when the king of Kashmir came out in a procession, the boy went out to watch. The king's elephant[1] raised his trunk to salute the boy. The king knew that the boy was of royal blood. So the king gave the boy his own daughter in marriage. He also gave the newlyweds the territory of Kishtwâr to govern on his behalf or so Ladakhi historians claim.

Shâkya's son, whose name is not known, had three sons from the princess of Kashmir while they were at Kishtwâr. During his stay in Kishtwâr he must have re-conquered neighbouring Zâñskâr. After a while he decided to shift to Zâñskâr, along with his wife and their two younger sons. He handed over the estate of Kishtwâr to his eldest son to govern. (Shâkya's son must have been in his forties, or maybe fifties, when he did so, because he was still young enough to start life anew. There is a tradition in many parts of Ladakh, certainly in Zâñskâr, for the parents to move into 'the little house' behind the main house, when they reach a certain age, normally sixty.)

Zâñskâr is partitioned, repeatedly

When Shâkya's son returned to Zâñskâr, his father's kingdom, he was accepted as the king. He had a long innings at Zâñskâr. Before he died he divided that enormous, though sparsely populated, land between his two sons. He gave the areas to the right of River Zâñskâr to Lobzâñg

1. Kashmir's own histories are full of references to elephants till around the 8th century AD. This is the first mention I have come across in a history written by a non-Kashmiri of elephants having lived in Kashmir. Present day Kashmir has no elephants, though the fossils of elephants have been found in the Valley. On the other hand, there is no allusion to this incident in any of Kashmir's own very detailed histories. By the 14th century, Kashmir had begun to be ruled by Muslims- initially a Muslim of Ladakhi origin. It is unlikely for any other Muslim ruler of Kashmir to have so readily offered his daughter to a non-Muslim, a homeless child at that. Kachu Sikander Khan, who has recorded this story, knows the Islamic position in this regard. And yet if the Kashmiri ruler in question was the newly-converted-to-Islam Rinchen Shah, who knows, he might have liked the idea of his daughter marrying back into the royalty of his native Guge-Ladakh. The story of the elephant's salute could be apocryphal. Shâkya's son might have gone over to Srinagar specifically to seek Rinchen's help against the Segbo clan.

Lozâñg Alday, and those on its left to Thînam Alday. Thus Thînam received Zañglâ and a village that the Kachu describes as Chhaydar but which I am not familiar with, despite my deep association with Zâñskâr[2].

During Lobzâñg's reign there came a gift-bearing man from Guge. His name was Cho Paltar. He plied the king with, well, gifts. Lobzâñg trusted him either because he was naïve, or because he hadn't heard the proverb, or because, strictly speaking, Cho wasn't an envoy. It must have been a combination of all three. Lobzâñg awarded this con man an estate of as many as three villages (or almost a quarter of his kingdom): Pipchâ, Châ(h) and Shon. (Present day Zâñskâr has all of 25 villages. Lobzâñg would have received, perhaps, half that number.)

After a while Cho Paltar decamped. He was wanted in Leh for the murder of a group of traders. Most of his estate was forfeited and returned to Lobzâñg. However, the king allowed Pipchâ to remain with Cho's son, Tang-so.

Lobzâñg had three sons. He divided his kingdom up between the three.

Thînam had no such compulsions, for he had just one son, Gyalpo Rinchen. However, even his kingdom got depleted on his death. His widow, Zampâ rGyâlmo donated three of the villages under her control. This was a funeral offering, for the peace of Thînam's soul.

Around then (the late 15th/ early 16th century) three lâmâs came over from Lhâsâ to propagate Buddhism. Rinchen helped them in their efforts. So did two of Lobzâñg's sons, namely Sañg rGyâlpo and Day-tsok Sakyâpâ. All three kings extended concessions (such as an exemption from state taxes) to gompas (monasteries).

1535: The invasion from Kâshghar

The first precise date that we have regarding Zâñskâr is AD 1535. That was the year when Sultan Abû Saeed Khan Waai, of Kâshghar, attacked and conquered Zâñskâr. Later, his Commander in Chief, Mirzâ Haider Dûghlât/ Gurgân, led a force of 3,000 through Zâñskâr. He was on his way from Leh to Kashmir (presumably through the Pâdar/ Kishtwâr route). In the year 2001, Zâñskâr had only around 2,500 male adults, half of whom would be in the age group that soldiers are drawn from. Not only were the Zâñskâris heavily outnumbered, they must have been

2. Even after this particular dynasty disappeared, the partition would keep cropping up. In the 19th century, when the Dogras annexed Zâñskâr, they found it was divided into three 'kingdoms', one based in Padam, the second in Zâñglâ and a few villages under Teesta. However, there were several spells when all of Zâñskâr was united, and ruled by a single king.

'outgunned,' too. (Even in the 21st century, the slingshot- catapult is the Zâñskâris' favourite weapon, augmented with bows and arrows. The Turkmen-Mughals' weapons and training would have been vastly superior.)

Sañg rGyâlpo must have wanted to put up some kind of a resistance. In any case, his supporters and he found it prudent to go into exile. The Turkmen-Mughals captured the Padam Fort (now in ruins).' There was no way that the Zâñskâris could have defeated the Turkmens in battle. So they spread the rumour that an army from Lhâsâ was on its way to Zâñskâr, through Lahoul, to rescue the Zâñskâris.

At Zâñskâr the Mirza received tokens of submission to the authority of the Sultan, as well as presents. Thereafter, his army and he left for the Sûrû valley. Maulvi Hashmat Ullah Khan, the historian, says that the Mirza's army shed no blood in Zâñskâr. The Zâñskâris gave presents to the Turkmens on their way back from Kashmir, too. This time Lâmâ Tonbâr Phasten submitted the tribute, which included three horses.

Zâñskâr is renowned for its short, but sure-footed and sturdy horses. More importantly, this incident reveals the Lâmâ's eminence. In status he clearly ranked equal to the king, if not higher. This trend continues to this day. My theory is that temporal authority in Zâñskâr was normally divided between the kings of Padam and Zâñglâ, with many villages independent of both. Therefore, the lâmâs were often the most powerful political force.

There is only one other non-royal whose name figures in the historical records of Zâñskâr. This is a scholar-saint whose real name was Lama Sherab or Phagspâ Sherab. However, he is best known as the Zâñskâr Lotsâvâ. He lived sometime between the 11th and 15th centuries AD. According to the local tradition he was a contemporary of Lotsâvâ Rinchen Zangpo. That would place him in the 11th century.

It is said that the Lotsâvâ's role in promoting Buddhism in Zâñskâr is next only to that of Guru Urgyen Padmâ [Padmâ Sambhav] and Lâmâ Naropâ. It is because of the efforts of these three that Zâñskâr has a special place among all Mahâyân Buddhists, who call it 'the land of religion.'

(During my year in Zâñskâr the lâmâ who wielded the greatest political power had an eye handicap and was clinically mentally challenged. The latter problem was something he was born with and not the result of a later trauma. In the religious hierarchy he was quite senior, but not at the very top. He was powerful because he was vocal, aggressive and would never compromise on his people's interests. He was also incorruptible.

Even in Leh, Kushoks and other major lâmâs there have often won elections on behalf of the Congress as well as the National Conference.)

In the event, Sañg rGyâlpo returned to power. He thanked those who had spread the story about the Lhâsâ army. He also gave presents to monasteries because of their role during the crisis.

Leh eyes- and, ultimately, annexes- Zâñskâr

Sañg rGyâlpo's brother, Râtok rGyâlpo, succeeded him. That's when the kings of Leh attacked Zâñskâr, asserting an ancestral claim to the land. They took Râtok hostage to Leh and released him after he had paid a ransom. He donated all his properties to a gompa.

It is not clear if all three of Lobzâñg's sons were childless, though that seems to be the case. They established the Pipiting gompa. Perhaps because they were childless they donated generously to charity. Maulvi Hashmat Ullah Khan, the historian, describes them as weak and ineffective. The Padam- based branch of the Alday dynasty that Shâkyâ had founded came to an end with these three.

Senge Namgyâl (1590-1620 or 1570-1642), king of Leh, took over all the territories that had been under the three brothers. He left Thinam's Zâñglâ-based kingdom alone, for a while. Senge then appointed his younger son Day-tsok Namgyâl the viceroy or governor of all Zâñskâr, including Zâñglâ.

This dynasty went on to rule Zâñskâr till the Dogras annexed it to the Punjab and, thus, India.

Islam in Zâñskâr

The city-bred Day-tsok got bored in Zâñskâr. So, Senge sent over two of Ladakh's most prominent Kashmiri traders to keep Day-tsok company. These were Razzak Joo and Fateh Joo. That's how the first Muslims came to Zâñskâr.

The Muslims of Padam told me that their ancestors had been brought over Kashmir and Kishtwâr by the then king because he needed scribes and bureaucrats who knew Persian and who knew how to run an administration. The company-for-the-prince theory is the Kachu's. Either way, it was big heart of a Ladakhi Buddhist king to prefer Kashmiri Muslims over fellow Buddhists. The result is a very literate community that is disproportionately represented in the administration and commerce of Zâñskâr and accounts for around a tenth of the population.

Zâñskâr's economy was mostly demonetised till even the 1990s. The little trade that took place consisted of barter. Tourism is changing much of that. Therefore, in the 17th century it made sense to introduce commerce in Zâñskâr through Kashmiri traders. The Joos proved equal to the task. They started buying Zâñskâr's famed short-but-sturdy horses and selling them in the neighbouring Suru valley (Kargil).

Razzâq and Fateh, like most Kashmiris, were Sunnis. As a result the small Muslim community of Padam and Pipiting (both in Zâñskâr) is Sunni. Almost all the other Muslims of Kargil, and most of Leh's Muslims, are Shia. Razzâq's younger brother decided to settle in Pânikhar/ Pranti. That is one reason why Pânikhar, too, has a Sunni community.

Suru-Kartse (Karchey): Conflicts—marital and martial

Tséwâng Namgyâl, king of Zâñskâr, was the great-grandson of Day-tsok Namgyâl. (This must have been around AD 1715.) He was married to the sister of Thee Muhammad, the Sultan of neighbouring Suru- Kartse (Karchey). (Tséwâng had an extremely illustrious ancestry. However, Suru-Kartse was far more populous, more prosperous and, arguably, at least as powerful as Zâñskâr, if not more. It is significant that Muslim royals voluntarily gave their daughters in marriage to Buddhists as recently as in the eighteenth century.)

At some stage Tséwâng and his wife fell out with each other. A popular folksong written by the queen gives us her version. In the song the queen of Zâñskâr prays to God to give her brother, the Sultan, a male child. She then prays that the Gyâlpo of Zâñskâr should either treat her better or divorce her.[3]

Tséwâng chose the latter option. He divorced his wife. Thee Muhammad was less than amused. He attacked Zâñskâr with a strong force. Tséwâng knew that it would be suicidal to fight back. So, he holed up inside the Padam fort. The gates of the Karshâ monastery were got locked from inside. Most important, Tséwâng got destroyed the bridge that linked Karshâ and Padam with the road from Suru valley.

With the bridge gone, Thee was unable to cross the river. He ordered his forces to turn back. They crossed the Penzi Lâ and reached Rangdum. He thus threw the Zâñskâr administration off its guard. Tséwâng and his advisors assumed that Thee had retreated and given up.

However, Thee and his army rushed back from Rangdum in a swift charge. They ransacked and devastated the villages to the right of the river. Kachu Sikander Khan and Maulvi Hashmat Ullah Khan write that they looted the Karshâ gompa.

Tséwâng had no choice but to take back Thee's sister.

3. The poetry of Kashmir's best-known poet, Habbâ Khâtoon (late 16th century), too, is a chronicle of her bad marriage. Even her poetry gives the person being addressed (in this case, her parents) options on how to save her life: '*Either* get me a new pitcher [to replace the one that I broke] *or* pay [my mother-in-law] the cost of the pitcher.'

Zâñskâr is attacked by neighbours—and others

After Tséwâng's death, Zâñskâr was partitioned between his three sons. The eldest son got Padam, the middle one Zâñglâ and the third son Teestâ. (Teestâ is close to Himachal Pradesh. For some reason, its hereditary chieftain came to be known by the title Thâkur, which is very Himachali/ Central Indian.)

Around the beginning of the 19th century, Ladakh came to be attacked from all sides, by its neighbours. This was mostly during the reign of the incompetent Tsespal Namgyâl (1808-30), king of Leh. (Kachu Sikander Khan says that the king was Tondup Namgyâl. All other sources use the name Tsespal/ Tshespal.)

During that period, Zâñskâr had matching problems of its own—internal strife and poor administrators. Padam was then ruled by Jaymor, Teestâ by Senge Phonsok, and Zâñglâ by Tonyot Samphel.

Hordes from the neighbouring Kulu, Girjâ (Lahaul) and Khûnu (Kinnaur) invaded Zâñskâr. They killed everyone who resisted them and looted places as deep inside Zâñskâr as Karshâ.

Then Rattan Sher Khan, king of Pâdar (Kishtwar), and his forces entered Zâñskâr through the Umâsi Lâ. They reached Padam, without meeting with any resistance. They destroyed villages along the way, and stole yâks and horses.

The people of Zâñskâr went to Leh to seek the help of their overlord, King Tsespal of Leh. Instead of helping them, he scolded the delegation and summoned the king of Padam to Leh to explain his conduct.

The third invasion was by the Malliks of Wârwan (also in Kishtwar). They had, for centuries, been trading with the various villages of Zâñskâr. They, too, decided to take advantage of the vacuum in Zâñskâr in particular and Ladakh in general.

Mukhtâ Mallik, Fateh Mallik and Dâyam Mallik led a force through the Bhot Kol pass and thence the Suru Valley. Every year, for three years, they plundered the villages that they passed through.

The final invasion, in 1834, was that of Zorâwar Singh, the Dogra general who conquered Zâñskâr on behalf of Mahâraja Ranjit Singh of the Punjab. That was how Zâñskâr came to be a part of India.

4

A History of Balâwaristân[1]

The ancient period

The Gilgit-Baltistân area was called Bolor (or Balaur or Balâwar) in ancient times.[2] The Indo-Aryan Dards were perhaps the first to settle in this belt (and for that matter in Leh, Kargil and Guge). Bon was the first religion to be practised in Balâwar (as in much of the rest of Ladâkh).

The Mons, also an Indo-Aryan group, came in the second century. During that period they dominated the region.

(For the ancient and early mediæval periods, see the chapters about the histories of Gilgit, Baltistân and other neighbouring areas.)

The coming of Islâm

The oldest Islâmic record[1] that mentions the area is an inscription found in Afghânistân. It dates to the period of Al Mâmûn, the Abbasid Caliph (A.D. 813-833) and reads thus:

'The Imâm (may Allâh bestow greater honour on him) made the green flag [of Islâm] travel on the land of Dhul Riyâsataiñ in Kashmîr and in the areas of Tibet. Allâh has given him victory in Bukhan and Bolor and over the chiefs Jahal Khagan and Jahal Tibet...'

Till A.D. 1320 there were very few Muslims anywhere in Kashmîr (including Balâwaristân). Islâm was very much an individual affair till then. Rinchen, the Ladâkhi/ Tibetan, was the first King of Kashmîr to accept Islâm, taking on the name and title of Sultan Sadr ud Din. (He was also called rGyalbu Rinchen and Rinchana Bhoti).

Why did Rinchen convert to Islâm? Jonarâj, himself a Kashmîri Hindu, says that (the Buddhist) Rinchen tried to become a Shaivite Hiñdu

1. Please also see the chapters on the histories of Baltistân, Gilgit and Hunzâ.
2. Several Dogrâ and British records used this name till as recently as the early 20th century.

but Shri Deva Swami and other ranking Hiñdu priests refused to accept him into their fold. Then Rinchen saw a dream in which he was advised to accept as his guide whoever he first saw the next day. This person turned out to be a Turkistani saint who identified himself as Abdur Rehman (d. 1327), but who is better known in Kashmîr as Bulbul Shâh.

Gilgit was part of the kingdom of Kashmîr's Sultan Shahab-ud-Din (A.D. 1356-74).

The first mass conversions to Islâm in Kashmîr, and then Baltistân, began during Rinchen's reign. Islâm now received state patronage. Soon Muslim mystics started coming from Iran to spread the message of Islâm.

Around the 15th or 16th century, Islâm rapidly became the dominant religion in the entire area. However, there was no sharp break with the past. The legendary Tibeto-Ladâkhi Gesar of Ling [called Gyâlam Késar in Leh] continued to be a hero and role-model for the Muslims of Baltistân (and Kargil).

Buddhists and Muslims continued to marry each other. The poor did this and so did royalty.

Tarik Ali Khân writes,[ii] "Buddhist kings took Muslim wives and raised some of their sons as Muslims. Even Baltistân's legendary Ali Shér Khân Anchan is said to have given his daughter Gul Khatoon (aka Mindoq rGyalmo) to the Ladâkhi King Jamyang Namgyâl (r.1560-1590).

"Arrangements between the two religions may have been flexible; official records are not so accepting. Ladâkhi songs in praise of its royal lineage are careful to omit the names of princes who converted to Islâm. A.H. Francke, a Moravian missionary writing in 1907, speculated that, in turn, the maqpons of Baltistân may have fabricated their pedigrees with more Muslim names in a firm attempt to erase pre-Islâmic history."

Proselytisation: The first major impetus that the propagation of Islâm received in Baltistân-Ladâkh-Purîg was the visit (around A.D. 1381-82) of Amîr Kabîr Mîr Syed Ali Hamadâni. (See also the chapters 'A History of Kargil' and 'Islâm in Leh and Zâñskâr,') The Amîr Kabîr had got people in large groups to convert to Islâm in Kashmîr. For some reason he did not induce mass conversions in Ladâkh.

Apparently it was his main disciple Syed Muhammad Nûr Bakhsh of Khurâsâñ who convinced a sizeable section of the people of Baltistân and Purîg to accept Islam. (Two caveats. Syed Muhammad was probably a disciple of Khwaja Ishaq of Khatlan and it was the Khwaja who was a khalifâ or disciple of the Amîr Kabîr. Secondly, according to some scholars[iii] Syed Muhammad Nûr Bakhsh had never visited either Baltistân or Purîg but had sent his disciples instead. Be that as it may, the Nûr Bakhshi sect has since had a very major presence in Baltistân and Ladâkh.)

Mir Shams ud Din was a saint from Iraq and a disciple of the son of the great Syed Muhammad Nûr Bakhsh. He visited the Baltistân-Purîg region in 1505, with fifty followers. Through his preaching and example he converted more or less every Balti and Purgi who had not accepted Islâm by then. The Mir advocated the Imamiya or Shia school in particular.

The march of Islâm then began into the neighbouring areas. William Moorcroft, who lived in Ladâkh from 1820 to 1822, wrote, 'Islâm is evidently making rapid strides...In the western provinces [of Ladâkh] and those bordering on Balti and Kashmîr, it is spreading rapidly, and affecting a material change in the habits and character of the people.'

Why did Islâm continue to spread, though not backed by any government?

Francke wrote, 'One doctrine of Mohammedanism attained popularity and influence amongst its adherents: the doctrine of One God Only, and of the vanity of idols. This is the great truth and strength of this religion. and on account of it Mohammedanism spreads also in those lands where it is not supported by arms.'[iv]

The neighbours' clout

Balâwaristân owed some sort of allegiance to the Shâhmîrî Sultanate of Kashmîr, at least for some time. When that empire unravelled (in the early 16th century), these maqpons asserted their independence. However, Ghâzi Chak of Kashmîr (1552-62 A.D) once again conquered or otherwise brought under his control principalities including Skardu, Gilgit, Pakhli and Mungli (near Pakhli), the latter two now being in the so-called Âzâd Jammu and Kashmîr. Ghâzi appointed good governors to administer these regions.

(See 'A History of Baltistân' for details about the subsequent history of the 16th century.)

The era of the Sikh-ruled kingdom of Lahore (Punjâb)

In the middle of the 19th century (mainly between 1834 and 1842), the Dogrâs of Jammû helped conquer Gilgit and Baltistân, on behalf of Mahârâjâ Ranjit Singh of Lahore. Baltistân was annexed in 1840, and Gilgit in 1842.

Till then the Balâwaristân area had been under small chieftains and kings. Some of these chiefs ruled half a dozen villages and some just one or two. However, each of these potentates ruled over a state that was sovereign in every respect. The chiefs often fought one another. These internal conflicts made it easy for the Sikh-Dogrâ army to conquer the area. Keeping the local chiefs down was another matter, though.

The chapter on the history of Gilgit, for instance, will show how bitter-and bloody-things had gotten between 1810 and 1842. And why the region was ripe for the plucking.

Gaor Rehmân of Yâsîn killed Shâh Sikañder of Puniâl and took over Gilgit. This was perhaps in 1840. Shâh Sikañder's brother, Karîm Khân, fled to the neighbouring republic of Gor. He sent an envoy to the Sikh rulers of Kashmîr and asked for help. By then Astor had accepted the Sikhs' nominal overlordship. So, the governor of Kashmîr agreed to Karîm's request. He sent some regiments of the Lahore army to Gilgit. Col. Nathû led them.[3]

Gaor Rehmân heard of the Punjâb army's advance. He immediately quit Gilgit proper. Nathû and his army vanquished him some five kilometres north at Basîn. Gaor withdrew to Puniâl.

Meanwhile, Mathrâ Dâs, who was of the same seniority as Col. Nathû, or slightly senior, promised the rulers of the Punjâb that he would conquer the entire Gilgit region for them. They gave him a few regiments, too. Gaor Rehmân was the most powerful military genius produced by Balâwaristân during that era. He hammered Mathrâ Dâs and his regiments in a battle in the Sharot-Gulpur area, and sent the survivors packing to Srînagar.

When Col. Nathû learnt of his ambitious colleague's rout, he marshalled his own soldiers and marched from Gilgit towards Gaor Rehmân's territory. They came face to face at the place where the borders of Gilgit and Gaor's territory met. King Ghazan Khân of Hunzâ and the Râjâ of Nagar were there with their forces to support Gaor Rehmân. They knew that their army could not match Nathû's. So, they asked for a truce before a single bullet had been fired. They conceded Gilgit to the Sikh kingdom and Gaor also gave his own daughter in marriage to Col. Nathû. Indeed, the kings of Hunzâ and Nagar also followed suit and married their daughters to Nathû.

Prince Karîm Khân reminded Col. Nathû that the latter was there basically to help him, Karîm, became the king of Gilgit. However, by then Col. Nathû knew exactly how powerful the Punjâb army had grown in the area. So, the best that he was prepared to give Karîm was joint control of Gilgit. Karîm would be the king and would receive some of the taxes. A section of the Punjâb army would stay on in Gilgit and collect the remaining taxes, which they would remit to Lahore.

3. Drew, who wrote in 1875, i.e. shortly after the event, says that Nathû Shâh was 'a Syed [from] Gujrâñwâlâ' [Punjâb]. Other histories give the colonel's name as Nathû Singh.

Raja Gaor Rehmân (or Gaor Aman) of Yâsîn

That Gaor Rehmân was a military genius is not in doubt. The only question is whether he put his brilliance to good use or bad. The Dards speak very ill of him, and recount several instances of his cruelty. Contemporary British writers called him 'bloodthirsty.' That he hated Gilgit and its rulers is true. However, stories about his getting people killed for niyâz every time that he fell ill, or of chopping up infants with his sword, seem to be legends of the kind that crop up around all disliked people.

In the chapter on the history of Gilgit we have seen how Gaor had conquered that land, only to be expelled from it just a year and a half later. He was the son of Malik Imân (or Aman), the king of Yâsîn-hence his other name. Gaor belonged to the Bakhte clan. He reinforced his royal credentials by marrying three princesses from the region—two from Chitrâl and one from Puniâl.

The Dogrâs

By the mid-1840s the Punjâb empire began to disintegrate. Balâwaristân (like all of Jammu and Kashmîr) became part of the newly created Dogrâ Empire. In 1846, Gulab Singh, the Dogrâ Mahârâjâ. obtained Gilgit, as part of the same Treaty of Amritsar that had given him Kashmîr, Ladâkh and Baltistân. Till then Nathu Singh (or Shâh) had been governing Gilgit on behalf of the Lahore Darbar. By 1850, Gulab Singh had become the king of Baltistân and Dardistân (including Gilgit). Nathu Singh/ Shâh switched his loyalties from the Sikh rulers of Lahore to the Dogrâs of Jammu.

Gilgit was only nominally under Mahârâjâ Gulâb Singh. He was never able to set up his own civil administration there. In 1851, the Rajas of Gilgit, Yâsîn, Hunzâ and Nagar rose against the Dogrâs.

Raja Gaor Aman (or Gaor Rehmân) of Yâsîn led the joint front. The tribes of Chilâs and other adjacent areas supported him. The redoubtable Raja Gaor Aman (or Gaor Rehmân) treated the well-trained Punjâb army with contempt and attacked it.

The Punjâb-Dogrâ garrison tried to resist this uprising. A battle followed in which the entire Punjâb-Dogrâ force at Gilgit was killed. According to a legend, the only survivor in the Punjâb-Dogrâ camp was a Gurkhâ woman who swam across the Indus and told Punjâbi-Dogrâ soldiers on the other side what had happened.

Gilgit ceased to be even a nominal part of the Dogrâ kingdom, for a while.

This showed that while the kings of Gilgit-Baltistân might have disliked each other, in the face of an external enemy they were united. They prized their independence far too much. (In the chapter 'A History of Hunzâ' we have recorded an equally brave resistance to the British-Dogrâ onslaught.)

The Dogrâs felt quite humiliated by their defeat in Gilgit. They started preparing to restore their honour.[4]

The return of the Dogrâs

Mahârâjâ Gulâb Singh's successor, Mahârâjâ Ranbir Singh (1857-1885), persuaded almost every Dogrâ family to contribute a soldier to a force that he raised to conquer Gilgit once again, and neighbouring kingdoms, too. Colonel Devi Singh commanded the force. Gen. Hoshiar Singh was the overall commander. The Dogrâ army set out in 1859. It succeeded in 1860. Mahârâjâ Ranbir Singh's army also brought Hunzâ, Nagar and Ishkoman (near Sinkiang) into the Dogrâ empire. Miâñ Jawâhir Singh was appointed the first Wazir e Wazârat.[5]

The Dogrâs placed Baltistân in Ladâkh district. However, Gilgit was made an administrative unit of Jammu and Kashmîr in its own right, instead of being put under Leh. Its headquarters were in Gilgit town.[6]

In 1876 Chitrâl accepted Dogrâ sovereignty.

However, for all practical purposes the local rulers continued to run the day to day administration of the land. Because the place was very inaccessible from Jammu, and even Srinagar, the Dogrâs' actual control was not very pervasive.

'The Great Game': A British presence

Soon, the British Government of India started getting paranoid nightmares about some 'Great Game' that they imagined the Russians were playing in the neighbourhood. The British convinced themselves that the Russians wanted to conquer South Asia someday, and would do so through Gilgit and the surrounding Himâlayan region. Gilgit had another major neighbour as well—China. Because of Gilgit's supposed strategic importance, the British started meddling in the affairs of the Mahârâjâ's northern territories.

4. Likewise, the people of Balâwaristân were inspired by the sacrifices made by Raja Gaor Aman. The Punjâb-Dogrâ army killed many members of the family of this brave king. It became an article of faith for the people of the area to some day avenge the martyrdom of this noble family.

5. According to the official revenue assessment record of 1916. Jawâhir had assessed the annual revenue of the region at Rs. 7,842.

6. This administrative arrangement continued till 1947.

The British erected a watchtower in Gilgit, to literally keep an eye on Russia. In 1868, they posted a British officer in Gilgit to gather intelligence reports. They started leaning on the Dogrâ government and, in 1877, got it to accept the creation of a British Political Agency in Gilgit.

A few years later the British withdrew their Political Agent. Gilgit is cut off from the rest of the world for eight months of the year. That is because snow blocks all the passes that lead into Gilgit. The British had not catered for this. Nor did they man their Agency adequately. The Kohistânîs decided to take advantage of this and almost conquered the Agency. The British decided that it was better to wind up the Agency than be outnumbered and face certain defeat. They quickly packed up and left in 1881, only to come back in 1889,[7] this time with a more elaborate administrative and military structure.

The British were convinced that Mahârâjâ Pratâp Singh (1885-1925) was in cahoots with the Russians. So, for a few decades they installed a Resident in the state capital, who oversaw the running of the administration. They also felt that they needed to secure the northern borders of India, especially in the Pamirs and in Chitrâl and Hunzâ. In particular they wanted to control the Mehtar (king) of Chitrâl.

In 1889, under British pressure, the Mahârâjâ created a full fledged Gilgit Agency (i.e. a Raj-style district). The Agency included Yâsîn, Puniâl, Koh-e-Ghizar, Ishkoman and Chilâs. The civil and administrative control of the region, however, continued to vest in the Mahârâjâ's Government of Jammu and Kashmîr. The soldiers stationed at the garrison were from the Mahârâjâ's army, and the civil officials posted in Gilgit were Dogrâs and Kashmîrîs from the Mahârâjâ's civil service.

The British allowed the princely states of Hunzâ and Nagar and the principalities of Yâsîn, Punyal, Ishkoman and Gupis to exercise a considerable degree of independence, so long as they pledged allegiance to the British Agent.

The Second British Agency was a success because by 1889, the track from Srinagar, through Astor, had been augmented and a telegraph link had been established.

The British stationed a substantial force in Gilgit. Using soldiers from the Dogrâ army they started subduing all the neighbouring kingdoms. Between 1889 and 1895, the Jammu and Kashmîr state army, led by British officers, conducted a series of military campaigns in the north. As a result the British assumed direct control over Chitrâl, though on paper Chitrâl continued to be a part of the state of Jammu and Kashmîr.

7. In 1892, according to some otherwise reliable sources. The year 1889 is a more likely date because that was when the Mahârâjâ had sanctioned an Agency.

In 1891, Algernon Durand led Dogrâ soldiers to victory over Hunzâ. In 1893, the British improved the fort at Chilâs in order to secure the newly built road through the Babusar Pass against the Kohistânis.

E. F. Knight had accompanied the British-Dogrâ force. In 1893, his book *Where Three Empires Meet*, being a memoir about the campaign, was published. It told the whole world about the supposed strategic importance of the Gilgit-Baltistân-Hunzâ-Chitrâl region. It also spoke glowingly of the heroic resistance put up by the people of Balâwaristân-Hunzâ as well as the bravery of the Dogrâ troops. (See 'A History of Hunzâ.')

In April 1895, five hundred soldiers from Gilgit trekked through the snow across the Shandur Pass to rescue the (British-Dogrâ) garrison that had been trapped by the snow at Chitrâl Fort. This daring feat further enhanced the already formidable martial reputation of the people of Gilgit-Balâwaristân.

The Gilgit Scouts

In 1913, the British created the Gilgit Scouts, a para-military force which had 600 officers and men,[8] who reported to the Political Agent. They were commanded by a Subédâr Major, who was normally the brother of one of the kings. This was a para-military force, the members of which were mainly the sons of the seven kings of the area. The British created this unit in order to patrol India's borders, which were imagined to be threatened by the Russians. The British trained some young men from the region's royal families and commissioned them as VCOs (Viceroy's Commissioned Officers).

The Scouts had a bagpipe band, which wore the Black Watch tartan. To this day the band rehearses its music in the Chinâr Bâgh near the river.

Hari Singh became the Mahârâjâ of Jammu and Kashmîr in 1925. He was irked by subtle British attempts to establish their own authority in Gilgit. He insisted on asserting J&K's sovereignty in Gilgit. He ordered that only the State flag would fly in Gilgit. Legally he was right. The British had to accept the Mahârâjâ's sovereign right to rule Gilgit.

The 60-year lease

However, by now Russia—and the nature of the Russian state—had changed in a way that the British found even more threatening. A socialist government had been established in Russia, and the Soviet Union now extended to India's northern borders. The British were infinitely more apprehensive of the communists than of a people who were merely

8. Six hundred was the approved number. In actual practice no force ever has its full sanctioned strength. In 1947, for instance, the Gilgit Scouts had 582 men.

Russian. The need to 'secure' these northern borders became more urgent than ever before.

The British seconded Col. Calvin to the Mahârâjâ's civil service. In 1932, they pressured the Mahârâjâ to appoint the good colonel as his Prime Minister. Col. Calvin started persuading Hari Singh to lease Gilgit out to the British Government in India.

In 1935, the British finally managed to force the Maharaja of Jammu and Kashmîr to give them the Gilgit wazârat (roughly: district) on a 60-year lease.

The Mahârâjâ buckled because, in 1931, a popular, nationalist, democratic movement had begun in Kashmîr. Led by Sheikh Mohammad Abdullah, it had fired the people's imagination. With the people demanding a representative government, the Mahârâjâ could not afford to alienate the British as well.

The lease deed was signed on the 26th March, 1935. Mahârâjâ Hari Singh and the British Resident in Kashmîr, L. E. Lang, were the two signatories to the deed. The Viceroy, Lord Wellington, ratified it on April 3, 1935.

The deed clearly stated that while taking over the *temporary* administration of the territory, the British Government explicitly accepted that the territory fell *within the boundaries* of the Mahârâjâ's domain and that the Mahârâjâ *continued to exercise sovereign rights* over the area. (All emphases are mine.)

Baltistân and Astor(e) were not a part of the lease.

The Assistant Political Agent at Chilâs administered the Diamir area like a tribal territory. The Astor(e) sub-division of Diamir was not included in this arrangement. The APA's official residence was called 'Journey's End' because it took the British officer a very difficult journey of several months to get to Chilâs.

In 1935, an airfield was built in Gilgit.

'Ultimately,' notes Geocities, 'the contest [with Russia] went for nothing; by 1931 the area had been surveyed and it became clear that there was no pass in the region over which the Russians could bring a detachment (let alone an army) to invade India.'

The British rapidly lost interest in the area.

The events of 1947-1949: How Pâkistân came to occupy Gilgit-Balâwaristân

The avowedly 'pro-Pâkistân' Maj. Brown

A fortnight before the partition (and independence) of India in 1947, the British terminated the lease of Gilgit. The region was given back to the

Maharaja of Jammû and Kashmîr. The Political Agent of Gilgit handed over his charge to Brig. Ghansârâ Singh, a governor appointed by the Mahârâjâ. By then it was clear that India was going to be partitioned into a Muslim Pâkistân and a secular, though Hiñdu-dominated, India.

At the time Major William Brown was the Commandant of the Gilgit Scouts. Brown was a British officer who had volunteered to preside over the transition from the British administrators to South Asian rulers. However, he had decided in advance who these new rulers should be. Significantly, he had by then opted to serve in the soon-to-be-created Pâkistân Army.

'Brown,' says a University of Cambrîdge website, 'and his second in command, Captain A.S. Mathieson, decided to use the Scouts to stage a coup d'etat and take complete control of the Agency and then offer it to Pâkistân.' (Centre Of South Asian Studies/ 'Handlist of Papers-Garrett.')

Major Brown was not a neutral army officer. He either had pre-conceived biases and prejudices of his own or he was acting on orders from above.[9] Qutubuddin Aziz writes, 'An intrepid Scottish soldier, Major **Brown was** ***fond of Pâkistân***[10] **and** ***hated the tyrannical Dogrâ*** **straps [satraps?] with Mahârâjâ Hari Singh's evil coterie in Srinagar... The anti-**Dogrâ rebellion in the Gilgit Agency, in which *pro-Pâkistân* Brown helped, **made it possible for Gilgit, Hunzâ, Nagar, Puniâl and their neighbouring territories in the lofty Kârâkoram mountains to be placed under Pâkistân's** control in the autumn of 1947 which saw the birth of Pâkistân.' (*The Dawn*, Karachi, 4 Sept, 02; emphases mine.)

Brown had, since August 1, 1947, been advising the Governor of the Gilgit and Baltistân agencies, Ghansârâ Singh, and the Mahârâjâ of Jammu and Kashmîr that the "correct course of action for Kashmîr would be to join Pâkistân" He certainly thought that the Muslim majority areas of Gilgit, Baltistân, Hunzâ, Nagar and Chitrâl should join Pâkistân, and he ensured that this happened.

There was absolutely no reference to the wishes of the people, who had a longstanding record of toleration in matters of religion. Gilgit-Baltistân had no history of anti-Hiñdu, anti-India or anti-Mahârâjâ rebellions or even public demonstrations. Col. Yahya Effendi, a noted defence analyst from Pâkistân, would later note, 'The news of Kashmîr's accession to India was received in Gilgit calmly.'

The following day Gilgit was declared 'the independent Repûblic of Gilgit', which later acceded to Pâkistân. The Gilgit Scouts and Muslim

9. Would a disciplined young, serving British Army officer dare take such a far-reaching decision on his own?

10. That is, he was fond of Pâkistân even before that nation had come into existence.

soldiers of the Kashmîri army were then made to join the war against India, winning Baltistân for Pâkistân.

How did this happen? And why, considering the region's fabled peacefulness—and aloofness from the 'Pâkistân Movement'?

The rumoured disbanding of Gilgit Scouts

In the first week of August 1947, word went around Gilgit that the Dogrâ government was planning to disband the Gilgit Scouts.[vi] It is not clear whether this was a rumour (possibly spread by Major Brown and Captain Mathieson) or a fact (given the Scouts' British Raj origin). However, this explains what incensed the otherwise disciplined, well-behaved and secular Scouts. Fair-minded scholars owe it to posterity to find out if such a disbanding had actually been planned, because this was what sparked the anti-Dogrâ reaction.

Most of the Scouts now wanted an independent Gilgit (or an independent hill state that included Baltistân and other neighbouring areas).

However, some Gilgit Scouts wanted to throw in their lot with their fellow Muslims. They were in favour of some kind of an alliance with Pâkistân. Between August and October 1947, this group got in touch with Mr. Muhammad Ali Jinnah, the founder of Pâkistân, who was quite unwell then. (He died a few months later.) Mr. Jinnah informed them that Pâkistân was not in a position to help them because of the innumerable problems facing the newly born state.

Thus, the pro-independence sentiment prevailed.

Meanwhile, the Wali of Swât attacked Chilâs—and the Mehtar of Chitrâl put together an army to seize Koh-e-Ghizar and Yâsîn. The Gilgit Scouts, forces from Chitrâl and soldiers from all over Gilgit-Baltistân were organised into an army.

Prominent among the officers and other ranks who participated in this force were Captain (later Colonel) Mirza Hassan Khân. Major (later Brigadier) Mohammad Aslam Khân, Major Ehsan Ali, Subédâr Major (later Captain) Bâbar Khân, Subédâr (later Group Capt.) Shâh Khân, Subédâr Shér Ali, Subédâr Safiullah and Bakhtawar Shâh.

Capt. Mirza Hassan Khân thus founded the revolutionary republican movement in Gilgit-Baltistân. Subédâr Muhammad Ali (Bârdo) of the Padam Party provided critical political support.

An independent republic is established

According to Pâkistâni histories, on the 31st October, Major Brown asked the Scouts to take the Governor, Brig. Ghansârâ Singh, into custody, ostensibly to protect him. (According to Geocities, Brown had asked the Scouts to 'arrest' the Governor.) *The Daily Excelsior* adds, 'On November 1, 1947, Major Brown declared that Hiñdu rule had come to an end and

Gilgit would join Pâkistân.'[vii, 11] The local leaders, however, favoured independence.

The fact is that Capt. Mirza Hassan Khân, Subédâr Major Babar Khân[12] (who was the brother of the Mîr of Nagar and the Commander of the Scouts), and Mirzada Shah Khân (the brother of the Mîr of Hunzâ), were the ones who had got Brig. Ghansârâ locked up. They did so through the Scouts and a Muslim company of the State Troops.

Then why does Pâkistân want everyone to believe that Brown did these things all by himself? That's because the Khâns had arrested the Brigadier on behalf of an independent hill state, 'The Independent Republic of Gilgit,' and not in order to enable Pâkistân to annex the area.

That independent state lasted sixteen days.

In any case, there can be no doubt that Major Brown and Captain Mathieson led their 582 officers and men against the Dogrâs—and ultimately in favour of Pâkistân.[13]

Such was the affection that the Dogrâs and Gilgitis had had for each other that Brigadier Ghansârâ Singh, the Dogrâ Governor, did not see the need to post any Kashmîr State Force troops at Gilgit, the capital of the Gilgit Agency, where he lived.

The 6th Jammu and Kashmîr Infantry Battalion, posted at Bunji, 36 miles away, was the nearest. It consisted of two companies of Poonch Muslims, one Dogrâ Hiñdu company and one Sikh company.[viii] This is an extremely telling commentary about the religious composition of the

11. The 1st November has since been commemorated as 'Liberation Day': liberation from a monarchy and not liberation from any religious or ethnic group. This is evident from the fact that the 16th November, the day Pâkistân annexed the region, does not hold any significance for the local people. (Strangely, Maj. Humayun Amin's otherwise impeccable, even-handed, gracious and large-hearted account puts the date of liberation at the 4th November.)

12. There is a memorial to Bâbar Khân in the Chinâr Bâgh.

13. Pâkistân did not forget its benefactor. Maj. Brown was posthumously awarded Pâkistân's highest national award, the Sitara-e-Pâkistân.

This act has infuriated the public of Gilgit-Baltistân, because they consider Maj. Brown 'a criminal and traitor who snatched the future of a free country.' (The quote is from NDTV's documentary 'Cry Freedom' [2003].)

Wajâhat Hassan Khân, a local notable, once said that 'every revolution had a hero and a villain: Maj. Brown is the villain of our history.'

The sight of Pâkistân's military ruler, Gen. Pervez Musharraf, with Maj. Brown's widow on television in 1994, angered them further, for it meant that Pâkistân's highest executive was conferring legitimacy on Maj. Brown's extremely unpopular, unilateral decision.

On the 1st November, 2002, the people of Balâwaristân celebrated their Independence Day by burning an effigy of Maj. Brown.

Kashmîr State Forces, and why the Gilgitis could not possibly have seen it as a Dogrâ or a Hiñdu army.

On the 2nd November, 1947, the Republicans formed a Provisional Independent Government for these areas.

The Scouts then captured Bunji without resistance. As mentioned, the Hiñdu-Sikh troops there were greatly outnumbered. They were also too demoralised to put up a fight. Some of them tried to escape to Skardu and others to Astor. Most of them either died on the way or were captured. Some surrendered.

The Gilgit Scouts had put the Dogrâ governor under house arrest. They took control of the local garrison. They had also set up a provisional local government. Raja Shâh Rais Khân, the scion of an erstwhile ruling dynasty of the area, was made its president.

Meanwhile, Major Brown sent Capt. Mathieson to Chilâs. Mathieson and another officer, Mr Muzaffaruddin Shah, herded the non-Muslims into the fort and placed them 'in protective custody.'

For two weeks, Gilgit and the neighbouring areas were a republic, **independent of the Dogrâs as well as Pâkistân. Being physically cut off from India, the region was ripe for the plucking by Pâkistân.**

The first differences with Pâkistân

"The men of Gilgit Scouts had no intention of joining Pâkistân. They declared an independent Republic," Maj. Agha Humayun Amin points out.[ix]

Then how did Balâwaristân come under Pâkistâni control?

Brown and Mathieson put together a 'Supreme Council' in the territories that are now in the so-called 'Northern Areas'. This Council ostensibly asked the Government of Pakistân to take over their territory.

Actually, it was Brown and Mathieson who were in touch with Pâkistân. On November 14, 1947, Major Brown (and not the republican leaders) received a message from the Chief Minister of the NWFP that Pâkistân had agreed to make Gilgit a part of that country.

The Government of Pakistân sent Sardar Mohammad Âlam Khân, a Tehsîldâr from the NWFP, to Gilgit, on the 16th November 1947, to be its first Political Agent there.

Major Aslam Khân of the Pâkistâni Army had distinguished[14] himself in Kashmîr a few months before, when some Pâkistâni 'tribals' and 'irregulars' had 'spontaneously' attacked the Valley. He was promoted as Lieutenant Colonel and, in December 1947, sent to Gilgit as the overall commander of military operations in Gilgit-Baltistân.

14. Under his leadership, Pâkistân had captured significant territory in the Valley of Kashmîr.

Mr. Âlam Khân, the Political Agent, interpreted the situation very differently from the local republican leaders. He assumed that Gilgit-Baltistân now belonged to Pâkistân, the way, say, the princely state of Bahawalpur did. So, he dissolved the Independent Government, claimed that it was only a 'provisional' government, and took over the administration of these areas.

The leaders of the mountain republic, on the other hand, had nationalist aspirations. Within days this difference of opinion developed into a very bitter row between the two parties. The Agent divested the local leaders of all their powers. The local chiefs refused to take this lying down. The Agent told the republican leaders that if they persisted with their nationalist ideas he would go back to Karachi, the then capital of Pâkistân.

Now this was something that the new republic could not afford. It needed outside help—especially supplies—very badly. The area still does not produce enough to provide adequate employment to its people. In 1947, it imported all manner of consumer goods and essential supplies, including fuel oil, from outside. There was no land route through which India could have sent help. Pâkistân was the only power that could send provisions to the Gilgit-Baltistân region. So the local leaders climbed down and asked the Agent to go ahead the way he wanted to.

'With [the] arrival [of Alam Khan], the defunct president Shah Rais Khan was relegated to the post of civil supply officer,' Gilgit-based social scientist Aziz Ali Dad wrote. 'It shows the insensitive and ungracious attitude of Pakistani establishment. Alam Khan laid the foundation of a bureaucratic regime which turned the people's dream of freedom into a nightmare. Since then the people of Gilgit-Baltistan have not been able to attain their fundamental rights, identity and political status.'

Pâkistân annexes Baltistân

Baltistân remained with the Dogrâ forces. The Pâkistânî army organised the people of Gilgit and some neighbouring areas and surrounded the Kharpocho fort. Most of the Dogrâ soldiers who were outside the fort were killed. The siege went on for weeks. The tiny Dogrâ force inside realised that it had no chance. The soldiers surrendered and were allowed to go home. This happened on the 14th August, 1948, which was the first anniversary of Pakistân's independence.

The local nationalists, mainly Balti irregulars, reached Skardu with matchlock rifles and laid siege to the Dogrâ soldiers garrisoned in the Cantonment. Others were sent to capture Leh and Kargil. These soldiers were ill equipped and had no rations. However, they were better armed than the general public of Ladâkh, which had no arms at all. They advanced during the winter of 1948, and captured Kargil, Dras and the vital Zoji-la Pass, which links Ladâkh with Kashmîr and, in those days, with the rest of India. One Gilgit-Baltistâni contingent was less than sixteen kilometres from Leh when Indian forces repulsed it. Another Gilgit-Baltistâni contingent captured Zâñskâr.

Pâkistân has consistently downplayed the role of Capt. Mirza Hassan Khân[15] and other local nationalists. This offends the people of Gilgit-Baltistân no end, because they don't like their heroes being treated as traitors by Pâkistân.

Therefore, let us go back a few months and look in some detail at the enormity of the achievement of these brave men.

1947-48: The Gilgit Scouts' remarkable victories

Humayun Amin writes, "It may be noted that in most Pâkistâni accounts written by officers [who belong to the Punjâb and other places outside Gilgit-Baltistân] all credit for the success of [the] operations in Northern Areas is heaped on Aslam Khân. [However] Aslam had [a] limited role in planning [and] executing these operations and the most active part in the planning and execution was played by Major Ehsan (Kashmîr State Forces) and Lieutenant Shâh Khân (Gilgit Scouts) but Aslam being a regular army officer, having excellent contacts, and because he was the overall commander, robbed both of all credit. Aslam had lobbied for the appointment and got it on the basis that his father had served the Dogrâs before 1947 and that he knew the area. Aslam was by caste/origin a Pathan, but Punjâbi speaking and was closer in ethnic terms to the men who were associated with [the] compilation of the official history [of the Pâkistâni Army] and Shaukat Riza, who in his books was subconsciously trying to project the Punjâbi Muslims as the only fighting race as far as Pâkistân Army was concerned."

The Gilgit Scouts started recruiting local men and their strength rose to 2,000. They divided themselves into three forces and fanned out in as many directions.

The Ibex Force, led by the insuperable Major Ehsan Khân, moved on the Gilgit-Skardu route in late January 1948, to wrest Skardu from a Dogrâ battalion. They surrounded the outnumbered and under-supplied Dogrâs at Skardu on the 12th February. Maj. Humayun Amin writes, "Despite [their small number and poor supplies], the Dogrâs led by Lieutenant Colonel Shér Jang Thapa, an extremely resolute commander and a very chivalrous human being as far as treatment of non-combatants was concerned, held on till 14th August, 1948 when 200 of his garrison broke out towards Kargil, while Shér Jang with the remainder 250 of his troops surrendered."

15. Capt. Mirza Hassan Khân's son, Wajahat Hassan, joined the Pâkistâni navy but was not allowed to rise to a senior rank. Today Cdr. Wajahat Hassan is spearheading a movement to liberate Gilgit-Baltistân from Pâkistânî occupation.

In the summer of 1948, some Indian detachments tried to regain Skardu. However, Major Ehsan Khân and his men worked out innovative strategies. They ambushed the Indian forces at various points on the Skardu-Kargil Road and won the battle.

Captain Hassan Khân led the Tiger Force which occupied the Bunji-Kamri-Gurez-Bandipura route in order to thwart any Indian attempt to recapture Gilgit-Baltistân in early 1948 after the snow on the passes had melted.

Lieutenant Shâh Khân led the Eskimo Force. They marched from Astor through the snow-covered and uninhabited Deosai Plain (which is at more than 10,000 feet). This force came up from behind and attacked the Dogrâ garrisons that controlled Drâss-Kargil and the dZoji Lâ Pass area. They snapped the communications of these garrisons, as well as of those at Leh, with the Valley of Kashmîr.

The Gilgit Scouts captured Drâss on the 6th June, 1948. This is a crucial village now on the Srinagar-Kargil-Leh highway. It was then on the Kargil-Skardu road. It is the last village in Ladâkh when driving down to Kashmîr (or the first major habitation in Ladâkh when driving up from Kashmîr),

The only way to drive up from Kashmîr (and, in those days, from any part of India) to Ladâkh is through the dZoji Lâ pass. He who controls this pass decides which country will administer Ladâkh. Therefore, it was critical for India to have this pass. Pâkistân can live without the dZoji Lâ, But for Pâkistân to concede this pass to India meant conceding most of Leh and Kargil. That is how important this pass is.

The able Lieutenant Shâh Khân and his brave men started moving towards the dZoji Lâ in June. On the 7th July, 1948, the Eskimo Force had got its prize. (The Indian Army recaptured it later through the efforts and sacrifices of its equally hardy men. But that is another story— an epic, in fact. It has been recounted in detail in Dr. S.S. Bloeria's book, *The Zoji Lâ Operations* (1997), Har Anand Publications, New Delhi.)

The Gilgit Scouts then started marching towards Leh. They conquered most of the territory up to Nimu, which is around ten miles short of Leh town, as the crow flies. (The Scouts could not hold on to this territory either.)

Maj. Agha Humayun Amin has very gallantly praised the Dogrâs who fought bravely despite being hopelessly outnumbered. (Indeed, his account hails the performance of every good Indian officer elsewhere in the state as well.)

Every Indian should likewise admire the valour of the Gilgit Scouts, who were similarly outnumbered in their battles with the Indian Army when they were defeated not only at the dZoji Lâ but also in the Nimu area. The Indian Army later took back Gurez-Bandipura, too. However, Captain Hassan Khân and his Tiger Force managed to hold on to many of the territories that they had captured.

The achievements of this tiny but incredibly courageous force should always be seen in the context of its very small numbers. The great martial traditions of Gilgit-Balâwaristân explain how so much was done by so few men. One can not but marvel at how the officers of Gilgit-Baltistân managed to inspire their handful of men to achieve such an enormous amount. After all, the Gilgit Scouts had come within knocking distance of the two most important towns in the province—Srinagar and Leh.

1949: Pâkistân obtains temporary administrative control...

The nationalists of Gilgit-Balâwaristân continued their efforts to conquer territory for their proposed republic. When a cease-fire was ordered on January 1, 1949, under the auspices of the United Nations, they had managed to conquer an expanse of as much 28,000 sq. miles in Gilgit, Hunzâ, Diamir and Baltistân. They imagined that they would establish an independent republic in this huge region. However, even after the cease-fire, Pâkistân continued to occupy the region. Indeed, it tightened its grip on it.

This has rankled with the people of the region ever since. At a rally held to celebrate their Independence Day on the 1st November, 2002,[x] nationalist leaders from the region reminded Pâkistân of the United Nations Resolutions [of the 13th August, 1948, and the 5th January, 1949, especially the latter]. These Resolutions had mandated that a plebiscite be held to determine the wishes of the people of Jammu and Kashmîr [i.e. which nation the people of the state wanted to join.] The leaders of Gilgit, Baltistân and 'Âzâd' Jammu and Kashmîr reiterated that the UN Resolutions required that the Pâkistân Army be totally withdrawn from all parts of Kashmîr while India was not obliged to withdraw its Army in Kashmîr in full.

(The speakers at the Independence Day rally, especially Wajahat Hassan Khân and Yusuf Ali Naushâd, rubbed in that last point. They pointed out, "[According to the UN Resolutions] Pâkistân can not keep a single soldier in this area. The Pâkistâni Army has to vacate [the occupied areas] within seven days...[On the other hand] India can retain some forces [in Jammu and Kashmîr] to maintain the law and order.")

On April 28, 1949, the Pâkistân Government signed what has come to be known as the Karachi Agreement. Kashmîr was 'represented' by Sardar M. Ibrahim Khân and Chaudhary Ghulam Abbas (of Jammu). The Agreement gave Pâkistân temporary administrative control over the occupied territories. Neither of these 'Kashmîrî' leaders was from Gilgit-Baltistân (or even from the Valley of Kashmîr). Besides, they had specified that what they were ceding to Pâkistân was only for a while.

The only legal document that Pâkistân has to justify its control of Gilgit-Baltistân-Hunzâ is a 1949 decision of the so-called Azâd Jammu and Kashmîr Government. This gave Pâkistân the power to administer 'AJK' as well as the so-called Northern Areas through a Political Agent. The colonial British Government in India had created the institution of a Political Agent to keep an eye on the natives. It is interesting that Pâkistân has retained this colonial system for the so-called Northern Areas, even though Pâkistân's own districts are administered by Deputy Commissioners and District Magistrates (as in India).

...and starts behaving like a colonial master

The colonial approach did not stop there. Baltistân and Gilgit were to be administered under the Frontier Crimes Regulations (FCR)-that's right, through a colonial Act meant to put down crime rather than through the developmental system that Pâkistân gave its own districts. The oppressive FCR was, as far as Pâkistân was concerned, a substitute for a national constitution for Gilgit-Balâwaristân.

"For almost five decades," Pâkistâni journalist, Ishtiaq Ali Mehkri, wrote in the widely respected *Dawn*, Karachi, "the area has been under virtual martial law. Under the Frontier Crime Regulations, framed by the British during the colonial days, every resident of the area has to report to the local police station once a month and all movements from one village to another have to be reported to the police station."[xi]

The so-called Northern Areas have never been governed like one of the four states of Pâkistân, each of which has its own Governor, Chief Minister and legislative assembly. Nor are they a part of the so-called 'Âzâd Jammu and Kashmîr.'

In the 1940s and '50s, the Government of Pâkistân administered the 'Northern Areas' through its North West Frontier Province (NWFP), with the help of the local râjâs. Later, Pâkistân started governing the area through its Ministry of Kashmîr Affairs and the 'Northern Areas' (KANA). A grade 19/20 bureaucrat used to head the local administration and doubled as a one-man head of judiciary.

What hurt the republican nationalists of Gilgit-Balâwaristân the most was that the local rajas and mirs were permitted to rule their fiefs and tax their people as they always had. Pâkistân, on the other hand, occasionally allowed its own citizens to enjoy spells of democracy. Pâkistân had rid itself of hereditary monarchs, while it permitted them to continue in Gilgit-Baltistân-Hunzâ. (Which is not to say that elected politicians and army generals are necessarily better than hereditary rulers. Several feudal chiefs of Hunzâ, Gilgit and Baltistân had indeed been benign and good to their subjects.)

Till 1974, the seven kings of the region along the Gilgit and Hunzâ rivers remained more or less autonomous. The mirs and rajas continued to run the civil administration, police and judiciary.

The bitterness towards Pâkistân continues

The partition of India into two hostile states hurt Baltistân like it did all of Ladâkh. Till 1948, this was an area without borders. People from Central Asia, especially Yârqañd, greater Ladâkh and Kashmîr would stream in and out of Baltistân. After India and Pâkistân stationed their armies on the borders of this region, these mutually enriching cultural and trade exchanges came to an end, perhaps forever.

The Pâkistân artillery routinely shells Indian Kargil, often killing civilians and destroying houses and mosques in the process. When India fires back in retaliation, unfortunately sometimes innocent Baltis, too, get hurt.

After a while, in the mid-1970s, Pâkistân started calling the region 'the Northern Areas.' For the first few decades Pâkistân accepted these as the 'Northern Areas' of Jammu and Kashmîr. However, over the years Pâkistân has been trying to pretend that portions of the region (notably Hunzâ, Chitrâl and Astor) were a part of British India and thus of Pâkistân proper and not of the princely state of Jammu and Kashmîr, which had acceded to India.

This has led to a hostile reaction from the people of the area. For one, they resent the name that Pâkistân has given their region, because it describes them in terms of their geographical position in respect to Pâkistâni Punjâb. "Will any Pâkistâni government call the Punjâb 'the Eastern Areas' or Sind 'the Southern Areas'?" they ask. The local people prefer to call their region Balâwaristân.[16]

They point out that while they are not ethnic Kashmîrîs, Balâwaristân is a disputed area, and was part of the princely state of Jammu and Kashmîr, which existed before the 1st Nov. 1947. Unlike the Pâkistânis, they are not very comfortable with the resolutions passed by the United Nations on Kashmîr in January 1949.

Balâwaristân, or Gilgit-Baltistân, is spread over roughly 28,000 square miles. Its people are almost entirely Muslim, and are from the Shia, Sunni, Ismâili and Nûr Bakhshi sects. In 1963, Pâkistân carved a 5,180

16. "Cries from Pâkistân occupied Kashmîr: Heart beats for India?" by Abdul Hamid Khân (The article is apparently from the *Kashmîr Telegraph*. I picked it off the Internet.)

sq. km. (roughly 2,700 sq. mile) chunk, in an area called Shaksgam (which is in Shimshal, Hunzâ) out of Balâwaristân and gifted it to China.

Some changes are made

The visionary, left-leaning, democratically elected Pâkistâni Prime Minister, Zulfiqâr Ali Bhutto, changed some of the more detestable aspects of Pâkistâni administration. For that reason he is the only Pâkistâni politician remembered fondly by the local people. Bhutto got rid of the offensive FCR and abolished the extortionate system of land revenue. Around that time the administrative unit now known as the 'Northern Areas' was created. It was made of Gilgit, Ghizar and Diamir, as well as the two districts of Baltistân—Skardu and Ganche.

The 'Râjâ system,' too, was abolished between 1972 and 1974. The Government of Pâkistân relieved the kings (mîrs) of most of their powers, and the kingdoms were incorporated into Pâkistân.

The 'Northern Areas' were stealthily (and offensively) divided into five administrative districts: Diamer (administered from Chilâs), Baltistân (Skardu), Ganche (Khaplu), Ghizar (Gakuch), and Gilgit (including Gilgit town, which is also the headquarters of the chief administrator of the so-called Northern Areas). What was offensive was that old identities, some of them several thousand years old, were sought to be erased. Hunzâ, for instance, was for a while incorporated into Gilgit District,

The two other major changes brought about by outside forces have been the construction of the Kârâkoram Highway (KKH) to Tibet in 1978, and the enormous developmental work done by the Aga Khân Foundation. Both changes are well meant and neither is intentionally malign. However, there are serious concerns about their long-term consequences—especially those of the KKH—on the fabled longevity of the region, not to mention the culture and ethnic composition of the seven kingdoms.

Pâkistân's position

Pâkistân now calls the occupied part of old Ladâkh the 'Northern Areas.' It feebly tries to pretend that only 'AJK' ('Azad' Jammû and Kashmîr) was a part of the original Jammû and Kashmîr. While Pâkistân maintains the fiction that 'AJK' is an independent/ semi-independent country, regarding the so-called Northern Areas it has no such pretence. It claims that some of the 'Northern Areas' are part of Pâkistân proper. It runs the 'Northern Areas' as a 'federally-administered area': or what we in India would call a Union Territory.

Pâkistân's position flies in the face of the facts. Pâkistân and India became independent of the British empire on the 14th and 15th August,

1947, respectively. The so-called Northern Areas (as well as Astor, Hunzâ, Bunji and Chitrâl) were very much a part of the Dogrâ Mahârâjâs' state of Jammû and Kashmîr on those two legally significant dates. (And for several months thereafter).

The Jammû and Kashmîr Liberation Front (JKLF) might have its differences with the Indian State on many issues, but on the status of the 'Northern Areas' (and Astor, Hunzâ, Bunji and Chitrâl) both agree wholeheartedly. Even from the point of Kashmîrî nationalists on both sides of the line of control, the 'Northern Areas' are an inseparable part of Jammû and Kashmîr.

Because of Pâkistân's strange position, the 'Northern Areas' are neither a province of Pâkistân nor a part of 'Azad Jammû and Kashmîr.' As a result they do not have a legislature, no adult franchise and no representative bodies. Islâmâbâd governs them directly through a Northern Areas Council which is headed by Pâkistân's Minister for Kashmîr Affairs. A chief executive, normally a retired Pâkistâni army officer, appointed by Islâmâbâd, is the local administrative head. The 'Northern Areas' Council is headed by the Minister of Kashmîr and Northern Areas and meets only when the minister convenes it. The respected Pâkistâni magazine the *Herald* calls the 'Northern Areas' 'The Last Colony.'[xii]

In contrast, the people of Leh and Kargil not only send their own representatives to the national parliament and state legislature, they have elected district councils of their own. Indeed, rules have been bent to the extreme in favour of sparsely populated Leh and Kargil to enable them to be represented in disproportionately higher numbers in the national and state legislatures.

(Incidentally, under Dogrâ rule, members from Gilgit and Baltistân were represented in the State Assembly.)

The 'Northern Areas' Legislative Council

In 1993-94, Pâkistân created the so-called Northern Areas Legislative Council (NALC). This is the highest elected body in all of Gilgit-Baltistân. Some judicial reforms, too, were introduced around the same time.

If the 'Northern Areas' have a Legislative Council, then what's the problem?

The NALC does not have the power to legislate. This rankles with the people, because even the municipalities and other local bodies of Pâkistâni cities have this power. To make things worse, the Minister of KANA, a Pâkistâni, has been imposed on Balâwaristân as the Chief Executive of the NALC and, thus, of the region. The highest position that an elected representative of the Gilgit-Baltistân area can aspire to remains that of the Deputy Chief Executive. The Minister of KANA is a bit like a viceroy. He presides over the NALC and has the power to dissolve and disband this elected body at will. He has the absolute power to enact laws through 'direct orders,' without consulting the NALC or any other native of Gilgit-Baltistân. All political, economic and administrative powers vest in the Minister of KANA. He can appoint anyone from Pâkistân as the chief of the judiciary of the so-called Northern Areas—on a contract. This last point hurts the local population enormously, because in the rest of South Asia the judiciary enjoys enormous security of tenure. That their judiciary is appointed on short-term contracts is considered extremely offensive. Besides, the executive can easily manipulate an insecure judiciary.

The NALC once passed a resolution to get rid of KANA's control. Pâkistân retaliated in a mediæval way. It prohibited all legislators who were party to the resolution from thenceforth entering any government office in Gilgit-Baltistân.

Legislatures in India and Pâkistân routinely take bureaucrats to task if they err in the performance of their duties. The NALC is debarred from such much as criticising Pâkistâni civil servants posted in the region.

The most celebrated case dates to the 1990s. The KANA Minister placed Amîr Hamzâ, a Senior Superintendent of Police of local origin, under suspension for a staggering twelve years. This was as good as dismissing him from his job, because he would have retired around the time that his suspension came to an end. Hamzâ's wife got elected to the NALC. She condemned her husband's suspension in the Legislative Council. This happens routinely in the legislatures of India and Pâkistân. However, right after the lady finished speaking, the offended KANA Minister issued an order formally dismissing Amîr Hamzâ from government service.

Saif-ur-Rehman, also a member of the NALC, had the temerity to tick off a Pâkistânî bureaucrat for his imperious and harsh attitude towards the local people. Politicians do this all the time in South Asia—rightly or wrongly. However, Mr. Saif-ur-Rehman was charged with treason and jailed for having dared to criticise a Pâkistâni civil servant.

On his release from prison, Mr. Rehman started trying to bring the then estranged Shias and Sunnis together. This was in the finest traditions of Balâwaristân, where harmony rather than discord has been the historical norm. However, a terrorist killed Mr. Rehman, allegedly at the behest of the ISI. Apparently some Pâkistâni army and police officers were alarmed at the prospect of Mr. Rehman succeeding in his efforts to bring about peace.

The Balâwaristân-Kârâkoram area thus remains in a political limbo. It is administered directly by Pâkistân's federal government. However, constitutionally it is attached to 'AJK.'

Economic development since 1947

The literacy rate in Gilgit-Balâwaristân is 14 per cent for men and 3.5 per cent for women. (In predominantly Muslim Kargil 73.38 per cent of the men and 40.95 per cent of the women are literate; Buddhist-majority Leh is even more literate.)

Some brick kilns are the only 'industry' in the area. According to the Pâkistânî daily, the *Muslim*,[17] there were just 162 km. of metalled roads in an area of 72,496 sq.km. in 1993. (On the other hand Leh and Kargil had 1,736 km. of roads in an area of 54,036 sq.km. in 2000.)

There are only two colleges for a population of almost 1.5 million (vs. two colleges for 0.2 million people in Leh and Kargil). There is not a single polytechnic in this huge land, which is bigger than several sovereign countries. The only newspaper of the region, *K-2*, carries on its masthead the legend "(The) Voice of a constitutionless land".

In Islâmâbâd and other affluent parts of Pâkistân, most of the domestic servants and pre-teen (*muñdû*) waiters in tea stalls are from Gilgit, Baltistân and Muzaffarâbâd. What a contrast with the parts actually under Indian administration. Far from serving in menial jobs outside Kashmîr, since the 1970s it has been very difficult to find Kashmîrî youths who are willing to work in private residences even within the Valley, because they have better paid jobs. In Kashmîr, construction labour for public roads and buildings and private brick kilns is almost entirely brought over from Central India. So are farmhands at the peak of the agriculture season. What a change from the situation before 1947, when Kashmîr was a net exporter of labour.

The average wage in Kashmîr has generally been twice India's national average and that in Ladâkh three times the Indian average. As a result, in Ladâkh there is migration of labour in the reverse direction. All cobblers, barbers, watch-repairers and *mithâi* (Indian sweets) makers in Ladâkh are from the Indian plains. So are almost all managers and some waiters in the better hotels.

Ladâkh's post-1970 prosperity owes partly to the twenty-five thousand or so tourists that visit it every year. However, Leh also happens to be the district that receives the highest per capita government developmental aid in all of India, which is the main reason for its relative affluence and almost full employment. As 'tribals,' the people of Leh and Kargil receive preferential treatment in matters of government employment as well as admission to medical and engineering colleges run by the state and national governments.

According to the same formula, Balâwaristân would have received the same per capita aid had it remained in India. Instead of its people

17. December 13, 1993.

serving as menials in Islâmâbâd and Karachi, it would have enjoyed near full employment and 'imported' labour from the plains, as Leh is doing.

The Mirpuris of 'AJK' migrated in large numbers to the West, to improve their economic lot. The people from the 'Northern Areas' are not even allowed to do this. They need an exit visa to go abroad, which is given only in the rarest of cases.

Loss of territory

In 1947-49, the brave nationalist soldiers of the Kârâkoram-Hiñdu Kush region were able to take control of more than 28,000 square miles in what used to be the Ladâkh district and Gilgit division of Jammu and Kashmîr. Pâkistân appropriated the land from them—and then started whittling down the size of the republic that the revolutionaries had tried to create.

This is one of the things that have embittered the people of Balâwaristân against Pâkistân. Yusuf Ali Naushâd of the Balâwaristân National Front has been speaking bitterly[xiii] about how under Pâkistân the size of the republic that their ancestors had established has consistently been shrinking. '[Pâkistân first] lost Kargil and Drâss [to India in 1947]. Then we lost the Kâpar mountain, which we call the *chowkidâr* [sentinel] mountain of the region. We lost Siâchen and then several villages in Khaplu. Those who let these territories go should be punished.'

The people feel that what Pâkistân lost to India in wars was bad enough. However, the voluntary cession of Shaksgam to China is the most resented part of the process.

Constitutional issues in a 'constitutionless' land

The government of Pâkistân, 'is never tired of speaking about accesses [excesses] against the Kashmiris by Indian government, but it is not ready to grant constitutional status to Gilgit-Baltistan. India has given representation to the people of Daras [Drass], Ladakh, Guraiz and Kargil, who belong to same racial, linguistic and cultural stock as the people of Gilgit-Baltistan. What is the wisdom behind keeping the people of [Gilgit-Baltistan] deprived of their fundamental rights? If India is not afraid of granting constitutional status to disputed territories, then what are the factors stopping Pakistan from doing the same?'

Aziz Ali Dad, Gilgit-based social scientist (Dawn, Karachi, October 2007)

The 'Northern Areas' do not have a High Court. They are thus deprived of the facility of (and the right to file) 'writ petitions' against arbitrary State action. The court of the Judicial Commissioner can confirm even a death sentence. The Gilgitis cannot appeal to the Supreme Court.

None of the constitutions of Pâkistân, adopted in 1956, 1962, 1972 and 1973, recognised that 'Northern Areas' as a part of the Pâkistân's territories. On the other hand, the 1974 Interim Constitution of 'Azad' Jammû and Kashmîr, too, did not include Gilgit and Baltistân in its territories. This resulted in a strange vacuum from the Pâkistânî point of view (and a happy one from India's: because if neither Pâkistân nor 'AJK' claims this fabled land, then surely it is a part of India by default, as it was till 1947-48).

The Pâkistânîs realised this. So they passed the 'Legal Framework Order' which placed the 'Northern Areas' under the total control of the Kashmîr Affairs Ministry. In 1982, General Zia-ul-Haq proclaimed that the people of the 'Northern Areas' were Pâkistânis and had nothing to do with the State of Jammu and Kashmîr.

Some residents of the 'Northern Areas' filed a writ petition under Section 44 of 'AJK's' Interim Constitution Act of 1974. They jointly invoked the writ jurisdiction of the 'AJK' High Court claiming that the petitioners were bona fide citizens of the State of Jammu and Kashmîr and were hence eligible to approach the 'AJK' High Court for redress. They challenged the Pâkistâni view that the 'Northern Areas' were not a part of Kashmîr but were a part of Pâkistân. They also contended that even the Sino-Pâkistân Agreement of 1963 conceded that the 'Northern Areas' were a part of the State of J&K.

The Government of Pâkistân put forth the specious argument that the Government of Pâkistân "was not functioning or operating within the territory of Azad Jammu & Kashmîr [and] as such it was not amenable **to the jurisdiction of this [AJK High] court".**

Pâkistân also denied the well-known Karachi Agreement of April 28, 1949, "whereby the administrative control of Northern Areas was delivered to the Government of Pâkistân". The High Court of 'AJK' however decided that the so-called Northern Areas were a part of 'AJK'. Pâkistân, of course, never implemented the 'AJK' High Court decision. It got the decision overruled by the Supreme Court of 'AJK' which said that the 'AJK' High Court did not have the jurisdiction to issue any order returning the 'Northern Areas' to 'AJK'.

In another case, the Al Jihad Trust and others filed a petition in the Supreme Court of Pâkistân. They demanded that fundamental rights be accorded to them, including representation in the Federal Legislatures and the right of self-determination. The Government of Pâkistân held that the Supreme Court of Pâkistân had no jurisdiction since the 'Northern Areas' were not, in terms of Pâkistân's constitution, a part of Pâkistân.

Again the same anomaly from Pâkistân's point of view, and a vindication of India's stand that the 'Northern Areas' are not a part of Pâkistân.

No political activity is permitted in the 'Northern Areas.' Some political parties like the United Jammu and Kashmîr People's National Party and the Balawaristan National Front and others have been demanding the right of self-determination, only to find their demonstrations crushed and their leaders arrested. Demonstrations by students in Gilgit seeking employment have been put down equally brutally. The Gilgit-Baltistân United Action Forum for Self-Rule has been demanding the right to self-rule under the UNCIP (United Nations Commission for India and Pâkistân) resolutions on Gilgit and Baltistân.

Leave alone self-determination or independence, Pâkistân does not allow the people of the so-called AJK and Northern Areas to get a government job or contest elections unless they sign an oath that says '*Kashmîr banégâ Pâkistân*' (Kashmîr will become a part of Pâkistân). In the 2001 elections several candidates were disqualified because they refused to sign such an oath.

Alienation from Pâkistân

Shia-Sunni riots

In 1988, the peace of this Shangri La was shattered. Bloody riots broke out between different sects of Muslims, perhaps for the first time in the history of the region. The non-Sunnis felt that the Sunni-dominated Government of Pâkistân was patronising only the local Sunnis.

The Pâkistâni establishment accused the intelligence agencies of neighbouring, overwhelmingly-Shia, Iran, of instigating the Shias of Gilgit to revolt against Pâkistân. This was because the Shias had demanded that a Shia province called 'Kârâkoram' be carved out of the so-called Northern Areas.

According to Rehman Faiz,[18] '[The then military dictator of Pâkistân, President] General Zia [ul Haq] inducted jihâdi [religious extremist] terrorist hordes into Gilgit, where they carried out a large-scale massacre of the Shias. Moreover, the SSP[19] of [Pâkistân's] Punjâb was allowed to open an office in Gilgit, to rally round the Sunnis in the area against the Shias. This resulted in the spread of sectarian terrorism to the Northern Areas, before which it [was] limited mainly to Punjâb and the NWFP.[20] [xiv]

18. Mr. Faiz is the president of the Lahore unit of Amnesty International and an internationally respected activist in the field of harmony between different sects.
19. Sipâh é Sahâbâ Pâkistân, an extremist Sunni organisation.
20. Mr. Faiz' interview was published three months after my volume on 'Kashmîr.' I had written in that book, 'Guns have been used to settle private disputes in Pâkistân's Punjâb and Frontier [NWFP] Provinces for several centuries now... The 1990s brought this culture to Kashmîr.'

    I beg the Pâkistâni establishment to take pity on the people of Kashmîr and Gilgit-Balâwaristân and leave them alone to their peaceful ways, instead of exporting the violent culture of the plains to these simple hill people. On the contrary, Pâkistân (and India) should import the paradise-like ethos of Kashmîr and Gilgit-Baltistân-Bunji-Hunzâ-Ladâkh.

Besides, the Lashkar é Jhañgvi ('the soldiers of Jhañg'), a militant Sunni organisation, was brought in to control the Shias.

Pâkistân's aggression in Kashmîr and Kargil

Pâkistân's sponsorship of militancy in Kashmîr from 1989 onwards is a major sore point with the people of the area. Pâkistân recruited impoverished and unemployed youths from Gilgit-Baltistân and sent them into Kashmîr to create mayhem. The Indian forces killed most of them.

Five major terrorist (all right, jehâdi) training camps have been functioning in Balâwaristân since 1989. They train not only local youths but also Afghans, Pâkistânis and the odd Kashmîri. Every time international pressure on Pâkistân becomes unbearable, it winds up all jehâdi camps operating from its own soil and shifts them to what it calls 'AJK.' When the international community wizens up to this technicality, the camps are moved to the so-called Northern Areas.

A decade and a half later, the people of the area started asking themsleves—and the Pâkistânî authorities, 'What have we go out of this jéhâd?'

Pâkistân's aggression in Kargil in 1999, is the sorest point of all. The Indian Army martyred a number of Pâkistânî soldiers. Pâkistân wanted to maintain the fiction that those killed were from the Valley of Kashmîr and not from any area controlled by Pâkistân. So, it refused to collect the bodies of its dead soldiers, many of whom were regular soldiers of the so-called 'Northern Areas Light Infantry.' Their relatives have never forgiven Pâkistân.

This bitter comment from Balâwaristân has appeared on the Internet, "Our youths (Northern Light Infantry) were sent to Kargil as mercenaries by Pâkistân[.] As a result more than 900 NLI youth lost their lives, 1000 were wounded and became disabled and 40 are missing. The most barbaric role of both Pâkistân and Indian Army was that the Indian Army caught more than 50 NLI soldiers at different places of Kargil in 1999 war and asked if Pâkistân Army accepts NLI soldiers, they will be treated prisoners of war [as] per Geneva convention. But Indian Army shot them on the spot when Pâkistân Army denied accepting [i.e. refused to accept] them. Indian Army buried 300 dead bodies of NLI soldiers on Kargil heights, when Pâkistân refused to accept their bodies but accepted 2 bodies of its own nationals."

Pâkistân, on its part, realised how bitter the people—and soldiers—of Gilgit-Baltistân were about this. It felt that it could no long trust soldiers recruited from the region. So, for the first time in the history of the NLI, soldiers from Pâkistân were sent to serve in the NLI.

Political manifestations of this alienation

Alienation from Sunni-dominated Pâkistân has begun to manifest itself politically as well. The goodwill that Mr. Bhutto had earned had, for almost two decades, ensured that his People's Party of Pâkistân (PPP) was a dominant presence in the region.

However, in the 1994 elections to the National Assembly Council, the Tehrîk-é-Jâffaria Pâkistân (TJP), which is an avowedly Shiite grouping, did remarkably well. By the turn of the millennium it accounted for just under half the seats in the Council and was thus as big as the PPP. The TJP has become very important in Skardu and Shigar, too. A land where the Shias and Sunnis never fought sectarian battles, where they had always lived in harmony, has, unfortunately, got divided along sectarian lines.

In the 1990s an agitation began for a change of the Islâmiat syllabus that had been imposed on the schools of the area. All top positions in government as well as business are dominated by people from Pâkistân. This, too, has fuelled resentment against Pâkistân.

Attempts to give vent to their grievances have been crushed with a heavy hand. More than a hundred political leaders and workers were charged with sedition in the 1990s. Many of them were sent to jail as well.

Many of the things that the nationalists of Gilgit-Baltistân have been saying about Pâkistân (and its Punjâbi majority) have a familiar ring throughout the sub-continent. For instance, Wajahat Hassan Khân alleged[xv] that whenever a Pâkistâni bureaucrat came to Gilgit-Baltistân, all that he brought with him was a 'worn-out [Pâkistâni] flag.' However, when the same officer completed his stint and was transferred back to Pâkistân, he would go home with truckloads of belongings.

The latter allegation is made against 'non-local' bureaucrats and engineers in many parts of India. However, the bit about coming to Balâwaristân with just a 'worn-out flag' is new, and has an ominous secessionist ring to it.

Similarly, Sardâr Ishtiâq Ahmed[xvi] of the All Parties National Alliance[21] estimated that Pâkistân owes Gilgit-Baltistân Rs.5,500 million a year as royalties for the electricity-generating waters of River Indus alone. He believes that in all Pâkistân drains Rs.14,700 million worth of wealth out of the so-called Northern Areas every year.

21. This is an alliance of the leaders of the two main occupied parts of Kashmîr, viz., the so-called Âzâd Jammu and Kashmîr (AJK) and the 'Northern Areas.'

The region is so rich in mineral and forest wealth that an entire chapter of this book is dedicated to documenting these resources. However, the Sardâr's calculations can be debated, because nationalists from all raw materials producing areas of the world (e.g. Sub Saharan Africa and India's desperately poor Bihâr) say similar things against the areas where value is added (notably Japan, Taiwan and South Korea).

However, Mr. Ahmed is on firmer ground when he points out that Pâkistân gives Gilgit-Baltistân a mere Rs.2,300 million a year for salaries and developmental works. In per capita terms this is less than a seventh of what India gives Leh and Kargil.[22] That probably explains why people from Gilgit-Baltistân-Hunzâ-Chitrâl go to all corners of Pâkistân looking for menial jobs, while Leh and Kargil import labour from all over India.

His colleague Yusuf Ali Naushâd of the Balâwaristân National Front added[xvii] that the 'Northern Areas' do not get their due share of Indus water, nor their share of electricity. Besides, he said, the doctors and engineers of the region were unemployed. This had forced many unemployed youths to commit suicide. (In contrast, not a single engineering or medical graduate is unemployed in Leh or Kargil, where almost all arts graduates get government jobs within two or three years, as do most men who get through higher secondary 'A level' school.)

A doubly enriched identity

The majority (almost 60 per cent) of the Baltîs are Shia (Shiite) Muslims. They share the values of Iran, but not its relative affluence, urbanisation and literacy. Therefore, they lead a life that is even more orthodox than in Iran. The Iranians, for instance, make some of the world's most respected feature films. However, an influential section of the Balti clergy has ensured that cinema houses do not come up in Baltistân. All forms of Westernisation—or deviation from pristine Islâm—are frowned upon.

And yet the Baltîs are a gentle, tolerant lot. They have imposed restrictions on themselves, not on others. They appreciate tourists who

22. In 2003-2004, for instance, the 'district plan' of Kargil was Rs.55 crore (550 million) for development, Rs.32 crore (320m.) for salaries, and roughly Rs.3 crore for maintenance. Thus Kargil received around Rs.90 crore in the 'district sector' alone. In addition, it would have received a few crore rupees under the 'state' and 'central' (i.e. national) 'sectors.' Leh received a similar amount. Its 2004-05 'annual district plan' was Rs. 62 crore for development and Rs. 39.3 crore for salaries and maintenance. In addition it got a direct central grant of Rs.15 crore because it is a 'border district.' The total works out to Rs.117 crore for Leh alone, and it does not include 'state' and 'district' sector schemes. Thus, with a population that is one seventh that of the 'Northern Areas,' Ladâkh receives a little more.

respect their views about exposed female flesh, but do not force their views on them.

Despite being conservative Muslims, the Baltîs are proud of their pre-Islâmic past. So, if they look to Iran for religion, they lean towards Tibet and Leh for culture. Thus, if they love Hazrat Ali, the Shiite hero and pioneer, they adore the Tibeto-Ladâkhi Gesar of Ling [called Gyâlam Késar in Leh].

Far from giving them an identity crisis, or a split identity, this has made the Balti identity twice as strong. It is exactly the same in Iran,[23] where they are proud to be Muslims, but are equally proud of their pre-Islâmic Persian past and culture.

Sensitive Baltîs are concerned that pre-Islâmic Balti festivals are fast vanishing. The fire-throwing Me-phang is the most colourful of these. A nationalist revival has been brewing since the 1990s to stem the tide. Scholars as well as college students are leading the movement. Syed Abbas Kazmi and Mohammad Hasnain are among its best-known leaders. Both have gone to great lengths to keep Baltistân's pre-Islâmic practices alive.

Kazmi, for instance, is striving to protect what is left of Skardu's ancient Buddhist sculptures. He has also helped excavate the ruins of a Buddhist gompa that had once existed near Shigar. Both Kazmi and Hasnain have gone to endearing extremes to identify themselves with Baltistân's composite Islâmo-Buddhist culture. Hasnain calls himself Senge Tshering, a name normally used by the Buddhists. Kazmi 'prefers to eat out of a *photoh*, a traditional wooden bowl that today one only finds in Skardu's antique shops.'[xviii]

Hasnain is also trying to reintroduce the Tibetan script in Baltistân. He points out that the Balti language can simply not be written in the Arabic script.[24]

Because of Kazmi's influence, the Baltistân Students Federation has adopted the yung drung (swastika), the ancient Bon symbol of prosperity, as their logo.

Dilution of the local population

In many parts of the world local people get angry when persons from other parts of the same country migrate to their region or state, especially when outsiders take away local jobs. Some South Asian provincial administrations have even passed laws to protect local jobs and, in the case of India's tribal areas, local land from being usurped by outsiders.

23. And in Indonesia, Central Asia and Bangladesh.

24. The Balti language has its own right to left script. The early 19th century professors A. Fischer and Hultzsch told G.T. Vigne (c.1835) that the script was 'not based on any form of Arabic character, but rather resembles the Indian form of script.'

In the early 20th century, the Mahârâjâ of Jammu and Kashmîr passed a law according to which people who did not belong to the state could not purchase land or take up employment in the state. The law was also enacted to ensure that outsiders did not swamp the tiny local population (as, say, the mainland Chinese have done to the Tibetans).

In the parts of Jammu and Kashmîr (including Ladâkh) actually administered by India, this law is a huge issue. The local people vigilantly enforce the law, always trying to ensure that it is not tampered with. Not so in the areas occupied by Pâkistân.

There is a widespread feeling in Gilgit-Baltistân, as well as in the other occupied areas, that the local population is being overwhelmed by outsiders, in order to convert the original residents of the area into a minority in their own homeland.

Iqbâl 'Advocate,' a leader of the All Parties National Alliance (APNA), alleged at a public rally in Gilgit, "The people [of Gilgit-Baltistân] are being compelled to sell land to the Punjâbis and Pathâns [and other] 'non-local' people [who do not belong to the region]."

On the Indian side, too, the right-wing wants people from all over India to be allowed to settle in Kashmîr. However, the state of Jammu and Kashmîr has iron-clad laws which ensure that this does not happen. Obviously the people of Gilgit-Baltistân-Hunzâ-Chitrâl-Astor have no such protection. So, even if the local people have not been 'compelled' to sell land to outsiders, the Pâkistâni state (like Israel in West Bank) is doing nothing to stop such sales.

Indeed, the Pâkistâni right-wing has been allowed to have its way. The Pâkistâni establishment saw the 1988 agitation as an Iran-inspired 'Shia revolt.' In fact it was an innocuous request for the upgradation of the administrative status of the region. (At present it is a federally administered area. The people had merely asked that this gigantic region—as big as several sovereign countries—be converted into a state, on a par with the four states of Pâkistân.

(Almost all such movements in post-1947 India have resulted in the agitated region being granted 'statehood'-the status of a state.)

Instead of looking into the legitimacy (or otherwise) of the demand, Pâkistân went in for the right-wing solution: Dilute the Shia population and 'solve' the problem once and for all.

In addition to the aforementioned SSP and Lashkar é Jhañgvi, ('the soldiers of Jhañg'), one Brigadier Parvez Musharraf brought in truckloads of Pushtûns ('Pathâns') to quell the agitation. He now rules Pakistan. Poor Balâwaristân

Ever since, the people of Gilgit-Baltistân have started viewing refugees from their troubled neighbour, Afghânistân, as hatchet men of the Pâkistâni establishment.

The beginnings of a freedom movement?

The 1st of November, as we have seen, is a particularly hallowed day in the entire Kârâkoram belt. In the year 2002, the day was celebrated in Gilgit with a procession which, as usual, was mammoth. Tens of thousands of people marched on the main road. A motorcade of a few hundred cars followed them. Considering that this is a sparsely populated region, the numbers were spectacular.

What was different that year was what the marchers were saying. Cries of 'We want freedom from Pâkistân!' went up everywhere. The procession ended in a political rally. The leaders of the region, who described the event as 'historic,' then addressed the massive crowd that had assembled there.

One of the speakers suggested that all citizens of Gilgit-Baltistân should reject Pâkistâni ID (identity) cards and start carrying 'Gilgit-Baltistân ID Cards' instead. This was a way of demonstrating that they were not Pâkistânis.

The struggle to get out of Pâkistân's clutches is unfortunately acquiring an anti-Punjâbi and anti-Urdu character. Wajâhat Hussain Khân, an APNA leader, said that Pâkistân really was 'Punjâbistân.' Iqbâl 'Advocate' and Haidar Shâh Rizvi spoke out against the imposition of Urdu and wanted it to be replaced by the region's own language.

Now, the fact that the Punjâbis are in a majority in Pâkistân is not their fault. Nor is the average Pâkistâni Punjâbi responsible for what their government has done to the Gilgit-Balâwaristân-Hunzâ region. Similarly, the multi-lingual region will always need a link language. In the very long run that language might be English. Till then, Urdu might be the only language acceptable to everyone. After all, the proceedings of the historic November 1, 2002, rally were carried out entirely in Urdu.

Of course, the rich indigenous culture of the region has to be preserved and allowed to grow once again.

Fortunately, the movement has not taken on a sectarian colour.

Haidar Shâh Rizvi of the Gilgit-Baltistân Youth Wing succinctly summed up why the people had been driven to demanding liberation from Pâkistân. He said, "We asked for 'statehood,' local [self-] government and representation in the National Assembly." Pâkistân rejected all three demands.

It was clear that Pâkistân was determined to repeat the mistakes that its rulers had made in 1971. Its neighbours (India and Sri Lañkâ), too, have made mistakes but not ones that admit as simple-and painless-solutions as these three.

Pâkistân's President (Gen.) Pervez Musharraf knew that something, even if cosmetic, had to be done. In October 2007 he announced that the Northern Areas council had been given the status of a legislative assembly with powers to debate and pass its budget. However, a minister from Pakistan's federal government would be the chairman of the Northern Areas government.

The region had thitherto been governed under the Northern Areas Legal Framework Order, 1994, which intellectuals like Farman Ali described as 'a controversial, if not draconian, law through which Islamabad administers the strategic area.'

The people of Gilgit-Baltistan dismissed the president's announcement as 'an eyewash' (*Dawn*, Karachi, October 24, 2007) as it left unresolved the fundamental question about the constitutional status of the region and because it was silent on the need for an independent judiciary (which was functioning as a department attached to the Ministry of KANA) and the right of adult franchise.

The main problem, writer Aziz Ali Dad feels, was that the Assembly would continue to 'function under the shadow of an omnipotent and unelected representative [the KANA minister] imposed by [Pâkistân] on the elective representatives of the region.'

References

i Sheikh, Abdul Ghani, 'Muslims in Ladâkh and Sufi Traditions,' *New Hope*, vol.4, no.1, January-February, 2003.

ii 'Baltistân Little Tibet: Renaissance and Resistance in Baltistân' by Tarik Ali Khân. I read the article on a website. However, the article perhaps first appeared in *Himal*, a journal published from Kathmandu, Nepal.

iii Sheikh, Abdul Ghani, 'Muslims in Ladâkh and Sufi Traditions,' *New Hope*, vol.4, no.1, January-February, 2003. Page 31.

iv Francke, A.H., *A History of Ladâkh*, Sterling Publishers, New Delhi. Page 166.

v 'Two British officers played anti-India role,' *Daily Excelsior*, Nov 2/ 3 (year not clear: perhaps 2001 or 2002: I got this from their website; the dateline is Nov.2, so the newspaper would be dated Nov. 3.) The *Daily Excelsior* has, in turn, quoted the *Dawn*, Karachi.

vi "The war of lost opportunities Maj (Retd) Agha Humayun Amin from Washington DC writes about the chances we [Pâkistân] missed in Kashmîr." (From the internet.)

vii Also from 'Two British officers played anti-India role,' *Daily Excelsior*, Nov 2/ 3, 200?.

viii Shaukat Riza, The Pâkistân Army-1947-49, Page 291, quoted by Amin, op cit.

ix Op. cit

x All references to speeches made at the 1 November, 2002, rally are based on 'Cry Freedom: Pâkistân Occupied Kashmîr,' a documentary film made and telecast by NDTV 24x7, an independent Indian TV channel. The NDTV anchor told viewers that video footage of that rally was smuggled out of Balâwaristân—to be telecast by NDTV all of ten months later. (c) NDTV 2003. All speeches had been in Urdu and their translations are by this author.

xi I picked this up from the internet.

xii The statistics and Pâkistânî press comments about the 'Northern Areas' in this and the next few paragraphs are based on a Government of India website. The statistics about and comparisons with Leh and Kargil are my own.

xiii For instance, at the aforesaid rally of November 1, 2002.

xiv 'Inter-religious relations in Pâkistân,' by Yoginder Sikand, *The Kashmîr Times*, 6 April, 2004.

xv On the 1st November, 2002, at the above mentioned rally in Gilgit.

xvi Speaking at the same 1st November, 2002, rally in Gilgit.

xvii Also at the same 1st November 2002, rally.

xviii 'LITTLE TIBET: Renaissance and Resistance in Baltistân' by Tarik Ali Khân. (I read the article on a website.)

5

A History of Baltistân

The Balti race deserves the highest glory and goodwill. The people of this nation are honest, cautious, humble and decent in their dealings. They are disciplined and law-abiding by nature. They are used to the most arduous kinds of work. The [Baltis] are an amazingly reasonable people, and are of frugal habits. [Above all,] they are a very cheerful lot.

—Filippo di Phillipi[i]

The ancient period

The Balti people are partly of Tibetan stock, with considerable Caucasoid ('Aryan') blood in their veins.[1] They speak an ancient form of the Tibetan language and share the same culture.

1. Francke writes, "the Dard [i.e. Aryan] element [in Baltistân] is somewhat stronger than in other parts of [Ladâkh].'
However, Balti nationalists do not share this opinion. They identify themselves more with their Tibetan cousins than with several Indo-Aryan communities. Gergan and Hassnain, too, disagree with Francke's 'unsubstantiated conjecture.' They write, '[The Tibetans] have classified known humanity into five major races-(1) Chinese, (2) Mongols, (3) Iranians, (4) Indians, and (5) Tibetans. The Sbalti (Balti) as a sub-race have not been included in the Tibetan race but have been grouped together under the Iranian ethnic group in spite of the fact that they speak Tibetan, and they had a Tibetan literary tradition before they adopted Islâm as their religion.
'The Sbalti is classified as a sub-ethnic group under 'Iranian'; the sub-groups are: Iranians, Taziks, Turks, Uigurs, Dards, Sbalti and two other sub-Turko Iranian groups. It may be noted that Sbalti is the only group who speaks Tibetan.'
-From the introduction to and the main text of Francke, A.H., *A History of Ladâkh*, Sterling Publishers, New Delhi, pp. 20-21.
In fact Gergan and Hassnain are in part saying what Francke did, because the Iranians are 'pire' Aryans. My own take is that the Baltis have a bit of both communities and it is pointless to argue which element is 'stronger.'

Ptolemy is the oldest known author to have mentioned the Byltæ people. Interestingly and significantly, the Mons (who are among the oldest residents of the region) used to call them Tu-ruk (Turk?). The old name of this land was sBalti-yul. All Tibetan-speaking people, including those in Kargil, used this name. The Chinese called the region Po-lo-lo, that being a mispronunciation of the ancient Dard name of the land. However, the Persians knew the area as Baltistân. When Muslim saints from Persia started coming over to spread the message of Islâm, native Baltis began to call their land by the Persian name, Baltistân.

Old rock carvings suggest that the ancient Baltis were animists and believed in shamans.

Buddhism came to Baltistân in the third or fourth century, almost certainly from Swât. At some stage the form of Buddhism practised in Baltistân became entirely Tibetan. Rock inscriptions, in the Tibetan script, suggest this. (The Baltis have their own ancient alphabet and script, too. It runs from right to left.)

Because of its good location, Baltistân started interacting with people from the west (the Arabs, as well as Nestorian Christians) much before Tibet or the rest of Ladâkh did.

The Sikañder (Alexander) legend

In the plains of Kashmîr and almost everywhere in Jammu province and Himâchal Pradésh every old monument is said to have been built by the Pâñdavs of the Mahâbhârat fame. In Ladâkh and Balâwaristân (and in parts of Jammu's Rajouri-Poonch belt) all people with light eyes and brown hair claim to have descended from Alexander the Great.[2]

Alexander's army did come to India in 325 BC but it certainly did not visit Ladâkh-Balâwaristân (or even the Valley of Kashmîr). Jammu's Rajouri-Poonch belt is the only part of Jammu and Kashmîr that his army had actually brought under its sway. Even the Rajouri-Poonch area was probably conquered in battles fought just outside that belt.

And yet, in Baltistân[3] the Sikañder (Alexander) legend becomes considerably more credible than elsewhere in the state. Its capital is called Skardu in English and Askardu in several Urdu texts. According to revisionists, the name is a contraction of Askañdriâ, which, without a doubt, is the Hiñdî-Urdû word for Alexandria, 'the town that Alexander

2. Considering that according to several theories Alexander was gay, he seems to have become remarkably fecund in the Himâlayas. Maybe it was the fresh mountain air. Or perhaps the herbs had aphrodisiac odours.
3. As in the Mendhar area of Jammu province, which is linked to the Greek Menander.

established.' Askañdriâ is one of the names of the fort at Skardu. However, it could well have been another Sikañder. My theory is that the fort (but not the town) is named after Sultân Sikañder of Kashmîr, the so-called But Shikan (iconoclast). This fourteenth century Sultân looms large in the imagination of some Baltis. One of the most important royal families of the area (that of Khaplu) claims that Sikañder had founded their clan. Therefore, it stands to reason that he might have established the said fort as well.

Repulsing the Chinese

In the seventh and eighth centuries A.D., the Chinese attacked Baltistân and the Baltis bravely repulsed all Chinese attacks. That is how things have always remained.

The oldest extant record about Baltistân, the land, dates to A.D. 717. This is a Chinese document about its army going to defend Ladâkh against the Tibetans.

The Chinese wanted to either subjugate Baltistân or at least control the passes of the Pamirs. However, they could never annex Baltistân. The Chinese succeeded in their second-best aim, though. They managed to keep the Baltis off Darkot, which was the western limit of their empire. They wanted to make sure that the Baltis (and Tibetans) remained on the left banks of the Indus and Gilgit rivers and did not cross over to the opposite bank.

'The Chinese wanted to keep the Darkot Pass, the Western Gate which controls Oxus, Kunar ChitrâlChitrâl(Chitrâl), Gilgit, the Pamirs, the Sin-Kiang valleys and the main Indus Valley,' historians Gergan and Hassnain write. 'In 678 A.D. ...the Chinese were not able to face the combined forces of Tibetans and Baltis... The Chinese did not dare cross over to the left Bank of the Indus, Baltistân, but they destroyed the suspension bridge to stop further attack by the Tibetans.'[4]

Half a century later, the Chinese were back. They tried to conquer all the lands that were immediately to their west. The various Tibetan kingdoms fought back bravely. However, writes Francke, 'the state which offered the most serious obstacle to the progress of the Chinese was Baltistân. Several expeditions became necessary against Po-liu, as Baltistân was then called, and the first of these took place some time between 736 and 747.'

4. Historically, the interests of the Tibetans and Baltis have coincided and there has been enormous affinity between the two. Kachu Sikander Khân, for instance, writes, 'The fact is that the Baltis and the Tibetans have a very large number of things in common. As a result their racial solidarity has endured and remained intact.' (*Qadeem Ladâkh*...page 263.)

Relations with Western Tibet (including Ladâkh)

As we have seen, the emperors of Tibet, Ladâkh and Kashmîr sometimes controlled these chieftains.[5] G.T. Vigne (c.1835) points out, 'During the times of the Great Tibetan empire (before Glan-dar-ma) Baltistân appears to have been part of it.' It was during this era that a great monastery was established in Skar-chun-rdo-dbyin (Skardu?). This was around A.D. 804, when Rgya was the capital of Ladâkh and Skar-chun-rdo-dbyin was under the jurisdiction of Rgya.

However, attacks on Baltistân had begun well before the era of Lang Tarmâ (Glan-dar-ma), the great Tibetan king. Mân Song Man Chen (A.D. 650-679), a Tibetan king, had extended the borders of the Tibetan empire right up to the Pamirs. Later, Kong Song Dorjé (679-705), also a king of Tibet, included in his dominions places as far apart as the Sind valley, Kharsang-Shigar and Nânag Gong-Gilgit

As far as Ladâkh was concerned, if there were times when Ladâkh ruled Baltistân, there were others when the Baltis conquered much of Ladâkh.

When did Baltistân actually come under the (West) Tibetans? Certainly by the tenth century. Some historians feel that the Tibetans had triumphed over Baltistân as early as in the eighth century, and continued to dominate Baltistân politically and culturally till the fifteenth century, when many Baltis accepted Islâm.

Around A.D. 842, the Tibetan monarchy disintegrated and the kingdom of Tibet started breaking into autonomous provinces. Gilgit and Baltistân regained their independence in the process, Almost a century later, Prince Skitde Nemagon (975-990 migrated from Tibet to a region that borders Ladakh on the east. This region probably was Guge, which he started ruling independently. According to Kâchu Sikander Khân, Nemagon (Nyimagon, actually) established an independent kingdom in Purânîg (Purâng?) and it included all of the present Leh district.

This was a turning point in the history of the external relations of Gilgit-Baltistân. Thenceforth the fortunes of Gilgit-Baltistân became linked with those of Western Tibet, and remained so till the advent of Islâm in the region. In any case, Gilgit-Baltistân ceased to have much to do with Tibet proper, a situation that continues to this day.

However, Nemagon's son, Lhâ Chen sPalgyî-gon (c.1000-1025), as well as the next four generations of rulers of Western Tibet, did not pay

5. Distances in the region being what they are, the chiefs of Baltistân were free to rule their principalities as they thought best, so long as they accepted that, at least in theory, there was an emperor above them.

much attention to Baltistân. This continued till the advent of Lhâ Chen Utpâlâ (c.1125-1150), who was the king of much of Ladâkh. He was the first West Tibetan ruler to conquer all territories up to Pasho Kajor. Thanks to his victories, his successors (i.e. the kings of Ladâkh) continued to rule over Athok (Kharmañg) till the era of Maqpon Gâzi Mîr.

Baltistân produced a very eminent—and influential—Buddhist priest, sBal-te-dgra-bûm. He was a ranking member of the Himâlayan Buddhist council of priests. Around A.D. 1168, he got the celebrated Skyor-lun monastery constructed near Skardu and Shigar (Shi-dKar), the latter being in the Basho valley.

King Lhâ Chen Porop[6] of Ladâkh (c.1290-1320), too, tried to subjugate the area. The people of Kâlâminâs (which was either in Kharmañg or in Parkutta) murdered this king.

The early mediæval era

Why were the Baltis often subordinate to outside powers?

Internal disunity was the main reason because, man for man, the Baltis are great fighters.

Whenever the Ladâkhis invaded one part of Baltistân, the chiefs of the other Balti regions supported the Ladâkhis and not their fellow Baltis in the region that was being attacked. It was, as we shall see, because of family feuds that India got its first foothold in this area (under the Mughals) and finally annexed the region (under the Sikhs and Dogrâs).

Baltistân consists of five broad valleys: Khaplu, Kharmañg, Ron[g]du, Shigar and Skardu. Each was generally ruled by a maqpon, a chieftain, who was occasionally subordinate to a bigger power.

(The rulers of Skardu and Kharmañg were called maqpons. That of Rondu or Rundou was known as a louncha. Khaplu was ruled by a yabgo and Shigar by an amacha. However, the rulers of all five were loosely called maqpons[7].)

The five valleys of Baltistân have traditionally been divided into four kingdoms (Skardu, Khaplu, Shigar and Ron[g]du) and four small fiefdoms (Kiris, Parkutta [later renamed Mediabad] Tolti and Kharmañg). The eight have sometimes been united into one kingdom, especially whenever one of the maqpons was powerful enough to assert himself over the other Balti chiefs. Around the 11th century, for instance, the greater Balâwaristân area was a strong, united independent kingdom.

6. Could this have been King Ngorub? Or Morup, which seems most likely? The dates of their reign are similar.

7. Phonetically, the word, in its singular form, should be spelt dMag-dPon. Mag rhymes with, and indeed sounds exactly like, 'mug.'

This gave the people—and rulers—of the area considerable power vis-a-vis their neighbours. Around A.D. 1320, the chief of Parkutta was emboldened to kill an important Ladâkhi-Tibetan prince of the area, a man whose son, Rinchen Shâh, went on to become the first Muslim ruler of Kashmîr and also helped effect Kashmîr's first ever mass conversions to Islâm. (Rinchen's father was not a Muslim.)

The advent of Islâm

That the Baltis converted to Islâm in the 15th century is a guess. If Sultân Sikañder were responsible then the conversions would have taken place between 1389 and 1413, which was the period of his reign. However, the problem with this assumption is that Sultân Sikañder was a pure Sunni while the Baltis are almost entirely Shia and have been so since at least the 16th or 17th century. And yet, Sikañder would have certainly have established a Muslim community, big or small, in Baltistân. Even if he did not get a single Balti converted to Islâm, he had definitely brought some Kashmîrî Muslims over with him, and they would have been Sunnis. Later, finding almost everyone else becoming Shias, they, too, might have accepted the Shiite sect.

Francke believes that the Baltis were 'the first Western Tibetans who became [Muslims].'

The kingdom of Skardu has traditionally been the dominant power in Baltistân. This is only partly because of its central location. The real reason is that it is the most prosperous part of the region. Khaplu has often ranked next. Its importance owes to its control of the main trade route to Ladâkh, the one that runs along the Shyok River and goes east. Its ruling family is considered 'the most important and probably most ancient [maqpon] family.'[ii] Shigar lies on the route that goes north to Xinjiang. Because the Kârâkorams have to be crossed, this is a very tough route.

The Maqpons (small kings) of Skardu started asserting themselves in the 16th century and united all of Baltistân once again.

A Balti presence in Leh: The united Baltistân became an assertive land. As we shall see below, it began to annex neighbouring kingdoms. Even at the individual level the Baltis began to project their power beyond their own borders. For instance, a Balti village was established at Chushot (near Leh town), perhaps in the sixteenth century. By then Baltistân had a bigger population than what its fields and orchards could feed. So, by 'exporting' some of its population, Baltistân reduced some of its responsibilities towards its own subjects.

A smooth transition—and a composite identity

The story about the shared ancestry of the rulers of Skardu—as well as those of Astor, Parkutta, Tolti, Rondu and Katakchund/ Khartaksha, illustrates the smooth transition from Gylfo (Gyâlpo) kings (presumably Buddhist) to râjâs and begums (obviously Muslim). As in Iran, all these rulers came from one, unbroken royal line, which once was non-Muslim (Buddhist in Baltistân, Zoroastrian in Iran) and which continued to rule after a gradual (not sudden) transition[8] to Islâm. It is for this reason that to this day the Baltis, like the Iranians, are as proud of their pre-Islâmic past as of their Islâmic present.

The last (Buddhist) gylfo of Baltistân died around the 15th century. There were no male royals left either who could have taken the dynasty forward, Only the Gylfo's daughter survived. As many as twelve viziers of the region proposed marriage to her.

Around that time a mystic (presumably a Muslim sufi) had earned a great name for his piety and spiritual powers. No one knew anything about his origins. He invariably sat on a large stone in Shikari village (Shigar). He held a purse full of gold in one hand and a rod made of gold in the other.

Everyone agreed that he would make the most suitable husband for the young princess (whom Vigne[9] refers to by the Muslim-sounding title 'begum'). Their descendants went on to found the dynasties that have since ruled the states mentioned above.[10]

The stone that the saint would sit on came to be called the Burdo Nest. Till the region became a republic (in stages, between 1947 and 1974), every crown prince of the region would be anointed on that stone.

Baltistân caught in a pincer

Tséwâñg Namgyâl, king of Ladâkh (c.1532-1555) was a great empire-builder. He was the first Ladâkhi king to conquer several regions in the west, especially Shigar and Khârkar or Kharko (which is in Chitrâl). He thus took the boundaries of Ladâkh right inside Chitrâl.

8. I have used the word transition rather than conversion, because no Buddhist gylfo/ gyâpo actually converted to Islâm. The last Buddhist princess married a Muslim saint and a Muslim line arose, with the blood of the old dynasty in its veins.
9. Ahmed Shah, who was the maqpon of Baltistân in 1835, told Vigne this story.
10. The story of the saint who founded a clan of rulers reminds Francke (*Antiquities of Indian Tibet*, Volume II, Page 186) of a similar legend about the Chiktan royal house. It reminds me of Shimshal and Gilgit. Obviously it is considered good for the Muslim kings of the region to have had saintly ancestors, or at least the blessings of a Muslim saint for their line.

Baltistân's own records do not mention Tséwâñg Namgyâl's attacks. They probably took place immediately after Sultân Saeed Wâî's assault on Shigar. There is a theory that Tséwâñg had felt obliged to do something to restore the prestige of the Ladâkh government after the blows that the government had received in Baltistân (as well as Ladâkh proper) because of Saeed Wâî's victories. So he attacked Baltistân to show that his army had plenty of muscle left.

At the time either Abdullâh Khân or Hamîd Khân ruled Shigar. The chief of Skardu was either Shér Khân or Alî Khân.

Emperor Ali Mîr Shér Khân, the Añchan (Great)

Balâwaristân has produced an eminent emperor—the Great Ali Mîr Shér Khân 'Añchan' (A.D. 1590-1625 or 1630). He belonged to a Maqpon dynasty[11] and unified all of BaltistânBaltistân and Gilgit. As we have seen in the histories of Kargil and Leh, for a short while this visionary controlled almost all of Ladâkh and Guge (Western Tibet) in the east, and Chitrâl in the west. (According to other historians it was his grandson Shâh Murâd [1650-1690] who had extended Baiti rule to Chitrâl.)

The Mughal princess: Some Balti historians claim that Ali Shér Khân Añchan had married the sister of the Mughal emperor Salîm (presumably the one better known as Jehângîr). What is certain is that he married the daughter of a top ranking Mughal from Agra-Delhi. A number of craftsmen and musicians came over to Baltistân with the bride. Among the high arts that they brought with them were *râg* of Hiñdustânî classical music. These musical genres have been a part of Balti music ever since.

The matrimonial alliance with the Mughals is seen by some as a move to keep 'the Mughal emperors at bay.' Ali Shér Khân certainly succeeded in keeping the Mughals away from Baltistân. However, it was his unquestioned hold on his empire and his administrative skills that ensured this, not his marriage. In the matrimonial politics of mediæval India, small kings fended off their bigger and more aggressive neighbours by offering their sisters and daughters in marriage, and not by deigning to marry the daughters of more powerful kings. Mughal emperors were famous for letting their sisters and daughters die unmarried because they believed that no clan in the world known to them was their equal.

However, even if Ali Shér Khân had married a minor Mughal princess, and not Salîm's own sister, it says a lot about how his might was perceived in Agra-Delhi.

11. Francke says that Ali Shér was the Duke (maqpon) of Kapulu (presumably Khaplu). According to Kâchu Sikander Khân he was of the Skardu royal family.

Victory over Leh: King Tsewâng (c.1530-1560 or 1532-1555) of Leh had defeated the Baltis. He died childless and his younger brother, Jamyang Namgyâl (1555 or 1560-1590), succeeded him. On Tsewâng's death, the Baltis asserted their independence. Jamyang decided to bring them back into the Leh empire. His astrologers told him that it would not be good for his army if it went to war before the New Year. Their advice was based not on superstition but on centuries-old knowledge of snow conditions at that time of the year. However, Jamyang simply changed the day when the New Year occurred and brought it forward by two months so that he could go ahead and attack Baltistân.[12]

What Jamyang could not change was the snowfall. When his army crossed the passes and entered Purîg, (Kargil), Ali Shér's soldiers formed a wide circle around it. This was when Ali Shér revealed his military genius. He kept postponing the battle to the next day. This went on for several weeks till snow blocked all the passes. Now Jamyang's army was trapped in hostile territory. They went to one pass after another hoping to escape back to Leh. However, not a single pass was dry enough to cross.

Jamyang and his army surrendered to the Baltis.

Rewarding the vanquished: For a while Jamyang was a prisoner of the Baltis. However, like all great men, Ali Shér was magnanimous in victory. He offered his beautiful daughter, Gyâl Kâtûn, in marriage to his royal captive. (The fair-skinned Gyâl Kâtûn's beauty and complexion were quite an issue in Leh, where the clergy declared that she was the incarnation of a Buddhist-Hiñdu deity, the White Târâ.)

Ali Shér's offer came with only one condition. Jamyang had to disinherit all his children born of an earlier marriage. The captive king agreed, upon which his army and he were set free. Jamyang was given back his throne and kingdom. (Some people believe that Islâm was imposed on the Hiñdus and Buddhists of undivided India. Therefore, it is significant that Ali Shér did not even hint that Jamyang should convert to Islâm, either in order to marry his daughter or to buy his freedom.)

A dream, a prophecy: The noble Ali Shér was a mystic and a man of enormous spiritual powers. Soon after his daughter's wedding he hosted a grand banquet for his soldiers. It has been recorded that Gyâl Kâtûn wore extremely fine jewellery at the feast. (This is an extremely important piece of information, considering that in the nineteenth and twentieth centuries, as well as in the first years of the twenty-first, co-ed dining has been unthinkable in the Kargil-Baltistân belt.)

12. Ever since, Losar has been celebrated in Ladâkh during the eleventh month of the Buddhist calendar.

It is said that Ali Shér asked his son-in-law to sit on the throne and announced, 'I had a dream last night. I saw a lion coming out of the river near the palace. The lion pounced on Gyâl Kâtûn and entered her body. Right then Gyâl Kâtûn conceived. My dream indicates that a son will be born to Gyâl Kâtûn. The boy will be like a lion (Senggé). Therefore, you should name him Senggé Namgyâl.' ('Namgyâl' was Jamyang's family name. It means 'he who rules over everybody.')

The dream came true. Senggé Namgyâl grew up to become one of the greatest kings (if not the greatest) that Leh has produced. (No Ladâkhi or Balti finds it unusual that a Muslim king had so effortlessly come up with an appropriate Buddhist name—and for his own grandson at that. That is the kind of harmonious relations—and composite culture—that they have always had. In the 1960s, lay Buddhists in Leh would often ask their much-loved District Commissioner, Mehmood ur Rehman, to suggest names for their children.)

A developmental genius: Ali Mîr Shér Khân had a great developmental vision. He got a stone aqueduct built,[13] which still brings water from the Satpur stream, all the way across the valley. A by-product of this masterpiece of engineering is that 'a quantity of useful soil that would otherwise be washed away is banked up and preserved.'[iii]

Ali Mîr also got a fort built on a rock, at an elevation from the town. In a splendid tribute to the (Buddhist) Gylfos of Baltistân, he got a high platform constructed near the fort. Trees were planted on the platform, on which were the tombs of the Gylfos who had gone before him.

Another Leh army attacks Baltistân

In the chapter 'A History of Leh,' in the section 'Deldan, the Mughals and Islâm,' we have seen how subsequent Ladâkhi attempts to subjugate Baltistân came to naught because the Mughals stepped in to help the Baltis. However, the Leh kingdom did have some successes, too.

King Deldan Namgyâl (1642-1670s) inherited more than a third of his father, Señggé's, empire: the present day Leh district. Because he controlled the capital and the most important part of Señggé's kingdom, he inherited his ancestors' foreign policy. He decided to bring Baltistân

13. Miss Duncan reported in 1904 that there had existed a similar aqueduct on at least a part of that site since the times of the last Buddhist ruler of Baltistân. (*Antiquities of Indian Tibet*, Vol.II, page 186.) So, Ali Mîr Shér Khân must have got a new structure built on the site of the ruined one, using materials from the old aqueduct. Miss Duncan reported that 'Buddhist images [had] been preserved on the barrage.' This is further proof of Baltistân's composite culture and the Baltis' famed religious tolerance. Some 4.5 miles (7km.) from the barrage are more ancient Buddhist sculptures and inscriptions.

back under Leh's control. He sent his army to invade Baltistân in the 'wood-tiger' year.

The Leh army met with immediate initial successes. It annexed the Chorbar and Tortsekar villages and replaced their original headmen with local nobles loyal to Leh.

The Baltis were alarmed. They rallied around the Maqpon of Skardu, who complained to 'the Nawâb,' who in turn 'induced' an army of 2,00,000 (all right, 20,000) Turks to invade Ladâkh.

But who was this nawâb? Francke's guess is that he was the Nawâb of Kashmîr. Now, 'nawâb' was a title given to rulers and dukes in Lucknow, Bengal, and some other parts of Mughal India—mainly in the Indo-Gangetic plains of central India, plus Hyderabad. However, to the best of my knowledge, none of the Mughal governors of Kashmîr was known by this title. And if it were the Mughals' governor whom the Baltis had appealed to, why would he 'induce' the Turks to attack Leh? He could have easily ordered the Mughal army stationed in Kashmîr to defend the Baltis.

In the section 'Deldan, the Mughals and Islâm' there is a similar incident in which an army of 5,000 Mughals defended the Baltis against Leh. Could the two incidents have been the same? Theoretically, yes, because the Mughals were also known as Turks. But the size of the two armies was so vastly different.

Besides, here is an important insight. The Gaor Aman rajas of Gilgit had once ruled over Guréz (Kashmîr), through a nawab. This is the only nawab that I have heard of in all of J&K. The Malik dynasty of nawabs must have begun around AD 1690 or 1700, which was around Deldan's time. So, could this have been the nawab in question, because Guréz is quite close to Baltistân? Perhaps, yes, because he was a minor nawab who did not have a big army under his command and who had to 'induce' Turks (presumably Turks from one of the neighbouring Central Asian states, or even from the Turkish community of Kashmîr) to defend the Baltis.

As we have seen, the ancient Mons used to call the Baltis by the name 'Tu-ruk.' So, could the Turks who came in to help have been part of the great Balti diaspora? (Or could the Baltis be part of the even greater Turk diaspora? The latter is more likely.)

Well, either way, Drug Namgyâl, an able general and nobleman from Leh, put up a brave fight against the Turks and killed many of them. Francke writes, 'They [the Leh army] took away their [Balti] flags and kettle-drums, and thus gained a complete victory over the enemy.'

However, that must have happened in one particular battle, or in one series of battles. Overall, the Mughals repulsed attempts by Leh to conquer all or even parts of Baltistân.

A Mughal intervention of a different kind: Ali Mîr Shér Khân was succeeded by his son Ahmed Khân (c.1625-1650). When Ahmed died, for a while power passed into the hands of his brothers (and Ali Mîr's sons), Abdul and Âdam Khân.

Abdul was a bit of a builder, like his illustrious father. He got stately city gates constructed, in the Islâmic tradition of South and Central Asia. However, his brother and he started fighting each other. Abdul also took to tyrannising the neighbouring states. The chiefs of these states complained to the Mughals. Either Shâh Jehân or his son Aurañgzéb (1658-1707) was the Delhi-based Emperor of India at the time, most probably the former, with the episode continuing into the latter's reign. The Mughal emperor asked his army stationed in Srînagar to march to Baltistân to protect Abdul's weaker neighbours.

According to Balti legends, the steeds of the Mughal army included elephants. The Mughals certainly brought with them advanced guns and arms, some of which they later left behind. In any case, Abdul knew better than to resist the mighty Mughal army. The brothers agreed to present themselves before Aurañgzéb. On his advice they resolved to carve up their father's vast empire, with each brother ruling over one half. However, neither came home alive. Both died natural deaths in Kashmîr, on their way back (presumably from Delhi). Ladâkh, which had come under Baltistân during Ali Mîr Shér Khân's time, once again became independent.

Ahmed Khân's son Shâh Murâd aka Shâmrâd (c.1650-80) succeeded his quarrelsome uncles. The Mughals granted him a jâgîr (estate; fief) in Kashmîr.[14] This says something about his importance in the eyes of the Mughals, or at least how much they liked him. The farmers who tilled the estate would give Murâd and his descendants an annual revenue.[15]

Shâh Murâd is said to have 'conquered' Ladâkh. Francke rightly argues that he must have led 'only a more or less successful plundering expedition.' (As we have seen, and will see later, it was normal for the Ladâkhis and Baltis to raid each other's territories once in every century or so.)

14. This was not unusual. A few decades later, around 1752, the Durrani rulers of Kashmîr gave King Ranjit Dev of Jammu a large jâgîr in Kashmir.

15. This practice came to an end in the early nineteenth century during the era when Kashmîr was a part of the Lahore-based Sikh empire.

After Shâh Murâd, the next ruler of most of Baltistân was Rafir Khân (c.1680-1700). Sultân Murâd (c.1700-30) succeeded him. He once again brought Ladâkh under Balti suzerainty. He tried to re-establish the empire that Ali Mîr Shér Khân had built. He subjugated Gilgit, Hunzâ, Nagar and Chitrâl as well. (In all these cases the local kings continued to rule much as before, but acknowledged the supremacy of the Balti king.) The construction of the bridge near the Chitrâl fort is credited to Sultân Murâd.

Zafar Khân (c.1730-60) was the next king. Apparently, when he was young a powerful family called Kelumcheh came over from what is now called Kargil. They wrested the kingdom from Zafar. Later Zafar recaptured the castle, and the kingdom. This earned him the title Ghâzi. However, in the process a fire broke out in the Skardu castle and reduced most of it (and its priceless antiques) to ash. Baltistân has a long tradition of literacy, and written records. According to Vigne, a contemporary writer, countless records of historical value perished in this fire.

Ali Shér-Khân (c.1760-1790) not only conquered Shigar, he also beat back invaders from Ladâkh -probably a bunch of raiders—and captured many of them.

Of Ali's two sons, the younger, Ghulân Shâh, was the King of Parkutta. Ahmed Shâh or Khân (c.1790-1841), the elder son, was based in Skardu and had a more considerable empire, which stretched from Chorbut to Astor. He controlled Khapalu, Keris, Katakchund, Rondu, Shigar and Tolti. His brother's Parkutta, too, was under his overall command. On the other hand, kingdoms that did not, at least at that stage, accept Balti control included Gilgit, Hunzâ and Nagar. As for Chitrâl, as Francke[iv] points out, this 'country of Shâh Kator has long been independent of ...Baltistân.'

The late eighteenth/ early nineteenth century: After the ill-fated attempt by King Deldan Namgyâl (1642-1670s) to conquer Baltistân, Ladâkhi kings did not ever repeat the mistake. However, conquest is one thing but raids are quite another. People from Khaltsé and other parts of Leh district continued to raid Baltistân. Historians mention the existence of a document in Khaltsé, which tells us that groups of people from Leh, acting on their own and not as soldiers of the official Leh army, would often raid Baltistân. The government of either Khaltsé or Leh seems to have tacitly encouraged this, because raiders were rewarded with plots of land.

The Sikh-Dogrâ conquest

A family feud

By 1840, the Dogrâ rulers of Jammu had annexed much of Ladâkh on behalf of the Lahore kingdom. At the time the royal family of Baltistân was going through an internal power struggle.

Ahmed Shâh/ Khân's talented and much-loved eldest son, probably called Shâh Murâd, died early. Ahmed sent another son, Muhammad Shâh, to govern Astor, so that he could be shown the ropes of administration while ruling over a small part of the empire. Muhammad Shah's mother was the princess of Katakchund. It was the Balti custom that the (eldest) son born to the king of Baltistân from a Katakchund princess would normally succeed him to the throne of Baltistân. However, Muhammad Shâh proved an inept administrator. He also annoyed his father with his ways.

So, Ahmed Khân decided that Muhammad Ali Khân, his 13-year-old son from the princess of Shigar, would inherit his throne. This offended his oldest surviving son, Muhammad Shâh, who left Baltistân with a few followers, and met Zorâwar Singh Kahluria, the Dogrâs' indomitable general, at Purîg (Kargil). This happened around 1835.

The Sikh-Dogrâ force is invited, and given a foothold in Baltistân

Zorâwar agreed to help Muhammad Shâh become the ruler (governor, to be precise) of Skardu. The chief of Parkutta (most probably Ali-Shér Khân,[16] c.1810-1840) agreed to help Zorâwar's army reach Skardu, by showing them the best way to get there. He was probably related to Muhammad Shâh from the latter's mother's side. He was, therefore, keen to help Muhammad, and, thus, the Dogrâ contingent of the Lahore army.

Meanwhile, the Dogrâs had recruited a large number of people from Leh and Kargil into their army. Actually, they more or less absorbed the armies of the conquered territories into their own. Bañkopâ, the Ladâkhi general, for instance, retained his rank and command. In turn, the Dogrâs' Ladâkhi soldiers were absolutely loyal to their newly enlarged nation. Such was the state of race-relations, and the concepts of honour and loyalty to the nation, in those remarkable times. The people of Leh and Kargil had only recently been absorbed into the Punjâb empire, and already they were loyal to it.

16. Not to be confused either with the Añchan or with the Balti chief who was the father of Ahmed Shâh.

When Zorâwar Singh marched to intervene in the dispute in Baltistân, he divided his army into two halves. Soldiers from Leh, led by Gen. Bañkopâ, were in one half and the Dogrâs and Kargilis in the other.

The deposed King Tsespal (or Tsépal) is said to have been one of the leaders of the Leh half of the army. This corps marched to Hânu, crossed the Chorbat Lâ (pass) and entered Baltistân. They met with no resistance and, in turn, neither killed nor hurt anyone as they arrived at Skardu.

Initial Balti successes

The Dogrâ-Kargili corps travelled along the rivers Drâss and Indus. This route was rocky and extremely difficult. The standard road to Skardu was on the left bank of the Indus whereas the invaders were on the inhospitable right bank. So, this group sent an advance party of five thousand men, led by Mîr Nidhân Singh, to identify the best route for them.

The Baltis attacked this advance party from a position of advantage. It is said that only four hundred of the Dogrâ-Kargili force managed to flee the battlefield. The rest were either killed or taken prisoner.

Meanwhile, such Dogrâ-Kargili soldiers as were still on the right bank were in a terrible state. They were running out of food and it was getting cold. Their leader Basti Râm, however, decided not to give up. He had heard that the Dards of Dâ could construct ice bridges—and in just a few hours at that. So, he went up and down the banks of the Indus looking for a suitable place.

The soldiers from Dâ found a good spot on the bank. There they fixed wooden beams at a right angle to the bank, so that the beams jutted into the slow moving river. Soon a thick coat of ice had formed on the logs, along their entire length. The soldiers could now walk on the logs, which they did. They fixed more logs at the end of the first set. The new logs, too, pointed to the other bank of the slow river. Once again, after ice had formed on the second set of logs, the Dards from Dâ walked to the end of this set and fitted a third set. This went on till they reached the opposite bank.

Soon, enough ice had formed on the ice bridge for the entire Dogrâ-Kargili force to walk upon. The invaders tiptoed to the left bank of the river at night. This time they had seized the initiative and thus had the advantage. The Balti contingent camping nearby was not expecting the attack, so its commanders had not so much as stationed night watchmen to raise an alarm.

The invaders caused the sleeping Balti soldiers to get up in a panic and run to Skardu. The Dogrâ-Ladâkhi army laid siege to the Skardu Fort. When the besieged Balti soldiers ran out of water, they had no option but to surrender. For a while, the invaders imprisoned the reigning raja, Ahmed Shah, and sent him to Leh, with some precious Balti jewellery.

Muhammad Shâh was crowned the maqpon of Baltistân. In return, the Dogrâs were allowed to build a fort and station a small contingent of their soldiers there.

Lack of British interest: The British did not consider Baltistân as strategically important as, say, Gilgit, Hunzâ or Chitrâl. Therefore, they left it alone.

(For the next part of the history of Baltistân, see 'A History of Balâwaristân.')

References

i Kâchu Sikander Khân, *Qadeem Ladâkh*, page 263. Translated from the Urdu by the author. The spelling of 'Filippo di Phillipi' could not be cross checked with other sources.

ii Francke, A.H., *A History of Ladâkh*, Sterling Publishers, New Delhi, p.109. (This is the 1977 edition of a book originally published in 1907 as *A History of Western Tibet.*)

iii G.T. Vigne, *Travels in Kashmîr*, Ladâk..., London, 1842, vol. ii, pp.251 onwards.

iv A.H.Francke, *Antiquities of Indian Tibet*, Calcutta, 1926 (Reprinted 1992, Asian Educational Services, Madras.) Page 185, Vol. II. The book is in two volumes.

6

A history of ancient and mediæval Gilgit

The earliest times

Archæological discoveries show that people have been living in Gilgit for thousands of years. Its earliest inhabitants were animists. Then for a few centuries they followed the Persian practice of fire worship.

In the chapter on the 'A History of Leh' we had looked at Reeve Heber's theory that Tibetan nomads were the first to go to Leh in particular and Ladâkh in general. There is reason to believe that these nomads would have gone as far as Gilgit, too. This was in the era when the Dards and Mons were still living in their original homelands.[1]

The now famous *Gilgit Manuscripts* were discovered in 1938. They shed light on the early history of the area. It seems that Hiñduism and Buddhism had once flourished in Balâwaristân. Gilgit had its own Brâhmins, too. They converted to Islâm several centuries ago. All the same, their descendants continue to be held in high esteem. They maintain ritual cleanliness and do not eat beef.

Buddhist missionaries brought the religion to Balâwar. Soon Balâwar became an important centre of Buddhism, and remained so between the 4th and 11th centuries A.D.

Mahâyân Buddhist scholars and missionaries from the Indian plains would come to Balâwar and from there branch out to Central Asia and China. In time, the Dards of Gilgit themselves became active Buddhist missionaries and took their faith to much of Western Tibet.

1 However, a few centuries later, perhaps after being defeated by later settlers, the Mons were relegated to the very bottom of the social ladder. They live in relative poverty to this day and serve as 'hand-workers' (i.e. craftsmen). They are mostly musicians and carpenters.

The Dards are, ethnically, different from the Mons and Mongols. They started settling in this region around the 2nd or 3rd century B.C. Scholars like Kâchu Sikander Khân have come to this conclusion after studying the ruins of ancient Dard settlements, their songs[2] and their Dévmâlâs.

In the 3rd century B.C. Gilgit was a part of the Khotan province of the empire of Ashok, the great Indian emperor.

Gilgit, as we shall see, has often been a part of Kashmîr. Kalhan's *Râjatarangini* informs us that Gilgit and much of Balâwaristân were included in the kingdom of the Kashmîrî Emperor Lalitâditya (AD 725-753 or 724-761).

When the Silk Route to China came into being, the valley of the Indus was one of its significant segments. By the first century B.C., Balâwar, like Kashgar, had a pivotal position on the Route. As a result the Chinese had some clout in the region. By the eighth century A.D. the Arabs and Tibetans began to compete with the Chinese for influence. The Tibetans tied up with the Kashmîrîs in the eighth and ninth centuries to keep the Arabs out of the region. They succeeded in Balâwaristân. However, the Arabs managed to reach Xinjiang (Sinkiang).

The very European Shîns conquered Gilgit in the tenth century. They probably were Hiñdus and spoke Shînâ. They displaced the native Burushaski speaking people, who fled to Hunzâ, Nagar and Yâsîn. To this day, Shînâ is the principal language of Gilgit valley.

The ancient home of the Dards

Today the Dards are found in a very wide arc of territory. However, Gilgit was one of their main homelands—if not their original home. (See the chapter 'Dâ-Hânu.')

These Dards had an advanced civilisation, and that is not a casual statement. They clearly saw themselves as a distinct people—dissimilar, for instance, to the Mons. While there might have been no bitterness between the Mons and the Dards, both were expansionist people. In other words, both were residents of mountainous deserts. Therefore, both were always looking for fertile patches to settle in, within that vast Himâlayan desert. And whenever either of them found a tract where food could be grown, a section of that community would migrate to that arable land. By and large, the other community would look for some other land rather than fight for the patch discovered by their rivals.

2. The chapter on Sports, pastimes and festivals' brifely explains how the Dards' folksongs are historical records.

I have a theory that three kinds of people tend to migrate in all directions in big numbers. At one end are the very poor, who seek menial employment wherever they can find it. (Think of Nepal, the Indian state of Bihâr and present-day 'Northern Areas.'.) At the other end are advanced civilisations that colonise already settled lands as well as empty tracts. (Think of Imperial Britain, France, Spain and even Holland.) In between are skilled, enterprising people, for whom the world is their canvas. (Think of the Indian and Chinese diasporas.)

The fact that the Dard diaspora—and thus the Dard civilisation—is spread over such a wide arc suggests the second kind of migration. The Dards were an empire-building and colonising power.

'As regards the religion of ancient Dards,' Francke[i] conjectures, 'it was probably the form of Buddhism which was prevalent in the days of emigration at Gilgit; the many stone images without date which are found all over Ladâkh testify to this, and many of them show a particularly strong resemblance to those found about Gilgit.'

When did the Dards of Gilgit migrate to Dâ? According to a nineteenth century British theory, this happened as recently as in the seventeenth century, i.e. just two or two hundred and fifty years before the theory had been put forth. The theory seems plausible because when the people of Dâ sing their eighteen songs, they do it with such feeling and so much detail that one gets the impressions that the tribe had been in Gilgit till only four or five generations before.

On the other hand the dialect of the Dâ people is very different from that spoken in Gilgit today. (The Dards of Drâss speak a dialect quite similar to that which modern Gilgit speaks.) So, obviously the Dards of Dâ left Gilgit many, many centuries ago, and then lost touch with their cousins in Gilgit.

The ancient Dard commonwealth—or empire[3]

The Dards' racial stock is very different from that of the Mons and Mongols. In the 2nd or 3rd century B.C. they started establishing settlements in what is now called Ladâkh That is what their folksongs, dévmâlâ records and, above all, ruins indicate.

3. The Dards' footprint covered an area bigger than several modern nation states. However, each Dard 'colony' ('settlement' might be more accurate) was independent of the other. There was no central command and no 'metropolis.' Therefore, much as I respect Kachu Sikander Khân's scholarship, I feel that what the ancient Dards had established was a formidable commonwealth, and not an empire. it was not even a confederation.

The Dards, as we have seen, kept fanning out in all directions, but mostly within Ladâkh-Baltistân-Gilgit and Kashmîr. They did so not in one go but over several centuries. They were the first humans to live in most parts of Baltistân, Purîg (Kargil) and Zâñskâr. The Mons, on the other hand, were the first to construct villages and towns in Western Tibet and the adjacent parts of Leh district. The Mons did not resist the new settlers—the Dards—in the region where they had already set up some colonies. Indeed, the two communities were great friends.

It is impossible to say which part of undivided Ladâkh-Gilgit was the first to be 'settled' by humans. In other words, we just can't say in which part of old Ladâkh the first villages and towns came up. However, it is generally believed that Baltistân was the first, because it is the warmest and most fertile part of the region.[4] Purîg probably came next, followed by Zâñskâr. Leh district was probably the last to be settled.

The earliest Dard kings and nobles had Tibetan titles such as Gyâpo, Cho and Lonchhey. This shows how deep the bonds between the Dards and Mongols were. They lived close to each other and influenced each other's culture.

The ancient Dards initially set up tribal governments in Baltistân. These later evolved into national governments—or were destroyed by people of Tibetan origin. The same thing later happened to the Dards' earliest tribal governments in Purîg and Zâñskâr as well.

In Purîg the ancient Dards were divided into three major clans—Shîn, Yashkun and Dom. The Mons and Mongols from Leh came to Purîg a while later. Yet another wave of Dards followed them into Purîg.

Rong Lochen of Gilgit settled in Lonchhey and his descendants in the upper parts of Suru valley (also in Kargil). The people of Rondu (Baltistân) settled in the Hamling village of Zâñskâr.

The precise names of the chiefs who led their clans out of Gilgit and the names of the villages that they founded around this time (the eighth century A.D., plus/ minus four centuries) were recorded and have survived to this day. The names are accurate. It's only the dates that could be off the mark by eight or nine hundred years. The names of places were often half Tibetan and half Shînâ (e.g. Hém Baps, Hamîr-lâ and Hans-ko).[ii]

Later, 'during the era of Sâral' (obviously some important chief), two tribes went from Gilgit to Purîg—those of Thâ Cho and Mughal Bég. They established Phokar village and constructed a fort at Dâ(h).

4 To this day, the Baltistân-Gilgit region is where the bulk (around 85%) of the population of Ladâkh-Gilgit lives. Leh and Kargil are huge in size but very thinly populated.

The Trakhân kings

At some stage there was a saint-king called Trakan. This great mystic possessed supernatural powers. He founded the Trakhân (or Trakane) dynasty of kings. His immediate descendants had Persian names such as Azar, Jamshed, Khusro and Firdaus. Persian culture came to influence most of the Indian sub-continent because of Persianised Muslims-rulers as well as mystics. However, in the case of Gilgit (and Baltistân) it is entirely possible that the influence was direct, and pre-Islâmic.

Then came a ruler called Gûrîtham. Drew[iii] reminds us that in Hunzâ 'tham' is the word for king. Gûrî is a word common to the region (which includes Astor and the Kishen Gañgâ valley). Gûrîtham's children Muhammad Khân and Abbâs were certainly Muslims.

The Trakhân line ended with Abbâs, and Gilgit ceased to be an independent kingdom—perhaps forever. This must have been around the end of the eighteenth century.

Gilgit's neighbours rule it by turns

Between A.D. 1810 and 1842, Gilgit was invaded and conquered by one short-lived neighbouring king after another. Each ruled for an average of five or six years.

The Bakhté clan of Yâsîn overthrew the Trakhân dynasty. Then the king of Puniâl killed Sulémân Shâh of Yâsîn and annexed Gilgit. The Nagar people killed Âzâd Khân of Puniâl and helped themselves to Gilgit. Gaor Rehmân of Yâsîn killed Shâh Sikañder of the Nagar dynasty and took over Gilgit. This was perhaps in 1840. A year and a half later Shâh Sikañder's brother, Karîm Khân, joined hands with the Sikh rulers of the Punjâb and Kashmîr, and ousted Gaor Rehmân.

That was when Gilgit became a part of Kashmîr, though not for the first time.

Incidentally, the king who lost Gilgit to the outside world was himself an outsider and interloper from Nagar. He was not a descendant of the old rulers of Gilgit.

Gilgit's earlier spells under Kashmîr

King Lalitaditya-Muktapida of Kashmîr (AD 725-753 or 724-761) had subdued Dardistân, which almost certainly included Gilgit even then.

The expression Dardistân includes Guréz, Astor, Bunji, Gilgit, Yâsîn and Ashkoman (Ishkoman/ Iskoman). People would regularly travel between these Dard regions. According to some historians, in ancient times the Dardistân region included the tributary states of Hunzâ, Nagar, Chilâs, Puniâl, Iskoman, Kuh and Ghizar. The Dards are close to the

Chitrâlis in matters of ethnic stock, culture and language. (Today many of them have joined the Ismâili sect of Muslims and owe allegiance to the Âgâ Khân.)

There is no doubt that Sultân Shihab ud Din of Kashmîr (1354-73) had conquered Gilgit. The region was independent for two or three generations, only to be brought back into Kashmîr's fold by Shihab ud Din's descendant Sultan Zain ul Abedin (Budshah) (1420-70).

When Kashmîr's Shahmîrî empire disintegrated, some time after Budshah's detah. Gilgit became independent for a while again. Sultân Ghazi Chak of Kashmîr (1555-63) was the next Kashmîrî king to conquer Gilgit. The Mughals of Âgrâ-Delhi conquered Kashmîr from the Chaks in 1596-89. but the Mughal empire itself started breaking up after 1707.

Even when Gilgit was nominally under Kashmîr, it was ruled by its own râjâs. These kings enjoyed enormous autonomy so long as they accepted that they were under a bigger power.

The chapter 'A history of Balâwaristân' has further details, especially about the modern period.

References

i Francke. A.H.. *A History of Ladakh*. Sterling Publishers. New Delhi.

ii From Kachu Sikander Khân's *Qadeem Ladâkh....* page 82.

iii Drew, Frederic. *The Jummoo and Kashmîr Territories* (1875; reprinted 1997) Capital Publishing House. New Delhi-110002. Page 435.

7

A history of Hunzâ

"I have often been asked, 'Why did you want to go to Hunzâ? There were a number of reasons, the first being that, scenically, it is one of the most spectacular strips of the earth's surface. The second was the desire to spend a while in a country where a wheeled vehicle was unknown[1] and where you could pass a lifetime without ever handling money.[2] Such places, like dream-islands, have attraction for almost everyone. Though a lot of them exist, it appears that there are few, if any, where the inhabitants have so much charm, so many virtues and so few faults."

Mrs. Barbara Hilda Mons, **High Road to Hunzâ** (1958)

The origins

The people of Hunzâ are called Hunzâkuts. It is said that they are the descendants of five[3] soldiers who came to India in the army of Alexander the Great[4]. They fell ill and were thus unable to accompany Alexander when he went to war along the Oxus. They married beautiful Persian

1. The Hunzâkuts have for centuries known how to make round millstones. Therefore, if they did not have wheeled vehicles it was not because their technology was primitive. Bicycles are hardly used to this day in places as advanced as Jammû city, which got its first motor car at the beginning of the twentieth century and has, since the 1970s, had the highest cars-per-miles-of-roads ratio in Asia, after Tokyo. Unmotorised wheeled vehicles (bicycles, carts, barrows) are simply very inconvenient to use in the hills.
2. This was true of most of rural Ladâkh till the 1960s. Even in 1981, very little of the economy of Zâñskâr, for instance, was monetised.
3. Three, according to a variant of this legend.
4. Either Alexander's army was particularly fecund, or a very large number of his soldiers decided to marry local women and stay behind in South Asia. That's because several communities, scattered all over the sub-continent, claim descent from his soldiers.

women[5]. The couples chanced upon this serene valley and decided to settle in it.

Hunzâkuts look more European than South Asian. So, there could well be something to these legends. The royal family almost certainly came from Persia. The Mîrs, as they are called, look different from their subjects. (Incidentally, Mîr is a Turkish title.)

Keays[i] describes the Hunzâkuts thus, "Blue eyes, fair skins and blonde or reddish hair were said to be commonplace amongst all the Dards. With features that were nothing if not European, was it possible that here were the long lost descendants of the Greeks who had crossed Asia with Alexander the Great? Or, since even Alexander's day there were reports of a similar people, were they perhaps remnants of the original Aryan race from which all the Indo-European peoples were descended?"

Serious historians believe that the ancestors of most Hunzâkuts came to Hunzâ in the 5th or 6th century A.D. The royal family came much later. There is much debate about when it did.

One theory is that the Mîrs of Hunzâ have been ruling Hunzâ since the 11th century A.D.—from A.D. 987 according to some. Another theory puts their ascension in Hunzâ to A.D. 1435. The only thing that is confirmed by records is that the State of Hunzâ existed in A.D. 1710. Marco Polo, the traveller, happened to be in the neighbourhood in A.D. 1273. He described the region as being 'Noisy with kingdoms.' According to some, the Baltit Fort (in present-day Karîmâbâd) had been built by his time.

The ruling families of Hunzâ and Nagar are perhaps descended from Gilgit's Trakhân dynasty. If the common Hunzâkuts has come down from Alexander's solders, the royalty of Hunzâ-Nagar claims descent from the great man himself.[6] Further into the past their family tree traces its origins to divinity. (As do so most South, South East and East Asian royal families—Hiñdu, Muslim, Sikh and Buddhist.)

In the 15th century, twin sons, Girkis and Maglot, were born to a royal couple from this dynasty. The royal couple happened to be cousins as well. As children Girkis and Maglot hated each other. They later went on to rule over (and found the royal families of) Hunzâ and Nagar respectively. When Girkis and Maglot became kings they got their people

5. They got married to fairies (in the old sense of the word) from the Hiñdu Kush, according to another version. But then there's no contradiction. The women of Persia and the Hiñdu Kush area do look like angels.

6. So, now you can dismiss any theories that you might have heard about the Great Conqueror having been a fairy. He merely married one.

to fight bloody battles with each other. Or so the story goes. The people of the two kingdoms inherited their founders' prejudices. The stand-off continues to this day though now bloodshed has been replaced by stereotypes of and jokes about each other.

Some western travellers invented generalisations of their own. G. W. Leitner wrote in 1830, "I do not palliate the old Hunzâ practice of lending one's wife to a guest or of kidnapping good looking strangers in order to improve the race."

The regional balance of power

The people of Hunzâ, thus, had a longstanding feud with neighbouring Nagar. Some British Raj historians tried to portray this as a conflict between the Ismâili Shiâs of Hunzâ and the non-Ismâili Shiâs of Nagar. Rubbish. The conflict was no more than the tension that exists between neighbouring regions throughout the third world (and pre 1945 Europe).[7]

The Hunzâkuts accepted Chinese overlordship (till the Dogrâs took over). But on the side they would play footsie with that other major neighbouring power, Russia. (That, I suppose, was what alarmed the British into imagining that a Great Game was being played in the region.)

Badakhshâñ, on the other hand, would sometimes pay tribute to the ruler of Hunzâ.

Before borders hardened (in 1947-48) the people of Hunzâ would trade with Kashmîr, Badakhshâñ and Yârqañd.

The 19th century

In the nineteenth century the Dogrâ rulers of Kashmîr tried to annex Hunzâ.[8] The hardy warriors of Hunzâ, led by their resolute chiefs, would

7. The tension between Hunzâ and Nagar always reminds me of the equally silly state of perpetual warfare that has for centuries existed between little Billâwar and tiny Bhaddû, both in the Jammu hills. Every few years 'warriors' from Billâwar and Bhaddû would clash (with canes and batons) on the vast fields that separate these neighbouring principalities. They would break each others' bones, and go home limping at night, normally with not a single death on either side. Both Billâwar and Bhaddû were ruled and populated by Hiñdu Râjpûts.

   The people-and rulers-of both Hunzâ and Nagar were and are Muslims. Within the Muslim community, both are Shias. It is ridiculous to look for Ismâili and other doctrinal angles in a conflict that dates to centuries before the region had even heard of the Ismâili sect.

8. In the chapter on the history of Balâwaristân we have seen that in the mid-nineteenth century (probably in 1842) Hunzâ and Nagar (and Puniâl and Gilgit) had accepted the overlordship of the Sikh kingdom of the Punjâb—through its Srînagar-based administrators. In turn they were allowed to rule their kingdoms as they had done before.

from time to time throw the Dogrâ army out. The Hunzâkuts intimidated Gilgit and cosied up to the rulers of Kashgar. Now the Russians were gaining ground in Kashgar. The British were alarmed by the possibility that Hunzâ, too, might come under Russia's sway. So, they took direct political control of Gilgit in 1889.

Besides, Hunzâ and Nagar would not stop squabbling with each other.

The Mîr of Hunzâ was not the kind to buckle under British pressure, or accommodate their interests. The British colonial project was one that the average Englishmen was uncomfortable about. The Englishman believed in decent Christian principles and fairplay. But he also wanted an empire. This meant depriving other nations of their independence. So, he had to find high-minded reasons to occupy other lands. In the case of Hunzâ the excuse was the safety of traffic on the caravan route. (For that reason, most Englishmen who wrote about the region in the late 19th century insisted on describing the people of Hunzâ and Nagar as bandits and highwaymen.)

The 19th century: Hunzâ, Nagar and the rest of the world

So, what was the political status of Hunzâ and Nagar at the time (1889)? E. F. Knight, who accompanied the British-Dogrâ force during the battle of Nilt, wrote in *Where Three Empires Meet* (1893):

'In name they were tributary to [the Dogrâ kings of] Kashmîr, the King of Hunzâ paying a yearly tribute of twenty ounces of gold dust, two horses and two hounds, the King of Nagir [sic] a certain quantity of gold-dust and two baskets of apricots.... But till now both States have been practically independent; for though the Kashmîr Durbar made repeated efforts to reduce them to submission, these proved entirely unsuccessful ...For thirty miles up the valley the forts of Hunzâ face those of Nagir, the defences being evidently intended as against each other; whereas, at the strong position which forms the gate of their country, by Nilt and Maiun [Mâyûn], a strong line of fortifications faces down the valley, ready for resistance to an invader from below. Hunzâ and Nagir, though they were at other times almost constantly at war with one another, always united their forces against a foreign enemy.

'These Hunzâ-Nagiris ...have for centuries been the terror of all the people between Afghânistân and Yar-Kand. Inhabiting these scarcely accessible defiles, they have been in the habit of making frequent raids across the Hindoo Koosh and earning their livelihood by a well-organized brigandage, the thums, or kings, of these two little States deriving the greater portion of their revenue from this source.'

Safdar Ali was the Mîr of Hunzâ at the time. In order to become the king he had shot dead his father, Ghazan Khân, and tossed two of his brothers down one of Hunzâ's tall and dreaded cliffs.[9] He then informed the Mahârâjâ of Jammû and Kashmîr,[10] about his newly-acquired promotion thus:

'Because God so willed and fate so decreed, my departed father and I lately developed some differences. I decided to make the first move to settle the matter. So, I have given to myself the throne of my forefathers.'

The 19th century: the British find an excuse

Nomadic Kirghiz tribes apparently asked the British Government of India to protect them from the 'piratical' people of Hunzâ and Nagar. The government asked Captain Francis Younghusband, who was then surveying the Pamirs, to go and check.

When Younghusband drew close to Hunzâ he was told that King Safdar Ali planned to receive him in state at Gulmit. So the captain put on his full-dress uniform. He also bade his Gurkhâ to do the same. He later wrote[ii] that the two found these costumes very inappropriate for crossing the '...nasty glacier at Pasu. I rode up through the village lands towards a large tent, in which the chief was to receive me. Thirteen guns were fired as a salute, and when they ceased a deafening tomtoming was set up...I dismounted from my pony, and advanced between the lines to meet the chief. I was astonished to find myself in the presence of a man with a complexion of almost European fairness, and with reddish hair. His features, too, were of an entirely European cast, and, dressed in European clothes, he might anywhere have been taken for a Greek or Italian. He was now dressed in a magnificent brocade robe and a handsome turban, presented by Colonel Lockhart. He had a sword and revolver fastened round his waist, and one man with a drawn sword and another with a repeating rifle stood behind him.'

Younghusband landed up at Baltit in 1889. He asked the Mîr to tell his people to stop looting the caravans that travelled between Central Asia and British India.

According to British sources, Safdar Ali was appalled by the suggestion. The Mîr apparently said, "But it's the only income that we have. If your Queen Victoria doesn't like what we are doing, we can give her a share of the loot."

9. A British writer calls this method of ascension to thrones 'the time-honoured Kârâkoram style.'

10. Why would he need to inform the Mahârâjâ, if Hunzâ was not under Dogrâ-ruled Kashmîr?

Younghusband was not amused. He left Hunzâ. Two years later he would send the British Army over to resume the conversation, this time by other means.

The Great Game: as seen from Hunzâ

Safdar Ali was under the illusion that every major power (especially Queen Victoria, the Tsar of Russia and the Emperor of China) was dying to get him on its side[11]. So, he thought that he could afford to tell the British where to get off and assert his right to levy his brand of 'taxes' on caravans passing by.

The pillaging of caravans by the Hunzâkuts was just an excuse. If that was the real reason, then what were the British doing in nearby Gilgit? After all, no one had accused the people of Gilgit of being highwaymen. In any case, soon the mask was off.

Colonel Durand was the British Political Agent in Gilgit at the time. He met Safdar Ali at Baltit and told him that the British did not intend to annex or take over what now are the occupied areas of Ladâkh. They only wished to ensure that their mailbags could travel between Kashgar and British India without let or hindrance. And yes, he added, almost as an afterthought, could the Hunzâkuts 'have no further dealings with the Russians'[iii]? As for giving Queen Victoria a share of the booty, instead she could give him an annual grant if he would lay off caravans and stay away from the Russians.

The British noticed that the Mîr was not biting. So they sent him a stern message through Colonel Durand that they planned to dominate the northern mountains and manage the area as long as they controlled the rest of India.

Safdar Ali had, in his infinite wisdom, decided to exempt one of his brothers, Muhammad Nâzim Khân, from having to walk the plank with their other brothers. Nâzim advised Safdar to avoid the Russians. Safdar did not agree. He kept up his contacts with the Russians.

So, when Colonel Gromchevski came to Baltit, twelve Cossacks in his tow, Safdar gave him a formal reception. From all accounts Gromchevski seems to have been a man of enormous charisma. Nâzim considered him very good-looking.[12]

Gromchevski was an envoy who bore gifts. During the week that he spent at Baltit he gave the Mîr some silk, a pony and two breech-loading

11. Countless others continue to suffer from the same delusion—about the supposed strategic importance of the region.

12. The colonel later met Younghusband in the Pamirs. The captain, too, seems to have been very impressed by him.

rifles. Safdar Ali then learnt why the Tsar had sent the colonel to Hunzâ. The Tsar had been told that Hunzâ was slipping into the British camp. He did not want that to happen. He wanted the Mîr on Russia's side.

According to Nâzim's memoirs, the Tsar planned to station an army unit at Baltit. The unit would have consisted of three hundred rifles and two guns. Hunzâkuts soldiers would be taught modern military techniques by a Russian officer, who would be posted at Baltit for the purpose. The Tsar's envoy advised Safdar to play along with the British till the Russian unit actually arrived.

Safdar seems to have been a stiff, straightforward Indian king of the old-type, incapable of artifice or subterfuge. No sooner had Gromchevski's words died down than he denied permission to a British letter to pass through the territory under his sway. The British were not merely offended. They got to know what had been going on between the Mîr and the Russians. Their Political Agent at Gilgit decided to attack Hunzâ. Safdar, ever the irrationally exuberant Indian potentate, let it be known that he had asked his army to bring him Col. Durand, dead or alive, preferably the former.

The British-Dogrâ attack on Hunzâ

On the 2nd December, 1891, the British-Dogrâ contingent reached Nilt, which is sixty kilometres ahead of the Diaynor Bridge. Nilt had almost impregnable fortifications. There were two walls around the village. The inner wall was between five and seven metres high and four metres thick. The outer wall was more than two and a half metres high. Both had narrow openings through which guns could fire. Tall cliffs surrounded the village on all sides—except for one small opening, through which people would go to the main gate.

With defences like those it was only natural that Safdar Ali had no fear of the British. He was confident that his army could resist even a year-long siege. On the other hand, the British had extremely limited access to water. Within days they started running out of drinking water.

Col. Durand felt that the only way out was to launch a strong, brief assault on Nilt and seize it swiftly—in half a day or so. The soldiers inside Nilt opened intense fire. The Lieutenants Boisragon and Badcock and a few Gurkhâs jumped on the outer wall. They chopped its wooden gate to splinters. Capt. Aylmer and his Pathan batman ran into the opening thus created.

Aylmer planted explosives on the ground below the main gate. A Hunzâ-Nagar soldier went right up to him and shot him in the leg. Despite the pain Aylmer lit the fuse. To shield himself against the explosion he went to the other side of the wall. However, there wasn't even a whimper. Aylmer went back to the gate. A Hunzâ-Nagar soldier threw a large stone from above, smashing the captain's hand. However, Aylmer kept trying to ignite the fuse.

At last he succeeded. The gun-cotton exploded. Without waiting for the dust to subside, Aylmer, Boisragon and Badcock, accompanied by six Gurkhâs, rushed into the fort. The soldiers in the British contingent were caught off guard by this achievement of their leader. They weren't sure which side their colleagues had entered the fort from. Lt. Boisragon understood their bewilderment. He left the fort all by himself, went to where his soldiers were and came back to the fort with a modest contingent[13].

The Hunzâ-Nagar army fought back extremely bravely. Knight says that they 'defended themselves like fanatical dervishes.' Same thing, really. Depends on which side you are on.

The British-Dogrâ combine won the battle. However, Baltit was still a long way off. The Nilt Nullah had yet to be crossed. This is a deep ravine with tall precipices on both sides. Many of its walls were made of sheer ice. Hunzâ-Nagar army shooters occupied all the vantage-points atop the cliffs. The Hunzâ-Nagar army did not need to waste their bullets. They could simply roll rocks down to crush the invading soldiers. So, Col. Durand's plan to seize the defences had to be abandoned. The Hunzâ-Nagar army's heroic resistance paralysed the British-Dogrâ force for eighteen days.

Nagdu, the brave Dogrâ

'The ultimate victory [of the British-led force],' writes Mrs. Mons, 'rested upon the daring idea of a young Dogrâ of the Kashmîr Bodyguard Regiment named Nagdu who, after a number of attempts made at night, found a way to scale the opposing cliff face.'

The British-Dogrâ force planned its assault very carefully. On the cold, dark, long night of December 19, Lieut. Manners Smith and a group of soldiers climbed down the cliff on their side and hid at the base of the gorge. Some soldiers, including E. F. Knight, on whose memoirs this account is based, took positions on the hill above the Nilt fort.

Early the next morning the second British-Dogrâ group started firing on the Nilt outpost on the cliff across the ravine. This went on for almost thirty minutes. That's when the group at the bottom of the cliff began its offensive on the cliff on the other side. Knight estimates that a vertical ascent of almost 1,200 feet was involved. However, when they had

13. Captain Aylmer and Lieutenant Boisragon won Victoria Crosses for their bravery.

climbed two-thirds of the way up, they came upon a rock-face that could simply not be scaled.

So, the group had to descend all the way down to the base of the gorge. Lieut. Manners Smith and his force of fifty Gurkhâs decided to look for another way up. That found, they started all over again. Lieut. Taylor and fifty Dogrâs followed. The invaders managed to reach the level of the Nilt fort. They took on the Hunzâ-Nagar army in hand-to-hand fighting. One by one they captured all the vantage-points.

The soldiers of Hunzâ-Nagar were shattered—and confused. Defeat was a word that did not exist in their dictionary. After all, they had never lost a war in their entire history. Safdar Ali escaped to China.

When E. F. Knight and the British-Dogrâ force reached Hunzâ after their victory, Knight asked some Hunzâkuts where Safdar was. The Hunzâkuts told him that when they last saw Safdar Ali he was going over the roof of the world. (The Pamirs are, in Hunzâ and other Persophone lands, known as the Bâm é Duniyâ [the Roof of the World].)

Merger with Jammû and Kashmîr—and the rest of India

The British replaced Safdar with his brother, Muhammad Nâzim Khân. Ever the prudent one, Nâzim threw in his lot wholly and unreservedly with the British. In turn they knighted him and gave him nice titles.

After they defeated the Hunzâ-Nagar army at Nil(i)t, the British stationed their army at Aliabad. It remained there till 1897. After that Hunzâ became a princely state protected by the British Government of India but part of the state of Jammû and Kashmîr.

In 1894, one George Nathaniel Curzon came calling. The Mîr and he climbed up to the Kilik Pass on the Tagh-dumbash Pamir. He measured the altitude of the pass, which, he discovered, was 15,870'. Thereafter, he sat on a rock and started composing a letter to the editor of *The Times*, London. He could have waited till he got back to the plains, for there's unlikely to have been a post-box nearby. Five years later he became the Viceroy of India and was better known as Lord Curzon,

Sir Muhammad Nâzim Khân, K.C.I.E., K.C.S.I., ruled Hunzâ for forty-six years. He died in 1938. British records speak glowingly of his reign. Humayun Beg was his celebrated Wazir. Sir Nâzim would on occasion attend the Delhi Durbar of Indian Rajahs. At one such durbar, he recorded, 'They asked me where my kingdom was, and I replied that it touched on the borders of China.'[14]

14. Thus, he considered Hunzâ as being below the border with China, and not on the Chinese side.

His son, Ghazan Khân, who ruled for the next seven years, succeeded Sir Nâzim. Ghazan's son, Muhammad Jamal Khân, assumed the throne in 1945.[15]

1947-and after

In 1947, India was partitioned into secular, but Hiñdû-dominated India and avowedly Muslim Pâkistân. The Hiñdû Mahârâjâ of Muslim-majority Jammû and Kashmîr had to choose between the two. The Mehtar of Chitrâl and the Mîr of Hunzâ sent telegrams to His Highness suggesting accession to Pâkistân and swearing loyalty to the Mahârâjâ if this was done.'

(See 'A history of Balâwaristân' for the events of 1947, and how Hunzâ landed up in Pâkistân.) More than five hundred princely states were incorporated into India, which began to rule them all[16] directly. Pâkistân, on the other hand, gave the rulers of some princely states, notably Hunzâ, the right to govern their kingdoms as they had before. The Republic of Pâkistân only controlled their defence, foreign affairs and a few like subjects.

Pâkistân altered Hunzâ's sovereign status on the 25th September, 1974. Mîr Muhammad Jamal Khân was the thum (king) of Hunzâ at the time. Regardless of whether they had ruled Hunzâ since the 11th century A.D. or the 15th, the Mîrs of Hunzâ were one of the longest lasting royal dynasties in the world.

Most analysts, western as well as Pâkistânî, attribute this to Hunzâ's remoteness and inaccessibility. However, dynasties are overthrown not only by invaders from outside but equally often for home-grown reasons. So, if the Mîrs lasted almost nine hundred years without a major internal rebellion or decadence, it says something about the wisdom with which they ruled that near-paradise.

After the forcible incorporation of their ancestral kingdom, the Mîrs of Hunzâ became active in the politics of the region.

References

i Quoted by Amaury Aubrée-Dauchez in a website

ii *In The Heart of a Continent*, by Captain Francis Younghusband, 1896.

iii The quote is from Mrs. Mons, op cit.

15. 1946, according to another version.
16. Except, for legal reasons, Arcot in South India, which had a different status for a while.

8

Hunzâkuts Royalty

A fecund dynasty: One reason why royal (and industrial) dynasties the world over die out is because at some stage there is no heir, or no male heir, to continue the line. Remember the Doctrine of Lapse enunciated by the British Raj? The Mîrs of Hunzâ, on the other hand, were a fecund lot. Muhammad Jamal Khân (1945-74), for instance, had nine children. (Some medical studies suggest that the infertility of several dynasties internationally has been due to the heavy meat content in their diet. The Hunzâkuts, on the other hand, are mainly vegetarian.)

Western influences: All over the Indian sub-continent men have been wearing western-style clothes, attending western-style schools and colleges and, in many cases, drinking western-style alcohol[1] since the late nineteenth century. However, considering Hunzâ's extreme remoteness, the extent of such influences elicits surprise—and comment.

By the mid-twentieth century the princesses had started cutting their hair the western way—short and with a fringe. The Wazir would drink Scotch whisky, neat. It was not uncommon for middle-class people from educated families to wear white trousers, shirt, tie and a blazer with the royal coat-of-arms embroidered on the pocket. There would often be a white British hat on the head.

However, as in the rest of South Asia, traditions were never forsaken. Hunzâkuts princesses would sit on the floor in a row on ceremonial occasions and not speak a word. The westernised Wazir, too, would sit on the ground. The Mîr would wear grand eastern-style robes and jewels, though his sword would be British. Lord Kitchener, the then Commander-in-Chief, had presented this sword, on which Edward VII's insignia had been etched, to Muhammad Nâzim Khân, when he (Kitchener) had visited Baltit. The Mîr's 'throne' (divân, really), too, was decorated in an Indo-Persian fashion.

1. As opposed to local brews.

At least by the twentieth century the Mîrs of Hunzâ started sending their children to the plains for their education. The boarding schools of Abbotâbâd were a particular favourite. Princesses and, sometimes, princes, too, would often be taught at home. Winston Mumby, an American tutor, for instance, lived in Baltit, with his wife Carol, in the 1950s.

While the women of Hunzâ have traditionally not worn the veil or lived in seclusion from the men, there were some restrictions on royal women. They would not be seen easily by their own male subjects. Nor would they let anyone photograph them till the early twentieth century. However, by the middle of that century they began to receive male guests within the palace.

By the first half of the twentieth century many men had given up their distinctive traditional dress for lifeless western-style clothes. Clothes stitched in Rawalpindi were considered very elite.

Matrimonial links: The Mîrs have often given their daughters in marriage to the princes of Yâsîn and Chitrâl. The royalties of Hunzâ and Nagar have longstanding matrimonial links—despite the enmity that existed on the surface.

Lots of gifts had to be exchanged during these royal weddings. So, the local people would chip in. Each village would give a present, brought by its notables on some festive occasion before the wedding. These presents would vary from sheep and ponies to gold dust in little bags. Kitchen utensils were as welcome as rifles. Some just gave cash.[2] Members of the royal family would note each gift in a register.

'Milk-parents': As soon as a child was born to the Hunzâ royals, it was handed over to foster-parents, who brought it up for several years. The foster-mother played wet-nurse to the child. The idea was to renew bonds between the Mîrs and the common folk. Once a set of commoners was chosen as a 'milk-family' for a royal baby, the foster couple could look forward to a life of relative comfort as long as they lived. They were lodged in small cottages behind the palace and got their food from the Mîrs' kitchen. This was in addition to what they earned from their own property.

These foster parents were chosen very carefully. The Wazir (minister), for instance, was a very likely candidate. This honour was bestowed not only on the nobility but on all kinds of respectable, educated, middle-class families, as well—a respected schoolteacher, for instance.

Some of these respectable families stayed in their own, well-built houses in the Shumâl Bâgh ('the northern garden') area, near the Baltit Fort.

2. A rarity in a largely cashless economy.

Royal children spent the first few years of their lives with their foster-parents. (The number of years was not fixed.) After they returned to the palace they continued to meet their milk-parents regularly. Princesses normally spent the weeks before their wedding at their milk-parents' home. They were, so to speak, given away from that house.

The royal palaces

The 15th century fort

Ayesho, a 14th century A.D. king of Hunzâ, married a princess of Baltistân. Her father, King Abdar Khân, sent five hundred craftsmen, architects and masons with her to Hunzâ. They constructed the famous 62-room Baltit Fort. It also served as a palace.

Some accounts dated to A.D. 1273, too, speak of a fort at Baltit. It, too, stood majestically above the town. Was it the same palace that is attributed to Ayesho's father-in-law, with the dates being askew by a few decades? Or was it an older fort that stood at the same site? As of now, no one knows. I suspect the former because an A.D. 1273 fort would not need to be rebuilt within a few decades.

The Mîrs of Hunzâ lived in this palace till the middle of the twentieth century. Like Hunzâ itself, no invader could capture or occupy the fort till 1891.

In that year, Mrs. Mons writes, 'the British took up their quarters [in the Baltit Fort] and systematically looted it. When I remarked upon this sad fact to the Mîr, he replied courteously that he was sure it was not the British but the Dogrâ troops under their command.'[3] However, as Mrs. Mons points out, Knight leaves us in no doubt. In the book *Where Three Empires Meet*, in the chapter 'Loot in the Thum's palace-a Treasure-Hunt', he writes:

'This massive fortress, which has been for hundreds of years the secure stronghold of the robber kings, inviolate until this day, stands boldly out, set in the midst of a sublime landscape ...Twigg, Boisragon and myself took up our quarters in the most comfortable chamber we could find, which we soon discovered to have been the apartment of the

3. Reminds me of Woody Allen's classic 1970s film *Sleeper*. The bumbling Allen character works out a plan on behalf of his group of young men and women. It succeeds. The film's heroine prefers Errol, a dashing hunk, to Allen, a skinny nerd. She exults, 'Errol's plan has worked.' Woody looks dumbfounded, because it was his plan. Later the same plan backfires. Everyone blames Woody for it. Today Pâkistân is trying to pretend that the Dogrâs had never ruled over Hunzâ and that they were incapable of conquering the fabled valley. However, ask them who took the old palace apart. and they will blame the Dogrâs.

ladies belonging to the Thum's harem. It was surrounded by a low, broad, wooden divan, on which our bedding was laid. Pillars of carved wood rose from the edge of the divan to the carved beams of the roof, blackened by the smoke of ages...A fire was lit in the open fireplace at one end of the floor, the smoke escaping through a square hole in the roof. Save for the Oriental pattern of the wooden carvings it was just such a hall, I imagine, as King Canute might have lived in...We enjoyed a delicious night's rest after our late fatigues.

'We were up betimes on December 23rd, and proceeded to rummage all the nooks and comers of the deserted palace. We had heard that the treasures of many a pillaged caravan ...were stored here, so the search was an exciting one. The tribesmen had been informed that, provided they gave up their arms, their property would be respected by us...But the possessions of the fugitive Thum were declared to be forfeited, so we set to work to collect together all the valuables that were to be found in the place, individual looting being of course forbidden...We were informed that the Thum had made all his preparations for flight long before his defeat at Nilt, and... had carried off the bulk of his wealth with him across the Hindoo Koosh...still, they had not taken all, and we raked together a curious and miscellaneous collection of odds and ends scattered about and secreted away in the various chambers and cellars!'

The new palace

After the British-Dogrâ force took the old fort-cum-palace apart, the Mîr built a new palace. This one combined local traditions with British influences. For instance, it had a western-style bathroom with a bathtub. The livery of the staff, too, coupled eastern cummerbunds with western-style brass buttons and breastplates.

In 1925, Sir Muhammad Nâzim Khân added a little guesthouse next to the palace. It has been built atop a huge boulder, near an orchard of flowering trees. The guesthouse, too, combined local decorations (the horns of animals such as the ibex) with European ones (stone carvings, as well as a spiral wooden staircase outside). The furniture, furnishings and decorations, too, were European. The old crockery and cutlery of the palace carefully balanced imports from Russia with those from England, playing a little Plate Game of their own. The blue dragon rice bowls were, appropriately, from China.

Among the eastern touches were the carved ceiling and elaborately etched door-lintels. The decorations included elegant swords and shields with exquisite Islâmic calligraphy and a 16th century Chinese matchlock gun.

The flag, protocol and ceremonials

Flag: The royal flag of Hunzâ depicted black mountains covered with snow. There was a green 'sky' above them. Against that green background was a white crescent and star, as well as a golden bow and arrow, which pointed towards the lower half.

As we saw in the section on the Kârâkorams, the name of that range has several possible meanings. 'Black mountains' is the one that fits best. It is also how the flag portrays that range. Green, of course, is the colour of Islâm, and the crescent and star its symbols.

Protocol: In 1912, the British Government of India ordered that the Hunzâkuts royalty would be accorded a 9-gun salute (out of a possible twenty-one guns). Later, in 1966, the Government of Pâkistân increased this to a 15-gun salute.

Titles: The king of Hunzâ was called the Mîr. The queen was known as the Rânî.

Regalia: The Mîrs owned several camels.

Customs: Whenever the Mîr came down the steps that led to his durbar (court), the people would bend down to kiss his hand as he walked past them.

Royal patronage of festivals

Eid[4]: The two main Eids (Eid ul Fitr and Eid uz Zuhâ) are, naturally, the biggest festivals of the year in any Muslim land. However, in Hunzâ these used to be major royal occasions.[5] Men, wearing their festive best, would gather at Baltit's town square. They would sit in neat rows all around the square (except the side that led to the palace). Mrs. Mons noted in 1958, that the rows would be 'ten deep... The oldest and most respected [men would sit] nearest to their ruler.'

A *shamiânâ* (large, colourful tent) would be erected for the royal women, on a ground at a higher level overlooking the square. Other women would (and in most of Kashmîr, Kargil and Leh still do) sit in a group of their own.

The morning meal for all spectators would be on the Mîr. It would be served to them during the festivity, in the rows in which they were sitting.

After the people had eaten, the band would start playing music suitable for dancing. 'Only men and boys take part,' Mrs. Mons wrote.

4. See also the chapter 'Sports and pastimes,' the section on 'Polo,' and the sub-section 'Ceremonies before the game.'
5. Somewhat like Dussehra which is one of the four most important festivals for all Hiñdûs, but in Mysore it receives royal patronage like nowhere else.

'It is said that in the past, when an intoxicating spirit was distilled from mulberries, men and women used to foregather in a dance that ended in an orgy, with the result that the Mîr forbade the spirit and frowned upon the custom of the two sexes dancing together. This ban still survives, in that dancing is considered unseemly for women.[6] To our western eyes this is no great loss to them, for the steps have little rhythm, being mainly of the hop-skip-and-jump variety.'

Each village would perform a dance. Some of the dancers would drink the famous Hunzâ *pani* (literally, 'water,' but this particular 'water' was somewhat stronger).

6. Across Ladâkh the intermingling of the sexes during a dance depends on religion as well as local tradition. The men and women dance together in all Buddhist areas, as well as in Dâ Hânû. In Muslim Kargil the record is mixed. In some parts, especially in and around the town, they do not dance at all. In other regions of Kargil they are, in the new millennium, being allowed to dance, in sororities, and, in some rare cases, with the boys.

9

Europeans in Ladakh

(And the books that they wrote)

Diogo d'Almeira (or d'Almeida), a Portuguese layman, who was in Ladakh for two years around AD 1600, is the first European in recorded history to have visited Ladakh. Two Jesuit priests, the Fathers Francesco de Azevedo and Giovanni de Oliveiro, are the next we hear of. They came in 1631, through Tsaparang (Guge, Tibet).

Another missionary, Ipolito Desideri, travelled from Srinagar to Ladâkh and thence Lhâsâ, in 1715, and wrote in some detail about the land. He was the last of the Jesuits in Lhâsâ. Missionary activity in Tibet ground to a halt after him. (An edited version of his *An Account of Tibet* was published in English in 1937. A little earlier, in 1924, *Early Jesuit Travellers in Central Asia* by C. Wessels, SJ, had been published in The Hague.)

The next recorded visitors, William Moorcroft, a veterinary surgeon, and George Trebeck, both being employees of the (British) East India Company, came more than a century later. They travelled through Ladakh between 1820 and 1822 and their writings are even more valuable. (In 1971, their *Travels in the Himalâyan Provinces of Hindustan and the Punjab,* 1837, was reprinted by a Delhi publisher.) This was among the first travelogues ever written about the region.

Alexander Csoma de Koros, a Hungarian, spent three years, most of them in Zâñglâ and Phugtâl, in Zâñskâr, around the same time. He came looking for the origins of the Magyar language, hoping that it might be linked to the Tibetan language. Magyar is one of the few languages in western or central Europe that are not Indo-Aryan. He could not prove the connection, but in the process he founded the discipline of Tibetology.

Next came G.T. Vigne (pron: veen or veen-yer) whose 1842 *Travels in Kashmir, Ladak, Iskardo* had a perfunctory section about Ladakh.

The Dogras conquered Ladakh in the nineteenth century, and the British Raj took a conscious decision to look the other way. However, after that a steady stream of colonial administrators started coming to Ladakh, mostly on work. Alexander Cunningham led a team that, in 1846 and 1847 respectively, demarcated the borders between Ladakh on the one hand and Tibet and Spiti on the other. His work, too, resulted in first rate publications, notably *Ladak. Physical, Statistical and Historical; with Notices of the Surrounding Countries*, 1854, reprinted in 1970.

Frederic Drew's *The Jummoo and Kashmir Territories* (1875, reprinted in 1976) is an equally invaluable work.

The Moravian mission came to Ladakh in 1885, and over the years some Ladakhis converted to Christianity. The mission set up churches in Leh and Shey.

In 1909, the (British) Government of India sponsored a cultural mission, the first of its kind, to Ladakh. Dr. A.H. Francke (pron. frank-kay) of the Moravian Mission Board, a German scholar, undertook this task on behalf of the Calcutta-based (British) Directorate General of Archaeology. Francke was an expert linguist who knew several Indian languages, as well as Tibetan. The scholarship produced by this cultural mission was of a high order and Dr. Francke's works (especially the second volume of *Antiquities of Indian Tibet,* 1926, as well as his 1905 translation of the epic Kesar Saga*)* are still among the best on the subject. Francke, along with his fellow Germans—Emil and Hermann von Schlangintweit and Karl Marx, put together, for the first time in any language (including Ladakhi itself) the history of the area. Their work is normally referred to as the Ladakh Chronicles.

The prolific Italian Professors Giuseppe Tucci who mainly wrote the 3 volume *Indo-Tibetica*, 1932-36*)* and Luciano Petech (mainly *A Study of the Chronicles of Ladakh,* 1939), have painstakingly put together the history of Guge (western Tibet) and Ladakh.

A somewhat later travelogue is *Peaks and Lâmâs* (London, 1939) by Marco Pallis. It was reprinted in 1975.

Almost everyone who has written about the history of Leh thereafter has relied on the writings of these Europeans. (For some reason European writers did not choose to write about the Shiite Muslim Kargil. The best histories of that area are by Kargil scholars themselves as well as other Indians like Hashmat Ullah Khan.)

After the Chinese invasion of Ladakh in 1962, the movements of foreigners in the region were severely restricted for the next twelve years. In 1974, Ladakh was thrown open to tourists. Along with Western tourists came writers- and books- of all sorts. Coffee table glossies and good scholarship (notably Snellgrove & Skorupski's *The Cultural Heritage of Ladakh*, 1977) as well as unintentionally hilarious, self congratulatory travelogues.

One Michel Peissel, for instance, claims that he 'discovered' the 'kingdom' of Zâñskâr. For one, Zâñskâr was not a kingdom; the valley consisted of *two* (sometimes three) kingdoms—if you can call them that—and several independent villages. Secondly, when was it lost or 'hidden' that it needed to be discovered? Countless non-Ladakhi Indian administrators preceded Peissel. He was not even the first European to visit—or write about—Zâñskâr, having been beaten to it by a Hungarian by more than a century and a half.

The best books written after 1974, are by Prof. Snellgrove & Skorupski, both of the University of London, and by Janet Rizvi (*Ladakh: Crossroads of High Asia*).

The role of some of these Europeans in the politics of Ladakh—and Guge—and that of the Moravian church in Leh is mentioned in greater detail in the section on Ladakh's history.

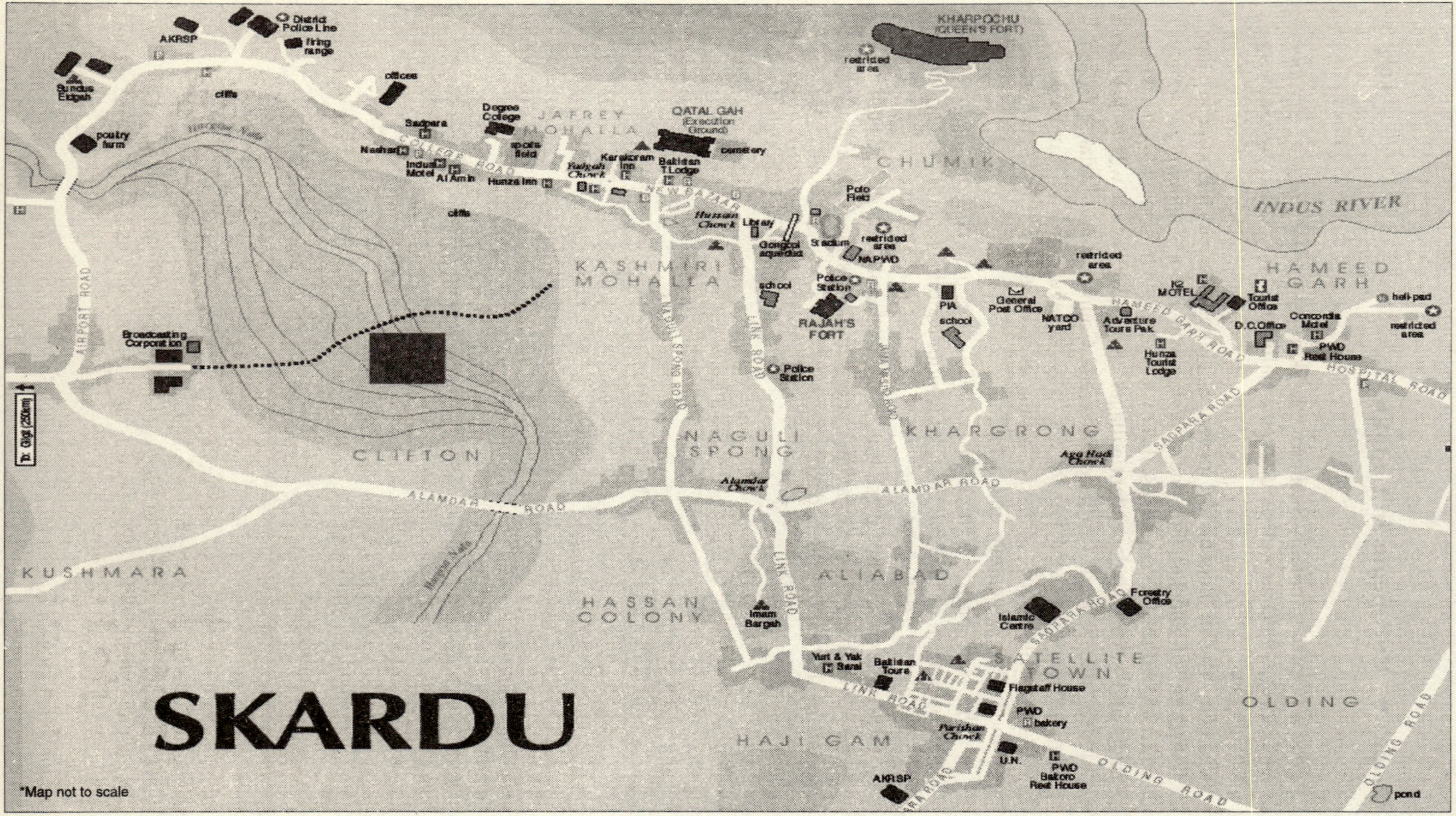
SKARDU
*Map not to scale
To Gilgit (250km)
AKRSP
District Police Line
firing range
Sundus Eidgah
poultry farm
cliffs
offices
Sadpara
Degree College
sports field
JAFREY MOHALLA
QATAL GAH (Execution Ground)
cemetery
KHARPOCHU (QUEEN'S FORT)
restricted area
Nashat
Indus Motel
Al Amin
COLLEGE ROAD
Hunza Inn
Yadgah Chowk
Karakoram Inn
Baltistan T.Lodge
NEW BAZAAR
CHUMIK
INDUS RIVER
Polo Field
Hussain Chowk
Library
Gongma aqueduct
Stadium
NAPWD
KASHMIRI MOHALLA
school
Police Station
RAJAH'S FORT
PIA
General Post Office
NATCO yard
Adventure Tours Pak
Hunza Tourist Lodge
K2 MOTEL
Tourist Office
HAMEED GARH
heli-pad
Concordia Motel
D.C.Office
PWD Rest House
HAMEED GARH ROAD
HOSPITAL ROAD
AIRPORT ROAD
Broadcasting Corporation
CLIFTON
NAGULI SPONG ROAD
LINK ROAD
NAGULI SPONG
Alamdar Chowk
KHARGRONG
Aga Hadi Chowk
SADPARA ROAD
ALAMDAR ROAD
KUSHMARA
HASSAN COLONY
ALIABAD
Imam Bargah
Islamic Centre
Forestry Office
Yurt & Yak Sarai
Baltistan Tours
SATELLITE TOWN
Flagstaff House
PWD
bakery
Parishan Chowk
U.N.
PWD Baltoro Rest House
OLDING
OLDING ROAD
HAJI GAM
pond

Places of Tourist Interest

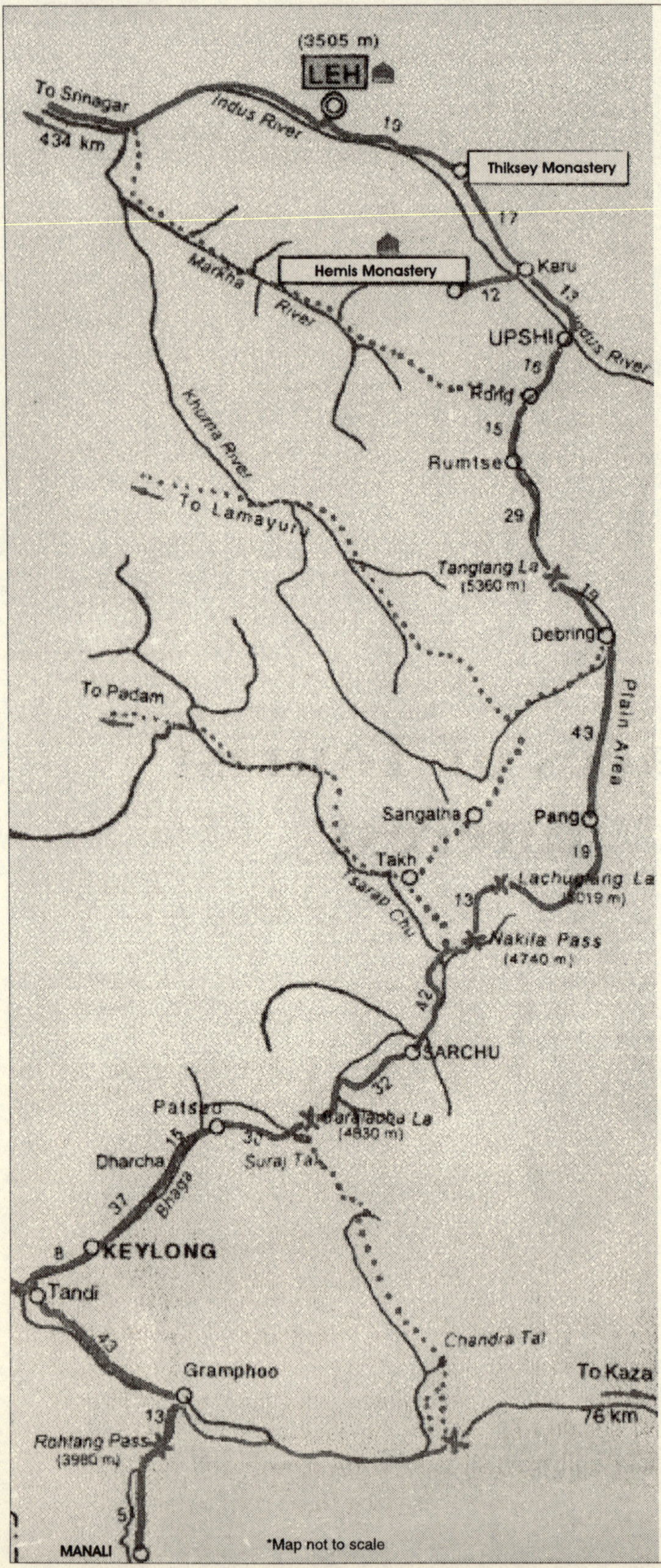

Manali-Leh Road

10

Ladakh

Frequently Asked Questions

Incredible Altitudes

Ladakh is the highest inhabited region in the world. It is also one of the coldest. Leh town is 3,522m./ 11,750' above the sea. So, if you live in, say, Bombay or New York, imagine a place at the end of a road that is three and a half kilometres long. Then look skywards and imagine that this place is now 3.5km. above you. That's how high Leh is, and with 22 metres to spare.

The average height of the Ladakh range is 6,000m. Peaks in the district, e.g. the Kang Lâ Cha and Kang Ya-tse, routinely go up to 6,400m. The highest mountain in Ladakh is the Saser Kâñgrî (7,680m.)

The lowest parts of Ladakh are around 9,000 feet above the sea.

Kargil is the highest inhabited region in the world. It is also one of the coldest. Kargil has traditionally been Leh's shy and retiring twin. However, in the summer of 1999 our friends across the border decided to make Kargil a household word by thrusting a war upon India. Now, suddenly, the world is waking up to the fact that the Kargil district of Ladakh holds most of the world's altitude-related records.

According to the French author Michel Peissel, Kargyâk (14,400') in Zâñskâr (Kargil) is the world's highest inhabited village. (Mining camps in the Andes don't count. Leh, too, has settlements that are higher than Kargyâk. Protagonists of Kargyâk say that those aren't full fledged villages, either.) Peaks in Kargil, e.g. the Nûn and Kun, rise to 7,135m. and 7,087m. respectively.

Drass, a roadside village in Kargil, is the second coldest inhabited place in the world, after Siberia.

Climate

The climate doesn't shape the lives of people in other parts of the world the way it does in Ladakh.

Winter: Temperatures fall to zero degrees (Celsius) by mid-October in most parts of Ladakh, including the towns and villages most favoured by tourists. In Leh proper this might be only for a brief part of the day. However, the year that I was in Zâñskâr (Kargil district) we plunged into all-day below zero temperatures from the 31st October, and remained below zero throughout the day till late February. After that, till the end of March, even some days in April, we would have sub-zero temperatures for at least a part of the day.

Leh and Kargil towns are slightly warmer. However, most inhabited areas of Ladakh (except Nubra and Dâ-Hânu, which are warmer) still follow the same pattern. In Zâñskâr, we'd be minus 12°C at the warmest time of the day from November to mid January. And at the coldest? We don't know. We had two thermometers. One of them was calibrated to go down to minus 35°C, and we routinely touched that mark. The other thermometer had to be activated physically and at 6 am it would equally often record minus 35°C. Perhaps it was lower still at, say, 5 am. Therefore, we can safely assume that for around two or three months a year temperatures in the inhabited parts of Zâñskâr go down to around minus forty degrees Celsius at night. (I am not aware of any studies other than ours conducted in Zâñskâr.)

Drâss is incredibly cold, even without windchill. Temperatures there drop to minus 45°C quite often during the winters. A government publication, however, asserts that Drâss can be as cold as minus 60°C in the winters. Leh and Kargil towns touch minus 30°C at night and around minus six to nine at noon during the worst period.

You find that forbidding? Adventure lovers find this the most exciting part. The rivers freeze over and some of them, for specific periods and at specific times of the day, become fit to walk on. That's how people travel from Kargil to Zâñskâr for a few weeks every year, on the *chadar* road, in parts of December, January and, sometimes, early February.

When the intensity of winter lessens, for a few weeks, it becomes possible to walk on the snow. This is called *kharass* and occurs in April (and may be March)

Precautions to be taken

You don't need to be athletic fit to survive Ladakhi winters. Unless you are already suffering from a major ailment or have breathing problems, you'll do fine. Just wear the right amount of clothes, eat vitamin C, drink lots of non-alcoholic liquids and make sure your room is heated. Bring plenty of vaseline along. Your skin can get parched because of the dryness. Sunglasses are recommended through the year to avoid the glare of the snow in winter and of the sand in summer. The sun ruins your skin and ages it rapidly. Since the 1980s, fashion-conscious girls in Leh town have taken to covering every millimetre of their faces and arms for this reason. A lotion to block the sun would help. If you are over 45 or have an existing medical problem, please consult a doctor before visiting Ladakh even in summer.

The best way to travel to Ladakh is by road from Srinagar. That way you get acclimatised gradually. If for some reason you *have* to fly to Leh, then it is recommended that on arrival you do nothing remotely strenuous for the rest of the day. Just rest in your hotel room for 24 to 48 hours. Don't even stroll in the market. Personally I never follow this precaution. Nor did Kuchipudi dancers Raja and Radha Reddy, who performed their vigorous dance on the very evening of their arrival. The dance made Raja sweat even though he was barechested on a cold September evening. But then the Reddys and I are fit as fit as athletes

The road journey from Srînagar to Leh takes sixteen to eighteen hours, spread over two days, with a night halt in Kargil. Tourists assume that they waste a day if they travel by road. Actually they don't, because if they fly to Leh they will waste the first day getting acclimatised anyway. And travelling by road has the added advantage of getting to see some of the most exciting parts of Ladâkh en route.

Summers: July is the hottest month and touches 38ºC on some days. Temperatures start falling (in both Ladakh and Kashmir) after the 15th August. 20ºC is the norm during the day in the summer.

The atmosphere: The air in Ladakh is thin. This means that there is far less oxygen in the air than there is in the plains. The concentration of carbon dioxide, too, is low. On the other hand, infra-red and ultra-violet radiation is very strong, which causes the local population to age prematurely. So keep your sunscreen handy. Apply it lavishly. Try to get a sun-block with a solar protection factor (SPF) of more than 30.

General: Ladakh is a dry, mountainous ('high altitude') desert. Annual precipitation is 9 cm in Leh district and, at 23.9 cm, slightly better in Kargil district. Kargil receives snow almost everywhere, including Zâñskâr. Leh town, as well as the plains of the district, have traditionally received almost no snowfall. The little snow that would fall was dry and got easily blown away. However, in the late 1990s, with the climate changing everywhere, Leh started getting real, moist snow—only an inch or two a year, but still.

Strong winds result in blizzards when there is snow and dust storms when there isn't.

Clothing

July is the warmest month: You can wear T-shirts even in the evenings. It's about the same during the last fortnight of June and the first fortnight of August. It starts getting nippy after the 15th August. From May to mid-June and mid-August to mid-September, days are pleasant but evenings can be somewhat cold. April and mid-September to mid-October are colder, but tolerably so. Normal woollens will do. It touches zero by mid- October in many parts of Ladakh. From November to the end of March you will need clothes fit for the second coldest inhabited region in the world, warmer only than Siberia. Quilted jackets and trousers, and thermal innerwear, are essential.

Kargil town is almost 800 metres lower than Leh town. However, several inhabited areas of the district are higher than the highest inhabited parts of Leh. Drâss, in Kargil, is colder than any village in Leh. And yet the availability of oxygen in the atmosphere is slightly more plentiful in most parts of Kargil than in Leh district. The same precautions apply to Kargil as to Leh.

Area

In terms of area, Ladakh used to be the biggest district in India—till 1979, when it was divided into Leh and Kargil. Not including the parts illegally occupied by China and Pakistan, at around 44,000 sq. km. Leh is still one of the biggest and Kargil still has an area of around 14,036 sq. km. (See also the last section of the chapter 'A paradise without a name.')

Both Pakistan and India claim that the state of Jammu and Kashmir is part of their nation. People have often wondered which of the two has the better case morally. Solomon would have offered to carve the state into two to see which the real mother was. India believes in the whole state staying together, not dividing it up. Pakistan sliced 5,180 sq. km. out of the state (all in Leh district) and gifted them to China. Shows how much it believes in its own claim to the state, leave alone the integrity of the state.

Ladakh before 1947: At one stage Ladakh district was bigger than several important countries. It consisted of three tehsils: Leh, Kargil and Skardu. Its area, including the Gilgit division, was 63,554 sq. miles. Its 1941 population was 3,11,915 (or 0.3 million). Its northern boundary then met the Pamirs. The world's second highest peak, K2/ Godwin- Austen (28,251'/ 8,611 metres), was part of undivided Ladakh.

In 1947, Pakistan annexed Skardu tehsil, which it has since converted into a federally administered unit called the Northern Areas.

Forests: Six square kilometres of Kargil's vast deserts are under forests, or 0.04% of the districtis. Leh is even worse off. It has no forests at all.

Literacy

Kargil is supposed to be the most conservative district of the state, perhaps of the country. People attribute this to the supposed stranglehold of the feudal Aghas and to 'ultra-orthodox' Shia Islam. For that reason the women of Kargil are supposed to be the most suppressed lot in the state, perhaps in India.

Given these highly flawed assumptions, the results of the 2001 census were a surprise (and, for me, a delight). 'Remote' Leh, it turns out, is the third most literate of the State's 14 districts. 'Ultra-backward' Kargil is no.5, almost on a par Srinagar (which is no.4). The shattering of myths doesn't stop there. The women of Kargil are the sixth most literate in the state. This is a huge achievement considering that according to the stereotype they are supposed to be no.13 or 14.

The perception of the public is not based on prejudice. It is merely outdated. After all, in 1981 just 19% of Kargil was literate. Leh, at 24.43%, was only slightly better.

District	2001: Total Literacy	Male	Female
Leh	59.81	69.16	49.66
Kargil	58.04	73.38	40.95

Religion

Leh: In 1981, 81.18% of the people of Leh were Buddhist and 15.31% Muslim. Apart from some Hindu settlers from outside the region, there were 156 Christians, who mostly subscrib to the Moravian church.

Most Muslims of Leh town and the surrounding villages are Argons. This is a community descended from Yarqandi (and, in some cases, Kashmiri) traders, who married local women. Thus, racially, they are part Ladakhi and part Central Asian. Unlike their neighbours in Kargil, all Argons are Sunni.

The Muslims of Bogdang, Nubra, Pheyang, Thiskey and Chichot are Shia.

In Ladakh as a whole there were around 68,000 Buddhists and 62,000 Muslims. (See also 'Islam in Leh and Zâñskâr.')

Kargil includes Zâñskâr, which is across the Penzi Lâ. Zâñskâr is predominantly Buddhist, with a small minority of Kashmiri Sunni Muslims from Kishtwâr. The people of Drâss are mainly Sunni. The rest of Kargil is almost entirely Shia Muslim, except some villages that border Leh, which have Buddhists as well.

In 1981, 77.9% of the people of Kargil were Muslim and 19.49% Buddhist (almost entirely in Zâñskâr and the areas where Kargil borders Leh). Apart from some Hindu settlers, there were 81 Christians.

Electricity and water below zero

Electricity: Theoretically, 75 of Leh's 112 villages and 79 of Kargil's 129 villages had been provided electricity by 1995. And yet the supply of actual electricity is inadequate.

Ladakh is the world's most difficult region to take electricity to. Its rivers are extremely shallow even in the months when there's water in them. During the long winters they are frozen- entirely or at least in part. Neither coal nor diesel is available locally, so these have to be transported from the Indian plains, over uncertain roads, at a huge cost. They are then stored at an even higher cost for the six or seven months that the passes are blocked.

Which is why, since 1981, I have been rooting for solar and wind electricity for Ladakh. There are more than 300 days of sunshine in a year. Wind is plentiful. Generation of electricity through both has been successfully demonstrated. The problem is of storage. How do we store for the night electricity generated from the sun? In car batteries? Too expensive and cumbersome.

In the 1990s the Stakna hydro- electric project was finally completed. It generates all of 4 megawatts of power. Kargil's 3.75 megawatt Iqbal Mini Hydel Project was commissioned in October 1995, but has not always functioned well.

Piped water: By 1995, as many as 102 villages in Leh and 126 in Kargil had been provided water connections.

I spent a whole year as the head of the Zâñskâr administration in 1981-82, and they couldn't provide piped water even to me. That's because water would freeze throughout the day for almost four months a year, and for a part of the day for another two. (In Leh town winter is slightly shorter.) Water pipes would crack because of this freezing or water would refuse to flow in them or both.

Therefore, please don't expect there to be actual water in these pipes throughout the year. (In Zâñskâr my *nono* [lit.: younger brother] would chop blocks of ice off the frozen river and melt them for me to drink, wash, bathe with, everything.)

Flushing toilets is an even bigger problem when temperatures drop below zero. The details are best left out. Suffice it to say that one stratagem is to pour a little kerosene after the water and set it on fire so that what goes down stays down.

How to get there/ When do the passes open?

By air: Leh town has an airport. There are flights to and from Delhi, Srinagar and Jammu. Sometimes there are flights to and from Chandigarh, Kargil has an airport but flights do not follow a fixed schedule.

On foot: Several trekking routes lead into Ladakh—from Kashmir (Anantnag and Srinagar districts), Jammu (Kishtwâr in Doda district), Himachal Pradesh (from Manali into Zâñskâr and Leh), Yarqand and Tibet. The route to Yarqand (Turkestan) is closed for reasons of security, as are all routes to Tibet. In the winters, snow blocks all trekking routes to and from Ladakh. (However, some routes within Ladakh remain open. The *chadar* and *kharas* routes to Zâñskâr open up for a few weeks each during the winter.)

By motorable road: Two motorable roads lead into Ladakh, one each from Kashmir and Himachal Pradesh. These are i) the National Highway from Srinagar (via the dZoji Lâ, Drâss and Kargil) and ii) the road from Manali in HP. The road from Srinagar gets blocked at the dZoji Lâ (pass) for around six to seven months every year. Thus, the Srinagar-dZoji Lâ-Leh road is open for five to five and a half months a year. The Manali- Leh road is open for an even briefer period i.e. between three and three and a half months a year.

A third motorable road exists, the one that leads from Leh to Kailash-Mansarovar in Tibet. However, it is in disuse because China does not allow Indians to use this all-weather road to go to Mansarovar. In 1994, at my request, the Government of India took the reopening of this road with China. There's a good chance that someday China will agree.)

The dZoji Lâ can get blocked as early as in the third week of October or as late as the last days of December. Engineers of the Indian Army try to keep the road open till the 15th November, even if there's been snow. After that, even if there is *no* snow you'll be using this pass at your own risk. (The rest of the road within Ladakh mostly remains open almost throughout the year. The dZoji Lâpass reopens in June[1] .

1. In 1998, 1999 and 2000 there was hardly any snow in winter. So the dZoji Lâ closed late and reopened much ahead of schedule.

(During the summers the roads to and within Ladakh behave better than does the Jammu-Srinagar National Highway, which gets blocked due to landslides whenever it rains heavily.)

So, air travel is your only option during the winters. The number of flights to Leh is far less than the number of people who want to go there. Therefore, getting air tickets is never easy, not even in the summers.

Apparently flying into Leh is extremely difficult for pilots, because of the clouds. As a result flights are often cancelled after you've even boarded the plane. Worse, sometimes they return to the base airport after flying more than half the distance.

Does that deter you? It shouldn't. Personally, I am grateful that in the last three decades of the 20th century it became possible at all to travel by aeroplane and automobile to the world's highest inhabited region. Before that the only way to go there was on foot or, maybe, on a pony. Cancelled flights are part of the adventure. After all it's not Disneyworld that we are going to.

(See also the chapter 'The Leh- Manali road.)

Tourism

Ladakh was opened to tourists in 1974, when 500 tourists- almost all of them foreigners- came visiting. The number went up to 24,000 in 1988. Thereafter, in 1990, the number of foreigners travelling to Ladakh through Kashmir suddenly plunged. It took almost a decade to get back to the 1988 level. By then the proportion of Indians travelling to Ladakh had gone up considerably, mainly thanks to the publicity we have been generating through the annual Ladakh (Tourism) Festival, which I introduced in 1993.

Before that the district administration would occasionally hold district level festivals. 1993 was the first year when we in the state government, through the Tourism Department headed by me, organised the Festival. We consciously chose to do so in the first fortnight of September. I chose these dates in order to extend the tourist season, which would otherwise start tapering off towards the end of August. My gamble paid off.

The tourist office in Leh is meant to help you with trekking routes and camping sites as well. Since 1998, the (state) Tourism department has been offering some rooms on rent at the 'Moonland' rest house (which is on the road between the airport and the town).

11

The Manali-Leh Road

The 474 km. Manali-Leh road remains open for just around three months in a year (mid-July to mid-September). Some people call it the 'Upshi-Manali road.' The landscape is barren and mostly uninhabited. There's just one place on this road, Tandi, where you can get petrol or diesel. It is between the Rohtang pass and Keylong. Do not expect hotels on the route either. However, during the tourist season, tented camps are put up at Sarchu, Pang and Brandi, where you can stay for a fee.

The road is good only for jeeps and that type of vehicle. The adventurous do it on motorcycles and bicycles, too. Buses are the cheapest. Coaches charge about 25% more than ordinary buses, per passenger. Gypsies/ Tata Sumos generally charge for the entire taxi around ten times the coach fare for a single passenger. The journey takes two days—about 12 hours on the first day and 10 on the next. Sarchu is the place that most people like to halt at for the intervening night. Tents with mattresses and quilts are available. So is food.

Details of the route: First, the all-important note of caution. This route is far more oxygen-starved and rugged than the dZoji Lâ route. Therefore, only the fit, the young and non-smokers should consider it.

The **Rohtang** is the first major pass on the road. It goes through the Pîr Panjal range of the Great Himalayas. Culturally we are now in Ladakh (though administratively we are still in Lahaul/ HP). The few houses that you will see have been built in the Ladakhi style—flat roofs, whitewashed walls and unbaked mud-bricks.

Gramphoo: This is a tri-junction. One road goes to Koksar-Leh and the other to Spiti.

Koksar: Lahaul begins here.

Sissu: This is the starting point for several treks.

Petrol, as mentioned, is available only at **Tandi**.

Keylong is the biggest 'town' on this road. It is the headquarters of the Lahaul-Spiti district. The road after Keylong travels along River Bhaga (which later becomes the Chenab), in the direction of its source. The Karding monastery is across the river.

Darchâ-Sumdo/ Jaspâ: This is the starting point for treks to Zâñskâr and the Shingo La. For the benefit of trekkers the Western Himalayan Mountaineering Institute has built a hostel at Jaspa.

The road winds uphill towards the **Bârâ Lachâ Lâ** pass (16,050'/ 4,892m.). A track from Spiti meets the main road at this pass. This is also where the Great Himalâyan Range is crossed. Travellers have used this pass for centuries precisely for this reason. The pass is also the watershed between the Chenab and the Indus rivers. We are now well above the tree line and into the bleak and rugged desert. Lake Yunân Tso is in the north.

The Zâñskâr range follows. The next two passes, the Lachalung Lâ (also spelt Lachulung) and the Tanglung Lâ (also spelt Taglang), enable us to cross this range. The Tanglung Lâ is the highest point on this road. The expanse between the two passes is almost entirely made up of rock, sand and twirling dust. The only people who live here- and that for a few months every year- are the Chang-pa nomads. Their sheep live off the few patches of green to be found. A few tents and tea stalls are set up during the season to cater to tourists.

It is mostly downhill after the Tanglung Lâ. Rumtse will be the first human habitation after the pass. The road now runs along River Gya, till it reaches Upshi village, where it meets the Indus. It goes past the Karu, Stakna, Thiksey, Shey and Choglamsar villages before reaching Leh town.

12

Leh and Kargil: Motorable routes

Road distances and routes

From	To	The route	See the Section/chapter on	Dist. in Km.
Pangong, Chushul	Dungti	Via the Chhaga La	'The Pangong-Dungti route.'	93
Kargil	Zâñskâr	Kargil, Suru Valley, Rangdum, Penzi La, Sani, Padam	'The Suru Valley' and 'Zâñskâr'	240
Kargil	Rangdum		'The Suru Valley.'	130
Kargil	Penzila	Suru Valley		160
Leh	Kargil	Leh, Khaltse, Lama Yuru, Fatu La, Namika La, Mulbek, Kargil	'The National Highway: *Leh to Kargil*' and 'The Leh-Kargil National Highway'	221
Leh	Pangong, Chushul	Leh, Chang La, Pangong Lake, Chushul	'Leh-Changthang-Tsomo Riri' covers some of this route.	198
Leh	Tsomo Riri	Leh, Upshi, Kurzok	'Leh-Changthang-Tsomo Riri'	215
Leh	The Rupshu Circular Route	Leh, Upshi, Sumdo, Pologongka pass, Debring, Upshi, Leh		360
Leh	Hanle, Demchok (Tibet border)	Leh, Upshi, Byoma, Loma, Dungti, Hanle, Demchok. (The road to Mansarovar, in Tibet, lies beyond.)	'Leh-Changthang-Tsomo Riri' covers much of this route.	336
Leh	Nubra (Panamik)	Leh, Khardung La, Khalsar, Panamik, Sasoma	'Nubra' covers much of this route.	165
Leh	Shyok Valley	Leh, Khardung La, Khalsar, Diskit, Hunder	'Nubra' covers some of this route.	124

Manali	Leh	Via three major passes: Rohtang, Bârâ Lachâ and Tanglang	'The Manali-Leh Road'	473
Rang-dum	Padam (Zâñskâr)	Via Penzila	'Zâñskâr.'	80
Srinagar	Leh	Srinagar, Sonamarg, dZoji La, Drass, Kargil, Khaltse, Leh	'The National Highway...'	423
Srinagar	Kargil	Srinagar, Sonamarg, dZoji La, Drass, Kargil	'The National Highway: *Srinagar to Kargil'* and The Kargil-Srinagar National Highway'	203

Leh district: Motorable routes

The routes have been arranged in the alphabetical order of the final destination, Leh town being common to all the routes. Routes within Leh town come first. All distances are in kilometres.

Leh town: on foot etcetra

(The first column has the cumulative distance and the second column the distance from the place last mentioned.)

i) The airport to the main bazar

(This section is best done in an automobile.)

0.0	0.0	The main road at the exit of the airport.
0.4	0.4	(Side road on left to Doordarshan, the national television)
1.2	0.8	(Side road on right to Agling.)
2.1	0.9	(Tourist Reception Centre on the left.)
2.2	0.1	Major tri-junction.
		(Right: Karu, Upshi, Manali, Stok, Hemis, Pangong, Tsomo Riri, etc.)
		Straight: Leh town, Nubra. We go straight.
3.1	0.9	(Bus terminus on the left.) The road travels uphill.
3.2	0.1	(Another road branches off to the bus stand, left.)
3.6	0.4	Crossroads.
		Right, straight ahead: Pologround, Leh Palace, Festival venue and important offices.
		Right (straight and, a few metres later, sharp right): To Nubra.
		Straight (left): To the main bazar. We go straight.
4.1	0.5	Straight ahead: Old road. No entry for vehicles.
		Right: The main bazar continues. We turn right.
4.4	0.3	The Jama Masjid is in front of us.
		The road turns left and the main bazar continues.
4.6	0.2	Tri-junction.
		Left, behind us: The Subzi Mandi.
		Right: The Zâñgsty road. We turn right.

4.7	0.1	Tri-junction. Turn left to go to Changspa. (See also 'The Circuit House to the Airport'.) The Changspâ area ends at the steps that lead to the Shanti Stupa, which is 1.2km. from here.

ii) The Circuit House to the Airport

(This essentially is a reversal of the 'Airport to main bazar' route. It is necessary to give this route separately because at times vehicular traffic in Leh is one-way. Besides, not all directions can be automatically reversed.

0.0	0.0	The Circuit House
0.2	0.2	LEDG (Ladakh Ecological Development Group)
0.25	0.05	Tri-junction. Left: The Sankar gompa. Right: The main market (and, beyond it, the Airport, Hemis, Srinagar, Kargil, Pangong, Tso Moriri etc.) We turn right.
0.4	0.15	Tri-junction Right: Changspa. Straight: The main market. We go straight. We ignore the minor side lane on the left a few metres later.
0.5	0.1	(Right: Side road to Upper Tukcha.)
0.52	0.02	(Right: Side road to Leh Fort.)
0.6	0.08	Major tri-junction. (Food Affair German Baker on left.) Left: Main market. Right: Subzi Mandi. We go right.
0.7	0.1	Crossroads. Straight ahead: Library Road. Left: The Main market (uphill). Right: The Leh Fort Road. We go left.
0.8	0.1	Straight: Main market ('no entry' for vehicles on certain days). Right: Taxi Stand. We take the road on the right.
1.0	0.2	Left: The main market, uphill. Right: Leh Old Road. We turn left.
1.1	0.1	Major tri-junction. Left: Main bazar. Right: Main bazar: this road leads to the airport. We turn right.
1.6	0.5	Major tri-junction. Left: To the polo ground. Right: To the airport (downhill). We go right.
2.2	0.6	(Right: Side lane to the bus terminus.) (Right: The Government Arts [Handicrafts] Emporium.)
2.4	0.2	(Left: All India Radio.)
2.6	0.2	(Right: The Sonam Narboo Memorial Hospital.)
2.8	0.2	(Left: The Navodaya Vidyalaya.)
3.0	0.2	Left: Petrol pump. Straight: The airport. Right (behind): The Leh Old Road

		Right (sharp right): Sakara Village and the Zorâwar Fort. We go straight.
3.1	0.3	Major intersection.
		Left: Choglamsar. Stok, Hemis, Pangong, Tsomo Riri, Manali, etc.
		Straight ahead: The airport, Kargil, Srinagar. We go straight.
5.3	2.2	Left: The airport.

iii) From the Zâñgsty/ main bazar tri-junction to Changspâ and the Shanti Stupa.

Changspâ is where the inexpensive guest houses, and some mid-market hotels, are.

0.0	0.0	The tri-junction (This is 4.7 point on route 'i' and 0.4 on route 'ii' above.) You have to turn left and right, repectively, on the above mentioned routes, at this point.
0.1	0.1	The Moravian Mission, right.
0.5	0.4	The road curves left. On the right is a lane leading to the Army's Alpha Mess. We turn left, with the road. We are in the Changspâ area.
1.2	0.7	The Changspâ road ends in a perpendicular.
		Left: To the Army Cantonment and the (Army's) General Hospital (GH).
		Right: Road to the Shanti Stupa, Nubra, the Sankar Monastery and the Lamdon School.
		Straight ahead: Steps lead uphill to the Shanti Stupa.

Leh-Hanle-Demchok

(Entries in **boldface** indicate that there are more details about those places elsewhere in this book.)

0	**Leh**
46	Upshi
146	Mahe
168	**Nyoma**
188	Dungti: Two roads emerge from here. One leads westwards to Hanle, and the other goes south to Demchok. *See 140/288 on "The Pangong-Chushul-Dungti route."*
214	Rongo
262	**Hanle**
280	Photi La
296	Koyul
310	Gankial La. A village on the old trade route to Tibet. Caravans would halt here.
336	Demchok: This is the last Indian administered village. Beyond it is Tibet. The road from here leads to the sacred Lake Mansarovar.

The Pangong-Chushul-Dungti route

Km.	*Continued from the end of the 'Karu-Pangong route.'* (below)
0/ 148	The Pangong Lake.
47/ 195	Chushul.
93/ 241	The Chhaga La.
115/ 263	The Loma bridge (on the Indus). This is a major crossroad. The Leh-Nyoma-Demchok road meets here.
140/ 288	Dungti: Two roads emerge from here. One leads westwards to Hanle, and the other goes south to Demchok. (after which the areas occupied by China begin)

The Manali-Leh route

0	Manali
	The Vashisht Hot Springs
	Marhi
52	The Rohtang Pass (13,000'/ 3,978m.)
71	Koksar (Chandra River).
107	Tandi ***(petrol!)***. Road junction. The other road leads to Udaipur.
115	Keylong
145	Darcha Sumdo
189	Bârâ Lachâ La
222	Sarchu *(night halt?)*
	The Lingti Plains
	The Tsarap Chu river
276	The Lachalung Lâ pass (16,900'/ 5,059m.)
298	Pang
364	The Tanglung Lâ pass (17,582'/ 5,325m.)
424	Upshi
	Thiksey
	Shey
	Choglamsar
470	Leh

Nubra: Nubra valley (Leh-Panamik)

0	**Leh**
25	South Polu. The ascent begins.
39	Khardung La. The highest motorable place in the world.
71	Khardung village.
95	Khalsar. Tri-junction. The road to the west goes along River Shyok. Durbuk is in this direction. (See **'Pangong Lake.'**) The northern road follows River Nubra. We go north.
106	Tirit.
128	**Sumur**
130	**Teggar**
150	**Panamik**
165	Sasoma

Nubra: Shyok valley (Leh-Hunder)

0	**Leh**
95	Khalsar. Tri-junction. We take the road that heads west.
118	**Deskit**
124	**Hunder**

The Karu-Pangong route

Km.	*Continued from km.35.1 of the 'The Leh-Châñgthâñg-Tsomo Riri route below.*
0/ 35	Karu
43/ 78	The Chang La (pass) top: 5288m. A young, but unfit, man in his early thirties and a middle aged lady in my team fainted when our bus went through the pass. After the pass the oxygen content gets better when the road descends towards a valley.
74/ 109	Durbuk: A village at the northern tip of the valley.
81/ 116	Tangtse: The last village before the lake. Some accommodation is available.
113/ 148	The Pangong Lake.

The Rupshu Circular route

0	Leh
146	Mahe bridge. Crossroads. The main road leads to Nyoma. We take the side road to Pologongka La and the Tsomo Riri. *See 160.9km of "The Leh-Châñgthâñg-Tsomo Riri route."*
170	Sumdo: hot-water springs. Crossroads. We take the road that goes west. The other road leads to the Tsomo.
179	Pologongka La: The eponymous peak can be seen from here. The road goes down in the direction of Lake Startsapuk and then along the Tso Kar.
216	Debring. Tri-junction. The **Manali-Leh road** bifurcates from here.
250	Tanglang La
279	Rumtse
296	Miru
310	Upshi. Major crossroad. The **Manali-Leh road** leads south, across the Indus. The road in the east leads to Chumathang and Nyoma.
356	Leh

Leh-Srinagar (The National Highway)

(See 'Leh-Kargil' and 'Kargil-Srinagar,' both under 'Kargil district: Motorable routes.')

Leh-Srinagar (The Treaty High Road)

The old Treaty High Road is much the same as the present Srinagar-Leh National Highway. Please note that distances have been given in miles for this historic route alone. 1 mile= 1.6km.

Miles	
0	Srinagar
12.5	Ganderbal
24	Kangan
37	Gund
51.5	Sonamarg
60.5	Baltal; people used to camp at Kani Pather at Mile 64; there was a dak shelter at Mile 64.5.
	dZoji La, 11,578'
75.5	Matâyan, 10,430'
88	Drass, 10,144'
95	Shimsa Kharbu, 9,250'
110	Kargil, 8,790'
132	Mulbek ('Maulba Chamba'), 10,500'
	Namika La, 12,200'
146.5	Bodh Kharbu, 11,200'
	Fotu La, 13,432'
161	Lama Yuru, 11,300'
179	Nyurla, 9,900'
193	Saspol, 10,200'
204	Nimu, 10,250'
232	Leh, 11,200'

The Leh-Chânĝthânĝ-Tsomo Riri route

Km.	
0	**Leh** town: major tri-junction. You are roughly at the '1.6km.' point of route (ii) above.
1.7	The same tri-junction. Straight ahead are the airport, Kargil and Srinagar. Turn left.
2.3	The Government Degree College, Leh
6.6	**Choglamsar**
7.6	The side road on the left leads to Tashi Thongsmon.
7.7	The Central Institute of Buddhist Studies
8.1	The major road on the right leads to **Stok.**
9.9	**Shey**: the Sindhu Darshan (lit. 'Behold the Indus') festival *ghat* (riverbank). The said festival takes place here.
13.8	The Shey palace (left)
14.0	The Shey gompâ (left)
16.1	**Thiksey** begins.
18.1	Thiksey monastery (left)
18.7	Road to the monastery
21.1	Path to the Nyirma gompâ (left)
24.3	Road to the **Stakna** monastery (left)
30.3	Stakna hydro-electric project

35.1	Karu: crossroads (There is a restaurant here.)
	Left (uphill): Tangtse, Sâkti, Pangong (*See 'The Karu-Pangong route.'*)
	Right: Manali, Upshi, Hemis, Tsomo Riri
	Take the road on the right.
36.1	Crossroads
	Right: To **Hemis** (6.9km./ 12minutes away; the road is quite bad for the first 3km.)
	Left To Tsomo Riri
	Take the road on the left.
40.7	Igu (saandy desert)
49.1	Major crossroads (with several restaurants)
	Right (across the bridge): Upshi (1.6km. away), Manali, Sarchu
	Left: Nyoma, Changthâñg, Tsomo Riri
	Take the road on the left.
50.7	The Changthâñg area begins. Upshi is across the river on the right.
58.0	In this area (called Shara) you can sight thick- tailed foxes even around 2pm.
69.6	Likché
76.8	Rani Bagh. Grove on the left. Cross over to the other bank of River Indus here.
80.1	Hémyâ (also Hamya). Village and monastery. There are wild flowers in spring and summer. Good for rock climbing.
80.6	Cross the Indus again, to return to the previous bank.
109.0	(The bridge and side road on the right lead to Kiari, ignore it.)
121.6	Nurnis/ Nee. (Restaurant. VCDs available on rent.)
139.1	Chumathâñg: the hot water springs are on the right. The springs are set amidst a small, moist, grassy patch. Fortunately no one has tried to enclose them within masonry. Their boiling waters leap upwards at several points. There's plenty of steam near the springs, which are ten or fifteen metres away from the road.
	A track from here leads to **Chushul.** The tall peak in the northeast is the Chakula.
139.7	(The side road on the left, uphill, leads to the village. So we take the lower road, right.)
160.9	Mahé bridge (right). From here it is 23km. to Nyoma, 43km. to Loma, 49km. to Rongo and 70km. to Dibiring. Pologongka La can be approached from here.
	Left, uphill: To Nyoma.
	Take the road on the right, i.e. cross the Indus. You need to give your 'inner line permit' to the sentry at the bridge. The 'road' is now a mud track.
172.6	Crossroads.
	Left, uphill: To Kurzok.
	Right, below: To Pûgâ and Sumdo (i.e. Sumdo Yogma). Puga/ Sumdo have famous hot-water springs.

Take the road on the left. You will almost certainly see marmots in season.

175.1 Sumdo Kangmo

190.3 Another stretch of sandy desert

192.7 Lake Thâchung (Tazang) Karu has been close to the road for the last kilometre or two. This point and km. 195.6 are about the closest that the road gets to this fairly large lake, which is more than twice as big as, say, the Naini Tal of Uttaranchal.

Ignore the mud track on the right, uphill. Take the road on the left, the one that goes towards the lake. (In this, and the next two directions, I have suggested that certain roads on the right be ignored. In 2004, a major road is being built on the right, almost parallel to the mud track. Therefore, some day that might be the more comfortable road to take. However, you can't go wrong with the directions about taking the road on the left.)

196.1 Ignore the road on the right, below. Take the road on the left, uphill.

199.3 Ignore the road on the right, below. Take the road on the left.

199.4 On the right is a large, permafrost ice-field. When its waters melt, they flow towards the Tsomo Riri. The stream that the melting waters form runs along the 'road.'

199.6 We get our first glimpse of the Tsomo, straight ahead, framed between two mountains.

204.9 Tented colony of **Changpa** tribals, mostly on the left. They live in some eight or nine ugly tents made of canvas or polythene. Plastic has reached other parts of their lives, too—their shoes, for instance. Their picturesque old tents and shoes are gone. On the 6th July the Tibetan nomads celebrate the Dalai Lama's birthday at a small lake a few kilometres from here. This is a seven-day festival.

209.0 The road finally draws close to the lake. There is an island near this point, referred to as 'km. 209' in the entry on Tsomo Riri.

214.0 The road starts pulling away from the lake.

215.1 Kurzok (the village closest to Tsomo Riri; where the guest houses are). From here you can trek westwards to Lahual (HP) or southwards to the Parang La.

Kargil district: Motorable routes

The Leh-Kargil National Highway

Km.	
0	Leh (Sonam Narbu Memorial Hospital, right)
0.1	Leh (Kendriya Vidyalaya, left)
0.6	Leh (Tourist Reception Centre, left)
2.3	Leh (Airport, left)
2.8	Leh (Moonland guest house, left)

6.1	A side road on the left climbs up, towards a hillock and a gompa.
8.1	Artificial lake, created by Army Engineers, on the left.
10.1	Side road to Phey, left below.
13.6	Side road to Pheyang, right.
23.3	Gurudwara Srî Patther Sâheb, Nimmu, right (on the highway itself).
33.0	Side road to Nimmu gompa, right.
33.9	Nimmu village
37.2	Large chorten; mânéy wall begins.
37.7	Mânéy wall ends
38.5	Basgo/ Bazgo
41.5	Side road to the Maitreya temples, right.
58.7	Saspol
62.1	Ignore the bridge and road left below. Proceed straight.
83.1	Side road to Temisgam, right.
85.2	Nurla
94.9	Khaltse bridge
95.2	Khaltse (automobile fuel available)
97.5	Major road branches off to the right, uphill, to Batâlik (74km. from this point), Da, Garkon and Baima. We go left, downhill.
102.8	Direct road, right, uphill to Lama Yûrû. We go straight ahead and take the bypass.
114.0	Lama Yûrû is to the right, above.
115.3	A road from the Lama Yûrû monastery meets the bypass here.
117.0	The bypass meets the direct Lama Yûrû road, which comes up from behind, right.
130.0	Fatu Lâ/ 13,479'
136.7	Small village. (Heniskut is 3km. from here.)
149.6	Path to Bodh Kharbu, right.
157.1	Major road to Bodh Kharbu, right, downhill.
176.6	Nâmikâ Lâ/ 12,198'
178.4	Wâkhâ (On a summer's night you can expect to sight at least half a dozen foxes between Wakha and Mulbek.)
180.9	Mulbek (Tourist Bungalow)
181.6	Mulbek (The Chamba statue.)
219.1	Kargil (The famous Zâñskâr/ Srinagar/ Leh crossroad)
220.3	Kargil (The main bazar; at this point there is a major side road on the left that leads uphill to the Tourist Bungalow and some of the better hotels.)

The Kargil-Srinagar National Highway

0	Kargil (The main bazar; at this point there is a major side road on the left that leads uphill to the Tourist Bungalow and some of the better hotels.) We go straight ahead.
23.7	The Shimsa Kharbu Wildlife Sanctuary is on the left.
55.8	Stekbu: ancient sculptures smack next to the highway, on the right
56.25	Side path to Goshan and Sando, on the left.
56.6	Umba wildlife sanctuary, left.
	Road to Sankoo, also left.
56.9	Drâss/ 10,660'
57.3	Drâss: Side road to Goshan, right. (This is the preferred road to Goshan: shorter and better maintained.)
57.4	Drâss (Outside the Tourist Bungalow.) (The Stekbu sculptures are are, thus, exactly 1.6km. from the gates of the TB.)
58.2	Side road to Braknak and Goshan, right.
58.4	Bridge and river. The Mushkoo valley is on the right. The river that comes down from the mountains on the right is River Mushkoo.
58.5	Side road to Murâd Bagh and Mushkoo, right.
59.3	Bridge and the confluence of rivers.
69.6	Pandrâss
75.7	Draupadi Kund, right.
77.3	Matâyan
82.8	Meenamarg. The uphill climb begins.
94.2	Gumri. The dZoji Lâ pass begins. (On the left is a path that leads to the holy Shri Amarnathji Cave.)
95.7	The bad portion of the road begins. Half way through the pass, Ladakh ends and Kashmir begins.
109.7	End of the bad portion of the road.
115.6	The dZoji Lâ pass ends.
119.6	Bridge over a confluence of rivers.
120.0	Sonamarg area begins.
122.2	Side road to the Thajawas glacier, left.
123.0	Sonamarg area ends.
163.0	Kangan
166.7	Side road to Nârâ Nâg, right.
180.6	Gânderbal
202.5	Srinagar: Lâl Chowk.

13

Leh District

Leh has traditionally been known for its rugged landscapes, some of the highest mountains in the world and gompas. As a result Western tourists have taken to Leh in a big way. In 2001, they voted Ladakh the second best attraction in India, after Agra. The Ladakhis, in turn, have used tourism very intelligently. Far from letting it ruin their heritage, they have used tourism to keep their culture alive. This is best seen in the architecture of their hotels, which are not poor imitations of Delhi's 'modern' houses (which in turn are kitsch copies of the West). Ladakhi hotels, and most of their modern houses, have been built in Ladakh's own architectural tradition. During the Ladakh Festival everyone dresses in the Ladakhi style. Indeed, the festival has led to a revival of many of Ladakh's dying traditions.

Leh, thus, is a unique example of an Indian region that has been able to benefit from modernity without losing its own traditions. The 2001 census revealed that Leh had emerged as the third most literate of the State's fourteen districts, ahead even of Srinagar.

Travelling within Ladakh: *Buses:* Buses are available from Leh for Kargil, Srinagar, Nubra, Manali and several places within Leh district. *Taxis:* Taxis are extremely expensive in Ladakh. Jeeps are dearer still and 'jongas' the costliest. That's because those high altitudes and bad roads tend to wear vehicles out fast and because all automobiles do far fewer kilometres per litre of fuel and because of an oligopoly. Despite that, taxis are the preferred mode of inter-village transport for tourists.

Where to stay: The people of Leh and Zâñskâr have taken to tourism like few other people in India. This is perhaps the only region where guest-houses have really taken root. People spruce up the best rooms of their houses, add western-style toilets and rent them out inexpensively. This has happened not just in Leh town but also in the villages. A very large number of hotels, too, have sprung up. This is the only part of the state (indeed, of India) where there was no pressure on the government to set up (ultimately unprofitable) public sector hotels. In fact, the owners of private hotels have asked the government not to step in. However, since 1998, a small government guest house, the *Moonland*, has been functioning near the Leh airport, in the direction of the town.

Outside Leh town: There are government-run, excellent value for money, inexpensive tourist bungalows at Khaltse, Sâkti and Saspol. Khaltse also has a PWD Rest House, but mainly for government servants. There are guest houses in all the important villages of Leh. (See the 'Appendix.')

Camping equipment: Apart from what the private sector might have in stock, the Tourist Officer, Leh has some sleeping bags, quilted jackets and other equipment to be hired out to tourists for a small fee.

Medical facilities: There is a district hospital at Leh, and dispensaries at Chachot, Khaltse, Sâkti, Saspol and Thiksey.

Foreign exchange: You can change money at the main branches of the State Bank of India and the Jammu & Kashmir Bank in Leh town.

Places of tourist interest

(Gompas are among the main attractions of Ladakh. They have been listed in the chapter 'The important gompas of Ladakh'.

(Places on the National Highway between Leh and Kargil have been listed in the chapter 'The highway: Leh to Kargil…' However, except for places with primitive and mediæval rock carvings, that chapter has relatively few details.

(All distances given below are from Leh town. Please allow for an error of up to ±2 km. because it all depends on where you measure from.)

Basgo: 39-42 km. downstream from and west of Leh. Also spelt Bazgo. It is famous for its ancient fort, which overlooks the only route into the Indus valley.

History: As will be seen in the chapter 'A History of Leh', Basgo is steeped in history. It was the capital of lower Ladakh (Basgo and Tingmosgang), when the region was partitioned around the 14th century. The earliest reference to Basgo in the *Ladakh Chronicles* is about the 15th century when it was the capital of King Grags-Pâ-'bum (who apparently was the same as Drags-pa bum-Lde). Some scholars feel that Basgo is probably an old Dard name. The village has a different name in the Tibetan language, which means the Divine Peak of Great Stability.

Trags-bum-de's grandson, Bhagan, reunited central (Leh-Shey) and lower (Basgo-Tingmosgang) Ladakh. He also founded the Namgyâl dynasty. This must have happened towards the end of the 15th century or early in the 16th.

The Portuguese merchant Diogo d'Almeira (or Almeida), the first European to write about Ladakh, visited Ladakh around AD 1600. He wrote that Basgo was the capital of Ladakh.

Later, the Basgo line of Namgyâls shifted to Leh. However, one branch of the Namgyâl line remained at Basgo, which is why the fort and the nearby Maitreya Temple continued to be in fairly good condition. King Tsewang Namgyâl built the temple in the 16th century. The monastery is atop a very tall rock. Murals and other artworks dating to the 16th century can still be seen.

Around AD 1680, the Tibetans, in alliance with the Mongols, laid siege to Basgo. The siege lasted three years till the Mughals came to the Ladakhis' rescue by sending in an army. Snellgrove and Skorupski call the Basgo fort 'certainly the most impressive of Ladakh's citadels despite its ruined state.' They rightly argue that 'in earlier times [the fort] must have been also well-nigh impregnable, as was illustrated by the three-year siege that it withstood.'

One reason why the Ladakhis could hold out for three years is that the fort then received water throughout the year, unusual for a desert.

The Namgyâl line that moved to Leh founded the dynasty that ruled much of Ladakh till the Dogras annexed the region for the Sikhs. Indeed, it was at Basgo that, in 1835, the Dogra General Zorâwar Singh formalised Sikh suzerainty.

The area: The nearby Chargyâl Thâñg is famous for its huge *chortens* and *mâney* walls. King Sengge Namgyâl had got the *mâney* constructed. (A *thâñg* is a plateau.) Basgo itself is in a hollow. Therefore, you have to descend from the arid, grassless Thâñg to the fertile and, thus, populous hollow. There are fields and fruit bearing trees, as well as a cluster of Buddhist monuments. The old polo ground (*shagharan*) has been in disuse since at least the nineteenth century.

The Basgo Rabtan Chartse-khar (or Rafstan Larchey-khar) (fort and palace): This legendary 16th century fort is made of unbacked clay bricks. It is now in ruins. Kings Jamyang Namgyâl and Sengge Namgyâl built it. Within the ruined fort are two large temples and a shrine, all with images of the Maitreya. The tallest of these, the Chambâ Lhâ Khang dates to the 16th century. It, was built by King Tsewang Namgyâl.

The highest tower of the fort has a *lhato* (altar). Writer Tashi Morup says that it 'appears to guard the three [above mentioned] shrines.'

The village is on the right bank of the Indus. Being in a hollow, it is the warmest winter residence in Ladakh. Which could be why it traditionally was the capital of lower Ladakh.

In the village there is an economy class guest house, the *Lagang*.

Choglamsar: A post-1960 suburb of Leh town. This area includes a Tibetan refugee settlement as well as educational and research institutes connected with Buddhism and Tibetology. It is known for its high-altitude plants and fragrant flowers. It is a good starting point for river-rafting.

In the village there are three economy class guest houses, the *Lhâsâ*, the *Buddha Garden* (ph. 44074) and the *Khangsar*.

Chumâthâng: See 'Hanle' in this section, below.

Chushul: 195km. This is a little village in a picturesque valley. The areas occupied by China are very close, in the east. Chushul is best known for the bloody battles of 1962. Its main landmark is 'India Gate,' a memorial to Indian soldiers. It has a low hillock, from atop which can be seen Lake Spanggur, in the Chinese-occupied territory.

Gaik: See 'Hanle' in this section, below.

Gurudwara: See 'Patther Sâheb' below.

Hanlé-Tsomo Riri-Chumâthâng-Nyomâ-Pûgâ: This is a vast, sparsely populated, desolate, desert belt in southeastern Leh, near India's border with Tibet. *Tsomo Riri* is a celebrated lake (see the section on 'Lakes' in this chapter).

Places on the road to Nyoma

The Kesar caves near **Chumâthâng** are the best- known landmark of that village. Some of these caves are two-storeyed. They are on the right bank of the Indus and on the route that leads to Nyoma.

Down the same road, in the direction of Nyoma, is a place called **Nor Nis**. Here old rock engravings have been found. Themes depicted include the usual hunters and ibexes, as well as yaks. What make these drawings unique (and significant) are the figures of camels and conical huts. Both are unknown in flat-roofed Ladakh. (See the chapter on 'Nubra' for Bactrian camels and how they got left behind in Ladakh.)

Gaik is the next major archæological site on this route. Traces of a pre-historic village were discovered here. The boulders here have engravings of ibexes and wild goats.

Kungyum is a village that occurs before Nyoma. Ruins of a Dard castle were found here, atop a massive rock. Boulders near the river have engravings of ibexes and wild goats.

Between Nyoma and Hanlé

Wild asses are the biggest attraction of these desert plains. Some rocks in this stretch have the figures of animals (ibexes, horses and yaks) as well as humans engraved on them.

Near **Nyoma**, at a place called **Rong**, are the ruins of an ancient settlement. It must have been a Dard village, because the Dards had lived in that area. However, some scholars say that the Mons might have lived here.

Hanle has a small gompa of the red hat sect atop a hillock. King Sengge Namgyâl got the mâney constructed. Hanlé has traditionally been known for its wild asses, birds and enormous plains. Now this tiny village is famous because it has the world's highest-located astronomical observatory. Much of its population consists of very poor Tibetan refugees. They simply crossed over from the other side of the border. (Tibetan refugees in Leh are better off and more enterprising. They came in through Delhi and, perhaps, Darjeeling.)

Pûgâ-Tsomo Riri

To reach this stretch you might need to cross River Indus at Myâ. Pûgâ is a valley known for its hot-water springs. Dr. Mani notes that boulders with engravings have been found near Pûgâ, near Kidwang and at the Tso Kar (salt lake). Kidwang is on the north-western side of the Tsomo Riri.

Kungyum: See 'Hanle' in this section, above.

Nor Nis: See 'Hanle' in this section, above.

Nubra: See the chapter on 'Nubra.'

Nyomâ: See 'Hanle' in this section, above.

Patther Sâheb: 24.5 km., on the highway national, in the direction of Kargil-Srinagar. This is a gurudwara, attributed to the sixth Sikh Guru.

Pûgâ: See 'Hanle' in this section, above.

rGyâ: There used to be an ancient Mon fort here. The gompâ has been built atop some of the ruins of that fort.

Sâbû: (See the 'Leh-Khalsar' trek.) *The Changal Khar fort:* Lha Chen Sherab (14th century AD) got this fort constructed. It is now in ruins. The mediæval Singay Zagâng village came up around the fort.

108 chortens: Lha Chen Thî-sug Lde got them constructed.

Sâkti: (Around 45km. from Leh. Near Chemray and Taktak.) There are ancient rock engravings as well as the ruins of a Mon fort at Sâkti.

Saspol: 62 km. before Leh on the Srinagar-Kargil-Leh highway. Saspol is on the right bank of River Indus and is famous for apricots. It has always been a halting place on the Srinagar-Leh route. The *Gazetteer* notes, 'At the end of June the river here was about 100 yards wide and unfordable.'

The village is known for its caves and for being near the Alchi monastery, which is 5 km. away. Likir, too, is close by.

Shey: 15 km. to the south/ upstream from Leh. Shey is where the first known king of Ladâkh set up his capital. Through much of history Shey, rather than the Leh town, was the capital of most of Ladakh. Then for a while it was the capital of just Maryul-Stot. This was before the reign of Gyapo Tsewang Namgyâl I (16th century).

Even after the capital shifted to Leh, in the 17th century, it was Shey that the kings thought of as home. Whenever a pregnant queen was thought to be carrying the heir appraent, she would be sent to Shey so that the prince was born at the ancestral home. Shey's pre-eminent position in old Leh can also be seen from the very large number of chortens there, especially near the palace.

Fort: The hilltop Shey fort that we see today, above the palace, was possibly built before the Tibetans migrated to and started ruling Ladakh. Lhâ Chen sPal Gyi Gon (990-1020), king of Guge, is believed to have got the fortress built. Much of what we see today is a tenth century AD structure.

Palace: King Deldan Namgyâl built this palace, around 1650. Inside the palace there is a three-storey, 7.5 metre, idol of Lord Buddha, perhaps the largest of its kind in Ladakh. This is the Sakya Muni Buddha, seated. The idol is made of copper and brass and plated with gold and silver. It is studded with gems and precious stones. There is no other statue of this kind anywhere in Ladâkh.

King Sengge Namgyâl (the 17th century) probably got this idol built. Some historians say that sPal Gyi Gon's father, the great Nemagon (c. 975), had got a sculpture executed at Leh. Could it be this? Other historians feel that King Deldan had built this idol, in honour of his father, Sengge.

The palace has the largest victory stupâ in Ladakh, the top of which is made of pure gold. Since this was mostly a summer palace, it used to be surrounded by a fine garden, much of which is still intact. The royal family shifted to Stok in 1834. Since then the palace has been in disuse, hence its poor condition. The small artificial lake below the palace has become a marsh. It is believed that it served the same function as a moat.

The Dresthang Monastery: Thiksey controls this monastery, and the hundreds of chortens near it. The Dresthang monastery is 'exclusive' in the sense that you need permission to enter it. So, please contact the head lâmâ in advance. It was built during the reign of Sengge Namgyâl.

The Dhyâni Buddhas: Shey has 11th century rock carvings of five standing Dhyâni Buddhas, also known as the Pañch Tathâgat. They are below the palace and can be seen from the road. In dating them to the 11th century, I have the authority of archæologist BR Mani. It is difficult to agree with accounts that date these carvings to Sengge's reign, let alone Deldan's (both mostly 17th century). SS Girgan says that this probably is the oldest known sculpture in Ladâkh. At least he rules out the Sengge/ Deldan theory. However, the engravings at Hunder and the sculptures at Kartse Khar and Mulbek date to between the 6th and 8th centuries. If we go along with Girgan then either the Shey Buddhas are older than that or the sculptures at these other places are not as old as Snellgrove, Skorupski and Mani say they are.

Mosque: Mir Syed Ali Hamadani is said to have built the small mosque of Shey. This would have been around AD 1381. He was a Sunni. And yet most of the Muslims of Shey are Shias. Kachu Sikander Khan's theory is that the mosque was built by the sultans of Kashmir in the fifteenth century around the time that they invaded Ladâkh. He adds that according to a local tradition the Shah of Hamadan had offered prayers at this mosque. The dates of the Shah's travels have been recorded quite accurately. Therefore, either the legend about his having performed the *namaz* here is wrong, or the mosque had been built at least by the 14th century.

Hotels: In the village there's a D class hotel, the *Shelkar* (phone: 47061), and two medium class guest houses, the *Deldan* and the *Akhoon*.

Siachen: See the chapter on 'Siachen.'

Târo: Some inscriptions have been found here. They probably date to the reign of Lha Chen Lha Rgyâl (13th century AD).

Temisgâm: (See the 'Leh-Kargil National Highway.')

Tingmosgang: 92km. from Leh. This historic village is famous for the treaty signed here. Its main attraction is its 15th century palace. *The Tingmosgâng palace:* Dragspâ Bum Lde, King of Sham (15th centuryAD), got the palace constructed. It was the seat of government of the Kings of Sham from the time that Ladâkh was partitioned till the reign of Gyapo Tsewang Namgyâl I.

The palace was built by Dragspâ Bum, the younger brother of Dragspâ Bum Lde, King of the Sham region of Leh. It is surrounded by fortifications.

The village is located in a valley on the trekking route between Khaltse and Likir.

There is a guest house in Tingmosgang, the *Namra*. Prices are not low at all.

Wânlâ: King Lhâ Chen Nuklok (12th century AD) is said to have built the Wanla fort, now in ruins.

Rivers

The Indus is the principal river of Ladakh and travels south to POK and Pakistan. However, before it leaves India it is joined by the rivers Suru, Shyok and Zâñskâr

Lakes

'Tso' means 'lake.'

Chang Chenmo: This is a large lake in northwest Ladâkh. Streams from the surrounding mountains, especially the northern slopes of the Karakoram Range, feed it. It has no outlet. Therefore, its water is brackish.

Lingzi Tang: This large lake is near Ladâkh's northwestern border with Tibet. It is near the southern mountains of the Karakoram Range. When snow melts on the mountains around the lake the water thus formed turns into streams. These streams flow into the Lingzi Tang. Its water is brackish.

Pangong Tso/ Lake: (13,936 feet[1] .) Also called Tso Monanglari ('the lake of the great hollow'). This L- shaped lake is around 148 km./ six hours from Leh by taxi. You should travel in the direction of Hemis, and turn left near Hemis. The last major village before the lake is Tangtse. Chushul is 47 km. ahead of the lake.

This is a salt water (brackish) lake, the highest of its kind in the world. The waters of the lake (or, correctly, this series of interconnected lakes) are mostly sapphire blue, with different shades of blue and green at different places. People claim to have counted as many as seven shades. The general formula is that the colour is green where it is shallow, blue where deep and other shades in between.

The lower lake is called Pangong Tso, is around 65 km. long, is the longest lake in Ladakh and is in Ladakh itself. (The upper lakes, on the other hand, are in Rudok. The Chinese have annexed parts of Pangong proper, too.) The total length of this series of lakes is 144 km. and almost three-quarters of this are under Chinese ownership or occupation. The lakes are 3 to 6 km. wide.

The Pangong is 142' (around 45m.) at its deepest, in the north-west. British officers reported around 1860, 'We looked in vain for fish, and, with the exception of a species of bug… we failed to see any animal or signs of life…' In September they noted that the temperature of the water was 55°F.

1. 'Tso' means 'lake'. If you can't say 'ts', just say 'so' or, maybe, 'cho'. You can do this with all Ladakhi words that begin with a 'ts'.

Local people told me that the lake freezes over punctually on the 14th November every year. This is one report I would like to check out personally, for I, too, have visited the lake only in September. It remains frozen for three months when it can be walked upon.

Till 1993, tourists, not just foreigners but even Indians, could visit the lake only if they obtained special permits. That year, as the Tourism Commissioner of Jammu and Kashmir, I was able to get the rules changed and this was one of seven thitherto-prohibited areas thrown open to tourists. A major Indian film, *Dil Se*, was shot at the Pangong.

There are barren, rocky mountains in the east and north-east, with peaks at between 18,000' and 19,500'. The mountains in the south-west are taller and go up to 21,500'. One of these peaks is always covered with snow. The glaciers on some of these mountains melt into little streams, some of which merge with the lake.

The *Gazetteer* notes, 'The Lukung stream enters the lake at its north-west end... The lake has no effluence, and shows signs of gradual subsidence. The waters of the western end are much more salt [sic] than those of the eastern end near Ot. In the stream connecting the Pangong Tso with the Tso Nyâk the water becomes drinkable... Wild geese are plentiful here, and in the Tso Nyâk there are fish, a species of tench.'

Lukung is at the northern edge of Pangong. You first get to see the lake from here. Two roads emerge at Lukung. One, leads to the lake. The other goes to Phobrang, which is next to the areas occupied by China.

Tangtse: There are old engravings on some boulders near Tangtse.

Durbuk: It is learnt that there is a large statue of the Chambâ Buddha.

Thukung: This is a place at the southern end of the lake. It is here that the lake turns at a right angle, towards the east, into Chinese occupation. In 1962, there were bloody battles here.

Accommodation: There are two rooms for certain categories of travellers near the lake. You would do well to take your own tent, though. The Tourism department has a two bedroom hut at Tangtse, a distance away. Or you can camp at Spangmik, the last village that you will be allowed to visit. You can not camp close to the lake.

How to get there: There are no buses to the lake. Jeep- taxis are the only option. Unless you plan to trek much of the way, from where the bus leaves you.

Spanggur: Now under Chinese occupation, this little lake can be seen from the Indian side. It is in the same area as the Pangong, and is to the southeast of Shyok. When snow melts in the surrounding mountains, the water flows into this lake. Its water is mainly brackish.

Tso Kar: (150km. from Leh; 75km. from Tsomo Riri.) 'Kar' means 'salt'. For that reason, many guidebooks refer to it as the Salt Lake. Over the centuries table salt has been extracted from this lake. This was stopped in 1959.

The lake is located in the Aksai Chin region, and is near the Indo-Tibetan border. The Tso Kar is also close to the Tsomo Riri. It is believed that in the distant past the Tso Kar and the Lingzi Tang were interconnected.

Indeed, there is a theory that thousands of years ago there was a small sea where the Tibetan plateau now is. Several salt lakes dot the Aksai Chin area now. They might be remnants of that sea.

It is more likely that they are not. That's because most of them, the Tso Kar included, receive fresh water from the streams that flow down from the surrounding mountains. In addition, a river flows into the Tso Kar from the Karakoram range, which is in the north.

Changpa nomads live on the pastures between and near these two lakes. So does a wealth of wildlife: the bharal, the kiyang, the lynx, the marmot, the nyan and the wolf.

Thukje monastery: This is a small monastery in a village close to the lake. It comes under the Kurzok monastery.

Tsomo Riri: (4,595m.) 215km. south-east of Leh town. This large, brackish water lake is 19km. long and 7km. wide. Its colours change as the sun moves during the day. In June it starts getting bright as early as 4.30am. There continues to be light till around 8.30pm. Tso means 'male lake' and a Tsomo is a female lake.

There are many glaciers uphill from this lake. When they melt their waters form little streams that flow to the flat land below. All these streams merge to make up the Tsomo Riri. However, there are no drains to take water out of the lake. So, because of the dryness all around, and the summer sun, the waters of this lake evaporate considerably, especially in summer. As a result the water left behind is brackish and saturated with salts and there are no living organisms inside the lake.

Outside the lake is a different matter altogether. There is an 80m. by 60m. island near its north-eastern shore. (In the road directions to the Tsomo, this point is at 'Km.209.') This island is where the bar-headed goose and brown-headed gull set up their nests. In season as many as three thousands birds congregate at the lake. Groups of as many as five hundred bar-headed geese at a time are common. The reason is obvious. When birds migrate southwards in April and May they have to fly over hundreds of miles of desert. Suddenly they see this huge expanse of water. They are naturally tempted to stay there for a while.

The rare and endangered black-necked crane is the lake's star attraction. Other visitors include the Craig Martin, the Horned Lark, the red-billed Chough, the Tibetan Snow-finch and several kinds of Wagtail.

Like the Pangong, the Tso is partly in China. For that reason, tourists were not allowed to visit the lake till 1993 when... well, you've read the story already. Except that I now regret my enthusiasm to get the ban on tourists lifted. The World Wildlife Fund considers this one of ten wetlands of global importance. But 'development' is scaring the birds away—mostly to Tso Kar. A couple of ugly buildings and camps have since come up near the lake. More ominously, so has a firing range where policemen learn how to use rifles. True, they fire on paper targets, not birds. But there's too much noise pollution. I am attempting to curb this. If I can't then I'm afraid I'll have to lobby for a ban on tourists visiting the lake, this time for reasons of ecology. The firing range, too, has to be shifted.

I last visited the lake in 2001, in the middle of June. Around eight in the morning there were around three dozen birds on the island itself. There were twenty or thirty Brahmini ducks on the marshy eastern banks of the lake, well away from the island.

'Km. 209' is where the lake is closest to the road. This is also where the road from Leh first meets the lake.. The island as well as the eastern banks, where the Brahmini ducks were, are both close to the 'Km.209' point. To reach either place you will have to trudge through half a kilometre of alluvium and occasionally jump over narrow streams. In the case of the island, a good long-jumper can jump over from the marsh to the island. With practice it is possible to walk noiselessly towards the birds without scaring them off. Tough sandals or floaters, neither of which I wear, are the recommended footwear. My shoes and socks were soggy for several hours thereafter.

The lake is too far for a day return from Leh town. I have travelled from Leh to the Tsomo in a 'Traveller' in as little as five hours and forty five minutes and, with several photography stops, in as much as eight hours. Accommodation during the tourist season: You can stay in tents that are, on order, set up by Snow Leopard Adventures, Zâñgsty, Leh.

Kurzok is a tiny village on a hillock close to the banks of the Tsomo. There are a couple of privately owned guest houses in the village. It has a medium-sized monastery that is said to have been built around 1650. *Reach Ladâkh,* a guidebook, disagrees with this oral account, which I picked up at the monastery. It says, instead, that Lama Kunga Lodos

Snyingpo founded the Thupstan Sningpo Druprgout Chosling (monastery) between 1851 and 1861. It adds that Tsering Tashi Namgyâl, the head of the Rupsho monastery, sponsored the construction.

The monastery has murals and a small library. Both are said to date to the seventeenth century. By the end of the twentieth century several sections of the monastery started falling apart because of poor maintenance. Therefore, in 2001, its management launched a major renovation and expansion of the lhakhang. It belongs to the same red hat Drug Pâ sect as Hemis, but is not subordinate to the latter. There are three prominent idols in the monastery.

There is a tall mountain behind Kurzok from which several little streams flow down towards the Tsomo. Southwest of the village, much too close to the banks of the lake, is the palatial, white, 20th century, summer residence of the head lama of a distant gompa. He comes over just once a year.

Hot-water springs

There are famous hot water springs at Chumâthâng, Panamik/ Panamic (Nubra), Pûgâ (Chang Thâñg) and near Zâñglâ (in Zâñskâr, Kargil district). An official publication describes all of them as sulphur-springs. I seem to remember from scholars I met in 1982, that the springs at Pûgâ had borax.

Ladakh has mineral water springs, too.

Leh town

Leh (3,522m.) is a charming, not so little, town built on a slope. it has a population of around 27,000. The colourful Leh bazar is one of its attractions. To their credit, the people of Leh have not succumbed to ugly 'modern' architecture the way people in the rest of the state (and, indeed, elsewhere in India) have. And yet a disproportionate number of shops in the bazar are owned by Punjabis and Kashmiris or claim (yes) German ancestry (countless bakeries do).

.However, in some ways tourism has taken its toll. A senior administrator estimated that in the year 2001, there were at least fifty *massage parlours* in Leh. Most of them sprang up after 2000. They offer a whole range of massages, from Ayurvedic to Thai (i.e. fully clothed).

The main attractions of Leh town are:-

Buddha's two-storey idol (inside the palace): King Deldan Namgyâl (17th century AD) got it constructed.

Chorten, five-storey: King Deldan Namgyâl got it constructed.

Chortens, 108: King Lha Chen Thî-sug Lde got the 108 chortens constructed.

Dard graves: There is a Dard cemetery near Leh town. Francke examined some skulls found there and came to the conclusion that they dated to between the 1st and 5th centuries AD.

Dukhang: King Deldan Namgyâl (17th century) got this assembly hall constructed.

Jamia Masjid: This large mosque was probably built in 1666, following the 1663 agreement between the Mughal Emperor Aurangzeb and Gyâlpo Deldan Namgyâl of Leh. (See 'A History of Leh'.) What you see today is a much renovated and changed version, with 'modern' masonry, and little of the original. It is located in what is now the main market of the town.

Kachu Sikander Khan's theory is that the construction of the mosque was started during Sengge's reign and completed during Deldan's 'on orders from Emperor Aurangzeb. The emperor sent over the architectural drawings and design for the mosque.' If Aurangzeb had sent the design then how could Sengge have started construction? (See also 'Islam in Leh'.)

Jokhang: This is a small monastery in the main market, across the road from the State Bank of India. The Ladâkh Buddhist Association built it in 1957. You can visit it at almost all hours. It has an idol of the Crowned Buddha (Joyo Rinpoché).

The Leh Palace (Léchen Pal-khar)**:** This is a nine-storeyed structure. It was built on a hillock overlooking the town by King Sengge Namgyâl in the 17th century. His father Jamyang might have laid the foundations and approved the architectural designs. (More in the chapter on 'History'.) It inspired—and preceded by half a century—the more famous, multi-storeyed Potala Palace of Lhâsâ. Now in ruins on the inside, its façade inspires awe at the technological skills of the Ladakhis.

The Ladakhis did not invent the multi-storeyed building. The official word is that New York did- in the late 19th century. Or Chicago did in 1871. (Buildings of more than five-storeys or a height of 22 metres are accepted as multi-storeyed.) However, the history of Kashmir tells us of the 12-storey, fourteenth-century palace of King Zain ul Abedin. While that palace no longer exists, Senge Namgyâl's nine-storey, 17th century Leh palace and the Potala of Tibet, do.

Of the two, the Leh palace is the older by around 60 years. Leh can thus boast of the oldest extant nine-storey building in the world. It is almost certain that the Leh palace inspired the Potala palace. The Leh palace rests on the slope of a hill, though. See also the entry on 'Thiksey' in this chapter. Thiksey is on terraces. The Leh palace has a wall that is nine storeys high.

There are old wall paintings inside, which depict the life of Lord Buddha. There is also a prayer room and library of old manuscripts inside. Some of the corridors have old *thankas*. There are also old arms and idols in the palace.

Also nearby is the Namgyâl Tsemo (victory) peak. On it are the ruins of the fort constructed in the 16th century by King Tashi Namgyâl. (More about the Lords of the Four Quarters under 'History'.)

Leh Namgyâl Tsemo Monastery: There is a small monastry in the complex.

Mâney Ringmo and chorten: King Deldan Namgyâl (17th century AD) got both constructed. The maney was for the peace of his mother's soul.

Maney Somâ (near the Ringmo Maney): King Tsetan Namgyâl (18th century) got the maney constructed.

Mâneys, Three large: King Deldan Namgyâl got them constructed.

Shanti Stupâ (above Changspa): This is a hilltop monastery just outside Leh town, in the direction of the Khardung Lâ. It was built with Japanese aid. The Dalai Lama inaugurated it in 1985. It embodies the powerful chant, Nam Myo Ho Reng Gey Kyo, which has been written in Roman letters at several places. The inner architecture is very East Asian. The exteriors blend classical Central Indian (Bihari) Buddhist architecture with East Asian influences.

Sankar monastery: This, perhaps, is the most important monastery in town.

Polo

(See also 'Polo' in the chapter on sports.)

King Jamyang Namgyâl (c.16th century) married a Balti princess (see 'A history of Leh'). Polo is a Balti game. Therefore, it probably came to Leh with Queen Gyal Khâtûn. On the other hand, it could well have come much before that—from neighbouring Kargil.

There are six players in each team. A match lasts an hour. There is a break of ten minutes in between. Each time a goal is scored, there is a burst of raucous music and the teams have to change sides.

The formerly restricted areas

There are several areas in Ladakh that are out of bounds for tourists, Indian as well as foreign. In 1993, I was able to get the ban lifted from nine of these areas (notably Pangong, Tsomo Riri, Dâ-Hânu and parts of Nubra). However, you still need a permit from the Deputy Commissioner (DC), Leh, which will contain your name, the number of your vehicle, etc. Take at least three photocopies of the permit along. You might need to give them to the security guards en route. These permits are for groups of four, valid for seven days and issued if you get a letter of introduction from a travel agent. You also need to submit a photocopy of the first page of your passport. (Citizens of Pakistan, Bangladesh, Srî Lanka and Myanmar need the prior clearance of the Ministry of Home Affairs in New Delhi.)

The "new" areas

The seven areas in which only 'restricted' tourist activity could take place between 1978 and 1993, but which were thrown open to tourists in 1994, are:

Khaltse sub-division:

Khaltse-Dumkhar-Skurbuchan-Hânu-Biama-Dâ

Nubrâ sub-division:

a)Leh-Kharduñg Lâ-Khalsar-Tirit up to Panamik

b)Leh-Kharduñg Lâ-Khalsar up to Hunder

c)Leh-Saboo-Digar Lâ-Digar-Labab-Khuñgru-Gampa-Tañgyar (only for treks conducted by approved tour operators and accompanied by state police personnel)

Nyumâ sub-division:

a)Leh-Upshi-Chumâthâñg-Mâné-Pugâ-Tsomo Riri (lake)-Kurzok

b)Leh-Upshi-Debling-Pugâ-Tsomo Riri (lake)-Kurzok

c)Leh-Kâru-Châñg Lâ-Durbuk-Tâñgtsé-Lukuñg-Spangmik (Lake Pangong, up to Spangmik).

14

Nubra Valley

(Also spelt Nobra.) Often called 'the valley of flowers,' Nubra is generally considered the most beautiful part of Leh district. It is an open valley, 2 to 3 miles. wide and 128 miles long. If we include the mountains, and not just the valley, Nubra is 72 miles wide. Together with what is under the illegal occupation of Pakistan and China, Nubra has an area of 9,200 square miles. The population is mostly Buddhist. There are some Muslim communities, mainly in the Turtuk Bogdang area, down the Shyok river in the north-west.

Deskit is the main village. You can stay at one of the many guest houses located within private residences. Western tourists often rate these guest houses better than hotels in the Indian plains, mainly because of personalised service. There are major monasteries in Deskit and Sumur. You can pitch tents at Tirit.

Vegetation: There are plantations of willow and poplar in most villages. Fruit bearing trees, too, grow here. There are ample clusters of the thorny, woody hypophae shrub on the floor of the valley. The shrub yields excellent firewood. (See also 'History' below.)

Geography: The Nubra valley is actually made up of two smaller river valleys, those of the Nubra and Shyok rivers, above as well as below the confluence of these rivers. The soil at this confluence is sandy and, thus, unfit for agriculture, despite the abundance of water (which is rare in a desert). The Shyok river cuts through the valley. The Saser sub-range of the Himalayas is drained on the east and west by the Shyok and Nubra rivers.

That Ladakh is really a desert of the Saharan kind hits you when you get to Hunder. There are sand dunes and, yes, camels—in fact, the famous double-humped Bactrian camel.

Climate: Nubra's climate is not as harsh as that of the rest of Leh. That's because its main village, Deskit, is, at 9,950', almost two thousand feet lower than Leh. Its other major village, Hunder, too, is at a mere 10,300'. And yet, the mean elevation of the inhabited portions of this valley is 12,760'. As a result, winter temperatures are never worse than minus 3°C during the day and minus 15°C at night. Summer temperatures go up to 28°C during the day and 15°C at night.

Precipitation is almost as low as in central Ladakh. In both regions almost all the available water comes down from the mountains when the snows melt.

Attractions: Siachen is Nubra's best known landmark. The hot water springs of Panamik (see below) are a close second. The valley is famous for its apricot orchards. Indeed, Nubra means 'green'. The ibex and the gurhel live here. So do a few snow leopards. (According to *Reach Ladâkh* the word Nubra means 'Ldomra' or 'the valley of flowers.')

The Bactrian camels: These shaggy camels were the main pack-animals of the caravans of Central Asia. Some would pass though Ladakh as well, and would go all the way up to Leh. Some wealthy landowners of Nubra and central Ladakh purchased a few of these camels, perhaps in the late 19th or early 20th century. None survived the extreme cold and high altitude of central Ladakh. The last central Asian caravans passed through Nubra in 1949. However, sixteen such camels remained in Nubra. By 1980, their number had swelled to 35. So by a quirk of history, Hunder in Nubra has become the only place in India where Bactrian two-humped camels live.

The officially approved routes: There are two approved routes:

i) The valley of the Nubra river: Leh-Khardung Lâ-Khalsar-Tirit-Teggar-Sumur-Panamik-back to Leh; and

ii) The valley of the Shyok river: Leh-Khardung Lâ-Khalsar-Deskit-Hunder-back to Leh.

The latter route might not seem impressive but it covers the two main places: Hunder which is famous for sand dunes and the Bactrian camel; and Deskit, which is the main village of Nubra. On the other hand, for the people of Ladakh and Yarqand (Turkestan) the main attraction is Panamik.

How to get there: There is a bus service from Leh to Nubra, twice a week. However, most tourists prefer to travel by taxi. Local tour operators offer pricey five-day Nubra packages. Buses leave the Leh bus stand at dawn and reach Deskit almost six hours later, just before noon. Tourists who can't wait three days for the next bus to leave find out which trucks are going their way the next morning and work out a paid lift with them.

Some tourists trek from Leh to Nubra (see 'Trekking'). With the coming of automobiles, this trek does seem pointless.

The route: Leave Leh town. Ganglas is 9 km ahead. It used to be a police checkpost. Another 16km. later (25km. from Leh) is South Polu. Before automobiles came to Ladâkh, this used to be the southern camp for travellers. The **Khardung Lâ** (pass) is another 14km. ahead. This is the highest place in the world (18,300'/ 5602m.) that you can go to in an automobile. It is 39km. from Leh town.

At the pass you are likely to find snow throughout the year. Guidebooks say that the Lâ (pass) is always covered with fog, too. Maybe I was unlucky whenever I went there for it was clear. My jeep took less than 90 minutes between Leh and the Khardung Lâ. Army soldiers have built a Hindu temple at the Khardung Lâ. The mountains you will see from here are the Zâñskâr range in the south and the Saser massif in the north.

Nubra lies beyond the pass. There is a tea stall at the Nubra end of the pass. Some 14km. later is North Polu, where the northern camp for travellers used to be.

Khalsar (c.10,000') is the first village in the valley. It is an hour's drive journey from the Khardung La and 95km. from Leh. From here you can trek to Sâkti. The river you will see is the Shyok and the picturesque village that can be seen is Tsati.

Khalsar has inexpensive- and basic- hotels and eating places. A while after Khalsar the road bifurcates—Deskit and Hunder are to the left (northwest) and Tirit, Sumur and Panamik to the right (north).

You can also stay in economy tents at the Samling campsite. The Samstaling moanstery owns the site.

The road from Deskit to Hunder runs along River Shyok.

The Tirit-Panamik route follows the course of the Nubra river instead. The area is picturesque and the order in which the villages appear is: Tirit, Lukung, Teggar, Sumur and Panamik.

History: People, mostly traders, who travelled from either Leh or Tibet to Yarqand had to pass through Nubra. It is estimated that ten thousand horses would pass through Nubra every year.

The valley grew naked barley (locally called *grim*) in abundance. Caravans travelling on this route would purchase *grim* in large quantities. Most of the villages of Nubra are built near low platforms of alluvium. Partly for this reason Nubra is very fertile. Most parts of Kashmir and Ladakh have traditionally grown just one crop, because in winter the fields are covered with snow and it is very cold. Lower Nubra, on the other hand, grew two crops centuries before modern agricultural practices were introduced. The lucerne (*chunpo*), apples and apricots that grew here, too, were in great demand with the caravans. As a result Nubra is relatively prosperous, and its villages are large.

But this very fertility earned Nubra the envy- and, thus, enmity- of neighbouring Turkestan, which raided Nubra many times.

In 1530 or 1531, Mirza Haidar Dughlat conquered Ladakh on behalf of the king of Andijan (Farghana), now in Uzbekistan. (Dughlat happened to be a cousin of Babar, who later became the emperor of India.) We know that in 1535, there was a rebellion against Dughlat's officers in Nubra. Therefore, at least for a while Nubra had come under the Farghana kingdom.

Some time after 1575, King Tsewang Namgyâl of Ladakh conquered several of the kingdoms that neighboured Ladakh. He then wanted to conquer some Central Asian kingdoms, which happened to be ruled by Muslims. The people of Nubra told him that their economy was totally dependent on the caravans of traders who passed through their land. To keep them coming they needed peace. No trader would transit through Nubra if there was a war on Ladakh's northern border. Tsewang bowed to Nubra's pressure and called off the planned military campaign.

In 1999, during the Kargil war, Pakistan attacked, and tried to occupy, the border villages, savagely, with modern weapons. (See also 'Siachen'.)

Restrictions: In 1993, I got much of thitherto restricted Nubra opened up for tourists. However, international tourists still can't travel to areas beyond the Hunder bridge and Panamik. Indian tourists can travel to a place in Turtuk that is almost smack on India's Line of Control with Pakistan. Siachen is not open to tourists from the Indian side. On the other hand the parts of Siachen that are under Pakistan's illegal control are, and have almost always been accessible to tourists. I hope that some day tourists will visit Siachen, from the Nubra side, too. Wish me luck.

Best season: The road to Nubra is open only from June to September, which happens to be the best season, too.

Principal attractions/ main villages: Apart from the landscape, Nubra's biggest attraction is its wildlife, notably the Bactrian double-humped camel. The important places Nubra are:

The Shyok Valley

Deskit (9,950'): The scenery leading to Deskit is spectacular. The village itself is on the sharply sloping left bank of the Shyok river. From here you can look across the point where River Shyok merges with River Nubra. Deskit is the administrative headquarters of Nubra.

The village has a 17th century gompa on a rocky spur above the village, and several apricot trees. There is a crust of soda on the surface of the plain. This is collected and sold. Some believe that there is a link between these deposits and the hot-water springs of Panamik.

There are several shops and a few basic to middling guest houses and eating places in Deskit, in the main village and near the gompa. The *Sand Dune*, the *Olthâñg* and the *Thachung* have all been classified as economy class guest houses. *Sunrise* is marginally more expensive and the *Karakoram* and *Khangsar* slightly cheaper. *Sangam* has a dormitory as well.

Detour for anthropologists and other social scientists: Bokdâñg is 120km. ahead of Deskit on the road to Turtuk. It is 60km. before Turtuk. All residents of this village subscribe to the Nur Bakhshi sect of Islam.

Buses leave Deskit for Panamik and Chamshen in the afternoon. They return from these two places in the morning. Sumur is served by both buses.

Hunder (10,300'/ 3,231m.): Hunder is an enjoyable seven-kilometre walk, through sand dunes, from Deskit. These dunes change their shape every time there is a strong wind. Hunder is by far the more scenic of the two, because of a profusion of apricot orchards, the pretty Hunder stream and bridges on the stream. The village has been built on the left bank of River Shyok. The river gets split into a number of channels, one of which is almost 100m. (300') wide in September/ October. These channels add to the beauty of the place.

Historically, people travelling from the Nubra valley to Skardu (now in POK), via the Shyok valley, would halt at Hunder. They would camp in an orchard. One rough road from here leads to Leh (through the Thâñglasgo pass). Another rough road goes to the Snimo and Likir valleys.

Today small population of double-humped camels in Hunder is used for joyrides and safaris for tourists- and some times as transport. When Nubra was on the trade route to Yarqand, the camels were used as pack animals. They cover the distance between Hunder and Deskit, through sand dunes, in two hours.

Antiquities: The ruins of an old fort can be seen above the village. King Sengge Namgyâl got a grave constructed here for his Muslim mother. It had a grand *rozâ* (low surrounding wall) but is now in ruins. There is also a small Ge Lugs Pa monastery near Hunder.

Rock carvings: In the nearby desert are rocks with some very exciting engravings. There are, of course, the usual ibexes and other animals. But there also are two carvings of the sitting Maitreya, from the sixth or seventh centuries AD. These are some of the oldest works of art in all Ladakh. Some scholars believe that they are the oldest.

Dr. Mani adds that there is a large cave on the left bank of the Hunder *nâlâ* 'about 4km. further towards south-west. Some stone pieces, supposed to be palæolithic tools, were also found in this area. Towards south at Hunder Dok on the left bank of the *nâlâ* there are four caves which were occupied by Buddhist monks at a later date as meditation caves.'

Where to stay: There are a few mid-priced guest houses in the village. The *Stobsal*, the *Hunder Moonland* and the *Rtab-Gyalpâ* are all economy class guest houses. The *Snow Leopard* is slightly more expensive.

***Skampoo*:** Cross the Hunder nullah at the place where the Hunder nullah and the Shyok river meet. 5km. west of here is a village called Skampoo. On the left bank of River Shyok are large rocks with old engravings of animals (ibexes, mostly) and humans.

A kilometre further ahead (in the direction of Skuru) is a place called Terche. Here the Maitreya has been etched on a large, flat rock.

The Nubra valley

Let us return to Khalsar and go to the other side of the river from there (i.e. eastwards). *Mane* is across the river from Deskit. It is north of the point where the Shyok and Nubra rivers merge. There are many large rocks with engravings on them in this area. The figures engraved include the usual humans and animals (ibexes, goats and deer). However, the engravings at *Tirit*, which is even further to the north, are very rewarding: because these are not just line drawings and because the themes go beyond the commonplace. These are on a rock on the left bank of River Nubra. Two of the three deities carved can still be seen, with most of their details intact. All three are standing. One of them has a sword and the second a rosary. Other rocks at Tirit have animals and humans engraved on them, but again with a difference. The ibexes' horns are more elaborate; in one figure they are shown fighting. The humans' arms are outstretched.

If you travel further north of Tirit you will reach Sumur.

Sumur*:* This beautiful village is on the left bank of River Nubra, just above its junction with River Shyok. It, too, is on the Leh-Yarqand caravan route. It is north of Tirit and Deskit. Sumur and Teggar are around 2.5km. each from the Sumur Gompa.

There are large rocks nearby with old engravings. As at Tirit, the quality of artwork is well above the average. The deer are better drawn than elsewhere. The ibexes are shown running, and are in a row. Dr. Mani writes that the 'remains of an ancient Buddhist stupâ [chorten?] were also noticed' at Sumur.

Where to stay: There are five guest houses in the Sumur-Sanistaling area. Three are basic and economy (*Tsewang Jorgais*, *Tashi Khangsar* and *LP*), one is fairly decent and mid-priced (*Staklay*) and the fifth (*Lhârgyâl*) is in between.

Teggar: Teggar has been built on a hill that overlooks Sumur. On boulders here are some old engravings of ibexes- not mere line drawings but fuller figures.

Where to stay: The *Yrab Tso* (phone 52046 Leh) is an expensive B-class hotel near Teggar. The *Lhârimo North Camp*, too, is expensive.

Samstaling: This mid-nineteenth century (c.1868) gompa is about six km. from Sumur by road, of which the last three km. are uphill. The distance is shorter if you walk. Lama Tsultin Nima founded the gompa. Its frescoes were restored painstakingly in the 1960s. Though middling by overall Ladakhi standards, it is, with Deskit, one of the two most important monasteries in Nubra.

On a very large rock at Samstaling have been engraved two Maitreyas (between 9 and 11 feet high) and a chorten. Over the centuries they have faded somewhat.

The gompâ is one of the most puritanical in all Ladâkh. It allows women in only during the daytime hours. Besides, one has to be decently dressed (i.e. most of one's body has to be covered.) Intoxicants are taboo every where near the monastery.

Tirsa is 15km. north of Samstaling. There are engraved boulders near Lake Tirsa, up the hill and east of the river. The figures include the usual ibexes but some of the drawings are better and more filled out than is the norm. One of the ibexes has a long neck.

Yansa is north west of Tirsa, and across the bridge from Panamik. The rocks on the right bank of the river have figures of ibexes and horse-riders. Dr. Mani writes that 'housed in a secluded room there is a sculpture of Padmapâni [Avalokiteshvar] on a stone slab in low relief near a chorten which can be dated to the period prior to the introduction of Tibetan Buddhism.' Which means that this slab is from the eighth or ninth century or even older, which makes it very rare.

Panamik (10,840'): *The caravan route:* Panamik, traditionally, used to be an important halting place on the summer route between Leh and Yarqand. It was the last major village before the traveller went into the Kârâkoram and Kun Lu (Ka-Lu) mountains. Caravans and individual travellers would have to walk for twelve days before they reached the next village.

Therefore, the government would keep a major stock of foodgrains at Panamik, for traders as well as their horses. The shopkeepers and farmers of Panamik would supplement these stocks, especially of fodder, with their own. Farmers would grow grass and fodder on designated fields, especially for these caravans. For a fee, the horses of the caravans would be allowed to graze on these fields. This resulted in considerable prosperity for the people of Panamik. When the caravan route was closed in 1949, Panamik lost its main source of income and shrank to its present state.

Hot water springs: The village has two famous hot water springs, at the exits of which the water is at 167°F. It is 155°F even in the baths. People from all over the district visit these springs for their supposed curative qualities. So did travellers from Yarqand, before borders hardened.These scalding waters are said to cure rheumatism and syphilis. (The last bit is interesting. I first visited Ladakh in 1981. That's before AIDS became widespread. In those days venereal disease (VD or STD) meant syphilis or gonorrhoea. STD was rampant in some of the neighbouring hills. However, STD was totally unknown in Ladakh. I was told that the viruses of these diseases couldn't survive Ladakh's incredible cold. Just as snakes can't. So, who were these people who came to get their syphilis cured? Yarqandis? Or is Panamik the reason why there's no syphilis in Ladakh?)

Other Attractions: The tiny, mid eighteenth century Ensa (Insa) gompa is across the river and a three or four hour trek from Panamik. There are large rocks around the monastery and some trees between these rocks. Ensa is not one of the major monasteries of Ladakh.

The Lobone Tso is a small but pretty lake. Being quite unknown, it hasn't been overrun by tourists. Not yet.

Restrictions: Panamik is more or less the last village that tourists are allowed to go up to. However, from here you can go to Sasoma, 15km. away. At Sasoma there are tracks in the direction of the Tulum Puti La and Saser La passes.

Where to stay: There are two moderately priced guest houses (the *Silk Route* and a nameless guest house) and a cheaper campsite (*Rimo North*) in the village.

Shopping: Handicraft shops sell woodwork and weavings.

Buses: There is a Leh-Sumur-Panamik bus service twice a week, and as many buses between Deskit and Panamik.

15

The Siachen Glacier

Geography

The Siachen glacier is in a valley in the Kârâkoram range of Ladakh, at its northernmost tip. It is 76km. long. (Another estimate puts the length at 72km.) Either way it is one of the longest in the world, arguably the biggest glacier outside the tundra. It is between 2 and 8km. wide. Every year it receives 10 metres of snow, of which two-thirds falls in winter. The glacier is frozen and snowbound throughout the year. It rises from 3,550m. above the sea to 5840m. Temperatures drop to minus 50 degrees Celsius at night for the greater part of the year and this does not include the wind-chill factor. At least on one occasion the Indian Army recorded a temperature as low as minus 78°C. Blizzards are frequent and cruel. They can reach speeds of up to 300km. per hour (150 knots).

The glacier consists of many peaks and side valleys. It flattens out ahead of its centre. The Indira Col, which divides Central Asia from South Asia, is at its northern end. It is also the northernmost point under Indian administration. The Shaksgam valley lies beyond the northern slopes of the Indira ridge. The Shyok basin, which borders China, is to the east of the glacier. (Shaksgam is that part of Jammu and Kashmir which Pakistan had illegally handed over to China.)

Siachen is drained by the Nubra river, which goes on to merge with the Shyok river near Khalsar. H. Strachey, a British explorer, wrote in the 19th century, 'The thickness of ice seemed at least 200 feet. Wild juniper trees grow all about the hill-sides along its lower part. It is remarkable for the extreme flatness of its level, and for the absence of moraine. The upper part is much crevassed.'

Getting there

From the Indian side the way to travel to the glacier is through Leh. The second and third week of June are normally the best time for an expedition.

By then the snow would have melted in the moraines, on which you will camp at least three times each way. You might like to spend a day or two in Leh to get used to the rarefied oxygen. The next stop will be the Nubra valley. Most expeditions spend a few days at Tigur (Teggar) village in Nubra to prepare for the difficult journey ahead. Then comes the Terong valley, which is to the east of Siachen. On entering this valley you will see the Gyong Lâ valley in the west. (It is also possible to enter Siachen through the Gyong Lâ (pass) and valley.)

Further ahead, you will see the Singhi Kâñgrî (7751m.) peak in the north-east. (Singhi means 'difficult'.) The name of nearby Afraz (6814 m.) apparently means 'the one that rises above the others'. It was named after Khan Sâheb Afraz Gul, an Indian who helped a Dutch team survey the region in 1929 and 1935. Harish Kapadia, Vice President of the Indian Mountaineering Federation writes, 'We decided to name this central peak of the glacier after (Afraz).' (I only have Mr. Kapadia's authority for the meaning of Afraz, or even 'Afraj', as spelt by him. I couldn't find either word in my Urdu dictionary. Could it be Afroz, which means 'inflaming, igniting'?)

Kapadia adds, 'From the middle of the glacier the view (is) stupendous. In one sweep (one can) see the upper Siachen glacier leading to Indi[R]a Saddle and Indira Col… In the east (lies) the gentle Teram Shehr glacier with Junction peak rising from the only green meadow on the edge of the glacier. To (the) immediate east (rise) the peaks at the edge of the Teram Shehr plateau… As Lord Vishnu is the god of preservation [and the husband of Indira or Laxmi Devi], we chose to give the names of Vishnu to some of the [thitherto unnamed] peaks on the Teram Shehr plateau.'

Till the political situation improves it might not be possible for you to go over to the Teram Shehr glacier, at the head of which is Col Italia. When it does, you would first go to the Kumar Camp. From there you would go through the wide gully that flows from the Teram Shehr glacier to the Siachen glacier. (The army base at Kumar is at 16,000'.) There are gentle slopes to the right of the gully. They are 'the only green (slopes) in the area,' Kapadia notes. He adds, 'These could possibly have been the site of the settlements mentioned by the Workmans.' From the gully you will go to 'the long turn-about approach from the main junction of the Teram Shehr glacier with the Siachen glacier.'

It is possible that the ruins of the settlement that Bullock-Workman found in 1912, were those of the Yarqandi village which the Baltis used to trade with.

The highest peak on the Teram Shehr plateau is at 7030m. and was named Padmanabh by Kapadia's team. It can be climbed only from the south ridge.

Because of the hostilities you should try to cross the Siachen glacier before seven in the morning. After that it is possible that the Pakistan Army might start firing on the 2.5km. stretch of the glacier which needs to be crossed to get to the Indira Col.

The trek from the roadhead to the Indira Col is just under 100km. and takes around 12 days of actual trekking each way.

The passes[i]

Eastern and northern passes

The Turkestan Lâ (North) (5720m.) is to the north of the main Turkestan Lâ. It leads to a portion of the Urdok glacier in the north.

The Indira Col (East) (5800m.) is on the Indira Saddle, between Indira Saddle and the Turkestan Lâ (North). It too leads to the Urdok glacier.

The Staghar pass (5800m.) is near the Staghar Tower on the eastern ridge of the Siachen glacier. It leads to the Singhi Kâñgrî (7,751m.) on the Staghar glacier.

These passes were first crossed in 1889, 1912, 1929 and 1976 respectively.

The Col Italia (5290m.) leads, in the east, to the Central Rimo glacier. This Col is at the head of the Teram Shehr glacier.

Western passes

The Gyong Lâ (5709m.) links the Gyong nallah in the west and east.

The Bilafond Lâ (5647m.) is the main pass that links the Ghyari nallah and the Siachen glacier.

The Saltoro pass (5700m.) links the Sherpikang glacier in the west. In the earliest days, climbers who approached the peak from the west would cross this pass. It is above the Peak 36 glacier and at the foot of the Saltoro Kâñgrî. There are two Saltoro Kâñgrî peaks: 'I' at 7,742m. and 'II' at 7,705m. The latter is one of the world's highest virgin peaks.

The Sia Lâ (5700m./ 21,100') links the Sia Lâ glacier (which is part of the Siachen glacier) with the Kondus glacier in the west.

The Conway Saddle (5793m.) is named after its pioneer, Martin Conway. This Col is at the head of the Abruzzi glacier and on a shoulder of the Sia Kâñgrî. Therefore it is used for climbing the Sia Kâñgrî. After a descent it leads to the Sia Lâ. Sia Kâñgrî I is 7,422m. high and Sia Kâñgrî II is 7,092m. The latter used to be called Handinge.

History/Early explorers

The Baltis knew the glacier as the Saicher Gharni. British writers called it the Saichar Ghainri. It later came to be known as the 'place' (chen) when 'roses' (sia) grew. That's because of the wild roses that grow in the lower valleys. A Yarqandi village existed near the Teram Shehr glacier at least in the second half of the 19th century, if not before. There the Yarqandis would trade with the Baltis.

Kapadia recounts an interesting legend, 'Once some… Yarkandis descended the Ghyari nala and took away a Balti woman… to their glacial village. To take revenge, the Baltis contacted an important mullah who gave them a tawiz (amulet) which was to be placed on the Bilafond Lâ. The mullah instructed them to return via the Nubra valley. However the Baltis, after placing the *tawiz* on the pass returned the way they had come. Soon afterwards a great storm visited the Siachen glacier and destroyed the settlements and only the rocky desolation remained.'

There is a 6,400m. peak near the glacier called Tawiz. It might possibly have got its name from the amulet of the legend.

William Moorcroft, who crossed an edge of the glacier in 1821, was the first to write about it for the world outside. G.T. Vigne (1835) was the next to go near the Siachen, in an attempt to get to Bilafond Lâ ('butterfly shaped'). Henry Strachey (1848) entered from the Nubra valley, climbed the glacier for three kilometres and was the first western writer to call it by a name (Saichar). Other westerners, notably Dr. Thomas Thomson (also 1848) and Frederic Drew (1850), were the next to visit some part of the glacier. The (British) Survey of India mapped a portion in 1861. However, the surveyor, E.C. Ryall, assumed that the glacier was 16 miles (25km.) long.

Francis Younghusband (1889), who went from the Urdok valley to the 'avalanche swept' northern Turkestan Lâ, and Dr. T.G. Longstaff (1909) concluded that this was where the main axis of the Kârâkoram was. Longstaff and his colleagues, Dr. Arthur Névé and Lt. Slingsby, are the first known outsiders to have travelled on the glacier, end to end. They first went through what is now known as the Bilafond Lâ (pass) and went back the same way. They next attempted the glacier through Nubra valley and succeeded. It was this team that gave names to the Teram Kâñgrî peaks. The name Teram Shehr means 'the destroyed city' and is based on a Balti legend. The trio also measured the Siachen glacier accurately and determined the boundaries of the Kârâkoram.

Significantly, Longstaff wrote, "We had [in the process of demarcating boundaries] stolen some 500 sq. miles from the Yarkand river systems of Chinese Turkestan, and joined it to the waters of the Indus and the Kingdom of Kashmir.'

The American couple, the Workmans came in 1911-12. Together with Grant Peterkin, a surveyor, they spent two months surveying the glacier in detail. Fanny Bullock-Workman named the now famous Indira Col and Indira Saddle after goddess Laxmi, the goddess of wealth and the wife of Lord Vishnu.

In 1929, two separate European teams took the process of mapping and surveying further. The Dutch group included Khan Sâheb Afraz Gul. The Duke of Spoleto's Italian expedition came from the north and discovered the Staghar and Singhi glaciers.

Another Italian survey team, headed by Prof. Giotto Dainelli (1930), gave the name Col Italia to the pass (6,200m.) that goes eastward from Teram Shehr to the Rimo glaciers.

The Indian government opened the glacier to tourists in 1972. It remained open till 1983. Since 1984, special permission has been needed.

Around 1972, several Japanese teams crossed over from the Bilafond La to the Siachen glacier. They climbed peaks like the Teram Kâñgrî I (7462m.). The first international group to be allowed into the area from the Indian side after the new rules was a Japanese expedition in 1984. They scaled Mamostong Kâñgrî I.

In 1985 and 1986, Western teams were allowed to climb the Rimo III peak and the Indira Col (West) respectively. Since then, international teams have been permitted to go the Terong valley, but not to the Siachen glacier itself. Officers of the Indian Army have climbed several peaks in the area.

However, peaks like Saltoro Kâñgrî I and II in the Siachen Muztagh are still an enigma and a challenge.

Superstitions

In the mid-1980s, an Indian artillery soldier, Om Prakash, was found missing from the glacier after a protracted spell of firing by the Pakistani army. Till at least January 2001, Indian soldiers posted at the glacier continued to believe that he was alive. They have included Om Prakash in the pantheon of Hindu saints and divines under the name 'O.P. Baba.' His picture has been placed next to icons of deities in an army-built temple on the glacier. Soldiers seek his blessings for their protection while they are posted at the glacier.

Partridges are found in abundance in and around the glacier in season. And yet Indian soldiers posted there do not kill them, or indeed other birds or even dogs. It is considered inauspicious to do so.

Indian soldiers also believe that women bring bad luck to the glacier. On the 13th April 2000, a woman visited the glacier. The same day an

Indian soldier was killed and thirteen others were wounded. Then, in August 2000, a lady-doctor of the Indian Army visited the Siachen Base Camp. Several Indian soldiers were wounded soon afterwards.

The conflict

The origin of the dispute

When the cease-fire line (CFL) was drawn up in 1949, as part of the Karachi Agreement between India and Pakistan, the Siachen glacier was not specifically mentioned. Nor was it in the Simla agreement of 1972, also between the two countries. Both times the line drawn came to an end at a point called NJ 9842. The 1949 agreement vaguely said that beyond NJ 9842 the line went 'thence north to the glaciers'. There was, and is, no delineation of the cease-fire line between NJ 9842 and the Chinese border. (For the events between 1947 and 1949, leading to the cease-fire, see 'A brief history of Kashmir'in the volume about 'Kashmir'.)

In both 1949 and 1972, the line of control (LoC) was described as moving from Nerlin (inclusive to India) and Brilman (inclusive to Pakistan), up to Chhorbat Lâ in the Turtuk sector. So far the language is precise. Beyond that vagueness takes over the agreed definition: 'From there the line of control runs northeastwards to Thâñg (inclusive to India) thence eastwards joining the glaciers'

Vagueness crept in because neither Pakistan nor India had any troops in this region. The Siachen glacier is often called the Third Pole because it is uninhabited, extremely cold and difficult to reach. That is why neither country felt the need to post troops there. NJ 9842 is near the Shyok river at the base of the Saltoro mountain range.

This vagueness resulted in each side having its own interpretation. In a joint paper, Samina Ahmed, a Pakistani scholar, and Varun Sahni, an Indian, noted, 'Pakistan draws a straight line in a northeasterly direction from NJ 9842 up to the Kârâkoram Pass, while India's line of claim moves north-northwest from NJ 9842 along the watershed line of the Saltoro Range, a southern offshoot of the Kârâkoram.' ('Frozen Frontline', *Himal*, December 1998.)

India occupies the glacier and most of the heights on Saltoro ridge facing Pakistan.

One of my own favourite theories is what I call the Nirula's School of Sovereignty. Nirula's is a salad bar in Delhi to which international tourists flock with their guidebooks. Over lunch they try to determine what places they should visit in India and how to go to these places. They read about Kashmir and some of them decide to visit Kashmir. They purchase tickets for Kashmir from an office in Delhi and, sometimes, book a room in a Kashmiri hotel or houseboat from an agent in Delhi. After completing their vacation in Kashmir they tell their friends back home that they had visited 'the Indian state of Kashmir'. Some say that in print, too.

Now, if they had been able to plan out an expedition to the Siachen glacier sitting in Delhi, they'd go back and talk of having been to 'an Indian glacier called Siachen'. India does not allow foreign mountaineers into its part of Siachen. Pakistan does.

In the Land Economics Department of Cambridge University there was a huge map of South Asia, showing the boundaries of Kashmir exactly the way India want them. Around the same time (1987-88), *The Guardian* carried a map of the Indian sub-continent, again reflecting the Indian point of view. Upon investigation I learnt that both maps had been picked up in Delhi. That was a time when India had a democratic government, with all the attendant freedoms. Most of its neighbours had military governments. So, scholars and journalists writing about South Asia found it more convenient to pick up materials for their research in Delhi.

As things turned out, in the 1950s Western mountain climbers, including some cartographers, planned out their expeditions to Siachen, perhaps sitting in a similar restaurant in Pakistan. They obtained permission to visit the glacier from Pakistani government. They went back and produced maps and atlases showing the entire area of Siachen within Pakistan's side of the LoC.

I hope I have made my point.

The Indian journalist, Rakshat Puri writes, 'After India realised [the strategic importance of Siachen], and learnt of Islamabad's presuming to give permission to foreign expeditions in Siachen, it raced Pakistan to occupy it.' (*The Hindustan Times,* 7 July 1999.) Pakistan's permissions to these expeditions and the maps subsequently prepared by those Western mountaineers left India with no choice but to act.

The view from Pakistan

Arif Jamal's recounting of the conflict over Siachen sums up how moderate elements in the Pakistani establishment view the issue. Writing in the multi-edition *News* (11 July, 1999) he recounted, '(T)he Indian forward policy in Siachin [sic] [was] launched by Prime Minister Indira Gandhi in the mid-1980s. Taking advantage of the incomplete delineation of the LoC under the Simla Agreement of 1972, which stopped at grid reference NJ 9842 beyond which lay the Siachin Glacier and the Kârâkoram pass leading to Chinese territory, India launched a military initiative code-named Meghdoot [on the 13th] April, 1984. The twin objective of the initiative was "to cut away Baltistan from Northern Areas of Pakistan" and "to cut off Pakistan from having direct links with China".

'Impelled by "Siachin consciousness", which stressed the region's strategic value, New Delhi decided to establish a permanent Indian picket at Bilafond Lâ. Pakistan reacted ...by launching its own operation Ababeel. In 1987, Indian troops attacked and captured the Quaid Post which Pakistan had established in the winter of 1986-87 and which dominated the Bilafond Lâ [18,200']. In 1993, India further extended its tentacles into Siachin by bringing Sia Lâ [21,000'] under its military control...

'New Delhi began to press for the "delimitation" of a line from map reference point NJ 9842 northward to the border with China "based on ground realities". Pakistan countered this Indian demand by stressing that India and Pakistan should redeploy their forces in Siachin to pre-Simla [Agreement of 1972] positions. During the technical talks on Siachin in November 1992, both sides agreed that (1) India would withdraw to Dzingrulma and Pakistan would withdraw to Goma, at the base of the Bilafond Glacier, and (2) surveillance was to be accomplished by helicopter.

'However, New Delhi soon wriggled out of this agreement by asserting that India's concessions would not go beyond minor adjustments on the Saltoro ridge. Indian military occupation of Siachin provoked frequent border skirmishes and artillery duels between Indian and Pakistani forces with many casualties on both sides.

'According to one intelligence estimate India has been spending $100 million annually on its military operations in Siachin. More than 300 Indian soldiers have been killed and 10,000 injured since 1984.'

Arif Jamal has been far more understanding of India's compulsions than most Western analysts. Brian Cloughley tells the story thus:

'[Why is there] such an absurd conflict? It began in 1984 when Mrs. Gandhi thought it would be a good thing to occupy the glacier. Actually, that isn't completely accurate. An Indian Army senior officer thought he would attract favourable attention and thus promotion (which he didn't get), by suggesting a stealthy deployment to the north, towards China, beyond the Line of Control dividing the areas of Kashmir administered by India and Pakistan, because there were no Pakistani troops there. Mrs. Gandhi agreed to his proposal. When Pakistan discovered the happening, it sent its own soldiers.' (*The News*, Pakistan, 2 May, 2000.)

June 1987: The battle for world's highest army post

At some stage around 1986 or 1987, the Pakistan army walked into an undefended stretch that was 21,153' above the sea. By deciding to station soldiers there, Pakistan made it the world's highest army 'post.' There were 1,500' high walls of ice on both sides. Therefore, it was also one of the world's most difficult posts to conquer. From the Pakistan's point of view it was only fitting that the world's highest army post be called the 'Quaid Post,' after the founder of Pakistan.

The Quaid is one of the many posts in the Bilafond Lâ (pass). To quote Indian journalist Vijay Kumar, it interfered with 'India's observation and logistics for the pass'.

A task force was created specially to get the post back for India. A young Indian officer, Naib Subedar (roughly, Corporal) Bana Singh, volunteered to join it. A battalion-size operation was launched on the 26th June, 1987, when the temperature was minus 40°C. Bana Singh led a group of soldiers of the 8th JAKLI Ladakhi (Jammu and Kashmir Light Infantry) through a difficult and hazardous route.

They moved from trench to trench, tossed grenades at the Pakistanis and charged at them with bayonets. They succeeded in evicting Pakistan's soldiers from the post. For this Bana Singh was awarded India's highest military honour, the Param Vir Chakra (PVC), an award normally given posthumously to those who display bravery of the highest kind during battle and lay down their lives in the process. Bana Singh is one of very few living soldiers to be awarded the PVC. The Quaid Post was renamed 'Bana Post.'

This is the only operation in Siachen in which either India or Pakistan has been able to wrest control of an occupied height from the other side. It is not as if Pakistan has not tried to get the Bana Post back. It tried in November 1987, and again on the 17th and 27th October, 1998. It lost a very large number of men in the first of these attempts. The other attempts, too, were unsuccessful, though with fewer casualties.

The two countries' positions

Robert Wirsing, an American scholar, quoted by KBK Infographics, summarises the two countries' positions thus. (The language used is entirely mine):

India wants Pakistan to correct its maps. It also wants a demilitarised zone. In a nutshell, India wants the ground realities to be accepted. The two countries should exchange maps showing existing military positions. The Line of Control (LoC) should be drawn north of NJ 9842 based on 'ground realities.' Which is another way of saying, You keep what you control and I keep what I have. The two countries should draw up ground rules to govern military operations. Finally, troops should be re-deployed to mutually agreed positions.

Pakistan, on the other hand, is not satisfied with the ground realities. It wants to change them, because it feels that India has taken too much land after 1971. It wants troops to be re-deployed to the pre-Simla

Agreement locations: positions as they stood immediately after the 1971 war. It wants the LoC to be determined north of NJ 9842 (i.e. based on its point of view, and not on the ground realities). It wants India to vacate the entire glacier before the two sides begin negotiations.

India vs. Pakistan: Who has the advantage?

Since 1984, Ahmed and Sahni note, 'Pakistan has tried innumerable times to displace the Indian forces, and has always had to withdraw with severe casualties. India has had to do nothing but sit tight and periodically repel a Pakistani assault.'

This flies contrary to the impression that most Indians have. The Indian public believes that Pakistan has got India trapped in Siachen, that the terrain favours Pakistan and that far more Indians than Pakistanis are getting killed in Siachen. This impression is both correct and wrong.

The Pakistan army's task is, indeed, easier. Its posts are at a much lower height. (See 'The bases,' below.) Roads, or at least tracks, reach all its base camps. On the other hand, Indian posts are located at extremely inaccessible places like the Saltoro Ridge. To reach these posts, soldiers have to trek through snow for several days, and also climb up sheer mountains. Food, weapons and fuel have to be carried to these posts by helicopter, adding to India's expenses. (See 'Provisioning' elsewhere in this chapter.)

However, these very heights give India an enormous military advantage. Except for Gyong Lâ (13,900'), all the heights are under Indian control. So, if Pakistan wants to dislodge the Indians from any of these heights, its soldiers will have to climb up very steep mountains. Each time they do so—and they have tried quite often—they are easy targets. Which is why they have never succeeded in Siachen.

The bases: Indian and Pakistani

The Indian base camp is at 12,000' above the m.s.l. The forward bases on the Saltoro Ridge are higher still. Kumar is at 16,000', Bila Top at 18,600', Pahalwan at 20,000' and Indira Col at 22,000. The Saltoro Range has a very steep gradient. Therefore, avalanches are frequent.

Pakistan's highest position is Conway Saddle, at 17,200'. This saddle controls the passage to the glacier from the Pakistani side. The remaining Pakistani posts are at between 9,000' and 15,000', and thus fairly comfortable to live in. Ahmed and Sahni note, 'Glaciers at the Pakistani frontlines begin at 9,440 feet and Pakistani troops are stationed on steep slopes, exposed to harsh weather.'

By Indian standards, 9,440' is a picnic, being only slightly higher than Gulmarg or Sonamarg. Even Leh's 11,250' and Padam's [Zâñskâr]

11,750' are quite comfortable in summer and bearable in winter. It's Kumar and above that are lethal.

Provisioning Indian soldiers

Part of the Siachen glacier is under the illegal occupation of Pakistan. The 110km. line that separates Indian territory from that occupied by Pakistan is called the AGPL (actual ground position line). This is a line and not a border, though it serves as one.

The glacier remains frozen throughout the year. In winter, for three to five months, snow covers the outposts of the Indian army.

Indian Army outposts are typically located at between 17,000' and 18,000' on the Saltoro ridge, with some higher still. Helicopters can not land on the glacier. If they could, life would have been so much simpler for the army officers and men stationed there, who could simply be dropped near their outpost. The nearest Army camp where helicopters can land is Gulab (15,000' above the msl).

The Indian Army has been guarding this 'highest battlefield in the world' since April 1984, under Operation Meghdoot which costs Rs. 3 crore ($ 0.6m) a day (all prices are as in 1999). And this figure does not include the cost of maintaining and servicing the aircraft that bring the supplies over.

Here is why things are so expensive—food and other supplies for the troops are carried by aircraft (IL 76 or AN 32) from Leh to Thoise, across the Khardung Lâ pass (18,380'). From there Cheetah helicopters ferry these supplies to Gulab. This helicopter has been built with French technology. Its normal carrying capacity is 225kg. However, at some of those heights a Cheetah can carry just 20 to 25 litres of water (or other liquid) at a time. This is particularly true of the Amar and Sonam bases, both of which are above 18,000'. Helicopter sorties cost Rs.48,000 an hour. Therefore, at Amar and Sonam the cost of drinking water works out to around Rs.2,400 per litre. (In the year 2000 a 121km. oil pipeline was laid from the base camp. This has made the transportation of oil somewhat more convenient and less expensive.)

These heroic sorties are made by the Leh-based 114 Helicopter Unit, better known as the Siachen Pioneers. Many helipads in Siachen are barely three metres by three metres in size. As soon as the helicopters fly within the range of Pakistan's troops, they are fired upon. This makes flying helicopters very difficult even during peacetime. Not that Siachen has known any peace since April 1984.

Other aircraft suffer from similar problems. An IL-76 carries 90 tonnes in central India but only 30 tonnes within Ladakh. (This aircraft flies up to Thoise, after which helicopters take over.) Mi-17 helicopters can transport four tonnes at a time in the plains, but only 1.2 tonnes in Ladakh. AN-32s can carry just four tonnes at a time in Ladakh.

Dinesh Kumar writes that every year Cheetah helicopters fly 500 tonnes of rations to various places on the glacier. Mi-17s transport 5,000 tonnes of goods annually. AN-32s and IL-76s make around 950 round trips every year between Leh and Thoise. ("Siachen operations will be listed in Guinness Book," *The Times of India*, 26 August, 1996.) Journalist Pamela Bhagat, whose husband is a senior Army officer, has published a very different estimate. She writes, 'About 60,000 tonnes of load is flown into Siach[e]n every year and an equal amount is air dropped by Air Force aircraft and helicopters.' ("Where nature is the enemy," *Daily Excelsior*, Jammu, 18 March, 2001.)

For all of Ladakh, supplies are brought from mainland India during the summer. They are stocked in godowns and depots and sold during the six winter months when the passes are blocked. For Siachen, goods are brought from Leh and stored at Gulab for the same period. Everything has to be carried manually from Gulab to the outpost that the item is meant for. Climbing up the glacier to the outpost is difficult enough. Carrying supplies makes it tougher still.

Letters, however, are placed in a small bag that is tied around the necks of local dogs trained for the purpose. The dogs are given some meat to eat and sent off to Gulab (as well as the other way around). Postman Bernard.

Casualties

As few as 3% of the Indian soldiers who have died at Siachen were killed by Pakistani guns. The situation on the Pakistani side is similar. Some 97% of the soldiers die because of the extreme cold, the altitude and the terrain. 'Combat casualties' are low because, as Samina Ahmed notes, 'troops are dug in, artillery fire over mountain peaks is generally inaccurate (as winds are erratic and difficult to predict in such terrains), and infantry assaults are seldom made in the harsh climate and difficult terrain'.

Pamela Bhagat writes, 'Since the summer of 1984, on an average one soldier has been killed every week and 10,500 have been injured so far [till March 2001].' She adds, 'Rifles and machine guns [have] to be thawed over kerosene stove[s] and relayed to posts. Firing at the enemy [is] quite futile since striking targets [is] almost impossible with trajectory, distance and speed of fire being so erratic.'

Strategic Importance

Frank Wisner, the then US Ambassador to India, delivered an address at the University of Jammu in early 1997. Apparently he asked India and Pakistan to give up their claims to the Siachen glacier. Defence analyst BK Mathur quoted him as saying, 'I believe India and Pakistan can agree that this patch of frozen earth has no strategic value worth the life of even one more of their sons.' ("Strategic relevance of Siachen Glacier," INFA, *Kashmir Times*, 21 March, 1997.) The majority of the Indian press and a number of Indian politicians have taken a similar view of this high altitude conflict

Then why is India sacrificing so many of its soldiers, and wasting so much money, on this cold, uninhabited place?

i) **The Chinese/ Central Asian angle:** The Indira ridge leads from the foot of the Sia Kâñgrî to the Turkestan Lâ (North). It then turns south to the Turkestan Lâ (East) (5,810). As of today it is India's northernmost ridge and stands between Central Asia and South Asia. That is its strategic importance.

Journalist Rakshat Puri writes, 'Going to the north-west of the Siachen glacier at Dzingrulma- as it does at present- the line moves from NJ 9842 through Bilafond, Saltoro Kâñgrî, Sia Lâ, Baltoro, to join the central part of the Shaksgam area of Jammu-Kashmir which Pakistan illegally ceded to China. But if it [the line] were to go north-eastward of the Siachen glacier from Dzingrulma, the line would move on to join the Indo-China boundary between the eastern corner of the Pakistani-ceded Shaksgam and the western corner of Chinese-occupied Aksai Chin. This is where the strategic Kârâkoram Pass is situated.

'Put it another way, the LoC would, if it went north-east of the Siachen glacier, keep the Kârâkoram Pass out of the Indian-administered side of Jammu-Kashmir and within Pakistani control...

'Can there be any doubt that Pakistani control of the strategically important pass would be China-managed?'

ii) **The Pakistani angle:** Pakistani troops captured much of Kargil in 1947-48. India recovered Kargil (and the dZoji Lâ (pass)) in November 1948, and Zâñskâr shortly afterwards. This ensured that the best route from mainland India to Ladakh remained with India. However, Gilgit, Baltistan and Hunzâ remained with Pakistan. So Pakistan responded by consolidating the northern route that runs parallel to the Indian highway. The Pakistani route passes through Hunzâ (in POK) and reaches the occupied areas near Nubra (across River Shyok).

And that is what gives Siachen additional strategic importance. If Pakistan were to capture or dominate Siachen, it can then terrorise the people of Nubra (as it does the people of Kargil town and Drâss where it controls the heights). It will also be in a better position to overrun Leh.

At present Pakistani's bases at Siachen are all in the foothills and lower slopes. India dominates the heights.

BK Mathur reminds us that 'the three major passes, Sia Lâ, Bilafo[n]d Lâ and Chugang Lâ, are firmly under the control of the Indian army... The Pakistani troops are thousands of feet below, along the lower slopes, and in mountain warfare troops below are always at a disadvantage... the Indian Army is in a strong position and it is difficult for Pakistan's Northern Light Infantry to come up from lower slopes... In 1984, they tried to capture [the vantage positions under Indian control] militarily. In April 1989, they launched a major assault and captured Chumik height near Chang Lâ.'

Pakistani journalist Arif Jamal summed up Siachen's strategic importance when he wrote that the twin objectives of Operation Meghdoot were "to cut away Baltistan from Northern Areas of Pakistan" and "to cut off Pakistan from having direct links with China."

Put simply, India can not give up the glacier. By controlling Siachen, India can prevent the Aksai Chin highway (under Chinese control) from being connected with the Kârâkoram pass. If Pakistan were to get Siachen, the two roads could be connected and Indian forces could possibly come under attack from both sides. Pakistani and Chinese forces would then move with ease between areas under their control. Also, by retaining the glacier, India can keep an eye on the Kârâkoram Highway and the Khunjerab Pass. Besides, if India were to give up its claim to the glacier, that would weaken India's position in its border negotiations with China.

FX: F for 'fake,' X for ''xecutions'

In the Greek epics, as in feel-good Filmistân[1] movies, a lot of people who are presumed dead actually did not die. They turn up alive in the last reel and there's happiness all around. (Gen. Odysseus is the most famous example.) In 2003 (and, perhaps, only during that summer), the hostilities in one portion of Siachen assumed that good feeling. Forty-six Pâkistâni soldiers, who were said to have been killed by an Indian unit, never died. (In fact they were never born.)

An Indian Colonel posted in Siachen told his juniors to show 'imagination and initiative.' The juniors took the orders of their

1. Filmistân is better known by the slavish term 'Bollywood.' Both refer to Bombay's commercial Hiñdî-Urdû cinema.

Commanding Officer literally. On the 29th July, an Indian Lieutenant claimed that his unit had killed an enemy soldier earlier that day. The problem with his report was that no Pâkistâni soldier had been spotted in that area—the Chandan complex—in the three preceding weeks, leave alone that day.

A fortnight later the same officer did one better. On the 8th August, he sent a video recording to prove that his unit had killed an enemy soldier. He got a Rifleman from his unit to play a dead Pâkistâni in that video film. Sixteen days later this imaginative unit created a video recording of three Pâkistâni soldiers being killed in action.

The Colonel was delighted, one would have thought, by the bravery of his men. However, it now seems that his delight was only about the quality of the video films. There seemed to be a *cinema verité* type of movie director lurking somewhere inside him, waiting to burst forth. The Colonel spoke to his junior, a Major, on the telephone the next day and 'asked him to ensure a "hazy video [recording]" in order to make "enemy activity" [look] realistic. [So, the officer in the Chandan area] decided to first construct an "enemy air defence bunker" and then destroy it. On September 21, the bunker—in India's territory—was destroyed by Indian rockets and mortar. A splinter hit [the Major], who was evacuated [from Siachen and recommended for a gallantry award]. The destruction of the enemy bunker was recorded on [video] tape.'[ii]

The unit stopped reporting such incidents after November 2003. That was the month when a ceasefire between India and Pâkistân came into force at Siachen—'for the first time in the Glacier area after 1984.'[iii]

The US Army has a full-fledged unit that helps Hollywood make patriotic war films. This enables the army to get its (and, hopefully, the nation's) point of view across. It benefits Hollywood even more. The co-operation of the US Army reduces the studio's costs and also ensures that the hardware shown is absolutely realistic. Since the 1980s, Filmistân has been receiving similar help in India—and rightly so. However, in the process a bit of stardust has, naturally, rubbed off on one or two officers in a million-strong army.

The talented unit at Chandan seems to have learnt an enormous lot from the film crews who have been shooting in Ladâkh since the year 2000.

Therefore, one can't really blame the Colonel for having been taken in by the video recordings. He told the Army's Court of Inquiry that 'the veracity of videos of other "kills" was authenticated by the "excitement and zeal" in the background voices.'[iv]

These videos were later screened for the benefit of middle ranking officers of the defence services at a premier training institute at Wellington in South India. A Major who has the brilliance to add to the soundtrack "excitement and zeal" in the voices of actors who are not on the screen certainly deserves an award—from *Filmfare* magazine, because the gallantry award is not likely to come through now. And this film deserves to be screened not at the (defence services) Staff College but at India's leading film institute at Puné instead.

That was a light break in an otherwise grim story—and should be taken as such. There are no press or television teams in Siachen to blow the whistle. It was the Indian Army that, to its credit, instituted a Court of Inquiry, exposed the scandal and released details to the press. It has punished the Colonel and two Majors, whose talent at special effects will ensure that they aren't without jobs after they leave the army. Three bad eggs in a million-strong army do not add up to a fraction of one per cent of the total. Their ham-handed (though technically superb) attempts 'to claim awards and citations for imagined gallantry'[v] should not be allowed to diminish the sacrifices made by their colleagues who have lost their lives or limbs—or at least a precious part of their youth—on that merciless battlefield.

Ecological damage

Indian glaciologist Syed Iqbal Hussain[vi] has been comparing satellite images of the Siâchen glacier, taken in 1978, 1994 and 2001. He notices that there has been a 'progressive retreat' in the glacier. In other words, it has been getting smaller and smaller. Dr. Hussain estimates that Siâchen glacier 'will vanish quicker than the Biofa [glacier] where there is no army presence.'

Hussain says, 'The military presence in Siâchen is a burden on the glacier. More than 1,000 kg. [of] human refuse is deposited in glacial crevices annually. With no bio-degradation because of the cold, melting snow washes [this waste] into the Indus [river] that feeds India and Pâkistân.'[vii]

So, what is likely to happen?

'With melting, initially the discharge hydrograph will go up,' Hussain says. (Translation: In the first few years there will be more water than normal in River Indus, because of abnormally fast melting of the glacier.) However, by the year 2050 there will be very little left to melt. Therefore, there will be that much *less* water in the Indus every year, once the Siâchen glacier is gone—or decimated. Water shortages in India and Pâkistân will become even worse. As it is, neither country has enough water for its people in the summer.

Negotiations

The governments of India and Pakistan held seven meetings between 1986 and November 1998, to discuss Siachen. However, neither side budged from its stand. Therefore, those meetings were unable to result in an agreement.

In 1984 and 1985, i.e. immediately after Operation Meghdoot, 'flag meetings' were held between the sector commanders of the two countries. Talks between the defence and foreign secretaries of the two countries were first held in January 1986. At two of the subsequent talks- those held in 1989 and 1992, especially the latter- it seemed as if the problem had been solved.

The 1989 agreement was between the two defence secretaries. They resolved 'to work towards... a comprehensive settlement, based on redeployment of forces... and the determination of future positions on the ground'.

The meeting of November 1992, was the sixth. It agreed on the mutual withdrawal of troops from key passes to new positions. They would thus create a 'zone of complete disengagement'. Pakistan would move to Goma and remove its artillery from Baltoro and Conway Saddle. India would move north of Dzingrulma (which is the base of the Siachen glacier). Apparently, both sides also pledged to refrain from reoccupying vacated positions. If this had been implemented, the conflict would have disappeared. However, not only was this agreement never implemented, one of the countries involved even said that no agreement had ever been reached.

The then Prime Minister of Pakistan, Mrs. Benazir Bhutto, complicated things further in 1992 by linking Siachen to the larger Kashmir issue.

In January 1994, India sent a 'non-paper' to Pakistan. Inter alia, despite being in a position of advantage, India offered to withdraw from Dzingrulma. There was no response from Pakistan.

The November 1998 talks got nowhere either. India said that it wanted an end to the situation in which Pakistani's forces fired upon Indian pickets almost every day. However, by then Pakistan's establishment had started saying that it had no interest in agreeing to a ceasefire, because that would legitimise India's position. Besides, Pakistan wanted a third party to monitor the ceasefire. (India's position is that there is no question of letting a third party in because the dispute is strictly bilateral.)

India wanted an immediate ceasefire and an exchange of military positions. It also pointed out that the conflict was not about Siachen at all, because the Siachen glacier was considerably east of the Saltoro

Ridge, where the Indian forces were, and thus well within Indian territory. Therefore, even the expression the 'Siachen conflict'.

Perhaps it should be called the Conway Conflict or something.

What has been termed 'the longest-running armed conflict between two regular armies in the twentieth century' now continues into the twenty-first century.

References

i. This section is based on Harish Kapadia, 'Siachen Glacier', *Indian Mountaineer*, Number 34, 1998.)

ii "Army admits 'cold lies' in Siachen operations," *The Kashmîr Times*, Jammu, May 8, 2004, page 12.

iii Ibid, page 1.

iv Ibid, page 12.

v Ibid, page 1.

Also see 'Siachen case: [Defence Minister] George wants guilty punished.' *The Times of India*, May 8, 2004. Page 9 of the 'Capital' edition.

vi Ganesh, Narayani, "Icy Retreat" *The Times of India*, June 5, 2004.

vii In my 'Afterword' to this book I have described in some detail how human and animal urine flows into rivers with the melting snow. I did not want to revolt the reader by talking of human and animal fæces. But, yes, if either is 'deposited' on snow or ice it will end up in the river.

16

The National Highway

Leh to Kargil and Srinagar

The National Highway: Leh to Kargil, and Srinagar to Kargil

(The traveller is likely to reach Srinagar or Leh by air, and then travel to Kargil, and beyond, by road. Since Kargil is midway between these two airports, the Srinagar-Kargil-Leh road journey has been broken into two segments: i) from Leh to Kargil, and ii) from Srinagar to Kargil. Please reverse the order and directions if travelling in the opposite direction.)

Leh to Kargil

The journey from Leh to Kargil town takes seven or eight hours in a light vehicle. It takes almost as long between Srinagar and Kargil. The Leh-Kargil 'National Highway' (NH) is a lot more rough and bumpy, though. However, on the Leh-Kargil road you don't have to go through a pass as exhausting as the dZoji Lâ. Besides, the Leh-Kargil road is open to traffic almost throughout the year. There are several villages, townships and monasteries on this route, most of them on the roadside itself.

The road passes through two districts, Leh and Kargil.

In Leh district

Within Leh district the National Highway goes somewhat like this: (All distances are from Leh town. There are entries about most of the places mentioned here in the chapter on 'Leh' district.)

• **Spituk (9km):** (Detour: Between Spituk and Nimu is a trekking route that branches off, on the right, for Pheyâng, Hunder and even Diskit.)

• **Pheyâng (17km):** Apart from a gompa, Pheyâng has some primitive engravings on large rocks. Dr.B.R. Mani writes that 'at a place 18km [after] Leh on the National Highway' there are more such engravings. These include the figures of animals (ibexes and horned goats) and hunters.

Patther Sâheb (24.5km from Leh city centre; 23.3km from SNM Hospital.) Guru Nânak Dév ji founded Sikhism. He then started travelling all over South and Central Asia on a series of now celebrated missionary tours.

During the 2nd Missionary Tour he visited and meditated in Nepal, Tibet, Yarqand and Ladakh. In AD 1517 he set up camp in Nimmu, on the bank of the river. He would meditate at the spot now known as Taposthân (on the right side on the highway).

A demon used to live on the hill across the road. He would terrorise the local people. When he saw the Guru meditate near the river he decided to kill him. So, he rolled a massive boulder down the hill, towards the Guru.

The demon saw the boulder hit Guru Nânak Dév ji. He came running down the hill, hoping to find the Guru dead. When he saw that the Guru was alive and unhurt, the demon knew that he had erred. He begged the Guru to forgive him. The demon then gave up his evil ways, reformed and dedicated the rest of his life to serving humanity.

When the boulder hit the Guru, not only did it come to a halt, the Guru's powerful body left a permanent imprint on the boulder at the place where it had touched him. The boulder with the imprint is now preserved inside the gurudwara, which is maintained by the 3rd Sikh Regiment of the Indian Army. There is a non-stop *kîrtan* (singing of Sikh devotional songs) at the Gurudwara from dawn to dusk, conducted by priests from the said regiment. There is also a Yatri Niwas (free guest house) inside the gurudwara complex.

The Nanak Hill is to the left of the highway.

- **Nimmu**
- **Basgo**
- **Likir** (61km) is at a short distance from the highway
- **Saspol** (62km)

Between Saspol and Alchi there is a bridge on the Indus. Near it are boulders with relatively recent (9th century) engravings. These are of Tibetan-style chortens, with inscriptions in the Tibetan language next to them.

- **Alchi** (70km)
- **Rizong** (74km, on a detour from the highway)

Nyurla: There are four large rocks at Nyurla on which are engraved the figures of animals (deer, goats and ibexes) and humans (hunters, group dancers and horse-riders). Burzahom, a neolithic site near Srinagar, is generally regarded as the oldest human settlement found in Kashmir. (Actually, it is the second oldest.) The stag hunt at Nyurla is similar in style to the one at Burzahom. So, could Nyurla's rock engravings be neolithic, too?

(Detour: The trekking route to **Tingmosgang** turns right from the highway near Nyurla and before Khaltse.)

Khaltse: The village is soaked in history, as you will notice if you manage to get through this book. Khalâchey, the capital of the ancient Dards, used to be where modern Khaltse is. There were two other Dard settlements nearby—at Skinding and across the river, at the feet of the mountain.

Inscriptions and forts: There used to be a Mon fort between Khaltse and Skinding, close to the river. It might even have been built in the Kushan era.

Francke, the great archæologist, found an ancient Brâhmi inscription near the old bridge. It mentions 'Uvima Kavithisa' (perhaps Vima Kadphises, the Kushân king) and the year 184 or 187 of some era.

According to one estimate this inscription dates to 200 BC. According to another view, the Kushans probably ruled between the 3rd and 5th centuries AD.

Near the Khaltse bridge are boulders with relatively late (9th century), as well as primitive, engravings.

There is a *Dard Castle* in the village, close to the chortens. Francke found many royal Tibetan inscriptions near them. He also found a very old Brâhmi inscription and a Gupta inscription.

The Braknak Khar (*fort*) is now in ruins. Apparently King Lhâ Chen Nuklok (12th century) had built it. This was the first fort that the Tibetans built in the Shâm area after displacing the Dards.

The Dards of ancient and mediæval Khaltse used to play polo on the vast ground between the bridge and the present village.

Plant fossils: The 30km stretch between Khaltse and Lama Yûrû is rich in plant fossils, mainly bryophites. Hobby-botanist SDS Jamwal, whose day job is as a senior police officer, estimates that many of these fossils are upto five million years old. They date to an age when there were no angiosperms. The theory is that peat got buried deep inside the earth because of frequent earthquakes. Clay metamorphosed into slate. Peat, on the other hand, decomposed because of the anaerobic conditions. It left behind precise imprints of plants.

Zabâlu Khar, near Khaltse, was a fortress where the ancient Dards used to collect customs duty. This duty was levied on the trade between

India and Central Asia. The fort is now in ruins. Apparently there was a bridge over the Indus at this point when the fort functioned as a customs post (*balutkar*). Later King Lhâ Chen Nuklok shifted the post to where the present bridge is.

There is a Tourist Bungalow and a PWD Rest House at Khaltse.

(Detour: To go to Da (of **Dâ-Hânu** fame) you can either take the metalled road that turns right just after Khaltse, or the trekking route that turns right from the highway, just after Bodh Kharbu.

(The Dâ-Hânu region is partly in Kargil and partly in Leh. See the chapter on 'Dâ-Hânu' and the Aryan Drokpâs for details.)

(Detour 2: **Batâlik** is a 75km. detour from Khaltse, along the Indus. You have to take the road that branches off to the right while travelling from Leh to Kargil. The Tourism Department has put up an overhead sign at this point, giving directions.

(***The Dangal Khar fort***, Samlamoon: There used to be an ancient Dard fort here. Only some ruins now remain.)

Some 13km after Khaltse on the NH you will come to kilometre-stone 324. Look at the mountain on the opposite side. Right in the middle of that sheer rockface is what looks like a **sculpture of the Buddha**, done in a Central Indian fashion. Surely no human could have reached there, leave alone sitting on some celestial scaffold to carve that icon. And yet it could hardly be the handiwork of the winds. (You can see this view from before and after 'Km. 324' as well.) This sculpture, surely, is one of the wonders of the world.

Lâmâ Yûrû (127km) is the next village. Francke found three inscriptions here, which date to between the 7th and 9th centuries AD.

A kitsch delight on the highway, before the Fotu Lâ, is the so-called *Jalebi Morh*. Engineers of the Indian army named it thus after the popular Indian sweet that consists, like the highway at this point, of an irregular spiral. There are eleven twists on the highway here. They make the 'Jalebi Morh' an object of much curiosity- and also much photographed. The road has to spiral upward because in just 32 km. it climbs 1,219m. (c.4,000'). From roughly 2,900m. (that being the level of the Indus at Khaltse) it quickly winds its way up to 4,094m. (i.e. to the Fotu Lâ).

The **Fotu Lâ** pass comes next. Like the Nâmikâ Lâ, shortly ahead, it is quite benign, despite being between 4094 and 4,108 metres (13,479 feet). It separates Leh district from Kargil. (Well, more or less. The exact boundary is 4km after the pass, when travelling in the direction of Kargil town.)

This pass is so benign that you won't even know that you are going through a pass it if you aren't told so. It is made up of some of the most beautifully coloured mountains in the world. If you are travelling from Leh to Kargil, these views start a kilometre or two before the pass. In the beginning the mountains are greenish. The best views start a kilometre after the pass and continue for another two kilometres- between kilometre-stones 294 and 292 to be precise. (Or km. 292 and 294, depending on your direction.) The stretch at the Nâmikâ Lâ is among the most majestic.

What gives these rocky mountains their colours? If the colours are sharp, then the cause is the minerals that the rocks are made up of. If the colours are soft, blurred or fuzzy, then it's grass, shrubs or even algae that you are looking at.

Across the canyon in the Nâmikâ Lâ area is Wâkhâ Reng. The stream here carries the seeds of several trees: mostly willow but also mericaria (locally called *umboo*). As a result there is a dense forest in that area.

In Kargil district:

After you enter Kargil district you will go past Bodh Kharbu, which is close to the Nâmikâ Lâ (3719 metres), and then past Mulbek and Pashkum before reaching Kargil town.

Bodh Kharbu (164km from Leh) is 70km before Kargil. Polo is popular in the area. Accommodation: There is a rest house, though mainly for government servants. (Khar means 'palace' and 'bu' means 'nine'. There used to be nine palaces here. Elsewhere in Kargil a building contractor dutifully wiped clean the ruins of ancient palaces in the late 20th century. He used the construction materials removed from the ruins in some engineering work.)

The Bodh Kharbu fort has been built on a mountainside at some distance from the present village. The kings of Leh and Baltistan and, in 1639, the Mughals, attacked it. It is believed that the Balti soldiers who died in those wars are buried here. The fort is now in ruins. In mediæval times the village used to be around the fort. This was one of the forward posts of the government of Chiktan. The mosque in the present village is contemporaneous with the fort.

(***Detour 1*** [strictly for those interested in *rock engravings*]: A little ahead of Bodh Kharbu is a place called Khangral. From here you can take a side road that leads to Shakar, the turtle peak and Chiktan Khar.

(After you have travelled 29km from Khangral you will come to **Skinbrisa**. Here, next to the stream, are several large rocks with mediæval as well as later engravings. The figures carved on these rocks include the ubiquitous ibexes, hunters with bows and arrows and buffalo-hunts. Dr.B.R. Mani, from whose fieldwork I have derived much information, estimates that there are 47 ibexes on a single boulder. The piece de resistance is a boulder with a fairly elaborate war scene. Warriors are shown riding horses. Significantly, in adition to the usual bows and arrows, some of the mounted soldiers carry long spears or lances.

(Sanjak, on River Indus, is two kilometres further down the same road, where the stream merges with the Indus. Another 2km. ahead is a place called Tilichang. Here you can see an old rock shelter with a bowl scooped out of a rock. The boulders here have more engravings. In addition to the usual ibexes, a deer and men with triangular bodies, there are also some group dances. [Remember, you are now iṇ Drokpâ country, and the Drokpâs, much as they deny it, love to dance and in groups.] The dancers are all in a row, the arms of each around the shoulders of the next dancer. The group dance has been drawn in the minimalist style used in signs inside airports. If you are familiar with the line drawings of The Saint series, you'll feel at home with the mediæval rock art of Kargil.

(Bémâ comes next, another 2km ahead. There is a rock shelter here, and two rocks with engravings. In the engravings we have more hunters, animals [probably wolves], ibexes [with penises] and group dances.

(Most of the engraved boulders of Rungdus, 2km. further ahead, were carelessly damaged while constructing the road. The figures that remain include hunters, ibexes, group dances, the *yâk* and, most significantly, a man wearing a crown. The lines of these drawing are made up of dots joined together. The artists had obviously used a hammer and a nail to make those dots.

(Da is around a kilometre away and Garkun yet another 3km. ahead. At Garkun there are more boulders with ibexes, and more rock shelters. Dr. Mani writes that 'ibex figures [have also] been found on boulders near village Darchicks [16km. from Sanjak] and at Benny Point [22km. from Sanjak and 5km. before Batâlik].

(From Sanjak you can proceed to Batâlik. From Batâlik you can return to Khangral-Bodh Kharbu, or go to Khaltse or to Kargil. End of this detour.)

(***Detour 2:*** **Chiktan** can be reached through the above detour.

(Janet Rizvi hails Chiktan as a fine example of the Buddhist-Muslim composite culture. I agree. Chiktan is one of the few villages in Ladâkh where Muslim women wear the perâk.

(Mrs. Rizvi adds that the greatest wealth of oral literature in Ladakh is perhaps to be found in Chiktan. This is especially so in the case of the epic *Kesar-lu*, which is best narrated by the bards of the Muslim villages of Chiktan.

(*Polo-ground:* Chiktan's historic- and celebrated- polo ground has been described in a folksong that is famous all over Ladakh. In fact, it is an enclosed stadium, about a kilometre from the present Khardûn neighbourhood and the palace. It is situated between the Thâchey and Mangli-tson neighbourhoods. Its mediæval- maybe ancient- walls are tall, made of stones and still mostly intact. Unfortunately, much of the Chiktan shagharan has been encroached upon.

(The *shagharan* is roughly 300 metres by 30 metres in size. As in Kishtwar [Jammu], the goal stones (*hazdo*) at the two ends are several centuries old and in a bad shape. There is an ancient grove near one of the walls of the stadium. There used to be a royal pavilion where the grove now is. After the gãme was over, Mon singers and dancers would perform on a platform facing this pavilion. Horses would be tethered to a wall away from the pavilion before the game and also later when the singing and dancing was going on.

(*The Râzî Khar palace*: King Tsering Malik (16th century AD) built this palace on the hillock of the present Khardûn hamlet. The architect was Chandan, a resident of Chhorbat or Khapalu. There is reason to believe that the palace included what remained of the 9th century AD palace of Tî-sok Gangâ-sok. It used to be one of the finest palaces in all Ladâkh. When Francke visited- and photographed- it in 1909, it was still mostly intact. Local citizens vandalised it during the course of the twentieth century. Kachu Sikander Khan says that they removed the woodwork and stones for their own use, and damaged the paintings. As he points out, now only the walls of some rooms on the lower floor remain.

(Remains of a mediæval mosque and of the ancient Chiktan village can be found around the palace.

(*Heritage building*: The Kachu notes with understandable sadness that a part of the house of Rahîm Khan, the Kalon, has been 'modernised.' It was in its original, mediæval condition till around 1985. It is located in Mangli-tson. The Kalon was the brother of King Muhammad Ali Khan of Chiktan.

(*Lhâ Khang:* This is one of the Kashmîirî/ Indian style Buddhist temples constructed by Lotsâvâ Rinchen Zangpo. It is in the Zagâñg neighbourhood and is now in a bad shape. A Lama looks after it. In ancient times, people would offer flowers here during the Snolâ festival.)

(***Detour 3:*** **Shakar**: *The palace* ruins are located on a hillock in the Mângrî hamlet. Ahmed Khan, King of Shakar-Chiktan (c.1735-1745), had built it. He began to live here after Shakar seceded from Chiktan during his reign. Gyalpo Deldan Namgyâl attacked it, but did not cause much damage.

(*The Bonpo Yul:* Yul means 'village.' The name suggests that the ancient Bons once lived here and that the Bon Chhos (religion) was once practised here. Close by, in the Sâkyat neighbourhood, are the ruins of the Manglâ Khar (fort) and the Namgyâl Tsemo. The Mangla Khar is one of the oldest tribal forts of Ladâkh. The Kings of Leh probably constructed the Tsemo, which might have been one of their army outposts. Leh town has a peak and a monastery by this name.

(The Gâsho dynasty ruled over the region through most of its known, i.e. mediæval, history. They, too, used the Tsemo as a fortress end of detours.)

Wâkhâ: *The palace and the ancient village of Wakha:* After the death of King Kunchok Sherab Stan (16th century AD), the kings of Wakha shifted their capital to Sûm Brâñ. This used to be a little hamlet to the left of present-day Wakha. It is on a hillock near the confluence of the Wakha Rong and Namika streams. The people of Wakha used to live around the palace. Only the ruins now remain.

King Babar Khan (18th century) was very fond of polo. There is a pologround across the river from the palace. He wanted to stay in touch with his favourite game even after he died. So he was, on his request, buried in a grave atop a large rock. This is on the bank of the river close to the palace.

Stadium: Wakha had a historical stadium (*chingrâ*) called Yar-Kyûm. Its ruins can be found at one end of the present village.

Mulbek(h) (3,230m.) is twenty-five kilometres after Bodh Kharbu, or 45km before and east of Kargil. (189km. from Leh.) This is a little valley. The village of the same name has a Buddhist population. Both are named after a stream that comes from the Zâñskâr range and merges with River Suru.

The Mulbek Khar sits atop the Halo-bark cliff. On occasion it was the capital of the kings of Ladâkh. The rest of the time, it was the headquarters of provincial governors. King Tashi Namgyâl (c.18th century) constructed this fort. It was set on fire during Zorawar Singh's invasion (c.1835). It is now in ruins. A monastery has been built within the precincts of the old fort. Near the cliff is a historic inscription etched at the behest of King Dragspâ Bum Lde. The remains of the graves of King Bum Lde, Chhoz Bum Lde and his Muslim queen can still be found.

There is a government-run 'tourist bungalow' in the village as well as some privately owned accommodation and eating places.

Shergol is another ten kilometres ahead, or 35km before Kargil. (199km. from Leh.) It is also spelt Shergole (the 'e' is silent). The village is on the right bank of the Wâkhâ brook. The village and the gompa are well off the highway. You are now on a side road that's on the left of the highway. (On the right, when you come up from Kargil.) Both Buddhists and Muslims live here.

Among the most celebrated sons of this village was Lungpo (minister) Rgpâ-chen (c.7th century AD). He was the prime minister of Songas Zangpo, King of Tibet.

An exciting four-day trek from Shergol leads, past the Safi Lâ and Rusi Lâ passes, into the Suru valley. Safi, a high-altitude village, has a mixed Muslim-Buddhist population and lies between the two passes. From the Rusi Lâ one can trek either to Sankoo or, southwards, through the glacier- rich Rangdum pass, to the Rangdum village and monastery.

Phokar (or Fokar) is 4km ahead of the Shergole monastery, on the side road that branches off left from the highway.

(For separate entries about the monasteries on this side road, please see the chapter 'The important gompas of Ladakh... Kargil district'.)

The National Highway between Shergole and Kargil is rewarding in more than one way. At night on this stretch I have seen foxes (minks?) with enormous bushy tails. Francke found primitive rock carvings.

The Chaq Shing Khar is located atop a hillock near Karambâ hamlet. It was the capital of a kingdom that included Suru-Karchey, Mulbek-Wâkhâ and Phokar. It remained so till the reign of (king) Kunchok Sherab Stan (16th century).

Kargil town (2,740m) is 234 km from Leh.

From Srinagar to Kargil town

On the night before you leave Srinagar for Ladakh (Kargil and Leh) by road please check if the dZoji Lâ pass is open on the day on which you plan to travel. (The pass, also spelt Zoji Lâ, is closed for almost six months in winter. During the rest of the year it is shut once a week for maintenance.) Please also check the hour when they'll let your vehicle through. Or else you'll wind up waiting at the pass for hours. (Please do this when travelling back from Leh, Kargil or Drâss to Srinagar, too.) The staff at the bus and taxi stands would know. So would the staff at Srinagar's TRC, Kargil's Tourist Office and the Drâss tourist bungalow.

Normally they allow private vehicles to leave Sonamarg (Srinagar district) for Kargil only at 2 pm. You can leave Srinagar around 9 am on such days

(In case they allow your vehicle to leave Sonamarg earlier, at, say, 9 am, you might have to leave Srinagar around 4 am or so. You'll be in Sonamarg by 7 am.)

Either way, you don't want to get stuck in the slow moving army convoy. Being sandwiched inside a convoy can be extremely frustrating.

You want to be among the first in the queue of vehicles at **Sonamarg**, waiting to be allowed to enter the dZoji Lâ. (Mornings and nights at Sonamarg are quite cold, even in the summer.)

The road after Sonamarg is surprisingly good. It remains so till the milestone that tells you that Gumri is 15km. ahead. Then the road gets bad and, after a while, terrible.

The **dZoji Lâ** (pass) on the Srinagar-Kargil-Leh National Highway gets blocked by snow every winter. This could happen as early as in the third week of October or as late as in the last week of December. The engineers of the Indian Army try to keep the road open till the 15th November, even if there's been snowfall. After that, even if there is *no* snow, you'll be using this pass at your own risk. (Not that you will be allowed to use it.) The pass reopens in mid-June.

The dZoji Lâ starts shortly after Sonamarg. It is an extremely rough, often unpaved, 7-kilometre road, which sometimes passes through mounds of ice. It is 3,530 metres at its highest and cuts through the mountain that stands between Kashmir and Ladakh. For those who have never seen ice or snow, the pass is a good introduction. Because of permafrost conditions, there'll be some fields of ice right next to the road at all times of the year. (The warming experienced between 1998 and 2002 changed that for a few years. Glaciers began to recede throughout the Indian Himalayas.) As you travel through the pass, on your right you will see the vegetation change rapidly—from the dense woods of Kashmir to the more stunted shrubs, barren hills and occasional pastures of Ladakh.

Once you're out of the pass, the road improves considerably. Or let's put it this way: inside the pass you'd been travelling on earth and stones. Now at least there'll be a road of sorts. It has been built on a path that was a historic trade route known as the Treaty Road. Central Asia is at its northern end and Tibet at the other (eastern) end.

The pass ends at **Gumri.** A path from here, on the right (south), leads to the holy Shri Amarnath ji cave.

Driving on this road, between Kargil and the dZoji Lâ, on an early morning, can be an incredibly rewarding experience because of the hundreds of birds you are likely to find on or near the road. Magpies come out in big numbers in late August/ early September. However, in mid-June the number of birds is much smaller: they come out in just one's and two's. You are likely to do this stretch in the morning when returning from Kargil to Srinagar.

Mînâmarg: In a way this pasture is a continuation of Kashmir. It has the meadows of Sonamarg, but not the trees. The hills in the north lead to the so-called Northern Areas of Occupied Kashmir. There is a greenish valley in the south.

Matâyan is 20km before Drâss/ 78km before Kargil town. It is the first village that you will come upon after the pass. Good rock climbing is possible on the hills between Matâyan and Drâss. The areas to the south (right) of the National Highway are a vast green expanse.

1.6 kilometres after Matâyan, right next to the highway, is the so-called **Draupadi Kund** (10,840'). It is now being said that Queen Draupadi of the *Mahâbharat* fame would bathe there. I suspect that the belief dates to after the 1830s, when the first Hindu soldiers arrived in Ladakh. What is certain is that the belief was quite well established in the late 19th and early twentieth centuries. The local Muslims of that era had heard that an ancient Hindu queen called Draupadi used to bathe and wash her clothes in that spring. Indeed, they would point to a fortress-like structure on a peak that no one had been able to climb. That is where Draupadi's family had lived, they were told. The Muslims of Drâss would even celebrate the legend at a festival which would be held every year near the Kund (pond), after the crop had been harvested, i.e. around October. There would be much singing and sport, mainly polo.

'When was the festival discontinued,' I asked.

'After the highway from Drâss to Srinagar was built, in the 1960s.'

'And why?'

'After the road was built no one had the time for festivals in October,' I was told.

Indeed, October has since become a month for extremely hectic economic activity. Everything that the Ladakhis need for the winter has to be purchased from Kashmir, Jammu or Delhi and stored for the next six months, when the road is be closed. These things range from soaps and matchboxes to kerosene, petrol, notebooks, photocopying paper, medicines, just everything. Naturally the people of Drâss now have things other than festivity in mind in the weeks that follow the harvest.

The drive between Matayan/ Draupadi Kund and Drass can be very fragrant, especially after a rain. Some army officers attributed this to the zeera (cumminseed) crop. Dr. Muhammad Deen has a more exciting explanation. The flowers that are abloom in June cause the fragrance, he says.

Murâd Bâgh: 18.8km after Matayan and 1.1km before the Tourist Bungalow at Drass, a road branches off to the left. It leads to a vast, open, green area. Murad Bagh is a charming little village in the middle of this green. The path then goes on to meet Mushkoo. This majestically located village is spread out between Mushkoo valley and Goshan. It is best approached from Drass, from which it is around 4km uphill.

Mushkoo, made famous by television reports of the 1999 war, is a large, green valley to the left (north) of the NH.

There used to be a Sikh-era (early 19th century) fort in the stretch between Mushkoo and Drass.

Drâss (3,230 metres) is a small town on the highway, 60km before Kargil. It is officially billed as the second coldest inhabited place in the world (after Siberia). Winter temperatures drop to minus 45°C. The windchill factor is even greater. (*Reach Ladâkh* claims that temperatures fall to minus 50°C.) In summer, however, Drâss can be quite pleasant. Till September, it can be positively hot at noon.

The people of Drâss are 'Aryans' of the Dard ethnic group. They had migrated here from Gilgit and speak Shina. Almost a dozen languages are spoken in Ladakh. Shina alone belongs to the Indo-European group. The rest have their roots in Tibet. The Tibetan name of the place is Hembabas.

The people of Drâss have for centuries known how to cross the snow-covered dZoji Lâ pass in early winter and spring. This gave them an unrivalled position as porters in the trade with Central Asia. Now that that route has been closed, they carry mail from the Kashmiri side of the pass to the Ladakhi side.

By 2005 or 2006, the national highway will change its present route and go over the Umba Lâ pass into the Suru valley before it reaches Kargil. Till then, the 3-day trek from Drâss to the Suru valley will remain quite popular.

Where to stay: There is a moderately priced, government run tourist bungalow. There also are even cheaper (but far more spartan) private guest houses like the *Snowland*. At the upper end are *Hill View* and *Dreamland*.

Being on the national highway, Drâss has a regular bus service to Kargil. Some buses to and from Srinagar halt here.

The Drass belt

Kargil has two regions where grass, some trees and other vegetation can be found. These are the Suru Valley and the Drass belt.

Drass village is at the centre of several little valleys, most of them green. Tourists often camp in Drass for several days. They explore the valleys around Drass during the day and return to their hotels in the evening. POK (mainly Baltistan) is in the north. Not only are the areas south of the National Highway open to tourists, they are also prettier.

- ***Mînaâmarg***, on the National Highway, is the first of these valleys when you drive up from Srinagar.
- ***Matayan*** valley comes next.
- ***Mushkoo*** follows.

Umba La is the pass that conects Drass with the Suru Valley. The areas around it, too, are green and picturesque.

A track leads from Drass to what the army and, increasingly, the public, call the *Sandow valley*. This valley leads to the Marpo La (POK). Tourists are not allowed inside this area. They are not missing very much.

A three-day trek from Drâss will take you to *Sankoo*, in the Suru valley (see 'Suru valley').

The local dance is called Dhani. Drâss also has a sword dance. The local culture- especially poetry and songs- is mainly Balti (as in Baltistan, POK). There are Kashmiri influences too: chhakri music, for instance. (See the volume on Kashmir: Culture.)

As the road proceeds towards Kargil, there will be tall mountains on the left. Baltistan is right behind these mountains. You will be able to see some of the peaks that Pakistan has illegally occupied. Seven kilometres of this road (and parts of Kargil town itself) are within the range of Pakistan's artillery. In 1998 and 1999, some of these peaks witnessed bloody fighting. In the winter of 1998, as per convention, both India and Pakistan withdrew their soldiers from these peaks. Pakistan took advantage of this and a few days later simply moved into several of the peaks that you can see here (and many that you can't). In the summer of 1999, the Indian army recaptured most of the recently-occupied peaks, sacrificing several of its bravest men in the process. The remaining peaks were recovered by the Indian government through diplomacy.

(See also the chapter on 'A History of Kargil,' and the section on 'War Sites' elsewhere in this book.)

Drâss itself is not pretty. **Goshan**, a suburb of Drâss, 2km uphill from the Drâss market, is a vast and stunning plain at around 11,250'. The war sites of Tololing, Tiger Hill and even the edge of the Mushkoo valley are best viewed from there. The Drass area can be very windy around noon (11.45 am to 2.30 pm). In Goshan these strong, sandy winds raise lots of dust.

You resume your drive to Kargil. The Suru river will often run parallel to the road.

Stekbu is one kilometre ahead of Drâss. It has a number of Buddhist stone sculptures. Many of them are primitive engravings on low stone slabs, the size of milestones. The figures represent the Maitreya Buddha, the Avalokiteshvar, a man on a horse, a lotus and a chorten.

Some of the slabs are right next to the highway. You don't even need to get out of your vehicle. Most of these intaglio sculptures were crafted around the same time as the Mulbek Chambâ. That could have been as early as in the eighth century. These sculptures and inscriptions have been declared protected national monuments.

Who got the stone sculptures of **Ranbir Por** made? According to a local tradition, the two squabbling queens of the Kharpon etched them themselves. (See 'Yulbo Drass' elsewhere in this book.) Others believe that they were part of Lotsâvâ Rinchen Zangpo's campaign.

Till the 15th century, the Drass region was predominantly, if not entirely, Buddhist.

(Incidentally, the Chinese occasionally claim all territory up to these icons as theirs. They argue thus: 'Tibet belongs to China. The Buddhist areas of Ladakh belong to Buddhist Tibet. These statues prove that Himalayan Buddhism had spread at least up to this place. Therefore, all Indian territory between Tibet and Stekbu belongs to China.'

(Other Chinese expansionists have a simpler formula. "All passes called 'Lâ' belong to the Tibetan continuum. Therefore, they belong to China." By that logic, even Drâss and Gumri, right up to the dZoji Lâ get included in the area claimed by some Chinese.)

More primitive engravings-on-rock have been found at Channi Gund and Dongga, all of them in the Dard area.

The road winds its way from Drâss to Stekbu, Bimbat, Kharbu, Kaksar [away from the highway] and finally Kargil, through the apricot- and apple- belt. Most of these are very minor villages. The first major human settlement on the road after Drâss is Kargil itself.

Bimbat: Like the Draupadi Kund this village has a Mahabharat connection. There are thick groves along the NH after Bimbat and pretty picnic spots nearby. The green stretch comes to an end shortly after Bimbat.

Greenery reappears at Chhani Gund, a longish village along the NH.

You can make it from Srinagar to **Kargil** town in just seven or eight hours of actual driving in a car or jeep. Most people do it in ten hours. Buses take ten to twelve hours.

17

Dâ-Hânu

Dâ-Hânu and the 'Aryan' Drokpâs

This is a substantial region that is partly in Leh and partly in Kargil. It lies between Hanu and Batâlik and is spread over 180 kilometres. Some Ladakhi writers call the area 'Brok-land'. It consists of four major villages, and some hamlets. It is as scenic as you would expect of a region of Ladakh be that is two thousand feet lower (and thus more green, less cold and less dry) than Leh or Zâñskâr. However, the tourists' main interest in Dâ-Hânu is cultural and anthropological.

The region is located in a narrow gorge of River Indus. The sun is so intense here that it is possible to grow two crops a year, Along with Nubra, Dâ-Hânu is one of the few places in Ladakh where this can be done.

The Brokpas/ Drokpâs

(Also spelt 'Dokpa' in Leh. In Kargil the name is spelt and pronounced 'Brokpa'. In this chapter, the names of the ethnic group, Dard, sub-group, Drokpâ, and region, Dâ-Hânu, have been used interchangeably.)

Brok/ Drok/ Dok mean 'the highlands.' Pâ means 'of' (or 'the people of'). The Drokpâs, thus, are 'the people of the highland [pastures]'. The women are called Drokmos or Brokmos. These, incidentally, are the names that other Ladakhis call the Dards of Dâ-Hânu by.

The Drokpâs almost certainly migrated here from Dardistan (POK). One of their songs talks about their migration from Gilgit (POK), led by Gil Sengge (the Lion of Gilgit). A set of eighteen songs, sung at the Bono-na festival, contains the history and value system of this tribe. Many of the songs are between sixty and ninety minutes long, each. Considering how detailed and encyclopædic they are, their length is not surprising.

According to these songs, several centuries ago the Drokpâs migrated from Gilgit to mountain pastures (called *drok*). Some scholars believe their original home was in the Bagrot valley of Gilgit. Their Lhâs (deities), too, migrated with them. For the Drokpâs dancing was something to be done only once in a while, during pauses in the real business of life-farming and hunting. The Lhâs were lotus-eaters who spent all their waking hours dancing. This began to tell on the pastures, which they (the deities) wore out by their constant dancing. To this day grass does not grow on the Mal Mal Khatu pasture at the place where the Lhâs would dance.

What is worse, the Lhâs wanted the Drokpâs to dance with them. For a while the Drokpâs went along with the Lhâs' demands. But soon this got to be a bit too much. Work began to suffer. And the Drokpâs could hardly refuse to obey the Lhâs. So they began to look for ways to get rid of their unwelcome celestial guests.

One of the Drokpâs had an idea. So, the next time that the gods and goddesses forced the Drokpâs to dance with them, the Drokpâs began to kiss them all, and kept at it. Now, the Lhâs were a bashful lot. They drew the line at being kissed by humans- en masse at that. They decided to pack up and leave. The Drokpâs cheered the Lhâs and even gave them a prolonged farewell.

Nice story. Might even be true. In any case, it has given every generation of Drokpâs an excuse to enact that last fateful dance, especially the ritual public kissing part. (Around the 1980s, the new generation of Drokpas started getting uncomfortable with outsiders' voyeuristic obsession with the mass kissing bit.)

The other songs

Not all Drokpâ songs are so dismissive of their divine guests. One of the songs describes the exodus of the Drokpas' ancestors from Gilgit to Dâ-Hânu, complete with details of the route. It expresses gratitude to the Lhâs for having conducted their ancestors safely across the mountains.

Another song is about pastoral duties. It talks about the life and duties of goat-herds, from tending the flock and feeding goats in the mountain pastures to the things that you can get from a goat i.e. milk, wool, horns and, above all, fine mutton.

A third song is about an ibex hunt. It describes in detail how the hunter scales the mountains, stalks his quarry, zeroes in on the prey and, the deities be praised, succeeds in killing the ibex. The Lhâs are thanked for their help. (See also the chapter on 'sports, pastimes and festivals.')

Racial 'purity'

The Drokpâs, who are supposed to be the purest 'Aryans' in the world, live in Dâ-Hânu. This author, like many others, believes that the Aryans are a linguistic group, not a race. Hence the quotes around the word Aryan.

And yet, racially the Drokpâs are totally different from the Mongoloid people of Leh. They number around three or four thousand. Their culture, religion and language, too, are very different from the rest of Leh.

This racial purity thing is getting diluted in Da and Hanu. The tract between these two villages is mainly in Leh district. In this region some 'Aryan' Drokpâs have intermarried with the Mongoloids.

The neighbouring tract, that between Garkun and Darchiks, is entirely in Kargil district. Drokpâs live there as well. They have guarded the 'purity' of their race more zealously there.

Inter-racial marriages: And yet, even Garkun can't claim absolute 'purity.' One of its families gave a daughter in marriage to a man from neighbouring Da (c.1960). Nothing unusual about that. Except that around 1930 his mother had come from as far away as Khardung. Thus, while the 'dilution' first came to Da, a generation later the 'dilution' travelled to Garkun. Da society had not held the mother's Khardung background against her. Nor did Garkun complain about the son being of mixed blood. Apparently, we outsiders are more concerned about 'racial purity' than at least these particular families.

Some of this 'dilution' was part of a conscious policy of the Gyâlpos (kings) of Leh. At some stage they sent three or four non-Dard families over to settle in Garkun. The Dards are Caucasoid/ Aryans, whereas the settlers were Mongoloid. This happened at some stage between the 10th and 18th centuries. As I said in the chapter on 'A History of Leh,' while dealing with historical events in Ladakh we should be prepared to be off the mark by a couple of centuries this way or that. Also, when we talk of people in Ladakh the numbers are so small that the migration of four families in a span of eight hundred years is historically significant. Especially when the community that they migrated to (and married into), and which this chapter is all about, numbers just around 3000.

Theories about the Drokpâs' origin

Some Drokpâs have blond hair and blue eyes. They are tall and fair. Therefore, some scholars have suggested that the Drokpâs might be the descendants of the army of Alexander, who is (incorrectly) believed to have gone to Gilgit/ Dardistan. Others feel that the Drokpâs might be the people who, according to Ptolemy and Megasthenes, possessed ants that dug up gold.

The Dards also live in Baltistan, Gilgit and Kalash, all in the 'Northern Areas' of Pakistan Occupied Kashmir. Their traditions and customs are, but for minor variations, the same as those in Dâ-Hânu.

Religion and customs

In Leh-Kargil, the Dards settled in two broad areas, Drâss (where they are entirely Muslim) and Dâ-Hânu. The people of Dâ-Hânu are mostly Buddhist by religion. They retain a way of life and culture that is totally different from that of the Buddhists of Leh or the Muslim Dards of Drâss. Their language is similar to that of the Muslim Dards of Drâss and Gilgit (POK), though. Their Buddhism, on the other hand, is nothing like that of the Buddhists of the rest of Ladakh. In fact many local people say that they are neither Buddhist nor Muslim.

In any case, they converted to Buddhism only around the 1820s or '30s, because of the efforts of Lâmâ Samphel of nearby Lâmâ. Yûrû. Before that the Drokpâs belonged to a religion called Bon-chos and worshipped animals, nature and ancestors. They still retain many Bon-chos rituals, including the great harvest festival, Bono-na or Chopo Srubla. Their shamanism, their songs and their cosmic system, too, are Bon-chos. ('Chos' means 'religion.' 'Bon' means 'animism' and includes the worship of fire and nature.)

Islam and the Drokpâs: The Brokpas of Chuli Chan and Da Da Do have converted to Islam. However, they live outside the areas covered in this chapter. They do not practice the customs described here. However, they speak the same language and often come over to watch the festivals of their Buddhist and animist cousins. The Dards of Drâss can not be called Drokpâ or Brokpa. However, even they sometimes participate in Bono-Na as spectators.

Eggs and dairy products are taboo: The Drokpâs abhor the cow as well as all dairy and other products obtained from it. This, as J&K Tourism's website notes, is 'most baffling for a people believed to be of Aryan descent.' On the other hand, they consider the ibex sacred and sing songs about ibex hunts. They worship the goat and consider it a symbol of fertility and prosperity.

The website adds that the goat is the Drokpâs' cult animal and is the 'preferred animal for offering as sacrifice [at the altar of Shringman Lhâmo, the Goddess of Wealth, on important occasions such as] Bono-na, held alternately in Garkun and [Da] villages, with a one-year break in between.' The sacrifice is conducted by the Lhâbdag-pa, 'who is the traditional officiant for this deity'. Indeed, the number of goats and sheep a family owns is a measure of its wealth. Many families have hundreds of each.

Regarding the cow, the website explans that it is only the Indian and Iranian Aryans who worship the cow. German Aryans, for instance, don't. E. Joldan has a better theory. Cattle are clumsy animals. The narrow and precipitous terrain of Dâ-Hânu is much too dangerous for them, for they routinely slip off and die. Besides, feeding them in winter is expensive and difficult. Goats, on the other hand, are sure-footed.

Eggs and fowls, too, are taboo. But men, being men, are bound to ignore taboos when away from the watchful eyes of women and elders. When visiting Kargil or Skardu they often eat eggs as well as dairy products. However, even they maintain the sanctity of their land. There is an auspicious Kagaaney Maaney three kilometres west of Da. The men eat up all the eggs and dairy products that they might have bought in Kargil before they reach this maaney, so that the area beyond it is undefiled by eggs, milk or butter.

The Zo (or dZo) is what is born when a cow mates with a yâk. It is the only cattle that the Drokpâs put up with, though quite unwillingly. They need this tough animal to plough their fields. As soon as ploughing is over, they drive the dZos away to the mountains above. They don't even use dZo dung as manure in their fields. (The dZo is male. The female is called Zomo or dZomo. The dZo is sterile, but the dZomo is not. In this respect they differ from that other crossbreed, the mule, both genders of which are sterile.)

Things are changing, at least in Hanu, where some families took to rearing cows in the 1980s.

Traditional dress: The easiest way to tell if someone is a Drokpâ is from the bunch of colourful flowers (increasingly made of paper or plastic) on top of that person's bonnet or hat. The said website says that the Drokpâs' dress consists of 'tight trousers made from the local coarse woollen tweed worn under a short upper tunic of the same cloth, both of which are richly decorated with geometric designs along the borders and seams. This colourful ensemble is topped off with a bonnet heavily bedecked with a variety of trinkets, beads, ribbons and rows... of needles, strings of cowry shells etc.' Most Drokpâ ornaments are beaded.

Astronomy: The Drokpâs have a rudimentary knowledge of astronomy. But they are fairly accurate at whatever little use they make of it. From the movements of the sun they can predict when the solstices and equinoxes will take place, dates that the rest of us take as a given.

Disputes: Like many other tribals (especially the Gujjars), the Drokpâs try to settle their disputes themselves, rather than in courts of law. (The same is true of most of Zâñskâr and much of rural Leh.) If neither party in a dispute can prove its case conclusively, both parties are taken to the village monastery (gompa). Both are asked to swear that they are telling the truth. Such is the fear of God that the liar rarely agrees to swear. He looks for excuses to wriggle out. The party that takes the oath wins.

The two are then kept away from each other on festive occasions, so that they don't start fighting again. A year later, by when the dispute would have been forgotten, the two are made to sit together and patch up.

Are the Drokpâs insular? In theory, yes. For centuries they tried to keep away from the other people of Leh and Kargil. And yet there is so much of Leh in their lives. In turn they have influenced the culture of Leh. Most importantly, they became Buddhists even if their practices are quite distinctive. Like other Buddhists they call their gods and goddesses Lhâ and Lhâmo, even if their main Lhâmo is entirely their own, as are several other deities. Their new year, too, is called Losar, though on a different day. They have a gompa, even if tiny and with just two or three lâmâs. They, too, have maaneys.

On the other hand, other Ladakhi Buddhists have adopted Drokpâ customs like throwing lit torches at a designated spot during Losar celebrations. Joldan argues that perhaps 'the Ladakhi custom[s] of making wild sheep from dough and decorating their kitchen walls with crescent and other designs, at Losar, have their origins in Brokpâ traditions. Tibetans don't do such things.' He adds that the bass drum (Dang Dang) of the Drokpâs was once part of Ladakh's royal orchestras. The Namgyâl Tsemo in Leh has a wall painting in which musicians play on such a drum for the king. Joldan also points out that 'the fashion among [other] Ladakhi ladies of wearing goat skin having long white hair, to cover their back comes from Brok-land [i.e. Dâ-Hânu].'

The people of Dâ-Hânu must surely have had some contacts with the Kashmiris, too. Several Drokpâ families possess elegant brass pitchers and other handicrafts of Kashmiri origin.

Language: The Drokpâs' language is very similar to Sheena, which, in turn, is much like Hindi-Urdu and, sometimes, English. ('Two' is 'du' and 'three' is 'tera/ tre.') I haven't rubbed in the Drokpâs' 'Aryanness' in this chapter thus far. Maybe it is time to do so, and remind the reader that this is their USP. Yes, their language is very Indo-Aryan. Actually, it is eerily close to Sanskrit. For instance, they call the sun 'suri' (from the Sanskrit 'surya'). Their word for 'hand' is 'hath.' However, over the years thousands of Ladakhi words have entered their vocabulary, perhaps a result of their 19th century conversion to Buddhism.

Joldan says that some of the Drokpâs' Ladakhification was because of pressure from a particular Ladakhi king. He adds that while the Dards of Hanu started speaking some Ladakhi, the women did not. 'If the idea was integration with the [other] Ladakhis...,' he writes, 'that did not happen.'

Funerals: The Drokpâs cremate their dead on pyres, on the banks of a river. This is very Hindu, and quite different from the anaerobic cremation of other Ladakhi Buddhists.

Flora: As mentioned, Dâ-Hânu, along with Nubra, is one of the few places in Ladakh where two crops can be grown in a year. Farmers grow apricots and grapes to sell in Leh and Kargil. They also grow flowers, especially their beloved Skalzâñg flower. The flower that they wear in their caps is called Shoklo and often grows on its own.

Washing/ bathing: Mrs. Janet Rizvi says that 'among the most striking of [the Drokpâs'] customs is a dread, and almost complete avoidance, of washing. For ceremonial purification they burn the fragrant twigs of the pencil cedar.'

As far as washing is concerned Mrs. Rizvi has been unfair to the Drokpâs because, this is true of many others in Ladakh as well. In fact, Mrs. Rizvi herself quotes Drew as saying, 'All [Ladakhis] have a rooted objection to washing. I was told that there was a custom of bathing once a year…'

It is true that even elite Ladakhis argue that there is no need for them to bathe frequently in winter because i) in winter they don't get dirty anyway, and ii) each time that you bathe a layer of your skin flows down with the water. Argument ii) above is true: but those are dead cells and get replaced immediately. The first assertion is totally incorrect. There's plenty of dust in the air even in regions like Zâñskâr, which are entirely covered with snow.

And yet this author would disagree with Drew and Rizvi. The Ladakhis bathe quite regularly in the summer and once a month or so in winter. Even Europeans wouldn't traditionally bathe more often than that in winter. At Cambridge there were no baths in the halls of residence at the University till the 19th century. The dons argued that baths weren't needed because students were never at the University for more than eight weeks at a time.

Besides, we should show more understanding of the Ladakhis' problems. Few parts of the world are as cold in the winter. Water is in short supply. It has to be heated with scarce wood. Even a health freak like this author would bathe only once a week (but wash twice a day) during his winter in Zâñskâr.

But I digress.

The Great Harvest Festival—Chopo Srupla

Shringman Lhâmo is the Drokpâs' Goddess of Wealth and Fertility. (Lhâ is exactly the same as the Hindu 'devata' or deity. Lhâmo in turn is the precise translation of 'Devi' or goddess.) The Lhâbdag-pâ or Lapdraks has been variously defined as 'the caretaker of the gods' and 'the traditional officiant for [the Lhâmo alone]'. Da and Garkun have one Lapdrak each.

The Drokpâs' Great Harvest Festival is called Chopo Srubla as well as Bono-na. It is held at Da and Garkun in alternate years. There is no festival in the third year. In the fourth year, the three-year cycle begins all over again. The festival lasts four or five days. It is normally held in October, in the first or second week. Apart from the religious rites performed at this festival, what strikes most outsiders (including people from the rest of Ladakh) is the ritual public kissing that takes place.

The dancing ground at Da is much bigger than the one at Garkun. Two large walnut trees, and some willows, grow over it. In both villages this is a largeish, circular patch of land in the open, and has been designated specially for this purpose. (The details given below are mainly about the festival when held at Da. The one at Garkun is almost identical.)

Warming up for the festival: At most Buddhist, and some Hindu, festivals, stories taken from religious lore are acted out in the form of plays or operas. The actors as well as the audience take these plays most seriously. At Basohli (Kathua district, Jammu province), for instance, actors who are supposed to play the deities lead a life of abstinence and purity for several weeks before the actual show.

In Da-Hanu, little boy is chosen to play the Lhâ. He has to be between eight and ten years old. There is a rock near Da. It has a designated section on which the boy lives for many days before the festival.

On the evening before the festival, 'warming up' exercises begin. The sweet smelling wood of the pencil cedar wood is burnt, a bass drum is played near the Da fort and a young goat is sacrificed, all to please the gods. Men gather in a room near the gompa and silently drink *chhang* as they listen to the music. (The chhang is sometimes served in elegant Kashmiri pitchers made of brass and designed in the Central Asian style.)

The procession: In the early afternoon of the first day, some meat from the sacrificed goats is given to each of the families assembled near the designated rock. The top people of the village, including the Lapdrak, then dance up to the rock, where the boy who plays the Lhâ (god) awaits them in 'divine clothes'. They bring him down, after which he leads a slow procession. They first go to a field, where they dance. The procession ends at the village square. After that the Lapdrak takes over.

On that and subsequent evenings, the Lapdrak sings the famous epic songs mentioned above. The men, and later the women, start dancing.

The dancing: Ladakhi dances must surely be the slowest in the world. My theory is that they take half an hour to do a pirouette, though on occasion it's known to have been done in as few as twenty-nine minutes. No, seriously, they take forever. Their own explanation is that because oxygen is in short supply at those incredibly high altitudes they have to move very slowly. I suppose they are right. But the fact also is that before the advent of electricity they used to have so much time on their hands in winter that they had to look for things to do. (For that reason, Ladakhi adults work all summer and don't tell their children fairy-, folk- or religious stories till after the first major snowfall.)

And yet other Ladakhis consider the Drokpâs' dances much too slow even by their standards. Dâ-Hânu is almost two thousand feet lower than the areas around Leh town, with far more oxygen all around. Therefore, they should have been dancing faster if the altitude/ oxygen theory was the right explanation.

The other difference is that in the rest of Leh the sexes intermingle while dancing—every other dancer will, for instance, be a woman. (Most Ladakhis, enter the dance floor in a single file. After that they generally form a wide circle. The circle goes around the dance-ground several times.) The Drokpâs, too, enter in a single file. However, the men come first and then do the women. Thirdly, most Ladakhi dances have three sections. The Drokpâs' dances have only two. Finally, unlike other Ladakhis, Drokpâ dancers cut an anti-clockwise circle when they go around the ground.

Mentog Stanmo- the flower dance: This joyous dance is popular in Darchiks (Dartsiks) and Garkun (both villages are in the Dâ-Hânu region). It is also the main dance of other places in Kargil and Leh, which are as far apart as Mulbek, Wâkhâ, Purîg and the Nubra valley.

Men and women hold bunches of flowers as they dance. Flowers cheer up people everywhere. They do the same here—the audience as well as the dancers.

The musicians: In most of Buddhist Ladakh (i.e. Leh and Zâñskâr) musicians form two specific castes, the Mons and the Bedas, which are considered socially inferior. In Dâ-Hânu any talented person can perform professionally in public on festive occasions, something that doesn't happen in most of rural, feudal South Asia. (Classical music is the preserve of the Brahmins and Khans of India, and traditionally they did not perform before the masses. Folk-artistes are given the same low status among pan-Indian—the Hindus and Muslims as among the Buddhists of Ladakh.)

E. Joldan says that the respect that is accorded to musicians is unique to the Buddhist Dards. Even the Muslims Dards of Gilgit (POK) have a separate, and socially inferior, caste of musicians, the Doms. My theory is that there's so few of them that the Buddhist Dards can't afford the luxury of having a separate caste of musicians.

But then having specialised castes of musicians has its advantages. The Mons and Bedas know as many as 350 different tunes. The music of Dâ-Hânu is quite basic in comparison.

Ritual public kissing: After it gets dark, the dancing picks up. The men are quite high by now. They start kissing their lady friends/ wives (Or they used to till recently). Joldan calls this 'mass kissing.' However, it is no orgy. The men normally kiss only their own beaux. Maybe I am making it sound a bit antiseptic. Oh, no. They all get their kicks, as in the rest of the world. They then go home for dinner, after which they come back for another round of dancing. (And yet they complain that the Lhâs were overly fond of dancing.)

Note: Educated Drokpas are embarrassed by all mention of this (mass kissing) custom. They even deny that it ever existed. This is an all India trend. Several Himalayan people will lynch you (or at least ban your book) if you remind them that their people practised polyandry till the 1990s and that some of them still do.

Other festivals

The Drokpâs have the same word for the New Year as other Buddhists—Losar. However, the date is not the same. The Drokpâs celebrate it shortly after the winter solstice. From Gilgit they brought the custom of lighting many wooden torches and collectively throwing them all at a designated place in the village. The custom was later adopted in Zâñskâr and the rest of Leh. ('Lo' means 'year'.)

The Drokpâs' calendar, like that of the Chinese, Tibetans and other Ladakhis, follows a twelve-year cycle. Each year is named after an animal. Lo-dron is the festival of completing a twelve-year cycle. Instead of celebrating birthdays every year, people do so after every twelve years. A feast is laid out on the occasion of Lo-dron. (The Lo-dron is often celebrated on the occasion of the Great Harvest Festival, and not on the precise date of birth.)

When girls complete their first 12-year cycle (i.e. turn thirteen), they normally attain puberty. During Losar all girls who celebrate their first Lo-dron that year have to perform a group dance.

Like the baker's dozen, the Drokpâs are deliberately inexact about the completion of the sixth Lo-dron cycle, except that they err on the other side. People are deemed to have completed six Lo-drons a year in advance, i.e. when they complete 71 years. This, too, calls for a major celebration.

The ban and its partial lifting

Around 1975, some neo-Nazi German women came over to Dâ-Hânu to collect the seed of these 'pure Aryans'. At the very least the women were Aryan-supermacists. Some killjoy government official in Delhi reacted by banning the entry of foreigners to this region. Venus envy.

This author got the ban removed in 1993—Well, substantially. Tourists have since been allowed to visit Da(h) and Biama. This region begins near Khaltse and is close to Likir-Alchi-Lâmâ Yûrû. Much of it is on the banks on the Indus.

Already tourism has caused ecological damage to some of the thitherto banned (or 'restricted') places that I had got "opened up". I would request tourists to stay away from the ritual public kissing, even if invited to by a section of the people, because other sections might be annoyed by this and might lobby to get the ban imposed all over again.

The officially approved route

Drive from Leh to Khaltse. From there follow the Indus and go past Domkhar, Skurbuchan and Achina Thâñg. These are pretty and fairly well to do villages. Achina Thâñg is the last non-Dard, Buddhist village before entering the Dard region. You will then reach Hanudo and finally Biama. Da and Biama are around 160km from Leh town. The road is good by Ladakhi standards.

Indians can also take the Batâlik-Darchiks-Garkun-Khaltse route along the Indus. This route passes through Da and Biama as well.

The villages of Dâ-Hânu

Da(h) (9,690') is on the right bank of River Indus, close to the region's boundary with Baltistan (now in POK). Buddhist Dards live in Da. The village has a mediæval fort. Joldan (1985) argues that it looks 'more like a Dogra than a Ladakhi structure.' Joldan's theory can't be right because records from 1890 specifically say that it had been constructed to protect the area from Balti invaders. The village also has a gompa. The village is below Hanu Yogma.

Joldan writes, 'Beyond Da, to the west, the Indus gorge gets narrower and the mountains on both sides steeper and higher. At several places in Da, the width of the village [is] hardly more than that of a football field.'

Da is a regional centre of sorts. The people of Bema, Larsand, Sanit and other hamlets celebrate all major festivals and social functions here.

In the village there are two economy class guest houses, the *Skabapâ* and the *Sheringman Lhâmo*. Da is 4km. from Garkun.

'Da' means arrow. There is a small tunnel near the village, out of which water flows into the fields. The people of Da say that their ancient leader, Gil Sengge, had created this tunnel by shooting a mighty arrow into the rock.

Hanu Goma and **Yogma** are twin villages on the Hanu stream. Hanu Goma is on the old Leh-Skardu road, which goes through the Chhorbat pass, also known as the Hanu pass. King Tsewang Namgyâl I (16th century AD) was the first to get this road constructed. The 19th century European explorer Vigne described the Hanu stream as 'an impetuous torrent, that in some places rolls along the large stones in its bed with a noise resembling the report of distant cannon, and afterwards leaps into the deep and more tranquil stream of the Indus in a cascade of some magnitude and beauty.' The stream rises near the Hanu pass.

Culturally, Hanu is quite different from Da and Garkun. True, the people speak the same language and are Drokpâs from Gilgit. However, they must have come from a different part of Gilgit and at a different time. They were brought here by an ancient hero called Tho Srali. Significantly, the Great Harvest Festival alternates between Da and Garkun, both of which were founded by Gil Sengge. It bypasses Hanu, which has a festival of its own.

The Ladakhi language is spoken more widely by the Hanu Drokpas than by the Drokpâs of the other villages. The people of Hanu also tend to marry within themselves, possibly to retain the purity of their race. As a result they tend to marry even first cousins. Other Buddhists, like the Hindus, tend to think of cousins as brothers and sisters. Therefore, marrying a cousin is seen as something like incest. (Some people of Hanu have married non-Drokpâs.)

Hanu had not been plagued by dance-loving, kiss-averse gods (Lhâs), either. Therefore, its harvest festival has to make do without the ritual public kissing.

Garkun*:* (Also spelt Garkon. 4km from Da.) The village has been named after Gan Dum, the village in Gilgit (POK) from which its inhabitants' ancestors had migrated here. The 19th century British explorer Drew wrote that this village was in Baltistan (almost all of which is now in POK). However, modern Garkun is very much in Indian Kargil.

Drew said about Garkun, 'It is most curious in its situation. It consists of very narrow strips or ledges of flat, watered ground, between separate stages of a great river-cliff, so that on one side there is a precipitous fall of ground, while on the other vertical cliffs overhang the narrow fields, which, receiving their radiated heat, quickly ripen their crops; *even at night the place does not lose its heat*...Apple trees, apricots, mulberry, and *vine* are cultivated, in company with the cereals, on the narrow space, and flourish well with the *combination of warmth and moisture*.' (All emphases are mine.)

The gorge in which Garkun is located is so narrow that for several days in winter the sun does not rise at all.

***The Minduk Khar*:** The Kalon of Mulbek used to live in this palace. He was a nominee of the kings of Leh.

The Gharâhar-do: This is a water-mill. It has been built atop an ancient water-mill that figures prominently in Ladakhi history. *History:* King rGyâlam Kesar is the number one legendary hero of all Ladâkhis—Buddhist as well as Muslim. The *Kesar-loo* (The story of Kesar) epic is supposed to be mostly legend. However, related stories indicate that some of it could be verifiable history. Nocho Bohar was Kesar's younger brother. The commander in chief of the Turks (Turkmens?), Shanthâ, murdered Nocho inside this water-mill. Queen Dogomâ is said to have asked Shanthâ to kill him. Nocho was cremated on the nearby Mosûmâ-ling Surû-chey Zagâng hill.

Darchiks or Dartsiks is the fourth large Drokpâ village. Non-Indians are not allowed into that tract.

New settlements and the Muslims: All of two Purgi Muslim families used to live in Garkun till the early 1980s. Then a new settlement came up at Da Da Do. Several Muslim families, Dard as well as Purgi, got plots of land there. The Purgis of Garkun shifted to Da Da Do. E. Joldan comments, 'So much the better... for all concerned, as they could not be integrated with the Buddhist Dards, in Garkun.' For sentimentalists like this author, on the other hand, the migration was the death of ideal- an ideal that had survived for centuries, during which Muslims and Buddhists lived together quite happily. (Purîg is the heartland of Kargil. 'Purgi' means 'of Purîg.')

18

The Kargil District

Not including the parts illegally occupied by Pakistan, Kargil district has an area of around 15,000 sq. km.

A guidebook says, 'In Kargil, one can see some of the finest examples of Turkish architecture… A stroll in the ancient bazaar might lead to a shop selling attractive flint and tobacco pouches, travelling hookahs and brass kettles- handcrafted items of everyday use… (turquoise) can be bought here at bargain prices. And who knows, perchance, you may brush shoulders with one of the Minaros (or Brokpas), a tribe that claims descent from the army of Alexander of Macedonia.'

Drâss in Kargil is the second coldest inhabited village in the world. (Siberia is the coldest.)

How safe is Kargil? It hurts that this question is asked at all. That's because of the 14 districts of the state, Kargil alone was singularly free of militancy, with not a single incidence of violence, in the entire 1990s. In that respect this overwhelmingly Muslim district was ahead even of Hindu-majority districts like Kathua and Udhampur, leave alone Jammu proper.

True, there was a war in 1999, and it had affected Drâss, parts of the national highway and Kargil town. There is as good a chance of that happening again in Kargil as on the Gujarat and Punjab borders or in New York City. Even during a war the Suru valley, Zâñskâr and the Mulbek area are quite insulated from Pakistani ammunition shells, except for a brief 1.5 km. stretch just after Kargil town. The precaution which the Kargilis would take during that war was to travel to Kargil down from Leh rather than up from Srinagar.

Brief history: During ancient and mediæval times the region consisting of the present Kargil district and the adjoining parts of Baltistan used to be called Purîg (spelt Puring by some scholars).

The name Kargil first appeared around the 14th century. Some believe that putting together the roots 'khar' (palace or fort) and 'rkil' (centre) derived the word. In that sense 'Kargil' means 'the palace in the centre' or even 'the kingdom in between.' Others say that the place has been named after its founder.

Yet others claim that the word 'Kargil' is a combination of the words 'gar'–meaning 'coming from any place'- and 'khil,' which means 'stop'. Thus, Kargil could mean 'stop [here] while coming from anywhere.' This could well be the true. For Kargil is at the centre of a circle, on the rim of which are Srinagar, Skardu, Leh town and Zâñskâr. It is at roughly the same distance from each of these towns. 'Kar-kil' can, according to one interpretation, mean 'equal distance.'

Racially the people of Kargil have descended from the Tibetans, the Dards of Central Asia and the Indo-Aryan Mon people. Some might even have Mongol ancestors. (Please also see the chapter on 'Leh' district.) Pashkum is believed to be the first village to have been inhabited in all of ancient Purîg.

The Dards of Drâss are Aryans. All of them are Muslim. They belong to both the Shia and the Sunni sects. (The rest of the district is almost totally Shia. Zâñskâri Muslims are entirely Sunni. In Pânikhar and Pranti both sects are to be found.)

The Brokpas of the Batalik area are mostly Buddhist.

The Tibetan population is Buddhist as well as Muslim. The Buddhist Tibetans live in Zâñskâr. The Muslim Tibetans are all Shias and live in the Kargil and Sankoo blocks. (There is more about the Mons in the chapter on 'A history of Leh.')

Geography: The district is surrounded by Kashmir, Kishtwâr, Kulu (H.P.) and Gigit-Baltistan. It has in turns influenced these neighbours and been influenced by them. A somewhat cerebral guidebook says that Kargil 'served as the initial receptacle of the cultural waves and ethnic movements that emanated from across the Greater Himalâyan wall.'

Kargil is somewhat greener than Leh. That's because a number of rivers, which originate in the Greater Himalayas, bring considerable amounts of water as they come down. So, even though Kargil, too, is in an arctic desert, places near these rivers are green. Villages in the Suru valley, as well as those on the highway, are, on average, at lower altitudes than the typical village in Leh. On the other hand, villages in Zâñskâr are normally higher than in Leh. Both groups of villages receive far more snow than Leh does. As a result there are considerable pastures in Zâñskâr, in the upper Suru valley and between Drâss and the dZoji Lâ pass. Bakerwal shepherds come all the way from Jammu to graze their flocks on these meadows in the summer.

The present Kargil town was never the capital of the Kargil/ Purîg area.

Purîg consisted of a number of small kingdoms in ancient times. These included Chiktan, Phokar/ Fokar, Sodh/ Sot and Suru Kartse (Karchey). These tiny principalities would sometimes go to 'war' (petty skirmishes, most of the time) with each other—often at the slightest excuse. Gasho Thâ-Thâ Khan, an exiled prince of the 9th century AD, was perhaps the first ruler who brought together the territories which comprise the present district. He first conquered the Chiktan area and later annexed Sot as well.

Another Sultan of Purîg extended his kingdom to include Zâñskâr, Pashkum and Sodh—pretty much the territory of the present Kargil district. He is referred to simply as 'the Purîg Sultan' in official histories. His capital was based at Karpokhar in the Suru valley,

Famous kings of Kargil include Boti Khan, Abdal Khan, Amrood Choo, Tsering Malik, Niathi Stan, Kunchok Sherab Stan and *Thî* Sultan.

Ali Sher Khan Anchan of Skardu (late 16th/ early 17th centuries) is arguably the king who left the deepest imprint on the area. This warrior from Baltistan conquered most of the principalities of Purîg and introduced his native Balti culture there. For example, he got an architect from Khapaloo in his native Baltistan to build the Chiktan Razi Khar (the Chiktan 'palace').

It was the lot of the Dogras to unite Baltistan, Purîg, Zâñskâr and the present Leh district, in the first half of the 19th century, to form undivided Ladakh. (After 1947, Pakistan grabbed a major chunk of Kargil. It continues to illegally occupy the so-called Northern Areas which comprise Gilgit, Baltistan, Hunzâ and Skardu. Besides, it gifted a portion of the land it had occupied to its Chinese masters.)

The people of Kargil, like those of neighbouring Leh district, were Buddhists till the 14th century, when *all* the people of present day Kargil, minus Zâñskâr and some areas bordering Leh, converted to (Shiite) Islam. In the centuries immediately preceding this conversion, Kargil's Buddhism, like Leh's, had come under the influence of Tibet.

Travelling within the district

There is a daily bus from Kargil to Sankoo.

The service to Zâñskâr is quite irregular, though. The Penzi Lâ, the pass that connects Kargil and Zâñskâr, is closed from around November to mid-June. It is not possible for any vehicle to travel between the two during this period. However, even when the Kargil-Zâñskâr 'road' (a mud-track at places) is at its best, buses ply between the two places at most twice a week.

Therefore, what most people- Ladakhis as well as tourists- do is to pay for a ride in one of the many trucks that operate between the two. The thing to do is to go to the yard where these trucks (or even buses) are parked the evening before you want to leave Kargil for Zâñskâr. Find out if there is a bus or truck going that way the next day. Reserve a place for yourself a day in advance. And find out the precise hour when the bus/ truck will leave and from which precise spot. (Most bus and truck drivers are non-Ladakhis.)

Will there be a bus/ truck for ... tomorrow?	kal kow-ee bus/ truck ... jã-é-gî?
At what hour will it leave?	kit-né ba-jé jã-é-gî?
How many hours will it take?	kit-né ghon-té la-géñ-gé?
Where will it leave from?	kis ja-gâ sé jã-é-gî?
Is there room (for us)?	(ha-mã-ré liyé) ja-gâ hai?
How much will it cost?	kit-nã pai-sã la-gé-gã?

Important places of tourist interest

How to get to Kargil town- and places en route

There is no airport (or railway station) in Kargil. The nearest airports are at Srinagar in the south-west and Leh in the east. So, till the Kargil airport is ready the only way to go there (or to Zâñskâr) is by road—from Srinagar or Leh.

The district is served by two major roads, the National Highway (Leh-Kargil-Srinagar) and the Kargil-Suru Valley-Zâñskâr road. Together they form a 'T.' Kargil town is in the almost exact middle of the National Highway. The road to Zâñskâr emerges from the National Highway, almost like a perpendicular, at Kargil town. This road first passes through the Suru Valley and then Zâñskâr. The Penzi La pass links the two.

The district can, thus, be divided into four sections with Kargil town at the centre of them all.

Route 1: Srinagar to Kargil town

(See the chapter 'The National Highway: Leh to Kargil and Srinagar- to Kargil.')

Route 2: Leh to Kargil town

(See the chapter 'The National Highway: Leh to Kargil and Srinagar- to Kargil.')

Route 3: The Suru Valley: Kargil town to the Suru valley (till Rangdum)

(See the section on the Suru Valley, pp 298-302)

Route 4: Zâñskâr (Penzi Lâ to Padam, Karshâ and Zâñglâ)

(See the chapter on 'Zâñskâr.')

Important places of tourist interest

Kokashu: ***Toto Khar and Pato Khar:*** These were the forts constructed by Tha-Tha Khan. He was the 9th century AD founder of the Gasho dynasty. These ruins are among the oldest-known man-made buildings in Kargil.

Yogmâ Kharbu: ***Khar Gok:*** *the old fort:* This was one of the army outposts of the kings of Chiktan. Much of the population of ancient Yogma Kharbu used to live within the fort. The ruined walls of the fort and some remnants of the old village can still be found. Muhammad Sultan, the King of Sot, attacked Chiktan, as a result of which Tsering Malik and Chinkhan Malik were killed. Chinkhan's sons Âdam Malik and Chhoszâñg Malik (c.1610-1635) were imprisoned here. King Ahmed Khan of Shakar (c.1735-1745) later captured the fort.

Muslim shrine: This is the tomb of Mîr Syed Hussain Shah (16th century). He propagated Islam in Kargil a generation or two after Hazrat Mîr Shams ud Dîn Irâqî. The original tomb is still intact- more or less. Every year, on the saints's anniversary, the people of the surrounding areas recite the *Fâtehâ* (a chapter from the Holy Quran) at the tomb. Devotees ask God for special boons. People give money and gifts in charity.

Kargî (Suru): *The Kargî Khar* was one of the forts of the kings of Suru-Karchey. It is now in ruins. The fort also served as a palace. ('Khar' means both 'fort' and 'palace.') Thi Sultan kept one of his queens here.

Lankarchey: *The Changî Khar* was one of the forts of the kings of Suru- Karchey. It is now in ruins. It was at its peak during the reign of Thi Sultan.

Timbas (Tambas?): *The Timbas polo ground:* This is one of the oldest shagharans of Kargil and is still usable.

Yor baltik (near Kokashu): *The Pisrî Khar palace and fort:* King Muhammad Sultan of Sot (17th century) probably got the fort and the palace constructed. This was the capital of the kings of Sot and was one of the best forts in all Kargil. It is now in ruins. Apparently the walls were set on fire during the Dogra invasion, on the orders of Hari Chand. Around four hundred families used to live under the protection of the fort.

The Khandûr Khar palace is older than the Pisri Khar. The Mughal and Leh armies attacked it in the seventeenth century, during the reign of King Muhammad Sultan. According to the local tradition both armies were repulsed. (The people of Bhaderwah in Jammu, too, believe that their king had defeated the Mughals.) It is said that water used to be conveyed to the palace through underground pipes made of clay. (This tradition might be on firmer ground. I have seen such clay pipes, some of them vertical, in the Basohli palace. Similar pipes also exist in Banni, which, too, is in Jammu.)

Muhammad Sultan's queen entered into secret negotiations with the Turkmens during the Mughal invasion. She was exploring the possibility of an alliance with them. There is a large rock near the palace. People say that the queen was buried alive, along with her horses and jewellery, under that rock.

The Feekar Khar: This was the first fort that the great Tha-Tha Khan (9th century AD) had built in Sot. Some ruins can still be seen. A mosque- *khânqâh* has been built at the site where the fort once was. The Feekar hamlet near the fort is extremely old and dates to the early mediæval (or late ancient) period. The word 'feekar khar' means both 'the fort that belongs to the Muslims' and 'the white fort.'

Akcha-mal: *The Chhû-bar Khar:* This was one of the army outposts of the Government of Sot. It is now in ruins.

Barchey: *The Pyû Khar:* This, too, was one of the army outposts of the Government of Sot. It is now in ruins.

Yulbo Drâss: *The Beero Khar and the Rgyâl Khar:* Both palaces are now in ruins. A Governor (*Kharpon*) had built them. The rulers of Leh had made him the Governor. He had two wives. They hated each other. So he had to keep them at a safe distance from each other. Kachu Sikander Khan writes that according to the local tradition he would keep his old queen at the Rgyâl Khar. His second wife, who was from Drass, would live in the Beero Khar.

Pashkum: *The Chûlî-Khar* fort was built by Habib Khan, King of Pashkum (1665- 1695). Its ruins can be seen atop a hillock in the Khardung hamlet. There used to be a polo ground at the foot of this hillock, by the banks of the river. People have built houses and fields on it.

The Broq Khar was built by Khévâ Khî Lde (Aldey), a Dard chieftain. This ancient fort is now in ruins.

Rgyâl Bom Lde (Aldey)'s Palace was built around the 15th century AD. It used to be on a hillock near the Lankor hamlet, where the graveyard now is. Some ruins can still be found.

Stakchey: This was one of the forward posts of the government of Chiktan. A representative of that government was stationed here. The post was later merged with Bodh Kharbu.

Byâmâ Khumbu has a rock carving of Padma-pâni Avalokitéshwar, with a goddess on either side. There is a two-line Tibetan inscription on the rock. As is the rule with Tibetan-style rock-carvings, this sculpture is in low relief. Put simply, the sculpture does not rise very much above the surface of the rock that it is on. My guess is that is that this carving dates to between the 12th and 14th centuries AD.

Near this carving is a rock with an ibex carved on it.

Dam(a)sna is a huge, flat, moist meadow by the river, 61km from Kargil town. It has a fine view of the Nûn-Kun peaks. (You first get to see Nûn at Thâñgbu, 5km before Damsna.) Apart from the fish that occur naturally in the river, there is a government-run fish hatchery. As a result Damsna is a favourite with anglers. For me, this cold, haunting, wind-swept meadow is what I assume the remoter parts Mongolia or southern Central Asia must be like.

Some of the tamest (and most comfortable) white water rafting I've ever done has been in this area. The 'river' is normally so shallow that even short people can stand on its bed without danger. You can jump out of the boat and then climb back in again. (It is different when the snow melts or when there are rains upstream, though.)

Kargil town: (2,740m) 204km from Srinagar; 234km from Leh. (The distance to Skardu, now in POK, too, is almost the same—about 230km) This district town is located at the junction where roads from Leh, Srinagar, Skardu and Zâñskâr meet. For that reason caravans from China, Turkey, Yarqand, Afghanistan and the Indian plains used to pass through Kargil. They would trade in silk, ivory, carpets and precious stones. All that now remains of that once-flourishing traffic are the ruins of caravanserais.

Kargil is the second biggest town in all Ladakh. (Popn. approx. 8,000.) It is in the lower basin of River Suru. The other two rivers that converge here are the Drâss and Wâkhâ Chu rivers. Kargil district is not even remotely as prosperous as Leh. All the same, a small construction boom took place after 1947, and the town was pock-marked with a number of ugly, 'modern' buildings.

Thus Kargil, the only hill station in all of Jammu and Kashmir, developed into a listless small town, instead of the charming hill resort that it could have been. The ancient Poin (Poyen) village, which is opposite Kargil town, on the other hand, is still unspoilt and is what Kargil proper must once have been like.

The town is well served by a large government tourist bungalow and several private hotels. In the 1980s the Welcomgroup, a major national chain that runs, for instance, the Maurya in Delhi, used to manage a fairly decent local hotel.

Flora: Not just the town but the district is famous for its apricots. They blossom in May/ June, when they give off a pleasant fragrance. The orange-coloured fruit ripens in August and is a pretty sight. You can buy apricats with or without preservatives. The former kind has a longer shelf-life and is slightly less expensive. However, you need to wash the preservatives off thoroughly before eating.

Mulberries and apples, too, are grown in the district. Poplars and willow trees are found everywhere. Cereals and vegetables grown in Kargil include barley, wheat and peas.

What to do in Kargil town: The only thing to do is to soak in the scenery, especially in Baru and Poin. There are picturesque walks to the river and to nearby Goma Kargil, 2km away. The town essentially is a halt on your way to Srinagar, Drâss, the 1999 war sites, Leh, Mulbek, the Suru valley or Zâñskâr. It is also the base camp for several trekking, river-rafting and mountaineering expeditions.

The *Baru Khânqâh:* There is a mediæval Muslim shrine here. It is very popular and famous. It was built during the era of either Hazrat Syed Muhammad Nûr Bakhshi or Hazrat Mîr Shams ud Dîn Irâqî.

The *Iqbal Bridge* and the eponymous hydro-electric project have been named after not Allama Iqbal, the great poet, but an engineer called Iqbal.

Shopping: Dried apricots and apricot jam are available throughout the year. Pashmina shawls made here are far more inexpensive than those made in Kashmir or even Basohli. However, they are quite crudely woven. Shops in the main market sell flint and tobacco pouches, brass kettles and hookahs. Some carpets are made in Kargil and are available at the Government Industries Centre.

Karpo Khar: *The 'White Palace':* This was the summer capital of the kings of Suru- Karchey (Kartse). It, too, was set on fire during Zorawar's attack. Only the ruins remain. From here, across River Suru, one can see what is left of the famous pologround (*shagharan*) of Sangrâ.

The tomb of King Thi Sultan: This ruined tomb is next to the Karpo palace (*khar*). At a short distance from here is the tomb of Thi's spiritual master, Syed Mir Hashim.

Kartse Khar: *Gigantic Maitreya:* There is a seven-metre, seventh-century[1] Chambâ/ Maitreya idol of the future Buddha near this village.

1. Snellgrove and Skorupski write that the Mulbek Chamba dates to the 7th century or later. (Page 1). Elsewhere (pages 7 and 9) they suggest that pre-Tibetan Buddhist rock-reliefs could date to the 8th century AD, and not much before. The relief at Kartse Khar is older than the one at Mulbek. Therefore, I have dated it to the 7th century. Scholars like Kachu Sikander Khan date both sculptures to as late as the 11th century—to the age of Lotsâvâ Rinchen Zângpo. Now, by the eleventh century AD Kashmîirî influences on Ladâkh's Buddhist art were more or less over. The Tibetan idiom had taken over. For that reason, too, the Chambâs/ Maiteryas of Kargil must have been carved in the 7th or 8th centuries AD.

This rock carving, in deep relief, is older than the one at Mulbek. It is slightly smaller than but as impressive as the one at Mulbek. There is a *gandharv* on each side of the deity. (The gandharvs are angels devoted to song, dance and the good life.) The sculpture faces River Itchi.

In 2001, the Taliban of Afghanistan destroyed similar (but larger) Buddhas that had been carved into rocky mountainsides. The very next week I launched a campaign through the media to promote 'India's own Bamiyan.' So far I have been able to identify five such Gândhâr-style gigantic Buddhas in Ladakh. The other two are at Durbuk and Apati (between Kargil and Batâlik). The one at Apati has been eroded by the winds.

After the destruction at Bamiyan, these perhaps are the only five Buddhas of their kind left in the world. If you are interested in sculpture and/ or Buddhism, or even just the spectacle of a large statue carved into a mountainside, I would very strongly recommend Kartse Khar and Mulbek. Durbuk in eastern Ladakh, too, is said to have a huge idol of the Chambâ-Maitreya.

Sani (Zâñskâr) has the fifth such sculpture, except that, at three metres, it is shorter. Besides, it is a roundel, and not carved into a mountainside.

Chambâ is the name that the Ladakhis know the Maitreya Buddha by.

To reach the idol, you can drive for the first seven kilometres from the main Suru Valley road and then walk for five or ten minutes. The trek can end at Shergol or at Mulbek(h), five kilometres away. The statue is located in the Thasgâm (Thangskam) hamlet of Kartse Khar.

Ruined palace: Kartse Khar used to be the winter capital of the kings of Suru- Kartse (Karchey). The old palace was burnt during Zorâwar's attack (19th century). There is an 18th century mosque nearby. It was constructed at the behest of the mother of King Thî Muhammad Sultan. Craftsmen and masons were brought over from Kashmir for its construction. The original mosque got burnt along with the palace around 1834-35. Later the Dogra government gave the local people some funds and tax reliefs to help rebuild the mosque atop the ruins. The mosque that was thus built was fairly ordinary. In the 1980s it was renovated extensively.

The shagharan (pologround) of Dambî-sâ used to be at a short distance to the north of the palace.

The tomb of Queen Rgyâl Bibi: Rgyâl was the wife of Thi Sultan. She was buried in a small forest, amidst rose bushes. It is said that her horse, her clothes and some of her other valuables were buried with her. The tomb is close to the palace and across the river. It is not far from the Maitreya idol.

Syed Mir Hashim: Thî Namgyâl, a Buddhist, was the king of the Suru area in the 16th century. His palace was at Karpo Khar. Thî converted to Islam. So he invited Syed Mir Hashim to come from Kashmir to teach him Islam. The Syed's shrine is nearby, on one of the routes to Drass.

Pânikhar: Buses ply between here and Kargil. On a good day the ride takes three hours each way. This is a charming village with open spaces, fields, ravines and a tree-lined road surrounded by mountains. These flat spaces descend in wide steps towards River Suru, which is more than a hundred feet below the village. The Chelung River merges with the Suru here. In summer several mountain flowers—and flowering trees- blossom here.

Trans-Himalâyan treks: From here you can trek to i) Pahalgam, through the Bhotkol pass (4,420m.), the Wârwan and Lidder valleys, and the Gulol pass. This is a seven-day trek. ii) Kishtwâr, through Wârwan valley. iii) Lehinwan (Kashmir), through the Margan pass.

(See also the chapter 'Trekking in Ladakh' for treks out of Pânikhar, including some easy day-return treks.)

Mountain climbing: Tangole, the base camp for the Nûn-Kun peaks, is six km away.

Accommodation: There is a tourist bungalow at Pânikhar. One of my juniors who belonged to the village told me that it was run down and primitive. Therefore, I was surprised to find clean sheets, plush new quilts, and a bathroom that was remarkably smart considering how far- and difficult to reach- we were from Delhi or even Srinagar. The other rooms were not as good. Still, nowhere in the world does one get a place like that for three dollars a day.

There are private hotels and tea stalls, too. Hotels *Snowland* and *Khayul* are economy hotels.

Parkachik: The base of the **Nûn** (7,135 metres/ 23,447') and **Kun** (7,087 metres/ 23,213') peaks is now within striking distance. Even for those who are not in a mood to scale two of the world's tallest (7,000m) peaks, Parkachik is an excellent place for adventure tourism. Rock climbing, for instance. Going up to the nearby and easy to reach Parkachik glacier in less than 45 minutes return, for another. (The base of the Nûn-Kun is called Gyâlmo Thâñgas and is 300 metres from the main road near 'km. 105'. The Sheep Husbandry Department holds a 'camp' for the benefit of shepherds and their flocks at this place every year.)

In 1998, I inaugurated a rather spartan, but also extremely inexpensive, government-owned dormitory at Parkachik, to help adventure groups which book these rooms in advance at Kargil. That same year I also inaugurated a slightly better equipped government tourist bungalow in

Rangdum village, which is the next halt, is 130km from Kargil and is the base camp for treks to

a) Heniskut and Lâmâ Yûrû. You have to cross the Kanji Lâ (pass) (5334 metres). The trek takes five days.

b) Kishtwâr (Doda district; Jammu province). This trek takes nine days, is more challenging, and involves crossing the difficult Chillung Lâ (pass). It is tough because the pass consists of a glacier. (The pass leads from the Suru valley to Warhwan, and is at the head of the Krish valley.

Pharuna: Near this village is a large boulder with primitive engravings. The figures that can be seen include an ibex, humans who are probably dancing and a man standing atop a horse.

B.R. Mani observes that 'There is a rock-cut cavity in a large boulder about 40m. south-east in which a man can easily sleep.' Such cavities have been created at several places in Ladakh, on all the old winter routes.

Sankoo has a Tourist Bungalow and also a rest house, the latter mainly for touring government servants. Ther are also some resraurants. Buses ply regularly from Kargil to Sankoo.

There is a thick man-made forest of myricarea, poplars and willows nearby. Wild roses also grow here. The architecture of religious buildings such as imambaras and mosques is part Turkish and part Tibetan.

A small 'rill' of water comes out of the green mountain slope here. Its mineral waters are incredible. They are light and dissolve grease without soap. Try washing dishes or greasy hands in them. Above all, they are very good for digestion.

Sangrâ: *Famous playgrounds:* The pologround (*shagharan*) of Sangrâ used to be one of the best in Kargil. Not far from this *shagharan* are the remains of Sangra's equally well-known stadium, 'Sangrî Nâran.'

Maqdoom Khar: To the west of the Nâran, at the outer limits of Sangrâ, is the Maqdoom neighbourhood. It used to be the capital of King Alday Choo of the Gasho dynasty.

Trespon: Its *Imâmbârâ* (Shiite place of worship), built atop a hillock, is an 'awesome fusion of Saracenic and Tibetan influences' in architecture and interior decoration- 'a real treat.' (The quotes are from *The Indian Express*.) Childless couples come here to pray for children in general and sons in particular. It is believed that their prayers are mostly answered. According to *The Times of India*, the Imam Bara was built in the 11th century. (I would put it at around the 16th century.)

Scythian bows: The Indian Express added that Trespone is 'one of the few places that has retained the traditional method of making the

Scythian bow from the ibex horn'. Of course, bows are now used only to shoot at targets made of mud. Because of its tradition with bows, Trespon is the headquarters of Kargil's archery sport.

Whitewater rafting is possible in and around Trespon. (See also the chapter on 'Rivers' for details about which stretches are safe for rafting.)

The Artseymo (or Seymo) Khar of Lonchhey: The legendary Tha-Tha Khan founded the Gasho dynasty, and much else. (See the chapter on 'History.') This was one of his forts or palaces. Remains can still be seen of what might be the oldest building in Kargil.

The War Sites

On the 30th September, 1997, the Pakistani army shelled Kargil town, killing 18 people. Several other Kargilis were crippled forever. Between 1997 and 1999, the Pakistan's artillery shelled various parts of the district, killing 39 civilians (non-combatants). The Pakistanis also destroyed the Jama Masjid and the Chaanchik Imam Bara. In the winter of 1998-99, reportedly around April 1999, Pakistani soldiers as well as mercenaries working under the command of the Pakistani army, occupied a 10km - wide, 140km long strip of 'unheld' (i.e. unguarded) Indian territory along the LoC in Kargil.

Among the mountain peaks and ridges that the Pakistanis had eased themselves into were Tiger Hill, Mushkoo, Tololing and Batâlik. The war was covered extensively by television as well as newspapers and magazines. The names of these war sites became household words all over India.

The people of Kargil had suffered terribly. They now needed recompense. I decided to put a positive spin on the publicity that Kargil had been receiving. I requested Raja Patil, a travel agent from Mumbai, to team up with the J&K Tourism Department, to bring tourists from all over India to Kargil. I mentioned Mr. Patil's efforts in an interview to *The Indian Express,* which is also published from Vijaywada in South India. This brought us tourists from that district in 1999 itself, within weeks of the end of the war.

Drâss now suddenly had a claim to fame other than being the second coldest inhabited place in the world, after Siberia. All the TV crews covering the 1999 war started reporting from Drâss, making it the best known place in Kargil.

Tiger Hill is a peak which you can see from the Drâss Tourist Bungalow itself. It is not the highest peak in the area. However, since there are no high hills around it, Tiger Hill stands out. Look north from the Tourist Bungalow. Then turn your gaze west at an angle of about 20°. This famous battle ground is the hill that is taller, and thus more majestic, than its neighbours. Please remember, this is a peak and not a ridge.

If tourists start insisting on going to this hill, it might interfere with the Army's work. Therefore, if you must go there, here is how. First, get the necessary permission from the Army. Then take the road that branches off from the National Highway, northwards, to Holiyal, which is around 4km away. The slopes of Tiger Hill are grazing grounds. They are situated between Holiyal and Mushkoo. The lower end of these pastures is roughly half a kilometre from the road that connects these two villages.

Mushkoo (3180m ; spelt Mushkoh in most press despatches) is a bit further ahead. The Mushkoo nallah (stream) meets the Drâss river 1km upstream from Drâss town (i.e. in the direction of Kashmir). The nallah is 25km long and terminates here. The Mushkoo valley begins here and goes uphill. Mushkoo village is 8km from Drâss town, via, of course, Holiyal.

Tololing (4590m), too, can be viewed from the Tourist Bungalow at Drâss. Look north and then turn your eyes east by roughly 30°. This is a ridge-line. The Army has given the peaks of this ridge names like 'Hump' and 'Three Pimples'. A fifty-minute trek will take you to the Tololing foothill nearest to the highway.

Batâlik can either be reached from Kargil town, (67km), or from a detour near Khaltse (Leh), (75 km along the Indus route.). One way of going there is to start from Kargil town, go to Baru (a suburb) and then drive some 4km. in the direction of Leh. You will reach Thang (television station), which, too, is a suburb of Kargil. A side road branches off at Thang towards Batalik, which is 57km from there.

From Batâlik Indian citizens can travel to the fabled Dâ-Hânu region.

In case you travel to Batâlik from the Kargil side, look out for village **Apati**, which is between the two. It is a must see for those interested in sculpture and/ or Buddhism. It has a large sculpture of the Maitreya, cut into the mountainside, in relief. It is not as well preserved as its counterparts at Mulbek and Kartse Khar. However, with the Bamiyan (Afghanistan) Buddhas gone, this is one of the few sculptures of its kind left in the world.

Other places of tourist interest in Kargil

The Suru Valley

The Suru valley begins in Kargil town itself, when one turns southward to the Baru section' of the town. A number of important government offices are in Baru.

There is no petrol pump (gas station) in the Suru valley.

The valley ends near Rangdum, at what is called the Penzi La watershed.

(It is possible to travel by jeep or bus from Kargil to Padam (Zâñskâr), 240km away, in a single 14-hour day. However, most people break journey at Pânikhar or Rangdum and cover the distance in two days.)

The valley is surprisingly fertile, considering that it is essentially in a desert. The almost linear road from one end of the valley to the other is almost 150km long. The valley itself is around 140km long. It is fertile because of alluvium and is the granary of Ladakh. Suru is, as mentioned, unusually green for a desert. It is set amidst some of the world's highest mountains—the Great Himalâyan Range. Together this makes it, especially the Damsna meadows, one of the most beautiful places in the world. Don't let me overstate my case. The greenery is limited to a thin, flat stretch along the river. The mountains around it are almost totally barren.

The children are mostly pink, very good looking and can be mistaken for Central Asians or even East Europeans. They are mostly Caucasoid Dards and Baltîs with some Mongoloid Tibetan blood. Their jewellery and costumes, too, are Central Asian/ East European. From Kargil town to Panikhar village the population is almost entirely Shiite Muslim. Panikhar has some Sunni Muslims. Zhuldo (near Rangdum), at the southern end of the valley, is the first Buddhist village.

In August and September the Suru valley acquires a haunting new attraction. The *sarsing* tree (elagnus hortensis) suddenly starts exuding a sweet scent. This is also the time when its cherry-sized fruit, also called sarsing, ripens. These trees line the road that runs through the valley. One tree is enough to envelope an entire village with its fragrance. The stretches that pass through Sankoo, Khachen and Grong-Minji in the valley, and Poyen and Shalikchay near Kargil town, are particularly fragrant. The perfume starts floating in the air well after sunset, normally around seven or eight at night. The scent is much like that which emerges from central Indian temples in the evenings.

(See also the chapter on 'Rivers.' It is the Suru River that defines the contours of the valley of the same name. However, the section on River Suru, naturally, covers the journey described below in the reverse direction—downstream, from Rangdum to Kargil town. In this chapter we start from Kargil town and move towards Rangdum.)

Minji Gund is the first major village in the Suru valley.

Trespon(e) is 22km ahead of Kargil town, when you travel into the Suru valley.

Seliskot comes next and has a brightly coloured mosque right next to the road. A 5km stretch begins at Trespon and goes up to Khumbathâng, in which there are trees on both sides of the road. Very unusual for what, after all, is a desert.

Khumbathâng is a huge plain. Langkârchay is the next village.

Pharuna (27km from Kargil) is a village in the Khumbathâng area.

Byâmâ Khumbu is 33km from Kargil.

Sankoo is eighteen kilometres ahead of Trespon on the road to Zâñskâr, or 40km from Kargil also on the same road.

By 2005, the national highway is likely to go from Drâss to the Umba Lâ and thence to Sankoo, abandoning the present route. (See also the 'Sankoo-Drâss' trek in the chapter 'Trekking in Ladakh'.)

The Kartse (Karchey) nalah flows in from the east and the Nakpochu from the west. Both are tributaries of River Suru and the two have created side-valleys respectively to the east and west of Sankoo. The Kartse (Karchey) river originates near the Rangdum pass.

[Detour: **Kartse Khar:** (Also spelt **Karcheykhar**) is roughly 8km. from Sankoo and 48km from Kargil, on a side road.]

(S(ha)angrâ, Karpo Khar [also on a side road], Bangialcha and Purtikchey are the next villages after Sankoo.)

There is a tall mountain opposite **Sangrâ** on which you can see a natural formation that looks like a snake. According to a legend there once was a smallpox epidemic in the region. A Muslim saint went over to that mountain to meditate and got rid of the pox by trapping it inside that snake like formation.

The road beyond Sangrâ is prone to avalanches between December and March. It is especially so in March when the weather starts getting warmer and the snow begins to melt. As a result the road to Pânikhar gets blocked and remains so for long spells.

Karpo Khar is the next village.

Thangbu is 16km from Sankoo and 56km from Kargil. The first views of Nun-Kun- and excellent views at that- are to be had from here.

Dam(a)sna, 21km. after Sankoo (61km from Kargil town), is one of Ladakh's least known treasures.

Taisuru is the next major village. It is famous for the architecture of its mosque and imambara.

Pânikhar is seven kilometres ahead of Damsna and 68km from Kargil town.

Pânikhar is the last major village before Nûn-Kun.

For the next ninety kilometres or so it's one vast, desolate, treeless expanse, often plain, surrounded by gigantic mountains. However, the roughness of the road is compensated by the Nûn-Kun and a small population at Parkachik, a few houses and a monastery at Rangdum, the Penzi Lâ pass and lake, and another stretch of majestic desolation till you reach Abran, the first village in Zâñskâr.

This route has an incredible presence and grandeur, very different from what you've seen in Leh. From June to September there's grass—at places there are pastures with the occasional herd of sheep—at those fantastic altitudes (11,700 feet above the sea). In a desert you are grateful for every spring you get to see, but this valley has a thin sliver of water flowing from one end to the other. Then you have marmots and the occasional migratory bird.

(Parkutse, the Shafat glacier near the Nûn-Kun massif, and Yulduk occur between Pânikhar and Rangdum.)

Parkachik, a very sparsely inhabited village, is the next major village after Pânikhar. Tangole, a minor village, is between the two. Gyalmo Thangas, the base of the Nun-Kun, comes next.

Kargil district is almost one hundred percent Shia (Shiite) Muslim, except for the Zâñskâr sub division and the villages mentioned in 'Route 2' above. Kargil town has a small Sunni population, though.

Though Rangdum is not a part of Zâñskâr, geographically or administratively, it is with this village that the Buddhist population—and monasteries, *maaney* walls and *chhortens*- begin.

On the Kargil-Zâñskâr road, 'km. 92' is where the heaviest snowfall takes place in winter. Therefore, as many as five 'passenger sheds' have been constructed near the road between 'km. 90' and 'km. 121'.

Rangdum (3,657 metres; 130km from Kargil, 65km from Pânikhar) is preceded by a huge- no, gigantic- plain, some pastures on the right and the habitat of hundreds of golden-fleeced marmots (see 'Wildlife') on the left. A tiny village (actually a cluster of half a dozen houses) comes first, where we have the aforementioned government-run tourist bungalow, a private hotel and a ground where we sometimes race horses, and trekkers pitch tents.

This open ground leads to the spectacularly situated 17th century **Rangdum Gompa**, three kilometres away, perched atop a hillock that rises suddenly from the plain. It is surrounded by some of the tallest and most stunning mountains in the world. (The plain itself is at 11,700 feet) International, professional photographers can't have enough of this panoramic sight.

The idea is to be as far from the gompa as possible if you want to capture the mountains, as well, but close enough to get the outlines of the gompa.

Several treks go through or begin at Rangdum. The most popular of these are the ones to Lâmâ Yûrû and Heniskut, through the Kanji valley. (See 'Trekking' in the 'Ladakh' as well as 'Kashmir'volumes of this series.)

After the gompa, begins the ascent to the Penzi Lâ begins. This slope leads from the Suru valley to the Zâñskâr sub-division.

19

Zâñskâr

The Penzi La: Two small, turquoise, high altitude lakes with camping sites nearby, and views of the surrounding permafrost mountains are the highlights of the Penzi Lâ pass, which is 160km from Kargil and, at 4,401-4,450 metres, is the highest point on the Kargil-Zâñskâr road. This pass is more of a tableland and, unlike the dZoji Lâ, has plenty of flat spaces and things to see. The Drangdrung, for instance. Kishtwâr (Jammu) is behind the mountains on the right.

You should expect the pass to be snowed under from November to the end of June. (For how to get to the Penzi Lâ, see the section 'The Suru Valley' in the chapter about Kargil.)

Zâñskâr begins half way through the pass, some 35km after Rangdum. The Zâñskar sub-division is spread over more than 5,000 sq. km., and is shaped like an inverted 'Y'. Padam, the capital, and Karshâ, the main monastic village, are at the centre of the 'Y'.

There are two valleys within Zâñskâr. The valley of the Doda Chu river is called Stod and the valley of River Tsarap Chu is called Luñgnak (or Lunak).

There are 25 villages in **Zâñskâr,** which had two 'kings', one each in Padam and Zâñglâ. Each ruled over six or seven villages, and there were several villages that were under neither 'king', though they might have allied with one or the other of them. It is doubtful if either 'king' ever had more than three thousand subjects. Even in 1981, all of Zâñskâr had a population of just 8,313, of which 396 were Muslims. My own impression, as the head of the Zâñskâr administration in that census year, based on estimates prepared by my staff, was that there were around 800 Muslims in Padam and Pipiting, but I'd rather go by the formal census.

From Abran to Padam and then onwards we have listed villages in the order that they occur on the road from Kargil-Rangdum-Penzi Lâ. Using Padam as the base you can go to

i) Karshâ, which can be seen from Padam (Kaisha is directly to the north);
ii) Zâñglâ, and the villages in between (i.e. to the north east of); and
iii) the Châr nallah (Phugtâl, Teestâ, Kargyâk and then Himachal) (i.e. directly south, veering slightly to the south east).
iv) The places between Padam and Abran, in case you did not enter Zâñskâr through the Penzi La and then Abran.

Zâñskâr is cut off from the rest of the world for almost eight months a year, because the Penzi Lâ gets blocked. Besides, there are no air services. A government publication says, 'The geographical inaccessibility and the esoteric nature of Buddhism practised here, gave its inhabitants the freedom to preserve and perpetuate their cultural identity. So that today Zâñskâr is one of the least interfered with microcosms of Ladakh and one of the last surviving cultural satellites of Tibet.'

Put simply, customs such as polyandry, which are more or less extinct in Leh town and in the more advanced villages of Leh district, still survive in some pockets of Zâñskâr. In 1999, around a quarter of Zâñskâr still practised polyandry. By then several shops had sprung up in Padam and you could actually buy things with money. I was the head of the administration in 1981-82. They hadn't even heard of barter till then. Each household had to make everything that it needed: even tweed, shoes, rice-beer, grains, everything. If you want to construct a house you still do it yourself. Members of your family provide the labour and make all the materials themselves. Neighbours might chip in on a reciprocal basis.

The only things that you needed to obtain through barter were salt, things made of brass, some wooden handicrafts and music. Salt was brought over by the Chañgpâ tribe. Similar underprivileged communities, at the bottom of or outside society, traded in items made of wood, brass and music.

Since the 1980s labour from Central India has started coming over in the summers. By then some Zâñskârîs had begun to get paid in cash. These were government servants, contractors for the government and those involved in tourism. They used the services of this migrant labour to build their houses and hotels.

The important places

From the Penzi La/ Abran to Padam

Not counting small clusters of houses here and there, **Abran** and then **Aksho** are the first major villages after the pass, followed by Hamiling, Shagam, Phey and Sani.

Hamiling (203km. from Kargil; 37km. before Padam): Engravings have been found on a boulder in this village. These are the figures of ibexes and wild goats, seven humans and symbols including, very significantly, the swastika.

Two kilometres down the same road there is a boulder near the road. A chorten/ stupâ has been engraved on it.

Shagam (209km. from Kargil; roughly 31km. before Padam): Here we have an ibex hunt engraved on a boulder. Hunters with bows and arrows, poised for a kill, have trapped the animal from both sides. A second ibex and a third man can also be seen.

Phey (215km. from Kargil; 25km. before Padam): This village has more than twenty large rocks with engravings on them. The art here ranges from primitive lines to relatively more sophisticated and fuller figures. Once again we have hunters with bows and arrows, ibexes and some symbols (e.g. the sun).

Dungri: Thus far the road had been on the left bank of the Doda Chu. It crosses the stream at this village. This is also the best place from which one can trek to the Zongkhul gompa. The gompâ is a three-hour trek from the motorable road.

The road turns south here. It leads first to Sani and then to Padam.

Sani (232km. from Kargil; 8km. before Padam; 11,560'; also spelt and pronounced 'Seni.'): This is a roadside village that has an ancient tree, a grove and a small spring, all of which are unusual in a desert. More important, Sani has a venerable monastery with ancient and mediæval frescoes, also right next to the road.

Sani is on the old trekking route from Kishtwâr to Leh, via the Umâsi Lâ. People still trek from here to Kishtwâr. It is on the right bank of a tributary of River Zâñskâr. Tangring village is on the other bank of the river.

There is a guest house in Sani.

Padam (3,505 metres; 240 km. from Kargil; sometimes spelt Padum; academics and purists spell it sPadam.) This, the headquarters of Zâñskâr, is 240km. from Kargil and almost eighty kilometres from the Penzi Lâ. It has a decent government tourist bungalow and several private hotels and restaurants. Today Zâñskâr has telephones with the ability to call any part of India- and perhaps the world, a facility not available in the Suru valley. The town's highlights include the mud 'palace' of the local 'raja'. There is also a small monastery in the town.

There are 8th century rock carvings and a rock shelter near the riverbank in Padam. On two large rocks the figures of ten Dhyâni Buddhas have been etched. Five of them are sitting while the other five are standing. Both are in low relief and, hence, Tibetan in style. There is also a five-metre Maitreya Buddha, devotees, chortens and also the animals associated with the Five Buddhas (Vairochan, Ratna Sambhav, Amitâbh, Amogh Siddhi and Akshobhay). My guess is that these carvings date to around the 12th or 13th century AD.

Elsewhere in Padam are two stone slabs with 13th/ 14th century engavings of the Buddha and the Maitreya.

The Padam fort: This used to be the seat of government of the kings of ancient and mediæval Zâñskâr. It is now in ruins. The Turkmen army of Mirza Haidar Gurgan captured and held it for a while. Kachu Sikander Khan has an interesting theory. He says that the fort was shaped like a bud. Therefore, it was called 'patum.' The word later changed to 'padam.' My theory is that the name of the town is derived from the Sanskrit-Tibetan-Ladakhi word 'padam,' which means 'lotus.' This flower is extremely important (and sacred) in Buddhism.

Inscriptions and icons: There are inscriptions and icons on a rock near the Padam fort. They perhaps date to the 8th or 9th century AD. They were probably etched by the Mons around the time that Buddhism was replacing the Bon religion in Zâñskâr.

Where to stay: As always the government's Tourist Bungalow is the best value for money. *Ibex* is several times more expensive, is better maintained and has better service. *Chorala* is mid-priced. *Haftal* is economy.

Near Padam

There are gompas in Pipiting and Stagrimo, both near Padam. It takes around an hour to climb up to **Stagrimo** (also referred to as Stagnimo), which is an good example of local architecture. It was built on a rock near the riverbank around the 10th century AD. It is arguably the oldest building in all Zâñskâr. It comes under the Stakna monastery. *Reach Ladâkh* says that the monastery 'provides epigraphic evidence that the region was influenced by Buddhism since ancient time[s].'

Towards Zangla

If Zâñglâ was Padam's rival for primacy within Zâñskâr in the past, today it is **Karshâ,** which is four to six kilometres away if you walk and

17km., if you insist on going in an automobile). The route is absolutely flat and it is a very pleasant and easy walk of not more than an hour and a half.

Karshâ itself has been built entirely on the steep slopes of a tall mountain. Therefore, you can see Karshâ quite clearly from Padam. The houses have all been painted white with lime from the nearby hill. What is unique about Karshâ- apart from the architecture- is that most of the people who live here are either monks or have something to do with Karsha's famous monastery. Since a monastery is also an educational institution, *The Indian Express* is not wrong in describing Karshâ as a university town.

The Tourism Department is getting a fairly big complex built at Karshâ for the accommodation of tourists. It is likely to be functional by 2005. Local people sometimes let out rooms. There are some restaurants near the stream.

Tongdé (correctly sTongdé) is around 15km. from Padam, via Pipiting. B.R. Mani writes that 15km. from Padam, 'on the right bank of River Zâñskâr in between Kumi and Thongde in a stretch of about 2km. near the confluence of [the] Doda and Zâñskâr [rivers] there are large number of boulders with rock engravings of primitive type.' The themes, again, are ibexes, strange looking animals, and hunters with bows and arrows. In one scene ibexes fight each other. Dr. Mani adds, 'Amongst these an interesting scene depicts five wild animals in a line, three moving to right and two to left. [One of these animals] is a tiger chasing a cattle [sic] and [two other animals] seem to be wild asses which are still found in Ladakh [especially in] Changthâñg.'

Zâñglâ is 35km. from Padam. The Zâñskâr river, which leads from Padam to Zâñglâ and then to Leh freezes so hard in the winter that for a few weeks one can walk on it. This is known as the *châdar*. The trek from Padam to the motorable road in Leh district can take a week. (See also the chapter on 'Trekking'.) There is a nunnery nearby. There are no formal hotels in the village, but some families take in guests. Zâñglâ is a base camp for trekkers in the summer.

The vinyl covered *chhaksa* toilet of the Zâñglâ 'palace' has been mentioned in some guidebooks. The blissful old fort atop a nearby hillock, however, is Zâñglâ's main attraction. Bliss? In all Ladakh my favourite shrine-on-a-hillock is Trespon; Zâñglâ is my number two favourite. It's a uniquely serene feeling that you get up there. And don't take my word for it. The eighteenth century Hungarian mystic-scholar Csoma Körös spent considerable time there meditating.

The Char nallah

Later, Körös went through Padam into the narrow Char 'nallah'. The Char gorge leads to Testa and finally to Kargyâk, which borders Himachal Pardesh and is the highest inhabited village in the world (not counting mining settlements in the Andes, which are not full-time villages). Between Padam and Testa is a huge cave called **Phugtâl** (also Phuktâl) inside which is a fairly big monastery. Körös spent considerable time in this cave monastery, writing his celebrated *Zâñşkâr Chronicles*. The only way to get to Phugtâl is on foot or horseback. The return trek can take the better part of a week.

How to get to Phugtâl: *The Padam-Phugtâl (Phugtâl) trek goes thus:*

Day 1: Walk from Padam to Mune: 6 hours.

Day 2: Walk from Mune to Purne: 8 hours.

Day 3: Purne to Phugtâl gompa: 4-5 hours.

Day 4. Phugtâl to Purne

Day 5: Purne to Mune

Day 6: Mune to Padam

On all six days you can begin your trek around 7 or 8 or even as late as 9 a.m.

Gilgit-Baltistan-Hunza-Chitral-Aksai Chin-Shimshal

The paradise across the line of control

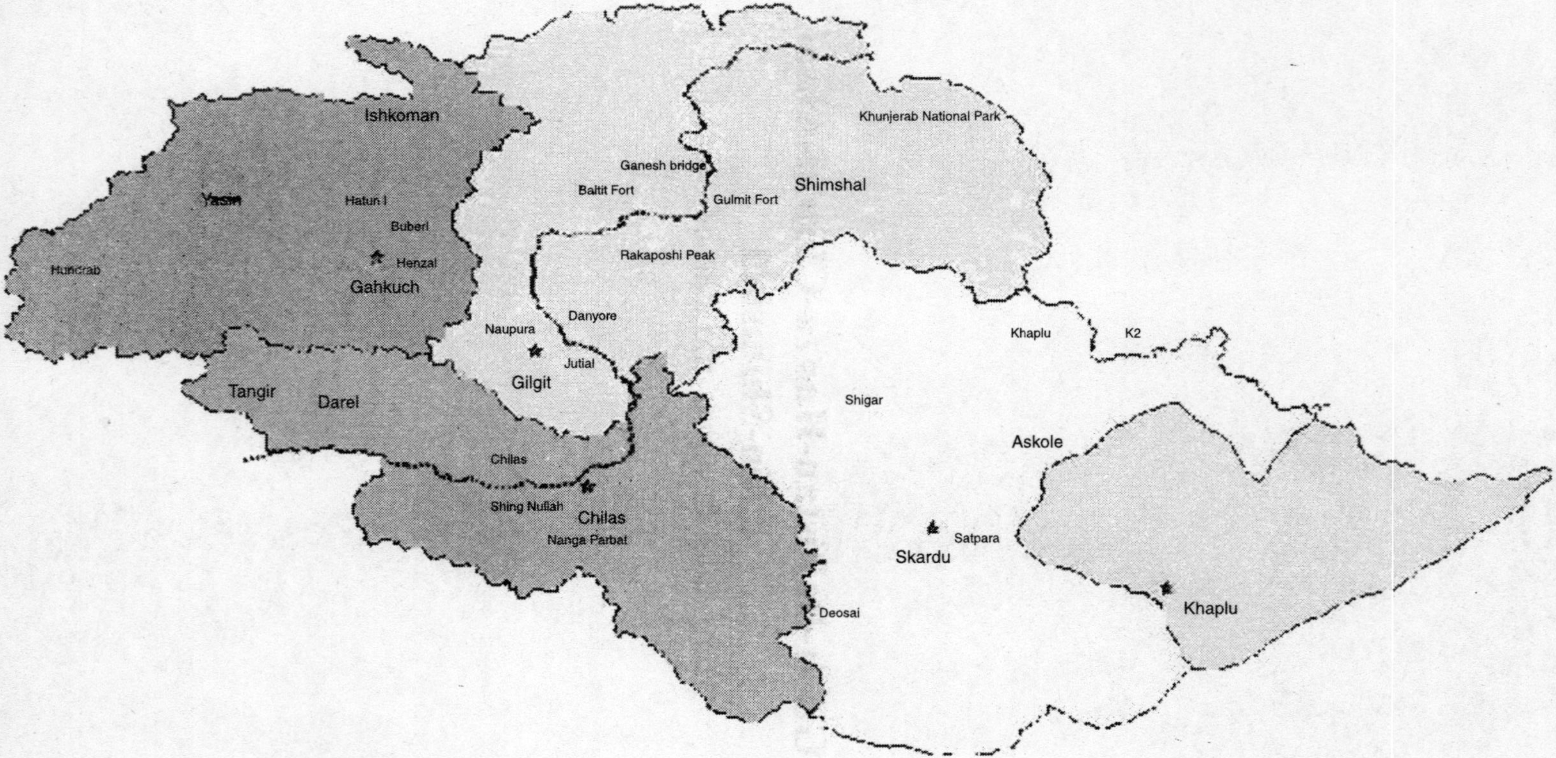

Across the LOC: Gilgit-Baltistan-Hunza-Shimshal-Chilas-Yasin

*Map not to scale

20

A paradise without a name

Once upon a time there was a Shangri La. It was nestled amidst the Kârâkoram and Hiñdu Kush ranges. Its people were (and still are) affectionate and hospitable. Crime was (and still is) virtually unknown. If the people had a fault it was their habit of lavishing on their guests hospitality of an order that they could not afford. The Shias, Sunnis and, till 1947, Hiñdus, lived in harmony. (This is one spell that has broken.)

This paradise included Baltistân, Gilgit. Chitrâl, Hunzâ-Nagar-Shimshal, Kohistân, Astor and Kaghan. In ancient times, much of it was called Balâwaristân. Till 1947, all these lands were a part of Ladâkh district and the Gilgit division. Therefore, the region had a name: Ladâkh (or Ladâkh-Gilgit).

In 1947-48, Pâkistân annexed the area. And as if that was not enough, Pâkistân chopped the land into pieces. While it put much of this paradise into an entity called 'The Northern Areas' (Shumâlî Ilâqâjât), it sliced entire kingdoms out of this region and merged them with the neighbouring provinces of Pâkistân. What is worse, it carved more than five thousand square kilometres of land from this region and gifted all of Shaksgam to China.

Today Pâkistân tries to pretend that these kingdoms and regions were never a part of the princely state of Jammu and Kashmîr. Perfectly decent and well meaning Pâkistânis have been brought up on this myth. All they need do is to go to old libraries in Lahore, Rawalpindi, Péshâwar, Abbotabad, Skardu, Gilgit or even distant Karachi, and look up pre-1947 British gazetteers and maps (in case they don't trust Dogrâ records or the writings of scholars like Maulvi Hashmatullâh Khân and other pre-1947 Muslim chroniclers).

Incidentally, whatever might be its other differences with the Indian State, the Jammu and Kashmîr Liberation Front (which is led by Mr. Amanullah Khân, who is from the so-called Northern Areas) agrees entirely with Indian maps regarding the areas that had constituted Jammu and Kashmîr on the 14th August, 1947.

People from within the occupied parts of Jammu and Kashmîr still consider themselves Kashmîrîs. For instance, Nâib Sardâr Ârif Shâhid of the 'AJK' Republican Party calls Gilgit-Baltistân the 'head' and 'crown' of Kashmîr. The Balâwaristân National Front and the Gilgit-Baltistân Association are among the countless political parties in the region which want 'a seat' for representatives of the region at 'any discussions about the future of Kashmîr.'

Giving the region a name: the options

Because Pâkistân has divided the occupied parts of Ladâkh-Gilgit into so many parts, it is impossible to give a name to this fabled region. Indian writers find this task the easiest. They simply call the area Pâkistân Occupied Kashmîr (POK). Technically they are right, except that there are several POKs, including the region called 'Âzâd' Jammu and Kashmîr and the areas of POK that have been illegally merged with Pâkistân.

Therefore, one could call this region 'Pâkistân Occupied Ladâkh-Gilgit.' Again, legally that would be correct because on the 14th August, 1947, all these areas were in the princely state of Jammu and Kashmîr, and were administratively within either Ladâkh district or the Gilgit division. However, this is a legal definition of the area, not a name.

The people of the so-called Northern Areas find the name given to them by Pâkistân most offensive, because it defines them in terms of their geographical location vis a vis Pâkistâni Punjâb. 'Would the Punjâbis like it if their state were to be called the Eastern Areas?' they ask.

Apart from being odious, the term 'The Northern Areas' does not cover several parts of old Ladâkh-Gilgit that have been illegally merged with Pâkistân or ceded to China.

One thing that struck me while writing this book was that most of the region was in the Kârâkoram range, some of it was in the Hiñdu Kush and the area around the Nañgâ Parbat was in the Himâlayas. Therefore, could the region be called Kârâkoram-Hiñdu Kush?

One possible name for the region is Balâwaristân. Nationalists from the region use this name. So have we in this book, though slightly cautiously. Are the people of Hunzâ, Gilgit, Astore, Kaghan, Chitrâl, Kohistân and Swât[1] comfortable with this name?[2] If they are then

1. Nationalists from Balâwaristân include Swât in their land.
2. Kachu Sikander Khân writes, 'Many European scholars have mistaken Balor [Balâwar] (Dardistân) for Baltistân.'

   If the Kachu is right, this confuses things even further, because in some parts of this book I, too, have identified Balâwar with Baltistân, relying on the works of local nationalists.On the other hand, perhaps because of this ambiguity Balâwaristân is the name that describes the Dardistân-Baltistân region the best.

Balâwaristân is the most appropriate name for the region. It has the sanction of history and ancient usage. What it awaits is the approval of all parts of the region.

The home of the majority

Till 1947, the area of Ladakh, including Kargil, Skardu, Hunza, Kaghan and the Gilgit division was 63,554 sq. miles (167,247 sq. km.). Its 1941 population was 3,11,915 (or 0.3 million). Since then Pakistan has been in occupation of around 72,496 sq. km./ 27,565 sq. miles of this territory (the figure has been shrinking). In addition, Pakistan occupies 13,297 sq. km./ roughly 5,134 sq. miles in what it calls 'Azad Jammû and Kashmîr' and has coughed up 5,180 sq. km. to China. China has illegally moved into another 37,555 sq. km. of Ladakhi territory.

After the initial success of 1947-49, which, in any case, was the doing of the indomitable republicans and Scouts of the region, Pakistan has made no territorial gains. India, on the other hand, theoretically administers 52,016 sq.km. of Ladakh. (This is not an official figure.) In actual practice, having regained villages like Turtuk, the Indian flag flies over a somewhat bigger area.

In the year 2001, Pâkistân Occupied Ladâkh-Gilgit had an estimated population of 15 lakh (1.5 million) while Leh and Kargil together had a population of 2,22,000.

The reader will notice that a very substantial portion of this book is about the occupied parts of Ladâkh-Gilgit. That is because a substantial portion of the territory of old Ladâkh-Gilgit and eighty-five per cent of its population are in Baltistân, Hunzâ, Gilgit, Astor, Kâghân, Chitrâl, Shaksgam, Aksai Chin and Kohistân.

Several chapters of this book, especially the ones about handicrafts, literature, culture, sports and pastimes, are common to both portions of this paradise perched on the roof of the world.

21

Gilgit-Baltistân-Chitrâl-Astor-Kâghân: an introduction

The region

Balâwaristân-Gilgit, which Pâkistân calls the 'Northern Areas,' is the northernmost part of Jammû and Kashmîr. This is a highly mountainous region that borders the Xinjiang Province of China. Chitrâl is in the west and the Kalam, Kohistân and Kâghân valleys are in the south. Kargil and the Valley of Kashmîr are in the east. The Republic of Tâjikistân is not very far away.

Put another way, the Hiñdu Kush range is in the west, the Himâlayas are in the south and east, the Kârâkoram is in the east, and the Pamirs are in the north.

Pâkistân, which is in occupation of this region, has divided the 'Northern Areas' into five districts: Gilgit, Skardu, Diamir, Ghizar and Ganche. The region has 650 villages, each being at a considerable distance from the next village.

Pâkistân has chopped occupied Kashmîr up into several parts. It calls the territories that it has occupied in the Kashmîr and Jammu provinces by the name 'Âzâd Jammu and Kashmîr.' Gilgit and Baltistân have been put into what it calls the 'Northern Areas.' It has gifted Shimshal to China. As far as places like Chitrâl and Hunzâ are concerned it has tried to merge them with Pâkistân-proper.

On the other hand, the mountains have their own ideas. They have divided the region into a number of valleys. Each valley has its own culture, history, language, sect of Islâm and sub-racial group of people. Often people from one valley can't understand the language of the other. So they either converse in Urdû and English, or grope for such words from the other man's dialect as they might know. (The same is true of valleys within Leh and Kargil.)

The Balâwaristân-Gilgit region was always an important hub of trade and travel between Central-and South-Asia.

The mountains are very high— so high that many of the attractions of the region are above the tree line. Thus, much of the region is a high-altitude desert. For that reason the people grow pretty gardens and orchards wherever they can. These expanses of greenery are infinitely more soothing at that altitude than in the plains, where vegetation can be taken for granted.

Today most of the international tourists who enter Pâkistân do so in order to go to the Gilgit-Balâwaristân-Hunzâ-Chitrâl region of occupied Kashmîr.

People, population and area: Pâkistân sliced 72,496 square kilometres out of the State and put them in the 'Northern Areas.' According to the 1981 census the region had a population of 0.574 million. In 2003, it had an estimated population of around 1.5 million. Traditional controls, which had held the population in check over the centuries, have disappeared. In just twenty years the population has almost tripled. In neighbouring Leh and Kargil, too, it has grown very fast since 1947, though not as rapidly.

Even today, the 'Northern Areas' have a very low population density—around 10 persons per square kilometre. However, much of this land is too barren to be cultivated. The people of the 'Northern Areas' own 0.124 hectares of agricultural land on an average.

The region has eight major ethnic groups—Balti, Shîn, Yashkun, Mughal, Kashmîrî, Pushtûn (Pathân), Ladâkhî and Turk. The languages and dialects that they speak are Balti, Burushaski, Khowar, Wakhi, Turki, Tibetan, Pushto, Urdu and Persian. The Muslims are divided into four broad sects—Shia, Sunni, Ismâili and Nûr Bakhshi.

This area has traditionally been a paradise, free of religious and sectarian conflict. However, with 'modernity,' since the 1980s there have been violent clashes between different Muslim sects. In all of South Asia, modern education has made young people organise themselves along sectarian, religious and other ethnic lines. The idyllic Gilgit-Baltistân region has not escaped this disease.

Traditional routes: There are eight mountain peaks of 24,000 feet or more, and a large number of glaciers, within a 65-mile radius of Gilgit. These include the Rakaposhi (26,050 feet), and Nañgâ Parbat (26,650 feet). Gilgit has traditionally been about 230 miles from Srinagar. A mountain track connects Srinagar with Gilgit. It goes over the 13,780' Burzil Pass.

The traditional route from Kashmîr later came to be called the Gilgit Road, and was in operation till 1947. With luck, this ancient route might become available to travellers soon. It leads from Srînagar to Bâñdîpur and thence to Guréz and the Burzil Pass. For at least two thousand years people have been using this route to travel between Kashmîr on the one hand and Dardistân, Yâsîn-Gilgit (the Great Poliu) and Chitrâl (the Smaller Poliu) on the other.

The other route to the Valley of Kashmîr is the Gilgit-Skardu track in the Indus valley. It has traditionally been only a mule track and is 118 miles long. All the rivers in the region are dangerous, because their waters flow very fast. They are unfordable and unnavigable except on inflated buffalo skins.

The Burzil and Tragbal passes are covered with several feet of snow for three or four months a year (from November to the middle of March), during which period it is not possible to travel across them.

In summer, people would travel from Kashmîr to Skardu through the Burzil Pass and then the Deosai plateau. This route is shorter than the one normally used but has no facilities and is uncomfortable.

The preferred route between Srînagar and Skardu is through the dZoji Lâ and then Kargil.

Terrorism and the tourist economy: The year 2001 was the best year ever for Pakistân's tourism industry. Almost 5,00,000 (0.5 million) international tourists visited Pakistân that year. That included an all-time high of 70 expeditions (consisting of 450 mountaineers) and 245 registered treks (made up of almost 1,300 trekkers).

The events of '9/11' took place after the tourist season of 2001 was over. However, the attacks on New York and Washington, which were financed by a Karachi-based émigré Pâkistânî, took their toll the next year. In 2002, the number of tourists and trekkers, as well as earnings from tourism, fell by more than 90%. The number of international tourists visiting Pakistân dropped to 45,000. This included 29 expeditions (consisting of around 200 mountaineers) and 42 registered treks (made up of 97 trekkers).

This devastated the tourist economy of Pâkistân in general and the Gilgit-Baltistân-Hunzâ-Chitrâl in particular. In 2001, the government of Pâkistân had collected US $617,000 as royalties from expeditions and treks. In 2002, this fell to US $141,000.

As in Leh and Kargil, the fears that led to this drop were greatly exaggerated. Since the 1960s, some 250 trekkers and climbers have died in mountain accidents in Pakistân. According to official Pâkistânî figures, during this period only three foreigners were killed in attacks, 'and these,' according to the Government of Pâkistân, 'were people travelling by themselves, without local support.'

The people: All over the world there are good and bad people, generous and miserly people and warm and cold people. However, when selecting people to send to Gilgit-Baltistân-Hunzâ-Chitrâl (and to most of Ladâkh and indeed Jammu and Kashmîr as a whole) God chose the first of each category. Every visitor to Gilgit-Baltistân-Hunzâ-Chitrâl talks about the simplicity of the people and their innate goodness. I wonder how much of this will survive 'modernity.' In Leh and Kargil, which have traditionally been free of crime and corruption, at least in the urban areas some corruption has started creeping in. Crime statistics mention highwaymen on the road to Chilâs. However, there is very little crime of any kind in most of Gilgit-Baltistân-Hunzâ-Chitrâl.

My remarks about the generosity of the people may please be taken very seriously. When people invite you home and offer you food it might cost them far more than they can afford. This is because of a value system where the guest has to be looked after no matter what the expense. So, unless you are certain that your host is well to do, it would be a good idea to minimise the burden on him.

The mountain ranges

If the Valley of Kashmîr is the prettiest part of the state and the most attractive for the recreational tourist, Gilgit-Baltistân-Hunzâ-Chitrâl have the most exciting mountains in the world, and a fascinating cultural diversity. When a place has mountains of that kind, it would naturally also have great valleys, meadows, springs and rivers.

The Kârâkoram Highway, made by Chinese engineers with Pâkistânî support, is a stunning achievement. It is no mean feat to build even an ordinary road at that altitude and in those enormously difficult mountains. And this highway is anything but ordinary.

Like many other Himâlayan roads that go through passes, parts of this highway get snowed under in winter. It is impossible to use these parts for five or six months every year. For that reason the Pâkistânis and the Chinese call it their 'seasonal border.' In a typical year the road reopens around May 1. In 2003, it opened as late as on the 15th June, but that was mainly because of an epidemic that had swamped China.

The Sost 'entry point' in the Khunjerab valley (near Gilgit) is among the important 'entry points' between occupied Kashmîr and China. Considerable trade takes place at this point. Men and materials for China-assisted developmental projects in Gilgit-Baltistân-Hunzâ-Chitrâl arrive through Sost.

Among the major projects that the Chinese are undertaking in Gilgit-Baltistân-Hunzâ-Chitrâl are i) the Rs.1.33 billion, 18 megawatt Naltar power project, ii) the 200km Kârâkoram Highway rehabilitation project near the occupied Kashmîr-China border, for which the Chinese government has approved Rs.6 billion. and iii) the 4 megawatt Guru power project (phase II). The Kârâkoram Highway rehabilitation project includes building and repairing bridges, and constructing protective walls along the landslide and mudslide-prone areas of upper Hunzâ.

The highest set of mountain peaks and ranges in the world: The second highest peak in the world, Mount Godwin Austen/ K-2 (8625 metres) is at the northern end of the region. Nañgâ Parbat (8126 metres) is in the south. Between the two are the Mounts Broadpeak, Haramosh, Masherbrum, Rakaposhi and almost thirty other peaks with a height of 20,000 feet or more.

This region is where the Western Himâlayas, the Kârâkoram and the Hiñdu Kush Ranges meet. The Pamirs and the Kun-Lun are not far away

A list of 169 peaks, which are of 7,000 metres or higher, is given in the chapter 'Balâwaristân-Gilgit: Mountain peaks of 7,000 metres and above.'

The Balâwaristân-Ladâkh region has the biggest glaciers in the world outside the poles. These include the 72-kilometre Siachen glacier, the Biafo, the Baltoro, the Batura and the Hispar.

Events: The three-day Shandur festival of Chitrâl takes place around July 7 in most years. Polo matches between the Chitrâl and Gilgit teams are the main attraction of the festival. There are many other folk games, too. (See the chapter on 'Chitrâl.')

The Lowari tunnel project: This proposed 8.5km tunnel is meant to link Dir and Chitrâl with Pâkistân by road throughout the year. At present the road gets snowed under in winter and is tricky during the rains. The proposed tunnel is located at an altitude of 10,500'. Work on the Lowari tunnel began in 1957, when its feasibility report was prepared. Later, some 200-metres of tunnelling was done in 1973, during the Prime Ministership of Mr. Zulfiqar Ali Bhutto. When completed, this Rs.6 billion ($130 million) tunnel will be Asia's longest. In 2003, the National Highway Authority (NHA) of Pâkistân awarded a contract to the Austria-based Geoconsult to look at the technical feasibility of the project once again.

The Astore-Gilgit road is prone to landslides, floods and earthquakes at around a hundred and fifty places. The Frontier Works Organization (FWO) of Pâkistân maintains the road. As in Ladâkh and Kashmîr, every time the road gets blocked because of these reasons, the Government of Pâkistân 'suspends traffic' on the road. (This is the South Asian way of saying that all vehicles are asked to freeze in their tracks wherever they might be on or near the affected parts of the road. This is routinely done on both sides of the line of control.) The FWO then swings into action and starts repairing the road. That done, they first let cars and jeeps travel. Buses and trucks are allowed much later. The exercise normally takes three to six days each time. During those days things become very difficult in Astore valley. Most foodstuffs, fuel and medicines needed in Astore are brought in from outside the valley whenever the road is 'open.' When the road gets blocked, stocks of all such commodities start running out.

The Kârâkoram Highway (KKH)

The all-weather 1,200 mile (1,900 km.) Kârâkoram Highway runs from Rawalpindi/ Islâmâbâd in Pâkistân's Punjâb province to Kashgar [Kashi] in China's Xinjiang Province. En route it passes through the part of occupied Kashmîr that Pâkistân calls the 'Northern Areas.' It goes over very difficult mountains, skims the Hiñdu Kush range, climbs up to the Himâlayas, and winds through the Kârâkoram and Pamir ranges before going down into China..

Havelian is 100km. from Islâmâbâd. That's where the 805km. dual-carriage road begins. It then passes through Abbotâbâd, Mansehra, Thakot, Besham, Pattan, Sazin, Chilâs (the first major town in the 'Northern Areas'), Bunji, Gilgit and Baltit/ Hunzâ before crossing the Khunjerab Pass (4,733m.) to reach the Chinese Frontier.

Chinese experts and Pâkistân Army engineers began work on the KKH around 1965. The road reached the edge of the 'Northern Areas' in 1980 and China in 1986. It was only in 1982, that it became possible for tourists to visit the 'Northern Areas.' Even if the KKH is not 'the highest paved highway on the planet' it is an engineering marvel by any yardstick, because it has been built on one of the world's most difficult terrains. The Khunjerab Pass itself must be one of God's most awesome creations on earth (see photograph). In the 'Glossary' to this book I have tried to define the word 'lâ' or 'mountain pass.' As the photograph shows, Khunjerab is a pass like no other in the world.

The motorable road at the Khardung Lâ (pass), 14km. from Leh town, is the highest in the world (18,300'/ 5602m.). Therefore, claims that the Khunjerab Pass holds this distinction might need to be reviewed.

True, the road at the Khardung Lâ is no autobahn. But then at places, even the KKH is only wide enough for two buses or trucks at a time. As with roads in several other parts of Balâwaristân-Ladâkh, at places the KKH is perched more than a hundred feet above the River Indus. One false move and the vehicle goes straight into the Indus, because it is a steep drop. However, the KKH also goes through waterfalls and gorges. As in the Banihal area of Jammû, and near the holy cave of Srî Amarnâth jî, the KKH is prone to 'shooting stones.' This means that at times stones (and even rocks) come hurtling down from the brittle hill above the highway.

The stretch near Chilâs poses a danger of a different kind—dacoits (highwaymen) hold cars up at gunpoint and rob travellers. However, they normally leave buses alone.

How to get there: The night bus from Rawalpindi to Gilgit does the journey in just under 20 hours, if there are no breakdowns or other delays. (In practice, 22 hours is the norm for old buses.) The bus leaves Rawalpindi around 10p.m. En route it passes through Murree and then Besham. Besham is a little town at which a side road branches off to Swât Valley. The bus and the KKH then pass through Kohistân, which is close to the Nañgâ Parbat (8,124m./ 26,656'). For several hours the bus will remain, so to speak, in the shadow of this, the ninth highest peak in the world. The mountain is best seen from the place where River Indus leaves the KKH and branches off into a side-gorge.

(Nañgâ Parbat: Of all the Himâlayan peaks of 8,000m peak or more, this peak is the westernmost.)

Chilâs is in the northern part of Kohistân. It has invaluable ancient rock carvings in which various Chinese Buddhist monks have recorded details of their travels. These missionaries travelled between China and India, learning and disseminating the message of Buddhism

You are now in a 'high-altitude desert.' The landscape is rocky, barren and majestic. At places there are sand dunes.

Bunji comes next, as the road continues its northward (northeastward, to be precise) ascent. Gilgit and then Hunzâ (Karîmâbâd/ Baltit) are further north still. Gojal in the Upper Hunzâ valley comes next. Indeed, Pasu is the last township in the the Gilgit-Balâwaristân-Hunzâ-Chitrâl region, indeed in the entire state, because if you go any further north, through the Khunjerab Pass, you will be in China's Xinjiang province.

Baltistân/ Skardu Valley

Skardu (2438m./ 7,440') is the headquarters of Baltistân, It is surrounded by tall peaks of the Kârâkoram range. In mediæval times Central Asians saw Ladâkh and Tibet as part of the same continuum. They believed that there were three Tibets: Tibet proper, central Tibet (Leh and Kargil) and Tibbatt-é-Khurd ('Tibet minor' or 'the little Tibet'). Baltistân was this 'Tibet minor.'

The Chinese province of Sinkiang is to the north-east of Baltistân. The Gilgit Agency of POK is in the north-west. Kargil district is in the south-east, and the Valley of Kashmîr in the south-west. Baltistân abounds in glaciers and tall mountain peaks. It has five valleys: Shigar, Skardu, Khaplu, Rondu and Kharmañg.

The name: The word Skardu is actually an abbreviation of the original Skar-mDo or Skar-mamDo, which either means 'a place that is enclosed' or 'the place where the stars are.' The weight of evidence supports the latter. The local people have traditionally used the word Skardu to refer to the entire Skardu valley, district and region. The neighbourhood around the fort and the office-district is called the Quilâ (fort). (See also 'A history of Baltistân' for revisionist theories.)

The town: Skardu has been built on an alluvial plain almost fifty metres above River Indus. There are mountains in the south. At one end of the town is a rock that towers almost 300 metres above the Indus.

The people: In addition to the native people, there has for centuries been a small Kashmîrî population in Skardu town. This included some Kashmîrî Pandits (they must either have converted to Islâm or returned to Kashmîr after 1947). The Kashmîrîs owned almost all the shops, in addition, of course, to running the pashmînâ trade.

The population of Baltistân is just under three hundred thousand. In the last census it was 272,000. These hardy people live in 230 villages. The average household consists of eight people.

Most families possess around ten goats and sheep, and two or three yaks or cows. Every tenth Balti family lives almost entirely off its cattle. Like the gaddis of Jammu and the chopâns of Kashmîr, they send a member of the family to a highland pasture in summer to look after the cattle.

Till the 1940s, the remoter villages of Baltistân ran a barter economy. Earlier still, butter was used as the currency. People would keep it in underground 'banks' for as many as fifty years and pull it out whenever they needed to buy something. Butter was also given out on loan.

The average farm in Baltistân is no bigger than an acre. Wheat, barley, millet, buckwheat and maize are the main traditional crops. Fruits, especially apricots, are an important crop. Almonds, apples, grapes, mulberries, peaches, pears, plums and walnuts grow in the area. Households spread plucked fruits and vegetables out in the summer sun to dehydrate them, so that they can be stored and eaten in winter.

There aren't enough jobs for everyone in Baltistân. So, every fifth household has someone working in Pâkistân, in jobs that the Pâkistânis themselves are now too well off to perform. The bread earner of almost every third Balti household is a 'temporary day labourer,' Working as a porter for visiting tourists pays better than many other forms of daily-wage labour.

Traditional architecture: The houses are made of what, in Kashmîr, are called Mahârâjî (sun-baked) bricks. However, the mud roofs are flat in the Ladâkhî style. Plenty of wood has been used in the old houses. Before glass became accessible to the common man, which was in the 20th century, people covered their latticed windows with mica or paper.

Aqueducts have been known in Skardu since at least the 19th century, if not much before.

Three forts and a palace: The oldest fort was built in the early mediæval era. It is atop a low hillock and now in ruins. So is the palace, which is at one end of the plain, near the rock. This is where the family that ruled Skardu till the mid-19th century. used to live. It was dismantled when the Dogrâs annexed Skardu. There is also an 18th/19th century fort, square in shape.

The best preserved of the lot is the rubble and mortar Dogrâ fort, which is perched in the middle of the Nausho hill. Its foundations were laid in 1888.

The tourist attractions of Baltistân

K-2 (8,611 m/28,253') is the world's second highest mountain peak. It is situated on Jammû and Kashmîr's border with China, in the Kârâkoram Region. Without doubt, this is the greatest tourist attraction of the entire Gilgit-Balâwaristân belt. K-2 is also known as Mt. Godwin Austen.

Kharpocho Fort: The great emperor Ali Sher Khân Anchan constructed this historic fort at Skardu. He had ruled over much of Ladâkh, and all the way up to Chitrâl, in the second half of the 16th century.

Khaplu Valley is 103km. from Skardu. Khaplu is the name of the scenic valley of River Shyok. It is home to some famous peaks, including the Masherbrum, Saltoro, Sia Gangri, K-6 and K-7.

Mountain Lakes: There are three high-altitude lakes in the neighbourhood—the Upper Kachura Lake, the Kachura Lake and the Sadpara Lake. All three are good for fishing. The Pâkistânî authorities have made arrangements for boat rides on these lakes. Lake Kachura is 29km. from Skardu and Lake Sadpara 8km.

Shigar valley is 32km. from Skardu. It is the base camp for the two most famous peaks of the Kârâkoram range—the Gasherbrum and the K-2. The road from Skardu to Shigar is 'jeepable.'

The Skardu plain is huge, being more than thirty kilometres long. It is between two and eight kilometres wide. However, it is rocky, sandy and mostly barren. This gives the place a rugged beauty of the kind that Ladâkh is famous for. The rivers Indus and Shigar merge with each other at one end of this crescent-shaped plain.

Some of the mountains near the plain rise to around 17,000' above the sea, or almost ten thousand feet above the plain.

The Buddhist Rock: This is a famous attraction on the road from Skardu to Sadpara. It is the only surviving Buddhist artefact in the district.

The Baltis

There are an estimated 388,000 Balti people in Gilgit-Baltistân. Of them 280,000 are in the Skardu Region and 98,000 in the Ganche Region. Some ten thousand have migrated to Pâkistâni cities like Karachi, Rawalpindi, and Multan.

In addition there is a sizeable Balti population in Kargil district.

The people of Baltistân call their own land Balti-yul. (Yul means 'village', 'town' and '-land'.) Baltistân is spread over 26,000 square kilometres (and, thus, is bigger than several independent countries). It has sixty mountain peaks of 21,000 feet (6,500 metres) or more. Four of them rise above 8,000 metres.

Baltistân is in the watershed of River Indus and its tributaries. It is a very dry, mostly treeless, land of rocky mountains and glaciers, punctuated by streams and some apricot orchards. There is very little rain and the place is almost a desert. Needless to say, Baltistân, like the rest of Ladâkh-Balâwaristân, is extremely cold.

The Baltis are a Mongoloid people of Tibetan origin. (They have an 'Aryan' inheritance, too, as has been discussed in the chapter on 'History.') They converted to Islâm perhaps in the 16th century. All Baltis are Shiites. In Ganche, however, they mainly belong to the Nûr Bakhshi sect, a denomination that had once tried to act as a bridge between the Shias and the Sunnis but is now seen as a sub-sect of the Shias.

The hospitable people of Baltistân are as proud of their religious identity as Muslims as they are of their racial identity as Tibetans. They still retain such of their Tibetan and animistic customs as are not disconsonant with Islâm.

Brasstacks

Best season: April to October, when the mean maximum temperature is 27°C and the minimum around 8°C.

The flight from Islâmâbâd to Skardu: Skardu has an airport, with a daily Boeing flight to Islâmâbâd. Most of the air route to Skardu is the same as the one to Gilgit. At some stage, the plane turns right and then flies through the narrow, rocky gorge of the Indus river. The faint-hearted should not look out of the window during this stretch.

Getting there by road: There is a gravel-top 241km. 'jeepable' track between Gilgit and Skardu. Jeeps cover the distance in between six and eight hours.

Accommodation: The Pâkistân Tourism Development Corporation runs the mid-market *K-2 Motel* at Skardu. There are government rest houses at Skardu, Lake Sadpara, Shigar Valley, Khaplu and Lake Kachura.

Handicrafts: Tourists often purchase the local tweed (pattû). Jackets and coats in which this homemade woollen cloth is used are quite warm. Pattu is made throughout Ladâkh, Doda (Jammû) and much of the Himâlayas,

Tourists also buy Baltistân's famous embroidered chugâs (gowns) and wooden spoons. All these are available in the Skardu bâzâr.

Fruit: Apricots, apples, peaches and pears grow in Baltistân.

'Balti' food

Most Balti nationalists are quite embarrassed by the international success of Baltistân's best-known cultural export: Balti food. The 'arctic' mountains of Baltistân have never known a prawn or a coconut tree. And yet both are used in the 'Balti' food being served in the outside world. What has been passing off as Balti food since the late 1980s perhaps originated among Pâkistânis in the English Midlands and certainly not in Baltistân. This cuisine has been a major hit in the UK, though.

Balti food is cooked in round-bottomed, cast iron cooking vessels. Apparently the 'Balti' pan came from China to Baltistân on the old silk route. By the time this cuisine reached the Punjâb the pan turned into a karhâî (a round-bottomed, cast iron vessel popular in the Punjâb).

Along the way Balti dishes absorbed aromatic Kashmîri spices, winter foods from mountain highlands, Mughal court cuisine, tribal food and, of course, Punjâbi influences.

Gilgit Valley

'The point of Gilgit, now as always, is strategic.[1] High above the snowline, somewhere midst the peaks and glaciers that wall in the Gilgit Valley, the long and jealously guarded frontiers of India, China, Russia, Afghânistân and Pâkistân meet. It is the hub, the crown's-nest, the fulcrum of Asia.'

-The Gilgit Game[i]

The Gilgit Valley (1,454m.) and its charming little headquarters of the same name are best known for their stunning mountain landscape. The

1. No, the point of Gilgit, now as always, is the goodness of its people. Even when Gilgit ceases to have any strategic importance, the generosity of the people and the beauty of the place will, God willing, remain.

town has decent hotels which serve good food. Since 1999, Gilgit has also had e-mail. Gilgit proper is at the centre of a large, wide valley. It is green and, thus, beautiful.

Tracks lead from Gilgit, mostly through mountain passes, to Chitrâl and Afghânistân (in the west), China and Central Asia (in the north), and Skardu, Tibet and the Valley of Kashmîr (in the east). In this respect it has a central position similar to that of Kargil town.

As a result people from different lands and cultures live in, or at least pass through, Gilgit. The town owes its importance partly to the fact that it is (and always was) a major transit and trade hub for the region. The people mainly speak Shînâ.

Gilgit is not at a very great height. Therefore, there is no shortage of oxygen. A short stay here helps acclimatise for the challenge of the higher mountains. Tourists like Gilgit for the scenery, and the relaxed walks in and around the town.

The air is crisp, clean and, in some parts, scented. In spring and summer, water flows in little streams all over the countryside. Chinârs, cypresses, eucalyptuses, many types of fruit trees, poplars and willows grow in the villages and along the road. Many of them blossom in spring. There are conifers in the higher mountains. And there are Persian lilacs and irises;

History: Gilgit and the neighbourhood were part of the Kushan Empire (1st-3rd centuries A.D.). Its other rulers included the Tibetans, some Chinese warlords, Afghans and the Dogrâs. Before the people converted en masse to Islâm around the 12th century, they were Buddhists and animists.

The goodness of the people: Writer Sheryl Shapiro[ii] recounts a very pleasant story about her arrival at the Gilgit airport. 'We had chosen a travelers [sic] hostel from our guidebook, but they were unrepresented among the jeeps waiting outside the small airport. No problem. A young man from a competing hotel offered to drive us to our destination, free of charge. This was the first indication that the people in the north were something special.'

I wonder if this kind of goodness exists anywhere else in the world.

The tourist attractions of Gilgit

Gahkuch: This is the headquarters of Ghizar district. It is also the staging post for travellers to Iskoman valley. It is popular with adventure tourists who come here for trekking, fishing and duck shooting. There are ancient ruins in and around Gahkuch, especially in nearby Hatoon. There are some private hotels and a government rest house in Gahkuch.

Naltar Valley is a three-hour drive from the Gilgit link road. The road from Nomal winds upwards through a rocky gorge.

After a few hours on a jeepable track, you will reach the roadhead. Some supplies might be available locally, for instance potatoes, cottage cheese and milk. The clear Naltar Lake yields good trout. You can trek up to the pass and, if it is clear, beyond.

Naltar's attractions include fertile, dense, high-altitude alpine meadows and pine forests at around 3,000 m./10,000'. There are tall mountains all around. Some of them have snow on their peaks throughout the year. In winter Naltar boasts of ski slopes. There are two ski-lifts at Naltar but both are meant for the army of occupation.

The valley also has several glaciers. The treks lead to Iskoman, Chalt and Puniâl valley. There are tiny lakes in the forest and trout in the lakes. The Naltar Lake is the best of the lot and people often walk up the sloping path to this lake, for its beauty as well as to fish there.

Indeed, walking on the mild slopes of Naltar's forests is the average tourist's favourite activity there. Sports lovers make Naltar the base camp for treks to the Naltar Pass (4,000m./ 13,000') and thence to the Iskoman Valley, or to Daintar Pass (4,800m./ 15,700') and from there to Chalt.

Because it is close to Gilgit (those with good vehicles do the return journey in a little more than four hours), most tourists go to Naltar for day trips. Those who choose to spend the night there either pitch their own tents or opt for the downmarket private hotel. The PWD (Public Works Department) rest-house is the best place to stay in Naltar, but not everyone is eligible to stay there.

Phander (177km./ 8 hours from Gilgit) is a scenic region with a trout-rich lake.

In and around Gilgit: i) There is a 7th century A.D. rock engraving of Lord Buddha 10km. from Gilgit town, at one end of the Kargah Nullah (see photograph). It should certainly rank among the wonders of the world. A large sculpture of Lord Buddha, in relief, has been carved in the middle of a sheer rocky precipice. One is left absolutely stunned by the feat, wondering how the sculptor(s) got there. Where did he (they?) place his (or their) feet? What kind of a scaffold did they use? Did they not feel dizzy? How did they lean back to view their creation while it was being done, to ensure that the proportions were right? The Kargah Buddha and its counterpart in Leh deserve far more international recognition than they have received. (See also the chapter 'The National Highway: Leh to Kargil, and Srinagar to Kargil.' Please see the lines just above the entry about 'Lâmâ Yûrû.')

ii) 30km. from Gilgit town, on a jeepable road, is the 14th century A.D. victory monument of Taj Mughal.

iii) The bridge across River Gilgit is the biggest suspension bridge in Asia (182m. long and 2m. wide).

Rama: (120km./ 6 hours from Gilgit.) There is a lake in the Rama region from which one can see the eastern side of Nañgâ Parbat (8126m.).

Shér Qilâ (40km./ 2 hours from Gilgit) is best known for being on the trekking route to Naltar valley, for its lake and for the trout found in the Shér Qilla Nullah (stream). Shér Qila is the headquarters of Puniâl, a pretty valley.

Singal (56km./ 3 hours from Gilgit) is in the Puniâl valley. Anglers go there to fish for trout.

Yâsîn (160km./ 7 hours from Gilgit): This valley is celebrated for hiking and trekking.

Adventure Sports

Polo is the best-loved sport in all of Ladâkh. Gilgit claims to have invented the game. (We in India agree that the game originated in Balâwaristân. Wherein Balâwaristân, no one is sure. It could well have been in Gilgit.) Gilgit has a very good polo team. As in the rest of Ladâkh, they follow no rules. An annual polo tournament is held between the 1st and 7th November.

Trout fishing: Trout is found in the following streams (distances from Gilgit proper have been given in brackets): Gahkuch (73km.), Kargah Nullah (10km.), Phander (117km.) and Singal (56km). For fishing permits contact the Assistant Director, Fisheries, Government of Pâkistân, Gilgit.

The Kargah Nullah, a picturesque mountain torrent, is a tributary of River Gilgit. Colonel Cobb, a British Political Agent, introduced trout in the Nullah in 1918. Ever since, its fishing stream has been celebrated for its trout.

Mountain climbing: For permits to climb the exciting mountains around Gilgit contact the Ministry of Tourism, Government of Pâkistân, Islâmâbâd.

An Austro-German expedition attempted the Nañgâ Parbat in July 1953. Hermann Buhl made it to the summit, alone. Rahbar Hassan had led the porters. That won him the sobriquet of 'The Tiger of Hunzâ.' (He was much like what Tenzing Norgay was to Sir Edmund Hillary.)

Trekking: International tourists are allowed to trek only in the 'open zone' of Gilgit. This means that they can not go to any place that is 16km. or less from the line of control with India or 50km. or less from the border with Afghânistân². However, even when travelling by bus within the open zone, 'throughout the Northern Areas, every hour or so the bus stops and all foreigners sign in with the military.'[iii]

Treks out of Gilgit: Fairy Meadows (11,000') is a picturesque alpine pasture. It has a green, fenced campsite. The dining hall and kitchen of the complex are in a pretty cabin. The toilet and washroom are equally charming. Sheryl Shapiro[iv] calls the toilet a "loo with a view" because it has a framed view of Nañgâ Parbat (26,658 ft.) through its window. The people of Gilgit have maintained the resort extremely well. There are forests of pine and larch nearby.

Brasstacks

Latitude 35.92°N; longitude 74.29°E.

In 1998, Gilgit town had a population of 82,000 and in 2003, all of 93,000.

Best season: May to October. The highest temperature in May is around 33°C and the minimum about 16°C. In September the maximum is 28°C and the minimum 11°C.

Getting there (and back): Apart from the Islâmâbâd-Gilgit bus service mentioned in the section on the 'Kârâkoram Highway,' it is also possible to travel between Islâmâbâd and Gilgit by helicopter.

The flight to Gilgit: The aeroplane flies over River Indus, which flows through rugged, barren gorges. The Nañgâ Parbat, 26,629', the westernmost peak of the Himâlayas, will be on the right. Its north face towers over the Indus Valley. Author Barbara Hilda Mons called 'it the greatest mountain wall in the world.' She pointed out, 'The river-bed is here only 3,000 feet above sea-level, so the summit of the mountain is over 23,000 feet above it.' Haramosh and then the Rakaposhi will be the next peaks that you are, on a clear day, likely see from your window.

To Chitrâl: From Gilgit it is an 18-hour drive, west, over the mountains, to Chitrâl.

Administration: The Political Agent (head of administration) of Gilgit has, after 1947, been a two-or three-star General of the Pâkistânî army. (His counterparts in Leh and Kargil have always been civil servants.) He lives in the stately Agency House of the British Raj.

2. As an Indian civil servant I find the implications of the two different yardsticks quite intriguing. Does this mean that the Pâkistânî authorities consider the line of control with India three times as safe (and less dangerous) than the border with Afghânistân? In other words, do they consider the threat from Afghânistân three times greater than that from India?

Accommodation: Travellers speak very highly of the *Medina* Guest House, Gilgit, for its facilities, for treating guests like family and for the high level of trust that they have in their guests.

The Wakhi People

There are an estimated 65,000 Wakhi-speaking people in all. Of these, 31,000 live in Gilgit, 13,000 in the northern parts of Chitrâl Valley, 9,000 in the Wakhân Corridor of Afghânistân, 10,000 in South East Tâjikistân and some 2,000 in the Xinjiang Province of China. In the so-called Northern Areas, there also are small Wakhi communities in Ishkoman and the Gojal district of Northern Hunzâ. Almost all Wakhis are Ismâili Muslims.

The Wakhi people belong to the same ethnic group as the Iranians. Their ancestors lived in what is now called the Wakhân Corridor of Afghânistân. This is the stretch between the Hiñdu Kush and the Pamir Mountains.

The Wakhi language is an ancient and crude ancestor of the Persian language. It is quite different from the Tâjik language. It has no script of its own and in modern times has been written in the Perso-Arabic script.

History: It is now being said that the Wakhis were among the earliest converts to Islâm. This assumption has been current ever since two 8th century manuscripts of the Arabic Umm-al-kitab were discovered in the Wakhân Corridor. These books, calligraphed in Iraq, were found in the early 20th century. Of course, it is possible that they reached the Wakhân Corridor several centuries after they had been written.

The Wakhi people have lived as small farmers and cowherds over the centuries, and live much the same life to this day. They were happy to reside in the Wakhân Corridor, despite its extremely meagre resources. However, around 1886, some of them migrated to Chitrâl. No one knows why, but it is assumed that they were driven there because of some extreme hardship at home. A famine seems to have been the cause of the next mass migration, which was around 1919. Then, in 1937, the government of Afghânistân started insisting on conscripting all able-bodied Wakhi men into their army. The Wakhis resisted. The government retaliated by putting pressure on them.

That was the last straw. All but a small group left the Wakhân Corridor, to migrate to the neighbouring regions.

In the 20th century, the Wakhi people decided to accept Prince Karîm Âgâ Khân as their spiritual leader and the Ismâili sect of Islâm as their creed. This being a liberal sect, the Wakhi people are more open to change and outside influences. Besides, the Âgâ Khân Foundation has undertaken major developmental activities in the area.

The Afghânistân-Tâjikistân region saw major upheavals from the 1970s onwards. This affected the livelihood of the Wakhis, impoverishing them further. In Gojal (Hunzâ) alone has this community done well. (See the chapter on 'Shimshal.') There, like the other people of Hunzâ, they have benefited from the enormous amount of work done by the Âgâ Khân Foundation, as well as their proximity to the Kârâkoram Highway.

Elsewhere, the Wakhis live in poverty. It is said that in Chitrâl, the Wakhân Corridor and High Pamir many of them have got addicted to opium. They have started neglecting their health as well work.

Which is a pity. A fine ancient community, which has a rich oral culture with an elaborate repertoire of folksongs and fairy tales, seems to have first got fragmented and then found itself on a path of economic and even demographic decline.

Chitrâl

Chitrâl is a valley in northwestern Jammu and Kashmîr, where the state borders Afghânistâṇ. This is where the steep Hiñdu Kush Mountains are. The Hiñdu Kush range is not as tall as the Himâlayas or the Kârâkorams, not being in the 8,000-metres-plus class. But it does have formidable peaks like the Tirich Mîr (7,788m./25,550'), which is the highest peak in the Hiñdu Kush range and can be seen from most parts of the valley. The other well known nearby peaks are the Noshaq (7492m), the Istoro Nal (7403m) and the Saraghrar (7338m).

Peaks in the 6,096m. to 7,315m. range (and preferred by mountaineers) include the Bunizem, Chosharso, Phal, Daser and Don.

Chitrâl valley is 322km. long. Afghânistân surrounds it from three sides—north, south and west. Tâjikistân is not very far either. The Wakhân 'corridor,' which is a thin strip of Afghân territory, is sandwiched between Chitrâl and Tâjikistân.

Tourists go to Chitrâl (1,128 m./ 3,700') as much for its beautiful mountains as to see its people, who are famous for their warmth, friendliness and unique culture. (See the chapter 'The 'infidel' Kafir Kalash clan of Chitrâl.') Anglers, anthropologists, hikers, hunters, mountaineers, nature lovers and trekkers are attracted to Chitrâl in summer.

Most of the people of Chitrâl are Muslims. However, there are three Valleys in the southern parts of Chitrâl where the 'Kafir' (infidel) Kalash people live. This is an animistic tribe of some 4,000 people that has, to quote countless Pâkistâni websites,[3] 'evaded' being converted to Islâm. (Many Pâkistâni websites[4] describe them as 'primitive pagans.') Members of the tribe are also known as 'the wearers of the Black Robe'. They live in the valleys of Birir, Bumburet and Rambur. As in Dâ-Hânû (Ladâkh), all men who wear the traditional Kalash dress affix a flower or two to their hats.

The (Muslim) Gujjars are nomadic tribesmen who live in—and migrate within—Chitrâl, as they do in the rest of Jammu and Kashmîr.

All these attractions have brought tens of thousands of tourists to Chitrâl, especially to the Kalash region—to Bumburet in particular. The benefits have been mixed. Apart for such employment that tourism has generated, it has also brought plastic and other non-degradeable wastes. A people who had only eaten fresh, organic fruits and vegetables before have started eating canned food. A pristine culture has begun to change.

Chitrâl is 365km/ 227 miles from Péshâwar and 405km/252 miles from Gilgit. The mean elevation of the valley is 1127.76 m./ 3,700'. This huge valley is spread over 14,504 sq. metres.

Phone Code: 0933

Languages: The people speak Khowar (Chitrâli) and Urdu.

Best season: June to September. The maximum temperature in June is 35°C (95°F) and the minimum around 20°C (67°F). In September, the maximum is 24°C (75°F) and the minimum 8°C (46°F).

Climate: Summer is pleasant but winter can be very cold. In spring the weather can be quite tricky in Chitrâl because it might suddenly start snowing or raining. Therefore, June to September is the best time to visit.

The cold of Chitrâl's winters is not the main reason why tourist arrivals suddenly dwindle from October to May. It is impossible to travel across the passes in winter, because all the major passes are buried under snow.

How to get there: By air: PIA (Pâkistân International Airlines) has a daily, 50-minute, Fokker flight between Péshâwar or Islâmâbâd on the one hand and Chitrâl on the other. As in most of Ladâkh, these flights are often cancelled when the weather gets bad. PIA has kept the fare low.

3. For instance, pakwatan.com, south-asia.com/pâkistân.Chitrâl.htm, home.online.no and victorynews.net.
4. khowar.com, pakvisit.com, northpak.8m.com, flypia.aero and cybercity-online.net were among the countless sites which, a Yahoo! search revealed, had used this brilliant phrase.

By road: Chitrâl is 227 miles/ 365km. from Péshâwar on a 'jeepable' road, which passes through Malakand, Dir and the Lowari Pass (3,200m).

There is a road from Islâmâbâd, too. It meets the Péshâwar road at Swât. After that the road goes to Dir and then to the Lowari Pass (see the chapter on 'Chitrâl...').

There is a third (405km./252 mile) 'jeepable' road between Chitrâl and Gilgit. It winds its way through the Shandur Pass (3719m).

The jeep drive will take between 15 and 25 hours, depending on the route and the state of the road. The Péshâwar route is shorter and faster.

It is possible to hire jeeps at any end of the routes mentioned: i.e. at Chitrâl, Gilgit, Islâmâbâd or Péshâwar. Those travelling from Chitrâl often like to spend the night at Mastuj. Travellers coming from Gilgit prefer to spend the night at Gupis.

Where to stay: The Pâkistân Tourism Development Corporation (PTDC) runs a motel in Chitrâl. There are also several rest houses and mid-market private hotels,

Permits: All international tourists need to obtain special permits if they wish to go to the Kalash valleys. They also have to pay a small toll tax of around US $1 per person. The permits are free and can be obtained from the office of the Deputy Commissioner, Chitrâl.

Permits for mountaineering are issued by the Tourism Division, Government of Pâkistân, Islâmâbâd.

Trekking: The valleys of Chitrâl are very popular with international trekkers. Most of the routes can also be covered by jeep. However, trekkers still do them on foot—for the exercise and to soak in the scenery, with the magnificent Tirich Mîr towering over the landscape.

The more popular trekking routes are: i) Drosh-Madaklasht-Golden-Kuguzi-Chitrâl (48km./ 30miles) and ii) Chitrâl-Shighore-Sassum-Ovir-Mroi.

There are no designated camping sites. The thing to do is to find an open space to pitch your tent and then request the owner of the land to let you spend the night there.

Fishing: The fishing season is from April to September. There is trout in the Golenbol and Shishi Kuh Nallâhs and brown trout in the River Lutkuh.

Anglers need to obtain permits, which are very inexpensive, from the Fisheries Department at Chitrâl.

Polo is the favourite sport of Chitrâl—as indeed of all of Ladâkh—Balâwaristân. There are polo matches on festive occasions. The Nowroze Polo Tournament is held in Gilgit from the 1st November every year; the Shandur Polo Tournament is held in the first or second week of July and the Skardu-Khaplu Polo tournament from the 5th to 10th September. The Chitrâl Polo Tournament is the fourth important fixture on the calendar. Its dates vary.

Places of tourist interest

Birmoghalasht: (2743 m./ 9,900'; 15km./ 9 miles from Chitrâl.) The exquisite summer palace of the former Mahtar (king) of Chitrâl is perched on this mountaintop. It directly overlooks—and in turn can be seen from—Chitrâl town. Awesome views of Tirich Mîr and the valleys below can be obtained from here. Till the late 20th century, the only way to go to this palace was on foot. However, a slim road that winds its way uphill has since been built. This narrow road is not meant for the faint hearted, for it always seems that the vehicle is about to jump off the road into the sharp drop below.

Chitrâl town: This is the district headquarters of the valley of the same name. Things to see in the town include its bazaar, the fort of the Mehtar of Chitrâl and the main mosque near the river.

Garm Chashmâ: (1859 m./ 6,100'; 45km./28 miles northwest of Chitrâl; 3 hours by jeep.) These are hot water sulphur springs located in a pretty, fertile valley famous for its orchards. People with skin diseases, chronic headaches, gout and rheumatism bathe in the boiling waters of these springs, which are known for their curative powers. There are tall, snow-capped mountains around the valley. Hamâms (baths) have been constructed near the springs. International tourists have to pay a small toll tax.

Lowari Top: (3,118m.) This is a picturesque, misty pass between Dir and Drosh (the first major habitation in Chitrâl). Because it is a relatively low pass, there is a small forest on it. For the same reason, clouds envelop the pass through most of the year. (Higher passes are dry and desert-like.) In winter (November-May) the pass is snowed under. From June to October it normally is possible to drive on the rugged, winding road that goes through this pass. (There are more details about Dir elsewhere in this book.)

Because of the state of the road, it takes around 31/2 hours in a tough vehicle to do the 70 km. between Dir town and Drosh. The journey from Péshâwar (Pâkistân) to Chitrâl, therefore, might take fifteen or sixteen hours.

The summit is extremely windy. If the mist isn't too thick, there are fine views to be had from the 'Top.' A customs check-post functions from a stone hut at Lowari.

Shandur Pass: (3,719m./ c.12,000') The jeep drive from Chitrâl to the pass and back is extremely rewarding, because you will pass through picturesque, far-flung mountain villages. As passes in the Ladâkh-Balâwaristân region go, Shandur is not very high. However, precisely for that reason it is perhaps the only pass in all Ladâkh-Balâwaristân that is a tourist destination in itself. Because the pass is as much as 1,250' long, it is big enough to be a destination. The views from the pass are, naturally, panoramic and reason enough to go there.

How to get there: Shandur Top is supposed to be 'midway' between Chitrâl and Gilgit on a rugged, 'jeepable' road, Actually, it is roughly 168 km./105 miles from Chitrâl and 237km./15 hours from Gilgit.

What to see: Like other Himâlayan passes, Shandur is an uninhabited wilderness for eleven and a half months a year. In winter it is snowed under. However, for two weeks in July the place suddenly comes alive. A vibrant tourist village of tents suddenly materialises to cater not only to international travellers but, more important, to tens of thousands of local visitors.

Also, unlike most other Himâlayan passes, Shandur is green in summer, with plenty of flowers all around. The clear water lakes near the pass have trout and are one of Shandur's biggest attractions.

Polo: Perhaps the grandest polo tournament in all Gilgit-Balâwaristân-Bunji is the one held at the Shandur Pass. At 3,719m. above the mean sea level, Shandur arguably is the highest place in the world where polo tournaments are organised.[5]

Passions run high at the annual Shandur Polo Tournament because this is when the finest polo players from Gilgit clash with the best from Chitrâl at this pass. It is an annual 'final' of sorts, because it is the culmination of countless 'league' matches that are played in Chitrâl and Gilgit to determine who will represent them at Shandur, People, often in their traditional clothes, travel for days to be at this colourful tournament. Even if you have no interest in the Himâlayan variety of polo (which originated in this region), you might want to be there for the spontaneous pageant of local culture, off the field.

Over the years many side events have sprung up around this tournament, which is spread over five days and four nights. There are

5. We in India believe that polo originated in Gilgit-Baltistân. However, many in Pâkistân claim that this sport was invented in Central Asia in the sixth century BC. According to this theory, polo was originally a war game, a mock-battle, with around a hundred horse riders on each side. Cavalry units were trained on the polo ground if they were being considered for the King's Guards and other elite units.

other equestrian events, too, and a festival of folk dances from all over the Gilgit-Baltistân-Chitrâl region. There sometimes is a trout fishing competition in the streams near the pass. Handicrafts from Chitrâl and Gilgit are sold at colourful shops set up for the occasion.

This is also the best time to watch the legendary—and infrequently performed—Chitrâli Dance. In the past this dance was performed mainly before battles, to boost the morale of the troops, and maybe for luck. (In case I've given you the wrong idea, I must hasten to add that only men take part in this dance.) If the home army won the war, then the dance was performed again—in celebration and thanksgiving.

This martial dance is an extremely graceful affair. Athletic men in white shalwar qameez outfits and red waistcoats twist and contort their shoulders and arms in ways that ordinary men would consider impossible. They wear elegantly curled, white hats called pakols in Afghânistân and Chitrâli hats in Gilgit-Balâwaristân.

Golf: The Shandur Golf Ground might well be the highest of its kind in the world. There is an annual golf tournament at Shandur.

Tirich Mîr: This is an extremely fertile and relatively populous valley. Every year, its lush vegetation breaks into a rich variety of midsummer colours. Imagine, for instance, orange and yellow apricots set against a background of green grass below, and snow covered mountains behind. Villages in Tirich Mîr are mostly small. The region has some celebrated glaciers.

Suggested trek: Drive up to Uthul. Then walk across the Zani Pass (3,886m) to a village called Shagram. (If you don't want to do the Zani Pass, you can drive directly from Chitrâl to Shagram.) From the pass you will be able to see the Hiñdu Kush range on one side and the Hiñdu Râj range on the other. The most striking thing about the two ranges is how different their colours are.

The track then passes through villages called Atak and Bandak and leads to the bottom of the Tirich Glacier. This base camp is called Shogor. The track comes to an end at the Lower Tirich Glacier.

Camp here. If you can spend a day exploring the area, you will be able to sight the majestic Tirich Mîr (7,708m), the Istoro Nal (7,403m) and the Upper Tirich Glacier.

It will take another two days to return to Shagram, trekking back on the same track.

Astor

Astor(e), the valley, also known as Hasorâ

Location: The Astor valley is to the north-west of Kashmîr and to the east of the Nañgâ Parbat. It is sandwiched between Kashmîr and

Gilgit. To its south are the Dorikûn and Kamri passes. The watershed of the rivers Neelum/ Kishan Gañgâ and Astor determines the southern limits of the valley. The watershed is at between 13,000' and 15,000' above the sea.

The valley of River Astor is around 105km. long. The valley is extremely narrow, especially at the bottom. Crops are grown many hundred feet above the river, wherever some flat, fertile land can be found.

The valley is somewhat broader two or three kilometres away from Dashkin. However, even there the bottom of the valley consists of slopes.

History: Some interesting work, which can be called 'agricultural archæology,' has been done in Astor. It reveals that crops were grown in the upper portion of Astor even in ancient times. Ruins of villages have been found there. Below Astor town, too, despoiled fields were found. They spoke of plunder and destruction.

According to a British account, "this state of things was brought about by the raids of the Chilâsîs, who, previous to 1850 [i.e. before the Dogrâ conquest], used to come over the Mazeno pass [18,500'] or by Hatu Pîr [10,254'] for the purpose of carrying off the cattle and making slaves of the women and children. It was on account of this that Gulâb Singh sent a punitive expedition to Chilâs about 1851-52, since when there has been no raiding. The present [c.1890] state of security is a great benefit to the inhabitants, but the country has not yet recovered from the ruin and depopulation of former times, though a few new settlements have arisen on old village sites."[v]

Hunzâ still has great watercourses. Those in Astor were ruined during such raids.

However, such were the defences of Astor, natural as well as human, that invaders could rarely conquer the valley. They had to limit themselves to raids.

Vegetation: Astor is not as green as neighbouring Guréz. Birch is abundant on some of Astor's mountains, though. Besides, areas below 8,500' have fine orchards. Many hills in Astor have barren patches where no grass grows. Pines are found only at some places and spruce is even less common.

There are dense forests in some parts.

Crops are grown at 10,000' and above.

Astor, the town

The town (7,840') has been built on an alluvial plateau on the left bank of the river. The plateau is a kilometre broad and around 150 metres above the river. On both sides of the town are ravines that are deep and narrow. Even though there is plenty of drinking water in the town, poplars are the only trees that grow there naturally.

The town has always been very small. Even though it once was a capital of Dard kings, it has no notable architecture. However, the bridge across River Astor was, even in the 19th century, one of the better ones in all of undivided Ladâkh-Balâwaristân. Equally, Astor's polo-ground has always been rated among the best in the entire region. There is an orchard near it. In the tradition of Ladâkh's smaller towns Astor traditionally had no marketplace, because most households were self-sufficient.

During the Dogrâ era the town was turned into a little cantonment. The Dogrâs called the town (and the valley around it) Hasorâ.

The fort is close to the ravine at the southern end. In its heyday it had three smart square towers made of wood and local masonry (mainly mud and rubble) on its eastern side and a round bastion in the west.

Kâghân Valley[6]

Kâghân is a wooded Himâlayan valley north-east of what is now the Hazârâ district of Pâkistân's North West Frontier Province. Nature has been extremely kind to it. This hauntingly beautiful mountain valley is dotted with meadows, little valleys, lakes, waterfalls, streams and glaciers. Mercifully much of its natural wealth is still intact (unlike what has happened in many parts of South Asia). The Kâghân valley is 155km. long. The lowest part of the valley is at 2,134m., and its highest, the Babusar Pass, is at 4,173m.

Best season: May to September. The highest temperature recorded in the mountainous parts of Kâghân in May is around 11°C and the lowest about 3°C. The road beyond Naran (23km. from Kâghân) gets snowed under in winter From mid-July to late September one can normally drive on it all the way to the Babusar Pass. As in the rest of Kashmîr and Ladâkh, the road packs up whenever there is heavy rainfall. People from the hot plains seek Kâghân out in summer, when the highest temperature never exceeds 51° Fahrenheit. The minimum temperature hovers around 37°F.

6. Was Kâghân ever a part of the Dogrâ state of Jammu and Kashmîr? The Dogrâ kingdom certainly extended up to the Babusar Pass. Therefore, it stands to reason that Kâghâm was part of Jammu and Kashmîr. The inclusion of this hauntingly beautiful valley in this book is based on Râj-era British accounts about and maps of Jammu and Kashmîr.

I have occasionally included Swât in this book on the authority of 21st century and late 20th century websites posted by Balâwaristân nationalists.

The journey to Kâghân: One can travel to Kâghân by road from Islâmâbâd and Péshâwar. The first major halt en route will be Abbotâbâd (122km. from Islâmâbâd/ 217km. from Peshâwâr). Buses ply on this stretch, and much of the way hereafter as well. Abbotâbâd is in the Hazârâ region. It has traditionally had a quiet and well maintained civil lines and cantonment. It has been built on a series of low, green hills.

Bâlâkot (72km from Abbotâbâd) will be the next important town. Kâghân valley lies just beyond this town. Its main spiritual attractions are the shrines of Syed Ahmed Shahîd and Ismail Shahîd Barelvî, the great freedom fighters of undivided India. The road gets bad after Bâlâkot. It isn't good enough for cars. The journey beyond, i.e. into Kâghân, can only be done in a jeep-type (sports utility) vehicle.

The first significant stop in the valley will be **Shogran** (2,362m./ 34 km. from Bâlâkot). Kâghân proper is a tiny village and is 61 km. from Bâlâkot.

Naran comes next. It is in the centre of the valley. Most tourists camp at Naran and use it as a base to explore the valley either by jeep, on foot or on horseback.

Kâghân is famous for its fish. The Fisheries Department at Naran issues fishing licenses. Brown Trout and the mahâseer are found in the cold waters between Kâghân and Naran. The local people believe that the trout of River Kunhar is the best in the Indian sub-continent. (This author's personal vote goes to the Tawâñg trout of India's Arunâchal Pradesh.)

Other attractions of the Balâwaristân-Gilgit region

Kârâkoram Mountains, the: This range is located at the western end of the great mountain chain of South Asia and Central Asia. The Kârâkoram range has the greatest concentration of high peaks in the world.

Swât valley: A pretty northern valley, easily accessible to the traveller. Swât has for centuries been the stuff of European legends, not the least because of its aristocratic religious cum temporal leaders, the Walis of Swât.

Saif ul maluk: This is a high-altitude lake.

Kallar Kahar is 40km from Bhera in the direction of Islâmâbâd on the motorway to the north of the salt range.

Brasstacks (for the areas occupied by Pakistan)

Air travel: Flying within Gilgit-Baltistân (as in all of Ladâkh) is an uncertain affair. Visibility gets reduced if thick clouds form anywhere on the aircraft's route. Even in Kashmîr, which is at a much lower altitude, at times one can't see more than a few feet away, and this happens in summer as well. Pâkistânî pilots (like their Indian counterparts) don't want to play with the lives of their passengers if the sky is not clear enough. So, they refuse to take off from Islâmâbâd[7]. This happens throughout the year. In winter, flights are cancelled for weeks on end.

Passengers of the first cancelled flight are the first to be taken when the weather clears up and when the aeroplane next goes to Gilgit. The next are the passengers of the second cancelled flight. So, backlogs of passengers start building up. To prevent backlogs of passengers with confirmed tickets, Pâkistânî airlines sell tickets for Gilgit flights only on the day before the scheduled departure.[8]

Therefore, if you have deadlines to meet, please do not count on always flying to or back from the 'Northern Areas' (or anywhere in Ladâkh) on time.

Road travel: During the rainy season, especially during the summer rains, the Kârâkoram Highway tends to get blocked whenever heavy rains trigger landslides. Traffic normally gets suspended for one day at a time, sometimes two. As soon as the engineers manage to clear some of the debris, they allow people (but not vehicles) to move from one side of the blockage to the other. People help each other carry luggage. Buses reverse the direction that they had been travelling in. A 'trans-shipment' of sorts is thus arranged.

On the other hand, bus fares are quite low.

Money and credit cards: Change as much of your money and travellers' cheques as you can in Islâmâbâd or Péshâwar. You will get a better rate. Only upmarket hotels in the so-called Northern Areas accept credit cards. Souvenir shops accept them only for high-end purchases. Visa is preferred over Mastercard by local establishments.

7. I have flown a few hundred times in those mountains, mostly as a helicopter-passenger. At least two of those sorties were touch and go affairs where we could have crashed. As the head of a Commission of Inquiry I have also probed the crash of a helicopter which ran into tall trees in an August fog.
   Therefore, I am on the pilots' side. Cynics in Ladâkh are not. They accuse pilots of cancelling flights even if there is a mere wisp in the sky. Actually, even I wonder why flights from Delhi (and Islâmâbâd) to Leh (and Gilgit) get cancelled so frequently. Because the return journey almost never does. Once an aircraft reaches Leh (or Gilgit) somehow the weather never seems to be so bad as to prevent the pilot from returning home to Delhi (or Islâmâbâd).
8. On other PIA flights you need to be reconfirm 72 hours (or more) before your departure. If you don't, your reservation will be cancelled.

Travellers' cheques and US dollars can be exchanged at certain banks. There are some money changers, too.

Communications: Gilgit and Chitrâl have a fairly good telephone system. Elsewhere in the 'Northern Areas' telephones are quite primitive. Gilgit is linked to the Internet through satellite telephones, which is why it is quite expensive.

Cultural sensitivities: Please remember that the people of Gilgit-Baltistân are conservative Muslims. People get wrong ideas if women smoke in public or wear revealing clothes.

The Gilgit, Hunzâ, Baltistan belt: the principal attractions

Gilgit/ Danyore: An 8th century AD stone inscription.

Gilgit/ Nagar: The Rakaposhi Peak (7,788 m).

Hunzâ: Sacred rocks of the Buddhist and post-Buddhist periods, near the Ganésh Bridge on the Karâkoram Highway.

Hunzâ/ Karîmâbâd: The 14th century Baltit Fort.

Hunzâ/ Gulmit: A 12th century AD fort and ancient settlement.

Khunjerab: A National Park near the Karâkoram Highway, close to Jammû and Kashmîr's border with China.

Gilgit/ Jutial: A Buddhist stupa (religious structure), near the water channel. It is around a hundred metres above the village.

Gilgit: The tower (minâr) of Taj Moghal.

Gilgit/ Naupura: A Buddhist monastery and a stunning rock sculpture of the standing Buddha, at the Kargah Nullah near Baseen.

Gilgit/ Henzal: A Buddhist stupa,

Ghizar/ Buber Punyal: Buddhist relics.

Ghizar/ Hatun (Ishkoman): A 7th century AD rock inscription.

Ghizar/ Hundrab: A National Park Near Shandoor border with Chitral.

Chilas/ Thalpan: A rock carving and the ruins of a pre-historic to post-Buddhist settlement. These are close to the mouth of the Kiner Gah.

Diamir/ Shing Nullah: Rock carvings, mostly Buddhist. Nañga Parbat Peak (8,125 meters) Can be approached from Raikot bridge on KKH.

Baltistan: The Shigar Fort and the 17th century AD Chimpa Village in Shigar Valley.

Satpara: Buddhist relics. These are located in Manthal Village and near Lake Satpara, southeast of Skardu Town.

K2: The world's 2nd highest peak (8,611 m).National Park; access from Skardu Town through Shigar or Husney valleys

Deosai: This is a high altitude plateau with a National Park: access from Skardu Town and Astore Town

Ghanche/ Khaplu: A 19th century fort.

References

i I picked this quote off the Internet.

ii Shapiro's article 'Hunzâ Hospitality' was posted on the Internet.

iii From the website Mango Grove (www.mango.itgo.com/northernareas)

iv Her article 'Hunzâ Hospitality' was posted on the Internet.

v Aylmer, *The Gazetteer*, 1890.

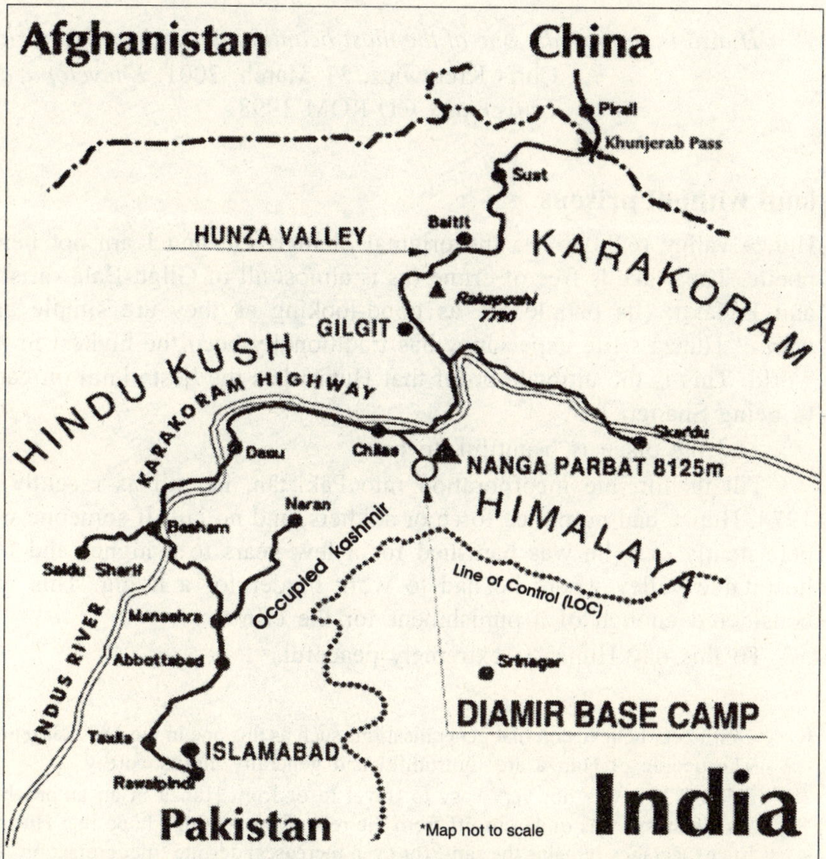

Across the LOC: Karakoram Highway

22

The Hunzâ Valley

'Hunzâ is supposedly one of the most beautiful corners of the world.'
Chris Kretowicz, 31 March, 2001. *Encyclopaedia Universalis* CD-ROM 1998.

A land without prisons

Hunzâ valley (c.8,000') is the original Shangri La, and I am not being poetic. The place is free of crime (as is almost all of Gilgit-Balâwaristân and Ladâkh). Its people are as good-looking as they are simple and warm.[1] Hunzâ's life expectancy has traditionally been the highest in the world. This is the ultimate proof that Hunzâ has the best claim on earth to being Shangri La[2].

And the place is beautiful, to boot.

Till its forcible incorporation into Pâkistân, i.e. till as recently as 1974, Hunzâ had no police force or soldiers, and no jail. If someone was persistently evil, he was banished for a few years to a higher and less hospitable valley where he had to work harder for a living. This was considered enough of a punishment for the crime.

To this day Hunzâ is extremely peaceful.

1. Don't ever believe colonial generalisations such as this one in the 1890 Gazetteer: The people of Hunzâ are 'untruthful and generally untrustworthy.'
2. Till 1982, it was not very easy to travel to or from Hunzâ in an automobile. As a result it was quite cut off from the rest of the world. I hope that Hunzâ's life expectancy remains the same (or even increases) despite 'modernisation' and contacts with the world beyond. I sound this note of caution because the equally decent Gujjar nomads used to live very long (and were tall, tough and disease-free) so long as they were nomads. Once they started settling down ('sedenterisation' is the word that academics use) the next generation was no longer as tall, sturdy, disease-free or long-lived.

The pretty valley

Hunzâ valley is surrounded by tall (24,000'/7.500m. high), snow covered mountains of the Kârâkoram Range. It is immediately to the north of Gilgit, where the Kârâkoram Highway follows River Hunzâ, as the road travels northwards into China

The valley has a haunting mien. The wind that wafts through the poplars smells sweet. And the valley is surprisingly green for its altitude.

Hunzâ valley rises in wide steps from the river to highland pastures. These steps are man-made terraced fields as well as natural mounds and hillocks. When the glaciers and ice formations in the mountains melt, they form little streams, flow down to the valley, and pour themselves into River Hunzâ. The river then flows south towards Gilgit. In summer shepherds take their flocks to mountain pastures to graze.

Hunzâkuts people have round faces, are fair skinned, have blond or fair hair and blue or green eyes. They top all this with glowing smiles. The women wear tall, colourful hats that are unique to Hunzâ. They sometimes have baskets on their backs.

Location: River Hunzâ forms the southern boundary of Hunzâ. It separates Hunzâ from the Nagar area. Attabâd and Mâyûn respectively are the villages on the eastern and western extremities of Hunzâ.

The tall Berber (or Barbar) range, which rises to 25,000' at places, is to the north of Hunzâ. The Budalas hill (c.15,000') is in the west and the Shimshal range (c.22,000' at places) in the east. The taller mountains are covered with snow throughout the year.

Hunzâ consists of three broad regions—Hunzâ proper (a group of sixteen traditional villages), Shimshal and Gojal.

The villages of Hunzâ have been built on a set of mountains that rise as one travels northwest of the central region, and go down when we go west of the centre. The difference in altitude between the highest and lowest villages is almost two thousand feet.

Getting there: The flight from Islâmabâd/ Rawalpindi to Gilgit takes around an hour. From Gilgit you can take a mini-van (normally a Suzuki) to Karîmabâd (Hunzâ). You can also drive from Islâmabâd/ Rawalpindi to Gilgit, Before the KKH this had to be done over the Babusar Pass, which would be open only for a few months in summer. Till the 1970s people flying from Islâmabâd/ Rawalpindi to Gilgit would be put in aircraft meant to carry freight. You sat in the space between the cargo. (The same was true to the flight from Chandigarh to Leh.)

Best season: May to October. The highest temperature recorded in May was 27°C and the minimum 14°C. In October the maximum hovers around 10°C and the minimum around 0°C. My favourite season in this region is spring. That's the time of the apricot blossom. The streams all bubble with clean water from the melting snow.

Mountain climbing: For permits to trek in and climb the majestic mountains of Hunzâ contact the Tourist Division/ Ministry of Tourism, Government of Pâkistân, Islâmâbâd.

Rivers: River Hunzâ originates at the Kilik pass. It then goes past Hunzâ, Nagar and Pisan (Nagar) before pouring itself into River Gilgit. It is roughly 200km. (125 miles) long. In spring, summer and early autumn it is impossible to cross. Its current is very strong. In emergencies the local people try to swim across with inflated bags made of goatskin. Its width fluctuates between 30 metres in winter and almost a hundred metres in summer. Its depth varies from around two feet in winter and six feet in summer.

River Nagar is the other major river in the neighbourhood.

Traditional bridges across the two are made of ropes in the Himâlayan tradition. But even by Himâlayan standards they are scary, because the ropes don't provide much of a foothold.

A prosperous land

Plentiful agriculture: Many of these villages have been built on the banks of the various streams that flow south from the Berber range to River Hunzâ. Glaciers melting uphill create these streams. As a result there is plenty of water to drink as well as to irrigate the fields.

Therefore, the people have always had plenty to eat. Obviously, that has contributed to their longevity.

Fruits and farm produce: Hunzâ is known for its apples, excellent apricots, almonds, cherries, grapes (and, hence, wine), mulberries, peaches, pears and several dry fruits (nuts). Its walnuts are among the best in the world. The people extract oil from the kernels of apricots and walnuts.

Other agricultural products include barley, corn, cabbage, onions, potatoes, other vegetables and wheat. Tobacco is grown in some places.

In most of Ladâkh sheep are emaciated and yield very little meat, especially in winter. Not so in Hunzâ where sheep are plentiful (and well-fed eight months a year).

And yet, Hunzâ is called 'The Land of the barely adequate.'' They have more or less all that they need, but no marketable surplus. As in much of rural Ladâkh (especially Zâñskâr) and pre-1947 Kashmîr they store dried food (including dried vegetables and dried fruits) for the long winter, when no fresh vegetation grows.

Animals: Yârqañdî horses are the norm in Hunzâ. Pattû, a local tweed, is made from the wool of sheep. The pashmînâ goat is found in

Hunzâ. The ibex is not very easy to catch. The orial, on the other hand, is not as difficult.

The extraction of sulphur... The people of Hunzâ have a very interesting method of extracting sulphur from a particular kind of mud. This mud is dark and hard. They put the mud into an iron cauldron. They add butter equal to a fifth of the weight of the mud. The mixture is then heated. The butter separates the sulphur from the rest of the mud. More than half the mud used thus becomes sulphur.

Another kind of mud yields saltpetre.

...and using it for parricide: So, what do they use sulphur and saltpetre for? Often, to make gunpowder. (Neighbouring China has been making gunpowder since at least the 11th century A.D. Immediately before the Dogrâs conquered Hunzâ, the valley was subordinate to China.)

And what is gunpowder doing in Shangri La? Well, on occasion it has been used to kill people.

The late-19th century ruler of Hunzâ, Mîr Safdar Alî Khân, pumped as many as twelve bullets into his father and thus wrested the throne from him. This act did not go down too badly with the public. They preferred him any day to his much-hated father.

Gold can, in tiny quantities, be sifted out of River Hunzâ.

Hunzâ proper

Hunzâ is at 2,438m./ c.8,800' above the sea.

What to see: Karîmâbâd is the headquarters of Hunzâ. It was called Baltit till the 1960s, when it was renamed after Prince Karim, the Âgâ Khân. At the turn of the millennium it had a population of around ten thousand.

From Karîmâbâd you can see the gigantic Rakaposhi (7,788m.). At night, moonbeams bounce off the snow that always covers this mountain, adding to the valley's mystique. The 15th century Baltit castle, perched several hundred feet above Karîmâbâd, has been built on thick stilts and has wooden bay windows. If tourist literature describes it as 'fairy-tale-like' for once the description is more than just lazy advertising copy. This used to be the palace of the kings of Hunzâ, who were known as Mîrs.

The Sacred Rock of Hunzâ is near the river, at the foot of the hill on which the fort has been built. It has pre-historic carvings and etchings, including the sketch on an ibex.

Karîmâbâd is a very sunny little town in summer, spring and autumn. In season the plentiful maize crop adds to the beauty of the region. So do its fruit-laden orchards. It has some celebrated trees, too. A mulberry tree in Karîmâbâd dates to around 1775. A walnut tree near the old fort belongs to the 16th century.

Karîmâbâd has charming old streets made of cobbled stone. Many of them are on slopes, and some are quite steep. The weather is always cool and the surroundings are fertile.

Why does everyone talk of Hunzâ's fields and orchards? Aren't such things commonplace everywhere in the world? No, not in the mountainous deserts of Balâwaristân-Ladâkh-Tibet. The inventive people of Hunzâ have, over the centuries, created brilliant little irrigation channels, changed a desert into a granary and made the area prosperous. This fascinating irrigation system is used to this day. The people who lived in this region in ancient times were as inventive as they were farsighted. There are glaciers uphill that start melting in spring. The ancestors of the Hunzâkuts carved channels into rocks. The melting water comes down to the fields in these channels.

Treks: One can trek up to nearby Duikar for its panoramic views.

The Ultar Meadow is a pasture where the people of Karîmâbâd take their sheep and goats to graze in summer. It takes around four hours of climbing up a stiff slope to reach the Ultar Glacier. The path is along the irrigation channel and the glacier's terminal moraine.

Wildlife: Snow leopards are found in Hunzâ.

Where to stay: Karîmâbâd has a number of reasonably good hotels.

Altit, a village near Karîmâbâd, has accommodation that international travellers speak of approvingly.

Pasu, Gojal Upper Hunzâ Valley

Location: Gojal is the region north of Attabâd, and goes all the way up to the Kilik pass. It is a group of sixteen villages, which have sub-divided somewhat over the decades,

Pasu (Gojal) is famous for the Pasu Glacier, which is the second longest in the world.

Pasu is the northernmost town on the South Asian section of the Kârâkoram Highway. If you go any further north, through the Khunjerab Pass, you will be in China's Xinjiang province. Because of its location on the frontier, Pasu receives quite a few international visitors. Therefore, it has more facilities than in many parts of the 'Northern Areas'.

Before you reach Gojal you will pass Gulmit. In 1992, a huge part of the glacier near Gulmit fell into River Indus. This obstructed the river's southward flow. As a result a huge lake got created and destroyed the splendid old Pasu town, as well as some villages.

This, too, is an Ismâili area. Therefore, the Âgâ Khân Foundation has built schools and other institutions in Pasu/ Gojal. Iranian culture, especially their radio network, is popular here.

Shimshal is prone to extremely terrible floods, which take place whenever 'glacier dams' burst. The flood of 1964 destroyed many terraced fields and half the original village. Pasu village was then rebuilt with houses that are dispersed rather than in a cluster. Since then the people have also been changing their agriculture. They have increased the extent of terraced fields and have brought a bigger area under cultivation. They have since been trying to improve their pastures and have also been developing plantations.

What to see: The Pasu Glacier, of course, is the main attraction. The Borit Lake is another.

Shimshal

Shimshal is a small sub-division of Hụnzâ. It has only two traditional villages (which consist of smaller hamlets).

The Shimshal area is on the left bank of the river that flows south from the Kilik pass.

The Great North Road

The pre-KKH route from Gilgit to Hunzâ: Sikañdarâbâd (60km. from Gilgit) used to be the 'roadhead' and is in Nagar.

The road from Gilgit town first crosses a bridge over River Gilgit. It stays with this river for some five kilometres till River Gilgit meets the Hunzâ River. There the road swerves northwards into the Hunzâ Valley and now runs precipitously above River Hunzâ.

The road then goes past the huge, landslide-prone Chaichar Parri cliff.

Chalt comes next. Barbara Hilda Mons calls it 'a large green oasis where the road is bordered with willow trees and the little streams with purple irises.' From there one had to cross a suspension bridge to get to Sikañdarâbâd. After Sikañdarâbâd one had to do the rest of the journey on foot or on ponies. Nagar and Hunzâ are on the opposite sides of the same gorge. Hunzâ is some eight kilometres upstream. A bridge connects the two.

Between Maiun and Murtazâbâd there is a place with imperfect millstones littered about everywhere. Mrs. Mons writes that this is the only place 'where the rock on both sides of the river is considered suitable for millstones, and the millers of Hunzâ and [Nagar] come to cut their stones on the spot. Should one attempt fail, they select another rock and start afresh.'

Stereotypes are always wrong. The women of Nagar are always supposed to be in black clothes. However, at all stages of history some of them have worn colourful clothes as well.

Maiun is 6.5km. ahead of Sikandrabad. It has a small rest-house. Many travellers spend the night there. The Rakaposhi can be seen through the poplar trees. Nilt, of the battle fame, is on the opposite side. This is a ledge high above the river. Apple and mulberry trees and vines grow on it.

Murtazâbâd comes next. The first glimpse of the Hunzâ valley is had from atop a hill fixture where the river takes a turn. From here one can see Aliabad as well as Ultar, the tall mountain behind Karîmâbâd. We next have to cross the Hasanabad Nullah by a bridge. Aliabad (6.5km. from Karîmâbâd) is next. At Aliabad, as elsewhere in Hunzâ, the traditional women wear red caps.

The snow-covered Rakaposhi towers over the scenery.

Bow cum catapult: In Hunzâ, as in all of Ladâkh-Balâwaristân, catapults are a favoured weapon (to kill animals and even men) The Hunzâkuts have a wooden bow that has two strings kept apart by thin blocks of wood, inserted near the ends. In the middle is a leather strip into which it seems that an arrow is to be fitted. However, these bows are, instead, used as catapults, with which small stones are shot accurately at animals.

23

Shimshal

Shimshal is a small valley (population: around 1,200) on the north-eastern border of Hunzâ. The Pâkistâni authorities have sliced it out of Hunzâ and placed it in the Gilgit district. Within Gilgit, this valley is in the Gojal area of Gulmit tehsil (i.e. sub-district). Gulmit is also where the nearest post office is. There is a village, also called Shimshal, in the upper part of this valley. The villages of Shimshal have mostly been built at altitudes between 3,000 and 3,300 metres above the sea level.

The Wakhi speaking parts of the upper Hunzâ valley are called 'Gojal.' Shimshal was where Wakhi-speaking people first settled in Hunzâ. The people of Shimshal, as we shall see, have Wakhi as well as Burusho blood in their veins. They are the descendants of mixed marriages that have been taking place since at least the 16th century. Even though the men who founded the community were Burusho, the culture of the place is pristine Wakhi, its purity obviously the result of the remoteness of this area.

A prosperous, surplus economy: The people of Shimshal are mostly farmers and herdsmen, and well to do ones at that. Shimshal is one of the very few places in the Balâwaristân-Gilgit-Hunzâ region that are self-sufficient in matters of food, even though they grow only one crop a year. Thanks to good irrigation and fertile soil, wheat, barley, potatoes, apricots, apples, peas and beans are grown in the area. Some people also grow vegetables in their kitchen garden—for their own family.

But the main reason why the region is so prosperous is also why it is so beautiful—it has huge pastures. There the people of Shimshal take their goats, sheep, yaks and other cattle to graze. Apart from milk and milk products, yak hair and sheep wool earn them good money. So do carpets made of yak hair.

Remittances are a major source of income. Almost every ninth Shimshali, or every fifth or sixth adult, lives away from the region—in

Pâkistân or even in the Gulf. The three Âgâ Khân Rural Support Programmes, which have been active in Shimshal since 1985, have helped develop the region enormously.

Adventure tourism—trekking, mainly—brings some money, too. The region has nine peaks that are at 7,000 metres or higher. These, and some famous glaciers, would, till the early 1990s, ensure almost a hundred tourists a year. However, in the mid-1990s this figure dropped to around thirty a year. And this was well before '9/11' hit international tourist arrivals even further.

Some of the world's best mountain climbers of the 20th and 21st centuries are Shimshalis—notably Rajab Shah, Mehrban Shah and Havildar Yusuf.

How to get there: The traditional way to reach Shimshal is to get off the Kârâkoram Highway, leave vehicles at Pasu and walk for two days (60 kilometres) along the Shimshal River to the village of the same name. That is how people from Hunzâ and beyond had been going to Shimshal since olden times.

However, a road from Pasu to Shimshal village, which took a decade and a half to make, was completed in the early years of the 21st century. So you need not do things the traditional way any more.

History: Mamu Singh founded the present village of Shimshal, perhaps in the 16th century. This Burusho noble belonged to a clan of viziers from Baltit (Hunzâ). He had a Wakhi wife called Khodija. Mamu was Hunzâ's ambassador to Sarikol (Central Asia) when bitterness developed between Sarikol and Hunzâ. So Khodija and he had to flee Sarikol. Soldiers from Sarikol chased the two right up to the Avgarch Pasture, which is in the hills of Qarun Pir in the Upper Hunzâ River Valley.

From Avgarch the middle-aged, childless couple went to Shimshal where Mamu found a huge slab of slate lying on the ground. One of Hunzâ's fabled ancient water channels lay in disuse nearby. It took great effort to lift the slab, but it was worth the while. The waters of a spring spurted out and poured into the water channel.[1] A very heavy slab was obviously needed to keep the water inside.

1. David Butz, who is one of the foremost authorities on Shimshal, feels that the 'channel that had been built by earlier travellers who had passed that way on their way over Pamir to Chinese Turkestan.' In my view, settlers, and not travellers, build channels. Especially channels as elaborate as those found in Hunzâ.

   In 1999, Butz was with the Department of Geography, Brock University, St. Catharines, ON, Canada, L2S 3A1. His 'Shimshal Nature Trust notes' have been posted on the Internet.

Mamu Singh was by then the owner of several hundred sheep and goats. Thanks to this channel, Mamu was able to establish a village there, on the ruins of an earlier civilisation.

Shams, a mystic, gave Khodija a blessing because of which a son, Sher, was born to her.

During Shér Singh's youth a dispute arose about whether the Pamir belonged to Shimshal or to an unnamed neighbouring power—some Chinese principality, perhaps. They decided to settle the issue over a game of polo. They used, writes David Butz, 'all Pamir as the playing field: if Shér drove the ball over Shimshal Pass toward Shuwert, he would win title to all territory from Shimshal to Raskam; if the Chinese succeeded in carrying the ball to Shuijerab, Shér must relinquish all lands from Pamir to the Hunzâ River.'

Shér won. Interestingly, he rode a yak and not a horse during the game. The vast principality that Shér established has always been on friendly terms with Hunzâ, and under its overall sway.

Like his father, Shér married a Wakhi woman, she being from Sarikol. The three royal clans of Shimshal are Bakhtikator, Baqikator and Gazikator. They are the descendants of Sher's three sons.

It is not clear when the people converted to Islâm. Khodija is a Muslim name. The names Mamu Singh and Shér Singh are pre-Islâmic and Hiñdu sounding. However, these could be part of the tradition followed by other Râjput princes in Jammu and Kashmîr—notably in Kishtwâr and Râjouri—where the princes continued to have Hiñdu—sounding names even after they had become Muslims. In the 19th century, the King of Hunzâ—and, later, his subjects—accepted the Ismâili sect of Islâm, under the influence of a saint from Sarikol.

The Khunjerab National Park (KNP): George Schaller, a field zoologist, surveyed the area briefly in 1974. The 2300 square kilometre KNP was established in 1975 on the basis of that survey. The idea was to ensure that the natural home of several rare species of Asian mountain wildlife, especially the endangered Marco Polo sheep (Ovis ammon polii), was left undisturbed.

However, in the bargain most of Shimshal's fabled pastures, as well as those belonging to another eight villages, got enclosed in this park. The importance of pastures to the economy of Shimshal has been pointed out above. But now whenever the people send their herds to their ancestral pastures they are committing a crime, for which the Pâkistâni authorities can jail them or at least impose a fine.[2] Pâkistân's National Council for

2. We face this dilemma in many parts of India.

Conservation of Nature (NCCN) and the World Wide Fund for Nature (WWF) have drawn up a plan that outlaws such grazing. As an administrator, and one of the pioneers of the Green student movement in Britain, this author understands the ecological ideals that have gone into this plan. However, the net result has been extremely hard on the Shimshalis. And it is likely to get worse.

Studies conducted in Shimshal show that endangered wildlife fares much better in the unrestricted parts of Shimshal than in the areas included in the park. This brings into question the very rationale for the park.

The Government of Pâkistân is now trying to establish the Central Kârâkoram National Park (CKNP), the areas under which also include much of Shimshali territory.

Hunting and its abolition: Shimshal's renowned hunters have a pedigree that dates back at least to the great Shér Singh, who was a quintessential hunter. However, hunting in Shimshal has never been allowed to be a wanton or socially irresponsible exercise. Butz writes, 'Most hunting has always been collective: at the high pastures. Hunters were required to distribute game among households, keeping only the breast and organ meat for themselves; in the village, game was hunted and eaten only on ceremonial occasions, or to feed volunteers working on community projects. Hunters were admonished to shoot only the oldest animals, only one animal per hunting excursion, and never pregnant or nursing females (on pain of divine retribution). Indeed, one of [Shimshal's] most treasured songs recounts a sad conversation between a baby ibex and her dying mother.'

Since 1997, the people of Shimshal have, on their own initiative, 'abolished all hunting, except for a small number of ibex to feed the men responsible for herding yaks through the winter at Pamir, and have instituted a system of fines to enforce this ban on hunting.'[i]

References

i. The quote is from Dr. Butz' website.

24

Nagar

The Shia Burusho People

Twin kingdoms: There have been traditionally been two kingdoms in Hunzâ Valley—the eponymous Hunzâ and the bigger but lesser known Nagar. The kingdom called Hunzâ dominated the valley even though it had far less people, less cultivable land and fewer water resources. The people of both kingdoms speak the Burushaski language. Native speakers of this unwritten language are called Burusho.

Unfortunately, the people of the two former princely states, Nagar and Hunzâ, have for centuries been barely on talking terms. The fact that the royal families of the two states would marry with each other did not make political relations between the two any better.

I do not believe that the people of different races or nations have different temperaments. However, at a given point of time one set of people might have a different set of values, a different ethos from another set of people. With time this ethos might change (as I believe has happened to Hunzâ-Nagar since the 1980s, when relations between the two have improved).

But just everybody agrees that the people of Nagar and Hunzâ are very different from each other. Barbara Hilda Mons, a sensitive British traveller, noted in the 1950s that 'the difference in temperament is often attributed to the effect of living respectively on the sunny and the shady side of the valley. Though richer and greener, watered by the inexhaustible glaciers of Rakaposhi, the north-facing slopes of Nagir scarcely see the sun in winter.'

A Shia Burusho people

The people of Nagar are called Nagroshis. Almost all of them are Shias. They have had traditional ties with the Shias of Baltistân. The

Shia Burusho people speak the Burushaski language, like their cousins in Hunzâ proper, across the river. There are minor differences of dialect between the two. However, they are Shia Muslims and not Ismâili Muslims. There are around 82,000 Shia Burusho people, of whom around two thousand are in Gilgit and the rest entirely in Nagar Valley.

Nagar consists of two groups of villages. One pocket is on the eastern bank of River Hunzâ and overlooks Hunzâ proper. The other pocket is south of Hunzâ, on the Kârâkoram Highway, up the Chalt valley on the opposite bank of the Hunzâ river.

The **Rakaposhi** (7,788 m.). is the main tourist attraction of the area. The people are small farmers and shepherds. Some of them have orchards.

As in Hunzâ, a dynasty of Mîrs ruled them over the centuries, right up to the 1970s. (In the 19th century they came under the Dogrâ sway.) After Pâkistâni occupation this family continued to enjoy a position of leadership in the area. The Mîrs were stripped of their powers in 1974.

As happens almost everywhere, and certainly in the Himâlayas (on both sides of the Line of Control) a senseless (and sometimes violent) rivalry between the two ethnically similar neighbours, Hunzâ and Nagar, has existed for centuries.

Hunzâ, though smaller, has always been the more glamorous neighbour. International travellers had to pass through Nagar to get to Hunzâ. And yet they ignored Nagar. The Hunzâkuts accepted a more open and development-oriented sect of Islâm. They welcomed writers and travellers from the West much before Nagar did. They took to education considerably earlier and thus have much higher literacy and standards of healthcare. Because the Hunzâkuts chose to be Ismâilis, the Aga Khân Foundation concentrated its substantial funds on the Hunzâkuts. The Nagroshis, a sympathetic American traveller observed, 'sadly have usually come out second best [in all matters, including] combat.'

Luck (or should we blame geography?) hasn't favoured the Nagroshis either. The Kârâkoram Highway has bypassed Nagar.

I chanced upon this perceptive comment in a website about the so-called Northern Areas: 'The Nagar people still remain small in their own eyes as an ethnic group. This poor self-image tends to dominate their perception of the world around them, and hinder[s] their development. Being Shiite Muslims, which [sect] itself has a poor stereotyped image,[1] has further discouraged many from active involvement in this people group. This fear needs to be overcome by [developmental agencies] before [they] can help the Nagar people face their particular spiritual and social problems.'

1. Shiite Kargil had the same image problem (self-image as well as stereotyping by others) till the 1980s. Then an unspoken, unorchestrated, uncoordinated determination ran through the youths of the area: to catch up with neighbouring, mostly Buddhist, more glamorous Leh. And in just two decades, as the 2001 census has revealed, they had done it. Today Kargil is one of the most advanced districts of Jammu and Kashmîr, indeed of all India, in terms of many developmental indicators. Thus, there is no reason why Shiite Nagar can't catch up with Hunzâ.

25

The 'infidel' Kafir-Kalash clan of Chitrâl

There are three Valleys in the southern parts of Chitrâl where the 'Kafir' (infidel) Kalash people live. This is an animistic tribe of some 4,000 people that has, to quote countless Pâkistâni websites,[1] 'evaded' being converted to Islâm. (Many Pâkistâni websites[2] describe them as 'primitive pagans.') Members of the tribe are mostly known as 'the wearers of the Black Robe'. They live in the valleys of Birir, Bumbure(e)t[3] and Rambur.

The Kafir-Kalash Tribe

History: No one knows how this tribe originated. The standard story is that they are the descendants of some soldiers of the army of Alexander of Macedonia who had settled in Chitrâl. Kalash means 'black' in the language of the tribe. There was a similar tribe on the Afghân side of the border. Its members would wear red robes and came to be called the Red Kafirs.

When the army of Alexander the Great marched from Afghanistan to India, it had to cut through the snows of the Hiñdu Kush. Parapamisus ('the mountain range over which no eagle can fly') is the name that the Greeks had given the range. The Greeks were not the only famous army to pass through this region. The Tartars, led by Ghengis Khân and Tamerlane, came next, though several centuries later. The Mehtars (kings) who have mostly ruled Chitrâl claim to be descendants of Tamerlane's

1. For instance, pakwatan.com, south-asia.com/pâkistân.Chitrâl.htm, home.online.no and victorynews.net.
2. Some examples are: khowar.com, pakvisit.com, northpak.8m.com, flypia.aero, cybercity-online.net and innumerable other sites that came up in a Yahoo! search.
3. Variously spelt Bumbureet, Bumburet and Bumboret.

dynasty. One of the branches of the Silk Route passed through the Baroghil Pass in Upper Chitrâl.

Because of its inaccessibility and strong defences, few outsiders have dared invade Chitrâl. Chitrâl came under the sway of the Dogrâs in the 19th century. The British took the kingdom on lease from the Dogrâs. They set up a garrison in Chitrâl in order to check any possible Russian attack on British India. The British later realised that there was no way that a Russian army could enter India through Chitrâl, so they left.

Pâkistân occupied Chitrâl in 1947. For the next twenty-seven years the Mehtars enjoyed considerable autonomy as far as day to day administration was concerned. However, in 1974, Pâkistân incorporated the kingdom into Pâkistân-proper, delinking it both from the so-called 'Âzâd' Jammu and Kashmîr and the 'Northern Areas.'

The Kalash region: Bumburet (40 km./ 25 miles from Chitrâl) is the biggest of the three valleys in which the Kafir-Kalash live. It is also the prettiest. There is a 'jeepable road' right up to Bumburet. One can also travel by jeep to Birir, which is 34km./ 21 miles from Bumburet. Till the 1990s, the 32km./ 20 mile road from Chitrâl to Rambur was 'jeepable' only up to Ayun, which is exactly half way between the two. One had to walk from Ayun to Rambur. However, now the entire stretch can be done in a sports-type vehicle.

The 4,000 or so Kalashis live in some twenty villages in these three valleys.

Religious Festivals: The principal festivals of the Kalash are Joshi Chilimjusht (14-15 May), Uchao (August), Phool (20-25 September) and Chaomas (18-21 December). There is much singing and dancing and general merriment on these occasions.

Joshi Chilimjusht is a spring festival. The people beseech God to protect their shepherds, who are then preparing to go to pastures in the high mountains. Uchao is a relatively little known summer festival that marks the harvesting of the cereal crop. The autumn festival of Phool is a celebration of the grape-and walnut-harvest. Chaomas, the mid-winter festival is held to welcome the New Year and purify the village.

These four festivals consist of prayer, music, dancing and general fun. Men gossip and drink wine. Women wear special clothes and dance. Dance halls have been built for such occasions. This distinguishes the Kalash from their Buddhist and Dard cousins, who dance in the open. Kalashi 'ballrooms' are dark. Their doors and pillars, like those of other public buildings in the Kalash region, have elegant carvings. There are goat-like figures right outside these 'ballrooms.'

Traditional clothes: The Kalash women mostly wear black gowns. Their summer gowns are made of coarse cotton. In winter they wear handspun tweed. Their black woollen headgear, the pool, is exquisite but extremely heavy: it weighs around two kilograms. The cowries, shells and buttons studded on the pool are responsible for its weight. A large coloured feather tops the turban. Their necklaces are large, with many strings of red beads.

The Kalash men wear Chitrâli woollen hats. However, unlike other Chitrâlis, they decorate these hats with feathers and little metal bells. That's one way of telling a Kalash man from a non-Kalash. Another is the beard—Kalash men normally do not have one, unlike many of their Muslim neighbours (who do). Most Kalash men settle for just a moustache.

In winter they wear long woollen gowns called shuqa. On festive occasions they wear gray, brown, green or blue dresses. The cloth, as in most of the Himâlayas, is made at home and is rough. These cloaks have a hole for the neck. The belts that they wear are long and made of wool. Their goatskin shoes have woollen or leather thongs for laces.

In the 20th century the women took to wearing the shalwâr-qameez.

Religion: The Kalashis call God "Deziao." They worship animals and, as in parts of China, their own ancestors as well. Much of their religion is Hiñdu . The Hiñdus use the term 'Dewalok' for 'the land of the [male and female] deities.' By 'Dewalok' the Kalashis mean 'male and female sacred spirits.' As in Hiñduism, these Dewalok perform specific kinds of tasks, which they have been allotted in advance. They also intercede with Deziao on behalf of their devotees.

The Kalashis believe that earth itself is heaven. Those who have been to Chitrâl will doubtless agree. The Kalashis are grateful to God for having given them food, accommodation, greenery, water and, indeed, life itself.

The Kalash call everything pure (e.g. men, mountain pastures and goats) by the name Onjesta. Pragata is their word for all things impure (e.g. women, especially when they are menstruating or giving birth to children, at which times they are sent to designated places called Bashali).

This pure-impure divide is central to the Kalash religion. So is nature.

Like the Hiñdus, the Kalash worship a large number of deities. Each deity has a specialised role. If one protects crops, another blesses animals. The Kalash beseech particular deities to protect their families, orchards and other aspects of life. Among the deities, Koda (Sajigor) ranks the highest. One of their deities is exactly like the Greek deity Pan.

Christian missionaries have been trying to convert the Kalashis. The Government of Pâkistân has, to its credit, outlawed attempts to convert the Kalashis to Islâm-or any other religion.

The women: The Kalash women do not observe the pardâh (veil). As in some parts of Jammu and Himâchal Pradésh, the women do most of the work, at home, as well as in the fields. The men are relatively inactive and often stay at home, to look after the children. As a result, the Kafir women have gained a reputation for their physical toughness.

Summer is when the women work in the fields and, in the evenings, cook, spin, and weave. In winter women, as well as men, tend to stay, and work, at home.

In the Jammu hills there is a scenic valley called Banni where the women do a disproportionate amount of work. But as a result they wield all the power and call the shots. Not so with the Kalash people. The Kalashis do not allow women (and that includes international tourists) to enter some of their temples. There is a stiff fine (usually a goat or its value in cash) for unintentionally violating this taboo. For deliberate acts of this kind, the fine is heavier still.

Women are often sent to Bashalis (see above) in the sixth or seventh month of their pregnancy. They stay in Bashalis for the next three or four months, till the child is born. Food and other essential commodities are sent to (or stored in) the Bashalis till then.

Death rites: The Kalashis put their dead in coffins, which is unusual for an Asian people who are neither Christian nor Jewish. Could this be a custom that they picked up from their Muslim neighbours? No, for South Asian Muslims do not use coffins made of wood. (The Muslim kafan is a shroud of cloth.)

The Kalash coffins are taken to designated cemeteries and left there. There are no lids on these coffins. And most important, the coffins are not lowered into a grave. Therefore, according to me this custom comes closest to that of the fire-worshipping Zoroastrians (Zarathustrians) who leave their dead to be eaten by vultures.

In the Kalash region all kinds of other animals eat up the dead, and what is left decomposes. As a result, Kalash cemeteries emit a strong odour. For that reason, at the instance of the Muslims of the area,[4] most of these cemeteries have shifted to the woods and other distant places.

4. Muslim-Kalash relations are excellent—certainly at the individual level. However, after Pâkistân occupied the area it did nothing to prevent non-Kalash people from settling in the three Kalash valleys. As a result the tiny Kalash community has been outnumbered in its own land. (In contrast, despite pressure from the right wing, India has not allowed any dilution of the Kashmîrî population. Migrants from other parts of India are not allowed to purchase land or get state government jobs in Jammu, Kashmîr or Ladâkh.)

Somewhat like ancient Egyptians and some other peoples, the Kalashis place the worldly possessions of the dead near the coffin. Poor people come at night and take these things away.

Architecture: Kalashi houses are made of timber. The empty spaces between logs are filled with mud and pebbles. Because Chitrâl is extremely cold, the people burn lots of wood to cook as well as for the heat. Therefore, there are holes in the Kalashis' wooden ceilings, to let the smoke out through.

The temples of the Kalash are made of wood. As in the rest of the Himâlayas, the doors, doorjambs, temple pillars and ceilings are normally carved exquisitely and in great detail.

Most houses have a wide verandah on the upper floor. This is the nerve centre of activity within the household, for this is where the women sit and work.

26

Aksai Chin

Aksai Chin is a barren, mostly unpopulated, ice desert in Ladâkh. It is a vast, flat plateau between Chãñgthãñg and Northern Tibet. A few tiny settlements scattered about this huge expanse are the only sign of human life that the traveller will get to see. At noon the sun can burn the skin, but nights are extremely cold.

Analysts, Indians as well as others, have often said that the region has 'little geographical, economic or military value.'[i] And yet, as Western writers have often commented, the region is a bone of contention between India and China 'for reasons of national pride.'

Aksai Chin has a population of around 15,000, or one person for every three kilometres. And even that is a floating population. There is no permanent habitation in the region.

History: In 1914, India was a part of the British Empire. The powerful British government in India wanted to demarcate the northern borders that India shared with China and Tibet. So they invited delegates from China and Tibet to Simla, which was the summer capital of British India, for discussions. Aksai Chin was one of the territories that the Dogrâ Mahârâjâs had conquered. Because the Dogrã Mahârâjâs were subordinate to the British, Aksai Chin was part of the British Empire.

The Chinese had atavistic memories of having ruled over this area at some stage in the past, when they were a stronger nation. They did not want to accept the reality of the Dogrâ, and hence Indian, conquest.

The British, on the other hand, pointed out that the Dogrâ Government of Jammu and Kashmîr was in physical possession of Aksai Chin, which, therefore was very much a part of British India. The British drew up India's northern borders on the basis of what was actually with them or with the Indian princes subordinate to them. This northern border is called the MacMahon line, and is defined along the Himalayan watershed.

The Tibetans and the Chinese did not want to accept the British interpretation. However, they had to lump the MacMahon line because they could hardly defy the world's biggest empire.

India ceased to be a British colony in 1947. Independent India assumed that the whole world would accept the borders that it had inherited from the Raj. Till 1962, relations between India and China were so good that India never thought it necessary to post an army on its border with China. So, at some stage in the 1950s, the Chinese simply moved into this vast region, which is one sixth (16.9%) of the entire princely state of Jammu and Kashmîr, and occupied it. In 1958, they built a motorable road from Gartok in Tibet via Rudok, through Aksai Chin, to southern Sinkiang [Xinjiang]. Nick Easen writes, "Regional analysts say that the area is so remote that India's intelligence service didn't learn that China had established a road through the area until the following decade."

Indeed, Aksai Chin is so far from the inhabited parts of Leh that Indian officials did not get to know of the Chinese occupation till much later, when, in 1962, some adventurous young men from India's Indo-Tibetan Border Force, who happened to be trekking in that area, found Chinese soldiers there.

Actually, as James A. Santuccii points out, "Tensions between the two countries over their disputed border had been building for three years. The Chinese *initiated the conflict*, striking the northeastern border of India [then called NEFA and now known as Arunâchal Pradésh] as a cover for the seizure of territory in Ladâkh ... China's offensive was initiated on October 20, 1962. The Chinese forces quickly ejected the ill-prepared Indian forces at the Kârâkoram Pass and from posts near Pangong Lake."

Easen adds, "A brief but brutal war in 1962 was precipitated by China's actions in this very sector. It culminated in China seizing about [37,555] square kilometres (14,670 sq miles) of *Indian territory* in Aksai Chin [and the Demchok/ Pangong area]." (Both emphases are mine.)

Earlier, Pâkistân had annexed some neighbouring parts of this region. In 1963, Pâkistân gifted 5,180 sq. km. in Shaksgam, which had thitherto been in its occupation, to China. This was equal to 2.33% of the original princely state. China is thus in occupation of 19.2%, or almost a fifth, of Jammu and Kashmîr.

Why does China need these areas if 'not a blade of grass grows on them'? According to Tibetan analysts, it appropriated the region "so that Beijing could link its two *rebellious provinces* of Tibet and Xinjiang and build the strategic Kârâkoram Highway from the Chinese town of Kashgar to the Pâkistâni capital of Islâmâbâd along the historic Silk Road."[ii] (Emphasis added.)

China has since placed the Aksai Chin area in the jurisdiction of western Tibet and calls it by the name 'Xizang province.'

How to get there: It takes more than eleven days from Lhasa, in a rugged 4x4 sports utility vehicle, to get to Aksai Chin. The terrain is rough.

Much of the highway that links Aksai Chin with Xinjiang is at altitudes of around 4,000 metres above the sea. The road is open throughout the year because it does not get snowed under. Nor does it go through avalanche prone areas. The road also links Lhasa (Tibet) with Kashgar.

Restrictions on tourists: The road from Lhasa to Aksai Chin is mainly meant for the Chinese army. Private trucks that ply on it mostly carry fruit and vegetables for that army. Therefore, tourism is restricted. Tourists who travel without valid permits or in vehicles that they are not supposed to be in, are likely to be fined at army check points.

What the region holds for tourists: A British writer once called Aksai Chin 'the ultimate isolation.' Because of the rarefied atmosphere, the colours are spectacular and the views panoramic. Travellers on the West Tibet road now have to pass through the region. The brackish-water lakes of Aksai Chin have a haunting charm.

There is one such lake, the Lungmo Co (c.5000m.) on the border that the so-called Tibetan Autonomous Region shares with Xinjiang. Sumish, a village on this border, has some roadside eateries and a small population that consists mostly of ethnic Uighurs. The Uighurs probably moved in after China annexed the region. They mainly dwell in tents and live in Sumish to look after the road.

'Co' means 'lake' and is the local equivalent of the Ladâkhi 'tso.' The road from Sumish to the picturesque Lungmo Co first winds downwards and then climbs up to the Changmar area where the lake is, at the feet of tall mountains that have permafrost snow on their peaks.

References

i From "Kashmîr: A Potential for a World War," an article posted on the Internet. Prof. Santucci is from the Department of Comparative Religion, California State University, Fullerton, CA 92834-6868

ii World Tibet Network News, Friday, October 29, 1993

27

Shaksgam

Shaksgam is an area south of the Mintaka Pass that used to belong to Hunzâ. It is to the north east of the Siachen glacier. China's insecure Sinkiang region is to the east of the Shaksgam valley. Shaksgam has a floating population of around 2,000, but no permanent villages or towns. With one person to every two and a half square kilometres, the region is virtually uninhabited.

On March 2, 1963, Pâkistân gifted 5,180 sq. km. of land in Shaksgam, which had thitherto been in its occupation, to China. Mr. B.R. Singh, an Indian civil servant who has specialised in the Kashmîr-Ladâkh area, told this author, "The Mîr of Hunzâ used to send his cattle to Shaksgam for grazing. [This showed that the land was his.] However, he used to pay a rent of sorts for it. This according to the Chinese proved that it was their land. The British Government used the Mîr's logic to claim this area for Jammû & Kashmîr [and thus India]. In 1935, the Chinese challenged the Mîr's rights and claimed that the land was theirs. [Three decades later,] Pâkistân conceded the Chinese point of view." Which is a pity, because Pakistan should have stood by the Mîr of Hunzâ.

As will be seen from the chapter on the Siachen Glacier in this book, nothing had been demarcated on the map beyond point NJ9842. It is true that Shaksgam valley was one of the areas that had not been demarcated between India and Pâkistân. But there can be no doubt that it belonged to Hunzâ and thus either to India or, for arguments' sake, to Pâkistân, but certainly not to China. Pâkistân should have sorted the matter out with India.

It is strange that Pâkistân accepted China's arguments rather than those of the Hunzâkuts people who, Pâkistân claims, are its citizens. I am sorry to repeat the Solomon metaphor, but the real mother would never have allowed its baby to be carved up. The people of the so-called Northern Areas were not consulted before such a major step was taken.

Pâkistân thus altered the borders of the princely state of Jammu and Kashmîr, perhaps forever. This is one of the reasons why the UN resolutions of 1948/49 on Kashmîr can no longer be implemented, even if India and Pâkistân want to.

As a face-saver for Pâkistân, Article 6 of the 1963 agreement between China and Pâkistân originally read: "The two parties have agreed that after the settlement of the Kashmîr dispute between Pâkistân and India, the sovereign authority concerned will reopen negotiations with the Government of the People's Republic of China on the boundary as described in Article Two of the present agreement, so as to sign a formal boundary treaty to replace the present agreement, provided that in the event of the sovereign authority being Pâkistân, the provisions of the present agreement and of the aforesaid protocol shall be maintained in the formal boundary treaty to be signed between the People's Republic of China and Pâkistân." This article clearly implies that Shaksgam was one of the territories included in 'the Kashmîr dispute.'

Significantly, China deleted this Article in 1987.[i]

Travelling in Shaksgam—the Kârâkorams and the K-2

The biggest tourist attraction of the Shaksgam area is the Base Camp for the world's second highest mountain peak, the K-2 or Qogeli (8,611 metres). Everyone who attempts to climb the K-2 from the area under Chinese occupation has to use this camp. Even those who have no intention to scale the K-2 go there to soak in that majestic peak.

The second reason to go to Shaksgam is to spend a few days amidst the great Kârâkoram range, which stands as a wall between China and India, and India and Central Asia.

There are other reasons, too, to journey through this bitingly cold and desolate area. The romance of the Silk Route (one of the tallest sections of it, to be precise) is one. Following the footsteps of legendary adventurers like Sir Francis Younghusband and Sir Eric Shipton is another. Getting to see some of the oases of the Silk Route is a reward in itself.

And, as in the rest of Ladâkh, the traveller goes past high altitude rivers, gorges, panoramic landscapes and valleys.

As long as Shaksgam remains under Chinese occupation, the only way to go there is through China. The standard 24-day trip goes something like this:

Day 1: Arrive Beijing; *Day 2*: Beijing to Urumqi; *Day 3*: Urumqi to Kashgar; *Day 4*: Kashgar; *Day 5*: Kashgar to Kargilik; *Day 6*: Kargilik to Kudi; *Day 7*: Kudi to Mazar; *Day 8*: Mazar to Ilik via Mazar Dulla; *Days 9 & 10*: Ilik to the Arghil Pass; *Day 11*: To the Shaksgam River; *Day 12*: The Shaksgam River; *Day 13*: To the Base Camp; *Days 14 & 15*: The

Base Camp; *Days 16-20*: Back to Mazar the way we came; *Day 21*: Kargilik to Kashgar; *Day 22*: Kashgar to Urumqi; *Day 23*: Urumqi to Hong Kong via Guangzhou; *Day 24*: Depart Hong Kong.

Tour operators normally add a 25th day in Beijing.

The boundaries of Shaksgam

China and Pâkistân, between themselves, decided that the 'boundary line' between China's Sinkiang (as it was then spelt) and the areas that would remain under Pâkistân's occupation would be as follows:

1) *The north western extremity*: The agreed 'boundary' begins here at a 5,630 metre high peak, the reference co-ordinates of which approximately are longitude 74 degrees 34 minutes east and latitude 37 degrees 3 minutes north. This illegal 'boundary line' first runs generally eastward and then south-eastward along the main watershed between the tributaries of the Tashkurgan river of the Tarim river system on the one hand and the tributaries of the Hunzâ river of the Indus river system on the other hand. It passes through the Kilik Daban (Dawan), the Mintake Daban (Mintaka pass), the Kharchanai Daban (named on the Chinese map only), the Mutsgila Daban (named on the Chinese map only) and the Parpik Pass (named on the Pâkistâni map only) and reaches the Khunjerab (Yutr) Daban (Pass).
2) After passing through the Khunjerab (Yutr) Daban (pass) the so-called 'boundary line' runs generally southward along the above-mentioned main watershed up to a mountain-top south of the Daban (pass). There it leaves the main watershed to follow the crest of a spur lying generally in a south-easterly direction, which is the watershed between the Akjilga river (a nameless corresponding river on the Pâkistân map) on the one hand, and the Taghumbash (Oprang) river and the Koliman Su (Orang Jilga) on the other hand. According to the map of the Chinese side, this illegal 'boundary line,' after leaving the south-eastern extremity of the spur, runs along a small section of the middle line of the bed of the Koliman Su to reach its confluence with the Elechin river. According to the map of the Pâkistân side, the boundary line, after leaving the south-eastern extremity of this spur, reaches the sharp bend of the Shaksgam or Muztagh river.
3) From the aforesaid point, the boundary lines runs up the Kelechin river (Shaksgam or Muztagh river) along the middle line of its bed to its confluence (reference co-ordinates approximately longitude 76 degrees 2 minutes east and latitude 36 degrees 26 minutes north) with the Shorbulak Daria (Shimshal river or Braldu river).
4) From the confluence of the aforesaid two rivers, the 'boundary line,' according to the map of the Chinese side, ascends the crest of a spur

and runs along it to join the main watershed of the Kârâkoram range at a mountain-top (reference co-ordinates approximately longitude 75 degrees 54 minutes east and latitude 36 degrees 15 minutes north). On the Chinese map this is shown as belonging to the Shorgulak mountain. According to the map of the Pâkistân side, the boundary line from the confluence of the above mentioned two rivers ascends the crest of a corresponding spur and runs along it, passing through a height of 6.520 metres (21,390 feet) till it joins the Kârâkoram range's main watershed at a peak (reference co-ordinates approximately longitude 75 degrees 57 minutes east and latitude 36 degrees 3 minutes north).

5) Thence, the 'boundary line,' running generally southward and then eastward strictly follows the Kârâkoram range main watershed. This watershed separates the Tarim river drainage system from the Indus river drainage system. It passes through the east Mustagh pass (Muztagh pass), the top of the Chogri peak (K-2) the top of the broad peak, the top of the Gasherbrum mountain (8,068), the Indirakoli pass (these names are found on the Chinese maps only) and the top of the Teramn Kankri (Teram Kangri) peak, and reaches its south-eastern extremity at the Kârâkoram pass.

Incidentally, the maps of the Chinese and Pâkistâni sides are not identical in their representation of topographical features.

References

i I picked this factoid up from an otherwise accurate website but have not been able to cross check it.

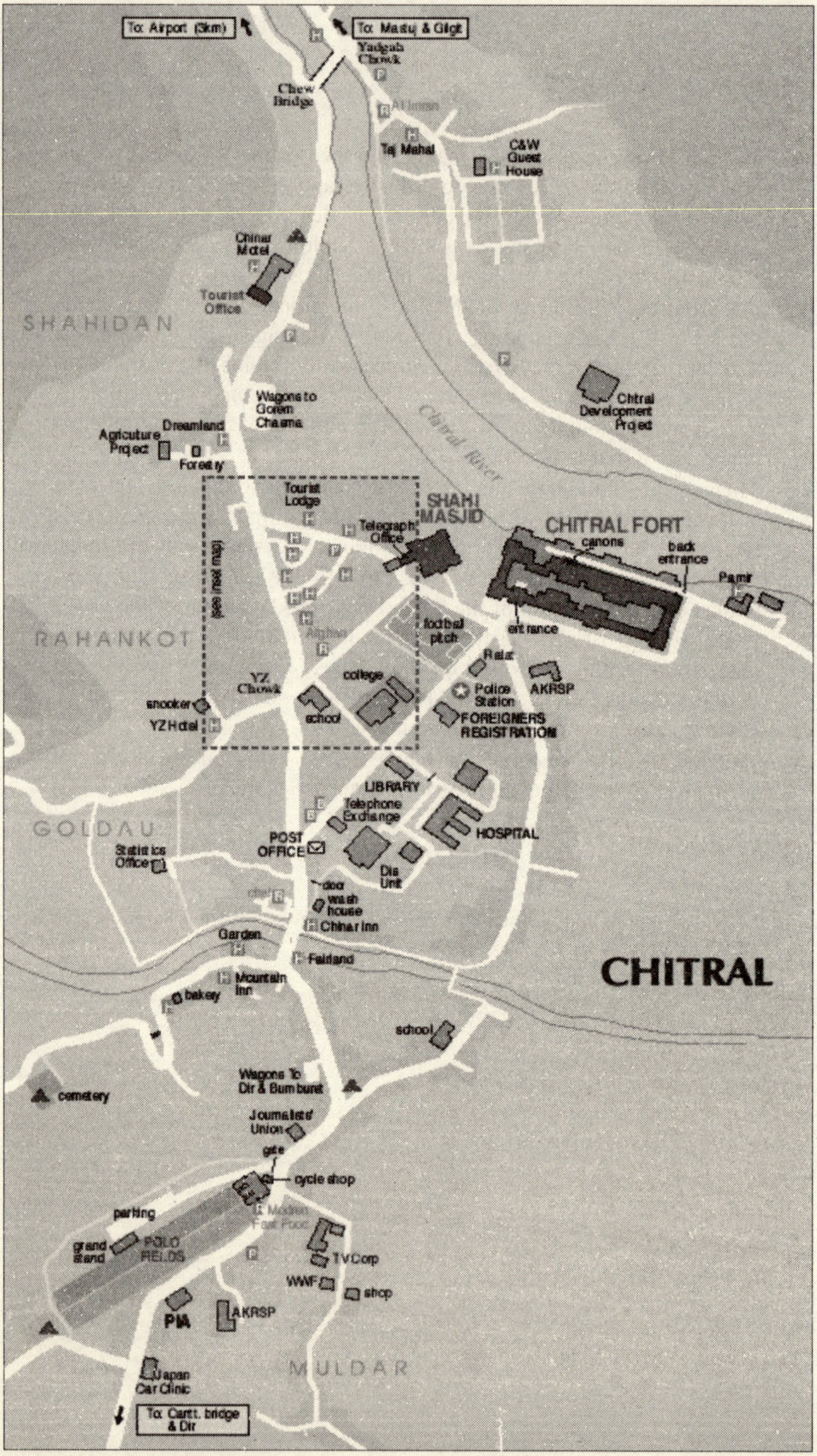
To: Airport (3km)
To: Mastuj & Gilgit
Yadgah Chowk
Chew Bridge
Al Hilal
Taj Mahal
C&W Guest House
Chinar Motel
Tourist Office
SHAHIDAN
Wagons to Garam Chashma
Dreamland
Agriculture Project
Forestry
Chitral Development Project
Chitral River
Tourist Lodge
SHAHI MASJID
Telegraph Office
CHITRAL FORT
canons
back entrance
Pamir
(see inset map)
RAHANKOT
Afghan
football pitch
entrance
Rafat
college
YZ Chowk
snooker
YZ Hotel
school
Police Station
AKRSP
FOREIGNERS REGISTRATION
LIBRARY
Telephone Exchange
HOSPITAL
GOLDAU
POST OFFICE
Statistics Office
Dis Unit
car wash house
Chinar Inn
Garden
Fairland
CHITRAL
Mountain Inn
bakery
school
Wagons To Dir & Bumburet
cemetery
Journalists' Union
gate
cycle shop
Modern Fast Food
parking
grand stand
POLO FIELDS
TV Corp
WWF
shop
PIA
AKRSP
MULDAR
Japan Car Clinic
To: Cantt. bridge & Dir

Religion

Zanskar

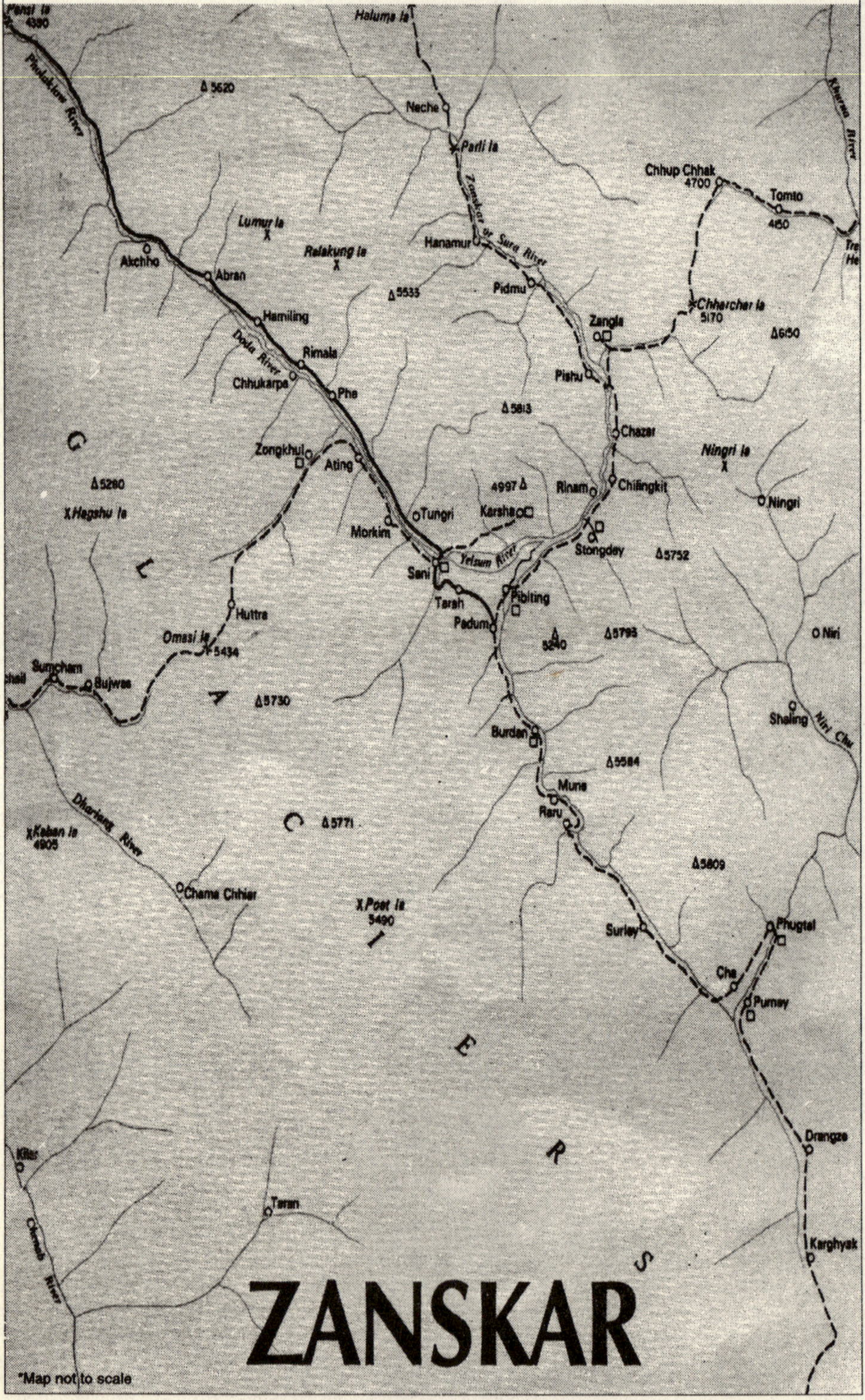

*Map not to scale

28

The important gompâs of Ladâkh

A gompâ is a Buddhist monastery. Buddhist nunneries are called chomo gompâs. 'Chomo' means 'nun' and 'lâmâ' means 'monk.'

There are gompas in Leh as well as Kargil. Within Kargil they are either on the National Highway between Leh and Kargil, or in Zâñskâr,

Leh district

(All distances are from Leh town. Please allow for an error of up to +2 km. because it all depends on where you are counting from.)

Alchi: 70km. from Leh. 5km. from Saspol village.

It is generally believed that the great scholar Lotsâvâ Rinchen (b)Zâñgpo (born AD 985) founded the monastery. However, he did not introduce a monastic community here. Instead he nominated four families as the caretakers of the Chos Khor. This made a take-over by another monastery inevitable. Since the 15th century the management of the Likir monastery has been looking after Alchi as well.

This 11th century gompa is arguably the oldest extant monastery in all Ladâkh—perhaps even the region's oldest extant building of any kind.

Basgo: 39-42km. from Leh. There are three shrines at Basgo, all dedicated to the Maitreya. King Senggé Namgyâl got most of them constructed. They belong to the red hat sect. Snellgrove and Skorupski write that 'this is probably the only temple in Ladâkh to have survived with some of its murals intact from the 16th century.'

The Maitreya Buddha: The management of the Maitreya temples at Basgo claims that these temples are 'a world heritage site' and one of the '100 most endangered' sites in the world. Actually UNESCO has included the 75-foot, copper-coated Maitreya (future) Buddha in the latter category. It sits atop a cliff, 300 metres above the village. King Senggé Namgyâl got it constructed to honour the memory of his father, King Jamyang Namgyâl.

Chemray: 45km. (11,800'). The great King Senggé Namgyâl died in 1645. This monastery was built as part of the funeral rites, to confer merit on the dead king.

Gongo Kargyat: There are eight places in Nubra where naturally formed Buddhist Arhats are found. Gongo Kargyat is the collective name of these eight places.

Deskit: Lama Shesrab Zangpo of Stod founded this monastery when Dragspâ Bum Lde (1400-40) was the king of Ladâkh.

Hemis: 49km. Hemis was probably built in 1630 at the behest of King Senggé Namgyâl. It is the best known—and thus the wealthiest—gompa in Ladâkh. Its fame owes to the fact that it is the headquarters of the red-hat Drukpa sect and, for that reason, Ladâkh's biggest gompa.

Lâmâ Yûrû: (2,957m.) 127km. west of Leh. Lâmâ Yûrû is the oldest monastery still in use. It possibly became a Buddhist gompa in the 10th century AD, apparently at the behest of Lama Mahâsiddh Nâropâ.

Leh: See 'Namgyâl...' below.

Likir: 61km. to the west. The earliest that the frescoes of Likir can be dated to is the 11th century. Lama Duwang Chosje established a monastery at this spot around AD 1065.

Matho: 27km. southeast. Lama Tungpâ Dorjay built the gompa in the early 16th century. It was named Thupstan-Sharling Choskor. The then king granted the monastery a large estate in the surrounding villages.

Mangyu(r): It is believed that Lotsâvâ Rinchen Zâñgpo, the great translator, built three monasteries in the 11th century, including Mangyu. Alchi and Sumdah are the other two.

Namgyâl Tsemo Monastery, Leh : This used to one of the royal monasteries of Ladâkh. It is located in the palace complex. King Dragspâ Bum Lde built it around AD 1430.

Phyâng. 17km. to the west. The Zagâñg Snon Krâshish Chhos Rizong monastery: Around fifty monks live in this monastery, which was built in the 15th or 16th century.

Rizong: 74km. west of Leh. Rizong is the most inaccessible monastery in all Ladâkh. In its strict adherence to principles, and in its seclusion, Rizong is unique in all Ladâkh.

Sankar: 3km. This is said to be the only monastery built on flat land, in the 'plains', so to speak. (But so are Mangyu and even Alchi.) Sankar is the seat of the Yellow Hat sect and, thus, linked to Spituk.

Spituk: 9km. to the southwest. The present Spituk gompa was built in the 15th century.

Stak(h)na: 26km. from Leh or a few kilometres upstream from Thiksey. This is one of the older monasteries in Ladâkh. The Drukpa monastery itself was built around 1580 by Chosje Jamyang Palkhar, a saint.

Stok: 17km. to the south-east/ a one-hour drive from Leh. In the 1830s the Dogrâs annexed Ladâkh to the kingdom of Jammu and Kashmîr. The Ladâkhi royal family then shifted to Stok and the palace at Stok was probably built then. The Gurphuk monastery is at a short distance from the palace. It is a branch of the Spituk monastery.

Sumdo: (Roughly 65km. southwest of Leh town.) There are three temples in the complex.

Taktak: 46km. east of Leh; a few kilometres from Chemray; right above village Sâkti. This monastery is the only one in Ladâkh that belongs to Nying ma pa, the oldest Tibetan sect of monks.

Thiksey: 20km. to the south. Sherab Zâñgpo built a monastery at Stakmo. His nephew, Paldan Sherab, shifted it to Thiksey. The gompâ is said to date to the 11th century, maybe the 12th.

Nyarmâ: Close to Thiksey are the ruins of Nyarma, a monastery and seminary founded by the great 10th century scholar Rinchen (b)Zâñgpo.

Urgyan Rizong: This is a 'meditational retreat' in a little valley.

Kargil district

On or near the Leh-Kargil Highway

Mulbek(h) (3,230m.) is 45km. before and east of Kargil. It is 190km. from Leh.

Right next to the road there is a nine metre deep relief idol of the Maitreya Buddha, carved out of a rock. This is the future Buddha.

Wâkhâ (Rgyâl) has a nunnery called the Jangchup Chosling monastery, very close to the highway.

Shargol(e) is another ten kilometres ahead of Mulbek, or 35km. before Kargil. Its small but old Ge Lugs pâ Buddhist monastery has few but interesting frescoes.

There is a tiny Buddhist nunnery nearby.

Phokar (also Fokar) is 4km. ahead of the Shargol monastery. A tall hill rises from the Phokar plain. You will have to climb it to get to the Phokar Rizong/ Urgyan Dzong.

In Suru Valley

Rangdum (3,657 metres; 130km. from Kargil town, 65km. from Pânikhar, on the road to Zâñskâr.) Around forty monks live in this 18th century gompa.

In Zâñskâr sub-division

Sani: (8km. from Padam.) Emperor Kanishka (aka Kanika) had got 108 chortens constructed in the first century. One of these 'Kanika chortens' is in Sani. Two 9th or 10th century stone slabs flank the entrance to the main hall.

Padam (240km. from Kargil town) has a monastery, but it is not one of the ranking gompas of Ladâkh. There are gompas in Pipiting and Stagrimo, both near Padam.

Karshâ (4-6km. from Padam): Around 150 monks live here, not in the gompa itself, but in houses scattered all over the town. Phagspâ Sherab (Zâñskâr Lotsâvâ) founded the gompa, perhaps in the eleventh century.

Stongdey: (20km. north of Padam on the way to Zangla.) The highlight of the Marpaling monastery is its gon khong (temple of guardian deities). Marpa, the saint, founded it.

Phugtâl/ Phuktâl is a stunning monastic village built inside a huge cave. Csoma Körös, the 18th century Hungarian mystic-scholar, wrote the *Zâñskâr Chronicles* here.

Zongkhul: The Zongkhul gompa is said to have been founded by Mahâsiddh Nâropâ. This legendary 10th century monk from Kashmîr had taught at the universities of Vikramshila and Nalanda.

29

A calendar of Buddhist Festivals

For the convenience of tourists the Department of Tourism, Jammu & Kashmir sought the services of Ladakhi astrologers, especially Mr. Thupstan Shanfan, who drew up the following schedule of festivals till the year 2009. Just as table diaries carry the previous year's calendar as well, the schedule of the immediately preceding years has been listed for reference.

Monastery/ Festival	**2000**	**2001**	**2002**	**2003**	**2004**
Stongde (in Zâñskâr)/ Gustor	Jan 4-5	Jan 22-23	Jan 11-12	Jan 30-31	Jan 19-20
Spituk/ Gustor	Jan 4-5	Jan 22-23	Jan 11-12	Jan 30-31	Jan 19-20
Deskit/ Dosmochey	Feb 3-4	Feb 21-22	Feb 10-11	Feb 28-Mar 1	Feb 18-19
Leh/ Dosmochey	Feb 3-4	Feb 21-22	Feb 10-11	Feb 28-Mar 1	Feb 18-19
Likir/ Dosmochey	Feb 3-4	Feb 21-22	Feb 10-11	Feb 28-Mar 1	Feb 18-19
Yarma-Gonbo/ Ltung-Shaks		not	available		
Stok/ Guru Tse Chu	Mar 14-15	Mar 4-5	Feb 21-22	Mar 12-13	Feb 29-Mar 1
Matho/Nagrang	Mar 20-21	Mar 9-10	Feb 26-27	Mar 17-18	Mar 5-6
Buddha Purnima	June 16	June 6	May 26	June 14	June 3
Hemis/ Tse Chu	July 11-12	June 30-Jul 1	June 20-21	July 9-10	June 27-28

Monastery/ Festival	2000	2001	2002	2003	2004
LamaYuru/ Kabgyat	July 18-19	July 7-8	June 26-27	July 15-16	July 4-5
Karshâ/Gustor	July 28-29	July 17-18	July 7-8	July 26-27	July 14-15
Phyâng/Tsedup	Aug 1-2	July 22-23	July 12-13	July 31-Aug 1	July 19-20
Korzok/Gustor	Aug 2-3	July 23-24	July 13-14	Aug 1-2	July 20-21
Dakthok/ Tse Chu	Aug 9-10	July 29-30	July 19-20	Aug 7-8	July 27-28
Sani/ Naro Nasjal	Aug 14-15	Aug 3-4	July 23-24	Aug 11-12	July 30-31
Shachukul/ Gustor	Aug 20-21	Aug 16-17	Aug 5-6	Aug 24-25	Aug 12-13
Thiksey/ Gustor	Nov 14-15	Nov 4-5	Oct 24-25	Nov 12-13	Oct31-Nov1
Chamday/ Angchok	Nov 23-24	Nov 13-14	Nov 2-3	Nov 21-22	Nov 10-11
Galdan Namchot	Dec 20	Dec 9	Dec 29	Dec 18	Dec 7
Losar	Dec 26	Dec 15	Jan 3, 2003	Dec 24	Dec 12

Monastery/ Festival	2005	2006	2007	2008	2009
Stongde (in Zâñskâr)/ Spituk Gustor	Jan 8-9	Jan 27-28	Jan 17-18	Jan 6-7	Jan 23-24
Deskit/ Dosmochey	Feb 6-7	Feb 26-27	Feb 15-16	Feb 4-5	Feb 22-23
Leh/ Dosmochey	Feb 6-7	Feb 26-27	Feb 15-16	Feb 4-5	Feb 22-23
Likir/ Dosmochey	Feb 6-7	Feb 26-27	Feb 15-16	Feb 4-5	Feb 22-23
Yarma-Gonbo/ Ltung-Shaks	Feb 12	Mar 3	Feb 21	Feb 10	Feb 28
Stok/ Guru Tse Chu	Feb 17-18	Mar 8-9	Feb 25-26	Feb 15-16	Mar 5-6
Matho/Nagrang	Feb 22-23	Mar 14-15	Mar 3-4	Feb 20-21	Mar 10-11
Buddha Purnima	May 23	June 11	May 31	June 18	June 6

Monastery/ Festival	2005	2006	2007	2008	2009
Hemis/ Tse Chu	June 17-18	July 6-7	June 25-26	July 12-13	July 1-2
LamaYuru/ Kabgyat	June 23-24	July 12-13	July 2-3	July 20-21	July 8-9
Karshâ/Gustor	July 3-4	July 22-23	July 11-12	July 29-30	July 18-19
Phyâng/Tsedup	Aug 7-8	July 27-28	July 16-17	Aug 3-4	July 22-23
Korzok/Gustor	Aug 8-9	July 28-29	July 17-18	Aug 4-5	July 23-24
Dakthok/ Tse Chu	Aug 15-16	Aug 4-5	July 24-25	Aug 11-12	July 30-31
Sani/ Naro Nasjal	Aug 18-19	Aug 8-9	July 29-30	Aug 15-16	Aug 3-4
Shachukul/ Gustor	Aug 31-Sep.1	Aug 20-21	Aug 10-11	Aug 27-28	Aug 16-17
Thiksey/ Gustor	Nov 18-19	Nov 8-9	Oct 28-29	Nov 15-16	Nov 4-5
Chamday/ Angchok	Nov 29-30	Nov 18-19	Nov 7-8	Nov 25-26	Nov 13-14
Galdan Namchot	Dec 26	Dec 15	Dec 4	Dec 21	Dec 10
Losar	Jan 1.2006	Dec 21	Dec 10	Dec 28	Dec 16

30

Islâm in Leh and Zâñskâr

Muslims live in Leh town and in twenty-five other villages of Leh district.[1] Before 1947, the Muslim population was greater. In the 1950s some Muslims[2] migrated to the areas occupied by Pâkistân. In Zâñskâr the Muslims live in Padum (the 'capital') and Pipiting.

The first Muslims—and mosques

The advent of Islâm: Hussain Mansûr Hallaj of Baghdad was among the first known Muslims to have travelled through Ladakh. This was in the 10th century. Historian Abdul Ghani Sheikhi asserts that 'the first Muslim set foot in the area as early as in the 7th or 8th century.'

By way of proof he mentions a group of boulders near Tangchey (Tângtsé?) on which a verse from the Holy Qurân and the names of some Arabs have been engraved in Arabic. These Arabs include Nâsir ibn Sâleh Abu Mansûr, Abul Âyat and Zakâriâ ibn Qâsim. On cross checking with Central Asian records, Sheikh found that these were Arab army commanders and administrators of the 7th//8th century. That, incidentally, was the first century of Islâm, internationally.

However, it was Amîr Kabîr Mîr Syed Ali Hamadâni who first propagated Islâm in Ladâkh. This great 14th century saint spent some time in Ladâkh while travelling between Kashmîr and Kâshghar (Chinese Turkestân).

The first mosques: Amîr Kabîr Mîr Syed Ali Hamadâni built the first mosque in Ladakh. He did so in Shey, perhaps in 1381. The mosques at Tiyaqshi and Padum are among the many said to have been built by

1. The district has 112 villages in all.
2. The entire Muslim populations of Sespol, Khâltsé and Nemo, and many from Bazgo left for the occupied territory.

him in Leh and Zâñskâr.[3] He also got several mosques constructed in Baltistân.

Chhushat Yoqmâ has an extremely old mosque and an almost equally old Imâmbârâ (Shiite place of worship). No one knows when either was built.

The Jâmia Masjid, Leh: For some reason most histories put the construction of the first mosque in Ladakh at more than two—even three—centuries after 1381. An official publication of the state government puts the date of the first mosque as 'later' than the '15th century'. Many books seem to indicate that Leh's Jâmia Masjid, built in 1594 or 1666, was the first mosque in Leh district.

However, evidence of the Shah é Hamadân's 1381 visit to Shey is overwhelming. Equally certainly it was he who got the first mosque (perhaps, mosques) built in Leh district.

Trying to put a date on when the Jâmia Masjid of Leh town was built has been an interesting exercise for this author. A publication of the J&K Tourism Department says that 'built in 1594 by Senggé Namgyâl [as] a tribute to his Muslim mother, the Leh mosque, an exquisite work of Turko-Iranian architecture, stands majestically in the main bazar.'

This belief is based on a folksong, which tells us that Senggé had donated land for the mosque.

The grand mosque that we see today is mainly in the Indo-Islâmic style. There is a smaller and older mosque close to it.

Now we know that Prince Nawâñg Namgyâl, too, had a Muslim mother, Queen Tsering rGyâlmo. (See 'A History of Kargil'). The mother and son were definitely alive in 1594. Senggé probably wasn't even born then. So Nawâñg could have got the mosque built. He was one of the sons of King Jamyâñg. But he never got to be king. Nor is there a belief in Leh that it was Nawâñg who built the mosque for his mother.

Ali Shér Khân Añchan, the emperor of Skardu, defeated Jamyâñg around 1600, imprisoned him and ransacked and briefly ruled over Leh. Jamyâñg married Ali's daughter, Gyâl Kâtûn. Jamyâñg died around 1616. His son Senggé was a minor then. Therefore, his Muslim mother Gyâl Kâtûn ruled as the regent for a while. According to many historians, all that she got built was one room in the Bazgo palace. (However, Sheikh says that she got mosques constructed at Hunder, Leh and Bazgo.)

Obviously the minor Senggé could not have built the mosque in 1594. On the other hand Ali Sher could, and there is some weak evidence

3. According to most historians the first Muslims went to Zâñskâr with Day-tsok (some time between 1570 and 1642). Therefore, would the Shah é Hamadân have built a mosque there in 1381-82?

that he might have. At one stage, his name, or that of his grandson, Shâh Murâd, had been inscribed on the mosque. But why would Ali Sher, a Shia, have got a Sunni mosque built? Even Nawâñg's mother was a Shiite.

However, Jamyâñg could have built the mosque for either or both of his Muslim wives. No one says that he did. Therefore, we have to accept the theory that the Jamia Masjid was built in 1666. This followed the 1663 agreement between the Sunni Mughal Emperor Aurangzeb and Gyâlpo Deldan Namgyâl of Leh. But then the question arises as to why the names of Ali Sher and/ or Shâh Murâd got to be written on a Sunni mosque.

(See 'A History of Leh' for details, especially regarding the settling of Kashmiri Muslims in Spituk.)

Other sects: The Muslim world is not divided neatly into Shîâs and Sunnîs, as simplistic accounts would have us believe. As I have shown in the volume on Kashmîr, there are sects that have tried to bridge this divide. The Nûr Bakhshîs are one such sect. (There is a major Nûr Bakhshî population in Turtuk which, since 1971, has been on the Indian side of the Line of Control in Leh district. For the almost two and a half decades before that it had been under Pâkistâni occupation.)

The Kelumcheh, a clan from Purîg (Kargil), which went over to Baltistân around 1730, were neither Shia nor Sunni. Like the Shîâs they did not accept the first three Righteous Caliphs of Islâm. However, they gave an extremely high place to Hazrat Abu Bâqar's daughter, Âyéshâ, and Hazrat Usmân's daughter, Hafzâ. (Both noble ladies were the wives of Hazrat Muhammad, peace be upon him, the prophet of Islâm.)

Apparently, there was a Muslim saint in Kashmîr who put his interpretation of Islâm down in a book. He probably migrated to Baltistân in the late seventeenth century. The Kelumcheh follow his principles.

Later mosques: In the 19th century, an Imâmiâ (Shiite) mosque was built in Leh.

Conversion and Migration

Conversions: The defeated Deldan, and his son, went through the motions of converting to Islâm. They went back to Buddhism immediately thereafter. No other conversions from Buddhism to Islâm took place in that era, certainly not in significant numbers. And yet almost 16% of the population of Leh (and 4.76% of Zâñskâr) is Muslim. How come?

Migrations: Since mediæval times Ladakh had extensive trading links with the neighbouring Muslim-majority Yârqañd. This came to an end in 1949. Over the centuries, some Yârqañdi traders settled in Leh and married local Buddhist women. Their descendants form a community that is now called the Argons. Most Argons are Sunnis and follow the Hanafiâ school.

Muslims from Yârqañd (and Tibet) continued to trickle into Leh (and Kashmir) even after 1949, like their Tibetan Buddhist counterparts. The head of one such Muslim family reached Leh through Darjeeling (where he married a Tibetan Buddhist). Another Yârqañdi family, including the women and children, did the difficult journey over the Kârâkorams on foot and horseback. Muslim or Buddhist, post-1949 immigrants have been very few.

Till the late 1970s there were almost two dozen Yârqañdi families in Leh. Many went over to Kashmir and settled there. One such family migrated to Kargil instead. Then the Government of Turkey invited all ethnic Turkestanis to return to Turkey. Almost all Yârqañdis living in Kashmir accepted the offer.

By the 21st century there were just two Yârqañdi families left in Leh.

However, the Argons as a whole make up only around a third of the Muslims of Leh district. The rest are Shia or, as in Turtuk, Nûr Bakhshî.

In 'A history of Leh' we saw how the pashmînâ trade of Ladâkh was controlled by Kashmîrî Muslims. This was commented upon by visiting Europeans as early as in 1715. That tells us why there is a small Kashmîrî population, dependent on the wool trade, in Leh district.

Today the Dogrâ contingent of the Sikh army that conquered Gilgit-Ladâkh for the Punjâb (and, thus, India) is sought to be painted as a Hiñdu (all right, Hiñdu-Sikh) force. However, as I have pointed out in 'A history of Balâwaristân,' it had a very substantial number of Muslim officers and soldiers. Some of them settled in Ladâkh.

Each of the Muslim queens mentioned earlier brought a small retinue of maids and musicians with her. These would be Muslims from her land.

A village of Balti Muslims was set up in Chushot, perhaps in the sixteenth century. (See 'A history of Baltistân.') Shiites from neighbouring Purig (Kargil), too, sometimes settled in Leh district: often to escape some natural calamity back home.

Migration by invitation: The Buddhist kings of Leh and Zâñskâr often invited talented Muslims to come and settle in their land. (King Ranjit Dev of Jammu would later follow their example. See also 'A history of Zâñskâr.') Some, like the Zargars of Kashmîr, were brought in to mint coins for the Government of Ladâkh.[4]

4. Ladâkh has a very old tradition of its kings inviting talented Kashmîrîs to settle in Ladâkh. Rinchen bZangpo, for instance, brought a hundred artists from Kashmîr to Ladâkh in the 11th century A.D. Of course, they were all Hiñdu-Buddhists.

The Persian language skills of yet others, notably the elite Khowjas of Leh, were in great demand in Ladâkh. As we have seen in 'A History of Leh,' in the 17th and 18th centuries the Lo Pchak religious and trade missions to Tibet were managed by Ladakhi Muslims. The Khowjas were often the Muslim family that controlled these missions.

King Jamyâñg Namgyal's favourite traders were a group of seven Kashmîrî Muslims. He gave them land to settle on, in and around Leh town. Each of them went on to found an important clan.

All over India, except in Sikh and Christian areas, butchers almost always are Muslims. The majority of Buddhists in Leh and Zâñskâr eat meat but do not kill animals themselves. So, Muslim butchers were requested to come to Leh.

Emigration: Over the same centuries Kashmîrî and Ladâkhi Muslims too went to Yârqañd and Tibet to trade. To this day there is a small community of two thousand Kashmîrî-Ladâkhi Muslims in Tibet,

A growing population: On the whole the population of Muslims in Leh has been rising consistently. P.H. Francky'[ii] wrote in the early 20th century, 'The Arghon population of Ladâkh (Leh in particular) is increasing more rapidly than the Buddhist population.'

This was at a time when Ladâkh (and the state) was supposedly ruled by Dogrâ Hiñdus.

The Argons

Most Argons are well educated. Some of them have risen to senior positions in the government and academics, though the odds are stacked against them.

Exclusion from affirmative action: In the 1980s the Government of India determined that all the people of Leh and Kargil, including the Gyâpo princes, the Lungpo nobility and the Kargil aristocracy, were tribals. All the people were tribals, except the Sunnis of Leh and Kargil. Tribals are entitled, by law, to several kinds of affirmative action, including a certain number of jobs at every level in the government.

The Argons have always distinguished themselves through hard work and high standards of honesty. They now have to redouble their efforts just to stay where they are.

The title: The Argons mainly live in and around Leh town. Till the 1980s 'Argon' was a very exalted title. Only the wealthiest Sunni Muslim businessmen, who traded goods in Lhâsa, Yârqañd and Kâshghar, were called Argons.

It's the politics of 'reservation' (affirmative action) that welded the Sunnis together. Till then they were known as Yârqañdis or Puriks

(Purgis), depending on where their male ancestors had migrated from. Now that they alone had been excluded from the benefits of 'reservation,' they had a common goal, and identity. They needed a name to call themselves, and the word 'Argon' came in handy. The entire community started using a title thitherto confined to the elite.

The Shias

As in Kargil, the Shias account for the majority of Muslims in Leh district. They live in the villages where the two districts meet, as well as in Bogdang, Nubra, Pheyang, Thiksey and Chechot.

References

i Sheikh, Abdul Ghani, 'Muslims in Ladâkh and Sufi Traditions', *New Hope*, vol.4, no.1, January-February, 2003.

ii Quoted by Sheikh, op. cit., p. 36.

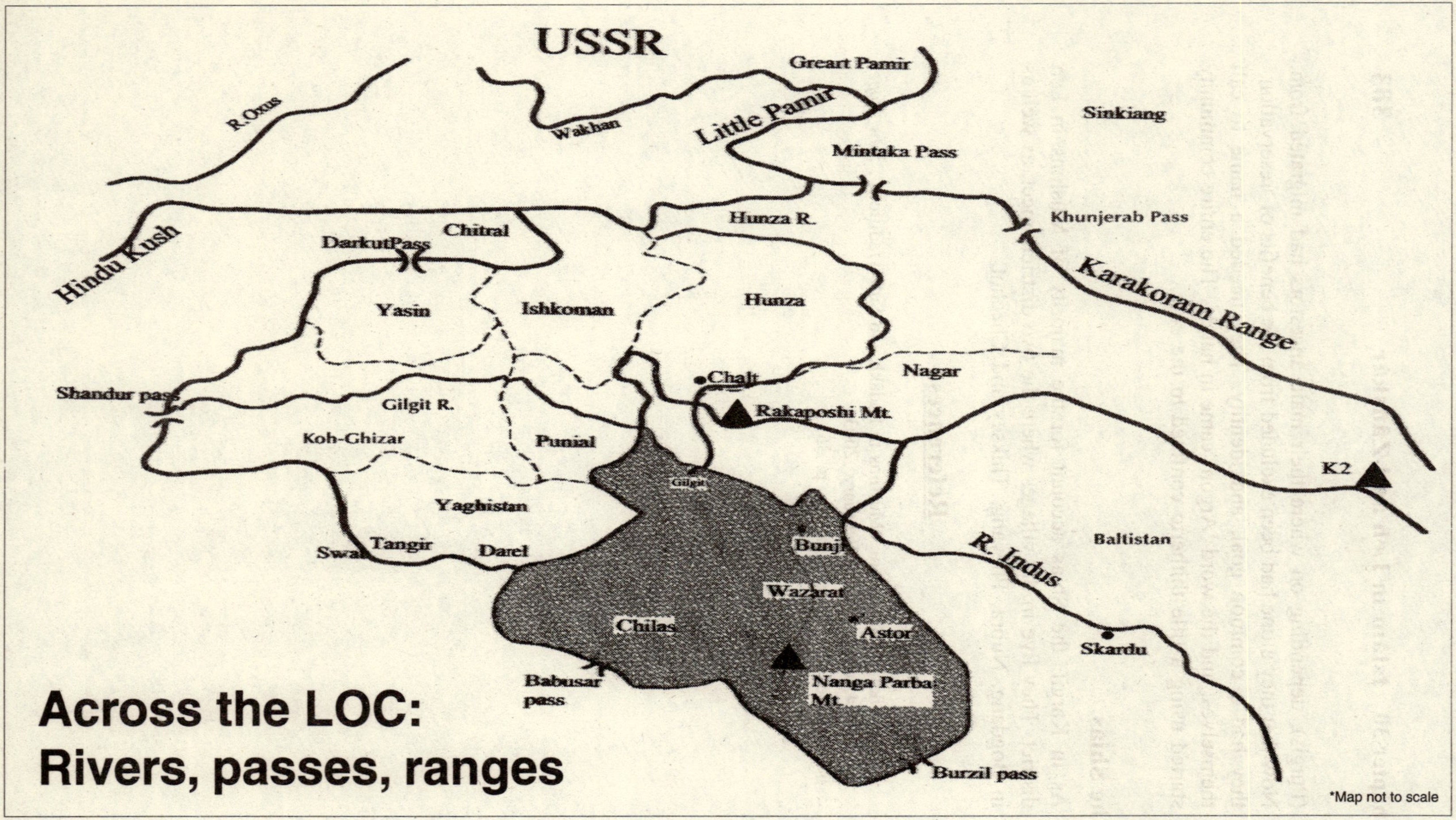

Across the LOC: Rivers, passes, ranges

Culture

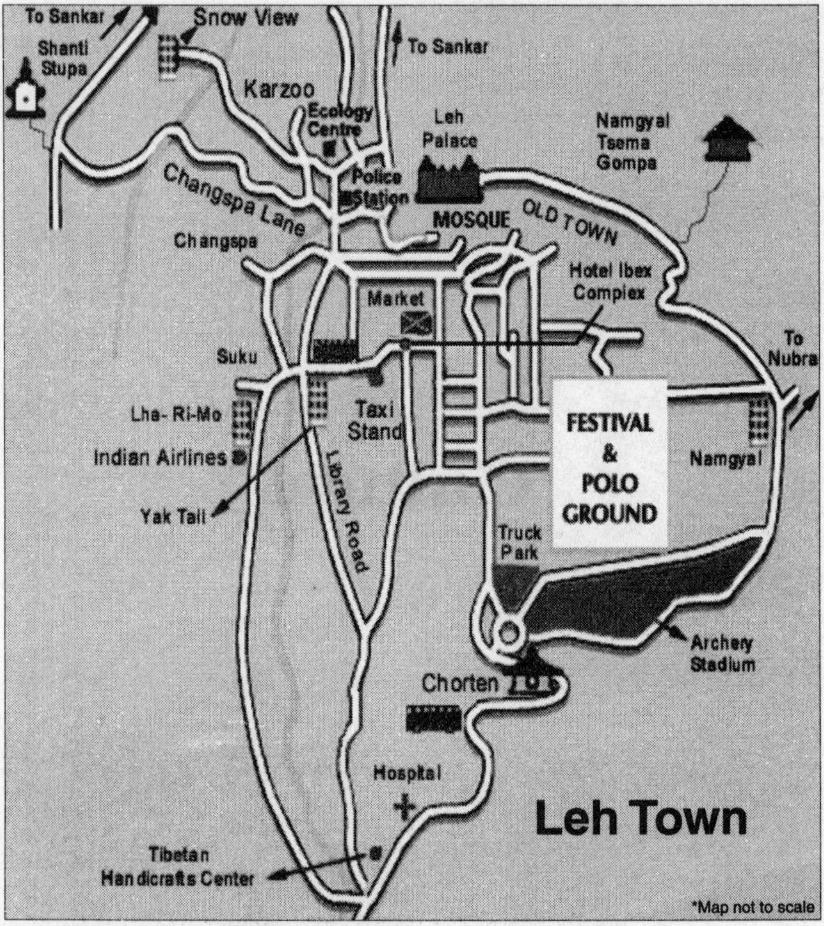
To Sankar
Snow View
Shanti
Stupa
To Sankar
Karzoo
Ecology
Centre
Leh
Palace
Namgyal
Tsema
Gompa
Police
Station
Changspa Lane
MOSQUE
OLD TOWN
Changspa
Hotel Ibex
Complex
Market
To
Nubra
Suku
Taxi
Stand
FESTIVAL
&
POLO
GROUND
Lha-Ri-Mo
Namgyal
Indian Airlines
Library Road
Yak Tail
Truck
Park
Archery
Stadium
Chorten
Hospital
Leh Town
Tibetan
Handicrafts Center
*Map not to scale

31

Sports, pastimes and festivity

Archery

Archery is a living tradition in all of Ladakh. It is taken quite seriously in the relatively sombre Kargil. Contests are held in the villages of Kargil when the snow begins to melt in early spring.

In Leh, writes Janet Rizvi, 'archery festivals seem to be little more than excuses for a summer party' with dancing and chhang (the local beer). Mrs. Rizvi adds that 'as with dance, a strict etiquette prevails. Each competing teams must be captained by someone from an aristocratic family, preferably the senior member present.' Targets are really a heap of mud not more than two or three feet high, placed at ground level. At least in Leh and Zâñskâr there's a lot of ribaldry attached. For instance, if an archer's arrow hits a particular spot on the target he'll be appreciatively ribbed by his friends that he will get a virgin as girlfriend.

Only particular families make the Scythian bow. The central shaft is made of mulberry wood. Slivers from the horns of the ibex goat are pasted on this shaft. This gives them great tensile strength. The craftsmen of Trespon village in Kargil sell these bows to almost all of Ladakh.

Related festivities: On the last day of the tournament a sheep or a goat is slaughtered and chopped into pieces. Its various parts are placed at the same level as the target. If an archer hits one of these pieces he gets to keep that portion and also scores a few points.

There is a mock battle of the sexes in the finale. It consists of hitting a melong, which is made of brass. Before glass reached Ladakh the melong was used as a mirror. Therefore, it is supposed to represent the fairer sex. The first challenge for the archers is to secretly persuade a newly married bride to give them her melong. Women in the audience feign disappointment if one of their ranks betrays them thus to the men.

The melong is then placed on the target. If the archers manage to hit, indeed smash, the melong, it is considered a victory for the men. Therefore, when archers aim at the target the women kick up a ruckus to distract them, so that their arrows miss the melong. If an archer hits the melong, he has to slaughter a sheep or goat and distribute its parts (or money, in lieu) among the other archers. This is a kind of prize-in-reverse. Instead of receiving a prize, the best archer celebrates his triumph by treating his colleagues.

When the players and audience leave the stadium, some of them shoot a few arrows in the direction of the edge of the village. They cry out, 'The arrows have gone to the land of the arrows' and 'The feathers have gone to the land of the feathers.' They also pray for the well being of everyone.

In some areas such as Shakar-Chiktan, archery is an excuse for several days of feasting. Groups, each consisting of three archers, organise and pay for these feasts. Villages elsewhere frown on feasting during the tournament. These include Sot-Pashkum, Suru-Karchey and Mulbek-Wakha. These villages have a feast at the end of the tournament.

In much of Leh district colourful tents are put up at the 'stadium' by the youths of the village. Archers who hit certain parts of the target are garlanded with white scarves made of silk (khataks). They also have to dance at the 'stadium' between rounds of archery. The local elders and notables are invited and given seats of honour.

In most parts of Ladâkh, there is feasting after the tournament is over. Everyone participates in these feasts, regardless of class or religion. Apart from dancing, short plays are staged on such occasions.

During the 20th century, song and dance gradually diappeared from the Shia Muslim areas and got replaced by devotional chants.

Hunting

Hunting in art and history: Rock carvings found all over Ladakh indicate an almost obsession with hunting. Most of them show hunters with bows and arrows chasing an ibex or two. Therefore, when historians say that the Ladakhis have been hunters since pre-historic times, they are stating more than just the obvious. (There is an entire chapter on 'Rock engravings...' in this book. For details of the villages where these ancient and mediæval engravings can be found please use the index.)

The code of the hunter: The ancients hunted with enormous politically-correct self-restraint. They followed three basic rules: i) Animals were to be hunted strictly on a need-to-kill basis, and not for pleasure or sport. ii) Animals of certain species were not to be killed at all. (To this day the Buddhists consider it a sin to kill or eat fish. Most Ladakhis do not kill marmots either.) iii) Young ibexes were not to be killed either.

Each tribe had its own hunting-grounds. It was against the rules to hunt in another tribe's beat. Some wealthy families had private hunting grounds till as recently as the 19th century.

Methods: Some early hunters would trap their prey with nets. Tourists with an interest in pre-historic archæology might like to visit the Mangshûn hunting grounds of Purîg (Kargil), where evidence of this kind of hunting is available.

Later, bows and arrows appeared. Falcons and hunting dogs were used, especially to pin down the ibex. This kind of hunting has been copiusly recorded in the rock-art of Ladakh.

Kachu Sikander Khan says that guns appeared as early as during the Mughal-era (the 17th century, in this case). He adds that remnants of old guns and cannon can be found at places like Chiktan Khar, Sot Khar and Khar Purchey. Rifles were the last in this succession of hunting-weapons. However, soon after their appearance also came various bans and restrictions on hunting.

The hunt: All able-bodied men from a group of villages would together surround the grounds where the prey was. They would raise a din. Some of them would occupy the heights and roll down boulders from there. The idea was to scare the quarry into coming out of hiding. The animal would start running helter-skelter in panic.

The hunters would then bring out their bows (and, in later times, guns) and kill the prey.

Favoured game: The other sought after game were wild sheep such as the shâpû, the ranâ and the sanyân, and birds like the chakor, the Râm chakor and the water-fowl. The king and nobles of Skardu famously liked to hunt the chakor.

Polo

Polo, which was popular throughout Kashmir and Ladakh in mediæval times, survives as a living tradition in Ladakh. The Drâss polo team is the best in all of Kargil, probably because Drâss has for centuries been the polo capital of Kargil. The Baltis of Chushot (a village between Stok and Stakna in Leh district) and the people of Chiktan are the other champions.

Popular in Leh and Kargil and among the Muslims and Buddhists alike, polo probably came to Ladakh from Baltistân. One theory is that King Jamyang Namgyâl brought it to Leh in the fifteenth century. His wife was a Balti princess. The Baltis indeed are very good at polo.

However, this theory does not take into account that polo is very popular in Kargil, which is closer to Baltistân. It was the game of kings in mediæval Kashmir as well. Therefore, polo is more likely to have come from Kargil, and maybe even from Kashmir.

There are six players in a team, each player atop a horse. The game lasts an hour, with an intermission of ten minutes. Every time a team scores a goal, musicians stationed nearby break into a loud musical cheer. The two teams exchange goalposts after each goal.

Where was the game invented? The game is so old that it is difficult to say when it came to Leh and Kargil, and from where. A good guess is that it came from Baltistân, which is a part of undivided Ladakh. It has been in Ladakh at least since the first millennium AD.

Frederic Drew says that the game was invented in Anatolia (Rome). If he is right then the Baltis/ Dards must have gotten the game from there. What is certain is that the Aryan or Scythian Dards brought the game to Leh and Kargil.

In the Ladakhi language (including its Balti variant), the word 'polo' means 'ball.' It is almost certain that the name of this game is of Ladakhi origin. Therefore, there is every reason to suspect that the people of Ladakh probably invented the game itself. Within Ladakh there is unanimity that the Baltis were the first.

From Baltistân the game spread northwards into Central Asia, and south into Kashmir. Ali Shah Chak, the Sultan of Kashmir (1570-79) died while playing the game at Srinagar's Idgah. When he bent down to hit the ball, a sharp part of his saddle pierced his stomach. This shows how well established this game was in Kashmir by the 16th century. The Chaks were ethnic Dards. They, thus, belonged to the same stock as the people of Drâss and Dâ-Hânu. Dardistân is close to Baltistân. Many Dards have settled in Baltistân. Therefore, it is understandable that these Dardic rulers of Kashmir were fond of polo.

The folksongs of ancient Tibet have much to say about horse racing, but do not mention polo. The later folksongs of Guge (the part of Tibet that borders Ladakh) and Leh even tell us of the general principles according to which the game is played.

Pologrounds: The game was at its peak when Leh was ruled by the gyâlpos (kings). Pologrounds, called shagharan in Ladakhi, sprang up in many villages during that era. The most famous traditional shagharans of Ladakh are at Chiktan, Sot and Lambtas (all in Kargil), Skardu, Chhorbat and Khapalu (in Baltistân) and Leh town and Chushot (in Leh). A British writer has described Rondu and Gilgit, especially the former, as 'polo-mad.' After 1947, illegal squatters encroached upon the shagharan of Chiktan.

Ceremonies before the game: A few hours before all major matches Mon singers would collect at a designated spot near the royal palace, if it was in a capital city. (In the villages they would gather near the house of whoever was most powerful. This would be a Kalon, a lungpo, a vazîr-goyâ or a trâng-po. These, incidentally, are the titles of Ladakhi nobility.) The percussion and woodwind ensemble would then start playing Lhârnâ ('music for the gods'). This was the musicians' salute to the king/ village chief. It would also convey to the other people of the village that there would be a polo match later that day.

The players: Every able-bodied adult in the village who has a horse and knows how to play polo can join the team. This is possible because there are no limits on the size of the team.

'Rules': There are no rules in Ladakhi polo. That's what endears it to the boisterous audience. There are no chukkers and If the ball drops into the audience, the spectators can throw the ball back in, and thus temporarily be part of the game. A player, too, can pick up the ball and carry it with him to the goal. But the rival team can retrieve the ball from him through all means short of murder. Ends are changed after each goal. The game is played in two parts. A part is completed when one of the teams has scored nine goals.

In the 1980s the Kargil polo team started playing against the Army's team. The Army has the finest horses, and some of the finest riders and polo players, in India. India, in turn, has sometimes been the world champion in polo. The Army plays according to international rules. The Kargilis found that too staid and boring for their liking. Therefore, the Kargilis went back to playing only with fellow Ladakhis.

Horses—in commerce, songs and superstition: Horses are expensive everywhere, polo horses more so. The outside world invaded Ladakh in the 1960s with automobiles and other expensive consumer goods. Before that a horse would be a household's costliest possession.

No wonder horses loom large in the songs and literature of Ladakh. Poets would go into raptures while talking about their favourite horses. 'That horse is as strong as a lion, as swift as a shâpû [wild sheep], swims like a fish...' Each limb and muscle of the horse would be eulogised. So would his fancy saddles and bridles. (There are several songs about great riders, too: 'Fearless, with the right riding posture...')

The people of Ladakh prefer horses with manes that are blue, black, pale yellow and 'the colour of the nightingale.' Like the Tibetans (and central Indians) they consider some horses lucky, some jinxed and others in between. They believe that you can tell from the colour of a horse's mane and according to the colour of its body whether or not it will prove lucky for its owner.

An ancient Tibetan king wrote a very well informed book about horses, their types and how to purchase a good horse. The ancient Ladakhis lapped up this book and have used it over the centuries with great profit.

The game: The game is played in the late afternoon. The Mons are the first to reach the pologround. Their music announces to the whole village that the game is about to begin.

The ball is made of the wood of the willow.

Ree-sair: ritual trekking, mountain climbing and nature-worship

Ree-sair means 'a stroll in the hills.' A Kargili teenager described this festival, which takes place during the spring, as a picnic. I see it as 'ritual trekking,' 'ritual mountain-climbing' and 'ritual worship of nature.' The Ladakhis probably invented this festival to make sure that their youths got to climb at least one mountain every year. The idea is also to get used to living at high altitudes, even higher than the villages people live in. This is also a means to make people aware of the beauty of the nature around them—the hills, the streams, the waterfalls, the flowers...

Ladakh has no grass, flowers, waterfalls or streams during its dry, six-month winter. Therefore, in spring the people of Ladakh need rituals like this and festivals like Snolâ—to savour the few blades of grass that grow in that desert, and the few streams that flow through it.

Men, women, young girls and young boys form separate groups. Each group goes up to a peak of its choice and camps in that area for several days. They are lost to the world for that period. Ree-sair is also designed to give people a break from the stresses of everyday life.

In most parts of Ladakh these groups are arranged according to gender and age alone. In ancient times groups were mixed. Today co-ed groups are to be found only among the Dards of Darchiks and Garkun. Nowhere are the groups organised by religion, race or class. Thus, barriers are consciously broken down.

In the old days Mon musicians would acompany the groups. There would, thus, be singing and dancing at camps in the Buddhist areas. Shiite Muslims avoid light-hearted songs. Instead, they recite religious poetry, sing of Muslim saints and chant verses about Karbala (Iraq) and its martyrs.

Snolâ/ Minduk stanmo: The festival of flowers

Snolâ (pron. snow-laa) is the spring-festival of Ladakh. People travel great distances, often on foot, to be with their families, friends and relatives during this festival.

Origin: This is almost certainly a Dard festival, brought to Ladakh by the earliest Dard settlers. It used to be celebrated by all communities. Now it is mainly celebrated in Buddhist villages. Different communities celebrate it differently. In Kargil they call it Minduk Stanmo.

Kachu Sikander Khan writes that Snola resembles the Sheenu-Bozânoo spring festival of Gilgit. In Gilgit, apart from merrymaking, people use the occasion to pray for a good crop.

The day before the festival: The youths of the village, girls as well as boys, go to nearby hills to collect flowers (minduk) on sticks. They spend the night in the hills, feasting and celebrating.

Day one: The 'flower people' come down from the hills early the next morning. They sing and dance on the way. Their staffs, now laden with flowers, are called chhâk ching. There would be flowers in their hats, too. Whenever they pass through a field, they crush the crop with their shod feet. The Ladakhis believe that crops that have been trampled upon in springtime are more bounteous.

The people of the village, and their guests, gather in the village playground (changrâh) to receive the 'flower people.' After they reach the village, the 'flower people' sing songs that celebrate the spring, while the others provide the beat.

Typically, the songs go thus, 'The festival of flowers is so exciting, ah, the festival of flowers! Flowers are a-blossom in the meadows, ah, the festival of flowers! We've just crushed the crop in the field outside my uncle's house, ah, the festival of flowers!'

Day two: The Buddhists take the flower-sticks to the temple of the local god or goddess. A goat is slaughtered to please the deity. These customs are later, Buddhist or Mon, additions to the festival.

The highlight of the second day is a fair at which there is singing, dancing and, sometimes, polo.

Strublâ

Strublâ or Stroblâ means 'festival' or even 'fair.' All festivals are called Strublâ. However, the word also refers to a particular festival, which is held in September or October, when the crops have ripened. The festivity is spread over three or four days. Strublâ is the descendant of a Dard festival of Gilgit. It was originally called Gânoni.

The first place in present Ladâkh to adopt the festival was Darchiks-Garkun. From there the custom spread to other Dard areas such as Sot and Shakar-Chiktan (in Purîg/ Kargil) and Khaltse (in Leh).

The celebration of Strublâ was at its peak during the era of the Gyâpos (Buddhist kings), i.e. till the mid-nineteenth century. The rich and the poor alike got new clothes stitched for the occasion. The people celebrated the festival with enthusiasm because they believed that it brought peace and prosperity wherever it was observed. Despite having got itself a new name in Ladâkh, the festival is still celebrated in some of the areas mentioned. Bereft of royal patronage it has lost much of the pomp described in this section.

Before the festival is formally inaugurated, a group of teenaged girls go up to the Head (or Chief Guest) of the Festival and give him some flowers. At the conclusion of the festival, people give him butter. In the days when the local king was invariably the Head of the Festival, he would, in turn, host a feast for the people after the festival was over.

The festival began with polo, as it still does. However, till the twentieth century, every evening, after the day's polo was over, one of the participating villages would—in its turn—play host and invite the men and women of the neighbouring villages. The guests would assemble at the pologround to sing and dance.

Co-ed processions would saunter at a leisurely pace between the village, the *shagran* and back. Local music would be played on drums and woodwinds. Every day the Mons would go from house to house playing the *lhârnâ*, before and after the festivity. (This custom is similar to the *dhambâlî* festival of Kashmîr's Bîjbehârâ town.) Every householder would give the Mon minstrels some money, uncooked foodstuffs or other useful gifts.

People would host feasts at their homes and groups of people would do so at the venue of the festival. They would serve snacks, rather than complete meals. This particular tradition (like the music) continues to this day. The foods served include tea, local cheese, local bread, butter and foods made of barley.

Strublâ in its entire, pristine form, like many of the pastimes mentioned in this chapter, has started disappearing from Purîg (Kargil), the population of which is almost entirely Muslim. However, it has survived to an extent in Buddhist-majority villages like Mulbék, Wâkhâ and Darchiks-Garkun.

Sham is perhaps the only part of Ladâkh where Strublâ is still celebrated substantially in its original form.

Sâkâ

Sâkâ is a festival which is celebrated when the Rabi crop is sown, normally on the 21st February. This, too, was a Dard festival that later became popular all over Ladâkh. Ethnic Tibetans (which term includes Balti Muslims as well as the Buddhists of Leh) gave it a whole new twist and soaked it in their very own style of singing and dancing.

In Purîg there is a special song that is sung mainly during the Sâkâ festival. It talks about the migration of the ancient Dards to what is now Purîg/ Kargil. It also informs us that the Dards of present day Ladâkh had migrated from that part of Dardistân which is now known as Bunji. The song also consists of questions and answers and traces the history of the Dard race right back to the creation of the world and mankind.

The song begins with the question, 'O daughter, in the beginning what was the World of Humans [i.e. Planet Earth] established on?' The worldview of the Dards and Purgîs is spelt out in these songs.

These views were modified somewhat after Islâm came to the region.

Mâni or Mamâni

This Dard festival occurs on the 21st January and marks the end of the worst part of winter. Officially it is the anniversary of the founding of the Bâniyân tribe. However, over the years all of Ladâkh has come to adopt the festival. People spend the evening feasting with family and friends.

In Shakar-Chiktan boys *and girls* skate and play games on ice, wearing indigenous 'skates.' That girls in a predominantly Muslim area should take part (or would, till the mid-20th century, take part) in co-ed sports is significant.

32

Rock-engravings and carvings

All over Ladakh there are boulders with ancient or mediæval figures engraved on them. You will find these in the Drâss area, in the Suru valley, in Zâñskâr, on and near the Leh-Kargil National Highway, in the Dâ-Hânu area, in south-eastern Ladakh, in Nubra and even in Baltistan and other areas under Pakistani occupation. Ladakh is a huge region, bigger than many countries. And yet the themes depicted are normally the same: ibexes, goats, hunters with bows and arows, horse-riders, deer… Even the style varies only slightly.

However, within this narrow range of themes there is some variety. The horns of goats and the necks of ibexes vary. Some regions (especially Batâlik, Dâ, etc.) have line drawings of groups of people dancing arm in arm. One engraving (at Skinbrisa) shows a man with a long sword (lance?). Another (at Nor Nis) shows a camel, which is essentially an animal unknown in Ladakh. Nor Nis also has sketches of conical huts, again unusual for flat-roofed Ladakh.

Why are there so many ibexes in Ladakhi rock engravings? A.H. Dani writes that the local people believe that if a male ibex is drawn on a rock, this act leads to human pregnancy. Dr. Dani is a Pakistani archæologist who has worked in neighbouring Baltistan. He notes that ibex hunting is called *thuma saling* in much of this region. The hunt, too, gets refelcted in many of these rock-engravings.

Please consult the index for the precise places where such engraved rocks can be found.

How old are these engravings? Unless I have specified otherwise in a particular entry, the non- Buddhist engravings (i.e. ibexes and hunters) date to the Dard era, i.e. between pre-history and the eighth century AD. There is a possibility that the engravings at Nyurla might even be neolithic. If that is true, then there is the possibility that some of the other rock engravings, too, are as old as that. The rest could date to between the neolithic age and the early centuries of the Christian era. It is because of their antiquity that I have devoted considerable space in this book to rock engravings.

We also find Buddhist themes in rock-engravings. The oldest such engravings are of non-Tibetan origin: therefore, they must be Kashmiri or Gândhâr art. Finally, (e.g. near the Saspol bridge) there are Tibetan-Buddhist engravings.

Carving on stone is an art that survives to this day (see the entry on 'Stone work...' in the chapter on 'Handicrafts').

33

The language and literature of Ladakh

The language: Ladâkh does not have much of a high literature.[1] That, Kachu Sikander feels, is partly because Ladakhi is essentially a regional language derived from the Tibetan language, with inputs from the languages of the Dards, Mongols and Mons. However, Ladâkh has two great epics[2] and a very sophisticated treasury of folksongs. Ladâkhi is an Aryo-Tibetan language, which has been influenced somewhat by the Kashmîrî and Sheena languages. In turn it has influenced the languages of Kashmir and Kishtwâr[3].

The base of the language, its sentence structure and the bulk of its vocabulary are Tibetan. Pronunciation, accent and even folksongs, on the other hand, are Indo-Aryan.

Script: The Ladakhi-Tibetan (Bodhi) script is very close to Devanagri (the script of North India and Nepal) and Bengali. The alphabet uses a grid identical to the *varg* system of Devanagri (*k, ch, t, T* and *p*). The letters look similar to their Hindi, Bengali and Assamese counterparts.

Of all the languages available to the Ladakhis, Tibetan alone had all the sounds used by them. Therefore, the Tibetan script was adopted. For the same reason, the Tibetan system of education became the Ladakhi system. It suited local needs the best.

Tibetophilia: This Aryo-Tibetan fusion enabled the Dards and Mons to adopt the language, and even the cultural heritage, of the Tibetans. A cultural interchange took place and a composite culture evolved.

Every generation of the Buddhists of Ladâkh needs to learn the Tibetan language afresh in order to be able to read their common scriptures.

1. For that matter nor did most Indian languages till the 19th century (apart from the epics), even though these languages are spoken by several times as many people.
2. '*Gyâlam Késar*' and 'Norbu Zâñgpo' (The latter has been translated into English by Parvez Diwan).
3. For instance, the people of Kishtwâr use the word 'zampa' for a particular kind of bridge. This is a Ladakhi word.

In the process they had developed a taste for Tibetan literature, too. This continued till the 14th or 15th century, when Islam became an important religion in Ladâkh.

The influence of Islam: Purig, Baltistan and parts of Leh converted to Islam. They turned their attention from Tibet to Iran and the Arab world. Now the epics, poetry, names, customs, beliefs, folk heroes and saints of the Middle East became those of the newly Islamised areas. Happily, though, they adopted Middle Eastern heroes (say, Yusuf- Zuleikha) without giving up Tibetan ones (e.g. Gyalam Kesar, Darpon and Api-so).

Balti poets began to write *hamds* (poems in praise of God), *naats* (songs in praise of Prophet Muhammad, peace be on him) and *sanaas*, all mostly in the Persian style. However, the language that they wrote in was Balti, a Tibetan language.

34

The Handicrafts of Ladakh

Leh and Zâñskâr

The Ladakhis make crafts for themselves, and not to sell in the marketplace. So, many of the handicrafts mentioned below are not easily found in shops. Leh town is different, though. It has got used to tourists. Therefore, some shops try to stock the local crafts.

On the other hand, some crafts, such as dragon carpets and thankhas, are made by Tibetan refugees specifically to sell in the market.

Baskets

Baskets made from the *chipkiang* reed are used by rural folk. This reed grows along the Indus.

Carpets, dragon-

The Ladakhis, like most South Asians, sit on the floor while dining or simply relaxing in the living room. In much of North India and Pakistan these floors are carpeted. In Ladakh, as in Tibet, the carpets are small (around 3' x 6', just big enough for a medium sized man to lie on), made of pure wool and have brightly coloured pictures of dragons woven on them. Several such carpets are placed on the floor along the walls of the room, i.e. in a rectangle, for people to sit on. (The centre of the room is either left bare or will have an inexpensive rug, normally non-Ladakhi.)

The Tibetan refugees of Choglamsar make the best dragon carpets in Ladakh.

Other designs: Buddhist deities, the snow-lion, chrysanthemums and lotuses are the other figures depicted in Ladakhi carpets. Often there are geometrical patterns on the borders.

Other kinds of floor coverings: The Tsukdan is a speciality of Chang Thâñg. Such carpets are made of the hair of yâks.

Copper and brass

Copper and brass are the metals most commonly used in Ladakhi handicrafts. Zâñskâr possibly derives its name from these metals. The word probably means 'white copper' or brass. Therefore, fittingly, Ladakh's best metalwork is done in Zâñskâr, in Chiling village in particular.

Objects used in worship, as well as fancy kettles and pots, are made of these two metals. Often medallions made of silver are affixed on them. Equally often, the main body of the craft might be made of copper or brass, but a few parts would be of silver. Pots in which *chhang* (beer) is served, as well as the cups that chhang is drunk from, bowls, ladles and teapots are among the metal utensils made in Ladakh.

Goncha

All Ladakhis and Tibetans, young or old, male or female, wear a double-breasted, calf-length gown throughout the year. A wide cloth belt ensures that the gown is tightly wrapped around the body. Brass buttons on the right side fasten the front flap on the fold beneath it. Traditionally the Buddhists used to wear a burnt red gown made of strips of local, home-made tweed, and the Shia Muslims of Kargil black. Since the 1980s things have been changing. The thick and rough local tweed has given way to 'finer' cloth made by mills in the Indian plains. Materials used range from worsted to synthetic fabrics. Women's gowns in fashion-conscious Leh have since come in all possible colours. Summer gowns have become been lighter than the *gonchas* worn in winter. Rich women wear gowns made of velvet on formal occasions. Women's gowns sometimes have a hoop below the belt.

The position of the belt varies from region to region. It is worn above the waist in Chiktan. The people of Leh tie it around the waist. In Sham/ Khaltse they wear it below the waist.

Jewellery

The perak is, of course, Ladakh's best known ornament. This is the elaborate, gem-studded hat-cum-cape worn by Ladakhi women. Not only are crude, uncut, precious stones affixed to the leather base, often so are beautifully designed little silver boxes. That apart Leh and Zâñskâr have little jewellery of their own. The little that there is is made and sold in the side-lanes that branch off the main market of Leh town.

Metalwork

Items made of iron might not appeal to the casual tourist, but they are much valued by Ladakhis. The locks and keys of Leh and Kargil are masterpieces of engineering, as well as being very good to look at. Neither looks or works anything like the conventional locks of the rest of India. Instead, the keys have holes and slots that open different levers. Together the lock and key are called *kulik*.

Iron stoves, too, can be very elegant, with artistic designs. Blacksmiths are called *gaaraa*s in Ladakhi. They also make conch-bangles and tools for agriculture.

Papiér Mâchè

The Ladakhis use papiér mâchè masks during religious celebrations at gompas (monasteries). These masks have the faces of demons as well as benign deities, and are used to portray particular characters in the dance-dramas performed at monastic festivals. The masks are made of mashed paper and come in bright colours. However, in terms of style and artistry, they are nothing like the delicately decorated, understated papiér mâchè of Kashmir.

Pappu shoes

(Also spelt and pronounced 'pabbu.') Local shoes are woven from a fibre and are not made of leather. They wear hard and offer protection from Ladakh's extreme cold and the snows of Zâñskâr. Kalpana Manglik points out that they are 'made out of hessian cloth, used wool felt, coarse hair of the yâk and goat, woollen tweed and leather for the sole.' Normally these shoes are made by members of the family for their own use and that of other members. They are normally not sold in shops.

Perâk

Pron. peraak. This is not a handicraft that you can purchase either. It is the head-dress of well to do women. The base is made of a tough, thick, long strip of leather dyed blue, wide and long enough to cover the hair, including the long plait. There are flaps to protect the ears from the cold. Over the generations, one by one, precious stones and silver jewellery are affixed on this blue base. Some gold, too, is used.

Peraks are, thus, not made in a week or a month. Each perak continues to grow over the decades—indeed, centuries, if any space is left on the leather base for even more gems.

Women wear them on festive occasions. By the time most women get to inherit their mother/ grandmother's peraak they would be middle aged or older. In rich families even young women have peraks all to themselves. The average perak costs Rs.1,00,000 (at 2004 prices, when turquoise prices were lower than in preceding years).

To untrained eyes all peraaks look similar. However, they change with the region. For instance, in Mulbek (Kargil) they have a small pill-box hat at the top. Most peraaks are long strips. However, some are shorter. Some have caps affixed atop the head. In other peraks the cap is above the back of the head. Yet others have no cap at all. Some peraaks have cobra hoods. Others have wing-like flaps behind the ears.

Male head-dresses, too, vary from region to region. In fact, throughout the Ladakh-Balawaristan region you can easily tell where a man is from by his hat.

Pottery

Earthenware made in Ladakh includes bowls, braziers, jugs, kettles and the *zoma* (the vessel in which *chhang* is stored). Water and curds are stored in clay pots. Some people still cook food in earthen pots. Likir is one village where pottery is made.

Stone-work and sculpture

Everywhere that you travel in the Buddhist parts of Ladakh (Leh, Zâñskâr and some other villages of east Kargil) you will find *maaney* walls. These are made up of slabs of stone on which the words 'Om maaney Padmey hum' have been carved, in intaglio, in elegant Bodhi letters. Such elegant calligraphy-on-stone is normally done on order. At least one calligrapher is normally attached to every major gompa, especially to gompas near villages with a large Buddhist population.

Lâmâ Stag tsang ras chen is said to have invented the mâné (maaney) wall. At the very least he brought this concept to Ladâkh. Stag tsang ras chen was one of the most eminent monks and authors of his time.[1] King Señggé Namgyâl (16th/17th century) had invited him to Ladâkh, presumably from Tibet. Francke wrote in 1907 that he had not seen a single mâné wall that dated to before Señggé's time.

Precious stones, turquoise in particular, are needed for the *perak* head-dress. They are also carved into cups and curios.

Thukmus, a village near Siksa in Nubra, specialises in making chhang pots, frying pans, griddles and lamps out of stone. As the Dastakari Haat Samiti points out, 'Cooking at extremely high altitudes is a lengthy process.' For instance, *rajma,* the red bean so popular in Jammu, takes almost two and a half hours to cook in a pressure cooker in Zâñskâr, and much longer in a normal pot. (In Jammu, on the other hand, it takes just around thirty minutes in a pressure cooker.) In at least one case in the 1970s, during the long process of cooking the pressure inside the cooker became so intense that its lid blew off and sliced away the head of the person for whom the food was being cooked. The cooking pots of

1. A Famous Travelogue, *a Journey to Shamba La,* is attributed to him.

Thukmus have heavy stone lids that do not fly off. These lids also exert the necessary pressure on the food to compensate for the low atmospheric pressure outside.

Tables, low and carved

(*Choktse* or *chogtse*) Most Asians sit cross-legged on the floor during meals. When food is served in most parts of South Asia, dishes and utensils are placed on a carpet, sheet or banana leaf spread on the floor. In Ladakh and Tibet (and parts of East Asia) dishes are placed on low wooden tables. Often there are dragons carved on the sides and top of these rectangular tables. These tables are placed on the above mentioned dragon carpets, one carpet and one table per person. During the rest of the day these brilliantly coloured tables double as desks and books and pens are placed on them. These tables are about two or two and a half feet long and about 15 inches high.

Than(g)kha

(Also spelt thankha, tangkha, tankha and tanka.) These are mostly cloth—normally silk or brocade—scrolls with Buddhist religious paintings on them. Sometimes thankhas are made of paper. The household thankha is usually a long rectangle the size of a large rock-star poster or small window. There could be wooden or brass rollers at the top and bottom, especially if the thankha is made of cloth.

You can get domestic thankhas on Delhi's Janpath and Srinagar's Boulevard. Other thankhas are big enough to cover the façade of a three-storey building. The bigger thankhas are the property of the major gompas (monasteries). The Hemis gompâ displays its famous thankha only once in twelve years.

Both kinds of thankhas have very colourful Buddhist religious pictures painted and/ or embroidered on them. Thankhas often depict tantric themes, Lord Buddha, his disciples, animals and 'the elements' (e.g. water, fire). As elsewhere in India, the colours used are extracted from minerals and plants.

Thankhas are painted (and sold) at various places in the district. Choglamsar has a major training centre for would-be artists.

Tweed

Till the 1960s, *all* families, rich as well as poor, would have a loom at home on which they would weave thick, rough tweed (*pattoo*) for the family. Each household wove its own tweed and made pappu shoes, there being no shops which (or craftsmen who) sold anything. The tweed is later dyed red.

So, every household had to be self-sufficient in everything. They had to make their own milk and butter, bricks if they wanted to add or repair a room, clothes, shoes, everything. The only things that craftsmen made for others were goods made of metal and wood. And music. Families were not expected to make their own music. These artisans belonged to the *lak-shes* (łak= hand; shes= worker) caste which, unfortunately, as in the rest of India, is placed at the bottom of society.

In places like Zâñskâr and the remoter villages of Leh, people still make their own tweed. The women spin the yarn while men weave the cloth. The middle-classes of Leh and Kargil towns have taken to purchasing cloth made by the mills of Mahârashtra and Gujarat, not just woollen cloth but also (blasphemy) synthetics.

Woodwork

The Ladakhis also make items of furniture other than the '*Choktse* tables' mentioned above. These items are based on principles similar to the *choktse* tables. The wood is painted in bright colours, mainly yellow, red, blue and green. Sometimes patterns are carved on the wood, in relief (i.e. raised figures). Dragons and demon-faces are popular motifs.

Colourful cupboards made in this manner, often with glass panes, are a traditional item, though the panes are a 20th century addition. Larger tables and bowls, too, are made of wood. Almost all gompas, and some private residences, have traditional bookshelves, with a separate shelf for each wood-bound book. These shelves could be made to order, though their design would need to be modified if modern, Western-style books are to be kept in them.

Kargil

Jewellery

Balti women wear jewellery that is heavy and complex. Silver is predominantly used. Elsewhere in the district, especially in Suru Valley, jewellery is very cheerful, Central Asian and subtle. Materials used include agate, corals, carnelians, pearls and turquoise.

Amulets and charm boxes with intricate patterns are some of the other specialities of Kargil's jewellers. Women often make crude necklaces at home.

Shawls, pashmina

There is a government-run handicrafts centre where inexpensive pashmina shawls are made, and sold. They are not as fine as their Kashmiri (or even Basohli) counterparts. But they are also the least expensive of the three varieties.

Rugs

The Tsuk tul can also be used as a rug or blanket. Therefore, it is made of soft wool. Like gonchas (see above), which are made of strips of tweed sewn together, Tsuk tuls are made of a number of 9" strips. These strips are placed side by side, lengthways, each stitched to the next one.

Wickerwork and willow-basketry

Willow (*malchang*) is one of the few trees that grow naturally in Ladakh. Willow baskets are inexpensive, made at several places in Ladakh and commonly used.

People

35

Ladakh: Rapid rise in population

In 1911, the population of Ladakh as a whole was 67,994. This went up in the next decade to 68,886, an increase of 1.3%. Even in 1931, the population was only 72,181, which meant that it had gone up by 4.8% in *ten* years. Higher than before, but still very low by international (leave alone South Asian) standards. In the next census (1941) the population was 76,030 and the increase 5.3%. The graph was rising. In 1951, it had risen to 82,340 and 8.29%, a huge increase by Ladakh's own standards, but low in absolute terms.

From well-below to way above the national average

Leh is one of India's smallest districts in terms of population. It also has one of the lowest population densities in the world—with around two people to a square kilometre. All right, 2.44 people. Over the centuries the population of the district did not grow much, because of a series of social arrangements that ensured this. They had to, because this arctic desert has very little cultivable land. The system under which one of the sons would become a *lâmâ* (monk)- and sometimes one of the daughters a *chomo* (nun)- was part of these arrangements. So was polyandry.

Between 1951 and 1961, the population of Leh (then a tehsil of Ladakh district) grew by a mere 9.2 percent, from 39,947 to 43,585. Its population thus grow at a rate that was less than *half* the national average. In 1971, the population was 51,891, i.e. an increase of 19%: dangerously close to, but still less than, the all - India growth rate. Modernisation and the breakdown of the old social arrangements had clearly swung into action.

The 1981 figures were even more dramatic: the population was 68,380, which meant an increase of 31.7% over the previous decade or almost *one and a half times* the national average. In 1991, it jumped further to an estimated 92,000—a leap of 34.6%, a little less than twice the national average and way ahead even of the increase in neighbouring

Muslim-majority Kargil. By 2001, it had increased to 1,07,777, an increase of 17.14%. (Or between 1981 and 2001 the population had increased by 57.61%.)

By way of comparison, in the decade between 1971 and 1981, India's population grew at 2.2% a year. The nation's growth rate fell to 2.1% a year in the decade between 1981 and 1991. There are indications that in the 1990s it fell further to 1.9% a year.

The situation in Leh is not alarming. Ladakh is still the country's—perhaps the world's—most sparsely populated region. However, in recent decades, because of social change Leh is being transformed, and more rapidly than elsewhere. Leh has perhaps just 4,393 hectares of 'cultivable vast land' where grains, vegetables or trees have been planted. It has another 25,274 hectares of 'barren cultivable land'.

Improved technology can accommodate growing populations. Since the 1970s Leh has been going through an economic boom, what with all the money provided in by the government (the highest in per capita terms for any region in India), tourism and the army. Affluence has percolated to the bottom. You have to pay unskilled labour much higher than the wage laid down by the Government of India for the nation. (In 1982, the minimum wage in Ladakh was three times the national average.) The labour that constructs roads in Ladakh comes from Central India. The Ladakhis are, thanks to this boom, too well off to work as unskilled labour.

However, the wisdom received through the ages in Ladakh has been that the land can only support so many people and no more.

(Population figures for the undivided Ladakh district: In 1951, the population was 82,340; in 1961, it was 88,651. This meant that Kargil-which is perhaps 88% Muslim- grew at a mere 6.3% in a decade when Leh's population increased by 9.2%. In 1971, the population of Ladakh as a whole was 105,201.)

***Kargil* district:** Compared to Leh, Kargil is overcrowded. It has all of nine people per square kilometre.

In 1951, the population of the areas now in Kargil district was 42,393. By 1961, this increased by 6.3% to 45,066. This growth was lower than that in Leh by a third, and way below the all India average. However, during the next decade there was an 18.3% jump to a 1971 population of 53,310.

Clearly something, some custom or control, which had kept the population in check over the centuries, had suddenly disappeared. However, the growth rate was still well below the national average, and marginally less than that in Leh. In 1981, the population grew to 65,992: this time there was an even steeper increase of 23.8%. Now arid Kargil's growth was dangerously close to India's shameful average, but way below Leh's 31.7%.

It is *estimated* that in 1991 Kargil's population was 81,067, an increase of 22.84% in a decade, close to the national level, much below Leh's 34.6%, but still too high by any standards, especially Ladakh's own tradition. By 2001, Kargil's population had swelled to 1,14,821—an alarming 41.63% increase. (All right, the 1991 figure is only an estimate. So the increase in 1991 might have been higher than 22.84% and therefore the increase in 2001, was less than 41.63%. Still, between 1981 and 2001, the increase was an extremely worrisome 73.99%.)

Urbanisation

One significant change that has taken place is that the rural: urban ratio suddenly changed in the 1971 and 1981 censuses. Let's leave the 1911 and 1921 censuses, because all over India they showed atypical results. Between 1931 and 1961, just under 96% of all Ladakhis were rural and the ratio 22:1. In 1971, the figures changed to 92% and 12:1. By 1981, the urban population had risen to 9.11% of the total and the ratio had fallen to 10:1, which was less than half the traditional figure.

Permanently Single

Almost half of all Ladakhis (51.7% in 1981) had 'never married'. Or so the census revealed. The figure is higher in predominantly Buddhist Leh (53.38%), understandable because of the system of monks and nuns. However, even in mostly Muslim Kargil the percentage is as high as 48.86%, which really needs to be investigated.

And investigate I did, though with a small sample. I studied Ladakh as a whole, and used 1981 figures. Firstly, the census department seems to have included children in these obviously ridiculous figures. Happily, *none* of the children in the 0-9 age group was married. Between 10 and 14 years about 0.76% of the boys and around 0.88% of the girls were. Since the figures indicated that it was not unusual for Ladakhis to marry even in their late thirties, I took two samples—the 40- 44 age group and those between 45 and 49 years old. In the first group 9.7% of the men and 6.24% of the women had 'never married'. The figures for the second group were 10.24% and 5.6% respectively. Now, that is closer to the truth than saying that more than half of all Ladakhis had never married.

In both districts the proportion of permanently single men is slightly higher than of similarly placed women. The reason is obvious: in both districts, as in all of India except Kerala and except among the Christians, men outnumber women. Again, as the South Asian trend has led us to expect, the position is bad in Buddhist-majority Leh (870 women for every 1000 men) but in Muslim-majority Kargil it is worse (853: 1000).

Divorce

Divorce is low but it exists. Interestingly, in Buddhist-majority Leh 0.69% of the population (which includes, I am convinced, children of age five) is divorced or separated. In Muslim-majority Kargil the figure is *lower*, even if marginally (0.63%). Among the Buddhists divorce used to be (and in the rural areas, unofficially, still is) granted by a council of village elders (and officially by the civil courts). Among the Muslims of Zâñskâr there are some cases of 'trial marriage'. If the marriage doesn't work out, the child born during the 'trial' will be assumed to be the child of whoever its mother finally marries. Divorce among Muslims follows the same procedures as elsewhere in India.

However, in Zâñskâr even women (Muslim) can divorce their husbands under the *khola* system. (Islam allows women to *seek* a divorce, called khola, for one of a few specified reasons such as adultery by the husband or his impotence. In Zâñskâr Muslim women divorce their husbands under customary law much in the same manner as Muslim men do elsewhere in South Asia.)

Linguistic groups

Some 56% of the people of Ladakh speak Ladakhi, including the Sham, Leh and Rong dialects, and 37% speak Balti, which isn't all that different, and is spoken in most of Kargil. ('Dragon', for instance, is druk in Leh, Bruk in Kargil and duk in Zâñskâr.) Another 4% speak Tibetan and 'Buddhi' (Bodhi?) and 1% Brokpâ and Kashmiri.

Low death rate

Leh has one of the lowest death rates in the country—1.5 for every 1,000 persons, vs. a national average of 6.1 per 1000, both in the year 2001. (*Kashmir Times,* 11 July 2004.)

36

The fabled longevity of the Hunzâkuts

Is the fabled longevity of the Hunzâkuts for real?

'What makes the Hunzâkuts[1] live so long?' the rest of the world is dying to know. 'Is it the food that they eat? Or is it their water?'

Scamsters in the West have made millions peddling 'Hunzâ Pie' and 'Hunzâ bread,' the latter as a miraculous way to lose weight. Neither has anything to do with Hunzâ. Indeed, the Hunzâkuts don't make pies of any sort, and their 'bread' is nothing like Western bread.

John Borthwick[i] represents the revisionist extreme. He believes that the whole thing is a myth concocted by commercial interests. He writes, 'During the 1960s and 70s, the people of Hunzâ briefly became famous in the West for supposedly living to over 100 years of age, sustained by pure, 2,400 metre air and (it was said) an equally pure vegetarian diet. Recent research reveals no particular longevity (in fact, there's evidence of inbreeding). It seems that the myth of spinach-powered centenarians was concocted, as it were, by the author of a Swiss vegetarian cookbook.'

This set me off on a trail of investigation. The first question that I asked myself was, 'Is the 'myth' only as old as the 1960s?' I had grown up with the belief that the Hunzâkuts lived the longest in the world. Though Pâkistân now occupies Hunzâ, we in India have very strong bonds of affection for the Hunzâkuts. As schoolchildren we were proud of the fact the distinction of being the longest lived people in the world belonged to our brothers and sisters in Hunzâ. Because we grew up in the '60s and '70s, as far as we were concerned this belief had always been there.

But in view of Borthwick's statement I had to check.

1. The word 'Hunzâkuts' is a singular as well as a plural: like kudos.

Indeed, the British Gazetteers don't mention the Hunzâkuts' longevity at all[2]. The Internet is at the other extreme. There are tens of thousands of references to it.

I have been able to find two references that date to a few years before the Swiss cookbook. Mrs. Barbara Hilda Mons' classic 1958 account, *The High Road to Hunzâ* contains a remark that implies that this belief was widespread even then. She writes, 'That they are abnormally long-lived is impossible to prove, for the simple reason that no record is kept of the date of a child's birth. They do not know how old they are.'

Now this is a problem with Muslims and Hiñdûs throughout the Indian sub-continent. The illiterate ones do not know how old they are. The Buddhists of Ladâkh are different. Like the Chinese, they have 12-year cycles, each year being named after an animal. So they know how many cycles ago they were born, and in the year of which animal.

But what is evident from Mrs. Mons' remark is that even before the Swiss cookbook it was believed that the Hunzâkuts were 'abnormally long-lived.' In the same vein she wrote, 'The Wazir, Inayat Ullah Beg, though his age had been given to us as anything up to ninety-four, with his virile looks it seemed impossible that he could be over seventy.' This, too, indicates that Hunzâ's reputation for long-lived people precedes the Swiss cookbook. It also gives substance to Mrs. Mons' explanation that the fault lay with how the Hunzâkuts kept track of their age. (An affluent and highly-educated Wazir's parents were likely to maintain an absolutely accurate record of the date his birth, as his descendants would of the date of his death.)

Hunzâ's reputation as a Shangri La-like[3] paradise, too, predates some real or imaginary vegetarian cookbook. Much before Hilton's novel there was a legend according to which the Garden of Eden was located in one of the valleys of the Hiñdû Kush. In the 1950s, shortly after Mrs. Mons

2. As must be obvious from this series of books, I have enormous respect for the British Gazetteers as far as the other parts of the state are concerned. But when it comes to Gilgit-Baltistân-Hunzâ-Chitrâl, the British Gazetteers seem to concentrate almost entirely on forts and how well fortified these forts are-whether their walls can withstand a determined attack and what angles they can be attacked from.

3. I have used the formulation 'Shangri La-like,' because there are many other claimants to being the inspiration for James Hilton's *Far Horizons* (1933). This work of fiction was set in a kingdom in the mountains where everyone was happy, healthy and lived long. The protagonists of Mustang, Bhutan and Zhongdian (China) all insist that the novel's fictitious Shangri La was based on their valley.

left, an American team went to Hunzâ to make a Cinerama[4] film about Hunzâ, *In Search of Paradise.*

Personally, I find nothing surprising about the Hunzâkuts living for a century or more. I have worked extensively with nomadic Gujjars in Kashmîr and Jammu, and hope to write a book about their lifestyle. They lead very healthy lives and routinely live to be eighty or ninety—the same as or better than Japan and Sweden, the two longest living countries in the world. The Gujjars, too, are mainly vegetarians and lead tension-free lives. Most of old Ladâkh and Kashmîr was free of serious crime. So was Hunzâ. Add Hunzâ's incredible water and the average life span goes up by another decade or two.

The Hunzâ water theory

'There are five places[5] on Earth where the people routinely live to over 120 years of age in good health with virtually no cancer, heart attacks, dental caries (decay of a bone or tooth) or other major diseases common to modern society. [In these five places] they remain robust and strong and are also able to bear children in old age. The most famous of these, Hunzâ in the Himalayas, has people who live to be 120-140 years old,' the websites www.cybertown.com and www.flantech.com note[ii].

Scientists working in rural France found some villages where people were healthy and others where they were not. Research suggested that the difference lay in the local water.[iii]

Dr. Henri Coanda, a Romanian, discovered fluid dynamics and held more than 600 patents. This much is verifiable fact.

It is said that Coanda spent six decades analysing the water of Hunzâ. He wanted to know what it was about this water that kept the Hunzâkuts so healthy. He found anomalous properties in the water. Its freezing and boiling points, viscosity and surface tension were different from ordinary water.

On his 78th birthday[iv] he met the then 17-year old Patrick Flanagan.[6] A few days later he handed over all his records to Dr. Flanagan. Patrick (and his wife Gael) spent another thirty years analysing the Hunzâ water sample. They used a 40-year-old sample of Hunzâ water (presumably

4. Cinerama was an early giant-screen ancestor of today's Imax. Each of three projectors would simultaneously cast a third of the image on the screen. The three portions would together form a gigantic single image. However, co-ordinating three images was a cumbersome affair. Therefore, this technology never caught on, even though some of the most expensive Hollywood films of the 1950s and '60s were screened in this format at selected theatres the world over.
5. These include Vilcabambia in Equador in Latin America.
6. *Life* magazine had apparently included Patrick Flanagan among the ten most promising scientists of America.

bequeathed them by the good Dr. Coanda) because Hunzâ is no longer as unpolluted as it once was.

Till then it was believed that the magic of Hunzâ's glacial water lay in the minerals that it contained. The Flanagans did not rule out the role of the minerals. However, they made a stunning revelation. The structure of Hunzâ's water was very different from ordinary water. Hunzâ water's molecule formed into clusters, they said.

Hydrogen is the world's best antioxidant. This is because it has just one electron.[7] Dr. Flanagan discovered that Hunzâ water contained large quantities of negatively charged hydrogen ions.

The Flanagans then invented slice-based Flanagan Microclusters in which they reproduced the properties of Hunzâ water. However, this artificial water was quite unstable. If it was shaken or stirred, it lost its health-giving qualities. The 40-year-old sample of Hunzâ water, on the other hand, lost none of its properties when shaken.

What made Hunzâ so stable? Tiny spherical minerals, only 5 nanometres in diameter, did. These minerals are called nano-colloids and have enormous electrical energy. They react with the hydrogen and oxygen molecules of Hunzâ water. Microscopic crystals are produced in the process. These crystals have a structure much like that of the fluid around and the protein inside the cells of our bodies. Every time we drink normal water our system tries to change the structure of this ordinary water to that which Hunzâ water has.

Why does the body have to change the structure of normal water? That's because only water with a surface tension of 45 dynes per centimetre can really enter and hydrate the cells of our body. Now, normal water has a surface tension of 73 dynes per centimetre. Therefore, it needs to be broken down. Hunzâ water already has what it takes.

This, according to the websites and articles that I have consulted, gives Hunzâ water that extra edge.

If the cells of our bodies get dehydrated, if they don't get all the water that they need, they start dying. They start eating each other in order to survive. That's when the immune system breaks down. Ageing begins. The body becomes more prone to disease.

Apparently, Hunzâ water makes sure that our cells get the right kind of 'hydration', and effortlessly.

Could the Hunzâ water theory be a hoax?

Henri Coanda was one of the greatest scientists that Romania has produced. According to several 'Hunzâ water'-related websites he won

7. It thus neutralises free radicals.

the Nobel prize. However, there is no such person in the Nobel Prize Internet Archive. Besides, none of this great scientist's standard biographies—and I have consulted three—mentions a Nobel Prize or any connection with Hunzâ.

So, could the whole thing be an elaborate Internet hoax? I wonder. The Nobel Prize part is certainly untrue. But too many websites mention his connections with Hunzâ, Flanagan and water.

One website that mentions Coanda in the same breath as Hunzâ is www.biophysica.com. It says, 'Dr Coanda realised that the secret [of the Hunzâkuts' longevity] lay in the unique water of these mountainous glacial regions and in the 1930's he visited some of these including Hunzâ... What he and later Patrick [Flanagan] discovered was that the whitish Hunzâ water (milk of the mountains) contained minerals in elemental pulverised form called a colloidal suspension with high concentrations of Silica and Silver. The minerals were not in the ionised salt form, presumably because the salt form would have been dissolved away long before. The powder particles were electrically charged and of submicron size, some as small as 1-5 nanometres.'

The work of Coanda and Flanagan is referred to on a few hundred websites—104 about the great Coanda and 345 about his protégé, the then 17-year-old prodigy Flanagan. Could all of them be part of an elaborate Geneva-Sicily plot to promote a Swiss cookbook? Certainly not. But at least some of these websites are backed by the Flanagans. And the Flanagans are not a disinterested party. They have a product, Flanagan's Hunzâ Water, which claims to reproduce some of the qualities of the water that flows naturally in Hunzâ's springs.

Vegetarian diet

The Hunzâ diet consists of a lot of almonds, apples, cherries and apricots. The Hunzâkuts, like the Gujjars, are not strict vegetarians (unlike the Jains and some Hiñdû communities, which are). The Hunzâkuts eat meat, but only rarely.

References

i. A slice of Hunzâ High, a website
ii. I have combined the broadly similar observations of the two websites into one quote.
iii. www.cybertown.com
iv. Or so we are informed by www.silica-hydride.com, a website that features an article by Patrick Flanagan, MD. (MA)& Gael Crystal Flanagan, MD. (MA).

37

Hunzâkuts Society

'Ever since I first saw it in 1937, I have thought of the Hunzâ Valley as the ultimate manifestation of mountain grandeur...It is difficult to describe this fantastic principality without indulging in superlatives. Both to look at and in character the people are worthy of the unique setting.'

Eric Shipton

The world view of the Hunzâkuts

Why is there a pot of gold at the end of every rainbow? Because there is this supernatural being who lives inside each rainbow. He drinks water from a golden bowl, which he leaves behind where the rainbow ends.

And why do earthquakes occur? Because the earth rests on the horns of a bull. If one of the horns gets tired, the bull moves the earth to the other horn. The earth trembles during the switchover.

Being Muslims, the Hunzâkuts' view of the world is substantially Islâmic. However, it has a heavy overlay of Hiñdûism, either obtained directly or through Buddhism. For instance, the world is called *duniyâ* and the universe *qâyénât*. Both are Perso-Arabic concepts. But supernatural beings, on the other hand, are known by the Hiñdû name *déu*[1].

And the belief about the crock of gold is very European, possibly Greek. Similarly, the story about earthquakes is closer to that of Atlas than Islâm. Yet, many Hunzâkut beliefs are uniquely their own.

They believe that supernatural people live beneath the surface of the earth. The Hiñdûs and Buddhists believe in such a *pâtâl*. So did the Greeks, who called it Hades.

1. Even in the Valley of Kashmîr déus occur in private conversation and in the hagiographies of Muslim saints.

The Muslims (and Christians like Dante) believe in the many heavens or skies. So do the Hunzâkuts. However, they add that curtains separate these worlds. Therefore, it is not possible to see between them.

Traditional Hunzâkuts are flat-earthers. Their views on creation have obviously been influenced by Judeo-Christian-Islâmic beliefs. God, thus, is *Khudâ* (a Persian Islâmic word). The story of Adam, Eve and Satan is much the same in Hunzâ, with minor modifications.

Religion: The Ismâili sect of Muslims predominates in Hunzâ. This sect owes allegiance to the Âgâ (or Âghâ) Khân. Everywhere you will find pictures of His Highness or Holiness (as the Âgâ Khân is known): including on necklace pendants worn by people. (The Ismâilis are locally known as Mughlî Shiâs-'Mughal Shiites'.)

In turn the Âgâ Khân Foundation has opened a number of schools (including, in 1987, an Academy for girls) and hospitals. As a result, literacy (especially female literacy) in Hunzâ is higher than in the other 'Northern Areas.' Indeed, higher even than in the plains of Pâkistân. All western travellers notice that women are given more respect in Hunzâ than elsewhere in the 'Northern Areas' or in Pâkistân. Mango Grove, a website, remarks, '[E]ven in Gilgit... the only women in the bazaars were Hunzâ women, having [travelled] to [the Gilgit] market via bus for the day. Everywhere we went, women were evident and friendly, evidence of the higher freedom and status given them in Hunzâ society.'

The women do not wear the veil either.

Despite being Muslims, the men of Hunzâ have traditionally been making and drinking wine. However, modern, conservative interpretations of Islâm, which have come in from Pâkistân, are slowly putting an end to this practice.

Language: Burushaski is the language of Hunzâ. As in the rest of Jammu and Kashmîr, Urdû is the official language and English the language of the elite. The Burusho people live mainly in central Hunzâ and have always tried to establish villages only where apricots, which are their favourite food, grow. They tend to avoid arid areas.

There are several Hindûstânî words in the vocabulary of the Hunzâkuts. The queen is called Rânî and water is called *pânî* (the headier kind certainly is).

Shînâ and Wakhi are spoken in parts of Hunzâ. The people of north Hunzâ, above Gulmit, mostly speak Wakhi, an Iranian language. The Wakhis of Hunzâ migrated here from Afghânistân. Their population is extremely small. Ethnically, they are totally different from the Burusho and Shînâ people. (See also 'Shimshal.')

The people of Hindi and Maiun, both being villages below Baltit, speak Shînâ. This language is similar to Sañskrit and Hiñdi-Urdû. There is no Wakhi population in what used to be the kingdom of Nagar, where Burushaski is spoken right down to Minapin. Below that the people are mainly Shînâ-speakers.

Burushaski is not a written language. That, Shapiro[i] writes, 'is perhaps as well, as it has the most complicated grammatical structure. It seems to be a strange language-island, found at the exact meeting point of the Indo-Európean, Turkish and Tibetan groups but not related to any of them. It is not spoken throughout Hunzâ, but only in a limited central position.'

Colonel Lorimer's theory[ii] is that Burushaski was not always a 'language-island.' He feels that the 'language [had] once covered a much larger area [but was] gradually driven in on its least assailable territory.'

Burushaski is a non Indo-European language, of the Dene Caucasian group of languages. It is the only such language in the so-called Northern Areas. Burushaski is also spoken in parts of the Gilgit (Ghizar) Valley in the Puniâl district, with minor changes.

Burushaski has only one dialect left. This is Werchikwar, which some people speak in one particular section of Yâsîn valley. This group of people belongs to the same ethnic stock as the Hunzâkuts and has similar religious beliefs.

The Ismâili Burusho people: There are around 91,000 Burusho people who belong to the Ismâili sect of Muslims. Of them, some 50,000 live in Hunzâ Valley and 27,000 in the Gilgit area. Thanks to the Âgâ Khân Foundation, some twelve thousand of these simple and straightforward people have found employment in Karachi—in schools, hospitals and cultural institutions run by the Foundation. The rest—an estimated two thousand work in places like Rawalpindi and Islâmâbâd.

Hospitality: When visitors return from Hunzâ, to the last person they rave about the warmth, bigheartedness and hospitality of the people. If you get into a conversation with the local people they are likely to invite you home, and feed you things that they might not be able to afford.

They give gifts and expect nothing in return. They can't afford to give these gifts, either, but that's how they have been brought up.

The 'caste-system: Despite protestations to the contrary, there has always been a caste-system in the entire Himâlayan Buddhist belt (and in Japan and Korea). At the top, among Ladâkhi Buddhists, is the Gyâpo caste of royalty. Next comes the Lungpo caste of viziers (ministers). At the bottom is the Lak-shes ('hand-worker') caste, the equivalent of the scheduled castes of Hiñdûism and Sikhism. It also corresponds to the Burakumin of Japan.

Each of these three castes is relatively small. The bulk of the Ladâkhi Buddhist population lies below the Lungpos but above the Lak-shes caste. This middle class belongs to no particular caste. Therefore an impression is sought to be created that the Buddhists of Ladâkh and the other Himâlayas are a casteless people.

Hunzâ, though Muslim, has a variant of the Himâlayan Buddhist caste-system.

Royalty is at the top even here. They form the Thamo caste. There are two kinds of Thamos. 'Pure royalty' (where both parents are Thamo) is called Kareli. Children of Thamo fathers and commoner mothers are called Arghundaro.

No Thamo can get married without the approval of the Mîr. Often it is the Mîr who decides which Thamo youth will marry whom.

In all there are seven castes in Hunzâ. That does not mean that the Hunzâkuts caste-system has as many layers. Some castes are the equal of others and I suspect that there are only three (maybe four) layers.

Customs: Whenever important guests are expected, three or four young men go to the edge of the village to greet the visitor. They stand with plates filled with dried apricots. This is the traditional Hunzâ offering meant for guests.

In Buddhist-majority Leh and Zâñskâr, wizened senior women perform this duty in the smaller villages. In addition to apricots, they might bring some flour, butter and even chhang (beer). It is the rare visitor who actually eats the apricots or butter. In the bigger villages and at gompas, powerful, middle-aged or young, men greet honoured visitors. They garland the visitor with a white silk scarf, the khatak.

Children in Hunzâ are extremely disciplined and well behaved. They don't throw tantrums. This is a trait that I have noticed among Kashmîrî children, too. In my volume on 'Kashmîr' I attributed this to the privations imposed by the unfortunate events of the 1990s. However, it seems that this has always been so. Mrs. Lorimer lived in Hunzâ in 1934-35. She wrote that in Hunzâ there were "no anxious mothers crying, 'Don't go near the edge, you will fall!' Hunzâ is made up of edges-roofs without parapets, fires without guards, streams and reservoirs without railings, not to speak of the cliff tracks [and yet children don't fall over]."[iii]

Clothes: Men wear ankle-length cloaks made of unbleached wool.

Salt: Till the KKH was built, it was extremely difficult to get salt in Hunzâ or, indeed, in most of the Kârâkorams. The local quip was that in Hunzâ salt was more precious than gold, because gold could be sifted out of the Hunzâ River.

Architecture and the layout of villages: The region must have once been subjected to attacks from outside, because most of the villages have been built like forts. This is unusual for rural India, rural Kashmîr, rural Ladâkh, indeed for any rural category in South Asia. Some old ruined villages in Kargil were like that, though. Houses within walled-villages are close to each other. The traditional ones have been built of wood and stone.

There are stone walls around the fields, too. Again this is unusual. However, perhaps here the idea is to keep the sheep and cattle out.

The old villages of Hunzâ, including Karîmâbâd, the capital, have narrow lanes, with stone walls on both sides. The houses have flat rooftops.

The people climb up to the upper floor by means of a ladder. As in much of Ladâkh, for some reason the rungs of the ladder have much wider spaces between them than in the plains. I have never understood why, considering that most Ladâkhîs are shorter than the people of the plains. (The Hunzâkuts are of average South Asian height, being neither taller nor shorter than, say, the Punjâbîs). Perhaps the people of Balâwaristân-Ladâkh try to economise on wood, which is in short supply in most of Ladâkh-Balâwaristân, by saving on the rungs.

Roofs are designed to direct rainwater into a hollow specially made for the purpose. Rainwater harvesting, thus, has a long history in Hunzâ.

References

i Sheryl Shapiro's article 'Hunzâ Hospitality' was posted on the Internet.

ii The Burushaski Language, (Oslo, 1935) published by the Norwegian Institute for Comparative Research in Human Culture, and cited by Shapiro.

iii The quote and the comment are both from Mrs. Mons.

Wildlife
&
Nature

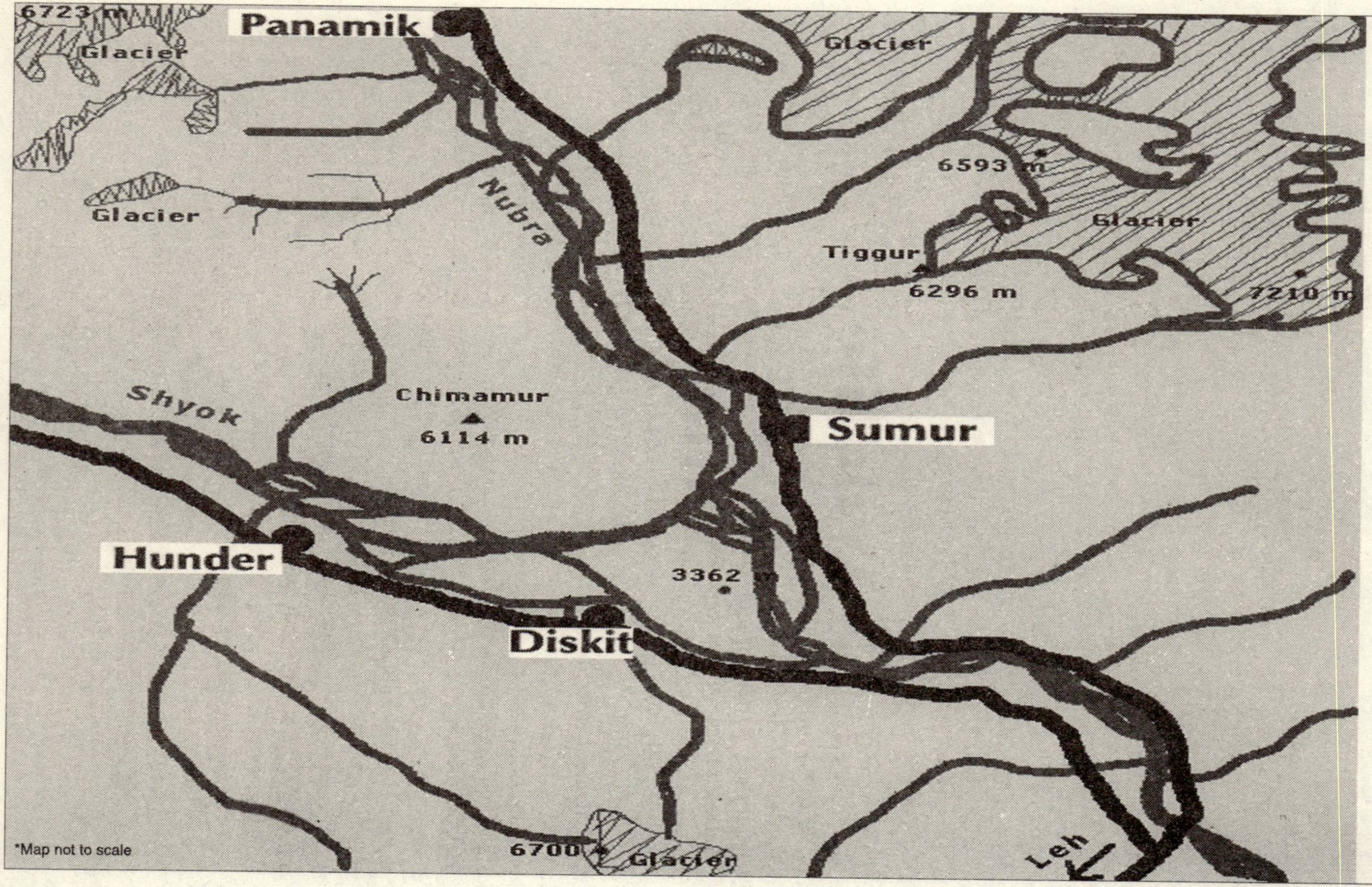
6723 m
Panamik
Glacier
Glacier
Nubra
Glacier
6593 m
Glacier
Tiggur
6296 m
7210 m
Shyok
Chimamur
6114 m
Sumur
Hunder
3362 m
Diskit
*Map not to scale
6700
Glacier
Leh

Nubra

38

Places where wildlife might be found

Some mountains were formed when two drifting continental plates collided. The relatively young Himâlayan range was born when the Indian and Asian plates rammed into each other. As a result, the Himâlayas have fauna from the oriental as well as palearctic regions. Ladâkh is in the northern part of the Himalayan range. Therefore, most of it is in the palearctic rather than oriental region.

Ladâkh is an arctic desert. It has hardly any shrubs, and other than at riverbanks and places where humans live, no trees or natural forests either.

The slopes of the lower mountains have very little vegetation. However, as the mountains rise higher, towards the snow line, their slopes start playing host to herbs, wild roses and willows. This is the alpine zone.

Trees and plants grow wherever the soil, wind, availability of water and 'exposure' are good. In Ladâkh not only is water very scarce and the ground rocky, the place is incredibly cold. As we go higher up the mountains, it gets chillier. Greenery becomes even more difficult to find. Amateur visitors assume that so does wildlife.

However, this is not true. Some animals have adjusted magnificently to these harsh conditions, including the biting cold, the insignificant amounts of greenery, the rocky earth and the lack of protective shelters. Almost all ungulates, and the majority of other animals, go down to lower and, thus, warmer altitudes in the autumn, and spend the winter and early spring there.

However, other animals, notably marmots and the brown bear stay on in the upper reaches, where they hibernate. We humans are not the only ones to be affected by "mountain sickness" in Ladâkh because of the shortage of oxygen. So are other animals. Their system responds to this problem by causing the number of red blood corpuscles in their body to increase, as does their blood acidity.

Nature has given some of the bigger mammals warm, shaggy coats for the winter.[2] That, according to the Department of Wildlife, Government of Jammu and Kashmîr, is perhaps why more species of goat and sheep live in the 'open country' in Ladâkh than anywhere else in the world.

Ladâkh is the highest inhabited region in the world. It is located where three 'zoogeographic' zones meet. Therefore, Ladâkh plays host to an incredible array of wildlife—over a hundred and fifty species of bird and more than a dozen major mammal species. Many of these animals are found only in Ladâkh, having become extinct elsewhere. One of the highest densities of ungulates in the region, thus, lives in the Karakoram-West Tibetan Plateau Alpine Steppe.

Parks and sanctuaries

It is advisable to wear khaki, green or camouflage in all these sanctuaries and national parks in Ladâkh. Please do not disturb the animals with loud noises, radios/ music playing systems, motorboats, diesel generators, etc. (I am thought of as a Luddite, an enemy of progress, because of my refusal to allow motorboats at many tourist destinations, whenever I am in a position to do so.) Please don't leave behind non-biodegradable garbage. Flash photography can irritate some animals into violence, and scare others needlessly.

National parks are a 'higher' category than sanctuaries.

The Hemis High Altitude National Park: This park covers an area of 600 sq. km. The dozen-odd species of mammal that live in this area include the snow leopard, the ibex and the great Tibetan sheep—the bharal and the shâpû. They are best seen between September and May. Rare birds, too, pass through the park. For example, the Himalayan snow cock. Best viewing season is March to May and September to December.

The Hemis park is spread over the catchment areas of two valleys, both of which drain into the Indus river. There are several camping sites in the park, which you can drive to from Leh. Permission to visit/ camp can be obtained from the Wildlife Warden, Leh.

Châñgthâñgi is an upland plateau in east Ladâkh. It borders Tibet and is a southwest extension of the Tibetan plateau. Châñgthâñg is best known for its large brackish water lakes, the Pangong, Tsomo Riri and the Tso Kar. If you actually manage to go through this book, you will notice repeated mention of this plateau in connection with some of the most exciting forms of wildlife in the world, including the black-necked crane, the Brahmini duck, the chîru goat, the kyâñg wild ass and the

2. In summer we humans shear this coat and use the hair as wool.

marmot. Sightings of the latter two are almost guaranteed, unless you are plain unlucky.

The reason why there are so many rare species in this area is that Châñgthâñg has a unique combination of huge marshes and sandy plains, flat deserts and lakes and streams (tributaries of the River Indus), some snowfall (unusual for a desert), some rainfall (60mm. to 70mm. a year), chilling temperatures (minus 40°C in winter) and very high altitudes (between 4,000m. and 7,000m.).

In 1993-94, I was able to get the three lakes opened for tourism but, fortunately, not the 4,000 square kilometre Châñgthâñg Wildlife Sanctuary. Tourists can't go to the sanctuary because it is close to the areas that the Chinese army has occupied illegally. China had invaded the area some time before 1962. This (and the subsequent response) has greatly upset the ecological balance of the area. I now regret my enthusiasm of 1993-94 to allow tourists into the area. They have further damaged the very tender ecology of Châñgthâñg. Therefore, it is just as well that tourists aren't allowed into the sanctuary. The area was notified as a wildlife sanctuary in 1987.

It is not as if tourists (and the border situation) are deliberately killing the kiângs (wild asses). What we humans do is that we construct buildings and roads on pastures and wear the scanty grass out by walking or driving on it. This reduces the amount of grass that the asses can eat. We have also been disturbing the animals of Châñgthâñg through noises that were never heard before in that quiet desert (including the sounds of vehicles and helicopters). We have at times taken away the places in which these animals, especially the kiâng, used to live. All this has naturally led to a depletion of the kiâng (and other animal) population in Châñgthâñg.

In 1995, the Zoological Survey of India observed that the highest density of kiângs was in the 'undisturbed' Dungti-Tsaka La sector of the Châñgthâñg Wildlife Sanctuary. The density, as well as absolute numbers, was low in the 'disturbed' sectors of Nyoma-Loma and Loma-Hânlé. Regions that were moderately disturbed, for example, Tsaka La-Chishul and Chishul-Lol Yogma, had moderate populations.

There were an estimated 188 kiangs in the sanctuary.

There, thus, is a direct correlation between disturbances and the number of kiângs (and other animals) in an area.

The flora of this desert region mainly consists of low thorny scrub (Loricera spinoide, Hippophae rhamnoides), Tibetan furze (Caragana sp.) and a number of grasses (Festuca sp., Carer sp.).

Protected areas in the Ladâkh-Baltistân-Gilgit region

The following areas have been 'protected' in the region, on both sides of the line of control, by declaring them as wildlife sanctuaries (WS) or game reserves (GR, a Pâkistâni category).

Kârâkoram, 1,790 square kilometres; Hemis National Park/WS, 1,400 square kilometres; Hemis National Park/WS, 3,890 square kilometres; Khunjerab II, 2,269 square kilometres; Gya-Meru WS, 80 square kilometres; Tingri WS, 50 square kilometres; Lungnag WS, 940 square kilometres; Rupshu WS, 190 square kilometres; Naltar WS, 210 square kilometres; Kargah WS, 240 square kilometres; Chassi/Bowshdar GR, 480 square kilometres; Naz Bar GR, 410 square kilometres; Sherqillah GR, 130 square kilometres; Danyor Nullah GR, 160 square kilometres; Pakura Nullah GR, 140 square kilometres; K2 National Park, 2,330 square kilometres; Nar Nullah GR, 160 square kilometres; Astore WS, 750 square kilometres; Baltistân, 330 square kilometres; Askor Nullah GR, 150 square kilometres; Kanji WS, 90 square kilometres; Bodh Kharbu WS, 100 square kilometres; Rangdum WS, 280 square kilometres; Agram Basti, 270 square kilometres.

The Wetlands of Ladâkh

Ladakh has three of the world's highest wetlands. These are the Tsomo Riri, Tso Kar and Pangong Tso lakes. Almost three hundred and seventy species of rare birds have been sighted in the area. They are the only places in India where the bar-headed geese breeds, the most important sites in Ladâkh for the waterfowl to breed and the only place outside China where the black-necked crane breeds. Mammals like the wild ass (kiâng), snow leopard, lynx and Himalayan blue sheep live in the vicinity.

Reference

i. Sources of information for this set of entries include JM, Julka, JRB Alfred, HS Mehta and R Paliwal of the High Altitude Zoology Field Station, Zoological Survey of India, Solan, Himachal Pradesh; and the Zoological Survey of India, 'M' Block, New Alipore, Calcutta-700 053.

39

The land (and some other) animals of Ladâkh

The following is a selective listing of species that spend at least a part of the year in Ladâkh (and, in a few cases, the rest of the state, especially the occupied areas). In some cases local names have been mentioned after the common English name but before the scientific name, for example in the headwords <<Antelope, Tibetan (Chiru, Tosh/ Pantholops hodgsoni)>>, Chiru and Tosh are the local names.

Mammals etcetera

Antelope, Tibetan *(Chiru, Tosh/* **Pantholops hodgsoni***)*: An ungulate. Conservation status: Critical. A considerable population of the Tibetan antelope lives in the Changchenmo area. It prefers to stay at altitudes between 14,500' and 19,000'. It is about a metre high and its horns are normally half a metre in length. Male antelopes vastly outnumber females. Bot worms live under the skin of these antelopes, and in considerable numbers.

This is a little goat that lives in the steppes of Kânji Nâlâ, a 'Tibetan' plateau. It also lives in Aksai Chin. At both it prefers altitudes above 5,000 metres. In summer it migrates in herds to the Dopsang Plains and the Changchenmo valley. The chîru has beautiful horns that can be as much as 69 cm. wide.

This delicate animal, described by some naturalists as 'strange,' often feels itchy when the weather is hot. It then rubs its woolly body against thorny bushes, where it leaves wisps of its extremely rare, and, thus, expensive, wool. People go from bush to bush looking for to collect for these wisps, which involves great effort and cost. Shahtoosh shawls are made of these wisps.

Would it not be simpler (and infinitely less expensive) to simply catch hold of a chîru, kill it and pull out all its hair for shawls? No. That would be killing the goat that lays the 'golden', in this case, hair. The hairs of chirus curl up as soon as they die and, therefore, can not be used in shawls.

The ban on shahtoosh shawls is, thus, totally misguided. The chiru is rare and perhaps endangered but shawls are not the reason, (The last two paragraphs are on the authority of chiru expert Chanda Narang.)

Argali, Tibetan: (*Nyan*/ Ovis ammon hodgsoni)An ungulate. Conservation status: Critical. Found in parts of the Ladâkh-Balâwaristân region.

Asses: Found in several parts of the state, including Ladâkh.

Ass, Tibetan wild: (Equus Kiang Moorcroft) An ungulate. Conservation status: Vulnerable. Known as the kiâng in Ladâkh, the Tibetan wild ass is, morphologically, more of a horse than an ass. Its ears, for instance, are longer than those of a horse but much shorter than what an ass would normally have.

Physical appearance: The kiâng is the biggest wild ass found in Africa and Asia. It is a sleek, handsome animal and is about '13 hands' tall. It normally is reddish-brown (rust coloured) all over and white on the stomach. In winter it turns dark brown. Its tails, like those of a zebra, have a long tuft of hair at the end.

Like a horse, its tail tuft is large and its hooves are broad. However, like other wild asses, its mane is short and upright. Along the back there is a black stripe, from one end to the other, from nape to tail. This is a characteristic of wild asses.

Habitat: The kiâng lives in the Hânlé valley, near the Pangong and Rupshu lakes, and in Changchenmo. It mostly lives above 14,000' and, therefore, tolerates the cold the way few animals can. It prefers the open sandy tablelands near the Tibet border and altitudes between 3950 and 4850 metres.

Kiângs live in herds in which there are adult males and females as well as their foals. A herd can have between two and nineteen members. Some herds have as many as forty-five members, some even more. (The Zoological Survey of India found a herd consisting of 84 members in September, 1994). Occasionally the ZSI also came upon some solitary adult males.

I have seen a report which says that in the higher plains of Rupshu you can sometimes see herds of as many as a hundred. In view of the ZSI's very meticulous survey I wonder if the figure of a hundred is a carefully considered one, or a casual observation. Ditto for my own encounter with kiângs, mentioned below.

There probably are 1,500 wild asses in all of Ladâkh, local experts feel. (The Zoological Survey of India[1] estimates the population at around two thousand, which seems more realistic considering the large numbers that this author saw at Hânlé alone.)

I had gone to Hânlé in 1995, in connection with the setting up of an observatory. I had the privilege of giving those pioneering scientists some humble assistance by way of land and clearances for that project. Our helicopter flew extremely low, which was possible because there were no trees, poles, mounds or other obstructions. It, unfortunately, caused some panic among the kiângs and made them run very fast. But we must have seen at least two, maybe even three, hundred wild asses in that single day.

However, all of us accept that the wild ass of the Indo-Tibetan Himâlayas is an endangered species. It mainly eats Festuca sp., a sturdy grass that grows in very, very small quantities.

There might be some kiângs in the Spiti region of neighbouring Himachal Pradesh and north Sikkim.

The kiâng is found in large herds on the highest flat grounds between the Kuenlun and the Kârâkoram. Wild asses like to live near fresh water lakes. The Tso Kar lake is particularly favoured.

Outside India, the kiâng lives in Tibet and the Tsinghai and Szechuan regions of China. To and fro migration takes place between Ladakh and the neighbouring Tibetan areas.

Sub-species: There are three subspecies of kiâng. They differ from each other in terms of colour and size, and live in different parts of the Himâlayas. The polyodon is the smallest of the three and is found in south Tibet and north Sikkim. The sub-species kiang is native to the Changthang area of east Ladakh and west Tibet. In terms of size it stands in the middle. The holdereri is the biggest sub-species and lives in east Tibet and Szechuan.

An easy slay: The kiâng does not run away from men, unless irritated by gesture or sound. In fact, wild asses come up to within 150 metres of visitors to give them the once over. (Yes, man is not the only curious species.) The Champas eat their flesh.

(See also the section on the Chãñgthãñg Wildlife Sanctuary on pages 426-427.)

1. In August 1995, the ZSI studied an area of 490 square kilometres, located at about 220 km south-east of Leh and covered the following sectors: Nyoma-Hânlé, Loma-Chishul through Tsaka La, Chishul-Lol Yogma, and Chishul-Mane along Pangong Tso.

Bears: They normally do not attack humans unless attacked or irritated first. Of course, when they attack they normally crush the victim to death.

Bears, Himalayan black: (Ursus Tibetanus) They waken in the spring, after their winter hibernation. These bears are found at altitudes lower than those in which brown bears live, and are smaller than the brown kind. They mainly eat herbs and fruit but can be carnivorous as well. To this extent they are infinitely more dangerous than brown bears. They move out after sunset. In my experience they venture out only when it is fairly dark. When fruits ripen, they visit the fields and create havoc there, destroying crops and corn-fields.

Bears, Himalayan black (medium-sized): (Šelenarctos tibetanus) This bear lives in forests at altitudes of around 4,500 metres in the summer. It sets up home in dug-out hollows and caves. This predator eats almost everything. from ripe corn and fruit to deer, goats, sheep and, yes, termites. Three or four black bear couples have been sighted in the inhabited parts of Kargil/ Zanskar in July-August when the apricot and apple fruit ripens.

Bears, brown: (Mainly, Denmo/ Ursus arctos; also the Ursus Isabelina) A large carnivore. Conservation status: Low Risk. The Ursus arctos lives at higher altitudes than its black cousin and is more capable of adjusting to difficult living conditions. There are some two hundred such bears in Ladâkh, mostly in Zanskar but some twenty in the rest of Kargil.

Bharal: (Napo/ Pseudois nayaur) An ungulate. Conservation status: Low Risk (Also spelt and pronounced 'barhal.') This is an 'enigmatic' mammal because it is not clear whether it is a sheep or a goat. It has some morphological traits of sheep and some traits of goats. It is found in Kashmîr as well as Ladâkh. In Ladâkhi it is called nâ or snâ.

This species of blue sheep is the most commonly found type of sheep in all Ladakh. Unlike the shâpû/ urial, the bharal is found in abundance. Its brownish-grey exterior is part of the reason, because its colour camouflages the animal and thus protects it to an extent. Bharals often stand absolutely still, which makes it very difficult for hunters to see them. When frightened, bharals run extremely fast to safe places.

The bharal is small and lives wild almost throughout Ladâkh, especially Zâñskâr, Tiri and Changchenmo, up to altitudes of around 15,000'. It has long horns, just under a metre long, and its flesh is considered a delicacy. The bharal is almost never found below 13,000' even in winter. In summer bharals go up, in large herds, to alpine meadows at 16,000', in fact, even higher. Some zoologists have spotted herds at between 18,000' and 19,000', on meadows where the summer grass is plenty.

Camel, Ferral Bactrian (*Nabong*/ Camelus Bactrian): An ungulate. The double-humped Bactrian camel is found in some parts of Leh district. (See the chapter on 'Nubra.')

Cattle: Common horned cattle are not at all common in Ladâkh. At most they might be found in the lower parts of Ladâkh. The Himalayan counterparts of common Indian oxen are widely found in Nubra and the warmer regions of Ladâkh. Yaks, or, more accurately, their descendants, are the type of cattle common to Ladâkh. (See 'Yaks' below.)

Deer, musk: This is a rare species, mostly because it has been hunted and killed through the centuries for its musk-pods. It is found in the lower parts of Ladâkh, especially in western Ladâkh.

The musk deer lives above the zone where pines grow. It prefers birch forests. When it comes down to the lower hills it seeks the safety and protection of dense forests.

Deer, Tibetan ravine: Called the goa locally and mainly found around Hânlé (Leh). Its horns are different from those of its mainland Indian counterpart and can be up to 35 cm. (14 inches) long.

Dogs: In particular the Bakerwals (shepherds), who live in the mountains, keep large, ferocious dogs that protect their flock as well as them from wild animals.

The 'toy-dogs' of Zâñskâr (Ladâkh), in particular those bred by the erstwhile royal family of Zangla, are much in demand outside Ladâkh. Apparently they even manage to survive in the much hotter plains of central India (perhaps with air conditioning).

Also found in Ladâkh is the Tibetan mastiff, which is considered an 'ill tempered' shepherd's dog.

Dog, Wild (*Phara*/ Cuon alpinus laniger): A large carnivore. Conservation status: Critical.

Fox: There is a fairly big population of the fox in Ladâkh. Western Ladakh is the best place to look for the fox. If you travel at night on the national highway between Kargil and Mulbek, or in the Suru valley, you are likely to drive past foxes with thick, bushy tails. Regrettably, many red foxes are trapped for this very fur, which is then smuggled out.

Fox, red (*Watse*/ **Vulpes vulpes or Vulpus vulpus**): A large carnivore. Conservation status: Low Risk. The Red Fox is found in Ladâkh. It prefers bush woodlands. There it digs a burrow under the ground to live in. Or it might live among rocks or under the cover of dense vegetation. It is a nocturnal animal. Hunger might force the stray Red Fox to come out during the day, though. It is a loner. Its diet changes with the season and depends on what is available. Also on what that particular fox has grown to like. The Red Fox preys on small rodents and birds—pheasants, partridges, marmots and voles. This monogamous animal is said to pair for life. Red Fox couples are known to live in the same place for years at an end. This home is often a burrow with more than one opening.

Gazelle, the Tibetan: (*Gowa*/ Procapra picticaudata) An ungulate. Conservation status: Critical. This small animal can be found in the steppes of the Kânji Nâlâ, a 'Tibetan' plateau. It normally moves in herds of five to ten. On some rare occasions it has been seen on the eastern fringe of Ladakh. Its horns typically measure 36 cm.

Goats: In Ladâkh goats have two important uses (other than meat): to transport materials on and, more commonly, for their wool. That is why the second kind are called 'shawl-goats' and are bred in Nubra, Zâñskâr and Rupshu. The latter are shorn once a year. The best hair is used for shawls and is called lena. Common wool is called bal. Hair is separated from the wool, is used for blankets, tents and ropes, and is called spu.

Hare: Common in Ladâkh, where its ears are larger than those of its British counterpart and where it is bluish grey in colour.

Hare, mouse: Found in Ladâkh.

Horse, domesticated/ ponies: Ladâkhi horses-horses, not ponies-are short but sturdy. The ones from Zâñskâr are among the best. In Leh they have traditionally been weaker. Horses and ponies from Drâss and Kargil are great load carriers. The Ladâkhis, too, play polo.

Horse, wild: Found in Ladâkh.

Ibex: (Capra ibex. '*Skin*' or '*sekin*' in Ladâkhi.) This goat can be found in the Suru and Warhwan (Doda, Jammu) valleys, Basgo, and POK's Astor and Baltistân regions. There are around 250 ibex in the steppes of Kânji Nâlâ, a 'Tibetan' plateau.

The size of ibex herds varies between ten and sixteen. In summer this gregarious animal moves from place to place grazing on grass, which, in that season. is everywhere. Their breeding season begins in November, and they deliver in late June, after a six-month pregnancy.

Ibexes prefer altitudes above the tree line. They thus climb to heights that are considerably higher than the ones that smaller wild goats go to. That is because they like to live amidst black precipitous rocks and cliffs. They seek shelter and security amidst sheer cliffs and ridges. In winter they come down to lower altitudes for food and shelter. Therefore, winter and spring are when it is easiest to find ibexes.

Ibexes are afraid of dogs. In Baltistân (POK), and in some other parts of the region, human hunters send dogs to drive ibexes up rocks. Thereafter the humans come over and shoot the ibexes.

Physical appearance: This is the best looking goat in all of Ladâkh. Besides, it can not be mistaken for any other kind of goat. It has a pair of elegant spiral horns. The biggest ibex horns on record measure 147 cm. The animal is large and stocky.

Ibex, Siberian (Skin/ Capra ibex sibirica) An ungulate. Conservation status: Vulnerable.

Leopard, snow: (*Shan*/ Uncia uncia) A large carnivore. Conservation status: Endangered. Also known as the white leopard and ounce, this is an elusive animal. It is very difficult to spot. Two Germans spent an entire winter with me in Zâñskâr trying to photograph this hard to get mammal. We spotted some rare ibexes instead, but even those not from close enough to photograph.

The snow leopard is a 'survivor from the frigid Pleistocene era,' as a government publication puts it. It is found throughout the Himalayan range i.e. the higher mountains of Kashmîr and Ladâkh being more favoured than most of the other Himalayas. It has been sighted often in the Suru, Warhwan (Doda, Jammu) and Nubra valleys. The snow leopard is believed to live in Zâñskâr, too. It eats the ibex, the bharal and the markhor.

The snow leopard also lives in Central Asia, and within India, in the Himâlayan mountains of Arunachal Pradesh, Sikkim, Uttar Pradesh and Himachal Pradesh.

In summer this solitary animal lives amidst rocks and cliffs, above the tree-line. It comes down to the villages in the lower valleys and hills in winter, when its prey does the same.

Physical appearance: The chest and under parts of this awesome animal are cream in colour. It has a thick coat of gray on which there are black rings or rosettes. This colour scheme camouflages it against rocks and the snow. But why would this supreme predator need to camouflage itself? Actually this is am offensive camouflage. The snow leopard does not want its prey to see it coming.

The snow leopard has large nostrils, because oxygen is scarce in the high mountains where it lives. It limbs are short and its chest muscles well-developed so that it can climb mountains the better. The snow leopard's hair is long and dense. Its tail is almost three feet long (that being equal to 75-90% of the length of its head and body measured together).

Its prey: In summer, while camping at high altitudes, it eats goats, the ibex, blue sheep and the shâpû. It follows its prey when they migrate uphill in spring and also when they come down in autumn. It also eats pikas (Ochotona spp.), hares (Lepus spp.) and gamebirds (chukar partridge and snowcocks). In winter, it terrorises domestic stock. It normally hunts in the early morning and late afternoons.

Population: It is estimated that there are some two hundred snow leopards in Ladâkh. A government website comments, 'With almost 40-50 skins smuggled out of Ladakh in the 1950's, 30-40 in the 1960's and 10-15 still [in the 1990s and '00s] being slipped out, the main enemy of this animal is, undoubtedly, man.'

The Chinese use the bones of snow leopards in their medicines as a substitute for tiger bones. Fur coats made of the skins of snow leopards are sold in China and Taiwan. Trophy hunters, however, remain the main threat.

Khunjerab II in Pâkistân Occupied Kashmîr and Taxkorgan IV in Occupied Tibet are the only two protected areas in the snow leopard's 'range' where viable populations (i.e. at least fifty breeding adults) of the animal can live. (A range is a region in which an animal can live. Most of Ladâkh-Balâwaristân and Tibet are within the snow leopard's range.) Eightyfive to ninety per cent of the areas in which the snow leopard lives are unprotected.

Lynx: (Felis lynx/ Lynx isabellina. Called eeh in Ladâkh.) A large carnivore. The lynx looks a bit like the wolf because its ear tufts stick out equally conspicuously. It is fawn and white in winter and somewhat darker in summer. Its tail is short and dark. The lynx eats marmots, snowcocks and hares.

This isabelline cat seeks shelter in forests and amidst tall grass and reeds. This good looking animal lives in the remoter parts of Ladâkh at altitudes of around 4,400 metres.

Markhor: (Capra falconeri) Called *Raphoche* in Ladâkhi. This 'serpent-eater' is a very large goat. The Astor (now POK) markhor has huge, flat horns, which rise with just one sweep. This migratory animal lives on 'dangerous ground' but not on the high mountains where the ibex does. Prefers dense birch and pine forests. Grazes on the grassy glens of these forests. Rarely goes above the snow-line.

Markhors travel in herds. They feel most secure from attack when housed amidst precipitous crag and rock. In December the older ones join the females and younger males. In spring they break company again.

Marmot, docile: Found in Ladâkh. Just before you reach the Rangdum gompa, travelling down from Kargil, there is a large expanse of land that teems with marmots. This cat-sized animal hibernates in underground burrows all through winter. During much of summer it is too groggy to react to hunters. Its responses are rather slow. Hence the epithet 'docile'. Even a child can walk up and grab a marmot, especially for its attractive golden brown skin. However, don't even try. You'll be causing major offence to local religious sentiment if you do. It's considered most sinful to kill a marmot. You can see why. The docile marmot is plentiful in places like Drâss, right on the highway, especially right after the dZoji Lâ opens (late May/ early June). You are almost guaranteed sightings while driving to Nubra.

Marten, stone: (Martes foina) This is a good looking and swift animal. It lives above the tree line, in forests as well as on barren mountains. It nestles in the hollows of trees, in holes in the ground and amidst rocks. Its looks make its fur much valued internationally. Therefore, hunters stalk this normally vigilant animal. It is estimated that four hundred skins of the Stone Marten are smuggled out of Ladâkh every year.

Mules: Mules, whether in the areas bordering Kulu, Kãñgrâ and other parts of HP, or those in regions neighbouring Yârqañd, have proved to be the sturdiest animals when it comes to carrying loads.

Nyan: See 'Sheep, wild' below.

Ovis Ammon: See 'Sheep, wild'

Ovis Orientalis/ *Urial*, Ladakhi (*Shâpû*/ Ovis orientalis vignii) An ungulate. Conservation status: Endangered. Known as the 'urial' in some parts of the Punjâb and greater Ladâkh. In the areas of Kargil under Pâkistâni occupation (Baltistân, Astor, Bunji) it is called the oorin. The shâpû is found in most parts of Ladâkh, mainly along the Indus. It lives on steep, grassy, hill slopes above forests.

The adult urial typically weighs around 85 kg. and the tips of its horns can be as much as a metre apart. (The Jammu and Kashmîr Forest Department's impeccable website very precisely says that the horns measure 99 cm.) This is perhaps the smallest sheep in East Asia. It normally is no taller than its horns. Urials live on grassy mountain slopes, normally between 3,000 and 4,000 metres. That, by Ladâkhi standards, is not a very great altitude and the majority of the human population lives in this zone. Therefore, it is quite common for hunters to kill urials.

As a result there are hardly five hundred urials left in the main inhabited areas of Ladâkh. There are another forty or fifty urials in the Markha and Rumbak valleys. For that reason all conservationists must unite to keep this dying species alive: not just by banning hunting but mainly by helping urials breed in greater numbers.

Urials, like most sheep, mate in December-January. Their offsprings are born in or around May.

Predators: In any eco-system there are many docile animals (and many species of docile animals). There also are a few predators (and even fewer species of predators) that eat the gentle ones. In Ladâkh the number of predators (and predator species) is smaller still because food is scarcer than elsewhere. Ladâkh's best known predators are the snow leopard, the brown bear, the wolf and the lynx.

Sheep, blue: See 'Bharal'' above.

Sheep, domesticated: In Ladâkh there are two kinds of sheep. i) The huniya has a large, black-face, and is used to transport materials, most notably salt, especially in Châñgthâñg and Rupshu. ii) In Kargil there is a smaller, prettier kind, which is eaten.

Sheep, Marco Polo: (Ovis ammon poli) An endangered species found in parts of the Kârâkoram-West Tibetan Plateau Alpine Steppe. This sheep is the largest of its genus.

Sheep, wild: The nyan is also known as the Great Tibetan Sheep (Ovis ammon). It is found near Shushal (the pass as well as the region), Hânlé and Rupshu. Its horns can be up to a metre and a half long (145 cm. is not unusual) and half a metre in girth.

All sheep, found anywhere in the world, are related very closely to each other. Even when they seem to look different, they are mere modifications of the same species. The nyan looks much like an antelope.

The Ovis ammon is the largest and grandest of all the wild sheep found in Ladâkh. It lives between 14,500' and 19,000' in summer. The nyan has a strong sense of smell, which alerts it if a hunter or an enemy is coming that way. The belief is that the nyan is a very difficult animal to get hold of. This is a view based on the terrain on which the nyan lives and the winds that blow there. However, the 1890 Gazetteer says that such 'difficulties ... are very much magnified'.

If we accept that the difficulties have been magnified, then the low probability of sighting this animal has to be attributed to its rarity. There is a population of some two hundred nyans in the easternmost part of Ladakh. This is an animal that migrates to wherever food and water are available but almost never goes down to altitudes below 4,500 metres.. It lives in the wilderness.

The gregarious Ladâkhi shâpû is found near and along River Indus. Its herds are not very big.

See also 'Bharal' above (==>).

Squirrel, woolly flying-: Some zoologists call this the 'single endemic mammal' found in the Kârâkoram-Himâlayan-Hiñdu Kush ecoregion. It lives at high altitudes in scanty pinus and picea forests.

Stone marten: See Marten, stone.

Ungulates: This is the most widespread set of species in Ladâkh-Balâwaristân. Most of them are endangered. See also the entries on

'Sheep, wild,' 'Sheep, Marco Polo,' 'Argali, Tibetan,' 'Markhor,' 'Ibex' and 'Ovis orientalis.'

Urial: See 'Ovis orientalis.'

Weasel, altai: (Mustela altaica) Found in the Ladâkh-Balâwaristân region.

Wolf, Tibetan (*Shangku*/ Canis lupus chanko) A large carnivore. Conservation status: Vulnerable

Wolves: (Canis lupus) Some three hundred wolves are found in Ladâkh. They eat sheep, to the distress of shepherds for whom this is a huge economic loss. This makes wolves the most detested predators in Ladakh.

When the shepherds move uphill to the mountain pastures for the summer, so do wolves. In winter they come down close to the lower valleys (and fairly close to the plains). In summer they live amidst thickets of reeds and scrub. In winter they seek shelter in caves and amidst rocks.

There are two broad varieties of wolf in Ladâkh. The kind found in the north are light fawn and brown. The ones in the south are darker. Wolves hunt in pairs and move over very long distances. One kind of wolf regularly moves across a narrow valley at dusk.

Yâk: The yâk is a kind of ox and is the biggest animal found in the cold Himâlayan desert of Ladâkh. Some kinds of yak weigh around a tonne. The tips of its curved horns can be as much as 90 cm. away from each other and can measure 76 cm. over the curves.

There are two kinds of yak.

Yak, domestic: When a yak mates with the common cow, the offspring thus produced is a hybrid called a dzo if male, and dzo-mo if female. The dzo-mo produces more and better milk than the female yak. The Ladâkhis convert most of the milk into butter, rarely consuming it directly, not even in tea (in which butter, rather than milk, is used). The next generation of cow-yak is called dimo in Leh-Zâñskâr and brimo in Kargil and is kept only for its milk.

The domesticated yak is not as tall as the wild variety, it is broad and strongly built, and is useful for carrying loads. However, this placid animal can not walk long distances. It gets footsore if it does. Therefore, it is quite useless at pulling the plough. The dzo-mo is used for the ploughing of fields as well as for carrying loads.

Nubra, being at a lower height, does not produce good yaks. Their dark hair is cut only when it almost reaches the ground.

Yak, wild: (Dong/ Bos grunniens) An ungulate. Conservation status: Critical. This kind is native only to Ladâkh where it is known as the dong in Leh-Zâñskâr, and brong in Kargil. It is a very rare animal and much larger and impressive than the domesticated variety. The bulls are much outnumbered by the cows.

Wild yaks are native only to the Kepsang and Polrang valleys. Therefore, they might even be seen in the Kubrung and Kepsang nallahs of the neighbouring Changchenmo valley, and in the nearby ravine, left of the Shyok. Indeed, this ravine is called the dongaylak, or 'the wild yaks' summer pastures'. Wild yaks are found in large herds on the highest flat grounds between the Kuenlun and the Kârâkoram. Favoured altitudes are between 15,000' and 16,000', normally the latter. Wild yaks spend their summers at altitudes above 6,000 metres. In winter they migrate in herds to the lakes, marshes and lower valleys.

Because of their inaccessibility to even the common Ladâkhi, wild yaks were first described only as recently as in the 1870s, by the great Russian explorer and horse-expert, Count Nikolay Mikhailovich Przhevalsky (1839-1888).

The Champa tribals eat the flesh of these yaks. Their horns can be thick and up to 77 cm/ 30 inches long. Their tails are greatly valued.

Physical appearance: Wild yaks are evenly black, with parts of the back and head sporting a slight tinge of rust. The tail is bushy, like that of a horse. They have a dense cover of long, shaggy hair, which is slightly grey at the muzzle. They resemble the bison, except that they are bigger.

Reptiles, insects etcetera

Amphibians: There are supposed to be no amphibians in Ladâkh. However, this is not strictly correct. Amphibians of the Bufonidae family have been reported in the Ladakh region. The species reported include:

Bufo viridi

Bufo latastii

Scutiger occidentalis

Annelida: Three species of Annelida from the cold desert of Ladakh were studied and recognized in the 1980s and 1990s.

Bees: The honey bee is not found in Ladâkh, though the black spotted bee, the bonga nakpo, as well as the wasp known as the golden bee (locally, the boni-ser), are. Since at least mediæval times the Ladâkhis have been making honey 'without the aid of bees'. (Which is the kind we'd have for lunch every Wednesday at our CU Green lunches at Cambrîdge University. Honey without cruelty. The Greens would love the Ladâkhis.)

Bluebottles: Common in Ladâkh at the peak of summer: July-August.

Fish: Fishing is taboo in the Buddhist parts of Ladâkh (Leh, and some parts of Kargil, especially Mulbek and Zâñskâr). Any attempts on your part to catch fish in the Buddhist areas will cause very deep offence. As soon as you are seen fishing, you will immediately be surrounded by a hostile mob.

Frogs: See 'Amphibians' above.

Ladâkh has few insects other than houseflies (and they only in July and August) and the insects mentioned in this section. No snakes.

Lepidoptera: Three species of Lepidoptera from the cold desert of Ladakh were studied and recognized in the 1980s and 1990s.

Lizards: There are at least three species of lizard in the region—Agama himalayan (common), Scincella ladacensis (sparse), and Phrynocephalus theobaldi (stone deserts).

Locusts: In Ladâkh found only in Zâñskâr.

Reptiles reported in the Ladakh region, in addition to those mentioned elsewhere in this section, include:

Family	**Species**
Agamidae	Phrynocephalus theobaldis
	Phrynocephalus recticulatus
	Laudakia himalayana
Geckonidae	Crytodactylus montium salsorum
	Crytodactylus stoliczkai
	Crytodactylus lawderanus
Scincidae	Scincella himalanum
	Scincella ladacense
Coluberidae	Coluber rhodorachis
	Elaphe hodgsoni
	Ptyas mucosus

Sand-flies: In Ladâkh found in swarms in Nubra and the lakes, especially the Tsomo Riri, where their huge presence can be uncomfortable for the visitor.

Scorpions: The puhur. Plentiful in the Cheshma Shahi-Pari Mahal-Raj Bhawan area of Srinagar city. Also in the Dachinpura and Lar areas. Their bite can be fatal.

Snakes: There are no snakes in Ladâkh, where the only reptile is a small lizard. It is said that Ladâkh is too cold for snakes to survive. I've never found one in any part of Ladâkh. British records, too, bear me out. However, the more recently published (around 1990) 'Gazetteer: Ladâkh Region' suggests that some non-poisonous species are found in the region. I still have my doubts.

40

The birds (avifauna) of Ladâkh

Jammû, Kashmîr and Ladâkh are located on the 'flyway route' of birds migrating from Siberia to the plains of India. Because the State has a large number of lakes and rivers, it plays host to many of these birds. In all 225 species of birds, representing 34 families, have been sighted in Ladakh. Around 110 of these species breed in Ladakh, mainly in the summer.

Very few birds live in Ladâkh throughout the year because the place is so cold and is a desert to boot. However, some parts of Ladâkh have water and others have trees and shelter of kinds. This is more than what some of the neighbouring regions can offer. Therefore, some birds spend some time in those parts Ladâkh. Thus, when we say 'Found in Ladâkh' below, we really mean 'found during the season, and then at particular places in Ladâkh.'

Partridges and snowcocks are the only birds that spend their whole lives in the upper reaches of Ladâkh.[1] Some birds live in the upper reaches in summer and the foothills in autumn, winter and spring. Most birds move to warmer parts of the world, after a halt in Ladâkh.

The following is a bare listing of some of the important species native to or found or seen in Ladâkh and, in some cases, the state.

Accentor, Brown (Prunella fulvescens): Found in Ladâkh.

Accentor, Robin: (Prunella rubeculoides) Found in the Ladâkh region. Interestingly, it 'winters' in this region.

Bluethroat (Luscinia svecica): Found in Ladâkh.

Bunting, Rock (Emberiza cia): Found in Ladâkh.

Chakor: The rekpa/ skekpa variety is found in Ladâkh. Sâbû in Ladâkh is a sanctuary for chakors. This is a village half way between

1. However, a zoologist asserts, 'There are *no* endemic bird species, and bird richness is low.' (Emphasis added.)

Leh and Choglamsar. To reach Sabu a detour to the left (east) needs to be take from the main road. Chakors fly in and out of people's houses because in Ladâkh the killing of chakors (and most other animals) is taboo.

The chakor is also found on the way from Leh to Nyoma and Upshi.

Chiffchaff, Mountain (Phylloscopus sindianus): Found in Ladâkh.

Chough: The chunka is common in the villages. Choughs are birds of prey. They go wherever humans and other animals go. They have been sighted at altitudes of as much as 6,150 metres.

Chough, Red-billed (Pyrrhocorax pyrrhocorax): Found in Ladâkh.

Chough, Yellow-billed (Pyrrhocorax graculus): Found in Ladâkh.

Chukar (Alectoris chukar): Found in Ladâkh.

Coot, Common (Fulica atra): Found in Ladâkh.

Crane, black necked: (Grus nigricollis): Count Nikolay Mikhailovich Przhevalsky (1839-1888), a great Russian explorer, ornithologist (and much more, including horse expert), was the first to study the black necked crane in 1876. The bird has still not been researched adequately.

Origin: There are fifteen species of crane in the world. Cranes, in general, were in existence sixty million years before man. They now seem to be headed for slow extinction, some scientists feel. Other ornithologists, who met in Moscow in 1982, felt that the BNC was no immediate danger. This optimism is partly based on the hunch that China has a big BNC population but is not letting the world know (or doesn't know itself). More important is the observation that since 1960 the BNC population in Ladâkh has remained exactly the same—three BNC couples a year.

Migration, breeding and routine life while in Ladâkh: Most cranes are migratory and travel thousands of miles every year. The black-necked crane flies up to very high altitudes to nest. It breeds only at altitudes that are between 3500 metres and 5500 metres. Three places in Ladâkh fit the bill.

In summer the BNCs, worldwide, are found in two distinct groups. The western group of BNCs goes to eastern Ladakh and the eastern group to southern Tibet. These are the two extremes of the Tibetan plateau. At other times BNCs have been spotted in Asian lands as far apart as Bhutan and India's Arunachal Pradesh in the west and Szechwan, Yunan and Vietnam in the east. If each of their winter homes is a dot on a map and all these dots are joined together, they will form an arc.

The BNC that we find in Ladâkh likes to live in open marshlands, wet plains, prairies and, sometimes, sandy flats.

Every year three BNC couples, sometimes more, come to Ladâkh, through the Indus valley, in mid-April or early May, normally the latter. They fly along the banks of River Indus as they head for marshes where they build their nests. BNC nests are large cushions of dead aquatic vegetation placed on shallow water up to two feet deep or even on open meadows. BNCs, thus, are 'ground nesting' birds. They prefer marshes because humans and other mammals can't reach there easily.

Apparently they need lots of space because these three couples live very, very far apart from each other. One BNC couple builds its nest in Chushul, one in Hânlé and the third near the Tso Kar. Even as the crane flies, there might be as many as ninety or a hundred kilometres between each of these three places. If there is a fourth (or fifth) couple in any particular year it would normally be only passing through.[2]

If snowfall had been poor in the immediately preceding winter, the marshes might be dry. In that case, BNCs have no option but to build nests on dry land where their eggs are in great danger.

Roughly three weeks after settling in the nest, the female lays an egg and then, 12 to 24 hours later, another. This generally happens in May. The size of each dull-white or brown egg is around 10cm. by 6cm. It weighs around 200 grams.

Predators try to eat these eggs. Humans collect them to sell to tourists. (You can help save the BNC from extinction by refusing to buy BNC eggs. All of us together should ensure that water is not diverted away from the marshes. We should also ensure that marshes are not 'developed' into pastures for cattle.)

If a unit of the Indian Army happens to be posted nearby they sometimes post a guard or two near the nesting sites to ward off both kinds of poachers.

Brahminy ducks and BNCs share the same marshes. Therefore, they don't always like each other. The ducks normally arrive a few weeks later. BNCs see the ducks as intruders and male cranes often chase them away with their large wings. Cranes are particularly aggressive if they find the ducks going near their nests. They don't stop at merely shooing the intruder away. BNCs might chase the intruder for almost an hour till he leaves the pond altogether. For that half-hour or more the incubation process gets disturbed because both parents leave the nest for the while that there is an intruder around.

2. Obviously Ladâkh is not the main breeding ground of the BNC. It has breeding places for just three BNC couples. The Tibetan plateau attracts a far greater number.

Both parents take turns to sit on the egg to incubate it. Naturalists of the Wildlife Department of Jammu and Kashmîr have observed that there are around ten such shifts during the course of a day. Each shift, thus, is of around two and a half hours.

After an incubation of eighteen to twenty-four days,[3] one live chick is born. (The other one always dies, even though more than two-thirds of the eggs hatch successfully. If it does not die a natural death, its other newborn sibling pecks it to death.)

The chicks are brown or gray and are very pretty when they are born. They start swimming within hours of their birth. In a day or two they are fairly developed.

Army guards remain around till the chicks are strong enough to defend themselves.

Towards the end of October or early November, the BNCs leave Ladâkh and fly away, with their newborn chicks, to eastern Tibet or South China.

Adult cranes keep these chicks with them for nine or nine and a half months in all, i.e. till the next mating season. After that they shoo their own children away. The young form a peer group and fly together till they are old enough to breed, which might be when they are three to five years old. Some precocious cranes start mating at two.

Physique: The black-necked crane is big, majestic and very good looking. Typically, it is four feet tall. However, its height can vary between two and five feet and its wingspread can be around seven or eight feet. Its body is pale gray, almost white. Its neck, head, feet and 'secondaries' are black and its bill green. There is a red patch on its beak.

Like other cranes, its legs are long and its bill and neck are long and straight. Its hind toe is raised. Apparently, this toe does not support any of the BNC's weight when the bird walks.

Cranes' windpipes are coiled, a bit like the coils of a trumpet, and for the same reason. As a result, cranes emit loud, throaty sounds that, on a quiet day, can be heard for miles. These notes can be quite musical and nice to the ear.

The BNC's flight: When the BNC flies, its head and neck point straight ahead. At times BNCs fly as high as five kilometres above the earth, and well above the ground even the rest of the time. Once up there they form a large 'V' and go around in fascinating circles. BNCs glide only when they descend.

3. Twentyeight to thirtysix days, according to another study.

Food: BNCs are enormous eaters and eat all kinds of berries, fruits, worms, insects, reptiles and, sometimes, birds. They rarely eat fish.

Song, dance and mating rituals: BNCs perform stylish dances in most months of the year, but more so during the breeding season. Sometimes entire flocks, including baby cranes, join in. (Yes, at times there are flocks.)

As in Spanish flamenco dances, the courting couple walks stiffly around each other, in brisk, stilted steps. Also as in flamenco, as they do so, they spread their wings only partly and hold their legs elegantly below them. They might even bow low. Then they might jump into the air, six to nine feet above the ground, as loud cries go out all around. Just one crane might do this, or a pair might, or even the whole flock might.

Scottish bandmasters toss their batons into the air and catch them on the way down. Cranes likewise toss twigs into the air with their bills and catch them also with their bills.

The cranes' 'unison calls' are another fascinating ritual when the entire flock squeals as one.

Crane, gigantic: Found in the marshes.

Crow, Carrion (Corvus corone):: Found in Ladâkh.

Crow, House (Corvus splendens): Found in Ladâkh.

Crow, Large-billed (Corvus macrorhynchos): Found in Ladâkh.

Cuckoo, Eurasian (Cuculus canorus): Found in Ladâkh.

Dipper, Brown (Cinelus pallasil): Found in Ladâkh.

Dipper, White-throated (Cinelus cinelus): Found in Ladâkh.

Dove, Oriental Turtle-(Streptopelia orientalis): Found in Ladâkh.

Duck, Tufted (Aythya fuligula): Found in Ladâkh.

Duck, wild: A water bird found in Ladâkh near the Rupshu lakes. Ducks are even more likely to be found near the bigger rivers.

Eagle, Golden (Aquila chrysaetos): Found in Ladâkh.

Finch: The varieties that visit Ladâkh include: Finch, Brandt's Mountain-(Leucosticte brandti)

Finch, Plain Mountain (Leucosticte nemoricola)

Finch, Plain-backed Snow-(Pyrgilauda blanford)

Finch, Streaked Rose-(Carpodacus rubicilloides)

Finch, Rose-: (Carpodacus spp.)

Rosefinch, Common (Carpodacus erythrinus).

Rosefinch, Great (Carpodacus rubicilla)

Finch, Tibetan Snow-(Montifringilla adamsi)

Finch, White-rumped Snow-(Pyrgilauda taczanowskii)

Fowl: The domestic fowl is reared in Leh and Nubra.

Gadwall (Anas strepera):: A water bird found in Ladâkh and Kashmîr.

Garganey (Anas querquedula): Found in Ladâkh.

Goldfinch, European (Carduelis carduelis): Found in Ladâkh.

Goose, bar headed: (Anser indicus) This bird is found, and breeds, in Ladâkh in alpine pastures just below the snowline. That's because insects, which this seasonal bird eats, are plentiful in those meadows, and so is this goose. Lake Tsomo Riri, the north and south banks of the lake, to be precise, is its biggest breeding colony in India.

Goose, grey: A water bird found in Ladâkh near the Rupshu lake.

Grebe, Great Crested (Podiceps cristatus): A water bird found in Ladâkh in autumn and winter.

Gull, Brown-headed (Larus brunnicephalus): This is one of the first birds to reach Ladâkh in summer.

Heron, Indian Pond (Ardeola grayif): Found in Ladâkh.

Hobby, Eurasian (Falco subbuteo): Found in Ladâkh.

Hoopoe, Common (Upupa epops): Found in Ladâkh.

Kestrel, Common (Falco tinnunculus): Found in Ladâkh.

Lammergeiers (Gypaetus barbatus) are bearded vultures. They are birds of prey. They go wherever humans and other animals go. They have been sighted at altitudes of as much as 6,150 metres. The wingspan of this majestic bird can be a stunning three metres. It is because of these huge wings that they can glide on high powerful upcurrents. Some awestruck rural Ladâkhis believe, incorrectly, that this vulture can scoop up young lambs and carry them away on its gigantic wings.

Lammergeiers always live close to mountains.

Lapwing, Red-wattled (Vanellus indicus): Found in Ladâkh.

Lark, Horned (Eremophila alpestris): Found in Ladâkh.

Lark, Hume's Short-toed (Calandrella acutirostris): Found in Ladâkh.

Magpie, Black-Billed (Pica pica): Found in Ladâkh.

Mallard (Anas platyrhynchos): A water bird found in Ladâkh near the Rupshu lake.

Martin, Eurasian Crag-(Hirundo rupestris): Found in Ladâkh.

Martin, Northern House-(Delichon urbica): Found in Ladâkh.

Martin, Pale (Riparia diluta): Found in Ladâkh.

Merganser, Common (Mergus merganser): Found in Ladâkh.

Monal, Himalayan: (Lophophorus impejanus) Found in Ladâkh.

Owl, Little (Athene noctua): Found in Ladâkh.

Partridge: Partridges breed at altitudes of around 5,000 metres. Along with snowcocks, they are the only birds that spend their whole lives in the upper reaches of Ladâkh.

Pelican: A small kind of pelican is found in the marshes.

Pigeon: The purgon is a small field pigeon, common in Ladâkh.

Pigeon, Hill (Columba rupestris): Found in Ladâkh.

Pigeon, Rock (Columba livia): Found in Ladâkh.

Pigeon, Snow (Columba leuconota): Found in Ladâkh.

Plover, Lesser Sand-(Charadrius mongolus): Found in Ladâkh.

Plover, Mongolian: This is a very rare bird, and one with a spellbinding act. Ladâkh is one of its few homes. Naturalists call its routine the 'distraction display.'

As soon as a male plover sights a predator he acts as if he has been wounded. He lets his wings droop towards the ground, on which he straggles as if with great effort. He goes through this act in order to catch the predator's eye, and invite the predator to come and attack him. While he is doing so, his female swiftly shepherds their child away from the predator. As soon as she has done so, the male, too, flies away, leaving the predator puzzled.

The Mongolian plover nests and brings up its young in July.

Pochard: A water bird.

Pochard, Common (Aythya retina): Found in Ladâkh.

Pochard, Ferruginous (Aythya nyroca): Found in Ladâkh.

Pochard, Red-crested (Rhodonessa rufina): Found in Ladâkh.

Raven: The large raven (porok) is very frequently found in the villages. Ravens are birds of prey. They go wherever humans and other animals go. They have been sighted at altitudes of as much as 6,150 metres.

Raven, Common (Corvus corax): Found in Ladâkh.

Raptor: Found in Ladâkh, in the upper reaches.

Redshank, Common (Tringa totanus): Found in Ladâkh.

Redstart, Black (Phoenicurus ochruros): Found in Ladâkh.

Redstart, Blue-capped (Phoenicurus coeruleocephalus): Found in Ladâkh.

Redstart, Guldenstadt's: (Phoenicurus erythrogaster) Found in the Ladâkh region.

Redstart, White-capped Water-(Chaimarrornis leucocephalus): Found in Ladâkh.

Redstart, White-winged (Phoenicurus erythrogaster): Found in Ladâkh.

Rosefinch, see 'Finch.'

Rubythroat, Siberian: (Ogla mamber) The other name of this bird means 'throat in flames.' It visits Ladâkh in large flocks.

Ruby throat, White-tailed (Luscinia pectoralis): Found in Ladâkh.

Sandgrouse, Tibetan: This is a handsome fawn and cream coloured bird. It visits Ladâkh in large flocks.

Sandpiper, Common (Actitis hypoleucos): Found in Ladâkh.

Sandpiper, Green (Tringa ochropus): Found in Ladâkh.

Serin, Fire-fronted (Serinus pusillus): Found in Ladâkh.

Shelduck, Ruddy (Tadorna ferruginea): Found in Ladâkh.

Shrike, Grey-backed (Lanius tephronotus): Found in Ladâkh.

Shrike, Long-tailed (Lanius schach): Found in Ladâkh.

Skylark, Oriental (Alauda gulgula): Found in Ladâkh.

Snowcocks, Himalayan and Tibetan, (Tetraogallus sp.): Found in Ladâkh.: These are large and majestic birds that spend the entire year—indeed, their whole lives—in Ladâkh. Therefore, humans as well as predatory animals hunt them for their meat.

Sparrow, House (Passer domesticus): Found in Ladâkh.

Sparrowhawk, Eurasian (Accipiter nisus): Found in Ladâkh.

Starling, Brahminy (Sturnus pagodarum): Found in Ladâkh.

Starts, red: Visits Ladâkh in large flocks.

Swallow, Barn (Hirundo rustica): Found in Ladâkh.

Swallow, sea: See 'Tern' below.

Swallow, Wire-tailed (Hirundo smithii): Found in Ladâkh.

Swift, Common (Apus apus): Found in Ladâkh.

Swift, Fork-tailed (Apus pacificus): Found in Ladâkh.

Teal: This is a water bird found in Ladâkh near the Rupshu lake. Even more likely to be found near the bigger rivers.

Tern, Common (Sterna hirundo): Found in Ladâkh.

Tern, Whiskered (Chlidonias hybridus): Found in Ladâkh.

Thrush, black-throated: (Turdus ruficollis) It visits the Ladâkh region. Interestingly, it 'winters' in this region.

Thrush, Blue Rock (Monticola solitarius): Found in Ladâkh.

Thrush, Blue Whistling (Myophonus caeruleus): Found in Ladâkh.

Tit, Great (Parus major): Found in Ladâkh.

Twite (Carduelis flavirostris): Found in Ladâkh.

Vultures: Species found in Ladâkh and Kashmîr include the Bearded Vulture. See 'Lammergeier' above.

Wagtail, Citrine (Motacilla citreola): Found in Ladâkh.

Wagtail, Grey (Motacilla cinerea): Found in Ladâkh.

Wagtail, White (Motacilla alba): Found in Ladâkh.

Wagtail, Yellow (Motacilla flava): Found in Ladâkh.

Wall creeper: Visits Ladâkh in large flocks.

Warbler, Hume's (Phylloscopus humel): Found in Ladâkh.

Warbler, Sulphur-bellied (Phylloscopus griseolus): Found in Ladâkh.

Warbler, Tickell's leaf (Phylloscopus affinis): Found in Ladâkh.

Water birds: Their biggest concentration in Ladâkh is near the Rupshu lakes, at altitudes of 14,000' and more. Please also see individual entries in this chapter. (See also 'Hunting' in the chapter on 'Adventure Sports'.)

Waterfowl: Every species of waterfowl is to be found in Kashmîr, and in plenty, in winter when they come down from the colder Yârqañd and Mughalistan. They leave when spring begins. In Ladâkh some species are found in the wetlands.

Wheeler: Visits Ladâkh in large flocks.

Wheatear, Desert (Oenanthe deserti): Found in Ladâkh.

Wheatear, Pied (Oenanthe pleschanka): Found in Ladâkh.

Wheatear, Variable (Oenanthe picata): Found in Ladâkh.

Whitethroat, lesser (Sylvia curruca): Found in Ladâkh.

Wigeon, Eurasian (Anas penelope): Found in Ladâkh.

Wren, Winter (Troglodytes troglodytes): Found in Ladâkh.

Wryneck, Eurasian (Jynx torquilla): Found in Ladâkh.

41

The flora of Ladâkh-Balâwaristân

There are around 880 species of flora (angiosperms, gymnosperms and pteridophytes) in the parts of Ladâkh that are under actual Indian administration.[i] (Kashmir has 3,054 species and Jammu district 506.) I have tried to list such plants, trees and flowers as grow in undivided Ladâkh and Gilgit, including Baltistân, Hunzâ, Astor and the other areas covered by this book. If those species grow in other parts of Jammu and Kashmîr (and adjacent areas), I have mentioned that as well.[1]

Ladâkh proper is an alpine (and, at places, arctic) desert. There is hardly any rainfall, snowfall or moisture in most parts of Leh district and only a little more in Kargil-Zanskar. This affects the vegetation of the region. Ladâkh proper is mostly a treeless desert. However, some plants grow along the banks of rivers and in the moist crevices of rocks. But within deserts there are oases. So, the flora of Ladâkh can be put in three broad categories: alpine, desertic and oasitic.

The alpine vegetation of Ladâkh includes several species that are also found in Kashmîr. Desert (or desertic) flora is mostly found at altitudes, especially barren mountain slopes, that are much higher than the plains of Ladâkh. This kind of vegetation has Tibetan and Siberian elements, is normally stunted and forms tufts. The vegetation of the oases grows along streams, rivulets and village ponds.

Many of the plants that grow in Ladâkh do so only when planted by men. Which means that they do not grow wild, on their own. These crops include barley, gram, lentils, onion, pea, potato and wheat.

1. The Râvi, the Chénâb and the Jehlum are the three big rivers of the state. (None of the three flows through Ladâkh.)

Tree species introduced by men in Ladâkh include apricot, mulberry, walnut and willow.[2] The government has brought in some species of salix and populus because they yield fodder and fuel. Small patches of the native Juniperus macropoda Boiss. are also found in some places.

In Ladâkh alpine vegetation grows mainly in small, confined strips of territory to which some of the melting snow water flows down. The upper beds of mountain streams, too, have alpine vegetation.

Temperatures fluctuate wildly over the months, and often even during the course of a single day. Thus, most of the inhabited parts of Ladâkh could be as hot as 38°C in summer and minus 30°C in winter. Similarly, in summer it could be 38°C at noon and around 10°C at night. As a result, rocks start cracking up and mountains crumble. Therefore, "rock ruin" is common in Ladâkh.

Most of the areas of Ladâkh-Gilgit under Pâkistâni occupation are similar to the ones administered by India. So is the Lahaul-Spiti region of neighbouring Himachal Pradesh. However, some parts of Pâkistân Occupied Ladâkh-Gilgit are greener and are in the temperate zone.

There are several high altitude (4,000 metres plus) lakes in Ladâkh (and in the Pir Panjal Range). Unlike lakes which are at lower altitudes, these lakes have no macro-phytic vegetation. There are twenty-six hotpots in India where rapid deforestation and 'endemicity' are taking place. Ladâkh (like Kashmîr and, indeed, the entire Himâlayas) is among this unfortunate twenty-six. Several species are endangered and will vanish unless all of us—residents as well as tourists—mend our ways.

Medicinal plants: Medicinal flowers are gathered only at midday, by hand, by the stem and carried in baskets. They should never be collected in the morning or cut mechanically (which includes the use of scissors and shears). The petals should never be touched and the plants should never be put in polythene or other synthetic bags.

A representative list is given below. The local name (in Ladâkhi and/ or Urdu-Persian) has often been given in italics, within brackets. The Ladâkhi name might be understood in Baltistân but the Urdu-Persian name will not be understood in Ladâkh. Urdu-Persian names are mainly used in the areas occupied by Pâkistân.

Acantholimon lycopodioides (*Girard*) Boiss (*Longze*): This is a rare and endangered medicinal plant species found on hill slopes in Ladâkh.

2. This sentence is on the authority of a leading botanist. However, apricot and willow, to the best of my knowledge as a historian, are native to several parts of Ladakh, especially Kargil and Hunzâ.

Achillea millefolium L. (*Gul-é-Biranjasif/ Chuang*) Flowers in August -March. Grows in Ladâkh, Gilgit, Swât,, Poonch, Medicinal property: hypotensive and haemostatic. Arrests bleeding.

Achyranthes aspera L. (*Gul-é-Charchitâ*) Flowers in September-April. Gilgit, Used for bleeding piles.

Aconitum balfourii Stapf. (*Bonga nakpo*): This is a rare and endangered medicinal plant species found in Ladâkh.

Aconitum heterophyllum (*Buma*): This is a rare and endangered medicinal plant species found in Ladâkh.

Aconitum rotundifolium (*Bonkar*): This is a rare and endangered medicinal plant species found in Ladâkh.

Aconitum violaceum (*Yangtso; zinba; dusi-lama*): This is a rare and endangered medicinal plant species found in Ladâkh.

Actinocarya tibetica: This is a medicinal plant species found in Ladâkh.

Adonis chrysocyathus (*Semshi*): This is a medicinal plant species found in Ladâkh.

Allium carolinianum (*Gogcheegma*): This is a medicinal plant species found in Ladâkh.

Allium humile Kunth. (*Pocha*): This is a medicinal plant species found in Ladâkh.

Althaea officinalis L. (*Gul-é-Khairo*) Flowers in July-October. Grows in the Muzaffarâbâd region, Medicinal property: demulcent, diuretic, emmolient Used in the treatment of bronchial catarrh and rheumatism.

Anaphalis contorta (*Telgang*): This is a rare and endangered medicinal plant species found in Ladâkh.

Anaphalis cuneifolia (*Simula*): This is a medicinal plant species found in Ladâkh.

Anaphalis nepalensis (*Tawa*): This is a medicinal plant species found in Ladâkh.

Anaphalis nubigena DC. Grows in the alpine parts of Ladâkh (and in Kashmîr).

Anaphalis triplinervis (*Phulu mentock*): This is a medicinal plant species found in Ladâkh.

Androsace aizoon (*Sgatik mugpo*): This is a medicinal plant species found in Ladâkh.

Androsace mucronifolia. (*Zigsolo*): This is a medicinal plant species found in Ladâkh.

Androsace rotundifolia (*Zigsolo*): This is a medicinal plant species found in Ladâkh.

Anemone rivularis (*Zupka*): This is a medicinal plant species found in Ladâkh.

Anemone rupicola (*Simaso*): This is a medicinal plant species found in Ladâkh.

Aquilegia fragrans (*Zadul-dorje*): This is a medicinal plant species found in Ladâkh.

Arabidopsis multiforum (*Imatso*): This is a medicinal plant species found in Ladâkh.

Arabis glandulosa (*Umnako*): This is a medicinal plant species found in Ladâkh.

Arctium lappa (*Miah*): This is a medicinal plant species found in Ladâkh.

Arenaria bryophylla (*Lekhum*): This is a medicinal plant species found in Ladâkh.

Arenaria griffithii (*Sokhtam*): This is a medicinal plant species found in Ladâkh.

Arenaria serpyllifolia L. Grows in the cold deserts of Ladâkh.

Arnebia banthamii Johnston (*Gul-é-Afsantin*) Flowers in October-November. Grows in Kâghân, Poonch Medicinal property: stomachic, tonic and vermifuge.

Arnebia euchroma (*Demok*): This is a rare and endangered medicinal plant species found in Ladâkh. The root, when soaked in (say, mustard) oil, colours the oil red. If applied to the hair, it is said to improve the health of the hair.

Artemisia biennis (*Khampa*): This is a medicinal plant species found in Ladâkh.

Artemisia brevifolia (*Khamchu*): This is a medicinal plant species found in Laḍâkh.

Artemisia desertorum (*Khamlol*): This is a medicinal plant species found in Ladâkh.

Artemisia dracunculus (*Burtse*): This is a medicinal plant species found in Ladâkh.

Artemisia gmelinii (*Khampa or shridhi*): This is a medicinal plant species found in Ladâkh.

Artemisia laciniata (*Bintso*): This is a medicinal plant species found in Ladâkh.

Artemisia maritima: Found in Ladâkh.

Artemisia maritima L. (*Gul-é-Kashmîrî/ Khamchu*) Flowers in August-September. Grows in Ladâkh, Astor, Chitrâl, Swât. Used in the treatment of cardiac problems, fever, and ailments of the throat and tongue. This is a rare and endangered species.

Artemisia maritime (*Phurnag*): This is a medicinal plant species found in Ladâkh.

Artemisia minor (*Phurnag*): This is a medicinal plant species found in Ladâkh.

Artemisia moarcroftiana (*Phurnag*): This is a medicinal plant species found in Ladâkh.

Artemisia parviflora (*Khamang*): This is a medicinal plant species found in Ladâkh.

Artemisia salsalaides (*Amango*): This is a medicinal plant species found in Ladâkh.

Artemisia scoparia (*Khamtso*): This is a medicinal plant species found in Ladâkh.

Artemisia sieversiana (*Khamchu*): This is a medicinal plant species found in Ladâkh.

Artemisia stracheyi (*Rumonlo*): This is a medicinal plant species found in Ladâkh.

Artemisia stricta Edgew. Grows in the cold deserts of Ladâkh.

Aster diplostephiodes (*Ba-sha-ka* or *Luqchunq*)

Aster flaccidus (*Lugmig, Chunwa:* small): This is a medicinal plant species found in Ladâkh.

Aster strachey (*Lugmig metura*): This is a medicinal plant species found in Ladâkh.

Astragalus rhizanthus (*Sarma*): This is a medicinal plant species found in Ladâkh.

Astragalus spp. Grows in the cold deserts of Ladâkh.

Astragalus strictus (*Serpang*): This is a medicinal plant species found in Ladâkh.

Astragalus thizanthus Royle ex Senth: Grows in the alpine parts of Ladâkh (and in Kashmîr).

Astragalus tribulifolia (*Vanglo*): This is a medicinal plant species found in Ladâkh.

Atelanthera perpusilla: This is a medicinal plant species found in Ladâkh.

Berberis pachyacantha: Grows on alpine slopes and in sheltered ravines in Ladâkh.

Berberis zabe (*Sherpa*): This is a medicinal plant species found in Ladâkh.

Bergenia stracheyi (*Dak-kya-hawo, gatikpa*): This is a rare and endangered medicinal plant species found in Ladâkh.

Betula utilis (*Takpa*): This is a rare and endangered medicinal plant species found in Ladâkh.

Biebersteinia odora (*Khardung*): This is a medicinal plant species found in Ladâkh.

Bistorta affinis (*Langna*): This is a medicinal plant species found in Ladâkh.

Bistorta vivipara (*Naram, Langangpa*): This is a medicinal plant species found in Ladâkh.

Blumea bifoliata (*Leuman*): This is a medicinal plant species found in Ladâkh.

Bupleurum himalayense (*Sah-kuchak*): This is a medicinal plant species found in Ladâkh.

Bupleurum marginatum (*Zira-sherpo*): This is a medicinal plant species found in Ladâkh.

C. wallichii DO: Grows on hill slopes in Ladâkh.

Capparis spinosa: Found in shrublands and patchy forests at the bottom of valleys.

Capsella bursa-pastoris (*Zokka*): This is a medicinal plant species found in Ladâkh.

Caragana gerardiana (*Zomosing*): This is a medicinal plant species found in Ladâkh.

Caragana versicolor (*Loosing*): This is a medicinal plant species found in Ladâkh.

Caragana versicolor Benth: Grows on hill slopes in Ladâkh.

Carum bulbocastanum (*Gosnyod*): This is a medicinal plant species found in Ladâkh.

Carum carvi (*Gonyot*): This is a medicinal plant species found in Ladâkh.

Centauria picris (*Konpa, Iqabskves*): This is a medicinal plant species found in Ladâkh.

Cerastium cerastoides· (*Spangian, kamo, panqien*): This is a medicinal plant species found in Ladâkh.

Chenopodium botrys (*Sanyek*): This is a medicinal plant species found in the cold deserts of Ladâkh.

Chenopodium foliolosum (*Sanyek*): This is a medicinal plant species found in Ladâkh.

Chenopodium hybridum (*Sanyek*): This is a medicinal plant species found in Ladâkh.

Christolea crassifolia: This is a medicinal plant species found in Ladâkh.

Chrysanthemum cinerarifolium (*Gul-é-Dâwoodi*): Flowers in March-July. Grows in Abbotâbâd Medicinal property: aperient. Used in the treatment of sore eyes, upset stomach.

Chrysanthemum griffithi. (*Serpan*): This is a medicinal plant species found in Ladâkh.

Chrysanthemum pyrethroides (*Serpan; bhurse-khampa*): This is a medicinal plant species found in Ladâkh.,

Chrysanthemum tibeticum (Hk. f. and Th. ex Cl.) (*Jerium, Phemantso*): This is a medicinal plant species found on hill slopes in Ladâkh.

Circium arvense (L.) Scop. *(Soh-chlia):* This is a medicinal plant species found on hill slopes in Ladâkh.

Circium wallichii (*Kakar*): This is a medicinal plant species found in Ladâkh.

Clematis orientalis. (*Emong nakpo*): This is a medicinal plant species found in Ladâkh.

Clematis tibetina (*Zakzic*): This is a medicinal plant species found in Ladâkh.

Codonopsis clematidea (*Ludut dorje*): This is a medicinal plant species found in Ladâkh.

Codonopsis ovata: This is a medicinal plant species found in Ladâkh.

Codonopsis rotundifolia (*Klupdud dorje*): This is a medicinal plant species found in Ladâkh.

Conringia planisiliqua (*Khaskar*): This is a medicinal plant species found in Ladâkh.

Convolvulus arvensis (*Grachi*): This is a medicinal plant species found in Ladâkh.

Corispermum hyssopifolium (*Seimso*): This is a medicinal plant species found in Ladâkh.

Corydalis diphylla L.: Grows in the alpine parts of Ladâkh (and in Kashmîr).

Corydalis govaniana (*Tongru-silva*): This is a medicinal plant species found in Ladâkh.

Corydalis meifolia (*Tonzil*): This is a medicinal plant species found in Ladâkh.

Corydalis rutifolia (*Chimlo*): This is a medicinal plant species found in Ladâkh.

Corydalis tibetica (*Stong zil*): This is a medicinal plant species found in Ladâkh.

Cousinia thomsonii (*Chansar; nag po; batsatsuak*): This is a medicinal plant species found in Ladâkh.

Cremanthodium arnicoides (*Rekonpa*): This is a medicinal plant species found in Ladâkh.

Cremanthodium ellisii (*Dariya kan*): This is a rare and endangered medicinal plant species found in Ladâkh.

Crepis flexuosa (*Remang*): This is a medicinal plant species found in Ladâkh.

Crepis stoliczkai Cl.: Grows on hill slopes in Ladâkh.

Crocus sativus: This is a medicinal plant species found in Ladâkh.

Cuscuta approximata (*Amarlata*): This is a medicinal plant species found in Ladâkh.

Cuscuta capitata (*Amarlata*): This is a medicinal plant species found in Ladâkh.

Cuscuta europaea (*Amarlata*): This is a medicinal plant species found in Ladâkh.

Cuscuta reflexa (*Amarlata*): This is a medicinal plant species found in Ladâkh.

Cymbopogon jwarancusa Schult (*Gul-é-Khawi*): Flowers in July-October. Grows in Chitrâl, Gilgit. Medicinal property: blood purifier, styptic and tonic.

Dactylorhiza hatagirea (*Sanchu; angbolakpa, wanoluk*): This is a rare and endangered medicinal plant species found in Ladâkh.

Daphne mucronate: This is a medicinal plant species found in Ladâkh.

Delphinium brunonianum (*Lunde-kaown*): This is a medicinal plant species found in Ladâkh.

Delphinium brunonianum (*Lunde-kaown*): This is a rare and endangered medicinal plant species found in Ladâkh.

Delphinium cashmerianum (*Lunde-kaown; cha-gotpa*): This is a rare and endangered medicinal plant species found above 4,500 metres in Ladâkh.

Delphinium cashmerianum Royle: Grows in the alpine parts of Ladâkh (and in Kashmîr).

Delphinium viscosum (*Bilamonokh*): This is a medicinal plant species found in Ladâkh.

Descurainia sophia (*Teri-latchij*): This is a medicinal plant species found in Ladâkh.

Dianthus anatolicus: Grows in Ladâkh.

Dianthus anatolicus Boiss: This is a medicinal plant species found in the cold deserts of Ladâkh.

Dioscorea deltoidea: Grows mainly in Kashmîr and Jammu. Its tubers are rich in diosgenin and yield cortisone, a steroid hormone.

Dracocephalum heterophyllum (*Zinkzer, driangu, priyanku*): This is a medicinal plant species found in Ladâkh.

Dracocephalum moldavicum (*Kirmir*): This is a medicinal plant species found in Ladâkh.

Dracocephalum staminium (*Ghiromanko*): This is a medicinal plant species found in Ladâkh.

Drumm. (*Gyamobdebyin*): This is a medicinal plant species found in Ladâkh.

Echinops cornigerus (*Ekzema*): This is a medicinal plant species found in Ladâkh.

Echinops niveus (*Ekzema*): This is a medicinal plant species found in Ladâkh.

Ephedra gerardiana (*Chhapat; tse*): This is a rare and endangered medicinal plant species found in Ladâkh.

Ephedra gerardiana Wall. ex Royle: Grows on hill slopes in Ladâkh.

Epilobium angustifolium. (*Utpal-wanbo*): This is a medicinal plant species found in Ladâkh.

Epipactis hēlleborine (*Penginlo*): This is a medicinal plant species found in Ladâkh.

Equisetum spp.: Grows near water bodies/ oases in Ladâkh.

Eragrostis poaeoides (*Gieng*): This is a medicinal plant species found in Ladâkh.

Erigeron alpinus (*Repan*): This is a medicinal plant species found in Ladâkh.

Eriobotrya japonica Lindley (*Gul-é-Lokât*) Flowers in July-August. Grows in the sub-Himâlayan Zone Medicinal property: Its flowers are expectorants.

Eritricum canam (*Changser, tukse*): This is a medicinal plant species found in Ladâkh.

Ermania lanuginosa (*Measlo*): This is a medicinal plant species found in Ladâkh.

Erodium tibetanum: This is a medicinal plant species found in Ladâkh.

Euphorbia stracheyi (*Tingling*): This is a medicinal plant species found in Ladâkh.

Euphorbia tibetica (*Tingling*): This is a medicinal plant species found in Ladâkh.

Euphrasia laxa (*Kianglo*): This is a medicinal plant species found in Ladâkh.

Ferula jaeschkeana: (*Thunak, risho*):This is a rare and endangered medicinal plant species found in Ladâkh.

Fritillaria roylei: (*Chikmo*): This is a rare and endangered medicinal plant species found in Ladâkh.

Galium boreale L.: Grows in the alpine parts of Ladâkh (and in Kashmîr).

Galium pauciflorum (*Phomongo*): This is a medicinal plant species found in Ladâkh.

Galium serpilloides (*Pemantso*): This is a medicinal plant species found in Ladâkh.

Gentiana algida (*Pungen carpov*): This is a medicinal plant species found in Ladâkh.

Gentiana carinata (*Ziang*): This is a medicinal plant species found in Ladâkh.

Gentiana decumbense L.: Grows near water bodies/ oases in Ladâkh.

Gentiana kurrooa (*Pangyin*): This is a rare and endangered medicinal plant species found in Ladâkh.

Gentiana nubigena (*Pangyin*): This is a medicinal plant species found in Ladâkh.

Gentiana olivieri (*Khilche nagpo*): This is a medicinal plant species found in Ladâkh.

Gentiana squarrosa (*Ziang*): This is a medicinal plant species found in Ladâkh.

Gentiana stracheyi (*Ziang*): This is a medicinal plant species found in Ladâkh.

Gentianella moorcroftiana (*Teekta*): This is a medicinal plant species found in Ladâkh.

Gentianella paludosa (*Pallutso*): This is a medicinal plant species found in Ladâkh.

Gentianopsis detonsa (*Shiti*): This is a medicinal plant species found in Ladâkh.

Geranium pratens Linn. (*Gagchuk; ngon-boo*): Grows in the alpine parts of Ladâkh (and in Kashmîr) and near water bodies/ oases in Ladâkh.

Geranium sibiricum (*Eyamlomentok*): This is a rare and endangered medicinal plant species found in Ladâkh.

Geranium tuberaria (*Yusiang*): This is a medicinal plant species found in Ladâkh.

GiGer microphyllum. (*Seri-jriboo*): This is a medicinal plant species found in Ladâkh.

Glechoma tibetica: Grows above 4,500 metres in Ladâkh.

Gnaphalium affine (*Gandha pattra*): This is a medicinal plant species found in Ladâkh.

Gnaphalium stewartii (*Peo*): This is a medicinal plant species found in Ladâkh.

Halepestes tricuspis: This is a medicinal plant species found in Ladâkh.

Heracieum pinnatum Cl.: Grows in the cold deserts of Ladâkh.

Heracleum lanatum (*Tunak, tukar*): This is a rare and endangered medicinal plant species found in Ladâkh.

Herminium monorchis: This is a rare and endangered medicinal plant species found in Ladâkh.

Hibiscus cannabinus L. (*Gul-é-Ambari*): Flowers in autumn-winter. Grows in Swât, Chitrâl Used in the treatment of Gastritis and constipation.

Hippophae rhamnoides (*Tar-ngoo, starbu, zino*): This is a rare and endangered medicinal plant species found in Ladâkh. It is found in shrublands and patchy forests at the bottom of valleys. See 'Seabuckthorn' below.

Hippuris vulgaris L.: Grows in the cold deserts of Ladâkh.

Humulus lupulus L. (*Gul-é-Junjul*): Flowers in July-August. Grows in Ladâkh, Pangi on the upper Chenab. Medicinal property: antiseptic, stomach tonic diuretic. Used in the treatment of hardness of uterus, female inflorescence (hop) and swellings.

Hyoscyamus niger (*Thangdum, langtang-tse*): This is a rare and endangered medicinal plant species found in Ladâkh.

Hypericum leptocarpus (*Meerang*): This is a medicinal plant species found in Ladâkh.

Hyssopus officinalis L. (*Gul-é-Zoffâ/ Jip-chi, chibu*): Flowers in June-September. This is a medicinal plant species found in Ladâkh, Kashmir, Pangi, Upper Chenab. Used in the treatment of chest congestions. A 'tea' made of its flowers is an expectorant.

Impatiens balsamina L. (*Gul-é-Mehñdiâ*): Flowers in July-October. Grows in Chitrâl, Medicinal property: antibiotic. Used in the treatment of intercostal neuralgia and lumbago.

Impatiens glandulifera Royle: Grows in the alpine parts of Ladâkh (and in Kashmîr).

Iniula rhizocephala (*Riamko*): This is a medicinal plant species found in Ladâkh.

Inula racemosa (*Manu*): This is a rare and endangered medicinal plant species found in Ladâkh.

Inula royleana. (*Ukchha*): This is a medicinal plant species found in Ladâkh.

Iris ensata (*Banpiaj*): This is a medicinal plant species found in Ladâkh.

Juglans regiaL. (*Akhrot*): This is a medicinal plant species found in Ladâkh.

Juniperus communis (*Shukpa*): This is a rare and endangered medicinal plant species found in Ladâkh.

Juniperus macropoda and J. indica: Found in steppe juniper forests in small patches on cliffs and sloping land.

Juniperus macropoda Boiss: Grows in very small quantities in some parts of the Ladâkhi desert.

Juniperus polycarpus: Grows on alpine slopes and in sheltered ravines in Ladâkh.

Juniperus recurva (*Shukpa*): This is a rare and endangered medicinal plant species found in Ladâkh.

Jurinea ceratocarpa (*Chholmong*): This is a medicinal plant species found in Ladâkh.

Koelpinia linearis (*Nodar*): This is a medicinal plant species found in Ladâkh.

Lactuca serriola (*Dudej*): This is a medicinal plant species found in Ladâkh.

Lagotis kunawurensis (*Tsermo*): This is a medicinal plant species found in Ladâkh.

Lancea tibetica (*Payak-tsa*): This is a rare and endangered medicinal plant species found in Ladâkh.

Lavatera kashmiriana Camb: Grows in the alpine parts of Ladâkh and Kasimîr.

Leontopodium nanum (Hk.f. and Th.) Hand.-Mazz. (*Palu*): This is a medicinal plant species found on hill slopes in Ladâkh.

Leontopodium nanum: Grows in Ladâkh.

Lepidium latifolium (*Shangshu*): This is a medicinal plant species found in Ladâkh.

Leucas aspera Spreng. (*Gul-é-Tumbâ*): Flowers in August-February. Grows in Jammu, Ravi, Chenab, Used in the treatment of children's coughs and colds.

Leucopoa albida (*Fukche*): This is a medicinal plant species found in Ladâkh.

LIoydia serafina: (*Kangkar; tsa-awa, anwa*): This is a rare and endangered medicinal plant species found in Ladâkh.

lnula falconeri (Hk.f.): Grows on hill slopes in Ladâkh.

Lomatogonium rotatum (*Tsemrang*): This is a medicinal plant species found in Ladâkh.

Lonicera spinosa (*Lamora*): This is a medicinal plant species found in Ladâkh.

Loontopodium spp.: Grows in the alpine parts of Ladâkh (and in Kashmîr).

Lotus corniculatus L.: Grows in the alpine parts of Ladâkh (and in Kashmîr).

Luppula barbata: This is a medicinal plant species found in Ladâkh.

Lychnis nutans (*Lappu*): This is a medicinal plant species found in Ladâkh.

Lycium ruthenicum (*Umila*): This is a medicinal plant species found in Ladâkh, in shrublands and patchy forests at the bottom of valleys.

Malva sylvestris. (*Sotsal*): This is a medicinal plant species found in Ladâkh.

Malva verticillala (*Chirati*): This is a medicinal plant species found in Ladâkh.

Marrubium vulgare (*Trapper*): This is a medicinal plant species found in Ladâkh.

Mattiastrum thomsonii: This is a medicinal plant species found in Ladâkh.

Meconopsis aculeata (*Serhun, tsenmon*): This is a medicinal plant species found in Ladâkh.

Meconopsis aculeata (*Serhun, tsergnon*): This is a rare and endangered medicinal plant species found in Ladâkh.

Meconopsis horridula (*Udpalsnogpo*): This is a medicinal plant species found in Ladâkh.

Meconopsis simplicifolia (*Udpalsnogpo*): This is a medicinal plant species found in Ladâkh.

Meconopsls sinuate (*Udpalsnogpo*): This is a medicinal plant species found in Ladâkh.

Medicago lupulina (*Gunyok*): This is a medicinal plant species found in Ladâkh.

Melica persica (*Tandi*): This is a medicinal plant species found in Ladâkh.

Mentha longifolia (*Phololing*): This is a medicinal plant species found in Ladâkh.

Mertensia tibetica: Grows on alpine slopes and in sheltered ravines in Ladâkh.

Mirabilis jalapa L. (*Gul-é-Abbâs*): Flowers in November-January. Grows in Hunzâ, Gilgit. Used in the treatment of haemarrhoids.

Morina coulteriana (*Khundaj, kare*): This is a medicinal plant species found in Ladâkh.

Morina longifolia (*Biskandara*): This is a medicinal plant species found in Ladâkh.

Myricaria elegans: Found in shrublands and patchy forests at the bottom of valleys.

Myricaria elegans Royle: Grows on hill slopes and near water bodies/ oases in Ladâkh.

Myricaria rose (*Hombuk*): This is a medicinal plant species found in Ladâkh.

Myricaria squamosa (*Ombu*): This is a medicinal plant species found in Ladâkh.

Nepeta cataria (*Gandhsoi*): This is a medicinal plant species found in Ladâkh.

Nepeta coerulenscens (*Neimlo*): This is a medicinal plant species found in Ladâkh.

Nepeta discolor (*Nyomalo*): This is a medicinal plant species found in Ladâkh.

Nepeta erecta (*Eripantso*): This is a medicinal plant species found in Ladâkh.

Nepeta eriostachia (*Zimthik Ie*): This is a medicinal plant species found in Ladâkh.

Nepeta flloccosa (*Shamalolo*): This is a medicinal plant species found in Ladâkh.

Nepeta glutinosa (*Gimanko*): This is a medicinal plant species found in Ladâkh.

Nepeta leucolaena (*Beimtso*): This is a medicinal plant species found in Ladâkh.

Nepeta longibracteata (*Teyanku*): This is a medicinal plant species found in Ladâkh.

Nepeta podostachys (*Shangukaram*): This is a medicinal plant species found in Ladâkh.

Nepeta spp.: Grows above 4,500 metres in Ladâkh.

Onosma hispidum Wall. (*Gul-é-Laljari*): Flowers in March-July. Grows in Landikotal, Swât, Chitrâl, Kâghân. Medicinal property: cardiac tonic, stimulant.

Origanum vulgare L. (*Lachung*): This is a medicinal plant species found near water bodies/ oases in Ladâkh.

Oxyfropis microphylla (*Stagsha nagpo*): This is a medicinal plant species found in Ladâkh.

Oxyria digyna (*Chur-tse, chum tse*): This is a medicinal plant species found in Ladâkh.

Oxytropis cachameriana Camb.: Grows in the alpine parts of Ladâkh (and in Kashmîr).

Oxytropis microphylla (*Taksha, rechakpa*): This is a medicinal plant species found in Ladâkh.

Oxytropis tatarica (*Sarkash*): This is a medicinal plant species found in Ladâkh.

Paeonia emodi Wall. (*Gul-é-Ud-Salap*): Flowers in May-June. Grows on moist ground in Kâghân, Chitrâl, Bahrin, Poonch. Used in the treatment of diarrhoea

Paraguilegia microphylla: This is a medicinal plant species found in Ladâkh.

Parnassia palustris L.: Grows in the alpine parts of Ladâkh (and in Kashmîr) and near water bodies/ oases in Ladâkh.

Pedicularis longifolia. (*Phakchang, lunori zarpo*): This is a medicinal plant species found in Ladâkh.

Pedicularis megalantha (*Lungruk makpo*): This is a medicinal plant species found in Ladâkh.

Pedicularis pectinata (*Lungri muppo*): This is a medicinal plant species found in Ladâkh.

Pedicularis cheilanthifolia (*Kikimo*): This is a medicinal plant species found in Ladâkh.

Pedicularis tongiflora Rudolph: Grows in the alpine parts of Ladâkh (and in Kashmîr).

Peganum harmala (*Sepan*): This is a medicinal plant species found in shrublands and patchy forests at the bottom of valleys in Ladâkh.

Pervoskia abrotanoides Karel (*Gul-é-Shanshohai*): Flowers in September-October. Grows in Chitrâl, Gilgit, Hunzâ, Ladâkh and Ziarat Used in the treatment of fevers.

Phragmites karka (*Retz.*) **Trin. ex Steud:** Grows near water bodies/ oases in Ladâkh.

Physochlaina praealta (*Langthang*): This is a rare and endangered medicinal plant species found in Laḍâkh.

Picrorhiza kurrooa Royle (*Honglen*): This is a rare and endangered medicinal plant species found in Ladâkh.

Plantago depressa (*Tharam*): This is a medicinal plant species found in Ladâkh.

Plantago erosa (*Tharam*): This is a medicinal plant species found in Ladâkh.

Plantago himalaica (*Karache, nikto*): This is a medicinal plant species found in Ladâkh.

Plantago major (*Riew kai*): This is a medicinal plant species found in Ladâkh.

Pleurospermum angelicoides (*Chhipi*): This is a medicinal plant species found in Ladâkh.

Poa annua L.: Grows in the alpine parts of Ladâkh (and in Kashmîr).

Podophyllum hexandrum (*Demobkusu, tandik*): This is a rare and endangered medicinal plant species found in Ladâkh.

Podophyllum hexandrum Royle ex Camb: Grows in the alpine parts of Ladâkh and Kashmîr.

Polygonum affine D. Don: Grows in the alpine parts of Ladâkh (and in Kashmîr).

Polygonum paronychioides (*Nhachu*): This is a medicinal plant species found in Ladâkh.

Polygonum polystachium (*Chutzi nagpo*): This is a medicinal plant species found in Ladâkh.

Polygonum viviparum: Grows on alpine slopes and in sheltered ravines in Ladâkh.

Potentilla anserine: This is a medicinal plant species found in Ladâkh.

Potentilla atrosanguinea (*Chisheng*): This is a medicinal plant species found in Ladâkh.

Potentilla bifurca L.: Grows in the alpine parts as well as deserts of Ladâkh (and in Kashmîr).

Potentilla desertorum: Grows on alpine slopes and in sheltered ravines in Ladâkh.

Potentilla fruticosa (*Khiamgar*): This is a medicinal plant species found in Ladâkh.

Potentilla fruticosa: Grows above 4,500 metres in Ladâkh.

Potentilla salesoviana. (*E-mong karvo*): This is a medicinal plant species found in Ladâkh.

Primula denticulata: This is a medicinal plant species found in Ladâkh.

Primula macrophylla (*Sulumentok, kilche*): This is a medicinal plant species found in Ladâkh.

Primula rosea (*Sulumentok*): This is a rare and endangered medicinal plant species found in Ladâkh.

Prunella vulgaris (*Syangave*): This is a medicinal plant species found in Ladâkh.

Psychrogeton andryaloides (*Lukchung ba*): This is a medicinal plant species found in Ladâkh.

Pterocephalus hookerii (*Spang-tsi-dowo*): This is a medicinal plant species found in Ladâkh.

Ranunculus brotherusii (*Maokiang*): This is a medicinal plant species found in Ladâkh.

Ranunculus laetus (*Sharchang*): This is a medicinal plant species found in Ladâkh.

Ranunculus lobatus (*Zamtso*): This is a medicinal plant species found in Ladâkh.

Rheum emodi (*Tukshu*): This is a rare and endangered medicinal plant species found in Ladâkh.

Rheum moorcroftianum (*Tukshu*): This is a rare and endangered medicinal plant species found in Ladâkh.

Rheum webbianum (*Tukshu*): This is a rare and endangered medicinal plant species found in Ladâkh.

Rhododendron anthopogon (*Balu*): This is a medicinal plant species found in Ladâkh.

Rhodiola heterodonta (*Sholo-marvo*): This is a medicinal plant species found in Ladâkh.

Rhodiola imbricate (*Shrolu*): This is a medicinal plant species found in Ladâkh.

Rhododendron anthopogon (*Balu*): This is a rare and endangered medicinal plant species found in Ladâkh.

Rosa foetida Herrm. (*Gul-é-Briar*): Flowers in January-July. Grows in Kurrum, Ziarat Used in the treatment of diarrhoea.

Rosa webbiana: Grows on alpine slopes and in sheltered ravines in Ladâkh.

Rosa, sericea (*Rongsal, syan, sib*): This is a medicinal plant species found in Ladâkh.

Salix denticulata: Grows on alpine slopes and in sheltered ravines in Ladâkh.

Salix viminalis: Found in shrublands and patchy forests at the bottom of valleys.

Salsola collina Pall.: Grows in the cold deserts of Ladâkh.

Sambucas nigra L. (*Gul-é-Uti-Khaman*): Flowers in March-April. Grows in Parachinar, Nathiagali, Medicinal property: laxative; stimulates blood circulation. Used in the treatment of skin irritation.

Saussurea bracteata. (*Pang-tsi dowo*): This is a rare and endangered medicinal plant species found in Ladâkh.

Saussurea gnaphaloides (*Yuliang, pang-tsi*): This is a rare and endangered medicinal plant species found in Ladâkh.

Saussurea lappa (*Kut*): This is a rare and endangered medicinal plant species found in Ladâkh.

Saussurea obvallata (*Spangsetobo*): This is a rare and endangered medicinal plant species found in Ladâkh.

Saussurea subulata Cl.: Grows in the cold deserts of Ladâkh.

Sedum ewersii. (*Churuppa*): This is a medicinal plant species found in Ladâkh.

Seabuckthorn (*Hippophae rhamnoides; chharma* in Ladâkhi) is the reigning superstar of Ladâkhi flora. The extracts of its berry are being credited with all kinds of miraculous medicinal properties, not least of which is this thorny shrub's ability to earn billions of dollars in foreign exchange for India, and neighbouring China. The shrub grows wild in various parts of the Indian Himâlayas, notably Ladâkh, Lahaul-Spiti (HP), Sikkim and Uttarânchal.[ii]

Miraculous properties: Seabuckthorn is a deciduous shrub. It is said to have the ability to absorb nitrogen from the air and 'fix' it in the soil. This enhances the fertility of the soil. It is being claimed that the Seabuckthorn fruit has more than a hundred nutrients essential for the functioning of the human body. Besides, it is full of a gas that all of us need very badly in Ladâkh—oxygen.

The shrub yields small golden berries, products of which are being marketed commercially as 'Leh berries' (because that name is less of a mouthful than either seabuckthorn or Hippophae rhamnoides.) Extracts from these berries are said to be rich in eight vitamins, including the vitamins A, B1, B2, E and K, as well as twenty four minerals, eighteen amino acids and several anti-oxidants. The seabuckthorn berry is supposed to have the highest concentration of vitamin C among all fruits. Its extracts are now being sold in the form of juice, jam and sauce.

As mentioned, the shrub is good not only for men but also for the soil. It has an elaborate root system and a 'compact canopy system,' which protect the soil from wind and water erosion. The shrub upgrades fragile and marginal mountain slopes by binding the soil softly.

And after we humans have sucked all the goodies out of the berry and the soil has been pumped with nitrogen, what do we do with its seeds, leaves, branches and bark? Obviously, they can't simply be thrown away. So, the local people use them as fuel and animal fodder.

Why does this wonder shrub grow only in the Indian and Chinese Himâlayas? Apparently that's because of the clean air, pure snow, extreme cold and awesome altitudes of the Himâlayas.

Phytochemical studies: Two of the scientists[3] who were posted in Ladâkh and have applied for a patent for a herbal beverage, teamed up with three scientists[4] based in Kerala, which is at the other end of the country. They conducted 'phytochemical investigations' on seabuckthorn samples collected from Ladâkh. They analysed the fruit, the seed and the leaves separately. They found:

i) carotenoids (mainly beta-carotene), tocopherols, fatty acids and steroids (mainly sitosterol) in the 'non-polar fractions;'
ii) terpenoids in the seed oil;
iii) phenolics and carbohydrates in the 'polar fractions;'
iv) plenty of beta-carotene (and some xanthophylls) in the fruit and the seeds;
v) decent quantities of ursolic acid in the seeds and leaves;
vi) beta-amyrin and uvaol as minor terpenoids; and
vii) palmitic acid, palmitoleic acid, stearic acid, oleic acid, linoleic acid and linolenic acid in the fatty acid;
viii) complex glycosides of flavonoids in the polar fractions.
ix) glycosides (mainly glucosides) of isorhamnetin and kaempferol;
x) the amounts of ascorbic acid and flavonoids were lower than the data contained in literature; and
xi) the levels of the phytochemicals varied enormously, depending on which part of Ladâkh the sample had been taken from, as well as on 'the physiological stage.'

Note of caution: In the chapter about the fabled longevity of the Hunzâkuts people I had sounded a note of caution. I had mentioned that a very large number of websites about the supposed elixir-like qualities of the water of Hunzâ had links to a commercial organisation. Now that seabuckthorn is being sought to be identified with the life-restoring Sañjîvani herb of the Hiñdu epics, I must say the same about the websites that tout the supposed wonders of seabuckthorn. Most of them uncritically quote the five scientists who discovered the berry's properties, and many of these websites have been sponsored by a Delhi-based corporation.

3. S. Dwivedi and O.P.Chaurasia, both of the Field Research Laboratory (DRDO), Ladakh. The other pioneering scientists who had, together with these two, applied for the patent are Col DP Attrey, Shri Basant Ballabh and Dr. Brahma Singh.

4. R. Kala, P.S. Hema and A. Banerji, all three of the Phytochemical Research Unit, Regional Research Laboratory, Trivandrum-695 019.

I do not have the qualifications to question the findings listed on the internet. Nor am I casting aspersions on them. However, in both cases it is my duty to point out the nature of the sponsorship of websites about the elixir-like water of Hunzâ and the wondrous berry of Leh. I should also mention that some Ladâkhi botanists, who do not have a direct commercial interest in the berry, are convinced that the berry's properties are every bit as good as they are cracked to be.

Mass appeal: Seabuckthorn's appeal transcends religious, and national, borders. Genghis Khan and his cavalrymen, it is said, ate seabuckthorn berries, seed and oil to improve the memory as well as physical strength. Obviously they overdosed on the noble berry. They could never forget a slight or an insult, and had the stamina and prowess to get even with everyone who had rubbed them the wrong way.

Russian cosmonauts, we are told, ate seabuckthorn products on. board the Mir because it gave them some extra oxygen. No wonder they did better than their American counterparts.

Personally, I love the taste of all seabuckthorn products. However, their labels point out that they have all been sweetened artificially.

It is possible that I might live an extra eleven minutes because I consumed a lot of delicious seabuckthorn juice, jam and sauce in my youth. Till then I will continue to need to wear a cap to look photogenic for the picture on the inside flap of the jacket of this book.

Selinum vaginatum: This is a rare and endangered medicinal plant species found in Ladâkh.

Senecio graciliflorus (*Zerjum*): This is a medicinal plant species found in Ladâkh.

Senecio leatus (*Hechiang*): This is a medicinal plant species found in Ladâkh.

Senecio tibeticus (*Niyamgar*): This is a medicinal plant species found in Ladâkh.

Silene indica (*Shukoa, luqsuk*): This is a medicinal plant species found in Ladâkh.

Silene longicarpophora: Grows above 4,500 metres in Ladâkh.

Silene moorcroftiana (*Timuksa*): This is a medicinal plant species found in Ladâkh.

Silybum marianum Gaertn. (*Holy thistle*): Flowers in March-April. Grows in Abbotâbâd, Mirpur, Its flower heads are used in the treatment of diabetes.

Sophora alopecuroides: Found in shrublands and patchy forests at the bottom of valleys.

Spiraea lycoides: Grows on alpine slopes and in sheltered ravines in Ladâkh.

Stachys sericea Wall: Grows in the alpine parts of Ladâkh (and in Kashmîr).

Stachys tibetica Vatck: Grows in the cold deserts of Ladâkh.

Swerlia petiolata (*Heising*): This is a medicinal plant species found in Ladâkh.

Swerlia thomsonii. (*Tikta*): This is a medicinal plant species found in Ladâkh.

T. tibeticum (Hk. f and Th. ex Cl.): Grows in the cold deserts of Ladâkh.

Tamaricaria elegans (*Hombuk*): This is a medicinal plant species found in Ladâkh.

Tanacetum dolichophyllum (*Seigmanlo*): This is a medicinal plant species found in Ladâkh.

Tanacetum gracile Hook.f. (*Gul-é-Tansy/ Khamchu*): This is a medicinal plant species found in Ladâkh and Hunzâ. Flowers in June-August. Used in the treatment of children's worms.

Tanacetum longifolium (*Bhurse-khampa*): This is a medicinal plant species found in Ladâkh.

Tanacetum nanam (*Phulumentok*): This is a rare and endangered medicinal plant species found in Ladâkh.

Tanacetum tenuifolium (*Autang*): This is a medicinal plant species found in Ladâkh.

Tanacetum tibeticum (*Khurmang*): This is a medicinal plant species found in Ladâkh.

Taraxacum officinale (*Han, khurmang*): This is a medicinal plant species found in Ladâkh.

Tenacetum fruticulosum Ledeb.: Grows in the cold deserts of Ladâkh.

Thalaspi alpestre L.: Grows in the alpine parts of Ladâkh (and in Kashmîr).

Thalictrum alpinum: This is a medicinal plant species found in Ladâkh.

Thalictrum foetidum. (*Haichinsah*): This is a medicinal plant species found in Ladâkh.

Thalictrum minus (*Chak-choo*): This is a medicinal plant species found in Ladâkh.

Thermopsis inflate (*Khymang; chudup*): This is a medicinal plant species found in Ladâkh.

Thlaspi arvense (*Bumak*): This is a medicinal plant species found in Ladâkh.

Thlaspt montanumL. (*Bumuk*): This is a medicinal plant species found in Ladâkh.

Thylacospermum caespitosum (Camb.) Schischk.: Grows on hill slopes in Ladâkh. This plant has the habit to form a cushion. One variety has a diminutive or miniature 'habit.' The 'bushy habit' is the common adaptation found in plants of the cold desert.

Thymus linearis (*Taksha nakpo*): This is a rare and endangered medicinal plant species found in Ladâkh.

Tragopogon gracilis (*Thar-noo, akhron*): This is a medicinal plant species found in Ladâkh.

Tribulus terrestris (*Zema rave*): This is a medicinal plant species found in in shrublands and patchy forests at the bottom of valleys Ladâkh.

Trifolium pratense L. (*Gul-é-Trepatrâ*): Flowers in February-April. Grows in Chitrâl, Astor,, Swât, Used in the treatment of asthma and spasmodic bronchitis. Medicinal property: expectorant.

Triglochin palustris. (*Puga, gaike*): This is a medicinal plant species found in Ladâkh.

Trigonella emodi (*Bhusu hung*): This is a medicinal plant species found in Ladâkh.

Urena lobata L. (*Gul-é-Bachitâ*): Flowers in Sept.-December. Grows in Changa Manga, Medicinal property: aphthosis, expectorant. Used in the treatment of sore throats.

Urtica hyperborean (*Pachoo, zasot*): This is a medicinal plant species found in Ladâkh.

Urtica urens (*Zabo, zatsut*): This is a medicinal plant species found in Ladâkh.

Verbascum thapsus L. (*Gul-é-Gidhar*) Flowers in June-August. Grows in Chitrâl, Mansehra Used in the treatment of coughs, diarrhoea, and throat irritation. Medicinal property: febrifuge, stimulant.

Veronica macrostemon (*Shimiogar*): This is a medicinal plant species found in Ladâkh.

Vinca major L. (*Gul-é-Periwinkle*): Flowers in December-March. Grows in Parachinar, Abbotâbâd, hills Medicinal property: its fresh flowers are laxative.

Viola biflora: This is a medicinal plant species found in Ladâkh.

Viola odorata L. (*Gul-é-Banafshâñ*): Flowers in March-May. Grows in Ladâkh, Nathia gali, Kâghân, Swât, Chitrâl Medicinal property: protects livers, soothes lung congestion. Used in the treatment of sinusitis, sore throats.

Vitex negundo L. (*Gul-é-Nirgundi*) Flowers in March-June. Grows in Thal, Swât, Mirpur Medicinal property: cardio tonic, Used in the treatment of cholera, diarrhoea, liver problems.

Waldheimia tomentosa (*Makungla, lugmik serpo*): This is a rare and endangered medicinal plant species found in Ladâkh.

Waldhemia glabra (*Sa-palu*): This is a rare and endangered medicinal plant species found in Ladâkh.

Waldhemia stoliczkai (*Cl.*) Ostenf. Grows in the cold deserts of Ladâkh.

Xanthium strumarium L. (*Gul-é-Cheero*): Flowers in July-August. Grows in Gilgit, Chitrâl, Swât, Its flowers are used in the treatment of toothaches.

Youngia tenufolia (*Stathis, jampa*): This is a medicinal plant species found in Ladâkh.

References

i. Sources of information for this chapter include

'Bio-diversity of Jammu and Kashmir' by A.H.M. Ali Reza with Hasan Z. Chowdhury.

'Medicinal flowers of Pâkistân,' an incredibly detailed paper by Mohammad Afzal Rizvi of the Bait al-Hikmah Research Institute.

'Floristic Diversity of Indian region' compiled By R. R. Rao.

'Country report -4. India: Lessons from Ladakh' Down to Earth (Volume 9, No. 23, April 30, 2001), published by the Centre for Science and Environment in Delhi.

All four papers have been posted on the Internet.

I have also consulted the book

'151 Healing Plants of Jammu and Kashmîr' by O.P. Sharma Vidyarthi (a government publication).

I am grateful to Mr. Jigmet Takpa, IFS, for the notes that he has very kindly given me.

ii. Sources for this entry include:

'Phytochemical studies on Indian Seabuckthorn (Hippophae rhamnoides)'by R.Kala, P.S.Hema, S. Dwivedi, O.P.Chaurasia and A.Banerji.

'DRDO develops herbal beverage for troops posted at high altitude' a government press release of December 24, 2001;

'Wonder berry from Ladakh' by A.S. Prashar; *Tribune* News Service, Chandigarh, April 19, 200?.

GILGIT
GILGIT RIVER
MUJAHID COLONY
DUMIAL
KASHIROT
SONIKOT BALLA
SONIKOT PAEEN
RESTRICTED AREA
Aerodrome
New Aerodrome
AIRPORT TERMINAL BUILDING
HAIDRY MOHALLA
MAGENI MOHALLA
SHEROT
YERKOT
BESHOT
DAMOT
JUTIAL
NAGRAL
BARMAS
KULCHINOT
AMPERI
G I L G I T
GILGIT PUL
JINNAH BRIDGES
CIVIL HOSPITAL
OLD POLO GROUND
FRONTIER CONSTABULARY
JAGLOT BUS STAND
THE NORTH INN
FOREIGNER REGISTRATION
GILGIT SCOUT MEMORIAL
Old Parade Ground
Baltit Hostel
RIVER VIEW ROAD
To: Chitral (300km)
To: Nomal (38km)
To: Napura Buddha
To: KKH
To: Serena Lodge
*Map not to scale

Trekking
Mountain climbing
River rafting

HUNZA
*Map not to scale
path to Ultar Glacier
Ghaimarsh
Buronghal
Aminabad
Shunukshal
Garabrees
KARIMABAD BALTIT
BALTIT FORT
Sultanabad Harchee
Aga Khan Monument
Altit Village
ALTIT FORT
Mominabad (Bericha)
Darandas
Molishkar
Chakarin
Faizabad
SACRED ROCKS
Coshee
cemetery
helicopter pads
disused mines
AHMEDABAD
Khaigram
Chandum
Hyderabad
Buldas
Shukroghal
Tsil Ganish
shrine
GANISH
PTDC Motel (Tourist Office)
Gareth
Chumarkhan
Karakoram Highway
Durkhan
Hospital
ALIABAD
Court
police
Sultanabad
Khan
Gulkhan
Shahyar Dome
Shahyar
Makanpura
Askur Das
Ancient Mosque
PCO
Sumayar Topkhan
rope bridge
Blork
Sumayar Khay
Manikhan
Phildiskay
Ulukhay
To: Silkiang Glacier
HUNZA RIVER
Hassanabad
MURTAZABAD
Pershal
polo
Dalgram
Masoot
Tamodas
Paeen
Borkish
Eagle Nest
quarry
Hot Springs
broken road
To: Gilgit (100km)
To: Sust (70km)
Karakoram Highway
To: Hispar (22km)
To: Hoppar (9km)
Batarkhan
OYUM NAGAR
Wutas
police
Tong
Rest House
Polo Field
Islamic school

42

Mountain climbing:

Leh and Kargil

There are five major ranges in Leh and Kargil districts (i.e. in the Ladâkh region). These are the Saser Range in the northwest, the East Karakoram in the north, the Ladâkh range in the middle and the Zâñskâr range in the south. The fifth, the Pangong range, is really an extension of the Ladâkh range. The two meet at the Kharduñg Lâ (pass).

Best season: 1st June to 30th September is the best time of the year to climb mountains in Ladakh. It is possible to climb many of these mountains as early as the 15th May and till as late as the 15th October.

Permissions required: Non-Indians may contact the Indian Mountaineering Foundation (IMF), Benito Juarez Road, New Delhi-110021, six to nine months before they plan to climb a peak. A fee has to be paid.

'Open peaks' in the Ladâkh Himalayas

The peaks listed below are open for climbing.

Areas A and B: International mountain climbers can climb these peaks, but only in joint expeditions with Indian mountaineers. Indian teams can climb these peaks alone as well.

Area C: These are peaks on or around the Sîachen glacier. International mountain climbers might find it difficult to obtain permission to climb these peaks.

'V' indicates a 'virgin' or 'unclimbed' peak.

The Kargil-Zâñskâr area

The peaks in the following box are mostly in the Zâñskâr range.

The Peak	Mtrs	Feet	Long.	Lat.	Remarks
Bien Guapa	6006				
Bobang	5971		76° 08'	33°25'	Beyond Nagdal Lake, via Kijal Nâllâh
D-41	5813				
Kun	7087	23,213	76°03'	34°01'	Beyond Pânîkhar
N-8	6392		76°07'	33°44'	
Nûn	7135	23,405	76°01'	33°59'	Beyond Pânîkhar
Pinnacle	6930		76°05'	34°01'	Beyond Pânîkhar
Ramjak	6318				Close to the Shingo Lâ
Unnamed peak (north of Gulmatang /Gyâlmo Thangas)	5934				
White Needle	6500		76° 02'	33° 59'	Beyond Pânîkhar
Z-1 or Zâñskâr 1	6181		76° 14'	33° 45'	Beyond the Haskira Glacier, via Gyâlmo Thangas (the base camp for Nûn-Kun)
Z-2 or Zâñskâr 2	6175				Beyond the Lalung Glacier, via Rangdum
Z-3 or Zâñskâr 3	6270				Beyond the Haskira Glacier, via Gyâlmo Thangas
Z-8 or Zâñskâr 8	6050		76° 20'	33° 50'	Beyond the Haskira Glacier, via Gyâlmo Thangass

Z-3 is at the edge of the Drangdrung glacier. The first to climb it was an Italian team in 1913. The second and third teams to succeed, too, were Italian, in 1981 and 1982, respectively. Small wonder then that, for a while, it was called Cima Italia.

The Leh area

The following box includes the Mamostong, Rimo and Saser Kangri groups of peaks. The rest are in the Ladâkh range.

The Peak	Mtrs	Feet	Long	Lat.	Remarks
Chaku Lâ	6529				Chumathang area
Chhamser Kangri	6622				Near the Tsomo Rîrî. Rupshu range
Cumberland	5227				
Golep (Gulup / Galeb) Kâñgrî	5900	19,352	76° 10'	33° 25'	It is beyond Stok. Harish Kapadia gives the coordinates as 77° 29' and 33° 57.'
Kakstet	6725				Near Pangong Lake
Kang Lâ Cha	6400	21,976	76° 51'	33° 25'	
Kang Ya-tse (Yatse) I	6400		76° 50'	33° 23'	S-W of Hemis
Kang Ya-tse (Yatse) II	6100				S-W of Hemis
Kantaka Kâñgrî	5275		77° 24'	33° 59'	
Kula	6546				Near Rupshu
Lapgo	6405				Near Rupshu
Lungsher Kangri	6666				Rupshu range. Near Tsomo Rîrî
Mashiro Kâñgrî	5367		77° 24'	33° 59'	
Mamostong Kâñgrî, East of	6025				Area B
Mamostong Kâñgrî	7518		77° 38'	35° 08'	Area B. Northwest of Saser Lâ
Matho West	5950				
Parcha Kâñgrî	6065		76° 12'	33° 47'	Beyond Stok. Harish Kapadia gives the coordinates as 77° 28' and 34° 00.'
Pologongka peak	6632				Near Rupshu
Rimo Peak I	7386		77° 26'	35° 20'	Area B. Terong valley. It is one of the 'painted mountains.'
Rimo Peak III	7233				Area B. North of Rimo I.
Sâser Kâñgrî I (peak)	7672	24,322	77° 52'	34° 52'	Area A. 'The Yellow Mountain.' Between the Nubra and Shayok rivers.
Sâser Kâñgrî II (peak)	7265	24,642	77° 50'	34° 48'	Area A. In the Saser Mustagh.

contd.

Sâser Kâñgrî III (peak)	7495		77° 55'	34° 50'	Area A
Sâser Kâñgrî area (Unnamed peak)	6210				Area B
Stok Kâñgrî	6153	20,172	76° 08'	33° 25'	Beyond Stok village. Harish Kapadia gives the coordinates as 77° 28' and 33° 59.'
Yan Kangri	6230		76° 04'	33° 00'	Beyond Nimaling and then Shangphu.

Kang Ya-tse/ Yissay: This peak is a great favourite with climbers. Harish Kapadia writes, '(T)he north face and the southwest ridge offer a very good challenge with great possibilities. The normal route via the northwest ridge leads to Kang Yissay II.'

Saser Kangri I: A team led by Roberts (UK) surveyed the 'Yellow Mountain' in 1946. British and Indian teams later made several unsuccessful attempts. Cdr. Joginder Singh of the Indo, Tibetan Border Police led the first team that scaled the peak (1973). In 1995, thirteen seasoned climbers died in an avalanche on their way back.

The Sîâchen Area

(All in Area C.)

The Peak	Mtrs	Long	Lat.
Apsarasas I	7245	77°10'	35°28'
Apsarasas II	7239	77°11'	35°28'
Apsarasas III	7236	77°13'	35°25'
Ghaint I	6587	76°55'	35°25'
Ghaint II	6537	76°56'	35°25'
Indra Col	5776	75°48'	35°42'
Sia Kâñgrî	7422	75°45'	35°39'
Singhi Kâñgrî	7751	76°59'	35°22'
Teram Kâñgrî I	7454	77°05'	35°31'
Teram Kâñgrî II	7407	77°06'	35°30'
Teram Kâñgrî III	7382	77°03'	35°33'

K-12: (7428m.) Shipton, in 1957, was the first to highlight the existence of this tall peak. In 1974, two Japanese climbers first climbed the peak. However, they did not return alive. The next year another Japanese team scaled the peak. The peak is to the west of the Sîâchen glacier.

7000m. plus: Virgin peaks in the Eastern Karakoram

(Source: 'Information Handbook' of the IMF.) *These peaks had not been climbed till 1998. I have modified altitudes and coordinates at places for consistency with other reliable sources.)*

The Peak	Mtrs	Long.	Lat.	Remarks
Sadbrao Kâñgrî II	7705	75° 47'	35° 28'	South of Saltoro Kâñgrî
Saser Kâñgrî II East	7518	77° 45'	34° 50'	
Saser Kâñgrî II North	7495	77° 45'	34° 50'	
Peak 7410	7410	77° 00'	35° 33'	Teram Kâñgrî group
Plateau peak	7287	77° 44'	35° 52'	
Peak 7280	7280	76° 48'	35° 32'	West of Kondus
Peak 7250	7250	77° 08'	35° 33'	Teram Kâñgrî group
Apsarasas II	7239	77° 11'	35° 28'	
Apsarasas III	7236	77° 13'	35° 25'	
Peak 7223	7223	76° 47'	35° 28'	
Peak 7195	7195	77° 00'	35° 33'	Teram Kâñgrî group
Peak 7150	7150	77° 03'	35° 18'	East of K-12
Peak 7140	7140	77° 08'	35° 31'	Apsarasas group
Peak 7130	7130	77° 08'	35° 31'	Apsarasas group
Sia Kâñgrî II	7093	76° 47'	35° 38'	
Padmanabh	7030	77° 12'	35° 27'	
Tughmo Zarpo	7017	77° 48'	34° 53'	
Chong Kumdan II	7004	77° 32'	35° 13'	

The Chong Kumdan group: Harish Kapadia's expedition of 1989, was the first to explore this group. He explains that 'chong' means 'big' and 'kumdan' means 'dam.' A large natural dam would in the big form near its snout. Hence its name. These peaks are located east of Saser Lâ. They range in altitude from 6520m. (Peaks IV and V) to 7071m. (Peak I). In between are Peaks II (7004m.) and III (6670m.)

Important Ladakhi passes

The pass	Feet	Metres	It connects
Bârâ Lachâ Lâ	16,050	4891	Lahaul and Zâñskâr.
Batkol	14,370		
Châdar	16,300		
Châng Lâ	17,370	5288	The Indus and Shyok valleys (Durbuk).
Charkhsay	16,700		
Digar	17,900		
Fatu Lâ	13,432		

contd.

Hingo Lâ	13,513		
Kârâkoram	18,550		
Kharduñg Lâ	18,380		Leh/ the Indus Valley and Khalsar/ Nubra
Lânak Lâ	18,100		
Nâkpo Gund	17,000		
NâmikâLâ	12,200		Leh and Kargil
Omâsi Lâ	17,370	5300	Zâñskâr and Kishtwâr- i.e Zongkhul gompa and Machail
Polo Kong Kâ	16,300		
Ribrau Lâ	16,100		
Sâser Lâ	17,820	5330	Nubra valley/ Sasoma and Shyok valley/ Saser Brangza
Shingo Lâ	16,728	5090	Darcha and Padam (Zâñskâr)
Singee Lâ	16,600	5060	Padam and Lama Yuru (in general); Boumtse and Yulchung (specifically)
Sir Sir Lâ		4975	Padam and Lama Yuru (in general); Hanupatta and Phutoksar (specifically)
Taklang Lâ	17,469		
Tanglang Lâ		5300	Manali and Leh
dZoji Lâ	11,500	3529	Kashmir and Kargil (Ladâkh)- i.e. Sonamarg and Drass

The most popular climbs

Name	Location	Base camp	Days Required	Remarks
The Stok Kâñgrî massif	South of Leh	Stok or Spituk	4-5	Extremely popular, perhaps because it is easy to reach. There are a number of peaks in this massif.
Gulup Kâñgrî	South of Leh		4-5	Close to Stok Kâñgrî
Matho Wesr	South of Leh		5-6	Close to Stok Kâñgrî
Kang Ya-tse (Yatse/Yisay)	Southeast of Leh	Hemis	6-7	
Kang Ya-tse	Southeast of Leh	Markha Valley/ Nimaling plateau	13-14	See the section on Markha valley in the chapter of 'Trekking.' There are several tall peaks in this area that can be climbed.
The Nûn-Kun massif	Between Kargil and Zâñskâr	Gyâlmo Thâñgas (near 'km. 105'), just before Rangdum		The base camp is just 300 metres from the main road. Nûn and Kun must be the

contd.

	Tangole, 6km. from Pânîkhar	only 7000m. + peaks in the world with base camp right next to a motorable road. *Reach Ladâkh* calls this massif, which has six known peaks, 'the most attractive climbing destination in the Great Himalayas.' The Nûn and Kun peaks are the tallest of the six.

General remarks

The Zâñskâr area

The three peaks named after Zâñskâr are easier than both Nûn and Kun. However, they are tall enough to provide adventure.

Restrictions: There are none. International teams can climb any peak that they choose to in this area.

The Leh area (other than the Eastern Karakorams)

i) Lake Pangong: The Kakstet peak (6442m.) is close to the lake.

ii) Lake Tsomo Rîrî: There are several tall peaks around the lake, in Rupshu valley. These include the Lungsher Kâñgrî (6600m.) and the Chhamser Kâñgrî (6622m.), both on the lake's eastern shore. They were once known as Thalda Kurmi. In 1995, Harish Kapadia led the team that first climbed these peaks. They also climbed the nearby Lapgo peak (6405m.)

iii) The Sîachen area/ Eastern Karakoram: See below.

iv) The Stok peak: This takes 5 days (return) in normal weather. *Stage 1:* Stok village to shepherds' camp, Mankarmo, in 5hrs. The route is mostly along the left bank of the stream. There are two minor passes en route. *Stage 2:* 4hrs. to the Base Camp. The path begins on the right bank. *Stage 3:* Half a day to the Advance Base Camp. *Stage 4:* 9hrs. to the Peak and back to the Advance Base Camp. *Stage 5:* 7hrs. to Stok village.

Restrictions: **i)** There are none in Southeastern Rupshu. This area includes peaks like Chhamser Kâñgrî, Kula and Lungser Kâñgrî.

ii) Eastern Ladâkh (Pangong and similar areas): This author got many of these areas 'opened up' to tourists in 1993-94. Special permits are required for international tourists.

The Eastern Karakorams

Part of the Great Karakoram Range is administered by India. This portion is called the Eastern Karakorams and is the northernmost tip of India. In turn the Eastern Karakorams are in three sections:

i) **The Sîâchen area:**
This group includes some of the tallest peaks in the world. Please also see the chapter on 'The Sîâchen Glacier.'

ii) **The Saser Kâñgrî group:**
Col. J.O.M. Roberts first approached this group. An Indian team finaly climbed it from the eastern side. Saser Kâñgrî II West (7518m.) was first climbed by a Japanese team. According to the IMF, the eastern peak of Saser Kâñgrî II (also 7518m.) remains one of the highest virgin peaks in the area.

iii) **The Rimo Muztagh:**
The historic trade route to Central Asia used to pass through this area. In 1991, an Indo-British expedition became the first to climb the Chong Kumdan I (7071m.). Chong Kumdan II (7004m.) has not yet been climbed.

Restrictions: **i)** Nubra and Shayok valleys: I got these areas, too, 'opened up' in 1993-94. International tourists can now travel upto Hunder and Panamik in groups of four. They can also go to the west base camp of the Saser Kâñgrî. Permission slips are required, though.

ii) It is relatively difficult- but possible- to get permission to go to Sîâchen or the Saser Lâ. International mountain climbers can go to the valleys of Eastern Karakoram in joint expeditions with Indians. Several peaks in the area can be climbed with special permission.

43

Balâwaristân-Gilgit-Hunzâ-Chitrâl-Bunji:

Mountain peaks of 7,000 metres and above

The following is an almost complete list of the mountain peaks of the Balâwaristân-Gilgit-Chitrâl-Hunzâ-Bunji region of old, undivided Ladâkh. The list includes some peaks that are under Indian administration but are close to the area occupied by Pâkistân. The peaks have been listed first in the descending order of their height and then in the alphabetical order.

The peak	Altitude (metres)	Altitude (feet)	Range	Group	Region/ district
K-2 Chogori	8611	28.268	'Kârâkoram	Baltoro	Skardu
Nañgâ Parbat	8125	26,652'	Himalaya	Diamir	Diamir
Gasherbrum I Hidden Peak	8068	26,470'	Kârâkoram	Baltoro	Skardu
Broad Peak Falchan Kâñgri	8047	26,444'	Kârâkoram	Baltoro	Skardu
Gasherbrum II	8035	26.362'	Kârâkoram	Baltoro	Skardu
Gasherbrum III	7952	26,087'	Kârâkoram	Baltoro	Skardu
Gasherbrum IV	7925	26.014'	Kârâkoram	Baltoro	Skardu
Distaghil Sar Main	7885	25.869'	Kârâkoram	Hisper	Gilgit
Kunyang Chhish Main	7852	25.761'	Kârâkoram	Hisper	Gilgit
Masherbrum NE K1	7821	25.660'	Kârâkoram	Bagrot	Gilgit
Rakaposhi Domani	7788	25.550'	Kârâkoram	Bagrot	Gilgit
Batura I	7785	25.541'	Kârâkoram	Batura Mustagh	Gilgit
Batura II	7762	25.459	Kârâkoram	Batura Mustagh	Gilgit

contd.

Distaghil Sar II	7760	25,452'	Kârâkoram	Hisper	Gilgit
Kanjut Sar I	7760	25,460'	Kârâkoram	Hisper	Gilgit
Masherbrum W	7750	25,400'	Kârâkoram	Chitrâl	Saser
Kâñgrî I	7672	25,400'	Kârâkoram	Siachen	Gaunché
Chogolisa I SW/E	7665	25,111'	Kârâkoram	Baltoro	Skardu
Chogolisa II NE	7654	25,111'	Kârâkoram	Baltoro	Skardu
Yukshin Garden Sar	7641	25,062	Kârâkoram	Hisper	Gilgit
Kunyang Chhish S	7620	24,993	Kârâkoram	Hisper	Gilgit
Shishpar Sar	7611	24,970'	Kârâkoram	Batura Mustagh	Gilgit
Batura IV	7594	24,908	Kârâkoram	Batura Mustagh	Gilgit
Skyang Kâñgrî I	7544	24,750'	Kârâkoram	Baltoro	Skardu
Batura V	7531	24,701'	Kârâkoram	Batura Mustagh	Gilgit
Yakshin Garden I	7530	24698'	Kârâkoram	Hisper	Gilgit
Mamostong Kâñgrî	7516	24652.48	Kârâkoram	Soltoro	Gaunché
Saser Kâñgrî E	7513	24642.64	Kârâkoram	Siachen	Gaunché
Tirich Mîr W II	7500	24600	Hiñdûkush	Hiñdûkush	Chitrâl
Skyang Kâñgrî II	7500	24600	Kârâkoram	Baltoro	Skardu
Kunyang Chhish W	7500	24600	Kârâkoram	Hisper	Gilgit
Saser Kâñgrî II W	7500	24600	Kârâkoram	Siachen	Gaunché
Saser Kâñgrî III	7495	24583.6	Kârâkoram	Siachen	Gaunché
Pumari Chhish W	7492	24573.76	Kârâkoram	Hispar	Gilgit
Tirich Mîr West I	7487	24557.36	Hiñdûkush	Hiñdûkush	Chitrâl
Pasu Massif M	7478	24527.84	Kârâkoram	Batura Mustagh	Gilgit
K 12	7469	24498.32	Kârâkoram·	Soltoro	Gaunché
Teram Kâñgrî I	7463	24478.64	Kârâkoram	Siachen	Gaunché
Muchu Chhish	7453	24445.84	Kârâkoram	Batura Mustagh	Gilgit
Malubiting W	7453	24445.84	Kârâkoram	Haramosh	Gilgit
Pumari Chhish N	7440	24403.2	Kârâkoram	Hisper	Gilgit
Yaghil Dome S	7440	24403.2	Kârâkoram	Hisper	Gilgit
Sia Kâñgrî I N	7422	24344.16	Kârâkoram	Baltoro	Skardu
Haramosh I	7409	24301.52	Kârâkoram	Haramosh	Gilgit
Teram Kâñgrî II	7406	24291.68	Kârâkoram	Siachen	Gaunché
Istro-Nal Main	7403	24281.84	Hiñdûkush	Hiñdûkush	Chitrâl
Tirich Mîr West III	7400	24272	Hiñdûkush	Hiñdûkush	Chitrâl
Kunyang Chhish E	7400	24272	Kârâkoram	Hisper	Gilgit
Pumari Chhish S	7400	24272	Kârâkoram	Hisper	Gilgit
Yazghil Dome N	7400	24272	Kârâkoram	Hisper	Gilgit
Ultar Sar I	7388	24232.64	Kârâkoram	Batura Mustagh	Gilgit

contd.

Rimo S I Peak 51	7385	24222.8	Kârâkoram	Siachen	Gaunché
Teram Kâñgrî III	7382	24212.96	Kârâkoram	Siachen	Gaunché
Sherpi Kâñgrî I Main	7380	24206.4	Kârâkoram	Saltoro	Gaunché
Istro-NalNorth I	7373	24183.44	Hiñdûkush	Hiñdûkush	Chitrâl
Rimo S II Peak 50	7373	24183.44	Kârâkoram	Siachen	Gaunché
Istro-NalNorth II	7372	24180.16	Hiñdûkush	Hiñdûkush	Chitrâl
Sherpi Kâñgrî II	7370	24173.6	Kârâkoram	Saltoro	Gaunché
Istro-NalNorth III	7365	24157.2	Hiñdûkush	Hiñdûkush	Chitrâl
Skil Burm	7360	24140.8	Kârâkoram	Baltoro	Skardu
Skyng Kâñgrî M	7357	24130.96	Kârâkoram	Baltoro	Skardu
Karun Kuh	7350	24108	Kârâkoram	Hisper	Gilgit
Kunyang Chhish W	7350	24108	Kârâkoram	Hisper	Gilgit
Pumari Chhish S	7350	24108	Kârâkoram	Hisper	Gilgit
Saragharar Main	7349	24104.72	Hiñdûkush	Hiñdûkush	Chitrâl
Skyang Kâñgrî W	7345	24091.6	Kârâkoram	Baltoro	Skardu
Momhil Sar Peak - 7	7343	24085.04	Kârâkoram	Hisper	Gilgit
Saraghrar Central	7330	24042.4	Hiñdûkush	Hiñdûkush	Gilgit
Yutmaru Sar S	7330	24042.4	Kârâkoram	Hisper	Gilgit
Bojohagur Duanasir	7329	24039.12	Kârâkoram	Batura Mustagh	Gilgit
Sia Kâñgrî II/E	7325	24026	Kârâkoram	Baltoro	Skardu
Yazghil Domes S	7324	24022.72	Kârâkoram	Baltoro	Skardu
Gasherbrum V	7321	24012.88	Kârâkoram	Baltoro	Skardu
Kunyang Chhish SE	7320	24009.6	Kârâkoram	Hisper	Gilgit
Malanghutti	7320	24009.6	Kârâkoram	Hisper	Gilgit
Baltoro Kâñgrî I	7312	23983.36	Kârâkoram	Baltoro	Skardu
Ultar Sar II	7310	23976.8	Kârâkoram	Batura Mustagh	Gilgit
Saragharar S	7307	23966.96	Hiñdûkush	Hiñdûkush	Chitrâl
Istro Nal South	7303	23953.84	Hiñdûkush	Hiñdûkush	Chitrâl
Istro Nal West I	7300	23944	Hiñdûkush	Hiñdûkush	Chitrâl
Saraghrar NW	7300	23944	Hiñdûkush	Hiñdûkush	Chitrâl
Baltoro Kâñgrî III	7300	23944	Kârâkoram	Baltoro	Skardu
Urdok I	7300	23944	Kârâkoram	Baltoro	Skardu
Malubiting NW	7300	23944	Kârâkoram	Haramosh	Gilgit
Yazghil Domes N	7300	23944	Kârâkoram	Hispar	Gilgit
Sherpi Kâñgrî III	7300	23944	Kârâkoram	Siachen	Gaunché
Teram Kâñgrî IV	7300	23944	Kârâkoram	Siachen	Gaunché
Malubiting Central	7291	23914.48	Kârâkoram	Haramosh	Gilgit
Rakaposhi E	7290	23911.2	Kârâkoram	Bagrot	Gilgit

Contd.

Savoia Kâñgrî	7286	23898.08	Kârâkoram	Baltoro	Skardu
Baintha Brakk Orge	7285	23894.8	Kârâkoram	Panmah	Skardu
Passu Peak 55	7284	23891.52	Kârâkoram	Batura Mustagh	Gilgit
Pasu Massif E	7284	23891.52	Kârâkoram	Batura Mustagh	Gilgit
K-6	7282	23884.96	Kârâkoram	Siachen	Gauncha
Istro Nal West II	7280	23878.4	Hidukush	Hiñdûkush	Chitrâl
Baltoro Kâñgrî III	7280	23878.4	Kârâkoram	Baltoro	Skardu
Istro Nal Northwest	7276	23865.28	Hiñdûkush	Hiñdûkush	Citral
Golden Throne SE	7275	23862	Kârâkoram	Baltoro	Skardu
Golden Throne NW	7274	23858.72	Kârâkoram	Baltoro	Skardu
Diran Minapin	7273	23855.44	Kârâkoram	Bagrot	Gilgit
Mustagh Tower E	7273	23855.44	Kârâkoram	Baltoro	Skardu
Sia Kâñgrî IV Central	7273	23855.44	Kârâkoram	Baltoro	Skardu
Golden Throne NE	7270	23845.6	Kârâkoram	Baltoro	Skardu
Mustagh Tower W	7270	23845.6	Kârâkoram	Baltoro	Skardu
Golden Throne SE	7265	23829.2	Kârâkoram	Baltoro	Skardu
Baltoro Kâñgrî V	7260	23812.8	Kârâkoram	Baltoro	Skardu
Baltoro Kâñgrî IV	7254	23793.12	Kârâkoram	Baltoro	Skardu
Saraghrar SW I	7250	23780	Hiñdûkush	Hiñdûkush	Chitrâl
Apsarasas I	7245	23763.6	Kârâkoram	Siachen	Gaunché
Apsarasas II	7239	23743.92	Kârâkoram	Siachen	Gaunché
Apsarasas III E	7336	24062.08	Kârâkoram	Siachen	Gaunché
Rimo II P 49	7233	23724.24	Kârâkoram	Siachen	Gaunché
Apsarasas IV	7227	23704.56	Kârâkoram	Siachen	Gaunché
Saraghrar SE I	7208	23642.24	Hiñdûkush	Hiñdûkush	Chitrâl
Mt. Rose Singhi Kan	7202	23622.56	Kârâkoram	Siachen	Gaunché
Istro Nal X	7200	23616	Hiñdûkush	Hiñdûkush	Chitrâl
Saraghar SW II	7200	23616	Hiñdûkush	Hiñdûkush	Chitrâl
Urdok Kâñgrî I	7200	23616	Kârâkoram	Baltoro	Skardu
Malubiting LC	7200	23616	Kârâkoram	Haramosh	Gilgit
Bularang Sar	7200	23616	Kârâkoram	Hisper	Gilgit
Lugpahur Sar MD	7200	23616	Kârâkoram	Hisper	Gilgit
Laupghar Sar E	7200	23616	Kârâkoram	Hisper	Gilgit
Apsarasas V	7187	23573.36	Kârâkoram	Siachen	Gaunché
Apsarasas III E	7184	23563.52	Kârâkoram	Siachen	Gaunché
Apsarasas III W	7181	23553.68	Kârâkoram	Siachen	Gaunché
Mustagh Tower NW	7180	23550.4	Kârâkoram	Baltoro	Skardu
Rimo III	7169	23514.32	Kârâkoram	Siachen	Gaunché

Contd.

Kampir Dior	7168	23511.04	Kârâkoram	Batura	Gilgit
Karun Koh	7164	23497.92	Kârâkoram	Khunjerab	Gilgit
Hachindar Chhish	7163	23494.64	Kârâkoram	Batura Mustagh	Gilgit
Yermanenbu Kâñgrî	7163	23494.64	Kârâkoram	Baltoro	Skardu
Unnamed Masherbrum	7163	23494.64	Kârâkoram	Siachen	Gaunché
Unnamed	7150	23452	Kârâkoram	Baltoro	Skardu
Deepak	7150	23452	Kârâkoram	Siachen	Gaunché
Latok I	7145	23435.6	Kârâkoram	Panmah	Skardu
Kampir Dior	7143	23429.04	Kârâkoram	Batura Muztagh	Gilgit
Gasherbrum V	7133	23396.24	Kârâkoram	Baltoro	Skardu
Sha Kawar	7125	23370	Hiñdûkush	Hiñdûkush	Chitrâl
Apsarasa S	7117	23343.76	Kârâkoram	Siachen	Gaunché
Koh Nadir Shah	7116	23340.48	Hiñdûkush	Hiñdûkush	Chitrâl
Udren Zom N	7108	23314.24	Hiñdûkush	Hiñdûkush	Chitrâl
Kunyang Chhish N	7108	23314.24	Kârâkoram	Hisper	Gilgit
Lagar Main	7100	23288	Hiñdûkush	Hiñdûkush	Chitrâl
Saraghrar SS	7100	23288	Hiñdûkush	Hiñdûkush	Chitrâl
Ghenta	7100	23288	Kârâkoram	Batura Mustagh	Gilgit
Lupghar II Central	7100	23288	Kârâkoram	Hisper	Gilgit
Yakshin Garden I (II?)	7100	23288	Kârâkoram	Hisper	Gilgit
Sherpi Kâñgrı	7100	23288	Kârâkoram	Siachen	Gaunché
Genta	7090	23255.2	Kârâkoram	Batura Muztagh	Gilgit
Urdok II	7082	23228.96	Kârâkoram	Baltoro	Skardu
Mandu PK	7081	23225.68	Kârâkoram	Baltoro	Skardu
Udren Zom Central	7080	23222.4	Hiñdûkush	Hiñdûkush	Chitrâl
Chogolisa Kâñgrî I	7071	23192.88	Kârâkoram	Baltoro	Skardu
Langar SE	7061	23160.08	Hiñdûkush	Hiñdûkush	Chitrâl
Pyramid Thyor	7058	23150.24	Kârâkoram	Baltoro	Skardu
Udren Zom S	7050	23124	Hiñdûkush	Hiñdûkush	Chitrâl
Link Sar	7041	23094.48	Kârâkoram	Siachen	Gaunché
Sraghrar N	7040	23091.2	Hiñdûkush	Hiñdûkush	Chitrâl
Spantik Ghenish Chish	7027	23048.56	Kârâkoram	Haramosh	Skardu
Akber Chioh Akher	7020	23025.6	Hiñdûkush	Hiñdûkush	Chitrâl
Chogolisa Kâñgrî II	7014	23005.92	Kârâkoram	Baltoro	Skardu
Rakaposhi E	7010	22992.8	Kârâkoram	Bagrot	Gilgit
Malubiting E	7010	22992.8	Kârâkoram	Haramosh	Gilgit
Gasherbrum VI	7004	22973.12	Kârâkoram	Baltoro	Skardu
Sangemer Mar	7000	22960	Kârâkoram	Batura Muztagh	Gilgit

Contd.

Lupghar Sar III E	7000	22960	Kârâkoram	Hisper	Gilgit
Apsarasa E Unnamed	7000	22960	Kârâkoram	Siachen	Gaunché
Chogolisa W Prupoo	7000	22960	Kârâkoram	Baltoro	Gaunché
Ghent III	7000	22960	Kârâkoram	Siachen	Gaunché
Kaberi Peak	7000	22960	Kârâkoram	Siachen	Gaunché

The names of the same 7000m.+ peaks, in the alphabetical order, are:

The peak	Altitude (Metres)
Akber Chioh Akher	7020
Apsarasa E Unnamed	7000
Apsarasa S	7117
Apsarasas I	7245
Apsarasas II	7239
Apsarasas III E	7336
Apsarasas III E	7184
Apsarasas III W	7181
Apsarasas IV	7227
Apsarasas V	7187
Baintha Brakk Orge	7285
Baltoro Kâñgrî I	7312
Baltoro Kâñgrî III	7300
Baltoro Kâñgrî III	7280
Baltoro Kâñgrî IV	7254
Baltoro Kâñgrî V	7260
Batura I	7785
Batura II	7762
Batura III	7729
Batura IV	7594
Batura V	7531
Bojohagur Duanasir	7329
Broad Peak Falchan Kâñgrî	8047
Bularang Sar	7200
Chogolisa I SW/E	7665
Chogolisa II NE	7654
Chogolisa Kâñgrî I	7071
Chogolisa Kâñgrî II	7014

Contd.

Chogolisa W Prupoo	7000
Deepak	7150
Diran Minapin	7273
Distaghil Sar II	7760
Distaghil Sar Main	7885
Gasherbrum I Hidden Peak	8068
Gasherbrum II	8035
Gasherbrum III	7952
Gasherbrum IV	7925
Gasherbrum V	7321
Gasherbrum V	7133
Gasherbrum VI	7004
Genta	7090
Ghent III	7000
Ghenta	7100
Golden Throne NE	7270
Golden Throne NW	7274
Golden Throne SE	7275
Golden Throne SE	7265
Hachindar Chish	7163
Haramosh I	7409
Istro Nal Christian	7200
Istro Nal Northwest	7276
Istro Nal South	7303
Istro Nal West I	7300
Istro Nal West II	7280
Istro-Nal Main	7403
Istro-NalNorth I	7373
Istro-NalNorth II	7372
Istro-NalNorth III	7365
K-2 Chogori	8611
Kaberi Peak	7000
Kampir Dior	7168
Kampir Dior	7143
Kanjut Sar I	7760
Karun Koh	7164
Karun Kuh	7350
K 6	7282

Contd.

K 12	7469
Koh Nadir Shah	7116
Kunyang Chhish S	7620
Kunyang Chhish E	7400
Kunyang Chhish Main	7852
Kunyang Chhish N	7108
Kunyang Chhish SE	7320
Kunyang Chhish W	7500
Kunyang Chhish W	7350
Lagar Main	7100
Langar SE	7061
Latok I	7145
Laupghar Sar E	7200
Link Sar	7041
Lugpahur Sar MD	7200
Lupghar II Central	7100
Lupghar Sar III E	7000
Malanghutti	7320
Malubiting Central	7291
Malubiting E	7010
Malubiting LC	7200
Malubiting NW	7300
Malubiting W	7453
Mamostong Kâñgrî	7516
Mandu PK	7081
Masherbrum NE K1	7821
Masherbrum W	7750
Momhil Sar Peak - 7	7343
Mt. Rose Singhi Kan	7202
Muchu Chhish	7453
Mustagh Tower E	7273
Mustagh Tower NW	7180
Mustagh Tower W	7270
Nañgâ Parbat	8125
Pasu Peak 55	7284
Pasu Massif E	7284
Pasu Massif M	7478
Pumari Chhish N	7440

Contd.

Pumari Chhish S	7400
Pumari Chhish S	7350
Pumari Chhish W	7492
Pyramid Thyor	7058
Rakaposhi Domani	7788
Rakaposhi E	7290
Rakaposhi E	7010
Rimo II P 49	7233
Rimo III	7169
Rimo S I Peak 51	7385
Rimo S II Peak 50	7373
Saltoro Kâñgrî I	7742
Sangemer Mar	7000
Saraghar SW II	7200
Saragharar Main	7349
Saragharar S	7307
Saraghrar Central	7330
Saraghrar NW	7300
Saraghrar SE I	7208
Saraghrar SS	7100
Saraghrar SW I	7250
Saser Kâñgrî E	7513
Saser Kâñgrî I	7672
Saser Kâñgrî II W	7500
Saser Kâñgrî III	7495
Savoia Kâñgrî	7286
Sha Kawar	7125
Sherpi Kâñgrî	7100
Sherpi Kâñgrî I Main	7380
Sherpi Kâñgrî II	7370
Sherpi Kâñgrî III	7300
Shishpar Sar	7611
Sia Kâñgrî I N	7422
Sia Kâñgrî II/E	7325
Sia Kâñgrî IV Central	7273
Skil Burm	7360
Skyang Kâñgrî I	7544
Skyang Kâñgrî II	7500

Contd.

Skyang Kâñgrî W	7345
Skyng Kâñgrî M	7357
Spantik Ghenish Chish	7027
Sraghrar N	7040
Teram Kâñgrî I	7463
Teram Kâñgrî II	7406
Teram Kâñgrî III	7382
Teram Kâñgrî IV	7300
Tirich Mîr	7708
Tirich Mîr West I	7487
Tirich Mîr West III	7400
Tirich Mîr W II	7500
Trivor Peak 8	7720
Udren Zom Central	7080
Udren Zom N	7108
Udren Zom S	7050
Ultar Sar I	7388
Ultar Sar II	7310
Unnamed	7150
Unnamed Masherbrum	7163
Urdok I	7300
Urdok II	7082
Urdok Kâñgrî I	7200
Yaghil Dome S	7440
Yakshin Garden I	7530
Yakshin Garden I (II?)	7100
Yakshin Garden Sar	7641
Yazghil Dome N	7400
Yazghil Domes N	7300
Yazghil Domes S	7324
Yermanenbu Kâñgrî	7163
Yutmaru Sar S	7330

44

Trekking in Ladakh

Please read the climate- and altitude- related precautions given in the introductory chapter on 'Ladakh'. Briefly, Ladakh is one of the coldest and highest inhabited places in the world. It is also a desert. You don't have to be an athlete or an Everest veteran to trek in Ladakh. However, you certainly need to be fit. Asthmatics, people with breathing or lung problems and heavy smokers might like to consider skipping treks in Ladakh.

Water is scarce. If you come upon a spring, its water is likely to be safe. On the other hand, water from rivers that carry melted snow can really throw your system out of gear. Thanks to tourism, some villages have started stocking up on supplies of the kind that trekkers need. However, transporting things from the Indian plains to Ladakh is extremely expensive and difficult. Therefore don't expect to find provisions except in the towns and touristy villages.

Rivers are likely to be in spate during much of the trekking season. The worst time to cross them is in the afternoon, when they carry all the snow that had melted that morning and noon. The best time is just before dawn, say 4 or 5 in the morning. Please do not cross rivers alone or without a rope anchor. Trekkers have died of drowning in these rivers.

The best season: This depends on the trek. The best weather in Ladakh is between June and August. However, some rivers are in spate in June. Treks that involve crossing rivers and streams are best undertaken after July. September and October are relatively safe from that angle. But October can be cold and in the higher mountains it sometimes snows quite heavily after mid-October.

Frostbite: Warm turnip water is said to be good first aid in cases of frostbite.

English Sentences(mostly used)	Ladakhi version
Where is ..., please?	... ka-ru yowt, lé?
I want to go to ..., please.	nga: ...-a: chhan-in rak, lé
In which direction is ..., please?	... ka: chhoks-la: yot, lé
Place to stay	duk sa:
Mountain pass	la:

Leh to Zâñskâr

Lâmâ Yûrû-Padam

This is a difficult trek. It could take between nine and ten days. The recommended season is July to September. Passes normally don't close till the last week of October. However, it gets very cold (even sub-zero) by mid-October. Therefore, while many trekkers continue to travel from Lama Yuru to Padan even in October, it's uncomfortable to do so.

You will have to climb up to 5,060m. It is possible to get ponies and porters at Lâmâ Yûrû.

Incidentally, the path to Zâñskâr through Hanupattâ is steeped in history. King Tsewang Namgyâl I had got the path it constructed in the 16th century.

Day 1: (To Chila) Your trek from Lâmâ Yûrû to Chila will take you through Wan Lâ (3,245 m., 9km. from Lâmâ Yûrû). Wan Lâ (10,900') can be 'oppressively' hot in summer. It is famous for its plentiful rose bushes, some of them five metres high. There is a gompa and an old castle at Chila.

Day 2: (To Hanupattâ) You will walk up a steep path, through loose rocks, to reach a steep pass at 4,265m. The river you'll see has saline water; so don't even consider drinking it untreated. However, half way through there's a well with fresh water. There's a small monastery in Hanupattâ (3,780m.)

Day 3: (To Photaksar) The first twelve kilometres or so are a gentle ascent to the Sisir Lâ (or Sirsir Lâ, 4,805m.). The path is fairly good. There are several river crossings. Be careful when you cross. There have been many accidents in the area. The descent to Photaksar is steep. This place is one of the few habitats of the yâk. There is a gompa in Photaksar (3,790m.). It is near a river.

Day 4: (To Shanpado Gongma, also spelt Chumpado Gongma.) At first the climb is gradual. Then an hour's steep descent follows. The climb resumes till the Singi Lâ (or Singey Lâ, 5,060m.). You can camp on the other side of the pass. Many trekkers do, but it can be very cold up there. So you might want to trek for another hour till you reach a village that consists of three houses.

Day 5: (To Lingshet, also spelt Linshat.) The path now runs along the side of a mountain as it gently goes up to the Lingshet gompa. Lingshet has sixty monks. It is the main seat of religion and culture in the area. You just might be able to get eggs and tsampâ in the village, but don't count on that. The gompa's annual festival, conveniently, is held in July (around the middle of the month).

Day 6: (41km. to Snertse) The track is not very well defined. Which makes things that much more difficult. Besides, you need to go up to the Hulum Lâ (4,710m.). After that you will go down through a valley which includes a glacier, snow and much water. Snertse is down below. Shepherds camp here in the summer.

Day 7: (24km. to Pidmu) You have to cross the four metre wide Omachu stream as you go down, through Hanumil, to the Zâñskâr valley. It was a comfortable trek today, and will remain so hereafter.

Day 8: (12km. to Pishu) Now the track follows the Zâñskâr river, upstream, and passes through Zâñglâ village (3,450m.). Zâñskâr traditionally consisted of two kingdoms—Padam and Zâñglâ. This was the headquarters of the latter. Apart from the Zâñglâ 'palace', a major attraction is the house in which **Csoma Koros** used to meditate. There is a very long rope bridge- almost 150 metres- near Zâñglâ. Several travelogues have written about it. However, it is much easier to walk on than many shorter rope bridges. Three kilometres later you will reach Pishu. Today's walk was mostly on flat land.

Day 9: (30km. To Padam or Karshâ) Keep following the Zâñskâr river as it goes upstream. After 16km. you will pass (S)tongde village (3,530m.), which has a major monastery. (In Zâñskâr the 's' is often silent if at the beginning or end of a word.) You can reach Padam (or Karshâ) today. (Both Padam and Karshâ have 'jeepable' roads that ultimately lead to Kargil town. Padam is, now, the bigger town with more facilities such as accommodation and communications. It is also the headquarters of all of Zâñskâr. Karshâ, on the other hand, used to be higher up in the traditional hierarchy.)

Padam-Lâmâ Yûrû: The last mention trek can be done in the reverse order, with slight variations, thus:

Day 1: Padam to Pishu. *Day 2:* To Hanamur. *Day 3:* To Snertse. *Day 4:* To Lingshet. *Day 5:* To the base of the Singey Lâ, 5100m. *Day 6:* To the Singey Lâ and then to Photaksar. *Day 7:* To the Sirsir Lâ, 4,100m. and then Hanupattâ. *Day 8:* To Phanji Lâ. *Day 9:* To Wan Lâ. *Day 10:* To the Pirkiting Lâ, 3,726m. and then Lâmâ Yûrû.

Padam-Lâmâ Yûrû: A third variant. This alternative slices off one day towards the end. *Day 1:* Padam to Pishu, 6hrs. *Day 2:* To Hanamur, 5hrs. *Day 3:* To Nyrtse/ Snertse, 6 hrs. En route you will cross the Parfi La, 4.450m. *Day 4:* To Lingshet, 8hrs. En route you will cross the Hanuma La, 4,450m. *Day 5:* To the base of the Singey Lâ, 5,100m., 7hrs. En route you will cross the Margo La, 4,500m. and the Kyukpâ La. *Day 6:* To the Singey Lâ, and then to Photaksar, 8hrs. *Day 7:* To the Sirsir Lâ, 4,100m. and then to Hanupattâ, 7hrs. *Day 8:* To Wan Lâ, 7hrs. *Day9:* To the Pirkiting Lâ, 3,726m. and then Lâmâ Yûrû, 5hrs.

Heniskut-Lâmâ Yûrû: (8 days, June to September) *Day 1:* (Heniskut to Kanji, 6hrs.) *Day 2:* (7hrs. to Shilakung; en route you will cross the Yogma La, 4900m.) *Day 3:* (7hrs. to Hanupattâ Drog; en route you will cross the Nyigutse La, 5,100m.) *Day 4:* (3hrs. to Hanupattâ proper) *Day 5:* (6hrs. to Wan La) *Day 6:* (5hrs. to Lâmâ Yûrû; en route you will cross the Pirkiting Lâ)

Lâmâ Yûrû-Mangyur: (5 or 6 days.) Lâmâ Yûrû is 106km. from Kargil, on the road to Leh. *Day 1:* (4 hours from Lâmâ Yûrû to Wan Lâ.) *Day 2:* (5-6 hrs. to Ursi/ Urtsi/ Urtse.) *Day 3:* (Night halt: Tar.) You will have to cross the Tar Lâ, 4,880m. to reach Tar. *Day 4:* (5 hrs. to Mangyur.) *Day 5:* (Trek to Saspol. Night halt at Saspol or, if you have a vehicle waiting, even in Leh town.)

Lâmâ Yûrû-Saspol: An alternat route: Lâmâ Yûrû-Pirkiting Lâ- Wan Lâ-Urtsi/ Ursi-Phanji Lâ-Tar Lâ-Mangyu(r)-Gyara-Alchi-Saspol. (The stages mentioned in this trek do not necessarily represent night-halts.)

Lâmâ Yûrû-Ule Tokpo (or Alchi): *Day 1:* (Lâmâ Yûrû to Pirkiting La, 3,726m., and then to Wan La, 5hrs.) *Day 2:* (6hrs. to Urtse) *Day 3:* (8hrs. through Tar La to Tar) *Day 4:* (7hrs. to Hepti La, then Mangyu La and finally Mangyu) *Day 5:* (3-4hrs. from Mangyu to Ule Tokpo). Or, a variant, *Day 5:* (6hrs. from Mangyu to Alchi).

Khaltse-Likir: *Day 1:* (From Khaltse to Skindiyang in 4 hours.) *Day 2:* (7hrs. to Ang) *Day 3:* (3hrs. to Hemis Shukpachan) *Day 4:* (3hrs. to Yangthang) *Day 5:* (To the Rizong monastery and back to Yangthang in 5hrs.) *Day 6:* (5hrs. to Likir)

The *châdar* route: Padam to Chiling

Zâñskâr is cut off from the rest of the world for almost eight months a year, when the passes are blocked by snow. However, during these eight months there are two brief periods when it is possible to leave Zâñskâr on foot. One of these is the *kharas* when for a fortnight or so the snow becomes hard enough to walk on.

The other is the *chadar.* This is when the river freezes over and develops a crust of ice so thick that people can walk on it. In Zâñskâr this happens from around mid-February to roughly mid-March in most years. People normally walk on this 'châdar' (crust) after sunset. However, before setting out, please check the exact time of the day when it will be safe. Also whether it will be possible to walk on the frozen river on the particular days that you want to travel.

Travellers camp at night in little caves near the frozen river. A fire is lit at the mouth of the cave to keep the people inside warm. Outside temperatures could be minus 30° Celsius at night and minus ten degrees even at noon. These caves are there all the way up to Tilat Sumdo.

It is not a comfortable journey. Whoever gave Chiling its name obviously knew English. His speling could do with some impovement, though. After Tilat Sumdo the chadar passes through a gorge.

In summer the distances given below will be covered in a different number of hours—normally in fewer hours, though in some cases more.

Day 1: (Padam to Karshâ, 5hours on the *chadar*) *Day 2:* (6hrs. to Pishu) *Day 3:* (7hrs. to Hanamur; it is possible to stay in the village) *Day 4:* (8hrs, to Deep Kongma) *Day 5:* (6hrs. to Dambu Baû) *Day 6:* (7hrs. to Markalak) *Day 7:* (7hrs. to Tilat Sumdo; you pass through a gorge) *Day 8:* (5hrs. to Chiling, the roadhead) *Day 9:* (From Chiling one can drive by jeep to Leh town).

Some adventure-tour operators specialise in Chadar Route treks, e.g. Glacier (Near Sabzi Mandi, Fort Road, Leh 194101; fax: 253638).

Padam-Hemis

This is a very difficult and long (13-day) trek. You have to climb as high as 5,300m. Best time of the year: July to Oct. Personally, I wouldn't do this trek after the end of September. Gets too cold.

There are very few villages en route. Please don't do this trek unless you are totally fit and fully equipped.

Day 1: (3 hours from Padam to [s]Tongde) Padam (3,600m.) is on the banks of River Zâñskâr. You need to cross the river using the rope bridge at the edge of the village. After a three-hour walk along the river you will reach (s)Tongde.

Day 2: (5 hours to Zâñglâ) Continue along the Zâñskâr river, still on mostly flat land, till you reach Zâñglâ.

Day 3: (6 hours to the base of the Sher Sher Lâ, 3,940m.) The track to the Zâñglâ gompa is steep uphill. After that you will enter the gorge of a knee-deep river. You will criss-cross the river at least fifteen or twenty times today, while travelling through the gorge. You will come to a place where two rivers meet. Take the left valley at this point. Walk till you reach the base of the Sher Sher Lâ (pass). (Also spelt Chhar Char Lâ. The pass itself is at 5,170m.) You will find a green camping ground, with water.

Day 4: (6½ hours to Chup Cha, 4,460m-4,700m) There will first be a very steep climb up to the Sher Sher Lâ (pass), on an uncomfortable, stony path, past boulders. After you cross the pass, you will go down to the green Chup Cha (or Chhup Chhak) plateau where two streams meet. The camping ground is quite good.

Day 5: (5 hours to Shang Kong Ma, 3,970m.) Today it will mainly be a descent to yet another meeting of two rivers. You will go down into a gorge and criss-cross the river more than ten times.

Day 6: (3½ hours to a nameless meadow, 3,800m.) Go down the valley. Criss-cross the waist-deep river several more times. Please be careful, and use a rope anchor. Don't even try to cross the river in the afternoon. It's just not possible. Once again you will find a meadow where two rivers meet. It's a good camping site. The water gets muddy in the afternoon, so store up in the morning.

Day 7: (4½ hours to Kurna Sumdo, 3,820m.-3,900m.) Start very early. First go down to Tilut (or Tilat) Sumdo, the point where the rivers meet. Then follow the right bank of River Kurna upstream (and uphill). There are bushes all along the route, in case you need wood. There will be several more river crossings. And much water, too, before you reach Kurna (or Khurna or Kurma) Sumdo. Here, too, the water gets muddy by the afternoon. The camping site is good.

Day 8: (6 hours to Nari Narsa, 4,270m.) Your trek today will begin with the little valley on the left. There will be a very steep climb, up a path of stones and boulders. (Can I still dissuade you from doing this trek? And today isn't even the toughest day.) If you don't unload the ponies, they might slip. Once again you will have to cross the water several times. Mercifully, though, the river is shallow today. Nari Narsa is a high-altitude valley. It has many camping sites. Water and bushes are plentiful.

Day 9: (6 hours to Lang Tang, 4,800m.) First climb through the valley to the Rubrung (or Rebrang) plateau. Take the valley on the right. There's a narrow gap in the range through which you will be able to cross it. This passage will take you to the Zalung Karpo Lâ (5,160m.). Go up the ridge (5,200m.). After that it's all the way down to the Lang Tang valley. There's a decent campsite to be found.

Day 10: (5 hours to Hankar, 4,200m.) Go down the valley till you reach River Markha. Hankar village is nearby. There's a campsite here. Hankar also has the ruins of a fort.

Wangchuk Chhenmo, the Amarnath of Ladâkh: (This is a slight detour from the main route.) Between Markha and Hankar is a little-known holy cave. I am confident that it will become a national phenomenon once this discovery is made public.

Inside the cave is a stone that looks like a Shiv Ling. Few Ladakhis have even heard of it. Fewer still have actually been there. Most of those who have are childless Buddhist women. Over the centuries such women have been visiting this cave to lick the stone, in the hope that they will then be able to bear children. Apparently it works. This cave is in a valley before Stok.

Wangchuk is the Ladakhi name of Lord Shiv. Chhenmo means 'the great.' Together, the name means 'the great Shiv.' Thus even in Ladakh the cave is associated with Lord Shiv and the lingam with fertility. This association and religious sanctity have been there for centuries. And yet neither Shaivites nor Western scholars are aware of the cave's existence. It has the potential of becoming another Amarnath or Mansarovar in terms of pilgrim traffic.

The cave is on the Junglam route. It is a steep 25 feet above the road. Therefore, the traveller is likely to miss the cave unless he is looking for it. It can be reached from the Hemis/ Markha (Leh) side as well as from the Zâñgla (Zâñskâr) side. People prefer the latter, because the climb is easier, and the walking portion shorter. From the Hemis/ Martselang side we have to cross two passes, which can be tiring. On the other hand, the journey by jeep from Leh (or Srinagar) to Zâñskâr takes at least two (but typically three) days.

Travelling from Zâñgla, there is a very narrow gorge after the Chhar Char La. It is colourfully called the Stâ Chhung Gâmî Chhung i.e. 'a horse can go through it [the gorge] but not the horse's saddle.' It is also called the dZo Chhung Rûmî Chhung i.e. 'a dZo (cattle) can pass through it, but not the dZo's horns.' Indeed, one can not stretch one's arms while passing through this gorge.

Detour 2/ branching off: From here you can trek to the Markha valley. You can then follow River Markha downstream and cross into the Indus valley at Spituk. For details see the 'Markha valley treks' later in this chapter.

Day 11: (5 hours to Nima Ling, 4,900m.) Go up the Markha valley. The path is good almost right up to the Nima Ling plateau. You'll find nomads and their small huts. You will not be welcome in case you want to stay in their huts. So just camp in the open. Water is available, but wood is not.

Day 12: (6 hours to Shakdo, 4,100m.) The climb up to the Kang Maru Lâ (5,030-5,300m.) is surprisingly easy, given the formidable height of the pass. Go down the gorge on the other side to get to Shakdo.

Day 13: (5 hours to Hemis, 3,760m.) It will be downhill till Martselang. After that it is a pleasant walk up to Hemis, which is on a motorable road.

Hemis-Zâñglâ-Padam: Here is a slight variant of the above trek, and in the reverse order:

Day 1: (4 to 5 hrs. from Hemis to Martselang (or Martselong) and Chhogdo (or Shakdo). *2:*4 hrs. to the base of the Kang Maru Lâ (or Kong Maru Lâ); the base is at 4,710m. *3:*3 hrs. to the Kang Maru Lâ (pass) and Nima Ling. *4:*4 hrs. to Umlung (3,900m.). *5:*5 hrs. to Thaltak Baho (4,450m.). *6:*5 hrs. to the Rebrang Lâ (3,900m.) and Rebrang. *7:*4 hrs. to Kurna (or Khurna) Sumdo (3,900m.). *8:*7 hrs. to Tilat Sumdo and Tomto (4,150m.). *9:*6 hrs. to Chhup Chhak (4,700m.). *10:*7 hrs. to Chhar Char Lâ (5,170m.) and then the base of the Chhar Char Lâ. *11:*3 hrs. to Zâñglâ. *12:*35 km. to Padam (Do the last stretch in one or two days on foot. Or do it in around two hours by jeep and thus save a day.)

Hemis-Zâñglâ-Padam (The Junglam route): Here is yet another variant of the above trek. This one is called the Junglam route. It is shorter than the other Hemis-Zâñgla-Padam trek by only one day, because it assumes that you will start from Martselang.

*Day 1:*6 hrs. from Martselang to Shang Sumdo. *2:*6 hrs. to Lartsa, the base of the Kang Maru Lâ *3:*6 hrs. to the Kang Maru Lâ (5,100m.) and then Thachungtse. *4:*6 hrs. to Yakrupal. *5:*7 hrs. to Kurna Sumdo (3,900m.). *6:*7 hrs. to Tilat Sumdo and Tomto (4,150m.). *7:*6 hrs. to Chhup Chhak (4,700m.). *8:*7 hrs. to Chhar Char Lâ (5,170m.) and then Zâñgla Sumdo. *9:*6 hrs. to Zâñglâ. *10:*35 km. to Padam.

The Markha valley: Treks to and through

It is possible to branch off from the 'Padam-Hemis' trek to the Markha valley.

Start from Spituk. (9 days to Hemis.) *Day 1:* (12 km./5hrs. from Spituk to Zingchen.) *Day 2:* (13 km./6hrs. to Yurutse.) *Day 3:* (14 km./ 7hrs. to Sku/ Skiu. En route you will cross the Kanda Lâ, 4,900m.) *Day 4:* (12 km./8hrs. to Markha.) *Day 5:* (11 km./ 5hrs. to Hankar. Several treks meet at Hankar. See, for instance, the 'Padam-Hemis' trek.) *Day 6:* (10 km./5hrs. to Nima Ling.) *Day 7:* (14 km./7hrs. to Shang Sumdo. En route you will go through the Kang Maru Lâ, 5,030-5,300m.) *Day 8:* (10 km./3hrs. to Martselang.) *Day 9:* (6 km./2hrs. to Hemis.)

Variant: On Day 5 you can travel from Markha to Thachungtse in about about 6hrs. and spend the night there. The next day, it will take around 5hrs. from Thachungtse to Nima Ling.

Start from Leh/ Stok. (9 days, Stok to Hemis.) Leave for Stok by taxi/ bus. If you feel up to it, you can start climbing the same day. If not, camp at Stok.

Day 1: (6 hours from stok to the Sto[c]k Lâ.) The gradient is mostly gentle. *Day 2:* (5½ to 6 hours to Umrutse.) The first stretch of about 1½ hours to the Rumbak pass is steep. You'll be able to see a small oasis from here. The last two hours' trek to Umrutse is up a gentle slope. *Day 3:* (4 hours to Shingo.) The first two hours' climb to the Kanda Lâ (4,900m.) is steep. After that begins an equally steep descent to the pretty Shingo oasis. *Day 4:* (5 hrs. to Skiu.) The Skiu gompa, with its long rows of *chortens*, is on the route.[1] *Day 5:* (5 hours to Shalak.) Today's trek is mostly a comfortable walk along River Markha. *Day 6:* (4 hours to Markha. Once again you will walk along the Markha river. Markha village (3,813m.) is located inside a green valley and has a monastery. Wood is plentiful. The Markha gompâ is built high on a cliff, owes allegiance to the Hemis gompa, and is open only early in the morning. *Day 7:* (8 hours to Nima Ling. You can do this stretch in two easy days; in that case the first night halt would be at Hankar.) A 4-hour walk along the Markha river will take you to Hankar. After that you will climb up a gentle to steep gradient for another four hours to get to Nima Ling. *Day 8:* (7½ hours to Sumdo, also spelt Sumda.) The first two hours are a climb up a steep, zig-zag gradient to the Kang Maru Lâ pass. Start early before clouds start building up and ruin your view. On a clear day, the view will include the Kang-Ya-tse peak (6,400m.) Also be careful when crossing streams, especially after a rainfall. Two of the

1. Chortens- properly mChortens, with an almost silent 'm'- are where the ashes of important people are buried. These are structures constructed in the open. There's no way you can miss them as you travel in any Buddhist part of Ladakh. They are along every road, even within Leh town. You will find long rows of them. Normally they are painted white. Almost invariably they have a tiered dome topped by a long, conical steeple. With modernity and wealth, these chortens have started becoming huge. The typical traditional chorten would be slightly smaller than a small room. You can't enter a chorten. They are solid inside.
   Hindus in most parts of India are placed in a horizontal position *atop* a pyre when they are cremated. Firewood is scarce in Ladakh. So the Ladakhi Buddhists are collapsed into a crouching posture when they die and cremated *inside* a chamber. The cremation is anaerobic: it uses only the air inside the chamber. If the person was important enough a chorten is later erected around this chamber.

downhill stretches are dangerous for the ponies. Travel mostly along the left bank of the river till you reach Chuskirmo. It will be 5½ hours from the pass to Sumdo. The Shang gompâ is nearby. The camp is in a grove. *Day 9:* (6 hours to Hemis.) go down the valley till you meet the Leh-Manali road. By now you would have crossed the river many times. It will take almost four hours to reach Martselang. Hemis is a dusty, steep, one- to two- hour climb ahead.

Start from Stok- a variant: (9 days to Hemis.) *Day 1:* (5 hours to a shepherd's camp.) Angora goats graze here in the summer. *Day 2:* (4 hours to Rumbak.) The first two hours are a steep climb to the Namlung Lâ (4570m.). After that you descend to Rumbak. *Day 3:* (5 hours to the bottom of the Kanda Lâ.) Climb up to Yurutse. Two hours later you will come to the bottom of the Kanda Lâ, where there is a spring and a flat ground to camp on. *Day 4:* (6 hours to Skiu.) The gradual ascent to the Kanda Lâ will take an hour and a half. It will take equally long to go down to Shingo village. From there to Skiu is another three hours. *Day 5:* (7 hours to Markha.) A third of the way through you'll need to cross the river by a bridge. Later, at Chaluk you will cross back to the other side. *Day 6:* (5 hours to Thachungtse, via Hankar.) When you have walked for around an hour, you will meet the track that comes from Zâñskâr. (See Day 10 of the 'Padam-Hemis' trek.) The Markha gompa is a little ahead. *Day 7:* (4 hours to Nima Ling.) It is an ascent, sometimes steep. *Day 8:* (6 hours to Sumdo, via the Kong Maru Lâ.) *Day 9:* (5-6 hours to Hemis.)

Add on i): If you have an extra day, spend it at Nima Ling. Yâks and goats graze here. Use the day to climb up the Kagyash peak (6,200m.). You can return to Nima Ling by the evening. It often snows in the area even in summer.

Add on ii): Or linger on at Skiu. Trek from here to the spectacular Zâñskâr gorges (around 4-5 hours each way). You will pass Kaya village, and its Drukpa gompa, which is run by Hemis.

Reversing directions: You could, of course, start from Hemis and end the trek at Stok. However, in terms of acclimatisation it would not be the same thing. In this case you would be ascending the tall Kang Maru Lâ on the second day itself.

Lama Yuru-Markha valley-Hemis: (11 or 12 days to Hemis.) *Day 1:* (4hrs. from Lama Yuru to the Wan La.) *Day 2:* (6hrs. to Hinju.) *Day 3:* (6hrs. to Sumda Chenmo Dorg; en route you will cross thê Kongski La, 4,900m.) *Day 4:* (6hrs. to Dundun Chan La) *Day 5:* (6hrs. to Chiling; En route you will cross the Lanak La, 4,850m.) *Day 6:* (5hrs. to Sku/ Skiu.) *Day 7:* (12km./8hrs. to Markha.) *Day 8:* (6hrs. to

Thachungtse.) *Day 9:* (10 km./5hrs. to Nima Ling.) *Day 10:* (14 km./ 7hrs. to Shang Sumdo. En route you will go through the Kang Maru Lâ, 5,030-5,300m.) *Day 11:* (10km./3hrs. to Martselang.) *Day 12:* (6 km./ 2hrs. to Hemis.)

Stok to Spituk: This is a three- or four- day trek.

The direct route. Day 1: (Stok to Rumbak, 6hrs.; en route you will cross the Stok La, 4,900m.) *Day 2:* (6hrs. to Zingchen) *Day 3:* (5hrs. to Spituk).

Through Mankarmo. Day 1: (Stok to Mankarmo, 6hrs.) *Day 2:* (6hrs. to Rumbak; en route you will cross the Stok La) *Day 3:* (6hrs. to Zingchen) *Day 3:* (5hrs. to Spituk).

Leh-Nubra

You can drive from Leh to many parts of Nubra. Therefore, you don't really need to do most of these treks, except for the exercise.

Leh-Panamik-Umlung: *Day 1:* (18km. from Leh to Sambog, by the bridle path.) You have to climb to around 15,000'. *Day 2:* (16km. to the Khardung village.) The gradient is steep till you reach around 17,000'. There's snow at some places even in August. I did this route around the 4th September when there was fresh snow. The descent to 15,000' is equally steep and, at times, dangerous. The area has a reputation for avalanches. After 15,000 you will descend along a rocky slope that is considerably less stiff. The valley that you will enter is generally quite green. *Day 3:* (15km. to Khalsar.) You will first descend for 8km. along a steep, narrow gorge to Shyok. The next 6 km. will be along the left bank of the river. *Day 4:* (23km. along River Shyok to Tagur.) The trek will be on the left bank of the river to begin with. After five kilometres you with cross to the right bank by a bridge. After that the track goes up the Nubra valley. The terrain is often plain, and almost always sandy, strewn with stones. Thorny bushes abound. After a while a long stretch of fields with crops begins. The small Ran Kralzung and Sumiur villages follow. Tagur is the largest, and most important, village of the area. The Santaling Gompa of the minority yellow hat Ge Lugs Pâ sect is nearby. *Day 5:* (19km. to Panamik.) To begin with you will go through flat, brown, sandy land. You will pass the occasional village and the odd cultivated field. You will have to cross a few fast-moving streams. Panamik is best known for its hot water springs. *Day 6:* (23km. to Camp Umlung.) There are cultivated fields in the first stretch. Brown, sandy and hard plains follow. More than half way through you will need to cross the Tillam Buti river. The trail then winds its way up a cliff, on a fairly steep slope. The descent will lead to Unlung and the river there.

As mentioned, you could have driven up to Unlung.

Leh- Khalsar: This is an alternate route that meets up with the 'Leh- Panamik- Umlung' route, above, on Day 3. There's no saving in terms of time, though. In fact it's the tougher route, and far more exciting.) *Day 1:* (24km.from Leh to Sabu. Bakaya estimated Sabu's altitude at 15,000' and the *Gazetteer* at 14,000'. Moorcroft-Montgomerie, writing in the late 19th century, did the Leh-Sabu stretch in 6 miles or 9.6 km.) Sabu is in a little valley, has terraced fields, several hamlets and a few trees. *Day 2:* (34km. to Digar.) The ascent to the 17,930' Digar Lâ pass is very steep and along a winding trail. There is a thick layer of snow on the pass, and continues for three kilometres to its north, almost throughout the year. That makes it a difficult pass to cross. The descent is somewhat easier. It is quite steep, down a long stony slope, to Polu camp. Then you go down a moorland amongst granite boulders and bogs for about 8km. Digar village (13,080' according to the *Gazetteer* and 15,000' according to Bakaya) has a huge figure of the Chambâ carved on a rock. The Digar stream flows nearby. *Day 3:* (40km. to Khalsar.) It is largely a descent to Shyok. You will mostly trek along the left bank.

The 'new' areas

I have, in this book, ensured that it doesn't escape the reader's notice that, in 1993-94, I had got seven thitherto 'prohibited' areas opened up for tourism. You could consider the following four unconventional treks in those areas:

i) Shachukul-Shara-Igu

ii) Shachukul-Kargyam

iii) Shachukul-Tukla-Hungyam-Tsomo Riri

iv) Darbuk-Itching valley-Tangyar-Nubra

Or you could do the more popular treks in these areas:

Rumtse-Tsomo Riri: 6 days, July to September. *Day 1:* (Rumtse to Kyamar, 5hrs.) *Day 2:* (6hrs. to Tisaling; en route you will cross Mandal Chan La, 4850m., and the Kumur La, 4000m.) *Day 3:* (6hrs. to Pangu Nagu; en route you will cross the Shingbuk La, 4850m.) *Day 4:* (7hrs. to Rachung Karu; en route you will cross the Horlam Kongkâ La, 5000m.) *Day 5:* (8hrs. to Gyama Gongma; en route you will cross the Kyama Yur La, 5200m.) *Day 6:* (8hrs. to Kurzok, the village closest to the Tsomo; en route you will cross the Nyalangnyugu La, 5100m.)

Rumtse-Tsomo Riri: This is a totally different route. You can go to the Tsomo by one route and return by the other. (11 days; July to September) *Day 1:* (Rumtse to Purang Sumdo, 3hrs.) *Day 2:* (6hrs. to Debring; en route you will cross the Taklang La, 17,500') *Day 3:* (6hrs.

to Spang Chendo) *Day 4:* (6hrs. to Pangmur) *Day 5:* (7hrs. to Numa; en route you will cross the Pangmur La, 4500m.) *Day 6:* (5hrs. to Daktago) *Day 7:* (6hrs. to Zozingo; en route you will cross the Thalakung La, 4900m.) *Day 8:* (6hrs. to Tharangang) *Day 9:* (6hrs. to Lato Gongma) *Day 10:* (6hrs to. Kyangdam) *Day 11:* (8hrs. to Kurzok, the village closest to the Tsomo).

Kibber-Tsomo Riri: (July-early Sept.) *Day 1:* (Kibber to Thangtak, 6hrs.) *Day 2:* (8hrs. to Kharsa Gongma; en route you will cross the Parang La, 5,500m.) *Day 3:* (8hrs. to Tharang Yokma) *Day 4:* (7hrs. to Polong Parak) *Day 5:* (7hrs. to Nurboo Sumdo) *Day 6:* (6hrs. to Kyangdam) *Day 7:* (8hrs. to Kurzok)

Tsomo Riri to Hemis (Rupsho Valley): *Day 1:* (From Kurzok/ Tsomo Riri to the Nyalangnygu Lâ, 5,100m., and then to Gyama in around 8hrs.) *Day 2:* (To the Lanyar Lâ, 5,500m., and then to Zozingo in roughly 7hrs.) *Day 3:* (To Thalakung La, 4,900m., and then Daktago in 6hrs.) *Day 4:* (6hrs. to Numa) *Day 5:* (6hrs. to Pangmur) *Day 6:* (6hrs. to Langmoche) *Day 7:* (To Yar La, 4,900m., and then to Dat in 7hrs.) *Day 8:* (6hrs. to Sogra) *Day 9:* (To the Zalung Karpo La, 5,100m., and then to Yakrupal in 7hrs.) *Day 10:* (6hrs. to Nima Ling) *Day 11:* (7hrs. to the Kang Maru La, 5,100m., and then to Chus Kurmo) *Day 12:* (6hrs. to Hemis)

Tso Kar (lake) to Hemis: *Day 1:* (6hrs. from Pangunagu to Nuruchan) *Day 2:* (6hrs. to Chabzâñg) *Day 3:* (6hrs. to Spangchendo) *Day 4:* (6hrs. to Langmoche) *Day 5:* (To Yar La, 4,900m., and then to Dat in 7hrs.) *Day 6:* (6hrs. to Sogra) *Day 7:* (To the Zalung Karpo La, 5,100m., and then to Yakrupal in 7hrs.) *Day 8:* (6hrs. to Nima Ling) *Day 9:* (7hrs. to the Kang Maru La, 5,100m., and then to Chus Kurmo) *Day 10:* (6hrs. to Hemis)

Kargil

Treks out of Sânkoo

Sankoo-Drâss: This is a three-day trek along the Nakpochu Black Water Nallah, across the Umba la (3380m.). The shrine of the saint Syed Mir Hashim, a popular pilgimage, is four kilometres away from Sankoo, in Karpo Khar village. The trek passes through pretty meadows, with flowers growing all over, and past pretty mountain villages like Umba.

Sankoo-Drâss: (Two days; a difficult trek, especially when the snow either falls or melts or becomes slippery.) There are buses from Kargil (and Padam) to Sankoo. *Day 1:* (3hrs. from Sankoo to Umba.) The track is bad. You have to ford a stream midway. *Day 2:* (10hrs./ 30km. to Drâss.) The first stretch involves a tough climb from around

11,500' all the way up to the Umba Lâ pass (14,800'). The 3-5 km. downhill trek on the other side is relatively comfortable, though. You will come to a greenish valley. After that, you will have to climb up to the Lamagus Lâ (c.14,000'), which towers over the Drâss valley. This stretch is quite easy. So is the gentle, two-hour descent to the Drâss valley.

Sankoo-Drass: *Day 1:* (4hrs. from Sankoo to Stakpâ Umba) *Day 2:* (5hrs. to the Umba La camp) *Day 3:* (4hrs. to Drâss, via Lamochan).

Sankoo-Rusi La-Shergol(e): This is a four-day trek over the Rusi Lâ (4950 metres), along the Kartse (Karchey) Nallah. It passes through the Ḳartse (Karchey) valley.

Sankoo-Barsoo-Shergol: *Day 1:* (6hrs. from Sankoo to Tikat) *Day 2:* (6hrs. to Pangher) *Day 3:* (6hrs. to Sapi/ Balti Khar, via the Rusi La) *Day 4:* (7hrs. to Shergol, via Sirzing)

Sankoo-Mulbek(h): This is a four day trek.. The route is much the same as for Shergol.

Treks out of Pânikhar

(See also the entry on Pânikhar in the chapter on Kargil district.) This village serves as a base camp for treks in all directions: within the Suru valley, to inner Ladakh and to Kashmir. i) The shortest satisfying trek, up the hill opposite the tourist bungalow, takes less than five hours, return. It takes us even closer to the twin Nûn-Kun peaks. ii) The 'Nûn-view saddle' (3,810m.) is a short, 3hr., trek from Pânikhar. It is on the Parkachik ridge. So, if you aren't up to going to the peaks themselves, trek to the 'saddle' from which you can get a fine view of the majestic peaks and the glacial valley around. iii) Or you can climb the Sentik ridge above Tangole village and go from the ridge to the glacial plateau. iv) and v) You can trek from here to Pahalgam in five days and Kishtwâr in six days.

Nûn-Kun: The Nûn is 7,135 metres/ 23,447' high and the Kun is at 7,035 metres/ 23,213'. These peaks are around 21km. east of the Bhot Kol pass and are roughly 1,000 metres/ 3,000' higher than the other mountains around them.

July and August are the best months to attempt the twin peaks. April can be very dangerous because a number of crevices would be open then. October is tricky, too, because of the likelihood of snowfall. The base from which the ascent begins is called Gyâlmo Throngos. It is located between the stones that mark the 112th and 115th kilometres (from Kargil). Don't always count on finding the milestones, though. They are buried under several feet of snow for almost half the year.

Nun and Kun are among the taller (7000 metres plus) peaks of the world. However, they aren't the tallest even in present-day Ladâkh. The two Saser peaks are. The USP of the Nun-Kun peaks is that they probably are the only 7000m.+ peaks in the world that jut out of the main, motorable road. You don't have to trek for days to reach just the base camp. You get out of your jeep or bus and walk for five minutes and you are at the base. Therefore, arguably, among all the 7000m.+ (23,000'+) peaks of the world, these must be the easiest to climb.

(Please see the chapters on 'Trekking in Jammu' and 'Trekking in Kashmir' in the respectivel volumes for treks from Kishtwâr [Jammu] and Pahalgam [Kashmir] to Pânikhar.)

Treks out of Mulbek

Mulbek-Sapi-Kanoor: (June-September) Mulbek is on the National Highway. *Day 1:* (From Mulbek to Phokar, 3hrs. En route you will pass Shergol and Sirzing.) *Day 2:* (5hrs. to Sapi/ Changyul) *Day 3:* (Optional detour: a 6hr. round trip to the Sapi Tso lake and cave and back) *Day 4:* (4hrs. from Sapi to Batambis) *Day 5:* (4hrs. to Kanoor). Kanoor is on the Kargil-Zâñskâr road. It is around 20km. from Kargil town.

Mulbek-Shergol: *Day 1:* (6hrs. from Mulbek to Sumdo. En route you will pass the Choron hot-water springs) *Day 2:* (4hrs. to Binaltsa) *Day 3:* (5hrs. to Shergol, via Phokar and a 13,000' pass).

Mulbek-Lotsum: *Day 1:* (5hrs. from Mulbek to Kuinglee) *Day 2:* (5hrs. to Tacha Brok) *Day 3:* (4hrs. to Tacha) *Day 4:* (3hrs. to Lotsum) Lotsum is on the National Highway and around 20km, from Kargil town.

Kargil: 'recreational peaks'

The men and women of Ladakh like climbing certain peaks as part of their annual Ree-sair (ritual trek). Kachu Sikander Khan has compiled a list of the favoured peaks and mountains of Purîg as well as the villages that patronise them.

Barban Chen: (c.17,500') This mountain is surrounded by Darchiks, Garkun and Shakar Chiktan. The people of these villages have been climbing up to the peak for centuries. In the foothills are ancient hunting grounds. From here, if you look south you will see the famous Nûn-Kun peaks.

Kyûñlî: (c.17,000') This is a peak in the Wâkhâ, Mulbek, Shakar Hagnas area.

Mang Styâng: (c.15,000') This mountain is between Sot and Tacha Karat. It is the peak favoured by the people of Barchey, Âpâti, Tomel, Akcha-mal, Kûkstey, Tacha Karat and the Pashkum area.

Nak Thul: (c.18,000') Phokar, Skambû and Syâyî are close to this peak.

Nindum Rârî (near the Fotu Lâ): (c.18,000') This mountain lies between Samrâ, Kokashu and Stakchey. Its name means 'Nindum, the divine mountain.' The Bons considered the mountain sacred. From its peak you get an incredible panoramic view of the surrounding valleys and villages for hundreds of kilometres, without many obstructions. In the east you can see upto Chânglâ, which is around 225km. away. In the west are the mountains of Zâñskâr. Baltistân is in the north and Lingshet in the south.

Panchoo (near Garkun): (c.18,000') This is one of the peaks that the people of Garkun climb.

rGyûn Khar: (c.18,000') This mountain is located between the villages Sot, Salmon Lâling, Sherchey Cholichen and Blârgo. Good views are to be had from the peak.

Ladakh-Himachal Pradesh

Padam-Darcha/ Manali: (9-10 days.) This trek can be done between July and September. The passes are blocked by snow in the other months. *Day 1:* (Around 6 hours/ 20km. from Padam to Money; another 2km. to Raru, 3,900m.) *Day 2:* (6 hours to Pupi Lâ/ Pepu La.) *Day 3:* (7 hours to Purne.) *Day 4:* (4 hours to Thâñgse.) You would certainly not want to go directly to Thâñgse and miss out on the exciting Phugtâl gompa which is inside a wide cave. (Also spelt Phugtâl.) The detour will take around 90 to 120 minutes each way. If you spend an hour an Phugtâl, you would have added another four or five hours to today's trek. *Day 5:* (3 hours to Kargyâk, also spelt and pronounced Kargiya.) Kargyâk is, arguably, the world's highest located village. It is also the last village in Jammu and Kashmir before you enter Himachal Pradesh. *Day 6:* (6 hours to Lakong/ Lhâkhang.) *Day 7:* (7 hours to Chemenopo.) *Day 8:* (5 hours to Zankar-Sumdo.) *Day 9:* (8 hours to Darcha, 3304m.) You can take a bus from Darcha to Manali, perhaps on Day 10. On Day 9 the last bus for Manali might have left by the time you get to Darcha.

A variant: Follow the above route till Day 6. Spend the night at Lhâkhang, as above. However, on (*Day 7*) head for Ramjak, where you should halt for the night. It takes around seven hours to trek from Lhâkhang to Ramjak, via the Shingkun La. *Day 8:* (6 hours from Ramjak to Palamo.) *Day 9:* (7 hours to Darcha Sumdo.)

Padam- Darcha/ Manali: A variant. (7-8 days.) *Day 1:* (22km. from Padam to Raru.) *Day 2:* (23km. to Cha, 3,901m.) *Day 3:* (25km. to Testa.) *Day 4:* (26km. to Kargyâk.) *Day 5:* (24km. to Lakhang Pulu.)

Day 6: (25km., via the Shingkun Lâ, 5,097m., to Zankar-Sumdo.) *Day 7:* (25km. to Darcha.) You can take a bus to Manali on Day 7 or 8.

Padam-Manali: Another variant. (7-8 days.) *Day 1:* (Padam to Raru, 22km.) *Day 2:* (22km. to Surley, 4,100m.) *Day 3:* (20km. to Purney, 3,900m., via Cha and Phugtâl.) *Day 4:* (20km. to Drangzay) *Day 5:* (19km. to Lartsa, via Kargyâk and Gombo Rangjon.) *Day 6:* (17km. to Gadi Shisa, via the Shingkun Lâ, also spelt Shingko Lâ and Shingo Lâ.) *Day 7:* (15km. to the Camp near Darcha) By bus from Darcha to Manali.

Padam-Manali: Yet another variant. (9 or 10 days.) *Day 1:* (12km. from Padam to Bardan)

The monastery at *Bardan* enjoys certain prestige in the area. Its large assembly hall contains idols and chortens made of copper, bronze, wood and clay. Dawa Gyatso founded it in the 17th century. It comes under the Stakna monastery. Around 40 monks live here. It overlooks River Lingti.

Day 2: (To Ichar/ Cha) *Day 3:* (To Phugtâl) *Day 4:* (To Purney) *Day 5:* (To Thâñgse) *Day 6:* (To Kargyâk) *Day 7:* (To a camp near the Shingkun Lâ) *Day 8:* (To Zampo) *Day 9:* (To Darcha) By bus to Manali, today or on *Day 10*.

Padam-Manali: Yet another alternative, with minor changes, combining many of the above routes: Padam-Bardan-Raru-Surley-Cha-Phugtâl-Purney-(S)Testa-Drangzay-Kargyâk-Lartsa-Shingkun Lâ-Gadi Shisa- Darcha -bus to Manali.

Ladakh (Kargil)- Jammu (Kishtwâr)

Padam- Galar (Kishtwâr): (7 days; an exhausting trek.) Start from Padam. *Day 1:* (12km. to Tungring.) Trek along River Doda but upstream.

Day 2: (12km. to Ating, 12,020'.) Leave the camp very early, around or before 5 am. if possible. That's because towards the end of today's trek you will need to ford a muddy glacial stream to get to Ating. Do this well before the sun is hot enough to melt the glacier anew.

Day 3: (24km. to Huttra.) Start walking along the left bank of the stream. After about 4 km. you will see the cave monastery of Zongkhul, atop a big rock. The track is not defined. It gets lost amidst the rock before vanishing into the river at the bottom of a cliff. However, the river is gentle and its bed firm. Around seven or eight kilometres after the monastery you will come to a large glacier. Around a kilometre after the glacier's snout you will cross the river using an extremely clever rock construction. A sharp uphill climb follows. You will come to a 'hanging valley'. Huttra has a fine camping site.

Day 4: (17km./ 13hours to Bujwas, also spelt Buswas.) It's a difficult trek today. In the beginning the track is vague and undefined, because it goes over hardened ice and snow, and through boulders and a moraine. After the track becomes clearer, it will be a long downhill trek to the Bhut Nadi valley. Local shepherds do this stretch in a single, long day. On the one hand they know the hills better than you do. On the other the sheep bring their speed down. So, you, too, should be able to do the stretch in around 13 hours. Buswas has a very good camping site.

The track from Buswas is clearly defined right up to Galar (Day 7). However, make sure you cross rivers at the correct points.

Day 5: (27km. to Machail.) It will take an entire day's trek to get to Machail. *Day 6:* (30km. to Atholi.) Again, a whole day's trek. *Day 7:* (32km. to Galar.) Another long day. Buses ply from Galar to Kishtwâr. However, the last one would have left by the time you get there. So, count on camping overnight at Galar.

Alternatives: You can combine Days 1 and 2 and make it from Padam to Ating in a single 22km. day. Secondly, the standard way of travelling between Huttra and Buswas is through the Omasi Lâ pass (5,434m).

45

Trekking in Balâwaristân-Gilgit-Chitrâl Hunzâ[1]

K-2 & Gondogoro La

This is a difficult, 21-day trek, including the round trip from Islâmâbâd back to Islâmâbâd. Gw, it is also one of the most sought after treks in the entire Himâlayan belt. The challenge of the K-2 and Gondogoro La is, without a doubt, what brings international travellers there. However, the incredible views that they see during the trip make them recommend this trek to friends back home. These views are unique to this part of the world.

K-2 Chogori (8611m./ 28,268'), of course, is the second highest mountain in the world . Broad Peak Falchan Kâñgrî (8047m./ 26,444') is the fourth highest in this region.

The route to Gondogoro La was discovered as recently as in the 1980s by a talented guide from Balâwaristân. He was leading a group of French trekkers at the time. He decided to take a risk and his resourcefulness paid off.

Day 1 Reach Islâmâbâd; Day 2 Day of rest (can be skipped) Day 2 or 3 Fly to Skardu; Day 4 Prepare for the trek and see Skardu; Day 5 Drive to Biansa, which is the roadhead; Day 6 to Day 12 Trek to Concordia; Days 13 and Day 14 Explore K-2 B.C and Broad Peak; Day 15 to Day 19 Cross Gondogoro La to Hushe; Day 20 Day of rest; Day 21 Drive to Skardu; Day 22 Fly to Islâmâbâd.

1. The region is in the illegal occupation of Pâkistân. Therefore, all routes begin with and end at Islâmâbâd because the airport of the Pâkistâni capital is the nearest in the plains with a regular service to the region.

Biafo and Hisper

This trip takes 21 days, from Islâmâbâd back to Islâmâbâd.

The Biafo and Hisper glaciers, together, constitute perhaps the mightiest and most spectacular passage in the Kârâkorams. Traders form Baltistân would travel to Hunzâ valley and Kashgar through the Biafo. Their ancient route is part of this trip.

Day 1: Reach Islâmâbâd; *Day 2*: Fly to Skardu; *Day 3*: Prepare for the trek and see Skardu; *Day 4*: Drive to Biansa, which is the roadhead; *Days 5 to 13*: Trek to the Hisper pass; *Days 14 to 18*: Cross the pass and descend to Huru; *Days 19 and 20:* Travel in a sports-type vehicle to Gilgit via Hunzâ; *Day 21*: Fly to Islâmâbâd.

Masherbrum and Hushe valley

This trip takes 16 days, from Islâmâbâd back to Islâmâbâd.

Masherbrum is a relatively green valley, which is a rarity in the deserts of the Himâlayas. That is one reason why it is considered one of the most beautiful parts of Baltistân. Within the valley the biggest tourist draw is the Masherbrum Peak (7821m./ 25,660'). It is a difficult peak. For that reason few mountaineers actually climb it. Most tourists are happy just to see the tenth highest mountain in the region, and one of the highest in the world.

Day 1: Reach Islâmâbâd; *Day 2*: Fly to Skardu; *Day 3*: Prepare for the trek and see Skardu; *Day 4*: Drive to Hushe Valley; *Days 5 to 13*: Trek to Masherbrum and Gondogoro base camp; *Day 14*: Drive to Khaplu; *Day 15*: Drive to Skardu; *Day 16*: Fly to Islâmâbâd.

Aling Valley and K-7

This trip takes 13 days, from Islâmâbâd back to Islâmâbâd.

Day 1: Reach Islâmâbâd; *Day 2*: Fly to Skardu; *Day 3*: Prepare for the trek and see Skardu; *Day 4*: Drive to Hushe Valley; *Days 5 to 11*: Trek to Aling valley and K-7 base camp; *Day 12*: Drive to Skardu; *Day 13*: Fly to Islâmâbâd.

Shimshal

This trip takes 15 days, from Islâmâbâd back to Islâmâbâd.

See the chapter on 'Shimshal.' This trip covers Hunzâ, which according to some is the original Shangri La, as well as Shimshal, a unique valley within Hunzâ/ Gilgit. The trip is a great favourite with those looking for serenity. The scenery is breathtaking and China is right across the border.

Day 1 Reach Islâmâbâd; Day 2 Drive to Chilâs; Day 3 Drive to Jurjur; Day 4 to Day 8 Trek up to Shimshal via Malanguti; Day 9 to Day 12 Trek to Pasu; Day 13 Drive to Hunzâ; Day 14 Drive to Besham; Day 15 Drive to Islâmâbâd.

The Golden Peak

This trip takes 19 days, from Islâmâbâd back to Islâmâbâd.

The Hopar region abounds in virgin peaks above the Barpu glacier.. Explorers seeking to go boldly where no man has ever set foot before often come here.

Day 1 Reach Islâmâbâd; Day 2 Fly to Gilgit; Day 3 Prepare for the trek and see Gilgit; Day 4 Drive to Hopar village; Day 5 to Day 11 Trek on the Barpu glacier the base camp; Day 12 to Day 16 Return to Hopar village; Day 17 Drive to Hunzâ; Day 18 Drive to Chilâs; Day 19 Drive to Islâmâbâd

The Nañgâ Parbat

This trip takes 14 days, from Islâmâbâd back to Islâmâbâd.

This tour will take you close to the "Killer Mountain," which is an extension of the greater Himâlayas. It is said that fairies (in the old sense) use to live where the base camp now is.

Day 1 Reach Islâmâbâd; Day 2 Fly to Chilâs; Day 3 Drive to Tato; Day 4 to Day 11 Trekking around the Nañgâ Parbat; Day 12 and Day 13 Trek to Raikot; Day 14 Drive to Islâmâbâd

The Hiñdu Kush

This trip takes 22 days, from Islâmâbâd back to Islâmâbâd. (Expect 3-4 extra days en route.)

Day 1 Reach Islâmâbâd; Day 2 Fly to Gilgit; Day 3 In Gilgit; Day 4 Drive to Gupis; Day 5 Drive to Nialti; Day 6 Trek over the Thui An Pass; Day 9 Day 10 Walk to Gazin village; Day 11 Trek to Dobargar village; Day 12 Trek to Lesht; Day 13 Trek to Ishpru; Day 14 Trek to Shah Jinali; Day 15 Trek to Istaro; Day 16 Drive to Chitrâl; Day 17 Chitrâl; Day 18 Drive to Péshâwar; Day 19 Drive to Islâmâbâd.

To the Hiñdu Kush-Kârâkoram in a rugged vehicle

This road trip takes 16 days, from Islâmâbâd back to Islâmâbâd.

Day 1 Reach Islâmâbâd; Day 2 Drive to Dir; Day 3 Drive to the Bumburet; camp in tents; Day 4 Drive to Rambur, return to the Bumburet camp; Day 5 Drive to Buni via Chitrâl; camp in tents; Day 6 Drive to the Phander Lake; camp in tents; Day 7 Drive to Puniâl; camp in tents; Day 8 Drive to Karîmâbâd and Gulmit; night halt in a hotel; Day 9 Drive to Batura and Gilgit; night halt in a hotel; Day 10 Drive to Astore and

Rama; camp in tents; Day 11 Drive to Rama Lake and return to Rama; camp in tents; Day 12 Drive to Babusar Village; camp in tents; Day 13 Drive to Naran; camp in tents; Day 14 Drive to Abbotâbâd; night halt in a hotel; Day 15 Drive to Péshâwar; night halt in a hotel; Day 16 Drive to Islâmâbâd.

The Hiñdu Kush-Ovir Pass Trek

This trip takes 16 days, from Islâmâbâd back to Islâmâbâd.

Day 1 Reach Islâmâbâd; Day 2 Fly to Chitrâl; Day 3 Drive to Chahbronz; Day 4 Trek to Shokorshall; Day 5 Trek to Junali; Day 6 Trek to Kani; Day 7 Trek to Bimis; Day 8 Trek to Duggas; Day 9 Trek to camp site below Ovir pass; Day 10 Crossing the Ovir pass; Day 11 Trek to River camp; Day 12 Drive to Chitrâl; Day 13 Visit to Kalash valleys; Day 14 Trek over the Chamboi pass; Day 15 Fly from Chitrâl to Péshâwar; Day 16 Drive to Islâmâbâd

The Silk Route: a sample of

This road trip takes 14 days, from Islâmâbâd back to Islâmâbâd.

Day 1 Reach Islâmâbâd; Day 2 Drive to Besham; Day 3 Drive to Gilgit, Day 4 Gilgit-sightseeing in the morning. Evening: drive to Karîmâbâd; Day 5 Karîmâbâd; Day 6 Drive to Sust and Taxkurgan; Day 7 Drive to Kashgar; Day 8 Kashgar; Day 9 Drive to Taxkurgan; Day 10 Drive to Karîmâbâd; Day 11 Drive to Gilgit and fly to Islâmâbâd. If the flight is cancelled, drive to Besham; Day 12 Drive to Swât; Day 13 Swât; Day 14 Drive to Islâmâbâd.

The Shandur Polo Festival

This trip takes 12 days, from Islâmâbâd back to Islâmâbâd.

Day 1 Reach Islâmâbâd; Day 2 Fly to Gilgit; Day 3 Gilgit; Day 4 Drive to Phander lake in a rugged vehicle; Day 5 Drive to Shandur Lake; Days 6 to 9: Soak in the polo, the dancing, the songs and general festivity. Days 10 and 11 Drive back to Gilgit or drive onward to Chitrâl; Day 12 Fly to Islâmâbâd

In the Kârâkorams on mountain bicycles

This trip takes 22 days, from Islâmâbâd back to Islâmâbâd.

Day 1 Reach Islâmâbâd; Day 2 Drive to Chilâs; Day 3 Drive to Tato and trek to Fairy Meadows. It is said that fairies (in the old sense) use to live on this beautiful pasture. Tourists walk about in the pine woods or bathe in the lake; camp in tents; Day 4 Trek back to Tato; camp in tents; Day 5 Drive to Chilâs; Day 6 Drive to Gilgit; in the afternoon go to Kargah to see the famous Buddha carved on a rock. Return to Gilgit for the night; Day 7 On mountain bikes to Karîmâbâd. See the Diran and Rakaposhi Peaks; Day 8 Karîmâbâd: See the Baltit Fort. Walk to Duekar;

Day 9 Drive to Skardu. The Kârâkoram range lies beyond Skardu; Day 10 On mountain bikes from Skardu to Shigar Valley, camp in tents; Day 11 Mountain bike from Shigar to Gol; camp in tents; Day 12 On mountain bikes to Khaplu. See the Raja's palace and the 300-year-old Chaq Chan mosque; Day 13 On mountain bike to Hushe; camp in tents; Day 14 Hushe-trek for a while to see the Masherbrum range; camp in tents; Day 15 Drive to Skardu; see the ancient Kharpocho fort built in the times of Ali Sher Khân Anchan. Go to the Kachura Lake; Day 16 On mountain bikes to Satapara village; camp in tents; Day 17 Mountain bike to Deosai Top; camp in tents; Day 18 On mountain bikes to Barra Pani; camp in tents; Day 19 On mountain bikes to Rama Lake. Overnight camping; Day 20 Mountain bike to Rama Lake; Day 21 Drive to Chilâs; camp in tents; Day 22 Drive to Islâmâbâd.

Chitrâl/ Kalash

This trip takes 26 days, from Islâmâbâd back to Islâmâbâd.

Day 1: Reach Islâmâbâd; Day 2: Drive to Péshâwar; Day 3: Drive to Swât: Day 4: Drive to Chitrâl; Day 5: Drive to the Kalash Valleys; Day 6: Drive to Rua; Day 7: Trek to Shah Ghari; Day 8: Trek to Shperdock; Day 9: Trek to Lusht; Day 10: Trek to the Kishmanja Camp; Day 11: Trek to Chikar; Day 12: Trek to the Darkot Glacier; Day 13: Trek to Lushkargoz; Day 14: Trek to Karamber and/ or the Kurumber Lake; Day 15: Trek to Shervjange; Day 16: Trek to the Chatboi Glacier-Sukhtarabad; Day 17: Trek to the Karambar Crossing/ Waghut; Day 18: Trek to the Chinllinji base camp; Day 19: Rest and soak in the scenery; Day 20: Trek to the Chipurson Ziarat; Day 21: Trek to Sost; Day 22: To the Khunjerab Pass and thence to Gulmit for the night; Day 23: Drive to Karîmâbâd; Day 24: Karîmâbâd; Day 25: Drive to Chilâs; Day 26: Drive to Islâmâbâd.

46

The rivers of Ladakh and river rafting

Leh/ the Indus Valley

The Indus

It is from this great river that India got its name. Several places—in Ladakh, near Sonamarg [Kashmir] and in Tibet—claim to be its source. Tibet wins. The place in Tibet where the Indus originates is around 17,000' above the sea and is at 32°N and 81°E. Thereafter the river flows north-west for 160 miles.

It is called the Singh-ka Bab during that stretch. According to a local belief, the river springs out of the mouth of a lion. Therefore, the Tibetans also call it the Sengge(y) Chhu, or the water body (chhu) that flows out of the mouth of a lion (senggey/ singh). The Ladakhis call it the Sanspo.

The Indus enters India from the east in southern Ladakh. The place where it does is at roughly 13,800' and at 33°02'N/ 79°09'E. The river continues to flow in a north-western direction. It begins its journey in India along an extended, flat, alluvial bed in Lungbale. The Indus is calm and serene during this stretch.

Details of the course of the river are given later in this section.

The river flows through a narrow passage for the seven miles after Nakjubukle. The constriction ends at Harlaput. The Indus remains unconstricted till Mahe. The Indus and River Hanle merge at Loma, five miles upstream of Harlaput. It is estimated that River Hanle rushes down at almost 60 miles per hour before the confluence.

The Indus enters the mountainous Pûgâ valley at Mahe. It continues to flow through the rugged terrain of this region till Karo. It opens up somewhat at Tarchit. At Karo the river enters the Leh valley. The valley is vast between here and Spituk (10,288'). From there the river is again pressed between narrow banks till it gets to Nimmu (10,150'). The blue waters of River Zâñskâr merge with the relatively dirty waters of the Indus above Nimmu. The Indus then widens somewhat between Nimmu and Khaltse (9,900').

The river remains under Indian administration till Garkun. After that it weaves through Pakistan Occupied Kashmir and finally leaves the state eleven kilometres downstream of Sazin. It enters Pakistan at 35°35'N and 73°23'E.

The more important towns that the Indus goes past in Pakistan include Attock (2,079'), Khushalgarh, Mianwali, Dera Ismail Khan, Dera Ghazi Khan, Mithankot, Rohri, Sukkur, Sehwan, Hyderabad, Kotri and Karachi. The river has a 160 km. delta that runs along the coast of the Arabian Sea.

The course of the Indus runs thus:

(A word about pronunciation: the 'e' at the end of the names given below is meant to be sounded, as if it were an 'é'. Thus the last two syllables of Nakjubukle are 'book-lay' and not like the English 'buckle'. Hanle is pronounced aan-lay. For some reason the 'h' is silent in this word alone.)

Lungbale 13,547'-Tagyarmale-Gangrale 13,547'	11 km.
Gangrale-Niuchele-Luzurma Yogma-Pemaririle-Nakjubukle 13.500'	23 km.
Nakjubukle-Khama Shishale/ Pema Laga-Tuble-Loma 13.500' (*confluence* with River Hanle)	8 km.
Loma-Harlaput 13,500'	8 km.
Harlaput-Nyoma Rap 13,500'	12 km.
Nyoma Rap-Yalapuk (L)-Rakaru (R)-Mahe 13,500'	19 km.
Mahe- Raldung-Yang-Chumâthâng 13,456'	18 km.
Chumâthâng-Jiro (hot spring)-Kidmang-Mudil/ Kesar-Nior Nis (or Nurnis) 13,161'	16 km.
Nior Nis (Nurnis)-Kangmar-Akeke-Kiari-Khatpâ Thâñgbo-Kumdok-Gaik 12,940'	16 km.
Gaik-Tirido-Thanka-Hémyâ 12,817'	19 km.
Hémyâ-Likché 12,707'	10 km.
Likché-Ikpadok-Khawâthâng-Tunah-Leh/ Manali road head 11,100'	17 km.
Roadhead-Igu-Karu 11,080'	15 km.
Karu-Changa-Stakna 11,060'	11 km.
Stakna-Ranbirpura-Thiksey-Shey	11 km.
Shey-Choglamsar Bridge (6.5 km. away from Leh town)	5 km.
Choglamsar-Spituk 10,286'	6 km.
Spituk (13 km. ahead is the *confluence* with River Zâñskâr)-Nimmu 10,150'	25 km.

Nimmu-Machakha-Umlung Gongma-Alchi Gompa-Saspol	19 km.
Saspol-Wuleh Tokbo	8 km.
Wuleh Tokbo-Nurla 10,130'	13 km.
Nurla-Chagri-Chokbu-Khaltse 9,900'	11 km.
Khaltse-Narmu	10 km.
Narmu-Skirbuchan	12 km.
Skirbuchan-Kanutse	23 km.
Kanutse-Sunnit	6 km.
Sunnit-Garkun (last Indian post)	5 km.
Garkun-Gurugurdu	12 km.
Gurugurdu-Marol (*confluence* with River Shingo)	15 km.
Marol-Kharmang (fort)	26 km.
Kharmang-Vaziri Gund	13 km.
Vaziri Gund-Mabrok	8 km.
Mabrok-Shokha	14 km.
Shokha-Sermi	7 km.
Sermi-Yagho (*confluence* with River Shyok)	6 km.
Yagho-Gol	3 km.
Gol-Goma Thurgon	18 km.
Goma Thurgon-Skardu 7,680' (*confluence* with River Shigar)	13 km.
Skardu-Ponedas	22 km.
Ponedas-Krabâthâng	13 km.
Krabâthâng-Kotmul	27 km.
Kotmul-Strongling	13 km.
Strongling-Juche	12 km.
Juche-Shingas	12 km.
Shingas-Burumdoir	14 km.
Burumdoir-Hanuchai	16 km.
Hanuchai-*confluence* with River Gilgit	16 km.
The confluence point-Bunji	12 km.
Bunji-Lichar	18 km.
Lichar-Drang	14 km.
Drang-Gunar	15 km.
Gunar-Chîlâs	27 km.
Chîlâs-Balugush	14 km.
Balugush-Sinai Much	17 km.
Sinai Much-Basha	17 km.
Basha-Harban	10 km.
Harban-Sazin	14 km.

The border between India and Pakistan is 11 km. downstream of Sazin at 35°35'N- 73°23'E. The first 4km. are under Indian administration and the next 7km. under Pakistani occupation.

Rafting: Gradient: (The grades are explained at the end of this chapter.)

(i) Karo to Choglamsar (including the stretch between Hemis and Choglamsar): Between Grade I and Grade II. The river is shallow and calm. It takes about three hours from Hemis to Choglamsar. En route are Stakna, Thiksey, Shey, Chushot and the Choglamsar bridge.

ii) Spituk to Nimmu: Between Grade II and Grade III, sometimes Grade IV. The stretch between Phay and Nimmu takes around four hours. The river is slightly faster here. Therefore, the rafting is far more exciting than in the previous stretch.

iii) Nimmu to Alchi: Grades III and IV. Not recommended for beginners. This stretch can take around 6-8 hours.

iv) At some places in Ladakh the gradient is of Grade V.

Considerable whitewater rafting has been done on several stretches of the Indus. Some stretches, like the one near Choglamsar, are easy enough for first-time rafters. Adventure tourism expert Asaf Mahmud writes, that 'The first ever and pioneering whitewater rafting feat in India was performed [on the Indus] in the autumn of 1975.' However, Asaf also offers a few words of caution. He says, 'The river has a tendency to shift its bed at various sections... It has some gorges as well... To run the entire river requires [an] expedition approach as most of its upper section [passes through a] wilderness.'

Foreigners can travel between Karo and Khaltse without any special permission.

The Hanlé river

This river originates close to India's desolate, sparsely populated border with Tibet. A number of little streams emerge from the Lokphuk Gongru Tso (14,400') lake and the melting glaciers west of the Imis Lâ (pass) (16,760'). The lake is 5km. upstream of Samdole. Asaf Mahmud says, 'The streams in this sub-region, clockwise, are, Pachatung, Tongongmalung, Tuang, Miksadiu, Nalung and Kuglung.' The streams join each other at various points to create River Hanlé.

A major source of the river is the Kongra Chu rivulet, which carries down the waters of the mountains east of the Tsomo Rîrî, extending to the Lanak pass in the south.

The river flows down northwards. Of its total length of 70 miles (112 km.), it spends around 30 miles (48 km.) winding through the vast and level Mangkâng plain. It merges with the Indus at Loma.

19th century British accounts, quoting Major Alexander Cunningham, the explorer, say that he called 'the above described swampy plain the Hanlé Tso (or lake), and [thought] it must be the largest sheet of fresh water in Ladák.'

Between Samdole and Loma it follows the course given below:

(The 'e' at the end of *almost* all the names given below is pronounced like an 'é'. Thus 'Shade' really is 'shaa-they,' 'they' being as in English. All altitudes are in feet and distances in miles. Both are approximations.)

From-to	Altitude	Distance
Samdole	14,900	0
Samdole-Ranksile	14,900	1
Ranksile-Zarser	14,900	1
Zarser-Hale	14,900	4
Hale-Ukdungle	14,412	8
Ukdungle-Zong	14,400	7
Zong-Shade	14,400	6
Shade-Hanle	14,270	7
Hanle-Târâkokpole	14,024	11
Târâkokpole-Nukzele	14,024	7
Nukzele-Tihrale	14,024	6
Tihrale-Loma	13,900	12
		Total:70 miles

How to get there: Every other day a bus or truck leaves Leh for Nyoma (almost 230 km. away). From Nyoma, which is the nearest town, you will either have to walk or, with luck, look for a lift if a vehicle happens to pass by.

Zâñskâr

The Zâñskâr river

River Zâñskâr is also called the Chiling Chu. Its headwaters include the Yunam, the Tsarap ('Serap') Lingti Chu and the Sarchu. The river then merges with the Sumgal, which comes down from near the Tsomo Rîrî lake. It takes 130 miles to reach Padam. In the process the river descends by almost 4,000'. It joins River Doda at Padam.

The river then turns north and travels 80 miles and falls another 1,500' (or 18.7' per mile) before it joins the Indus at Nimmu (Snimo).

Thus, in all, the river is 210 miles long, and falls a little less than 6,000' (or 28.5' per mile).

River Zâñskâr winds its way through some gorges that are so deep that they are in the shade almost throughout the day. It goes past Thonde (Stongde) 11,460', Rinam 11,224', Pishu, Zâñglâ 11,050', Pidmu, Hanumil, Purfi Lâ, Niraq 11,000', Chiling and Nimmu 10,160'.

Cunningham, the British explorer, estimates its discharge at 1,000 cubic feet in winter, 3,000 cu. ft. in May and 9,000 cu. ft. in August.

Rafting: Much of the river freezes over for a few weeks in the winter. Travellers walk on this *chadar* (sheet) road at night—when it is least likely to melt and, thus, give way. It takes almost a week of walking on the chadar to travel from Padam to the roadhead in Leh district. (See also the chapter on 'Trekking.'

In summer, rafters take roughly the same amount of time, a little more than a week, to run the river. The going is not always easy. The river abounds in pools, drops and rapids. Some of the rocks that you will encounter have jagged edges.

Several teams have rafted down from Karshâ all the way to Nimmu, where River Zâñskâr merges with the Indus. M. Asaf Mahmud says, 'The characteristics of River Zâñskâr call for an expedition approach. Detailed logistics based on complete self-sufficiency should be adhered to for running the river. Provisions for 7-10 days, including fuel for cooking, must be taken along, of course, in dry bags.'

The river is of Grade III. Some adventure groups organise rafting in mid-August.

The Doda river

The source of River Doda is at the bottom of the Nûn-Kun Massif, where it is formed by the melting of the Drungdrung glaciers. As the 70 km. long river travels south, a number of streams join it. These include the Chinzum (left), Chumu (l), Hagshu (right), Bardur (r), Kyala (l), Shimiling (r) and Seni/ Sani (r). The Kargil-Zâñskâr (Padam) road runs along the river.

Rafting: It is possible to raft on the stretch between Abring (Abran) and Upti-Karshâ.

The Tsarap Lingti Chu

The Tsarap Lingti Chu originates at Purne. The Niri (Tsarap Chu) and Kargyâk streams emerge from the Tso Tak Phu Lake (33°21' N- 77°18' E), which is upstream of the Phugtâl monastery and the Shingo Lâ (pass).

As the Tsarap Lingti Chu goes down, it passes Char, Abnop, Dorzong, Ichar, Raru, the Bardan monastery, Trakkar, Chila, Kissara, Pipiting (a suburb of Padam), the Upti Fort and Karshâ. River Tema comes down from the Poat Lâ (18,752'), which is south of Padam. It joins the Tsarap Lingti Chu at Money.

Rafting: It is possible to raft on the stretch between Phugtâl and Padam. Some rafters start near the Purne monastery, run the course of the river till it joins River Zâñskâr and then continue rafting on River Zâñskâr till Nimmu, where the latter river merges with the Indus.

The Markha

River Markha flows towards the west briefly before joining River Zâñskâr. In spring and summer it is in spate. People trek along the river in autumn and winter.

Kargil

The Shigar

The Shigar originates in the Bara Deosai plateau and flows southeast.

River Drass

River Drass emerges from near the dZoji Lâ. The Mushkoo and Gamru streams join it before it merges with River Shingo.

The Shingo

The Shingo flows east from the Chhota Deosai plains (West Karakoram). The Shigar and Drass rivers merge with it. It then joins the Suru north of Kargil and later merges with the Indus.

The Suru

The Karcha stream trickles down from Rangdum (34°03'N, 76°23'E), which is the place where the Suru valley meets Zâñskâr. The stream joins the substantial waters of the melting Shafat glaciers (which are at the bottom of the Nûn-Kun massif). River Suru forms when the two merge.

The river then travels west, draining the stunning valley of the same name, till it reaches Kargil town. En route it picks up three major tributaries. The Chalong stream, which comes from the Babong glacier, merges with it at Pânikhar. The Phulangma, the source of which is in Itchu, joins it at Sâñkoo. The Wâkhâ Chu combines with the Suru at Kargil town.

The Suru, in turn, merges with River Shingo at Yogmayul, near Kargil town. From there they travel together. They first go through an area where tourists are not allowed and then through POK. They finally reach Chathalung, where the Indus subsumes them.

There are further details about the Suru valley in the chapter on Kargil district. However, villages have been arranged in the reverse (upstream) order in that chapter.

The course of the Suru runs thus:

The altitudes given are of the place mentioned second and are in feet. Distances are in miles. 1 mile= 1.6 km. The distances and altitudes given are mostly approximate.)

From-to	Altitude (feet)	Distance (miles)
Rangdum	12,150	0
Rangdum-Zuliduk	12,000	3
Zuliduk-Shama Kurpo	11,970	5
Shama Kurpo-Gulmatonga	11,810	7
Gulmatonga-Parkachik	11,500	10
Parkachik-Tangol	11,000	5
Tangol-Achambar	10,700	2
Achambar-Pânikhar (Suru)	10,500	5
Pânikhar-Damsna	10,300	5
Damsna-Thama/ Mangdom	10,200	3
Thama-Karpokhar	10,000	5
Karpokhar-Sâñkoo	9,800	2
Sâñkoo-Pharona	9,500	8
Pharona-Chaliskot	9,300	4
Chaliskot-Grantung	9,214	6
Grantung-Titichumig	9,000	5
Titichumig-Kargil	8,987	4
Kargil-Yogmayul	8,814	3
	Total	82 miles

Rafting: M. Asaf Mahmud has calculated that the drop works out to 40.68 feet per mile. The river is already a great favourite of international rafters. There's a 'jeepable' road (Kargil-Zâñskâr) running close to, if not along, the river, throughout. There are villages, and thus supplies, all along the route. There are no restrictions on tourists, Indian or international. The scenery is spectacular and the mountains are greener than in the rest of Ladakh. (The moist plains of Damsna, so reminiscent of Mongolia, are a personal favourite.) And in the second half of the river, rafting is sometimes so safe that if you jump out of the raft in, say, early September, the water won't reach your hip.

Some stretches are rough, though.

(Kilometre references given below indicate the nearest corresponding point on the road that runs along or near the river.)

The fall is very steep between Rangdum and Parkachik ('km. 101' to 'km. 90'). Rafting is not advisable on this stretch. In general, the section between 'km. 87' (Parkachik) and 'km. 42' (near Sâñkoo) is meant for experienced and skilled river rafters.

The 8 km. stretch between Parkachik and Tangole(e) is good for rafting. It is followed by a steep- and dangerous- gorge. The approximately 10 km. stretch from below Tangol(e) to Damsna is good.

Then there is a bad section that begins near the '52 km.' point (roughly Purtikchey) to the '46 km.' point (roughly Sangrâ). In other words, the stretch on either side of the bridge at 'km. 48' should be avoided.

The section between 'km. 46' (Sangra) to 'km. 43' is all right. But 'km. 43' to 'km. 42' is to be avoided. It is quite safe from 'km. 42' (two kilometres upstream of Sâñkoo) almost till 'km. 2' (the Iqbal Hydel Project).

The eastern Karakorams

The Shyok (or Shayaok) river

The Shyok is often called 'the river of death' because of what it did in 1929. It has behaved since then.

The Rimo glacier, which is east of Sîâchen, is the main source of the Shyok (aka River Khumdan). The stream from the Rimo flows south and joins River Chip Chap at Gapshang (Yapchan). The Chip Chap, in turn, flows along the northern limit of the Depsang plains to reach Gapshang (15,710'). Together they form River Shyok. The waters of other glaciers join it as it flows down. These glaciers include the Chong Kumdan, the Kichik Kumdan, the Aq Tash and the Kunchang.

Till 1929, the Chong Kumdan blocked the flow of the river and acted as a natural dam. That year the river cut through the glacier and destroyed several villages downstream.

Once the river leaves the Depsang plains, the Shyok goes through deep, and narrow, gorges. When it reaches the southern tip of the Saser

Muztagh, which is the eastern extremity of the Great Kârâkorams, the river almost turns around to go back the way it came. Its course turns from N-S to N-W.

It widens near the Saser Brangsa. Between Chhong Jangal and Shoma and again between Asham and Tirit its bed is anything between 1.5 km and 2.5 km. And yet in its last leg, between Yaglung and the point in Baltistan where it merges with the Indus, it narrows once again.

The course: The Shyok mainly flows through the Nubra sub-division of Leh. It joins the Indus at Yagho (35°22'N, 75°22'E) in Baltistan.

(Altitudes in feet, distances in miles.)

From- to	Altitude	Distance
Gapshan	15,710	0
Gapshan-Saser Brangsa	15,200	19
Saser Brangsa-Sultan Chhushka	15,000	15
Sultan Chhushka-Kataklik	13,860	9
Kataklik-Mandultang	13,430	16
Mandultang-Yarguluk	13,200	4
Yarguluk-Mundro	13,000	4
Mundro-Neya Yâkmik	12,500	15
Neya Yâkmik-Dong Yailak	12,300	3
Dong Yailak-Shukpâ Kunzâñg	12,200	6
Shukpâ Kunzâñg-Chhong Jangal	12,000	14
Chhong Jangal-Sirshak	11,860	7
Sirshak-Shyok	11,500	8
Shyok-Shama	11,000	17
Shama-Agham	10,500	13
Agham-Rongau	10,490	8
Rongau-Satti	10,480	7
Satti-Tirit	10,200	8
Tirit-Deskit	9,950	9
Deskit-Hunder	9,900	4
Hunder-Rakhura	9,900	7
Rakhura-Kharu	9,700	6
Kharu-Yaglung	9,600	12
Yaglung-Malakcha	9,400	7
Malakcha-Chalunka	9,200	10
Chalunka-Turtuk	9,000	6

After Turtuk the river enters POK.

History: Till the 1940s the river was the main link between north India and Central Asia, through Ladakh and Yarqand. The Shyok freezes over in winter. Traders and others would walk on it. In summer, caravans would ply on the old Central Asian Trade Route, part of which ran along the river from Shyok village to Sultan Chhushka. The river is known for sudden and terrible floods. As a result there are hardly any villages near it.

How to get there: i)To Shyok village: Travel by vehicle from Leh, across the Chang Lâ (17,400') to Tangkse (Durbuk). From there you can reach the picturesque Shyok village in a day's trek along the Tangkse Nâllâh.

i-a) It is possible to travel by vehicle right up to Shyok village.

ii) To Gapshan: Trek across Skyangpoche, the Saser Pass and Saser Brangas, through Sasoma (Nubra) to get to Gapshan, where the river forms.

ii-a) Travel by vehicle, across the Kharduñg Lâ and over River Shyok, to get to Sasoma.

Non-Indians may please note that they require special permission to travel through much of the area.

Rafting: Not yet attempted by anyone.

The Nubra river

The Nubra emerges from the southern tip of the massive Sîâchen glacier. Various streams get together to constitute River Nubra at Tsamskangchan (12,170'). The river descends in a south-eastern direction through a valley. On its left is the Great Kârâkoram Range and on its right the Saltoro Range. It is an enormous river, with islands within, throughout its 160 km. course. It merges with the Shyok at Lughzhum, opposite Deskit (9,950').

In September the river is less than a metre deep at its deepest, opposite Charasa. It freezes over by November and can be crossed at several places, including where it joins the Shyok. In summer, travellers use the route along the left bank till Changlung (10,760'). There are hares and considerable brushwood in much of the gravelly, 2-3 km. wide, Lower Nubra valley.

There are a number of villages downstream of Panamik. They are huddled together and live off agriculture. Apricots and the juicy little apples that Nubra is famous for grow in these villages.

The course: The river goes past the following villages and areas:

Tsamskangchan
Lhâyul
Warshi
Jardongsa
Nyungstet
Stongstet
Henache
Kimi
Changlung
Sasoma
Aranu
Ayi
Takshai
Panamik
Pulithañg
Kuri
Yulskam
Chamshing
Pinchimik
Charbagh
Markala
Lughzhum

There is a monastery near Warshi, on the right bank of the river. On the bank opposite Panamik there is a hot water spring. From Sasoma you can trek along the right bank of River Shyok, through the Saser Lâ, across the Kârâkoram Range, to Saser Brangsa.

How to get there: You can drive from Leh, across the Kharduñg Lâ, over River Shyok, to Changlung. The road more or less follows the course of the river.

Restrictions: Tourists need special permits to travel to certain parts of Nubra.

River Chip Chap: The river emerges from near the Aksai Chin plateau. It then flows west and joins the Shyok.

River Galwan: The river emerges from near the Aksai Chin plateau. It then flows west and joins the Shyok..

River Chang Chenmo: The river emerges from near the Aksai Chin plateau. It then flows west and joins the Shyok.

The gradation of rivers

The rivers of Ladâkh have been graded according to gradient, the intensity of waves, obstacles (such as rocks), the width (or narrowness) of the passage, difficulties encountered and the ease of manoeuvring.

There are six grades.

The Grades: I: Easy. II: Slightly difficult. III: Difficult. Irregular waves. IV: Very difficult. Strong waves. V: For experts only. Violent waves. VI: Not possible to do any rafting on such stretches.

Everything
(*almost*)

47

The annual cycle of life, the privations of winter

(An afterword)

Should Ladâkh become a museum piece?

A European Union diplomat had lately returned from a memorable vacation in Ladâkh. (But then all visits to that unique land are unforgettable. No one can ever erase from the mind the rugged weeks spent in Ladâkh, even after memories of international casinos, shopping malls, luxury hotels and pleasure spots become a blur and merge into each other.)

My friend pleaded with me not to let Ladâkh be 'spoiled' by television and other mod cons, and to let it remain pure, 'Like Bhutân has done,' his wife added.

It is an old debate, at least in India. Modern tribal leaders, most of them with advanced educational degrees acquired in Delhi and other Indian metropolises, often resent being 'preserved as museum pieces.'

On the other hand, romantics like that EU diplomat (and, secretly, even I) trot out one hundred reasons-some of them extremely sophisticated-why the 'pristine' state of tribal areas like Ladâkh should be 'retained.' (In the chapter on 'The Fabled Longevity of the Hunzâkuts' I have referred to my work with nomadic Gujjar cowherds, whose life expectancy and health standards, including average height, drop sharply whenever they give up their traditional ways. At Cambridge, not just at the Green Party's bland vegan lunches but also in the classroom, we would discuss studies about how 'development' had destroyed tribal societies.)

The diplomat was saying things that I have never had the courage to, outside my own thoughts. So I felt that it was my duty to take the line that many Indian tribal leaders have since the 1960s: "It is unfair to deny the people of places like Ladâkh things that the people of the plains consider good enough for themselves—roads, allopathic medicine, electricity, telephones and, yes, television. It is like the nuclear powers preaching to India.'

Over the years I have devised a formula, a method, that balances 'development' with the romantic/ Green approach to the world: Let the tribal people decide what is good for them and what is not. Outsiders have no business to either impose 'development' on Ladâkh or keep it backward in the name of pristine purity.

I believe that the Ladâkh Festival is the best example of this approach. The publicity that it generates brings in tourists, and thus money, throughout the year. However, it is also one of the reasons why the Ladâkhis have started taking greater pride in their traditional clothes, architecture, culture and frescoes.

A place where real people live.

Ladâkh is a great place for an adventurous summer vacation. But it is also a place where real people spend the entire year. While this book is meant for the visitor, it is about the real Ladâkh—where people with a rich history and even richer culture live. Even in the choice of trekking routes, I have included all the tracks that the Ladâkhi people themselves travel on, not for exercise but to actually get somewhere.

I hope that this has been a cheerful, optimistic, positive book. If 'yes' then perhaps I am entitled to give you some tragic relief. Let me tell you why it is positively sinful to deprive Ladâkh of the things that we in the plains take for granted.

So let me tell you about Queen It Thoq Lhâmo[1] of the epics-and about the first year that I spent in Zâñskâr, a place that, even by Ladâkh's own very daunting standards, is extremely remote.

How snow on the passes destroys hope

It Thoq, a beautiful angel, once came down from heaven to see Planet Earth. Here she fell in love with Norbu Zâñgpo, who was the king of Tibet-Ladâkh. They got married, but not everyone was pleased. The Bad People manoeuvred to get King Norbu Zâñgpo to leave Ladâkh in late autumn.

The king crossed the passes and went to the world beyond. In that age it took two weeks of travelling on horseback or foot just to reach the outermost passes of Ladâkh. In many parts of Ladâkh, especially Zâñskâr, it takes as long even today.

1. Lhâmo means 'female deity.' It is the exact equivalent of the Hiñdî-Sañskrit word 'dévî.'

A few weeks later, in November, snow began to fall on the passes. It Thoq was crushed. She knew that now her husband would not be able to return to Ladâkh for another seven months, because the snow on the passes would melt only in May (or June). And for those seven months not only would she be alone on Earth, she would also be at the mercy of the Bad People.

A moving—and very long—passage in the Ladâkhi epic "The Story of Norbu, the King, and It Thoq, the Angel[2]" describes the sadness that gripped the angel-queen. Of course, it is possible that I found that passage needlessly poignant.

I was posted to Zâñskâr as the head of its administration in late October. The rules require all postings to Ladâkh to be effected by June, so that the officer has time to acclimatise himself and also study the land while it is still possible to move about. Being a non-smoker and an exercise buff, I had absolutely no complaints about the lack of oxygen. (Many people who fly into Leh—instead of driving up from Kashmîr—tend to have breathing and other medical difficulties on the first day.) That I am from warm Delhi and night temperatures in Zâñskâr by then were somewhat below zero—the freezing point—was also not the issue because, as I just said, I am a fitness freak.

But reaching Zâñskâr on a 29th October brought with it problems of many other kinds. The biggest of these was leaving the place in December, when all the roads and passes were blocked by snow. My brother, Prasun, then a graduate student at the University of Wisconsin, Madison, had been saving for years to make his first trip home after he left India. We had planned to meet in Delhi in December, when my annual vacation was due. However, my senior was desperate to find a fall guy who would not resist a posting in Zâñskâr.[3] So he told me sweet lies about sending a helicopter to fetch me from there in December.

A shopless, self-sufficient economy

And then there was the issue of supplies. Not only does Ladâkh not make any consumer goods, in the 1980s Zâñskâr had no shops either.[4] That's right, like some other inaccessible parts of Ladâkh-Balâwaristân, it did not have a market economy. The remoter parts of Kashmîr, Jammu and neighbouring Himâchal Pradésh at least had a barter system. In Zâñskâr

2. Translated into English by Parvéz Dewân.

3. This was in the 1980s. Since then only two other officers of the national civil service, the IAS, have held office in Zâñskâr. I was the first IAS officer to be posted there.

4. A few shops would spring up in summer to cater to tourists.

(and parts of Baltistân-Hunzâ) every family had to make everything that it needed, including tweed and shoes and bricks and houses.

As part of my iron-pumping regime I drink huge quantities of milk and eat (all right, ate) lots of animal flesh. I mean, have a heart. I was freshly out of college—and a mountain climbing guy in his early twenties needs lots of milk and meat.

But in Zâñskâr there was no way that I could purchase milk. Things were simply not sold. Yes, I could get milk, free of charge, from the people who came to my office for work related to the government. In most of Jammu and Kashmîr, including Gilgit-Baltistân-Hunzâ-Chitrâl, there is no private sector worth talking about. So, everyone depends on the government. Therefore, I could get all the free milk that I needed.

'No, it won't be a bribe,' I was assured. But that's the way I saw it.[5] Besides, it was extremely humiliating to have to depend on a new person every day for the day's requirements of milk.

Absolutely no vegetables grow in that desert in winter. Indeed, several kinds of summer vegetables were introduced into Leh as recently as in the 1970s, and had not then reached Zâñskâr. So, people would place the few summer vegetables that grew in their kitchen gardens out to dry ('dehydrate') on their flat rooftops. In winter they would boil ('rehydrate') the dried vegetables and then cook them as normal. (Because there was no electricity then—and only for a few hours a day now—there was no question of refrigeration. Not that any was needed in winter. Thanks to sub-zero temperatures throughout the day, that huge valley becomes one big deep freeze in winter.)

Now, on the 29th October, I could hardly start drying vegetables to last me seven and a half months. 'No problem,' my senior, the Liar, said. 'Take over your new assignment. Assume charge and go to Kargil or Srînagar to purchase winter supplies for yourself.' He assured me that I had all of November (and maybe the first week of December) before snow blocked the passes.

But I had an even more important thing to do before snow fell—I had to tour the area of which I was now the SDM or Sub-divisional Magistrate. (A good district officer should visit every village in his jurisdiction at least once a year. I was able to this in the valley of Kashmîr and in Jammu district, both of which are huge. In Basohli [Jammu] I tried to go to each village twice a year, or more.)

5. Levels of corruption in Ladâkh (again including Gilgit-Baltistân-Hunzâ-Chitrâl) are among the lowest in the sub-continent. Government officials normally don't expect bribes, and the people don't like offering any either.

So, on reaching Padum, the headquarters of Zâñskâr, I dumped my bags in the incomplete (but smart, clean and spacious) house (made of mud-masonry) that was to be my official residence for the next one year. Two days later I headed off for the one part of Zâñskâr that was impossible to tour after snowfall—the Châr Nâllâh (gorge).

When I awoke on the morning of the 1st November, my fourth day in Zâñskâr, I saw nice, clean snowflakes descend to the earth. Pretty sight, I thought. I was lodged in a large, comfortable house in a village called Châ. However, soon it began to dawn on me that this was no mere snowfall. It was the big one, which blocked the passes and covered the roads and made them impossible to drive (or even walk) on. (For that reason the government did not allot me a jeep—making me the only officer of my rank in all of India who had to trek—or hire a pony—if I wanted to tour my area. Needless to say, there were no buses or taxis in all of Zâñskâr, leave alone privately owned vehicles. And no petrol pump either.)

There, I realised, went my plans of meeting my brother after several years. There was no saying when he would be able to save enough from his student grant to travel to India again. There, also, went my hope of purchasing dried vegetables and other supplies from Kargil or Srînagar.

My favourite uncle, then a bachelor in his forties, had finally decided to get married that winter. Now there was no way that I could attend the wedding, which we had been looking forward to for years.

Besides, I had won—through a draw of lots—the right to purchase a flat in an upmarket part of New Delhi. This had been a huge stroke of luck, because most people had to wait for a decade or more before they were allotted such a flat. I had to go to Delhi to sign a set of agreements with the public sector agency that built these flats—and this normally took at least a week. Besides, I had to raise money to pay the first two instalments, and getting a housing loan was a nightmare in India till the beginning of the 21st century.

I now saw all hopes of getting that flat vanish.[6]

Which is why I knew exactly how the angel It Thoq felt as she watched the first snowflakes of November waft down towards the passes. She was devastated—as, several centuries later, was I.

6. In the event, my no-longer-young parents in Delhi bailed me out by going through the nerve-wracking process of signing the agreement. They paid the instalments from their own savings.

Winter festivity

Hey, cheer up! Only people who have loved ones outside Ladâkh have to go through this. For most local people winters are a time for lots of fun.

Winters are when all but a few monasteries have their colourful annual fair. Monks put on exotic masks and act out religious plays and dance-dramas. Winters are also a time for feasting. Till the 1960s and early 1970s, wealthy people would host dinners for a couple of consecutive days. If there was no rich patron around, the women would pool money together and organise a hen party, as they still do. Or young men of a particular age group would throw a 'peer group' party.

In all three cases, the guests would eat noiselessly, because the host would have paid a professional 'remembrancer'[7] to recite, in daily instalments, either of the two ancient epics dear to Buddhists and Muslims, Ladâkhis and Baltis, alike: "The Story of King [Gyâlam] Késar" and "The story of Norbu, the King, and It Thoq, the Angel." Most remembrancers would complete the recitation of an epic over four or five dinners.

By the time I was posted in Ladâkh—the 1980s—the tradition of remembrancers was dying out. With growing affluence it was no longer worth the while for the Mon community to memorise bulky epics, when the government paid so handsomely to join even its juniormost ranks. (Some Mons are Muslims while others are Buddhist.) Besides, in some parts of Ladâkh it was the women who did this. There were just two or three teenaged girls in the area that I was in who were keeping this tradition alive when I was there. Conservatism comes with material well-being. The people were no longer willing to let their women recite stories at dinners where men would be among the guests.

On the other hand, some housewives discover that after several years of listening to Mon storytellers, they have managed to memorise the entire text of one or both of the epics. The skills of such women are in great demand within the extended family. They recite either of the epics for the benefit of a family audience, over a series of winter dinners.

Winters are the only time of the year when tradition permits grandmothers (and others) to tell stories to the children. The superstition is that if anyone in Ladâkh recounts stories before the first major snowfall of the season—the one that blocks the passes—this act will cause a wayfarer somewhere in Ladâkh to lose his way.

7. I have borrowed this term from an English-language translation of the word *hifz*. This is the Islâmic (and also Hiñdu -Buddhist) tradition of learning entire holy texts and epics by heart—memorised accurately to the last comma.

There is an almost identical superstition in the plains of North India. The difference is that out there people are not allowed to tell tales before sunset—for if they do a traveller somewhere will inadvertently take the wrong road. My mother and grandmother believe that this superstition was invented so that people could work all day and get down to telling and listening to stories only after it was dark. That way they could utilise the hours of precious sunlight tilling the fields and doing useful things, and not waste them on talk.

The Ladâkhis do not want to fritter away the precious months of summer, spring and autumn. But once there's enough snow to block the passes, there's nothing to be done in the fields, again due to the snow. And, because very few villages have electricity even as in the year 2004, there's little to be done elsewhere either.

Winter privations

With no electricity anywhere in Zâñskâr, we had to read by the light of 'petromaxes'-lamps filled with kerosene. I had brought just two books with me. So I decided to ravish the little library that my predecessor had built up. While it had an Emile Zola and the *Shâhnâmâ*, a Persian classic (both of which I quickly devoured), it mostly consisted of, um, middle-brow stuff like Dale Carnegie. They would had ostracised me at Delhi's St. Stephen's had they caught me reading *How to win friends*... But I read Mr. C all the same, and with great benefit.

I was so desperate for reading material that I would have been grateful even for railway timetables. Naturally, no newspapers or magazines were published in or imported into Zâñskâr (not even in summer). And no bookshop, either. someone had one copy of the *National Geographic.* I read it over and over again.

The reason why there's no electricity in most parts of Ladâkh is that the rivers are mostly too shallow, especially in winter, to generate hydro-electricity. While I am one of the pioneers of solar and wind energy in Zâñskâr—and one of the first in India—the problem with the sun, as someone put it, is that it doesn't come out at night when we need it the most. And storing solar and wind electricity is a major problem to this day.

The reason why winters in Ladâkh are so difficult is only in part because of the incredible cold of the region.[8]

8. Drâss, a village in Ladâkh—yes, the one on the highway from Kashmîr, is the world's second coldest inhabited place after Siberia. As a whole, Ladâkh is one of the coldest places in the world.

Ladâkh is a series of valleys surrounded by some of the highest mountains in the world. Only two roads link it with the rest of India—the Srînagar road, through the dZoji Lâ pass and the Manâli road, through the Bârâ Lachâ Lâ and Rohtang passes. There are several feet of snow on both sets of passes between November-December and May-June. India does not have the wherewithal to clear this snow, I wonder if any country in the world does. Similarly, it is impossible to travel northwards to Yârqañd in winter.

Zâñskâr is cut off even from the rest of Ladâkh in winter because of snow on the Penzi Lâ.

Therefore, the Ladâkhis spend all of October in Kashmîr, Jammu and Delhi purchasing seven months' worth of petrol, kerosene, pencils, battery cells, paper, spare parts for everything, biscuits, canned food, medicines—in short, all kinds of manufactured goods, plus rice, wheat and lentils.

That entire winter all that I ate was chapatis smeared with pasteurised butter (of which supplies were fairly adequate in the government-run cooperative store, because the local people preferred homemade butter) and a huge bowl of lentils. That's what I ate for lunch and dinner, day after day, from late-October to mid-June.

I bought huge polythene bags filled with some awful tasting milk powder. The boy who cooked my food—my nono (lit. 'younger brother')—did not know how to convert it into milk. So, twice a day I would chew the required number of spoonfuls to make a kilogram of milk a day, and wash it down with boiled water. That was my breakfast and evening 'tea' for the entire year—a few spoons of milk powder and boiled water.

A seasonal local shop that catered to tourists had one can of curried chicken left. I promptly purchased it, as well as the six or seven bottles of jam that hadn't been sold. I also discovered two little cans of condensed milk in that shop. Its keeper was delighted to get rid of all the leftovers, and begin the new tourist season with a zero inventory. For me it was like finding a hoard of caviar—even though back home my family would have dismissed all these as junk food.

At home, as a teenager (which hadn't been very long before) I would avoid all vegetables, except perhaps peas and ladies' fingers. That's because I had a choice. In Zâñskâr, being forced to live without meat and vegetables, I was constantly wracked by visions of Christopher Columbus (or was it HMS Bounty?) and his sailors dying of scurvy, and boiling their shoes to eat the leather.

My father in Delhi panicked when he learnt about the lack of vegetables. He wrote (and I received his letter seven months later, in

May) asking me to boil grass and eat it rather than risk scurvy. I was about to eat any grass that I could spot (and by May a few tufts of grass can be found near human habitations) when a local officer told me how to identify edible grass.[9]

As a sporty young man with high levels of testosterone, and with lots of time on my hands, I would naturally spend all my spare time fantasising about young ladies. And in every single romantic fantasy of mine during that year I would take those beauties to my favourite gourmet eatery in Delhi, and then gorge on delicately cooked meat.

There were no butchers' shops in Zâñskâr. So a colleague and I would try to purchase one sheep a month and share it half and half. Because there wasn't any grass around in winter, the sheep would be emaciated and would yield only around four kilos of mutton. My colleague and I would each get two kilograms, which had to last a month, or an average of less than seventy grams a day. During the entire winter we were able to purchase sheep only twice, from someone who had use for paper currency. And both these occasions were towards the end of the winter, in May and June.

That June I weighed myself as soon as I reached Srînagar (on a week's visit, to get my housing loan sanctioned). I had lost twenty-two pounds, on an already slim frame.

For the eight previous months the entire world around me had been a six-foot thick cushion of snow. During the drive from Zâñskâr to Srînagar, I got to see the first flowers and trees and leaves—and streams—since October. This was in Kargil's Suru valley, which I am strongly attached to for that reason.

At Srînagar's Lal Chowk I also saw something that I hadn't in ages—human crowds. What a treat it was for the eye. (Zâñskâr has a population density of roughly one and a half person for every square kilometre.)

But let us return to winter life in Ladâkh.

If there wasn't any electricity in Zâñskâr, there was naturally no television either, not that I watch much television when in the plains. In the days before I went to Zâñskâr I would spend an hour or two every day listening to the radio—Radio Australia, Netherlands, VOA's Now Music and the BBC. But I had taken no battery cells with me to Zâñskâr, apart from the six inside my powerful, battery-guzzling FM radio. I had

9. In that desert, tufts of grass grow—for some five months a year—wherever humans and other animals have been urinating and defecating. That's a nice thought to keep in the mind while eating that grass.

to make these six cells last all of seven months. So I cut down my radio-listening very drastically. All battery cells lose their effectiveness because of the sub-zero cold. So, I would remove the batteries from the transistor radio and put them in the sun every morning, to heat and rejuvenate them.

Water was another issue. Needless to say, there was no running water even in the house of the SDM. My nono would go down to the frozen river every morning, cut some ice with a pick, crush it and stuff it into a 'gerrycan' and bring it up to my hut. There he would boil enough water for me to drink all day.

Why did we need to boil the water? After all there was no industrial waste to pollute it in those pristine mountains.

In Ladâkh all human and cattle urine freezes into icicles in winter. When it melts it necessarily flows down to the river. For that reason, at least half a dozen people died because of gastric problems that winter. (In summer, on the other hand, urine might get absorbed by the earth.)

The rest of the water in the gerrycan was for washing and cleaning. I was one of the handful of people who would wash every day and bathe once a week. I taught myself how to clean every pore with exactly one bucket of water. (I can do it with even less now. The trick is to stand absolutely straight, pour water slowly on the head and let it flow down to the feet. Keep varying the spot on the head where you pour the water. You can wet every millimetre of your body this way. Only the arms have to be washed separately.)

Sometimes when I switched on my FM radio during the day, I would hear the telephone ring—and one end of the conversation. Some lucky person in Leh town, who had access to a telephone, would be talking to his relatives in the rest of India. Naturally, there were no telephones in Zâñskâr, a region spread over five thousand square kilometres, and bigger than many city-states.

Because the roads were all blocked and there were no air services, there was no post office either. In June, when the passes opened, I found three wedding invitations lying for me in the Kargil post office. Apart from the favourite uncle, two of my dearest first cousins had got married. People commented on my absence at these weddings. They asked my parents, 'Have you had a fight with your elder son? If your son who is a student in the USA can be in Delhi, why not your older son who lives in India and is in the "all powerful" IAS?'

To this day people in the plains can't understand that there are places in Ladâkh if you enter which in November, you can't get out of till June.

If you live in India you simply can not help reading vicious stories, planted by FLs (frustrated losers), about how privileged the Indian Administrative Service (IAS) is.

No 'gazetted' (covenanted) officer of the national police service (the IPS), the Indian Army or any national para-military force has ever been posted to Zâñskâr. Doctors, who had been given much-coveted seats in medical colleges on the Ladâkh quota, refused to serve in Zâñskâr, preferring to fly off to Libya instead. Engineers posted to Zâñskâr spent the winter in Kargil. The highest-ranking para-military force officials in Zâñskâr those days were two sub-inspectors of the Indo-Tibetan Border Force. And they were sent vegetables, fresh and canned fruit, medicines, meat-on-hoof (live sheep), newspapers, battery cells, a wireless set that received messages in Morse-code, magazines, condensed milk... You see, they did not belong to the pampered IAS.

Of course, we in the IAS are spoilt silly. After not getting to see a blade of grass for seven months, we could, in the summer, choose between eating edible grass and non-edible grass.

Ladâkh and the perfect balance

So, is this the paradise which should be spared the 'scars of development' so that we can maintain its 'purity'? Today there are telephones in Zâñskâr and, in the summer, running water in bathrooms.[10] Thank heavens for that.

I am an inveterate traveller. I love Indian Ocean lagoons like the one in Minicoy which have been left untouched by oil spills. Since my childhood I have had Gauguin-inspired dreams of idyllic islands in the Pacific where people still live as they did a thousand years ago. James Hilton made me fantasise about Shâñgri Lâs in the Himâlayas.

However, surely it isn't fair to make the local people live in hell so that we vacationers can spend a few weeks in an unspoilt paradise.

10. Ah, but I haven't even told you about Ladâkhi toilets. Except for luxury hotels everywhere in Ladâkh, and the homes of the well to do in Leh town and Kargil town, they are exactly as they have been for centuries.
Michel Peissel, the French writer, went into raptures about the 'royal' loo at Zânglâ's mud palace. It was like other Ladâkhi loos, except that there was synthetic linoleum on the floor, instead of loose mud (to be thrown into the pit after the act). But it was such a change from what he had been seing (and smelling) that it merited a mention in his book.
Let me not nauseate you with the details. You will see those toilets for yourself when you go to the various tourist attractions. And you will drive past them all the time.

Appendix

Note: (Note: While efforts have been made to update information to early 2004, all telephone numbers, tariffs/ rates/ fares, timings and even the availability of facilities mentioned in this chapter, indeed in this book, are subject to change.)

The main resorts: hotels, transport, hospitals, shopping & c

Fact file

Place	Area (sq.km.)	Popn.	Best Time	Temp Max Celsius	Temp Min Celsius	Rainfall in mm
Kargil town	14,036 sq km. (not including POK)	6,000	May-Oct			Snowfall: 2' to 5'. The town, Suru valley, and the villages around Wâkhâ and the Kanji Nâllâh receive around 3' a year. Drâss and Zâñskâr get around 5' each.
Leh town	44,000 sq.km. (if we include POK and China -occupied Kashmir then: 82,665)	27,000	May-Oct		38-20 (approx)	

Leh

Area: In terms of area Ladakh used to be the biggest district in India till 1979, when it was divided into Leh and Kargil. At around 44,000 sq.

km. Leh is still one of the biggest. And that is after Pakistan and China have respectively occupied, through military aggression, 78,114 and 37,555 sq. km. of the state (mostly in Leh and Kargil). Pakistan carved 5,180 sq. km. out of the state (all in Leh district) and gifted them to China.

Rainfall: Ladakh, especially Leh town and the surrounding valley, is a desert. Annual precipitation is 9 cm in Leh *district;* in Leh town it is closer to 5 cm.

Temperature: July is the hottest month and touches 38°C on some days. January is the coldest month. The lowest temperature goes down to around minus 21°C.

Population: The town has an estimated population of 27,000. The district's population was estimated at 92,000 in 1991, and 1,07,000 in 2001.

Languages spoken: Ladakhi, Urdu

Telephone (STD) code: 01982.

Religions: 81% of the population is Buddhist and 15% Muslim. There is a tiny Christian community (with 156 members at last count), belongs to the Moravian church.

Medical facilities: The Sonam Narbu Memorial Hospital in Leh town (on the Airport Road) is as advanced a hospital as can be expected under the circumstances. There are a number of private doctors, too. The adventurous can try out the Tibeto-Ladakhi system of medicine, *Amchi.*

Name	Address	Phone
Sonam Narbu Memorial Hospital	Airport Road	252014
TB Hospital	Main Bazar	252759
Chief Medical Officer		252102
<u>Some other doctors are:</u>		
Ladakh Medicate Dr Ishey Sonam		252136
ENT Dr Namgial		252601
Dental Surgeon Dr Smanla		252488
Child Specialist Dr S Angchok		252026
Eye Specialist Dr ST Angchok		252683
Amchi Dr ST Phunchok		252449
Amchi Dr Tsering Rigzin	Old Bus Stand	252801

Location: Kargil is immediately west of Leh. (The Valley of Kashmir is in the distant south-west.) Himachal Pradesh (Manali) is directly south. The Guge province of Tibet is in the east. In the north is Yarqand. In the north-west are areas illegally occupied by Pakistan and in the north-east a region (Shaksgam) illegally gifted by Pakistan to China.

Leh is 434km. from Srinagar, 230km. from Kargil and 473km. from Manali.

Theatre and folk songs: During the tourist season, two rival theatre groups, CATS and LAS (aka LASOL), stage cultural shows every evening. The Cultural and Traditional Society does so at Bharat Bagh, near the Yak Tail Hotel. The Ladakh Artists' Society's proscenium is the courtyard of the Leh Palace. Shows are held a little before sunset (normally between 6 and 7 pm.) Please check show timings beforehand. Admission tickets are priced at around Rs.250 each.

Movies: There are two cinema halls in town. *Delite* has one show a day, at 7 pm in summer and around 5 pm in winter. The *Trishul* is owned by the army and is open to all Indians. On Sundays there are two shows at the *Trishul*, and just one show on other days.

Foreign exchange: One can encash currency and travellers' cheques at the main branch of the State Bank of India.

Tours and transport

There are no fixed organised tours. Travel agents, however, organise tours in taxis on demand, mainly for groups. If there are vacant seats, individuals can join, but have to pay more per seat than they would in a group. Custom-made tours will be organised for you at the taxi stand (ph.252723).

Packages: The Tour and Travel Division of the JKTDC offers 'packages' that cover everything from arrival at airport to departure, and accommodation, meals and sightseeing in between. Outside the state the JKTDC's offices are the same as those of J&K Tourism. In Srinagar and Jammu its offices are in the TRC.

Srinagar: Ph-0194- 2456670, 2457930, 2472644. Fax: 2457927, 2476107.

Jammu: Ph-0194- 2549065. Fax: 2546412.

The 'packages' offered by the JKTDC include: i) 'Kashmir- Ladakh" (US $295 per person; each group must consist of at least 4 persons) 8 days/ 7 nights (Arrive at Srinagar, see Gulmarg and Kargil, and depart from Leh). ii) Leh special: 4 days/ 3 nights. US $125 per person. (Leh-Sankar-Phyâng-Hemis-Thiksey-Shey.)

Most 'packages' include reception (and send-off) at the airport, accommodation on twin sharing basis, meals, local transport and sightseeing. In case a you are put up in a 'hut' (holiday cottage) rather than a hotel, there would still be two persons per bedroom. Thus there would be twice as many persons in a hut as there are bedrooms. In some economy packages there might be as many as 4 persons per room.

economy packages there might be as many as 4 persons per room. Children under 12 get a 50% discount. Some packages require groups to consist of a certain minimum number of persons. The JKTDC wants reservations to be confirmed 20 days in advance in some cases and 30 days in others.

Taxi rates: (all fares in Indian rupees)

Route	One way	Return
Leh-Alchi-Likir-Lâmâ Yûrû	2447	2904
Leh-Alchi-Likir-Rizong-Temisgam	1600	1900*
Leh-Shey-Thiksey-Hemis-Stok	1017	1150
Leh-Shey-Thiksey-Hemis-Stok-Matho		1512
Leh-Shey-Thiksey-Hemis-Stok-S-takna-Matho-Chemday-Taktok (one day)		1950*
Leh-Tsomo Rîrî-Tso Kar-via Mahi Bridge Taglangla (in 2/3 days)		8100*
Leh-Alchi-Lâmâ Yûrû	2660	2475*
Leh-Alchi-Likir	1400	1620
Leh-Alchi-Likir-Rizong	1640	1815
Leh-Deskit (Nubra)	3355	4425*
Leh-Kargil	4059	5376
Leh-Khardungla Top		1390
Leh-Manâli	11143	15400
Leh-Panamik (Nubra)	3520	4700*
Leh-Pangong		5250*
Leh-Sankar-Spituk-Phyâng		720
Leh-Shey-Thiksey-Hemis	863	995
Leh-Srinagar	7320	9982
Leh-Tso Kar via Taglangla	3500	4500*
Leh-Tsomo Rîrî via Mahi Bridge	4630	6500*

(The * indicates that a lower fare might be possible, depending on the route and duration of the tour. However all fares are subject to change from time to time)

Where to stay:

Ladakhis have taken to tourism like few other people in India. This is perhaps the only region where the concept of guest houses has really struck roots. People spruce up the best rooms of their houses, add western-style toilets and rent them out inexpensively. This has happened not just in Leh town but also in the villages.

A very large number of hotels, too, have sprung up. This is the only part of the state (indeed, of India) where there were no pressures on the government to set up (ultimately unprofitable) public-sector hotels. In fact, the owners of private hotels told the government that it should not step in at all. However, since 1998, a small government guest- house, the *Moonland*, has been functioning near the Leh airport, in the direction of the town.

The government has approved ('American plan') tariffs, given below for the year 2003-2004. They are likely to be revised upwards in mid-2004. Most hotels charge *less.* Hotel tariffs include three meals and are for one day. Guest house tariffs don't, include meals, though they normally give free tea/ coffee and a breakfast of sorts. SBRs are a rarity at most hotels.

Tip: 'American plan' tariffs make no sense if you are going to be out all day and not likely to eat all three meals. You can negotiate a substantially lower rate minus the meals. The difference that you negotiate should be enough to pay for the same number of meals at cafes outside. That way there will be variety in your meals. In any case, if you are not going to be in for lunch, at the very least insist on a *decent* packed lunch. We did so at one of the most expensive 'A class' hotels in Leh (deliberately omitted from the list below). The tiny lunch that they packed for us was so inadequate that it led to severely frayed tempers. (Phone numbers have been given in brackets after the names of most hotels.)

A class	**AP**	**EP**
Suite	2,625	1,875
Double bedroom	2,325	1,575
Single bedroom	1,820	1,445
B class		
Double bedroom	1,550	950
Single bedroom	1,110	800
C class		
Double bedroom	1,000	525
Single bedroom	700	400
D-class		
Double bedroom	625	375
Single bedroom	400	275

All hotel tariffs, AP (American Plan) as well as EP (European Plan), are in rupees.

A-class hotels:

- Bijoo (252131), Near Public Library: Good location. Indifferent service.
- Dewa Chan (253178): Located in Agling village, near River Indus, hence away from the main city. For that reason it offers substantial discounts. Good for a long stay.
- Dragon (253620), Old Leh Road: Used to be a C-class hotel. Upgraded to A-class in the 1990s. The rooms are small. The plus is that the rooms have been arranged in a genuinely Ladakhi style.
- Ga Ldan Continental (254436; 252436): Located near the vegetable market. Expensive. Charges more than the above-mentioned rate for suites. More popular with Indian tourists than with foreigners.
- Kangla Chan (252144), Karzoo Road: Good location. Good hotel.
- Kesar (K Sar) Palace (252348), Fort Road: Service has deteriorated and become impersonal ever since the giant Indian corporate, Peerless, took over the management from the owner.
- Khangri (252051; fax: 252762, 252311), near vegetable market: Centrally located. The diesel generator in the front is a nuisance.
- Ladakh Sarai (in Stok, outside Leh) (252777): Very expensive, Mongolian-style tents with attached bath. Rarely accepts custom on the spot. Most of its guests reserve rooms in advance at its Delhi office (1/1 Rani Jhansi Road; 27525357, fax 27777483).
- Lasermo (253349), Chululungs, Old Road.
- Lhârimo (252101), Fort Road: Personalised service. Has a sister concern, the Alchi Resort.
- Lingzi (252029), opp. Vegetable Market: Excellent location (near the German bakeries). The rooms in the front block are good. The ones behind receive little sunshine, value for money.
- Mandala (252222), Fort Road: Good hotel.
- Omasila (252119), Changspa: Good location- 1.5 km. from the main market. Good service.
- Rafica (252258), Fort Road: Built in 1999. Behind Lhârimo, on the ring road that leads to Lower Tulcha.
- Sîâchen (252586; 252037): Near the old bus stand. Noisy location.
- Sun n Sand (52468) Changspa area.
- Tsemo- la (252726; 252790), Karzoo: Good, peaceful location. The rooms are small.
- Yak Tail (252118): Near the Old Fort Road. Congested.

B-class hotels:

- Bimla (252754) Fort Road.
- Choskor (252746) Old Road. (A little cheaper than others in this category.)
- Himalaya (252104) Juma Bagh
- Ibex: Good location, near the market.
- Lungse Jung (252193), Tukcha: Offers substantial discounts because it has started going downmarket.
- Rockland (252589) Fort Road.
- Snow View (252136) Changspa area.

C-class hotels:

- Kang Lâ (252506): On Library Road. Satisfactory.

D-class hotels:

- De(h)lux (252755), Fort Road: Near Instyle German Bakery. Good.
- Firdous: Near the pologround. Satisfactory.
- Hills View: Library Road. Satisfactory.

Guest houses: There are three classes of guest houses(GH): upper, medium and economy.

- **Tariffs:** Upper-class (U): DBR: Rs.300; Single room: Rs.200-250.
- Medium-class (M): DBR: Rs.175; Single room: Rs.150.
- Economy-class (E): DBR: Rs.150; Single room: Rs.100.

There are a number of decent guest-houses in the old town, between the foot of the Leh Palace and the Sankar Gompa:

- All View (U; 252132), Sankar Road: Almost as good as a B-class hotel.
- Antelope (U; 252086), Chubi Road: Very good.
- Kailash: Satisfactory.
- Old Ladakh GH, Old Leh Road: Poor maintenance. However, it is very popular because it is inexpensive.
- Sabila: Near the pologround. Good rooms.
- Shalimar: Satisfactory.
- Tak: Satisfactory.

The guest-houses in the Changspa area are inexpensive and mostly good value for money:

- Asia. Good.
- Eagle (E): Good.
- Larchang: Good.
- Otsal (E): Good.
- Tsavo (E): Good.

There are good guest houses just outside the town, on the road to the Shanti Stupa:

- Manzoor (E): Satisfactory.
- Oriental (E), Changspa: Good.
- Rainbow (E), Changspa: Good. However, the presence of the Alpha Mess of the Army nearby is an inconvenience.
- Rinchens (U; 252486), Changspa: Good.
- Two-star (E), Karzoo: Satisfactory.

Elsewhere in town:

- Pangong: On Library Road. Satisfactory.
- Nezer (Nazir) View (E): Near Spic n Span hotel. Satisfactory.
- Ti Sei (M, 252404), Zâñgsti: Near German Bakery. Good.

Public sector: The Moonland, run by J&K Tourism, is on the road between the airport and the town. It is incredibly inexpensive (*Rs.250 a room on the average*) for the quality offered. However, it is way away from town.

Outside Leh town: There are government-run, excellent value for money, inexpensive tourist bungalows at Khaltse, Rumtse, Sâkti and Saspol. *Tariff: Rs. 150 and Rs.250 a room*. Khaltse also has a PWD Rest House, but mainly for government servants.

Winters: The following hotels and guest-houses continue to function in winter:

- *A- class hotels:*
- Khangri; Rs.900;
- Yak Tail: Rs.800
- Sîachen: Rs.600
- *B- class hotels:*
- Gypsy's Panorama: Rs.700
- Bimla: Rs.500.
- *Guest houses:*
- Indus (ph: 252502): Rs.500
- Khan Manzil (ph.252681): Rs.200.

Winter tariff includes heating charges. (They normally use *bukharis* fired with coal or kerosene oil.) Omasila, Lasermo and Gypsy Panorama have central heating.

Food

Leh has its own distinct cuisine, totally different from Chinese food. However, when some Tibetans migrated to Leh in the 1960s, they started making flat, tape-like noodles in Leh. The noodles became extremely popular wherever available. (Which means that they still haven't permeated the cuisine of, say, Zâñskâr.) Mo-mo dumplings, so popular in nearby Manali, too, are hesitantly entering Ladakhi kitchens.

The main Ladakhi dish, the *thukpa*, is a stew of meat and vegetables. In most parts of Ladakh it is thickened with barley flour. While Ladakhi food is available at most eating places, interestingly none of them bills itself as a 'Ladakhi restaurant'. You are far more likely to find 'Tibetan restaurants'. Tibetan refugees normally run them.

Price levels in Leh, and not just for food, are much higher than at corresponding places in the rest of India. This is partly because it costs that much more to transport things from the Indian plains to Ladakh. And partly because Ladakh has got used to very high wage levels, thanks to government spending and absence of taxes.

Tibetan food: The good places, most of them in the main market, are the two Amdo restaurants, Lâ Montessori and Kokonoor. Dreamland, too, is good. The Tibetan Kitchen on Fort Road, the Wok Tibetan Kitchen in the main market, the Tibetan Friends Corner Restaurant (near the Taxi stand) and the Devi Tibetan Restaurant (near the State Bank of India) are a notch lower.

- ***Kashmiri food:*** The Budshah Inn, near the mosque, is good.
- ***Mughlai ('Indian') cuisine:*** The Mughal Darbar in the main market is value for money.
- ***Western food:*** Yak Tail is expensive but one of the best.

Confectioneries: There are two 'German' Bakeries close to each other and uphill from the Lingzi Hotel, on the Old Fort Road. Expensive by the standards of the rest of India, both are good for the taste buds. They also sell sandwiches for your packed lunch, *momos*, lasagne and a fixed-price breakfast. The other good bakery is Mona Lisa (near the State Bank of India), which is also a restaurant.

Tourist information centres: There is a government-run TRC (Tourist Reception Centre) on the road between the airport and the town.

Address: Tourist Reception Centre, Leh 194101 (Jammu & Kashmir) India

Phones: 254497; 252094; Fax: 252297.

(Telephone area code: 01982)

Apart from information, the TRC also hires out sleeping bags, quilted jackets, shoes etc.

Kargil

All the statistics given below are about Kargil district. The altitude and STD code are of Kargil town.

Area	14,036 sq. km.
Population	65,990 (1981 census); 91,670 (1996 estimate); 1,15000 (2001 census)
Altitude	2,676 to 2,740m. (8,780' plus)
STD code	01985
Languages spoken	Purgi, Balti, Dard(i), Ladakhi, Zâñskâri and Sheena.
Religions	Islam; Buddhism. Kargil includes Zâñskâr, which is across the Penzi Lâ. Zâñskâr is predominantly Buddhist, with a small minority of Kashmiri, Sunni Muslims from Kishtwâr. The rest of Kargil is almost entirely Shia Muslim, except some villages that border Leh, where Buddhists live.
Annual mean rainfall	26 cm
Average temperatures	Drâss, currently the district's main attraction (because of in different seasons the war sites of Tololing, Mushkoo and Tiger Hill), is the second coldest inhabited place in the world. Winter temperatures drop to minus 45°C at night. Including wind-chill it could plunge to as low as minus 60°C. Zâñskâr is not as cold. Night temperatures in winter merely drop to minus 35°C. In both Drâss and Zâñskâr it is several degrees below zero even during the day from November to March. In summer, nights are cool- a light woollen sweater is sometimes needed. Sunny summer days can be quite hot: T-shirts are sufficient. The rest of the district is slightly warmer. Winters are colder than in most of Europe, but it rarely drops below minus 12°C. Summer nights warrant a light woollen sweater- except perhaps for a few days in July. Even in July, if it rains or gets cloudy, a sweater is required in the afternoons as well.
Annual snowfall	2 to 5 feet

Tours and transport

Taxis: Fares are as under

From - to	One way	Return
Leh-Kargil	Rs3400	Rs4700*
Kargil-Rangdum	Rs3850	Rs5100
Kargil-Padam (Zâñskâr)Error!	Rs7400	Rs9800
Kargil-Srinagar	Rs3500	Rs4500

Taxis charge Rs.300 extra for every extra night that you detain them. They charge Rs.900 for a 'full-day' booking.

*This fare, quoted by the Kargil Taxi Union, is lower than that given by the Leh Taxi Union for the same route for the same period.

Tourist buses: There is a daily (except Monday and Thursday) bus service from the Tourist Reception Centre, Srinagar, to Kargil at 0730 hours. The fare is Rs.250 (deluxe) and Rs 145 to 190 (semi- deluxe) per passenger each way. The journey takes 10 hours.

Packages: The Tour and Travel Division of the JKTDC offers 'packages' that cover everything from arrival at the nearest airport to departure, and accommodation, meals and sightseeing in between. Outside the state the JKTDC's offices are the same as those of J&K Tourism. In Srinagar and Jammu its offices are in the TRC.

- Srinagar: Ph. 2456670, 2457930, 2472644. Fax: 2457927, 2476107.
- Jammu: Ph. 2549065. Fax: 546412.
- The 'packages' offered by JKTDC include:

For Rs.6,999/ per person, ex- Jammu, the J&K TDC provides 2 nights in Kargil and 5 nights in Kashmir on a twin-sharing, MAP basis, for groups of 7 or more, in an A-class hotel (normally at the D Zoji Lâ). The package includes transportation (normally in a Tata Sumo taxi) from the Jammu railway station (or airport) to Srinagar, Kargil and back. You can increase the number of nights in Kargil and decrease those in Kashmir, if you wish.

JKTDC also has a number of Leh-related packages, which pass through Drâss and Kargil.

The JKTDC wants reservations to be confirmed 20 days in advance in some cases and 30 days in others.

Access:

The only way to reach landlocked Kargil is by road. You can take a taxi or bus (see 'Tours and Transport') from Leh or Srinagar to Kargil.

Route 1: The main pass between Srinagar and Kargil is likely to be blocked by snow from November to May. However, the road between Kargil and Drâss is open almost throughout the year. *Route 2:* The road between Leh and Kargil, too, is open almost throughout the year. *Route 3a:* The road into Suru valley is functional around the year till Sangra. After Sangra it is prone to landslides between December and March. *Route 3b:* The main pass to Zâñskâr is blocked from November to mid-June. During that period, it is possible to walk on the snow (or the frozen river) between Kargil and Zâñskâr depending on weather conditions.

In summer, you can trek to Kargil from Kashmir, Jammu, Leh or Himachal Pradesh.

When the roads are functional, government buses ply between Kargil and Padam (Zâñskâr) on alternate days, to most places in Suru valley (up to Pânikhar) twice a day and to places on the national highway at least once a day. The bus to Zâñskâr serves Rangdum as well. The road to Sangra-Pânikhar-Rangdum-Zâñskâr is closed between November and June. The other roads are functional more or less throughout the year.

Bus fares from Kargil to:

The Suru valley:

Sangra Rs30
Sâñkoo Rs26
Faroona Rs13 (a place near Khumbâthâng)

The road to Leh:

Mulbek Rs26
Phokar Rs25
Shergol(e) Rs24

Where to stay:

Kargil town

None of the hotels in Kargil has a website or an e- mail address. If the town has hotels at all it is because the town is a critical halting point for those going to Srinagar, Leh or the Suru Valley. The hotels are mostly quite basic. The D Zoji Lâ is located in Baru, a suburb of Kargil where all the government offices are. The Caravan Sarai is close to the Tourist Reception Centre and is perched atop the town.

Name	Location	Tel	AP Dble	AP SIngle	AP Suite bed	AP Extra	EP Dble	EP Sngle
Caravan Sarai	Lantook	232278	2000	1500				
D dZoji Lâ	Baru	232360	2484	2064		900		
Kargil Continental	Near the Tourist Reception Centre	232320	2277	1898	5000	850		
Sîâchen	Chanchik (near the Taxi Stand)	232221	2000	1500				
Greenland	Near the Tourist Reception Centre	232324	800	600		200	400	300
Tourist Marjina		2333293					400 - 500	200
Ruby		232343					200	
Crown	Near the Bus Stand	232371					120	60

Credit cards are not accepted.

Outside Kargil town

There are tourist bungalows (TBs) on the National Highway at Drâss, Heniskuts and Mulbek. In the Suru valley TBs are located at Sâñkoo, Pânikhar, Puntikchey Parkachik, Tangole and Rangdum.

At Drâss and Rangdum there are rooms in the Rs.100 range as well, and in Kargil town in the Rs.150 range, too. Private hotels in Kargil can charge up to Rs.1000 a night and in Padam around Rs.400.

Most hotels in the upper- and upper-middle price range serve Chinese, Continental and Indian food.

Camping equipment:

Apart from what the private sector might have in stock, the Tourist Officer at the Tourist Reception Centre has some sleeping bags, quilted jackets etc., to be hired out to tourists for a small fee.

Travel resources

The main Tourist Reception Centre is in the Tourist Bungalow, Kargil. Padam, the headquarter of Zâñskâr, too, has a tourist office. The Tourism Department's bungalows have helpful and knowledgeable staff, even though they are not meant to provide information.

There are no ATMs in Kargil.

The State Bank of India in Kargil proper has been authorised to deal in foreign exchange.

Hospitals

The government-run district hospital is in Kargil proper, on the slope that leads to the Tourist Bungalow. It is the best in the district. Hospitals of the next level are called PHCs (primary health centres). You will find them at Drâss, Padam (Zâñskâr) and Sâñkoo. Then come the dispensaries, which are located at Pânikhar, Tambas and Trespon. In addition, there are first aid centres at Karshâ (Zâñskâr), Minji, Mansuru, Parkachik, Phe, Rangdum, Sani (Zâñskâr), Stongchey, Tangri and Youlyuk.

The weather

Month	Recommended clothing
November-March	From November to the end of March just remember that you are in the second coldest region in the world, after Siberia.
April-May	April to mid-May it can be tolerably cold: normal woollens will do.
May	From May to mid-June days are pleasant but evenings can be cool.
June-July	July is the warmest month. You can wear T-Augustshirts even in the evenings. It's about the same during the last fortnight of June and the first fortnight of August. It starts getting nippy after the 15th August
September	From mid-August to mid-September days are pleasant but evenings can be cool to cold.
October	It touches zero by mid-October in many parts of Ladakh.

Tourist information centres

Offices of Jammu & Kashmir Tourism are at:

***Delhi*:** 210-203, Kanishka (hotel) Shopping Plaza, 19 Ashoka Road (opposite Meridien Hotel, Janpath crossing). Ph: 23345373; fax: 23367881.

jaktour@ndf.vsnl.net.in

***Mumbai* (Bombay):** 25, North Wing, World Trade Centre, Cuffe Parade, Colaba. Ph: 22189040. Fax: 22186172.

jaktour2@bol.net.in

Calcutta: 12, Chowringhee. Ph: 22285791; Tele/fax: 22281950.

***Chennai* (Madras):** II Floor, 36/36- A, North Usman Road. Telefax: 8235958.

jaktour1@nd4.vsnl.net.in

Ahmedabad: Airlines House, Lal Darwaza. Telefax: 25503551.

Hyderabad: 5th Floor, Left Wing, Chandra Vihar Complex, MJ Road. Telefax: 24734806.

Bibliography

Articles in journals and periodicals

Anon, "Army admits 'cold lies' in Siachen operations," *The Kashmîr Times*, Jammu, May 8, 2004.

Indian Mountaineer, Number 34(Journal of the Indian Mountaineering Federation) 1998

Manglik, Kalpana, Crafts map of Kashmîr (a folder published in 2000 by the Dastkâri Hât Samiti, New Delhi)

Mani, Dr. B.R., 'Rock carvings and engravings in Ladâkh: New Discoveries,' *Prâgdhârâ*, no. 9 (Journal of the U.P. State Archæology Department) 1998- 99.

Sheikh, Abdul Ghani, 'History of Leh- A New Perspective,' *New Hope*, Srînagar, November-December, 2002,

Sheikh, Abdul Ghani, 'Muslims in Ladâkh and Sufi Traditions,' *New Hope*, vol.4, no.1, January-February, 2003.

Sikand, Yoginder, 'Inter-religious relations in Pâkistân,' *The Kashmîr Times*, 6 April 2004.

World Tibet Network News, Friday, October 29, 1993

Books

Drew, Frederic, *The Jummoo and Kashmîr Territories,* Capital Publishing House, New Delhi-110002. (1875; reprinted 1997)

Francke, A.H., *A History of Ladâkh*, Sterling Publishers, New Delhi. (This is the 1977 edition of a book originally published in 1907 as *A History of Western Tibet*.).

Francke, A.H., *Antiquities of Indian Tibet*, Calcutta, Asian Educational Services, Madras.) Vol. II. The book is in two volumes. 1926 (Reprinted 1992,)

Information Department, Government of Jammu & Kashmîr, *District Profiles*. (Internal publication, not for sale)1998

Joldan, E, Harvest, *Festival of Buddhist Dards of Ladâkh and Other Essays*, Kapoor Brothers, Srinagar, 1985.

Kâchu Sikander Khân 'Sikander,' *Qadeem Ladâkh: Târîkh o Tamaddan,* Kâchu Publishers, Leh. (Year not stated, but around 1990.)

Kapadia, Harish, *Across Peaks & Passes in Ladâkh, Zâñskâr and East Karakoram*, Indus Publishing Company, New Delhi, 1999.

Khân, Sikander (see 'Kâchu Sikander Khân,' above.)

Negi, SS, *Himâlayan Rivers, Lakes and Glaciers*, Indus Publishing Company, New Delhi, 1991.

Rizvi, Janet, *Ladâkh: Crossroads of High Asia*, Oxford, Delhi, 1989 edition

Sharma Vidyarthi O.P., *151 Healing Plants of Jammu and Kashmîr* (a government publication).c.2000.

Snellgrove, David L. and Skorupski, Tadeusz, *The Cultural Heritage of Ladâkh*, Vikas, Delhi, 1977

Sufi, Dr. GMD: *Kashîr*, vols. 1 &2, written 1948; Light & Life Publishers, New Delhi, 1974

Vigne, G.T., *Travels in Kashmîr, Ladâk...*, London, 1842.

Weare, Gary, *Trekking in the Indian Himalaya*, Lonely Planet, Victoria (Australia), 1986

Younghusband, Captain Francis, *The Heart of a Continent*, 1896.

From the Internet

A Slice of Hunzâ High, a website

Amin, Maj (Retd) Agha Humayun, *The war of lost opportunities*

Anon, 'Country report -4. *India: Lessons from Ladakh, Down to Earth* (Volume 9, No. 23, April 30, 2001), published by the Centre for Science and Environment in Delhi.

Anon, 'Two British officers played anti-India role,' *The Daily Excelsior*, Nov 2/ 3 (year not clear: perhaps 2001 or 2002; I got this from their website; the dateline is Nov.2, so the newspaper would be dated Nov. 3.) *The Daily Excelsior* has, in turn, quoted the *Dawn*, Karachi.

Kala, R., Hema, P.S., Dwivedi, S., Chaurasia, O.P.and Banerji, *Phytochemical studies on Indian Seabuckthorn* (Hippophae rhamnoides)

Khân, Tarik Ali, *'Baltistân LITTLE TIBET: Renaissance and Resistance in Baltistân;* The article perhaps first appeared in *Himal*, a journal published in Kathmandu, Nepal.

Mango Grove (www.mango.itgo.com/northernareas)

Prashar A.S., *Wonder berry from Ladakh*; Tribune News Service, Chandigarh, April 19, 200?.

Rao, R. R. *Floristic Diversity of Indian Region*

Reza, A.H.M. Ali with Chowdhury, Hasan Z. *Bio-diversity of Jammu and Kashmir*

Rizvi, Mohammad Afzal, *Medicinal flowers of Pâkistân*, The Bait al-Hikmah Research Institute

Santucci, Prof. James A., *"Kashmîr: A Potential for a World War,"* Department of Comparative Religion, California State University, Fullerton, CA 92834-6868

Shapiro, Sheryl, *'Hunzâ Hospitality'*

www.cybertown.com

www.silica-hydride.com. This website features an article by Patrick Flanagan, MD. (MA)& Gael Crystal Flanagan, MD. (MA).

Index

(Page numbers in boldface indicate the main entry on that subject. Italics suggest a picture.)

Errata

Maps: The map of 'Kargil district' is on page 29; 'Across the LoC: roads' is on page 30; and 'Siachen' on page 32.

Picture captions: *Page 34 (unnumbered):* (Drokpâ): The third line should have read: 'As bloodlines go, the Drokpâs are the purest Aryans…'

Page 47 (unnumbered): Both pictures are of the Kargâh Buddha. The lower photograph is a close up.

Map 'Across the LoC: roads'**:** This is essentially a map of roads in Pâkistan Occupied Kashmîr. However, some of the towns to the south and southwest of Abbotabad (e.g. Murree, Islâmâbâd and Râwalpiñdi) are in Pâkistan. The so-called Âzâd Kashmîr (east) and areas north of Abbotabad have been illegally occupied by Pâkistan.

Page 17: The Sindhu Darshan Festival of Leh is held every June. There are indications that it might be renamed the Senggé Chhu or Sâñspo Festival in 2005.

Page 100: The centered headline should have read 'The mediæval (or medieval) era.'

Pages 109-111: Gen. Musharraf spells his first name as 'Pervez.'

Page 148: It may be pointed out that since the Indian rupee is stronger than its Pâkistani counterpart, in effect the people of the Leh and Kargil districts receive, per capita, nine or ten times as many government grants that their brethren do in the so-called Northern Areas.

Page 174: Reference i is from Francke, A.H., *A history of Ladâkh*, Sterling Publishers, New Delhi.

Francke, A.H., *Antiquities of Indian Tibet*, Calcutta, Asian Educational services, Madras.) Vol. II. (1926)

Page 217 (bottom): The motorable routes to the Surû Valley and Zâñskâr are, respectively, on pages 299-302 and 305.

Page 289: The 3rd line from the bottom should have read, 'See the *section* on the Surû Valley' (pp. 299-302).

Page 315: *Population…* In just twenty years the population has almost *tripled.*

Page 431: The sentence at the bottom should have read 'See also the section on the Chãñgthâñg Wildlife Sanctuary on pages 426-427.'

Pages 485 to 490: All altitudes in Column 2 are in metres and those in Column 3 are in feet.

Page 547: The * indicates that a lower fare might be possible, depending on the route and the duration of the tour.

Page 548: All hotel tariffs, AP (American Plan) as well as EP (European Plan), are in Indian rupees.

